ICONS OF MODERN CULTURE

Series Editor: David Ellis

Faust

Mephistopheles and Faust in Harry Clarke, Forest and Cavern, 1925

Faust:
Icon of
Modern Culture

Osman Durrani

HELM INFORMATION LTD

I dedicate this volume to RAE, TQA and PPR
'With friends such as these ...'
O.D.

© Osman Durrani, 2004

A CIP catalogue record for this book is available from the
British Library.

Published in Great Britain in 2004 by
Helm Information Ltd,
The Banks, Mountfield,
near Robertsbridge,
East Sussex TN32 5JY
U.K.

ISBN 1-903206-15-4

Jacket illustration: Felix Zakar, *Doctor Faustus*,
              Ink and gum arabic on paper, 2003

Printed on acid-free paper and bound by
   Antony Rowe Ltd, Chippenham, Wiltshire

Contents

List of Illustrations

Notes on the Author
and Contributors

Osman Durrani holds a D.Phil. from the University of Oxford, where he completed a thesis on *Faust and the Bible*. He lectured at Durham, UK, before becoming Professor of German at the University of Kent at Canterbury. His research has focused on many aspects of the Enlightenment, Romanticism and the twentieth century, and includes Anglo-German relations, popular culture, cabaret, and computer-assisted learning. *Fictions of Germany. Images of the Nation in the Modern Novel* was published by Edinburgh University Press in 1994.

Rolf Hellebust is an Associate Professor in the Department of Germanic, Slavic and East Asian Studies at the University of Calgary. He has written articles on Russian literature and culture for journals including *Style*, the *Slavic Review*, the *Russian Review*, and the *Slavic and East European Journal*. His book *Flesh to Metal: Soviet Literature and the Alchemy of Revolution* was published by Cornell University Press in 2003, and he is currently completing a monograph on the nineteenth-century literary tradition in Russia.

Derek Katz is an Assistant Professor of Music History at the University of California, Santa Barbara. He has specialised in Czech music and culture, especially the operas of Leoš Janáček. He has written on music for *The New York Times*, the Bard Festival, the San Francisco Opera and Lincoln Center in New York, and has given pre-concert lectures at venues across America, including the Ojai Festival in California and at the Lincoln Center and Carnegie Hall in New York.

Paul M. Malone is an Associate Professor of German in the Department of Germanic and Slavic Studies at the University of Waterloo, Canada. He holds a Ph.D. in Interdisciplinary Studies from the University of British Columbia and is a certified translator. In addition to his book, *Franz Kafka's* The Trial: *Four Stage Adaptations* (2003), he has published on literature, film, theatre-performance theory, and virtual reality computer technology, and is the current editor of *Germano-Slavica: A Canadian Journal of Germanic and Slavic Comparative and Interdisciplinary Studies*.

Yoko Riley holds an M.A. from Seijo University in Tokyo and a B.L.S. from the University of Ottawa. She now works in the Department of Germanic, Slavic and East Asian Studies at the University of Calgary, where she teaches courses in Japanese civilisation, language and film. She has co-written a two-volume multimedia Japanese language course. Her research has been on pre-twentieth-century Japanese history and civilisation, with a focus on the Sengoku and Tokugawa periods and their influence on present-day Japanese culture and society.

Derek Sellen lives and works in Canterbury, where he teaches English language and literature to foreign students. His poems have been published in various magazines and anthologies and have won national and international awards. He has read from his works on BBC Radio Three, and his plays have been performed in Canterbury and Brighton.

Series Editor's Preface

EVERY CULTURE has its icons, figures who populate the collective consciousness and provide it with essential points of reference. Any two members of the culture in question might well have different ideas as to what particular figures represent but both will recognise them as items in a common currency. It is in part through the different and sometimes competing meanings we give to the prevailing icons that we organise our knowledge and evince our views of the world.

In some instances the birth of an icon is an historical event, one which took place around 1412 in the case of Joan of Arc, for example, but more certainly in 1855 as far as Ned Kelly is concerned. Falstaff's first appearance in the world is also a matter of historical record but in a very different sense while that of Faust or Robin Hood is far less determinate. As these examples illustrate our icons are a varied band. They come in all shapes and sizes, quite what shape or size depending partly of course on the social or cultural position from which they are viewed, as well as the tastes and temperament of the viewer. Their essential heterogeneity and their vulnerability to private, idiosyncratic appropriation make them difficult to talk about in general, but if they have one characteristic in common it is that they have left their real, literary or mythical origins well behind. They have transcended those origins in order to represent for us qualities we admire or detest, facets of human failure or achievement which it would be uncomfortable to discuss in the abstract. It is through these figures that we often prefer to do our thinking. Close study of history is for the majority of a population esoteric, and however much 'celebrities' may temporarily engage public attention everyone is aware that they are fleeting phenomena, that they come and go. Icons on the other hand are deeply embedded. They provide a link with the generations which went before and characterise what we are quite as much as our clothes, our food or our anthems.

Each volume in this series describes and above all illustrates the process whereby a certain figure became iconic. It aims to show the different ways that figure has functioned for different interest groups and what role it plays in our culture now. Much of the illustration is literary but attention is also paid to music, painting,

1

photography and film (how people visualise their icons can be as significant as how they write or read about them). A few recent essays of an analytic nature may also be included and the authors of individual volumes will offer their comments on some of the controversial aspects of their subject, but the chief intention is to provide a descriptive context for the *display* of material. In that way readers can watch the sometimes chequered history of an icon develop and see for themselves how the figure concerned came to play such an important role in our common awareness.

DAVID ELLIS

Introduction

Myth tries to explain the inexplicable. Since it comes out of a fundamental truth it has to end in the inexplicable.—Franz Kafka

T O WRITE about Dr Faustus is in itself nothing less than a Faustian endeavour. Johann Wolfgang von Goethe, arguably the last of that now defunct breed of *uomini universali*, a true 'Renaissance Man' of omni-directional learning, constructed his most ambitious drama around this kaleidoscopic figure and left us with a profusion of contradictory images of a restless character and his heroic but often futile actions. To chronicle them as they have been portrayed from their literary beginnings in the sixteenth century to the present day has been to trace the vicissitudes of a culture that was central European in its origins, but rapidly spread across the continent and eventually across the globe. From his origins in Reformation Germany, where mother-directed Catholicism was losing ground to a sterner, father-oriented Protestantism, Faust has become a familiar figure with a strong claim to iconicity not only in his homeland and elsewhere in Europe but equally so in the western hemisphere and in Japan. The reason for this lies in the unique empowerment experienced in recent times by two vital media: transportation and communication. It is no coincidence that Faustus' birth coincides approximately with the discovery of America and the invention of printing. Dr Faustus was portrayed from earliest times as a great traveller. He was also associated with the invention of movable type, through a false identification with Johann Fust of Mainz. He is from the outset a 'man of letters' who travels the world and, as a further, no less central quality, indulges in a string of fleeting affairs with beautiful women, culminating in a technically impossible union with Helen of Troy. No one, it seems, not even Faustus himself, could tell whether she was a real woman or a phantasmagorical apparition. Our passion for virtual reality begins here. Faustus is the polymath, the globe-trotter, and the serial seducer. These are his three determining qualities, and in the eyes of his original biographer, the anonymous author of the sixteenth-century *Historia*, he could only fulfil his aspirations (to know all there is to know, to travel the globe at will, and to fulfil his

3

sexual desires) through a diabolical association which would, once the twenty-four years of pleasure had passed, lead to an inevitable day of reckoning.

All subsequent Fausts have shared this predicament to some degree. In doing so, they have combined the qualities of two other figures who acquired iconic status at the same time: Don Quixote and Don Juan, the one rich in imagination and longing, the other a tragic playboy. Some Fausts have been altruistically concerned to assist their fellow men by spreading knowledge and sharing their wealth, others have pursued beauty not merely as lovers but as poets and musicians. All have had a diabolical assistant or alter ego, a Mephistophelean helper who remains unstable and evasive: a servant, a guiding spirit, a friend, but all too often a derisive mocker, a rogue, a fiend in many disguises. In some versions of Faust's life, he remains in the background, in others he occupies the limelight and can become more important than Faust himself. The story seems to have been designed to allow for unlimited variety, endless permutation, surprise at every turn. This has given it longevity and permitted it to adapt itself to new social, cultural and national environments. Faustus was a heretic in the sixteenth century, an entertainer in the seventeenth century. In the eighteenth, he became a striver for self-fulfilment, a role most authors deemed worthy of forgiveness. Once the previously unthinkable option of salvation was introduced, the story's appeal increased, not least because its outcome had become controversial. The nineteenth-century Fausts frequently aspired, like their authors, to become great artists intent on creating something of permanent value; Lenau's is a painter, Spielhagen's a dramatist. Later on, however, they develop political ambitions, when demands for greater equality and social change were heard; this is true of Lunacharski's *Faust in the City* no less than of Avenarius' drama, both written at the time of World War I. In the twentieth century, Faust was an emblem of man's lot under socialism, of hero-worship and fascism, of the supremacy of science and of all aspects of a technically evolving modernity and a role-playing post-modernity. The observation of ever-changing transplantations of the theme into successive cultures is part of the enduring fascination of the material.

Yet the multiplicity of Fausts in book form, in music, on stage, on film and on canvas, in verse and prose, in ballet and opera, in cartoons and advertising, makes this investigation a well-nigh impossible task. In 1980 Günther Mahal conjectured that three million printed pages had so far been devoted to Faust, an estimate based on a crude assumption of 20,000 books averaging 150 pages apiece (Mahal (1980), 15). It now seems to me that this may have been an understatement even then, and that the number has in any case greatly increased since. On-stage productions of *Faust* number something in the region of three hundred per night world-wide, which may not be all that many by comparison with *Hamlet* or *Romeo and Juliet*, but in contrast to these and most other iconic evergreens, the Faust myth exists in a huge number of variant versions and is always retold differently. Even Goethe, who did more than anyone to stabilise an unstable original, produced no fewer than four separate but related *Fausts* in the course of his career as a writer. The present study will be noted as much for its omissions as for what it was able to document. Many major works languish in obscurity; others are being performed or re-issued as I write. To include more would have been to sacrifice analysis to data-collection for its own sake, an approach I have tended to eschew but which this compendium nonetheless exemplifies in places. In its capacity as a guide to Faust's unsystematic trail through five centuries, some material is placed before the reader with little or no further comment. Each chapter is followed by an extensive bibliography that includes recent work in the area.

The figure with whom this book is concerned goes by two names, Faustus and Faust, for which there are several explanations. 'Faustus' may be a surname or a nickname. It would appear to reflect the sixteenth-century's tendency to Latinise German proper names; it may denote the 'favoured' one, or it may refer to his putative birthplace in Knittlingen, as Latin *fustis* equates to German *Knittel*, a 'club' or 'stick'. The modern noun *Faust* means 'fist' and thus signals defiant strength and vitality. Roger Shattuck notes the similarity with Shakespeare's 'Prospero', and recommends reading *The Tempest* as a 'modified Faust play' (Shattuck, 80). A superficial similarity between the names Faust and Fust has led to confusion between the doctor and the printer, who was seen in some quarters as a magician (Meek, 139–41; Smeed, 99–109). We also encounter the appellation Sabellicus. His putative given name, Johann, or John, is but one of several. Jörg ('George') occurs beside Heinrich ('Henry'), the latter in all probability a not uncontroversial invention by Goethe. The name of his adversary is subject to much variation and corruption. Goethe confessed to ignorance of its origins and meaning (Letter to Zelter, 20 November 1829). Most recent authors follow his spelling, Mephistopheles. Marlowe, as far as we can judge, used either Mephastophilis or Mephostophilis. Besides these, there are less common variants: Mephistophilus (Shakespeare), Mephistophles (puppet plays) and many others (Meek, 142–50). It was tempting to shorten all of these to Mephisto, a form I prefer to use in the possessive case in preference to the unwieldy formation Mephistopheles's. The name's meaning has never been resolved and the morphology invites corruption; 'a sinister ambiguity haunts the syllables of the demon's name' (Butler, 132). I have attempted to copy the preferred form as used by each individual author. Recent versions display great variety; from 'Mr Scratch' in *The Devil and Daniel Webster* to Bulgakov's 'Voland'. Stanley Donen's *Bedazzled* features a 'George Spigott' and the Jones Brothers' *The Adventure of Faustus Bidgood* introduces a 'Fred Bonia-Coombs', but alternative names were applied to the tempter from the eighteenth century onwards; Klinger places his Faust beside a 'Leviathan'.

Faust and Mephistopheles are in their very different ways supremely ambiguous, ever-changing figures. This is true over the centuries as it is within individual works. There are times in their relationship when Faust seems to be in charge of what is happening, and there are other times when he is utterly at Mephisto's mercy. The devil, too, shifts from a position of total control to one of abject servitude. Faust may appear heroic or despicable, Mephistopheles may inspire terror, sympathy or ridicule. This diversity reflects the church's ambiguous position in regard to evil, which, while utterly deplorable, provides a useful instrument of social control.

Towering behind Mephistopheles is his 'master' Lucifer, who is acknowledged as Mephisto's superior, although he rarely stoops to intervene in the action.

Faustus' paramours go unnamed in many of the early versions, always excepting Helen of Troy, 'Helena' in Goethe, and 'Elena' in Boito. A romantic association with the Duchess of Parma is recorded in early implementations of the myth. She survives as Faust's episodic consort in many recent versions. Yet the most celebrated of all his loves made a relatively recent appearance in the legend. It was Goethe's idea to associate the great scholar with an unassuming small-town teenager whom he called both 'Margarete' and, using a homely diminutive of the same name, 'Gretchen'. She rapidly won hearts and minds and became an icon of wholesome Germanic femininity in her own right, inspiring artists, designers and hairdressers, haberdashers and milliners, to create images of flaxen-haired, plaited, dirndl-wearing maidens who could be broadcast to the world as emblems of unsullied maidenhood. Until recently, it was anathema to suggest that this might have run counter to Goethe's intentions; yet the text describes her as *schnippisch* ('cheeky', F 2612), and the name was commonly associated with prostitution in the eighteenth century, so that calling her Gretchen ('Little Madge'), far from endearing her to the audience, might actually serve as a mark of her degradation (Gaier, 113). Two recent novelists, Robert Nye and Michael Swanwick, have provided radically different explanations as to why this figure is known by two names (see below, 357). There is no less ambiguity in this figure than there is in Faust himself. In literature and painting, Gretchen has been everything from a willing sexual partner to an icon of saintliness. Her duality is well captured in René Clair's film *La Beauté du diable* by the figure of Marguerite, an apparently chaste gypsy girl who just happens to be decked out like the man-eating Carmen of Bizet's opera. In the visual arts, she may be depicted as a shy young maiden or a sultry courtesan. The girl upon whom the scholar becomes fixated goes by many names; initially these are variants of 'Margaret' (Margareta, Margarete, Gretchen, Marguerite, Margherita, Magrita and others), and while it was tempting to anglicise them all as 'Margaret', I have again endeavoured to follow each author's preference, however much the frequently similar nomenclature may cause confusion. Goethe provided her with a jealous brother, Valentin/Valentine, whom Faust eliminates, and whose story is developed in several operas.

The fourth figure who appears with a relatively high degree of consistency is that of Faust's *famulus* ('academic assistant') Christoph/Christopher Wagner. He varies from a self-aggrandising but incompetent acolyte to a well-meaning if literal-minded trainee. In early versions of the story, he can be found seizing the initiative himself and striking his own bargain with the devil. In later texts, we are more likely to find him attempting to restrain the doctor from his evil pursuits. Goethe shows us both sides; his Wagner is a dry-as-dust intellectual neophyte with a somewhat coy disposition in Part I, only to be transformed into a power-hungry gene-manipulator in Part II. The scholar, one might argue, has shifted from being a quiet observer of nature into a ruthless adventurer who delights in playing god. Yet both before and after Goethe, Wagner pursued an intriguing life of his own.

No sooner had the public read the Faust Book than 'Wagner Books' flooded onto the market as timely sequels. There are several English and German examples extant; they contain accounts of the adventures Wagner had after his master's demise, when he, too, travelled the world with Mephistopheles and an attendant spirit. Modern authors like Werner Schwab and Michael Swanwick have continued to make extensive use of him, and he assumes the role of narrator in Robert Nye's novel *Faust*. A number of other attendants and acolytes (Rafe and Robin in Marlowe) and spirits (Auerhahn in the Wagner Books) crop up in later derivations.

Some of the oldest texts provide the doctor with a good and an evil angel to stand by him and either encourage virtue or stimulate wickedness. These accessories are soon dropped, although Goethe surrounds his Faust with numerous emissaries from the spirit world whose role could be either benign or destructive. More importantly, he appears to put God himself on stage, and to make him condone the temptation that is about to come his way. Of all the apparent additions that Goethe made, this must be the most controversial. He was slated for his arrogance in doing so by many of his readers and critics. Sir Walter Scott remarked, 'Nobody but a German would ever have provoked a comparison with the Book of Job, the grandest poem that was ever written' (Hauhart, 76). Yet perhaps this was not quite as radical an innovation as one might think. Readings of little-known early eighteenth-century Fausts show that it was quite common to begin in heaven – a classical heaven, admittedly, but a heaven nonetheless. Jupiter would invite one of his minions to go down to earth and investigate what was amiss there. And on close inspection, Goethe's heaven turns out to be something very similar: a mock heaven, manipulated by machinery of the type used in mediaeval miracle plays, and an Olympian Zeus who had grown a bit older and, as Mephistopheles puts it, got out of the habit of laughing. This Lord is neither Greek nor Christian, but rather a leftover from both traditions, just as Faust himself is a leftover from an earlier epoch that had created him to illustrate its own ethical preoccupations. It is these that we need to set out to investigate before the subsequent implementations of the myth of Faust the Magus can be appreciated.

The present book begins with a look at the literary sources of the Faust theme. Here the focus will be on distinct epochs: the period up to the sixteenth century when the story was first committed to paper, the early chapbooks, the Enlightenment, Romanticism and the later nineteenth century, the twentieth century, and modern Fausts in English and other languages. Later chapters will consider stage productions, music, the visual arts, and film as media in which Faust has played a decisive iconic role. Finally, there is a survey of Faust's presence in contemporary life: in folk art and design, advertising and games. A section on Faustian dichotomies in contemporary political discourse was a tempting proposition for a further chapter, and some thoughts on this were incorporated elsewhere. The successive chapter-headings impose an apparent logic on the structure of this book, but generate their own confusion, given that there is much mixing of media, resulting in imaginative if confusing interplay between the various modes and genres in which Faust's story has been told. Estanislao del Campo's hilarious poem *Fausto* is included under 'Musical Fausts', as it relates to Gounod's opera; and Ophaboom's *Faustus* appears in the chapter on stage productions, but both of these could equally well have been included among the international or literary or modern popular variants. Eisler's opera might have been included among the dramatisations, Heine's ballet, on the other hand, could claim a place among the musical treatments; both these and many other works straddle the genres in complex ways. The same is true of many of the Faust films, nowhere more so than that of Gustaf Gründgens' Hamburg production, of which the director himself claimed that it was precisely halfway between a recording of a theatre performance and a film made for cinema audiences. It thus merits discussion in both 'film' and 'theatre' sections, albeit from different viewpoints. An opera by the Czech composer Luboš Fišer, *Věčný Faust,* was composed for television and, abounding as it does in surreal effects, is closer in spirit to other Faust films, notably Jan Švankmajer's, than to opera. I hope the reader will bear with these and several other inconsistencies in my approach, all of which are symptomatic of material which eludes easy classification.

Such illogicalities may seem a small matter beside the many omissions of which the author of this undertaking has made himself guilty. The present volume does not attempt to 'cover' all aspects of the theme, but merely to open them up to further investigation within the wider context of the theme. A huge number of Fausts have had to be omitted, through ignorance on my part, lack of space, or simply because information on them has been hard to come by. I would have liked to say more about several recent films, including the grimly futuristic *Fausto 5.0* by Isidro Ortiz and the Fura dels Baus team (Barcelona, 2001), which is distinguished by innovative camera-work and won awards in Sitges and Cannes. Ion Popescu-Gopo's *Faust* has proved impossible to locate. The same goes for many of the operas that have been based on the theme. Texts, too, have shifted in and out of print with the passing of years. All I have been able to provide were, in many cases, tantalising glimpses of a rich seam of creativity.

There was one area in which I found a huge surplus: English translations of Goethe's masterpiece. From the 1820s to the present day, this text has attracted several hundred translators of widely varying levels of competence, in prose, verse and, also, all too often in doggerel. Lina Baumann's dissertation of 1907 discusses thirty-five, although by 1885 more than fifty had been published. Every major publisher appears to have commissioned a new English *Faust*, so that, like Buridan's donkey, I felt unable to select the one that was just right for my purpose. Modern translators have been known to use trendy-sounding prose for the purpose, which entirely destroys the flavour of the original and only partly preserves its significance; older attempts often result in a quaintly antique pseudo-Shakespearian idiom, whose uncomfortable linguistic contortions raise too many smiles to be taken seriously. Whether my reluctant decision to try my luck with a version of my own manufacture has been any more successful is very doubtful. In this, I strove to provide a readable text that followed the original rhymes, rhythms and diction as closely as possible. Goethe is both extremely difficult and surprisingly easy to translate. His puns are rarely complex or obscure, but many words, beginning with the name of 'Faust', have double meanings and special uses. On the other hand, this poet is quite happy to use 'impure' rhymes, colloquialisms and dialect, and metrical imperfections are among the tools of his trade, as he strove to recreate the imperfect, 'woodcut' effect of sixteenth-century poetry which has a decidedly homespun feel to it. All other translations are mine, unless specifically acknowledged.

There is one area of activity that is bypassed in this volume. The book deliberately ignores the prolific 'Faust industry' as nurtured by academia over the past two centuries. Its findings have helped to corroborate or dismiss many opinions held by lay people, as frequent references within my text will demonstrate, but no attempt will be made to survey the vast swathes of books, articles, conference papers and the like, all of which attempt to cast light on the Faust phenomenon through the familiar strategies of interpretation and criticism. The icon of Faust must come first and stand alone, and it is thus with primary material in mind rather than with the products critical endeavour of that I offer this survey.

OSMAN DURRANI,
Canterbury, UK,
September 2004

Cited Works

Lina Baumann, *Die englischen Faustübersetzungen*. PhD Dissertation, Halle, 1907.

E[liza] M. Butler, *The Myth of the Magus*. Cambridge: University Press, 1948.

Ulrich Gaier, *Goethes Faust-Dichtungen. Ein Kommentar. Urfaust*. Stuttgart: Reclam, 1989.

William Frederic Hauhart, *The Reception of Goethe's Faust in England in the First Half of the Nineteenth Century*. New York: Columbia University Press, 1909.

Günther Mahal (ed.), *Faust-Museum Knittlingen. Exponate, Materialien, Kommentare*. Stuttgart: Paul Daxer, 1980.

Harold Meek, *Johann Faust. The Man and the Myth*. London: Oxford University Press, 1930.

Roger Shattuck, *Forbidden Knowledge. From Prometheus to Pornography*. New York: St Martin's Press, 1996.

J[ohn] W. Smeed, *Faust in Literature*. London: Oxford University Press, 1975.

Acknowledgements

T HE PRESENT compilation evolved during a difficult period in my career when
time and energy were consumed by 'academic programme reviews' and
'institutional audits' at my home university, leaving proportionately less
space for research than is called for by a project of this type. Although time was
always short, a generous grant from the British Academy financed travel to
Knittlingen, Wittenberg, Leipzig, Vienna, Munich, and Calgary, all undertaken
during busy teaching periods. Staff in the many libraries I visited were extremely
helpful, and I would particularly like to record my thanks to Tim Lörke and Heike
Hamberger of the Faust-Archiv in Knittlingen for their repeated hospitality and
unflagging willingness to help; to Susanne de Ponte, Andrea Hauer and Gabriele
Jäckl of the Munich Theater-Museum for assistance in selecting and preparing
illustrations and in tracing reviews of many theatre productions; to Jürgen Weber
and Caterina Anrecht at the Herzogin Anna Amalia Bibliothek Weimar, for tracing
materials in their collections; to Apollonia Steele of Special Collections, University
of Calgary, for enabling me to access rare editions of the texts; to Susan Reed of
the British Library, London, for extending that outstanding library's already
excellent holdings of *Faustiana*, and to Susan Crabtree of the Special Collections
at the Templeman Library, University of Kent, for helping me to track down many
rare nineteenth-century playbills and early editions and manuscripts of English-
language Fausts. The Library of the Institute of Germanic Studies in London
provided further material that had proved hard to find elsewhere. Eva Leithoff of
the Wittenberg Tourist Information Office gave useful advice on local Faustian
traditions.

   I am grateful to my colleague David Ellis for initiating and facilitating the
growth of the 'Icons' series, and to many researchers for their stimulating
comments. Especially, I wish to thank Jörg Esleben of the University of Calgary
for organising the Calgary *Faustival* during April 2003, which I was privileged to
attend and from which my own project derived renewed stimulus. This was a
landmark in Faust studies, not only in terms of its high level of scholarship, but
also by virtue of its fringe events, especially the many productions of and readings
from familiar and unfamiliar versions of the Faust material. It yielded vibrant proof,

if such were required, of the iconicity of its subject in the New World as well as in the Old. Many people who attended that conference allowed themselves to be included in this survey and gave generously of their time in helping to ensure a measure of completeness which this volume would otherwise have lacked. Here I was able to meet and engage in debates with leading scholars from North America, especially Jane K. Brown of Washington State University and Arnd Bohm of Carleton University, Ottawa, and to witness the first ever production of the two parts of Goethe's *Faust* in Canada on a single day, thanks to the magnificent efforts of the Drama Department of the host university.

The Knittlingen Faust-Archiv has already been mentioned. I owe a special debt of gratitude to its staff and to the Mayor of Knittlingen for their generous hospitality on three occasions during 2002/3, and was fortunate to attend the first symposium to be held at this venue under its current management, which concentrated on Hanns Eisler's opera, *Johann Faustus*, in November 2003. Here I met Andreas Maier, Joachim Lucchesi, and other experts on the musical aspects of the legend and am grateful to them for a number of helpful comments and suggestions. Another scholar to whom I am indebted is Bernd Mahl of Tübingen, President of the International Faust Society and author of an excellent study of Faust on the German stage, who gave me permission to quote extensively from his study of theatre productions of Goethe between 1806 and 1998.

Various theatrical groups helped to extend my first-hand experience of Goethe's and Marlowe's plays, and others introduced me to new versions of the legend. These include the Fundus Marionettentheater of Dresden, the Maple Salsa Theatre of Calgary, and the Merlin's Sun Theatre of Quebec. I am grateful to Dr Olaf Bernstengel of Fundus and to Tim Gosley of Merlin's Sun for much information about their productions, and to the latter for making the as yet unpublished script of *Faust through the Shadows* available to me. The work of Barry Yzereef (director) and Brian Smith (mask coach) of the University of Calgary's Drama Department was instrumental in ensuring the success of the above-mentioned staging of *Faust I* and *II*, as was the input of a cast too numerous to mention; Jamie Konchak's outstanding Mephistopheles must suffice for the labours of many. I also owe a big debt to Howard Gayton of the Ophaboom Theatre Company for supplying me with much information about their *Faustus*, to Mark Irwin of the Citizens' Theatre, Glasgow, as well as to Moray McGowan, for information relating to the Glasgow production of *Faust I* and *II* in 1986, to Maria Adriana Verdaasdonk of 66b/cell in Tokyo, and to Ulrike Mahr, who has for many years played the role of Mephisto in the outdoor theatre at Kronach. Another performing artist whom I wish to thank for supplying me with information about his work is Granville Taylor, who toured the world for many years as an illusionist working under the name of Faust.

Mike Jones was extremely helpful in providing me with a rare copy of his film *The Adventure of Faustus Bidgood* and I am grateful to him for this and for sending me some critical evaluations of and images from the film. Michael Billington, theatre critic of *The Guardian*, kindly made his reviews available to me. For this I thank him and his newspaper. Dr Nicholas Gevers of *Infinity Plus* also helped in various ways, and I thank him for permission to include a portion of his interview with Michael Swanwick that was concerned with the novel *Jack Faust*.

I was given assistance by several contemporary painters, and am particularly grateful to those who permitted their work to be included here. Jens Rusch and Heinz Zander kindly permitted me to reproduce material from their cycles, Beate Musch welcomed me to her gallery in Göppingen and generously made the work of her late mother, Margret Hofheinz-Döring, available to me. Dr Rudolf Volz, who has spent many years working on his two rock operas *Faust I* (1997) and *Faust II* (2002), showed great interest in this project and provided illustrations and recordings. My thanks also go to 'Flix' for permission to include a cover illustration in the volume.

Closer to home, I received help, advice and encouragement from Julian Preece, John Flower, Martina Lauster, Frank Finlay and many others. I was privileged to meet the creative artists who exhibited their work in the recent 'Doctor Faustus' exhibition in The Gallery in The Friars, Canterbury, in October 2003, and wish to record my admiration for Neville Pundole who provided the venue and organised this timely event, and to Felix Zakar, Ros and Roger Cockram, Clive Soord, Avis Murray and all the other contributors who shared their experiences of the Faust myth with me and gave permission for samples of their work to be reproduced in this volume. A special 'thank you' goes out to Derek Sellen for allowing me to reprint his short story 'Faustus and the Potters' from the exhibition catalogue in which it had originally appeared.

Last but by no means least, I should like to express my sincere thanks to Amanda Helm, my obliging publisher, to the creator and editor of the 'Icons' series, David Ellis, and to the four specialist contributors, Yoko Riley, Rolf Hellebust, Derek Katz and Paul M. Malone for their kind permission to incorporate their unpublished research papers in this volume and thus to extend its scope into several areas of interest beyond those originally envisaged. Paul's many helpful comments, not just on his own topic, deserve a special mention.

All possible care has been taken to trace ownership of copyright material and to make full acknowledgement. Listed below are details received at the time of going to press. In some cases it has not been possible to locate or even to identify the owner of copyright and Helm Information would be pleased to hear from any copyright holder not acknowledged so that appropriate arrangments can be made.

Helm Information would like to thank everyone who has provided help, information and material and in particular Yoko Riley, Rolf Hellebust, Derek Katz, Paul M. Malone and Derek Sellen for their contributions and Rudolf Volz, Michael Billington and Moray McGowan for allowing us to use their work.

We would also like to thank the following for permission to reprint the following illustrations:

The Munich Theatre Museum for permission to reprint photographs by Abisag Tüllmann: *Branko Samarowski is transformed into Mephistopheles* (no. 19) and of *Gretchen (Therese Affolter) goes the Full Monty*, Stuttgart, 1977 (no. 30). Also for Edward Grützner's *Mephisto vor und hinter den Kulissen* ('Mephisto on and off Stage') Pen and ink, 1872 (no. 61), Otto Devrient's mystery-play, 1876 (no. 22) and for *Paul Wegener as Mephistopheles*, Berlin 1909 (no. 24).

The Dulwich Picture Gallery for the portrait of Edward Alleyn, 1626 (no. 20), by Permission of the Trustees of Dulwich Picture Gallery.

Dr Bettina Clausen for two photographs from the Rosemarie Clausen Archive in the Centre for Theatre Studies, University of Hamburg: Will Quadflieg in Gustaf Gründgens' Hamburg Production, 1958 (no. 29) and of Peter Gorski's *Faust*, 1960 (no. 84).

Ruth Walz for her photograph of Faust (Bruno Ganz) and Mephistopheles (Adam Oest) arguing about the pact in Faust's study, in Peter Stein's production, Hanover 2000 (no. 31).

Dr Olaf Bernstengel for demonstrating his puppet theatre (no. 32).

Howard Gayton for supplying the photograph from the 2000 Ophaboom production of *Faustus* (no. 33).

Tim Gosley for the photograph and text of his *Faust through the Shadows*, 2003 (no. 34).

Dr Rudolf Volz for photographs from his rock opera *Faust I*, 1997 (nos 41 and 42).

To the Mayor of Knittlingen and the Faust-Archiv for the poster, *One Hundred Faces of Faust* designed by E. Peter Moosman (no. 42) and the Knittlingen Town Logo (no. 92).

Suhrkamp Verlag for the image of Rembrandt's Faust, 1639 (no. 47) and for the image 'A stout and coarse libertine, confronting the world with a satiated stare,' 1725 (no. 49).

The Stiftung Weimarer Klassik und Kunstsammlungen for Goethe's sketches of his *Prologue in Heaven* (no. 51) and his *Earth Spirit* (no. 52) and for the John de Yongh designs for Mephistopheles (no. 71).

Kehrer Verlag Heidelberg for *Faust's Study* and *Faust's First Encounter with Gretchen* by Eugène Delacriox , 1827 (nos. 57 and 58).

Heinz Zander for *Helen of Troy* from his edition of the chapbook, 1980 (no. 75).

Jens Rusch for *Walpurgis Night*, 1988 (no. 76).

Beate Musch for Margret Hofheinz-Döring's *Faust converses with the Earth Spirit*, 1969 (no. 77).

John Hansen for the photograph from his *Faust/The Lost Feminine*, 2000 (no. 78) and for the poster for the film (no. 88).

Photofest for Klaus Maria Brandauer as Höfgen in István Szabó's *Mephisto*, 1981 (no. 86).

Mike Jones for the photograph from his film *The Adventure of Faustus Bidgood* (no. 87).

Ulrike Mahr for supplying the photograph from the 1995 production of *Faust* in Kronach (no. 98).

Graville Taylor for his publicity poster (no. 108).

Roger Cockram for posing with his bowl (no. 109) and Clive Soords for the display of his Devil Jugs and sculptures (no. 110) and to Neville Pundole of The Gallery where the work was exhibited.

Oscar Zarate for his cartoon illustration from *Christopher Marlowe: Dr Faustus* (no. 113).

'Flix' for the cover of his book *Who the Fuck is Faust* © Flix/Ctm-Com GmbH, 2003 (no. 115).

We would especially like to thank Felix Zakar for allowing us to use his painting on the jacket.

Chapter One

Faust's Ancestors:
The Earliest Sources

The Faust of history, like a magnet, may unconsciously have drawn to himself the fabled adventures of earlier magicians. Trittheim's and Agrippa's feats were precedents for the evocation of Alexander's and Helen's ghosts; Simon Magus taught Faust to fly; Agrippa gave him a Dog-Familiar; Merlin also built castles; Master Vergil's Eastern adventures suggested Faust's trip to Constantinople; Zyto foreshadowed his magic meals and much of his 'leg-pulling'; and lastly Theophilus and Giles of Portugal showed him how to sign a pact with the Devil.—Harold Meek

The Myth is Born

THE QUESTION of whether to approach Doctor Faustus as a historical personality or as a literary construct has puzzled readers for centuries. The only near-contemporary biography is the original Faust Book, a *Volksbuch* ('chapbook') that was printed in Frankfurt in 1587, by which time half a century had passed since the assumed date of his death. The Faust Book is a compelling narrative that was published anonymously under the banner heading *Historia von D. Johann Fausten*. The German original consists of 68 chapters on 227 pages, and presents what purports to be the life story of a scholar who taught at the University of Wittenberg, became dissatisfied with academic learning and summoned a spirit bearing the outlandish but academic-sounding name of Mephostophilis. A pact is promptly struck between them. Its formal conditions are based on the principle of reciprocity: Mephostophilis will serve Faustus for twenty-four years precisely, and thereafter the situation will be reversed: Faustus voluntarily commits himself to serving the devil for all eternity. The imbalance of the time-scale is enough to signal to the reader that it is a monstrously unequal deal. A document is signed in the doctor's blood, and after twenty-four years of wild exploits, marked by increasing debauchery and facilitated by ready access to magic powers, Faustus dies an ignominious death, not before finding time to warn his students of the perils of following his example. It is implied that he will suffer unending misery in hell as a just recompense for his voluntary association with evil, and that the devil will have won a great victory through having corrupted a man of towering intellectual ability.

Although it is sometimes assumed that there must have been a single individual upon whose life the cautionary tale was based, current scholarship inclines to the view that literary and cultural influences played a greater part in the genesis of the Faust-myth than verifiable historical fact. Yet there are also those who claim to know precisely where Faust was born and where he died, although all such data is at variance with the Faust Book. Hans Mayer argued that because Faustus originated from peasant stock, there would have been little interest in compiling his biography while he was alive; his 'lowly rank' must be held responsible for the lack reliable data (Mayer, 10). Agreement on the origin and movements of this elusive figure will never be achieved, and besides, it seems a trifle improbable that a story as rich in extravagant details and as profound in its moral implications could have been derived from the coincidences of a single individual's life. Although there are realistic details like names of places and people, its underlying ideas are complex and reflect older traditions concerning sorcery, as well as the more recent perceptions of Christian ethics that were gaining currency in the sixteenth century. The beginnings of the Reformation coincide precisely with the appearance of Faustus in documentary sources, giving him an iconic status comparable to that of Martin Luther.

In order to appreciate the background to the legendary magician, it will be helpful to explore some ancient traditions of supernaturally assisted miracle-working. Sixteenth-century attitudes to several key issues in theology, especially the nature and power of witchcraft, the relationship between faith and remorse, and the question of grace and redemption, are relevant. This introductory survey will consider four types of source: the biblical magus, references to itinerant fortune-tellers, Lutheran theology, and the demand for devil books in the sixteenth century.

The Rise of the Magus

It is self-evident that some of the raw details of Faustus' life derive from ancient accounts of miracle-workers both good and evil. Belief in magically gifted individuals is sanctioned in many canonical writings. The Old Testament credits Solomon with supernatural powers, and in the New Testament, beside the obvious example of the Saviour, there are others who have special gifts of an inexplicable nature. The three 'Magi' are encountered early in the gospels (Matthew 2: 1–12) in their capacity as divinely guided sages; it was only with the advent of secularisation that they became known as the Three Kings for reasons that were largely political. The Greek word from which magus is derived refers not to royalty but to practitioners of oriental magic. As astrologers, they are directed by a star towards Bethlehem, where they worship the Lord with instinctive devotion before fading from history. The Bible tells of lesser figures that use supernatural talents for harmful purposes. One of these is Simon Magus, whose brief appearance (Acts of the Apostles 8: 9–24) spawned many graphic commentaries in later texts such as the fourth-century *Clementine Homilies*. He appears as a magic-working rival to the Lord in several apocryphal gospels, and much of what he promises to do is in direct imitation of Christ himself. It is for this reason that the Church identified him as 'the father of all heretics' (Irenæus in the Preface of *Against Heresies III*). Eusebius' *Ecclesiastical History* is equally outspoken. What will have particularly irked the Church Fathers is the fact that Simon had been baptised and was temporarily accepted as a member of the apostles before lapsing into major heresy. Here, too, there is a parallel with Faustus, who was not only a member of the Christian community but held the title of Doctor of Theology.

1. *The fall of Simon Magus carved by Gislebertus on Autun Cathedral, c. 1130. Apostles Peter and Paul witness the fall whilst a devil waits to claim his soul.*

Then Simon, having gone in to Nero, said: Hear, O good emperor: I am the son of God come down from heaven. Until now I have endured Peter only calling himself an apostle; but now he has doubled the evil: for Paul also himself teaches the same things, and having his mind turned against me, is said to preach along with him; in reference to whom, if thou shalt not contrive their destruction, it is very plain that thy kingdom cannot stand.

Simon said: I wonder, O good emperor, that you reckon this man of any consequence – a man uneducated, a fisherman of the poorest, and endowed with power neither in word nor by rank. But, that I may not long endure him as an enemy, I shall forthwith order my angels to come and avenge me upon him. Peter said: I am not afraid of thy angels; but they shall be much more afraid of me in the power and trust of my Lord Jesus Christ, whom thou falsely declarest thyself to be.

Nero said: Art thou not afraid, Peter, of Simon, who confirms his godhead by deeds? Peter said: Godhead is in Him who searcheth the hidden things of the heart.

Now then, tell me what I am thinking about, or what I am doing. I disclose to thy servants who are here what my thought is, before he tells lies about it, in order that he may not dare to lie as to what I am thinking about. Nero said: Come hither, and tell me what thou art thinking about. Peter said: Order a barley loaf to be brought, and to be given to me secretly. And when he ordered it to be brought, and secretly given to Peter, Peter said: Now tell us, Simon, what has been thought about, or what said, or what done.

Nero said: Do you mean me to believe that Simon does not know these things, who both raised a dead man, and presented himself on the third day after he had been beheaded, and who has done whatever he said he would do? Peter said: But he did not do it before me. Nero said: But he did all these before me. For assuredly he ordered angels to come to him, and they came. Peter said: If he has done what is very great, why does he not do what is very small? Let him tell what I had in my mind, and what I have done. Nero said: Between you, I do not know myself. Simon said: Let Peter say what I am thinking of, or what I am doing. Peter said: What Simon has in his mind I shall show that I know, by my doing what he is thinking about. Simon said: Know this, O emperor, that no one knows the thoughts of men, but God alone. Is not, therefore, Peter lying? Peter said: Do thou, then, who sayest that thou art the Son of God, tell what I have in my mind; disclose, if thou canst, what I have just done in secret. For Peter, having blessed the barley loaf which he had received, and having broken it with his right hand and his left, had heaped it up in his sleeves. Then Simon, enraged that he was not able to tell the secret of the apostle, cried out, saying: Let great dogs come forth and eat him up before Caesar. And suddenly there appeared great dogs, and rushed at Peter. But Peter, stretching forth his hands to pray, showed to the dogs the loaf which he had blessed; which the dogs seeing, no longer appeared. Then Peter said to Nero: Behold, I have shown thee that I knew what Simon was thinking of, not by words, but by deeds; for he, having promised that he would bring angels against me, has brought dogs, in order that he might show that he had not god-like but dog-like angels.

Simon said: Dost thou believe, O good emperor, that I who was dead, and rose again, am a magician? For it had been brought about by his own cleverness that the unbelieving Simon had said to Nero: Order me to be beheaded in a dark place, and there to be left slain; and if I do not rise on the third day, know that I am a magician; but if I rise again, know that I am the Son of God.

And Nero having ordered this, in the dark, by his magic art he managed that a ram should be beheaded. And for so long did the ram appear to be Simon until he was beheaded. And when he had been beheaded in the dark, he that had beheaded him, taking the head, found it to be that of a ram; but he would not say anything to the emperor, lest he should scourge him, having ordered this to be done in secret. Thereafter, accordingly, Simon said that he had risen on the third day, because he took away the head of the ram and the limbs – but the blood had been there congealed – and on the third day he showed himself to Nero, and said: Cause to be wiped away my blood that has been poured out; for, behold, having been beheaded, as I promised, I have risen again on the third day (*Acts of the Holy Apostles Peter and Paul*, Palmer/More, 30–2).

Several features in this passage are so closely linked to the Faust tradition that Simon Magus is sometimes seen as its 'actual originator' (Kahler, 79). Not only does he usurp the Lord's role as a miracle-worker, but he also portrays himself as a sage and scholar, deriding the simplicity of St Peter, 'a man uneducated, a fisherman of the poorest, and endowed with power neither in word nor by rank'.

He anticipates the arrogant doctor who claims to know more than the common man and repeatedly mocks and deludes ordinary peasants and tradesmen. Simon's magic is also shown to be bogus, as in the trick with the beheaded ram. On other occasions it is reliant on low forms of nature, such as the wild dogs in the cited passage. Faustus was also rumoured to be accompanied by a ferocious dog that was in some ways instrumental in assisting its master to perform his deeds. Simon Magus is specifically mentioned in chapter 52 of the Faust Book, as if the author wanted to stress the parallels.

A far larger body of writings arose during the Middle Ages in support of a more benign form of magic. This incorporates the lives of the Church Fathers and saints who came to be venerated across Europe not merely for their inherent goodness but also for the inexplicable deeds that they were able to perform. Many had knowledge of evil as well as good, either through visions and temptations or by having lived through a period of debauchery and heresy before conversion.

One of the saints whose name has been linked with that of Faustus is Cyprian of Antioch, believed to have been martyred in 280 AD. The importance of this figure as an antecedent of Faustus has long been acknowledged: 'From the sixteenth century [Cyprian] bears the name of Faust and will continue to do so' (Zahn, 132). Cyprian's life falls, like that of many saints, into two halves: a pre- and a post-conversion phase. In the following passage, the devils struggle to do his bidding, but ultimately fail to satisfy him as their powers desert them. There is evidence of a hierarchy in which the lower and less successful devils are weak and prone to fail when confronted with virtue. They resort to ruses such as disguises, but the keen-eyed magician is able to see through their ploys. The magic routines turn out to have two sources, as they do in the Faust Book, involving a mixture of the inexplicable and of elementary conjuring. Cyprian is, in the end, wise enough to identify the devil's involvement. The following passage presents a catalogue of failures, and eventually the most powerful of demons is obliged to admit that he can achieve nothing in the presence of the Crucified One.

Cyprian had been a magician from childhood: when he was seven years old, his parents consecrated him to the devil. He practised the arts of magic, often being seen to change women into beasts of burden and performing many other marvels. He became enamoured of Justina, and put his magic to work in order to have her for himself or for a man named Acladius, who also lusted after her. He therefore invoked the demon to come to him and enable him to win the virgin. The demon came and asked him: 'Why did you call me?' Cyprian answered: 'I love a maiden who is of the Galilean sect. Can you make it possible for me to have her and work my will with her?' The demon: 'I was able to throw man out of paradise, I induced Cain to kill his brother, I caused the Jews to put Christ to death; I have brought every kind of disorder among men! How could I not be able to let you have one mere girl and do what you please with her? Take this lotion and sprinkle it around the outside of her house, and I will come and set her heart afire with love for you, and compel her to consent to you.'

The following night the demon came to Justina and tried to awaken an illicit love in her heart. Sensing what was happening, she devoutly commended herself to the Lord and covered her whole body with the sign of the cross. Seeing that sign, the devil fled in terror and went and stood before Cyprian. 'Why haven't you brought that maiden to me?' Cyprian asked. 'I saw a certain sign on her,' the demon answered, 'and I weakened and all power left me.' Cyprian dismissed that demon and called for a stronger one. This one told Cyprian: 'I heard your orders and I saw why that other could do nothing, but I will do better and will carry out your will. I will go to her and wound her heart with lustful love, and you will enjoy her as you wish to.' So the devil went to Justina and did his best to win her over and inflame her soul with sinful desire. But Justina again devoutly commended herself to God and dispelled all temptation with the sign of the cross, then blew upon the devil and drove him away. The spirit departed in confusion and fled to Cyprian. Cyprian: 'Where is the virgin I sent you after?' The demon: 'I admit I'm beaten, and I'm afraid to say how! I saw a certain terrible sign on her and at once lost all my strength!'

Cyprian scoffed at him and sent him away. Then he summoned the prince of demons and, when he came, said to him: 'What is this power of yours that's so low that a mere girl can overcome it?' Said the devil: 'I will visit her and disturb her with various fevers. I will inflame her spirit with hotter passion and spread hot spasms throughout her body. I'll get her in a frenzy and put fearful phantasms before her eyes. And in the middle of the night I will bring her to you.'

Then the devil gave himself the appearance of a young woman and went to Justina, saying: 'I come to you because I want to live in chastity with you; but tell me, I beg of you, what will be the reward of our effort?' The holy virgin answered: 'The reward is great, the labour light.' 'Then,' said the devil, 'what about God's command to increase and multiply and fill the earth? I fear, my good friend, that if we persist in virginity, we shall nullify God's word. By being disdainful and disobedient we shall bring grievous judgment upon ourselves, and while we expected a reward, we will incur torment!' The virgin began to have serious doubts, induced by the devil, and she felt more strongly stirred by the heat of concupiscence, so much so that she rose and was on the verge of going out. But then she came to herself and recognised who it was that was speaking to her, so she shielded herself with the sign of the cross, then blew on the devil, causing him to melt like a candle. Thereupon she felt herself freed of all temptation. [...]

Now the devil, seeing that he was making no headway, changed himself to look like Justina in order to besmirch her good name, and deceived Cyprian, boasting that he would bring Justina to him. Then, but this time looking like the virgin, he came running to Cyprian as if languishing with love for him and wanting to kiss him. Cyprian, thinking of course that it was Justina, was overwhelmed with joy and said: 'Welcome, Justina, loveliest of women!' But the minute he pronounced the name of Justina, the devil could not bear it and vanished in a puff of smoke. [...]

All these apparitions, of course, were nothing but devilish artifices, and none of them served the devil's purpose; so, defeated and confused, he went back and stood before Cyprian. Cyprian said to him: 'So you too are beaten? What kind of power do you have, you wretch, that you can't overcome a simple girl or have any control over her? To the contrary, she defeats all of you and lays you low! But tell me one thing, I beg of you: where does her greatest strength come from?' The demon answered: 'If you will swear never to desert me, I will reveal to you the power behind her victory.' Cyprian: 'What shall I swear by?' The demon: 'Swear to me by my great powers that you will never desert me!' Cyprian: 'By your great powers I swear to you that I will never desert you.'

Now the devil, being reassured, told Cyprian, 'That young woman made the sign of the cross, and at once all my strength ebbed away. I could do nothing, and like wax melting at a fire I melted away.' Cyprian: 'Therefore the Crucified is greater than you?' The demon: 'Greater than all! And all of us and all those we deceive he turns over to be tormented in the fire that never dies out!' Cyprian: 'Therefore I too should become a friend of the Crucified, so as not to incur so awful a punishment!' The devil: 'You swore to me by the power of my army, by which no one can swear falsely, that you would never desert me!' Cyprian answered, 'I despise you and all your devils, and I arm myself with the saving sign of the Crucified!' Instantly the devil fled in confusion. (Voragine, II, 192–5)

The Golden Legend is the dominant text in western hagiographical literature and is renowned for its influential depictions of saintliness and of temptation. Jacobus de Voragine, Archbishop of Genoa, compiled it between about 1260 and 1275. From 1470 to 1530 it was the most frequently reprinted book and its content was well known to sixteenth-century authors. It is a source for the miracles as well as for the gruesome death of Faustus (Meek, 152f; Allen, 588–92). Cyprian begins as a lecher but then takes the devils to task for their inadequacy and by a process of interrogation gains vital information about the supremacy of Christ. The temptation of the Christian Justina is explicitly sanctioned by God. In many subsequent versions of the Faustus myth, the learned doctor questions his demons about heaven and hell in similar fashion, and is given no less earnest warnings regarding the perilous path he is embarked upon. The differences are significant. Faustus is willing to be satisfied by some of the transient sweeteners which his tempter obtains for his delectation, his arrogance is such that he becomes inured to any threats that are put to him, and, unlike the saints whose stories often take a similar course at the outset, he perseveres and does not relent. Rather than merely swearing allegiance to the devil, Faust must sign a pact in his own blood. It is his blindness in the face of grave danger that makes him a tragic rather than a pathetic figure. This, too, is a literary quality which points to a background in tradition rather than in life. The story was a major source not only for successive Fausts, but also, more immediately, for Pedro Calderón's seventeenth-century play *El mágico prodigioso* (Spivack, 943).

A third, no less significant antecedent to Faustus from religious tradition is the penitent sinner Saint Theophilus of Adana, whose life story is loosely associated with the cult of the Virgin Mary. Theophilus remained a popular figure until the early sixteenth century. His biography was composed in Greek at some point between 650 and 850 AD, and there were, by the end of the Middle Ages, more than 25 distinct versions in Latin alone, of which that in *The Golden Legend* was more than sufficient to ensure wide knowledge of the material (Palmer/More 58 f.). The life of Theophilus exemplifies the fragility of human nature. Even men of sound character who have been practising virtue from their earliest days are vulnerable. After serving as the old bishop's steward, Theophilus is dismissed when the latter dies and is replaced by the new incumbent.

Then after the bishop was ordained and they had returned to their own city, certain of the clergy urged that Theophilus be removed from his office and that the bishop ordain a new steward. When this was done Theophilus, having retired from his former office, took care of his own house only. Therefore the cunning enemy and envious foe of the human race, seeing this man living modestly and passing the time in good deeds, made his heart to beat with perverse thoughts, instilling into him jealousy of the steward's power and the desire of honour, and inclined him toward such abominable and wicked counsels that he sought not for divine but human glory and strove for vain and transitory honour more than divine – so much so that he even demanded the aid of sorcerers.

Now there was in that city a certain wicked Jew, a practitioner of all sorts of diabolical arts, who had already plunged many into the deep pit of perdition by his unchristian counsels. And the wretched steward, incited by vain glory, fell to turning over in his mind confusedly the lust of this world and was consumed by the desire of honour. So with all haste he proceeded by night to the aforesaid Jew and, knocking at the door, sought admission. Then the Jew, hateful to God, seeing him thus broken, called him into the house and said to him: 'Why hast thou come to me?' And Theophilus ran up and threw himself at his feet and answered: 'I beseech thee to aid me, for my bishop has disgraced me and has wrought this against me.' The detestable Jew replied: 'Come to me tomorrow evening at this hour and I will lead thee to my master and he will help thee in that thou hast desired.' Hearing this the vicar was rejoiced and did as he was told, going to him in the middle of the night. And in truth the wicked Jew did lead him to the Circus of the city and said to him: 'Whatsoever thou seest or whatsoever sound thou hearest, be not afraid and do not make the sign of the cross.' After Theophilus on his part had promised this, the Jew showed him suddenly creatures clad in white robes, with a multitude of candlesticks, uttering loud cries, and, seated in their midst, the prince. It was the devil and his minions. The hapless Jew, holding the steward by the hand, led him to this infamous assembly. And the devil said to him: 'Why hast thou brought this man to us?' He replied: 'My master, I have brought him because he has been falsely judged by his bishop and has asked for thy help.' The devil then said: 'How shall I give help to him, a man serving his God? But if he will be my servant and be counted among our hosts, I will aid him so that he may do more than before and rule over all, even the bishop.' And the perverted Jew said to the wretched steward: 'Didst thou hear what he hath said to thee?' And he replied: 'I have heard and whatsoever he shall say to me, I will do so long as he helps me.' And he began to kiss the feet of the prince and to implore him. The devil said to the Jew: 'Let him deny the son of Mary and those things which are offensive to me, and let him set down in writing that he denieth absolutely, and whatsoever he may desire he shall obtain from me, so long as he denieth.' Then Satan entered into the steward and he replied: 'I deny Christ and His mother.' And making a written statement and putting wax on it, he sealed it with his own ring and the two went away rejoicing greatly at his perdition. [...]

And when he had remained a short time in such vanity and in the deep pit of denial, God, the Creator of all and our Redeemer, who doth not desire the death of sinners but rather their conversion and life, mindful of his former way of living and in what manner he had served God's holy church, and that he had ministered abundantly to the widows, the orphans and the needy, did not despise His creature but granted him the conversion of repentance. And having turned away in his heart from such arrogance and denial and having regained a state of sober-mindedness, he began to humble his spirit and to be troubled by the things which he had done and he devoted himself to fasting, prayers, and vigils, – reflecting on many things and seeing himself cheated of salvation, meditating on the torments of eternal fire and the fire that is not quenched and the passing of the soul, the gnashing of teeth and the worm that dieth not. Turning over all these things in his mind, with fearful apprehension, groaning and with bitter tears he said: 'Oh miserable wretch that I am, what have I done and what have I wrought? Whither shall I turn now, I who am laden with luxury, in order that I may make my soul safe? Where shall I, unhappy sinner, go, I who have denied my Christ and His holy mother and have made myself a servant of the devil through an impious pact in my own handwriting? Who, thinkest thou, will be able to retrieve that from the hand of the destroyer, the devil, and succour me? Why did I have to become acquainted with that vilest of Jews who should be burned? – For this same Jew had been condemned a short time before by law and judge. – Why indeed? Thus they are rewarded, who forsake our Lord and Master and follow after the devil. For what did it profit me, the temporal advantage and the vain arrogance of this world? Woe to me wretch, in what manner have I lost the light and entered into darkness? I was well off, when I had retired to the management of mine own affairs. Why have I sought for the sake of vain glory and empty fame to consign my wretched soul to Gehenna? What aid shall I pray for, who am cheated of aid by the devil? I, who am guilty of this thing, I am the cause of my soul's perdition, the betrayer of my salvation. Woe to me, in what manner I am carried off I do not know. Woe to me, what shall I do? To whom shall I go? What shall I reply on the Day of Judgment when all shall be naked and open? What shall I say in that hour when the just will be crowned while I will be condemned? And with what assurance shall I stand before that royal and awful tribunal? Whom shall I implore? Whom shall I entreat in that tribulation? Or on whom may I call in that hour of need, when all are concerned with their own affairs and not those of others? Who will pity me? Who will aid me? Who will protect me? Who will be my patron? Verily no one. There no one helps but all render an account for themselves. Woe to my wretched soul! By what means hast thou been enslaved? How hast thou been cast down? In what way alienated and shaken? By what sort of ruin art thou fallen?' (Palmer/More, 61–5)

Theophilus is tempted by the 'cunning enemy and envious foe of the human race', assisted by a Jew who leads Christian men astray. This intermediary takes him into the presence of the devil in a setting that could be mistaken for the Eucharist ('creatures clad in white robes, with a multitude of candlesticks'). The erstwhile steward is promised power over men, if he agrees to become the devil's servant. The relationship between the two is characterised by the same paradox that informs the Faust legend: Theophilus must serve the devil in order to be served by him. This pact, which disguises itself as an inversion of the baptismal contract, is concluded in writing and sealed in the manner of a legal document. In some versions of the *Golden Legend*, Theophilus signs his contract in his own blood, a detail that appears to have entered the legend in the thirteenth century (Palmer/More, 76, n10).

The story does not end here. It is typical of the mediaeval approach to sin that man is accorded assistance by God to recognise his error and repent. Theophilus may reap temporary benefits but cannot enjoy the fruits of his apostasy; he is wracked by feelings of guilt and is helped by divine intervention to acknowledge his sin. As so often in mediaeval miraculous literature, the outcome is a triumph of virtue over temporary aberration; there are parallels in the story of Giles of Portugal, Proterius (from the *Life of Basil*), Mary of Antioch and elsewhere (Zahn, 14).

The legend of Theophilus merged into that of Faustus, so much so that the name Mephistopheles may be an antithetical formulation ('No Friend of Light' as opposed to 'Friend of God'). But there is one crucial difference: the seeds of evil do not wither in the face of good but seize hold of Faustus' soul. The *Golden Legend* assumes that God 'doth not desire the death of sinners, but rather their conversion and life' (Palmer/More, 64). God was soon to become sterner, less willing to forgive. By the sixteenth century when Faustus makes his début, the intellectual climate had changed in several key respects. The factors behind this transition range from the impact of the Black Death to the influence of the heretical movements such as that of the Cathars. By the time of Martin Luther, the view was gaining ground that man had to work harder for his salvation than had been assumed in the Middle Ages.

The most telling evidence of this new pessimism is the fact that the Faust Book's author can dwell to a much greater extent on the sinner's wickedness. Faustus seeks contact with the devil directly, needing no intermediary. The narrator multiplies his arrogant and nefarious exploits, only to refuse him the opportunity to confess and be saved. Or rather, the opportunity is dangled in tantalising fashion before the deluded sinner, and we see him struggling to grasp it, but a stronger, more malign force is at work that prevents him from recognising the lifeline. These two details reveal the innovatory approach of an author describing a man unable in his blindness to find the way out of a self-inflicted dilemma. This despite being gifted with the mind of a scholar and having recourse to all branches of knowledge available to the best-educated men of the day. Another important aspect of Faustus' entrapment is the signed pact. This written document closes off the escape route that Theophilus' oath had left open.

The pact with the devil is perhaps the most distinctive development of the plot, and it is a detail characteristic of the post-mediaeval approach to sin. Man is no longer free to say one thing and do another; his promises, even to the devil, are binding. This for two reasons: society's increasingly codified and ritualised legal system in which a man's spoken word is subordinate to his written pledge, and a changing view of evil as an independent force that is stronger than the transient absence of good. The story of *Doctor Faustus* builds on and reverses the earlier narratives in which the devil complains about the fickleness of sinners who turn to him in their need but abandon him as soon as their wishes have been granted. As the devil emerges from his mediaeval torpor to become as wily as his victims, he can and will demand a solemn written denial of the Christian faith that will be binding up to the hour of their death.

The mediaeval morality theatre is an abundant source of dramatic plots involving sinners and their contacts with the powers of hell. The plays are complemented by legends such as those considered above and, increasingly, by prose and verse narratives about sinners and penitents written for entertainment and edification. The differences between these and the Faustian material are substantial. They demarcate the world of late mediaeval Catholic Christianity with its acceptance of aberration from the uncompromising Lutheran view that was to gain ground during the sixteenth century. A typical character of this type, sometimes seen as a kind of female Faustus, is Mary of Nijmegen, or Nemmegen, whose story was first printed in Antwerp in or around 1518 and circulated both in Dutch and in English.

24

> Having been ill-treated by a cruel aunt, Mary calls out that she cares not 'whether ye dyuell or god come to me and helpe me I kare nat whether of them two it be'. The Devil, in the guise of a young man, offers his services, introduces himself as 'a master of many scyances' and promises to teach her these sciences if she will be his paramour. She is also requested to give up her name, Mary, but refuses to do this. She is allowed to keep part of her name and is now known as 'Emmekyn' ('Mariken' in Dutch). She learns many secret arts, and murders are committed on her account. Yet she never loses sight of eternity, and after seven years she returns to Nijmegen on the day of Our Lady's procession and recognises her sinfulness. The devil tries but fails to break her neck, and she confesses her sins to the Pope, who gives her a heavy penance. She has to wear three iron rings around her neck, but after two years, these fall away as a sign of God's forgiveness. (Summarised from De Bruyn, 5-7; see also Barnouw, 69-84)

Here, too, are some remarkable similarities with the Faust legend. Mary and Faustus are both tempted by the promise of knowledge ('scyance'), yet both move quickly away from pursuing wisdom to indulging their sensuality and performing their rudimentary tricks. Faustus may well ask for a book of spells and incantations so that he may raise up spirits as he pleases, yet this aspiration quickly yields to voluptuousness, just as Mary's desire for learning gives way to the no less strong urge to flatter her vanity. The Faust tradition arose as a subversion of those mediaeval sources in which sinners were depicted in pursuit of forbidden knowledge, only to be saved by a mixture of grace and self-recognition, not least with the assistance of the Virgin Mary (De Bruyn, 12).

An Itinerant Fortune-Teller

The story of Faustus is rooted in a climate of transition from naïve faith in redemption to increasing focus on sinfulness that required hard work if it was to be overcome. In these turbulent times, the legendary doctor's life cannot be satisfactorily mapped or reconstructed. His itinerary is a confusing one that criss-crosses Germany and resembles that of a travelling huckster, fortune-teller and lowly apothecary. Many scholars have attempted to inquire into his biography and examine the possibility that there may be specific and verifiable events at the root of the tradition. Could there have been a single individual on whom the Faust legend was largely or exclusively based? This is an intriguing question that has been answered in many different ways; Hans Henning's bibliography lists 183 articles and books purporting to give information about the historical figure. Two groups of scholars believe that Faust's identity can be pinned down: those who follow Günther Mahal in locating his birthplace in the south-western town of Knittlingen in 1480, and those who, with Frank Baron, take it to have been Helmstadt near Heidelberg some fifteen years earlier. The name of Knittlingen, sometimes spelt 'Kundling', occurs in manuscripts by Johann Mennel [also Manlius] and Johann Wier [also Wierus, Piscinarius], as well as in Philip Melanchthon's table-talk; these date from the 1560s (Meek, 36-40). By contrast, the literary Faust Book has him see the light of the world in the eastern province

2. Statue of Faust in Knittlingen by Hanne Schorp-Pflumm, 1954.
Photograph by Osman Durrani

of Saxony, but without hinting at his dates. It is probable that stories about many different savants and magicians, including Johannes Tritheim, Georg Helmstetter, and Cornelius Agrippa, had some effect on the content of the later chapbook. One critic actually suggests that they must have been a team or a family business, a hypothesis that neatly gets round the two names (Johann and Georg) and incompatible dates. That there were father-and-son teams of this type operating in the field of 'alternative therapy' is easily proven (Peukert, 55–74).

If there was a single Faustus, this person must have been widely travelled and have laid claim to an array of different skills, given the contradictory material that has been recorded. The sixteenth-century documents that refer to him vary in scope and reliability. To judge by the picture they convey, one or several figures were touring Europe under the name of 'Faustus' between 1500 and 1540. It has proved impossible to pin him down to a single individual with a recognisable biography. He is 'the classic outsider, rootless, a will o' the wisp, passing, like Socrates and Jesus Christ, without a personally written legacy to assert his true identity' (Jones, 3). All the evidence we have is in the form of isolated snippets, *Faustsplitter* or 'splinters'. The incomplete and contradictory records were first collected in large numbers by Alexander Tille in a compilation entitled *Die Faustsplitter in der Literatur des sechzehnten bis achtzehnten Jahrhunderts* ('The Faust fragments in the literature of

3. According to the chapbook and the Wolfenbüttel manuscript, Faust was born in Roda near Weimar. His supposed birthplace was demolished in the early twentieth century.
Photo: Leipziger Illustrierte Zeitung, 26 December 1896.

the sixteenth to eighteenth century'), a portion of which was translated into English by Philip Palmer and Robert More. The 'evidence' that is advanced by several German towns (Simmern, Heidelberg, Knittlingen, Roda, Wittenberg, Leipzig, Staufen) that they were the magician's birthplace or temporary domicile must remain suspect, though later authorities have used such contradictory data to provide a stimulus to the local tourist industry. A largish number of locations (Nuremberg, Ingolstadt, Erfurt, Bad Kreuznach, Gelnhausen, Rebdorf) rely on manuscript references to support their claims to have been visited by him. An association with the University of Heidelberg, where one 'Georg Faust' matriculated in 1505, is unreliable. The name was entered in the records, but there is nothing to suggest that this individual was identical with the magician. The literary text on which later Faust traditions are based gives a birthplace (Roda) and names a university (Wittenberg), yet there are no references in the chronicles of either to the magician's birth or employment there. Marlowe turns Roda into 'Rhodes', which led Victor Hugo to assume the Mediterranean island to have been his birthplace (Meek, 63).

What remains is a multitude of short, strangely unconnected and incompatible statements that provide tantalising glimpses of an itinerant charlatan's reception in various German towns, castles and monasteries. Baron regards eight of these as authentic, Mahal seven; both scholars use them to support conflicting theories as to the man's provenance. Yet ultimately, 'There can be no coherent biography of the historical Faust. The image we have of him is a colourful mosaic, patched together from the incidental and sharply contradictory statements of his contemporaries. Here, it often happens that legend and reality are closely inter-twined' (Reske, 10). It is a short step to the contention, first put forward in 1808 by Joseph Görres and later taken up by Friedrich Engels, that the Faust stories were the invention of the common people, the *Volk*, and that the chapbook (*Volksbuch* or 'folk-book') was like a folksong in that it had no individual author. Just as in Britain stories about various outlaws were assimilated into the 'iconic' figure of Robin Hood, Faust has a stereotypical dimension that shows the influence of magicians and tricksters like Friar Bacon and Till Eulenspiegel. What is clear is that, from its inception, the legend incorporates many incongruous beliefs and prejudices typical of the age through a kind of 'montage technique' (Baron (1989), 13f; Burke, 171; Allen, 583). It also shows how people imagined progress to be achievable by diabolical intervention. In the following extract, we have two examples of such 'magical' powers:

> When Dr Faust was based in Heilbronn, performing his unedifying arts throughout the region, he often went to Boxberg Castle, where he was always treated as an honoured guest.
> One cold winter's day, when he was strolling with the lords and ladies along the garden paths on the east side of the castle and the ladies began complaining about the frost, he immediately caused the sun to shine warmly, the snow-covered ground to turn green, and a mass of violets and all kinds of pretty flowers to emerge from the soil. Then he commanded the trees to blossom, and – in accordance with the wishes of the group – apples, plums, peaches, and other noble fruits ripened on the branches. Finally he caused vines to grow and bear grapes, and invited each of his companions to cut off a grape, but not before he gave them the sign to do so. When all of them were ready to start cutting, he removed the deception from their eyes, and everyone recognised that he was holding a knife beside his companion's nose. The area where this took place has been known ever since as 'the violet garden'.
> Another time Faust set off from Boxberg Castle at a quarter past eleven with the intention of reaching a banquet in Heilbronn at precisely the last strike of twelve o'clock. He got into a carriage drawn by four black horses and drove like the wind, and he did indeed arrive in Heilbronn punctually at the strike of twelve. A man working in a field saw how spirits with horns on their heads paved the way for his carriage, while others pulled up the paving stones behind it and removed them, so that no trace of this type of paving would remain. (Based on an oral tradition; Schnezler, II, 613f.)

The magic is explained in two different ways, firstly as an optical illusion, and secondly, as the accelerated work of a team of slave-like demons. The production of summer fruits out of season recurs in many accounts of Faustus. In Christopher Marlowe's play, the fruits are produced not through deception, but through the work of devils who are able to fly round the world and obtain goods from places where it is summer rather than winter, much as happens today thanks to the air-freight system (*Doctor Faustus*, 'A' Text, scene 11, lines 19–24). The other example of an innovation, a journey from Boxberg to Heilbronn in three quarters of an hour, could also be achieved within the same time-span today with the help of a paved road. In those days, that would have required the unimaginably vast resource of literally millions of cobblestones. So the author imagined, instead, a supernatural force that would lay cobbles with lightning speed and then dig them up again as soon as they had been passed over by a stagecoach – a fittingly diabolical, if frustrating, labour.

4. Doctor Faust's Gässchen ('Alleyway') in Erfurt. Photograph by W. Lorenz in Franz Neubert, Vom Doktor Faustus, *1932, 13*

The renowned Dr Faust lived in Erfurt among other places. He lived in Michelsgasse next to the great College. As a learned professor, he had permission from the academic senate to lecture on Greek poets in the main hall of the College Building. Here he explained Homer to his student audience, describing the heroic figures of the *Iliad* and the *Odyssey* so vividly that the students expressed a desire to see them with their own eyes. This he did by conjuring them up from the underworld, but when the students saw the mighty giant Polyphemus, they all became terrified and wanted to see or hear nothing more from him.

He drove two horses through the narrowest alley in Erfurt with a load of hay, for which reason this street has ever since been called 'Doctor Faust's Alleyway.' Once he came riding a horse that ate and ate and could never be satisfied. Another time he might produce all kinds of wine from a wooden table or make the inebriated company think that they saw grapes, which they would attempt to cut from the vine, but when he put a stop to their hallucinations, each one had someone else's nose between his fingers instead of grapes. A house in Schössergasse is still said to have a gap in the roof that can never be closed with tiles because Faust used to fly out of it on his magic cloak. He is said to have created a magnificent garden in midwinter and provided delicious meals for numerous noble guests, which greatly enhanced his reputation. Soon people in Erfurt were talking of nothing but Dr Faust, and it was feared that too many people would be vulnerable to his devilish arts. Thus a learned monk by the name of Dr Klinge was sent to convert him. But Faust did not want to be converted and in response to the monk's offer to say masses and prayers designed to tear him away from the devil, Dr Faust said, 'No, my dear Dr Klinge, it would be churlish of me to break the contract that I signed with my blood. That would be dishonest. The devil has kept the promises he made to me, and I intend to observe my part of the bargain.'

'Then get thee to the devil, thou accursed conspirator, thou morsel of meat ready for roasting by the devil!' cried the monk in anger. 'Go to the eternal fires that have been prepared for the devil and his fallen angels!' Then the monk ran to worshipful Rector and reported to him that Dr Faustus was an utterly incorrigible sinner. Faust was thereafter banished from the city, and it is said that no sorcerer has ever set foot there since. (Taken from a local anthology; Grässe, I, 339f.)

This summary of the magician's activities in the city of Erfurt contains numerous strands that at first sight appear to be contradictory. Faustus is initially presented as a learned doctor who knows his classics and is invited to lecture at the university. Here he proves himself able to describe the Homeric heroes in such vivid detail that his students are totally convinced and terrified by the apparent authenticity of his accounts. Yet he comes across as something of a hooligan, driving carts of hay like a yokel and riding on a ravenous horse like a boy racer, his demeanour utterly incompatible with that of the erudite classicist. He exits through the roof with little concern for the property of others. Yet he can be productive and generous, as is seen when he provides fruit in winter and supplies his companions with delicious fare. Here he is applauded for his skills in the same breath as he is unmasked as an illusionist for deceiving drunkards into thinking they are in a vineyard. This episode found its way into Goethe's play, where the drunkards in Auerbach's Cellar are caught up in a similar predicament.

The narrative alludes to the published Faust legend again when the question of his damnation is broached at the end. There is honour in his disgrace; Faust refuses to break his word to one who has, it would seem, delivered the goods he promised when the deal was struck. Thus three aspects of his career are sketched into this short passage: Faust is a scholar, a charlatan, and a man of honour bound by his oath. The fascination of the story derives to no small extent from the way in which these themes mesh with each other.

Even in these early and fragmentary accounts, Faust is rarely presented in a cultural vacuum. He is tied to a specific environment, which includes a named university. It is no coincidence that the two establishments with which he is most often associated are Erfurt and Wittenberg, where Martin Luther studied and taught. His career is in radical opposition to that of the great reformer. Faustus turns not to, but away from, theology. The subject furthest removed from theology was classical literature, which at that time was still seen by many as liable to corrupt innocent minds. To study Homer was by definition an idle pursuit, since it replaces the Bible with fantasy. This is one of several indications that Faustus has aspirations to be something more than a purveyor of cheap remedies and fanciful horoscopes. He has an interest in the classics, in physics, in science, in travel. He knows the ancient heroes. He serves the nobility. He admires beauty. These qualities are fleetingly glimpsed even in the shortest fragments.

But side by side with what can be seen as positive and progressive, and in stark contrast to the inquiring qualities of his mind, there is a different Faustus, a cheapskate, an impostor, a fun-loving prankster who has adventures in which the prejudices of the age surface in considerable clarity. This is the Faustus who outwits the tradespeople of the time and plays his pranks on horse-dealers and moneylenders, Jews and clerics. These two sides to the one man cannot be reconciled, and this very duality led to Faust becoming a cipher for the instability of the inwardly 'torn' character, the 'man with two souls'.

In addition to the anecdotes, there are several short documents bearing witness to the activities of one or more 'Faust types' in the first half of the sixteenth century. They range from sharp condemnation to grudging approval.

> Eight days ago there came to Erfurt a certain soothsayer by the name of Georgius Faustus, the Helmitheus of Hedeberg [*Hemi-theos* ('*demigod*') *of Heidelberg?*], a mere braggart and fool. His claims, like those of all diviners, are idle and such physiognomy has no more weight than that of a water spider. The ignorant marvel at him. Let the theologians rise against him and not try to destroy the philosopher Reuchlin. I heard him babbling at an inn, but I did not reprove his boastfulness. What is the foolishness of other people to me? (Letter by the Humanist Conrad Mutianus Rufus, Canon of the Marienkirche in Gotha, to Heinrich Urbanus, his student, a steward of the Cistercian monastery at Erfurt, 3 October 1513, Palmer/More 87f.)

This is a dismissive account of an itinerant braggart. Conrad Rufus gives a snapshot of public opinion in this letter, and while conceding that the ignorant may marvel at the lightweight babblings of certain self-opinionated persons, he also alludes to what must have been a growing debate in theological circles. There were genuine Humanists around at the time; he mentions one of them by name, Johann Reuchlin, who was a professor of Greek and Hebrew at Ingolstadt and later at Tübingen. His writings attracted opposition from members of the clergy. What Rufus is saying in this passage, therefore, is that the clergy would be much better advised to attack boastful soothsayers who prey on the minds of the ignorant than to get into disputes with genuine scholars and academics such as Reuchlin and Erasmus.

The phrase 'Helmitheus Hedebergensis' is evidently corrupt and has led to several interpretations, including one that would suggest Faustus came from 'Helmstett [or Helmstadt] near Heidelberg'. Frank Baron has shown that a Georg Helmstetter matriculated at Heidelberg University in 1483, received a bachelor's degree in the following year, and graduated as a Master in 1487 (Baron (1978), 15–18; *Ibid.* (2003), 91). Baron is convinced that this is the real Faust, born in

Helmstadt near Heidelberg around 1466. The problem with this is that all 'sightings' date from 1507 onwards and that it took the graduate twenty years to emerge as 'Faust', and a further twenty to carry out some of his major exploits. Records from a twelve-year period between 1520 and 1532 suggest that he was then travelling in southern Germany, putting in appearances in Nuremberg, Bamberg, Eichstätt and Ingolstadt. This would make a birth date of 1480, as suggested by Mahal, somewhat more credible. Yet all of this data is at variance with narratives from the second half of the century, which place Faustus firmly in the central and eastern part of the country in the area around Leipzig, but without providing a time frame.

As the legend developed, the dividing line between the scholar and the braggart, so clearly drawn in Rufus' letter, became blurred, and Faustus was eventually made to represent both the man of learning and the cheap trickster, a combination that has confused and disoriented those readers who prefer to see him as either one or the other. There is a tendency to blame censors or meddling interpolators for the low-life scenes in subsequent accounts of Faustus' life as William Empson does in his study of Marlowe (see below, 80). Yet when we turn to the records, it seems that some of the coarser elements regularly associated with him are more authentic than the doctor's academic credentials.

> Miscellaneous Items. Ten *gulden* given and presented as a testimonial to Doctor Faust the philosopher, who made for my master a horoscope or prognostication. Paid on the Sunday after Saint Scholastica's Day [12 February 1520] by order of His Reverence (From the accounts of Bishop George III, Georg Schenk of Limburg, Bishop of Bamberg from 1502 to 1522, as recorded by his Chamberlain, Hans Muller; Palmer/ More 88f.).

Even high-ranking members of the Catholic Church had recourse to the services of sorcerers, as this entry in the Episcopal accounts of Bamberg demonstrates. It is also interesting in that it reveals the precise fee paid to Faustus for his prognostications. Ten *gulden* ('guilders') was, for the times, a princely sum of money, equal to a full year's manual wages. The high level of remuneration and the credulity of the superstitious bishop indicate that Faustus' vocation was a profitable one for which a demand existed in high places. Large numbers of incantations attributed to sundry magicians circulated in Germany during the following century (Kiesewetter 263–371). They were often richly illustrated with red and black diagrams covered in pseudo-astrological ideograms. Yet the records of several southern towns demonstrate that the magician was not always welcome.

There is evidence that on at least one occasion, Faustus appears to have got his facts right, although his prophesy was ignored, much to the detriment of those concerned. In 1785, a German newspaper printed the letters which the explorer Philipp von Hutten (1511–1546) wrote to his family; these included a passing reference to a prediction advising against his ill-fated expedition to Venezuela in 1534:

5. *Eighteenth-century circular spell attributed to Faustus. Illustration from Kiesewetter, 419.*

Here you have a little about the provinces so that you may see that we are not the only ones who have been unfortunate in Venezuela up to this time; that all the above-mentioned expeditions which left Seville before and after us perished within three months. Therefore I must confess that the philosopher Faust hit the nail on the head, for we struck a very bad year. (Palmer/More, 95f.)

Whether this warning had been based on astrological calculations, as Baron argues, or was simply the result of common sense, can no longer be established. What is more interesting is that it enhanced Faust's stature in Venezuela, where Herrera Luque's fictional account of these events, *La Luna de Fausto*, is based (Arcaya, 20; Herrera Luque, 413; see below, 363).

Today, the Wednesday after St Vitus's Day, 1528. The soothsayer shall be ordered to leave the city and to spend his penny elsewhere.
Record of those banished from Ingolstadt. On Wednesday after St Vitus's Day, 1528, a certain man who called himself Dr George [Jörg] Faust of Heidelberg was told to spend his penny elsewhere and he pledged himself not to take vengeance on or make fools of the authorities for this order (From the Records of the City of Ingolstadt, 17 June 1528. Palmer/More, 90).

Safe Conduct to Dr Faust, the great sodomite and necromancer, at Fürth [or: henceforth], refused. By order of the Junior Burgomaster (From the Records of the City Council of Nuremberg, 10 May 1532. Palmer/More, 90).

These two terse entries show us a different Faustus, one who is unwelcome to the point of being declared an outlaw. Ingolstadt and Nuremberg speak with one voice in banishing him. Yet the tone is very different. The city fathers of Ingolstadt are cautious in condemning the man. He is merely ordered to leave quietly. So great is the fear of retribution that this order is accompanied by a sworn statement from the banished soothsayer to the effect that he will neither seek vengeance nor mock the city fathers for their decision. It must have been a delicate task to banish a man suspected of having supernatural powers that could be turned against those who ordered him out of their city. On this occasion, the man styling himself Faustus appears to have been willing to submit to their decision and go quietly.

The deputy burgomaster of Nuremberg takes a harsher line in his description of the magician as a sodomite and necromancer, alluding to crimes which would have placed him outside of the protection of the law. It may be that he had entered the city with a promise that he would not be harmed, and that this document revokes the earlier promise; the text is ambiguous. The very real danger that such men faced, not merely from the church but also from the secular authorities, is exemplified in these two extracts. That Faustus is credited with two of the most heinous crimes, sodomy and necromancy, may result from an attempt to heap all manner of perversions on the unwelcome visitor. His sexual activities provide another dimension to the adventures of Faustus and will come to occupy a determining role in the later versions of the myth.

The extracts from official papers would be of little significance, were it not for the presence of comments on and reactions to Faustus in the writings of some of the major figures of the time. The earliest of these is the Benedictine Abbot of St James at Würzburg, Johannes Tritheim [also Trittheim, Trithemius], a 'paradoxical figure' (Baron (1978), 23) who was a member of the Humanist circle and a man of great learning. Yet he had also acquired the reputation of a magician and developed a sophisticated system of cryptography. In this letter to his friend Johannes Virdung, he gives a detailed assessment of a man who must have figured as a rival. Both Tritheim and Virdung were themselves representatives of what one would nowadays see as a 'fringe' culture. Virdung somehow managed to combine the role of professor of mathematics at Heidelberg with that of astrologer to the Elector of the Palatinate.

The man of whom you wrote to me, George Sabellicus, who has presumed to call himself the prince of necromancers, is a vagabond, a babbler and a rogue, who deserves to be thrashed so that he may not henceforth rashly venture to profess in public things so execrable and so hostile to the Holy Church. For what, other than symptoms of a very foolish and insane mind, are the titles assumed by this man, who shows himself to be a fool and not a philosopher? For thus he has formulated the title befitting him: 'Master George Sabellicus, the younger Faust, the chief of necromancers, astrologer, the second magus, palmist, diviner with earth and fire, second in the art of divination with water'. Behold the foolish temerity of the man, the madness by which he is possessed, in that he dares to call himself the source of necromancy, when in truth, in his ignorance of all good letters, he ought to call himself a fool rather than a master. But his wickedness is not hidden from me. When I was returning last year from the Mark Brandenburg, I happened upon this same man in the town of Gelnhausen, and many silly things were told me about him at the inn – things promised by him with great rashness on his part. As soon as he heard that I was there, he fled from the inn and could not be persuaded to come into my presence. The description of his folly, such as he gave to you and which we have mentioned, he also sent to me through a certain citizen. Certain priests in the same town told me that he had said, in the presence of many people, that he had acquired such knowledge of all wisdom and such a memory, that if all the books of Plato and Aristotle, together with their whole philosophy, had totally passed from the memory of man, he himself, through his own genius, like another Hebrew Ezra, would be able to restore them all with increased beauty. Afterwards, while I was at Speyer, he came to Würzburg and, impelled by the same vanity, is reported to have said in the presence of many that the miracles of Christ the Saviour were not so wonderful, that he himself could do all the things which Christ had done, as often and whenever he wished. Towards the end of Lent of the present year he came to Kreuznach and with like folly and boastfulness made great promises, saying that in alchemy he was the most learned man of all times and that by his knowledge and ability, he could do whatever anyone might wish. In the meantime there was vacant in the same town the position of schoolmaster, to which he was appointed through the influence of Franz von Sickingen, the magistrate of your prince and a man very fond of mystical lore. Then he began to indulge in the most dastardly kind of lewdness with the boys and when this was suddenly discovered, he avoided by flight the punishment that awaited him. These are the things which I know through very definite evidence concerning the man whose coming you await with such anticipation. When he comes to you, you will find him to be not a philosopher but a fool with an overabundance of rashness. – Würzburg, the 20th day of August, AD 1507 (Palmer/ More, 83-6).

Tritheim's letter, which was submitted to close analysis by Baron and Auernheimer in 2003, is of great importance for several distinct reasons. It remains the most detailed early sixteenth-century account of a person who was known to be using the name of Faustus, along with that of Sabellicus, to legitimise his vocation. Again we have immoderate claims and references to wicked practices, such as 'the most dastardly kind of lewdness with the boys'. The manner in which this alleged charlatan advertises himself is revealing; 'the younger Faust' strongly suggests that the name was in use by more than one self-appointed magus and that the current magician was able to look back to an older patron for endorsement. It is evident that learned men of the time were exchanging letters about such seemingly trivial goings-on. Tritheim freely admits that his information is based on hearsay and that he has been receiving intelligence from 'a certain citizen' who in turn has drawn on reports from 'certain priests'. The appropriation of third-hand reports devalues what might otherwise have been a more reliable source for the man at the heart of the legend.

Tritheim has no sympathy for Faustus. Yet it also transpires that other luminaries of the period, notably the influential Imperial knight Franz von

6. *Johannes Tritheim, author of the earliest specific comment on Faustus, from Dullinger, (1616).*

Sickingen and even the powerful the Elector of the Palatinate, were prepared to intercede for this man and find him employment as, of all things, a schoolmaster! It is unlikely that such men would have been persuaded by vainglorious boasting alone. True, there is no evidence of tangible achievements in this document. The author restricts himself to giving instances of the would-be magician's arrogance. His negative comments betray the scepticism of an enlightened rationalist, but it is possible that they were tinged by jealousy, given that Tritheim was himself a noted astrologer who had been denied a university education. Tales of magical feats and of dealings with Emperor Maximilian suggest that Tritheim himself was a ready-made model for some of the literary Faustus' activities and may himself have invented the Faust myth (McLean, 5; Baron/Auernheimer, 9f.). His claims merit careful consideration, for they contain a number of telling pointers.

The first part of Tritheim's letter ridicules a man who claims to be the prince of necromancers, a second magus, a palmist, a diviner with earth and fire (*chiromanticus, agromanticus, pyromanticus*). Temerity, folly, and indeed madness are cited as his reasons for making these claims. The name 'Sabellicus' may refer to an area north of Rome noted for the practice of magic (Baron (1978), 14). But it is evident that Faustus has gone further than merely dabble in witchcraft. He is beginning to encroach on ground that the Humanists aimed to cover when he asserts that he would be able to restore the works of Plato and Aristotle, were they suddenly to pass into oblivion. No ordinary confidence trickster would make such a claim. It is more than a feat of memory, since Faustus suggests that he can not only reproduce but also embellish the texts, insinuating that the canonical works of the philosophers – as available to scholars at this time – were less than complete and perfect. The ability to conjure up the image of Helen of Troy is a reminder of the link between the titillations of sorcery and the high-minded quest for the treasures of classical antiquity, a central preoccupation of post-mediaeval man and one that formed the very essence of the Renaissance.

Faustus does not limit himself to emulating the ancients. He derides the gospels, claiming that 'the miracles of Christ the Saviour were not so wonderful, that he himself could do all the things which Christ had done, as often and whenever he wished.' It is unlikely that any man would have survived unscathed for long in sixteenth-century Europe after making such sacrilegious comparisons between himself and Christ. Yet it was logical that someone who believed in his supernatural ability should claim to be able to perform miracles. The wrath of the Church was inevitable. Part of Faustus' tragedy is that he is suspended in an intellectual limbo somewhere between the dominant ideologies of his age, and neither properly at home in Humanism or Christendom, both of whose discourses he mimics.

A duality of purpose strengthened his iconic properties for future generations. Yet his story is one of failure. At a time when the intellectual world was divided between Humanists on the one hand and a dogmatic Christian clergy on the other, Faustus occupies a position approximately half-way between the two, championing the classical authors while simultaneously contriving to negotiate with those very diabolical forces that were the product of late mediaeval religious hysteria, trapped between two camps equally reluctant to accept him. To the Humanist he was steeped in superstition and bigotry, while any Christian would have to abhor a man so recklessly extravagant as to forge a pact with hell. Faustus found himself in an inescapable dilemma. This is what made his story so attractive to subsequent generations of poets and tragedians.

By the 1530s, there is mounting evidence that his very name had become a by-word for illicit knowledge and sorcery. Martin Luther refers to him twice in his table talk. Several short references indicate that the father of the Reformation regarded the magician's art not as a curiosity or a pompous boast but as a direct threat to Christian faith. Faustus is a dangerous magician who, according to Luther's associate Philip Melanchthon, had attempted to fly in Venice and was accompanied by devils in dog form (Baron/Auernheimer, 98). Another relevant detail is that Luther defined himself with reference to this figure, drawing a clear distinction between Faustus who succumbed and himself who resisted evil blandishments.

> When one evening at the table a sorcerer named Faust was mentioned, Doctor Martin said in a serious tone: 'The devil does not make use of the services of sorcerers against me. If he had been able to do me any harm, he would have done it long ago. To be sure he has often had hold of me by the head, but he had to let me go again.'
>
> Mention was made of magicians and the magic art, and how Satan blinded men. Much was said about Faust, who called the devil his brother-in-law, and the remark was made: 'If I, Martin Luther, had given him even my hand, he would have destroyed

me; but I would not have been afraid of him, – with God as my protector, I would have given him my hand in the name of the Lord.' (Palmer/More, 92 f.)

Faustus was evidently discussed in Luther's immediate circle as a topical news item. The subject was of interest to them for several reasons. Luther was an academic 'doctor', as Faustus claimed to be. Like Faustus, he had become disenchanted with the evidently limited range of knowledge which the universities of the time were able to supply to their students. Like Faustus, he had undergone a radical change of heart that had put him in touch with a different and more spiritually oriented plane of existence. Luther's claims to understand the word of God more directly than the established clergy of his day struck many observers as the apex of folly and arrogance. Neither of the two doctors had use for compromise.

The parallels between Doctor Faustus and Doctor Luther go far beyond their personal conversion experiences and their uncompromising attitude. They will be explored further in the context of the intellectual background to the Faust Book. For the moment, it should be adequate to signal that Martin Luther had an intense personal belief in a devil who was so close that actual physical contact with him was a frequent occurrence: 'He has often had hold of me by the head, but he had to let me go again.'

By the middle of the sixteenth century, short narratives about Faustus began to be published. The first of these appeared in Johannes Gast's *Sermones Conviviales*, a popular anthology of anecdotes written by a protestant clergyman from Basle.

> He puts up at night at a certain very rich monastery, intending to spend the night there. A brother places before him some ordinary wine of indifferent quality and without flavour. Faust requests that he draw from another cask a better wine, which it was the custom to give to nobles. Then the brother said: 'I do not have the keys, the prior is sleeping, and it is a sin to awaken him.' Faust said: 'The keys are lying in that corner. Take them and open that cask on the left and give me a drink.' The brother objected that he had no orders from the prior to place any other wine before guests. When Faust heard this he became very angry and said: 'In a short time you shall see marvels, you inhospitable brother.' Burning with rage he left early in the morning without saying farewell and sent a certain raging devil who made a great stir in the monastery by day and by night and moved things about both in the church and in the cells of the monks, so that they could not get any rest, no matter what they did. Finally they deliberated whether they should leave the monastery or destroy it altogether. And so they wrote to the Count Palatine concerning the misfortune in which they were involved. He took the monastery under his own protection and ejected the monks to whom he furnishes supplies from year to year and uses what is left for himself. It is said that to this very day, if monks enter the monastery, such great disturbances arise that those who live there can have no peace. This the devil was able to bring to pass.

Another story concerns Faust's demise:

> At Basle I dined with him in the great college and he gave to the cook various kinds of birds to roast. I do not know where he bought them or who gave them to him, since there were none on sale at the time. Moreover I never saw any like them in our

38

regions. He had with him a dog and a horse which I believe to have been demons and which were ready for any service. I was told that the dog at times assumed the form of a servant and served the food. However, the wretch was destined to come to a deplorable end, for he was strangled by the devil and his body on its bier kept turning face downward even though it was five times turned on its back. God preserve us lest we become slaves of the devil (Johannes Gast, *Sermones Conviviales*, volume II, first published in 1548. Palmer/More, 96–8).

In the first of these two anecdotes, 'the Necromancer' is implicated in a situation that has a clear moral. Far from practising necromancy among the dead, he turns up at a monastery which is identified as being 'very rich'. The reception he receives is not in keeping with the high standing of the establishment; the wine they place before him is 'of indifferent quality and without flavour', and the brother lies to him about the keys. He even declares that waking the sleeping prior is a sin. This should suffice to give the attentive reader an impression of the state of affairs at this establishment. The moral decline is matched by the meanness of the occupants. Faustus performs a valuable service in cleansing the monastery of parasites. Although he avails himself of a devil to create havoc in the building, his role is ultimately beneficial. Like Christ among the moneylenders in the Temple, the doctor succeeds in cleansing a religious building. The ultimate beneficiary of this exercise is the Count Palatine, who immediately initiates a process of secularisation. Thus the dissolution of the monasteries, as experienced all over Protestant Europe at the time, is effected through the agency of Faustus, here portrayed as a convenient instrument of social change.

The second anecdote claims to be an eyewitness account of an event at Basle. Faustus is able to produce a variety of victuals that are exotic or out of season, as he did in several earlier tales. He is accompanied by animals that are rumoured to be embodiments of evil spirits sent to serve him, part of the traditional iconography of witchcraft. There is mention of his death and of attempts to turn over his corpse, stretched out face downwards as an indication of his damnation. No matter how hard they try, the body turns over again. This grizzly detail will have sufficed to convince credulous readers of his unpardonable guilt.

The fullest account of Faustus' death is to be found in Johannes Manlius' *Locorum Communium Collectanea* (Latin 1563, German 1565):

I know a certain man by the name of Faust from Kundling [assumed to be present-day Knittlingen], which is a small place near my birthplace. When he was a student at Cracow he studied magic, for there was formerly much practice of the art in that city and in that place too there were public lectures in that art. He wandered about everywhere and talked of many mysterious things. When he wished to provide a spectacle at Venice he said he would fly to heaven. So the devil raised him up and then cast him down so that he was dashed to the ground and almost killed. But he did not die.

A few years ago the same Johannes Faust was very downcast in a village in Württemberg on the day before his death. The innkeeper asked him why he was so sad, as this was contrary to his usual demeanour (for he was normally a complete rascal and prone to great wickedness, so much so that he almost died as a result of his great whoring). Whereupon he said to the innkeeper, if he should hear anything during the night, then he should not be afraid. At midnight there was a great disturbance. In the morning, Faust did not appear. And when midday came, the innkeeper in the company of several men broke into his room and found him lying dead beside his bed, the devil having turned his head around to face his back (Mahal (1986), 11; Palmer/More, 101f.).

Harold Meek's attempts to diagnose the cause of Faustus' death produced some unexpected if fanciful results; after considering epidemics, murder, accidental explosions, arteriosclerosis, kidney failure, syphilis and suicide by strychnine poisoning, he concludes that the latter two were decisive: 'he had suffered from Syphilis for years, which produced a degeneration of his brilliance and intensified his natural bombast; finally, in a state of great depression he took a strong dose of Strychnine' (Meek, 56). Those who see him as a literary figure will, by contrast, be struck by the tragedy of his demise. What makes it so is the fact that he knows precisely when it will occur and yet can do nothing to put off the hour. In most literary accounts, given that the period of pleasure granted to him had been twenty-four years, Faustus knows the precise moment when the fiend will strike, and gathers his students and companions around him in order to prepare them. Here he merely informs the innkeeper to expect a great disturbance. Foreknowledge of a terrible fate is a powerful method by which Faustus' plight is enhanced. It is a subject waiting to be exploited by subsequent writers.

Luther's Demons

For all his undisputed intellectual qualities as a thinker and reformer, Martin Luther was a profoundly superstitious individual. Far from overcoming the mediaeval beliefs in hobgoblins and demons, he deepened them and made them more acute (Oberman, 109; Strauss, 30f.). Much has been written about his obsessive character, which may have predisposed him to accept without question the physical reality of the devil and his direct intervention in human life as axiomatic facts. Luther expatiates on this theme in his table talk, and his letters and sermons frequently focus on physical manifestations of evil on earth. He records that the devil paid him repeated visits. The best known of these took place in Wartburg Castle, where the rebellious monk had been offered shelter after being declared an outlaw in 1521. He was in his study, working on his translation of the New Testament, when the devil is said to have appeared in his room. Luther threw an inkpot at his uninvited guest and the apparition vanished. For many years it was possible to view the ink stain that resulted from this encounter.

The apparition in Wartburg Castle was not an isolated incident. Luther was convinced that the devil was doing everything in his power to stop him from completing his mission of reform. He would make his presence felt in a number of disagreeable ways. He would produce terrifying noises and smells, or assume a variety of disguises. He would rattle around behind the stove in Luther's room, pelt the

7. A room in Wartburg Castle, where Martin Luther threw an inkpot at the devil while working on his translation of the Bible. Generations of souvenir-hunters have removed most of the plaster around the stove where the inkpot hit the wall. Photograph by Osman Durrani.

roof over his head with nuts, and roll heavy casks down the stairway. He appeared as a serpent or a star, and could even lodge himself in Luther's bowels, where he would grunt like a pig and emit terrible stenches (Oberman, 232–4; Osborn, 5f.).

It may seem paradoxical that a man who devoted his life to banishing ancient superstitions and heresy from religious life should have been so enthralled by a mediaeval demonology that was on its way out at the time. Luther inveighed against letters of indulgence and bizarre cults involving saints and their miracle-working relics, but persisted in warning against a fiend who was forever lurking in the vicinity, waiting for an opportunity to pounce on his victims in a theatrical manner, rather like the stage demons who were an essential component of every mediaeval morality play. The devil, as Luther saw him, derived his distinctive traits from the theatre and the popular imagination (stenches, rattling noises, crafty tricks), and the 'Mephistopheles' of Faust literature betrays many signs of his roots in a mediaeval commonplace.

The underlying question is why, at the start of the modern era, the devil should enter the literary culture of Europe, be it as Luther's antagonist, as Faustus' tempter, or as one of the many minor demons who were written about in the 'devil-books' that began to circulate at the time. The availability of the text of the Bible in new translations was the major factor. The scriptures now acquired greater vividness and more direct appeal than they had possessed for earlier generations, who relied on obscure Latin texts. The Bible upholds belief in the devil's physical presence on earth. An intriguing example is provided in the Old Testament, when

41

God and Satan enter into a kind of wager on the subject of Satan's ability to pervert a just man, Job.

> Now there was a day when the sons of God came to present themselves before the LORD, and Satan came also among them. And the LORD said unto Satan, Whence comest thou? Then Satan answered the LORD, and said, From going to and fro in the earth, and from walking up and down in it. And the LORD said unto Satan, Hast thou considered my servant Job, that there is none like him in the earth, a perfect and an upright man, one that feareth God, and escheweth evil? Then Satan answered the LORD, and said, Doth Job fear God for nought? Hast not thou made an hedge about him, and about his house, and about all that he hath on every side? Thou hast blessed the work of his hands, and his substance is increased in the land. But put forth thine hand now, and touch all that he hath, and he will curse thee to thy face. And the LORD said unto Satan, Behold, all that he hath is in thy power; only upon himself put not forth thine hand. So Satan went forth from the presence of the LORD (Job 1:6-12, King James Version).

This is the most important biblical source for the Faust legend. It outlines a celestial wager, in which the powers of Good and Evil are in dispute over the fate of a man's soul. Satan claims that he will be able to corrupt an upright man, Job, and the Lord appears to sanction the bet. The career of one man becomes a battle-ground between these hostile forces, and although the subsequent developments prove the Lord right, it is quite remarkable that the devil's labour of temptation and corruption should be approved by the supreme moral authority. The wager in heaven is just one instance among many of the Lord mocking his opponents: in the Old Testament, the supreme authority allows itself to be provoked for no other reason than to demonstrate its invincibility.

There are approximately one hundred references to the devil in the New Testament, but there are relatively few dramatic encounters between the opposing forces of good and evil. The best known is the temptation of Christ, which reveals that the Son of God is no less vulnerable in this respect than ordinary mortals. Again, Satan hopes to persuade Jesus to renounce righteousness; again, his hopes are in vain.

> Then was Jesus led up of the spirit into the wilderness to be tempted of the devil. And when he had fasted forty days and forty nights, he was afterwards an hungered. And when the tempter came to him, he said, If thou be the Son of God, command that these stones be made bread. But he answered and said, It is written, Man shall not live by bread alone but by every word that proceedeth out of the mouth of God. Then the devil taketh him up into the holy city, and setteth him on a pinnacle of the temple, and saith unto him, If thou be the Son of God, cast thyself down: for it is written, He shall give his angels charge concerning thee: and in their hands they shall bear thee up, lest at any time thou dash thy foot against a stone. Jesus said unto him, It is written again, Thou shalt not tempt the Lord thy God. Again, the devil taketh him up into an exceeding high mountain, and sheweth him all the kingdoms of the world, and the glory of them; and saith unto him, All these things will I give thee, if thou wilt fall down and worship me. Then saith Jesus unto him, Get thee hence, Satan: for it is written, Thou shalt worship the Lord thy God, and him only shalt thou serve. Then the devil leaveth him, and, behold, angels came and ministered unto him. (Matthew 4:1-11)

If the 'Son of God' is exposed to the blandishments of the tempter, how much more vulnerable must ordinary men and women be? The theme of temptation is broached on many occasions in the scriptures and passed rapidly into canonical belief and popular superstition. Martin Luther, whose whole life was an odyssey through the books of both Testaments in search of direct access to truth, could not escape the influence of so many references to direct interaction between man and devils. Not only does the devil cajole and persuade, but he also employs force to obtain power over men. His strategies are twofold; he attempts to overcome natural goodness by inflicting pain and grief, as he does on Job, but also appeals to logic, as happens both with Eve and with Christ (Spivack, 941).

Notwithstanding the attested failures with Job and Jesus, there are instances of at least temporary success. There are tales of possession, involving individuals whose minds and bodies have been taken over by demons. A large part of Christ's work is to do with the expulsion of such demons from the bodies of their human hosts. So the devil does not merely tempt but also gains violent possession of individuals. The number of such conquests alluded to in the New Testament strengthened popular belief in witchcraft and led to horrendous witch trials and exorcisms. Even people subsequently viewed as saints, such as Joan of Arc, were deemed to have colluded with the powers of hell. The ascendancy of Faustus in the sixteenth century must be due in part to the neat way in which his story meshed with the superstitions of the time. Two books that were popular at the turn of the century were overtly concerned with the persecution of vice: the notorious manual *Malleus maleficarum* ('Hammer of Witches') by Sprenger and Insistoris of 1485, and the comic exposure of vice by Sebastian Brant, *The Ship of Fools*, published in 1494. Yet it was, ironically, a Pope, Innocent VIII, who helped to spark off the witch-hunts that swept Europe in the sixteenth and seventeenth centuries with his 'Bull' *Summis desiderantes*, which targets the spread of sorcery in Germany.

The theme of folly was a major component of the cultural life of the fifteenth and sixteenth centuries. Not only moralists and poets, but painters, too, delighted in depicting the follies of humankind. Hieronymus Bosch and Pieter Brueghel are best known for the emphasis they place on the connection between folly, sin, and damnation. Erasmus of Rotterdam's *Praise of Folly* of 1512 combined Brant's approach with the satirical manner of Lucian to demonstrate that humankind owes its very existence to Folly. Through the mouth of Folly herself, the reader learns that not only procreation and all other human exertions, but also the work of the Holy Church, the activities of monks no less than those of popes, stem from this one source.

Brant and Erasmus supply richly documented collages of vice-ridden and foolhardy behaviour. From their different perspectives, they mock moral aberrations as rigorously as they chide the ordinary pleasures of life: robbery and hypocrisy are treated in the same way as dancing and communal merry-making. No allowances were made for 'innocent' fun at the time. All comedy in *Doctor Faustus* must be read in this light: it is placed there to indicate depravity, and little distinction is made between trivial misconduct and heinous sin.

An area that one might expect to have escaped castigation from the satirist was university life. Far from it. There are texts that suggest that the universities of the sixteenth century were no better than the monasteries and the alehouses. The anonymous satire *Letters of Obscure Men* gives a unique insight into the preoccupations of magisters and professors in pre-Reformation Europe. This compilation of fictitious letters reproduces a world of crumbling scholastic values and numerous abuses of privilege, which, despite the obvious exaggeration of a wickedly satirical mind, reveal a specifically Teutonic form of Christianity that is on the point of being swept away. It is Faustian in its evocation of a dreary wilderness that passed itself off as a source of wisdom.

> The other day a *Feast of Aristotle* was celebrated here – the Doctors, the Licentiates, and the Magisters were in high feather, and I too was present. To begin with, by way of a whet, we drank three bumpers of Malmsey, and for the first course we had fresh wastel-bread and made sops; and then we had six dishes of meat, and chicken, and capons – and one of fish; and between the dishes we ceased not to drink Kotzberger and Rhine wine, and beer of Eimbeck, and Torgau, and Naumburg; and the Magisters were full pleased, and vowed that the new-fledged graduates had acquitted themselves right well, and greatly to their credit.
>
> Then began the Doctors over their cups to argue canonically concerning profundities. And the question arose, whether 'magister nostrandus' or 'noster magistrandus' is the fitter to denote a candidate eligible for the degree of Doctor of Divinity. (Stokes, 291f.)

There has been much speculation about the authorship of these letters, which appeared in several volumes between 1514 and 1517. What is important is that they concentrate on an area in which Faustus is also supposed to have been active (Leipzig in particular) at the very time of his alleged public appearances and strongly hint that corruption was rife among local purveyors of knowledge. The chapbook about the doctor who sold his soul to the devil was thus no isolated statement about an untypical event. Any reader of the *Letters of Obscure Men* must have quickly formed the opinion that university doctors and sages had every chance of ending up in the devil's clutches.

Tritheim and Virdung were not the only men of learning who took a positive view of some of the more dubious arts. The English scholar John Dee (1527–1608) was a shadowy figure whose life-story echoes that of Faustus in many respects. Some authorities have associated him with the Faust Book and even argued that it was Dee who supplied the English translation. This will be discussed in more detail below (60).

Unlike Faustus, Dee was a man of great Christian and humility, yet he was also inspired by pagan beliefs in conjuring and magical practices, and while he claimed to be in contact with 'angels', there is in Dee's thought a hope that magic would somehow restore an increasingly mad world to its senses. Dee studied at Cambridge in 1542 and proceeded to Louvain, where he attracted the interest of men associated with Emperor Charles V. Invitations to visit princes and kings, including the Russian Czar, often came his way, and he was treated both as a favourite and

8. Martin Luther, (statue by Johann Gottfried Schadow, canopy by Karl Friedrich Schinkel, 1812) in Wittenberg Market Place. Photograph by Osman Durrani.

as an impostor, much as Faustus was. In 1555, under the reign of Mary, he was imprisoned on the grounds of 'lewd vayne practices of calculing and conjuring' in a manner that again recalls Faustus. And he was a great traveller. Six years spent on the continent between 1583 and 1589 ended on the recommendation of Pope Sixtus V. He became a favourite of and enjoyed the protection of Elizabeth I. Like Marlowe, he may have worked as a secret agent. In many of his activities, there is a strange resemblance to Faustus' apparent enjoyment of esteem in aristocratic circles while facing charges of necromancy from religious quarters. Like Faustus, he travelled widely and made great promises; like Faustus, he began his career as a rational scholar of a scientific bent but he went beyond science to recommend angel-magic as a complement to scholarship. He even seems to have tried to engineer his own death by petitioning James I to put him on trial (French, 6, 120–25, 10).

The sixteenth century was uncommonly rich in such parallels and precedents to Faustus, yet it was the literature of the period that was to supply the final incentive to write up the story of his life. What this introduction has shown is that the literature on folly grew steadily in significance during the first half of the century, and this led to a desire for ever more specific accounts of specific follies. The focus on the devil in Luther's sermons and writings speeded up the process. The final consequence was the emergence of a sub-genre of books aimed to shock and edify: the 'devil books' [*Teufelbücher* or *Teufelsbücher*], of which *Doctor Faustus* has proved to be the most enduring example.

Literary Devils

It remains a paradox that at a time when thinkers and churchmen were freeing themselves from the heavy burden of mediaeval superstition, there was growing interest in the interaction of humans with demons – a topic that strikes us as mediaeval rather than modern. Yet Martin Luther's 'rational' approach to Christianity was bound to encourage rather than to dispel such beliefs, however paradoxical this may seem to the modern observer. His strategy was to strip away what he saw as the inventions of the Church and return to the Bible itself, which he diligently studied and translated. And since the Bible describes several apparitions of Satan, it follows that such events are exemplary occurrences that explain man's misery and yet also hold a promise of redemption. In the Old Testament, Satan causes Adam and Eve to be banished, but he also fights in vain for the soul of the more steadfast Job. He makes few other appearances. In the New Testament, he is also rarely mentioned. True, the Lord is tempted, but resists, while lesser men, such as Simon Magus, succumb to the lure of evil. Satan is referred to as the 'Prince of this World' (John 12:31, 14:30, 16:11) and uses the promise of untold riches as his instrument when he temps Christ: 'All these I will give you, if you will only fall down and do me homage' (Matthew 4:9). These few biblical precedents set off a powerful chain reaction whose ultimate consequence was the fabrication of latter-day stories of human enslavement to personalised devils and thus established the underlying recipe for the Faust legend.

Luther was enough of a psychologist to recognise that temptation was never a simple matter. He speaks of different types of seduction, and assesses the individual's chances of escape in the following passage. What is worth noting in the context of Faustus is that Luther sees no chance of salvation for those whose minds the devil has taken over. This explains why reformed Christianity was unwilling to accept the idea of belated repentance as a liberating force.

> Humans are possessed by the devil in two different ways: some physically, by virtue of their external appearance and rank, others spiritually, through their minds and souls, as is the case with all godless people. In imbeciles and madmen, who have been possessed in body alone, the devil has merely taken over their outward physique and restricts himself to torturing their bodies, not their minds or souls, which remain unaffected and undamaged. Their devils can be driven out through prayer and fasting. But the enemies of God and the blasphemers are possessed in their minds, and they cannot be helped, nor can they be saved (Martin Luther, *Table Talk*, cited Roos, 17).

For Luther, once the mind had become infected, the chances of redemption were reduced to zero. Given this approach, Faustus, despite gaining insight into his wrongdoing and regardless of any attempts by friends to save him, can do no other than persevere in his wickedness. The Faust Book stands as a monument to the rigidly uncompromising attitude to evil that characterises the early Reformation.

The devil of Reformation Christianity is a different animal from the mediaeval devil of miracle plays and saints' legends. The disease which he inflicts on his victims is incurable. Not only is he an important figure in the canonical texts recognised by the reformers, but his presence as the Prince of this World obliges every individual to opt for or against association with him. The story of Doctor Faustus was central to the intellectual life of the sixteenth century and differed from that of the figures who were tempted in the miracle plays of preceding centuries. These normally resulted in defeat for the tempter and the consequent salvation of his intended victim. Faustus cannot fight off the pernicious influence because the devil's power has been upgraded. Faustus himself is now the instigator of the pact and not a mere victim of seduction. To understand why the author presented him in this way requires an introduction to the devil books that were appearing in large numbers at the time.

9. *Andreas Musculus' devil homes in on fashionable leg wear, 1555.*

Many factors combined to give these tracts their unique identity. They may, in part, be a result of age-old pagan beliefs that lingered on among the populace. It has been claimed that the old Germanic heroes were transformed into demons as Christianity gained ground in these territories, with the result that the Church had a ready-made and multifarious 'infernal court' composed of ancient gods, giants, and harmless nature-spirits. All these could be targeted in sermons. The decline of mediaeval courtly poetry may also have led to a literary vacuum that was later filled with humorous tales and anecdotes in which the Prince of Hell came to play a part. It has been estimated that around a quarter of a million copies of such books were in circulation at the end of the sixteenth century, and that they were part of a deliberate attempt to reinforce Lutheran orthodoxy in areas of the country where people still preferred spells to prayers and soothsayers to priests (Roos, 108f; Strauss, 29–31).

It is for this reason that the devil, traditionally assumed to be a master of disguise, appears in so many different forms in these booklets. Their fascination lies in the manner in which an essentially similar story can be varied to encompass virtually all forms of human behaviour. The devil tracts can be read as case studies of follies like the ones pilloried in Brant's *Ship of Fools* and in earlier works like Chaucer's *Canterbury Tales* and Boccaccio's *Decameron*. They revolve around a motley crew of demons, each with his own private portfolio of sins.

Another reason for this variety can be found in the hierarchical organisation of hell. Just as there were assumed to be many gradations among the angels ('cherubim', 'seraphim', 'thrones'), separate classes of devil were envisaged, each responsible for a distinctive transgression. The *Eheteufel* would specialise in the disruption of fond relations between husband and wife, encouraging deceit, adultery, and promiscuity. Another such spirit, graphically evoked by Andreas Musculus (*Vom Hosen-Teuffel*, 1555), would encourage fashion-conscious young men to spend inordinate sums on silken leggings. There were cohorts of distinct devils, eager to promote gluttony, dancing, swearing and other putative vices. These devils were attracting interest not least because they were moving with the times; they were interested in contemporary vices; they homed in on vulnerable individuals; they were 'homocentric' (Russell (1986), 63). With multifarious interests and contradictory qualities, they were modern emblems of the human vices they effectively mimicked.

> Many consider and regard it as proven that every country has its own native devil, every city its city devil, every village its village devil, every court its court devil and every household its own domestic devil; indeed, each social class, each person has a devil that causes torment and encourages us to commit sins. This is evident in that every country, social class, household and person has a specific vice which is greater than all others. And thus Germany is and always has been plagued, more than all other countries, by the devil that drives people to drink, as happens to us Germans by day and by night, and he leaves us no peace until we are full up and completely mad (Matthäus Friedrich, *Sauffteuffel*, 1552, dedication, cited by Roos, 54).

For all the emphasis on separate devils for separate nations, Friedrich does not hesitate to name more than a dozen other devils worthy of attention, including in their number many stock types of fools familiar from Brant's compendium of follies. Friedrich lists arrogance, anger, carping, swearing, excessive sorrow, envy, hatred, murder, mockery, insults, scandals, whoring, avarice, theft, usury, gluttony, gambling, despair, and deceit as having their own instigator in hell. It is characteristic of the period that no attempt is made to list them according to the

48

severity of the offence, murder occurring side by side with buffoonery and grief, nor is there a sharp demarcation between what we would nowadays see as sins, crimes, or bad habits. Faustus is similarly unselective; he will foreswear God, fornicate and insult innkeepers, each act, however petty, signalling a fresh instance of moral degeneracy.

An important aspect of the devil's work is to reverse the natural order of things. Infernal activity thus manifests itself in a state of affairs akin to the mediaeval literary motif of 'The world upside down'.

> Thus drunkenness makes the healthy lame while the lame jump and dance, the hearing grow deaf and the speaking fall silent [...] the seeing go blind and the sensitive lose their sensitivity, the healthy fall sick [...] the old become children, the modest become ruthless, the decorous become indiscreet, the silent begin to shout [...] night becomes day, day becomes night, boards and houses begin to move around, and one becomes two. (Matthias Friedrich, *Sauffteuffel*, 1552, dedication, Roos 75)

The devil books derive much of their fascination from the manner in which they succeed in updating older literary topoi. Man is foolish, he turns his world upside down, and the devil assists him in this, enabling the clear-sighted satirist to do his work. Faustus is just another example of folly and role-reversal: the doctor is less wise than his students or the meanest of his associates; his books are of no avail to him, his knowledge of Latin and of the Scriptures is not put to effective use. The doctor of medicine cuts off his own leg for fun. The university is a hotbed of ignorance. The devil appears as a monk. Here, too, there is a contemporary reference. The sudden decline in the influence of the mediaeval church led people to seek a more immediate relationship with their maker, which was patently open to disruption by evil forces. For many, it made sense to view the recently abandoned Catholic faith as the devil's construct, which explains why Faust's adversary often acts like a monk. It is now appreciated that witch trials and exorcism rituals were an important part of the cultural background to the literature of the period (Roskoff, II, 293–314; Baron (1992), 129–46; Schöne 186). It has even been suggested that the figure of Faust was created in order to protect women from trials as witches, by showing that educated men who practised wizardry were the real menace of the time (Baron (2003), 102).

Two books that came to serve as models of Protestant devil literature in general concern characteristically disparate misdeeds: excessively baggy trousers, and adultery. They are *Vom Hosen-Teuffel* ('On the Trouser Devil', 1555) and *Wider den Eheteuffel* ('Against the Marital Demon', 1556), both from the pen of Andreas Musculus, a university teacher from Frankfurt/Oder who may have studied under Luther at Wittenberg. What all these treatises have in common is their complaining tone. They offer no real stories other than the occasional anecdote, and read like sermons:

> All nations, Italians, Spaniards, French, Poles, Hungarians, Tatars and Turks have preserved their clothes and what they ordinarily use to cover their bodies as they

were instructed by their parents; Germany alone has been completely possessed and invaded by the devil, so that there is more modesty and honour in Venus Mountain and in the back yards of olden times than amongst us Germans of today, who describe and call ourselves honourable, decent and constant, yet have no more honour, decency and modesty than a fly is able to transport on its tail (Andreas Musculus, *Vom Hosen-Teuffel*, 1555, Roos 81).

Musculus provides a powerful invective against what he sees as a modern plague: trousers of the *Pluderhosen* variety ('baggy breeches consisting of slit silk') stimulate wicked desires, cause embarrassment and are horrendously expensive, requiring as they do one hundred yards of fine cloth. Although not a narrative, there are occasional anecdotes in the booklet, such as the one about the soldier who thought 'ninety-nine' yards of silk would be more prestigious than 'a hundred', as the word was longer and sounded more soldierly.

These texts would probably have been consigned to oblivion, had not later editors collected and republished them, as Sigmund Feyerabend, a bookseller from Frankfurt/Main, did in his highly successful compendium *Theatrum Diabolorum* ('Devils' Theatre') of 1569. This was a veritable encyclopaedia of demonology, containing no fewer than twenty devil books in its first edition, and later extended by the addition of eleven others. At a cost of three thalers, it was expensive, but as it capitalised on the reading and churchgoing public's thirst for information and provided end-to-end coverage of the topic, it did well and put an end to the publication of individual tracts on specific vices. From now on, any author wishing to make his mark in this field would have to offer a new approach and not confine himself to a verbal diatribe based on a catalogue of misdemeanours. It is here that the author of *Doctor Faustus* spotted an opportunity for a new type of book that combined a very specific account of a very specific devil with the sermonising strategy so prevalent among Reformation authors. The chapbook about Doctor Faustus that saw the light of print in Frankfurt/Main in 1587 is thus both the last of a long line of Lutheran devil-books and the first of a new type of narrative whose concise format and linear structure bore within it a viable blueprint for later dramas and novels.

Cited Works and Further Reading

Marguerite de Huszar Allen, 'The Reception of the *Historia von D. Johann Fausten*', *German Quarterly* 59 (1986), 582–94.

Pedro Manuel Arcaya, *Historia del Estado Falcón*. Caracas: La Nación, 1953.

A.J. Barnouw, 'Mary of Nimmegen', *Germanic Review* 6 (1930), 69–84.

Frank Baron, *Doctor Faustus from History to Legend*. Munich: Wilhelm Fink, 1978.

——, *Faustus on Trial. The Origins of Johann Spies's 'Historia' in an Age of Witch Hunting*. Tübingen: Niemeyer, 1992.

——, 'Der historische Faustus im Spiegel der Quellen des 16. Jahrhunderts. Von der Astrologie zum Teufelspakt', in Baron/Auernheimer, 84–107.

——, 'Georg Lukács on the Origins of the Faust Legend', in Boerner/Johnson, 13–25.

Frank Baron and Richard Auernheimer (eds), *War Dr Faustus in Kreuznach? Realität und*

Fiktion im Faust-Bild des Abtes Johannes Trithemius. Alzey: Verlag der Rheinhessischen Druckwerkstätte, 2003.

Peter Boerner and Sidney Johnson (eds), *Faust through Four Centuries. Retrospect and Analysis. Vierhundert Jahre Faust. Rückblick und Analyse.* Tübingen: Niemeyer, 1989.

Lucy de Bruyn, *Woman and the Devil in sixteenth-century literature.* Tisbury: Compton Press, 1979.

Peter Burke, *Popular Culture in Early Modern Europe.* London: Temple Smith, 1978.

George L. Burr (ed.), *The Witch Persecutions. Translations and Reprints from the Original Sources of European History.* 6 volumes. Philadelphia: University of Pennsylvania History Department, 1898–1912.

E.M. Butler, *The Myth of the Magus.* Cambridge: University Press, 1948.

—, *The Fortunes of Faust.* Cambridge: University Press, 1952.

Carsten Colpe, 'Aus der Geschichte des Teufels im Abendland', in Carsten Colpe and Wilhelm Schmidt-Biggemann (eds), *Das Böse. Eine historische Phänomenologie des Unerklärlichen.* Frankfurt: Suhrkamp, 1993, 63–89.

Sigismundus Dullinger, *Trithemius sui ipsius vindex [...].* Ingolstadt: Angermaria, 1616.

William Empson, *Faustus and the Censor. The English Faust-book and Marlowe's Doctor Faustus.* Recovered and edited, with an Introduction and Postscript, by John Henry Jones. Oxford: Basil Blackwell, 1987.

Desiderius Erasmus, *The Praise of Folly.* Translated by John Wilson, 1668. Ann Arbour: University of Michigan Press, 1958.

Peter J. French, *John Dee. The World of an Elizabethan Magus.* London: Routledge and Kegan Paul, 1972.

Johann Georg Theodor Grässe (ed.), *Sagenbuch des Preussischen Staats,* 2 volumes. Glogau: Carl Flemming, 1868–71.

Reinhold Grimm and Jost Hermand (eds), *Our Faust? Roots and Ramifications of a Modern German Myth.* Madison: University of Wisconsin Press, 1987.

Erich Kahler, 'Doctor Faustus from Adam to Sartre', *Comparative Drama* 1 (1967), 75–83.

John Henry Jones (ed.), *The English Faust Book. A critical edition based on the text of 1592.* Cambridge: University Press, 1994.

Carl Kiesewetter, *Faust in der Geschichte und Tradition, mit besonderer Berücksichtigung des occulten Phänomenalismus und des mittelalterlichen Zauberwesens.* Leipzig: Spohr, 1893.

Günther Mahal (ed.), *Der historische Faust. Ein wissenschaftliches Symposium.* Knittlingen: Faust Archiv, 1982.

—, *Faust starb in Staufen. Nachforschungen über ein verschwiegenes Faktum.* Vaihingen: Wilfried Melchior, 1986.

—, *Faust. Die Spuren eines geheimnisvollen Lebens.* Reinbek: Rowohlt, 1995.

Hans Mayer, *Doktor Faustus und Don Juan.* Frankfurt/M: Suhrkamp, 1979.

Adam McLean (ed.), *The Steganographia of Johannes Trithemius.* Edinburgh: Magnum Opus, 1982.

Harold Meek, *Johann Faust. The Man and the Myth.* London: Oxford University Press, 1930.

Heiko A. Oberman, *Luther: Mensch zwischen Gott und Teufel.* Berlin: Severin und Siedler, 1983.

Max Osborn, *Die Teufelliteratur des 16. Jahrhunderts.* Berlin: Meyer und Müller, 1893. Rptd Hildesheim: Olms, 1965.

Philip Mason Palmer and Robert Pattison More: *The Sources of the Faust Tradition from Simon Magus to Lessing.* New York: Oxford University Press, 1936. Rptd New York: Octagon, 1966.

Will-Erich Peukert, 'Dr Faustus', *Zeitschrift für deutsche Philologie* 70 (1947), 55–74.

Hermann Reske, *Faust: eine Einführung.* Stuttgart: Kohlhammer, 1971.

Richard Rohde, *Das englische Faustbuch und Marlowes Tragödie.* Halle: Niemeyer, 1910.

Keith L. Roos, *The Devil in sixteenth-century German Literature: The Teufelsbücher.* Berne: Herbert Lang, 1972.

Jeffrey Burton Russell, *Witchcraft in the Middle Ages*. Ithaca: Cornell University Press, 1972.

—, *The Life of Lucifer. The Devil in the Middle Ages*. Ithaca: Cornell University Press, 1984.

—, *Mephistopheles. The Devil in the Modern World*. Ithaca: Cornell University Press, 1986.

Dorothy L. Sayers, 'The Faust Legend and the Idea of the Devil', *Publications of the English Goethe Society* (1946), 1–20.

August Schnezler (ed.), *Badisches Sagenbuch. Eine Sammlung der schönsten Sagen, Geschichten, Märchen und Legenden des badischen Landes aus Schrifturkunden, dem Munde des Volkes und der Dichter*. 2 volumes. Karlsruhe: W. Creuzbauer, 1846. Rptd Leipzig: Zentral-antiquariat der Deutschen Demokratischen Republik, 1976.

Charlotte Spivack, 'Pact with the Devil', in Jean-Charles Seigneuret (ed.), *Dictionary of Literary Themes and Motifs*. 2 volumes. New York: Greenwood Press, 1988, II, 941–48.

Francis Griffin Stokes (ed.), *Epistolæ obscurorum virorum: The Latin Text with an English Rendering, Notes and an Historical Introduction*. London: Chatto & Windus, 1909.

Gerald Strauss, 'The Faust Book of 1587', in Boerner/Johnson, 27–39.

Alexander Tille (ed.), *Die Faustsplitter in der Literatur des sechzehnten bis achtzehnten Jahrhunderts*. 4 volumes. Berlin: Emil Felber, 1898–1901.

John Van Cleve (ed.), *Sebastian Brant's 'The Ship of Fools' in Critical Perspective, 1800–1991*. Columbia/SC: Camden House, 1993.

Jacobus de Voragine, *The Golden Legend. Readings on the Saints*. Translated by William Granger Ryan. 2 volumes. Princeton: Princeton University Press, 1993.

Theodor Zahn, *Cyprian von Antiochien und die deutsche Faustsage*. Erlangen: Andreas Deichert, 1882.

Theodore Ziolkowski, *The Sin of Knowledge. Ancient Themes and Modern Variations*. Princeton: University Press, 2000.

Chapter Two

From Superstition to Scepticism

Heroes are the exception among men, and Faust is the exception among heroes.
—Henry Levin

The Scholar as Villain

The two hundred years from 1570 to 1770 saw the legend of Faustus establish itself as a major landmark in world literature. The first printed chapbook appeared in 1587, some fifty years after the last of its subject's alleged sightings; an earlier manuscript from the mid-1570s was discovered in Wolfenbüttel Library and edited by Gustav Milchsack. The success of the Faust Book is astounding. It was quickly distributed across Europe. The attention-grabbing title of the German original reads: *The History of Dr Johann Faustus, the World-Renowned Magician and Master of the Black Arts, relating how he pledged himself to the Devil for a fixed period of time, and the strange adventures that he experienced, brought about and committed, until he finally received the wages that he had earned. Collected in several parts from among his own surviving papers and prepared for publication as a terrifying example, a case-study of debauchery and a well-intentioned warning for the benefit of all arrogant, overbearing and godless individuals.* The title says it all: the book was launched as a case-study of debauchery intended as a warning to the Christian reader.

Considering the reputation it was to enjoy in subsequent years, the slim volume began its career as a surprisingly inconspicuous-looking booklet with many irritating features. It is plodding and repetitive in its approach and contains confusing digressions. The sermonising is obtrusive. It offers cheap jokes beside sententious warnings, and the tale is cloaked in, at times even choked by, borrowed quotations from a variety of religious and secular sources. Its ethical content can be summed up in a single quotation from chapter 68: 'Always struggle against the devil and never stop trying to defeat him.' In pursuing his didactic aim, the author showed little creativity, but had recourse to homilies and catechisms for the theological content, to earlier joke books and folk traditions for the entertaining sections, and did not shrink from lifting entire passages from encyclopaedias in order to supply descriptions of the many cities and countries that Faustus claims to visit on his extensive travels. The readership, used to homilies and saints'

10. *Title page of the first printed chapbook, 1587.*

biographies that were likewise littered with improbable incidents, will have assumed the story to be no less authentic than these.

We do not know for certain who the author was, although there have been a variety of conjectures as to his identity: Andreas Frei, a schoolteacher from Speyer, a local pastor, or even the publisher himself, Johann Spiess [or Spies] of Frankfurt. Different scholars have put forward their own particular theories as to its provenance and ethos, all of them in some ways convincing, in others less so. It can be safely assumed that the 'History' was originally written as a Protestant religious tract containing clear evidence of anti-Catholic bias, for example in its condemnation of monasticism and celibacy and its emphasis on the futility of last-minute conversions. Yet the wide circulation of the text would indicate that there was something in it that could appeal to both parties and attract the interest of moderates as well as that of hard-liners. Robert Petsch argued somewhat implausibly in 1911 that the Faust Book was based at least in part on a superior but no longer extant Renaissance novel in Latin, of which the surviving vernacular text is a corrupt and defective derivative. Others argue in support of a Catholic and a Protestant source coming together in the Spiess compilation. Recent investigations show that the material was influenced by the witch trials that were current in Europe at the time (Allen, 582–94; Noll-Wiemann, 97; Baron (1989), 15–23).

11. Wittenberg University. Illustration from the Matriculation Register, 1644.

The location of the story at Wittenberg is of some significance. That university was a foundation that coincided in time with the earliest records naming Doctor Faustus. Wittenberg was the first German university to have arisen not out of an earlier monastic centre of learning but by Imperial edict at the behest of the local ruler, Elector Frederick the Wise of Saxony. It opened its doors in 1502 and rapidly gained fame as a result of the presence of Martin Luther, who took up a teaching post there in 1508 and promulgated his famous 95 theses from there in 1517. Although in abeyance today, the University of Wittenberg was the most popular German university between 1530 and 1620, making it virtually synonymous with progressive and innovative thought in higher education at the time. Faustus is placed there not only because he is a part of the world of idle speculation that was to be swept away by Martin Luther, but perhaps also because its more liberal charter would have permitted an eccentric mind to flourish there.

The narrative is divided into three sections, describing how the pact came to be signed, what benefits Faustus enjoyed in consequence, and how his life became more miserable as the hour of reckoning approached. These are chapters 1–17, 18–32 and 33–68. After a brief biographical sketch that stresses Faustus' origins as 'the son of a peasant', his entry into an urban world above his god-given station in life, thanks to the intervention of a wealthy cousin, and his discontent with conventional learning, there follows an account of his conjuration of the devil, which involves drawing magical circles at a cross-roads in a lonely forest. The devil who eventually responds to his spells introduces himself as 'Mephostophiles' and promises to grant Faustus twenty-four years of service in return for possession of his immortal soul thereafter. A pact is concluded along these lines and signed in blood. Faustus immediately questions the spirit about matters concerning heaven, hell and salvation, and is given answers that coincide in all essentials with opinions current at the time. The question of repentance is presented from a Protestant angle, in that deathbed conversions are held to be insufficient to secure divine grace. Faustus has damned himself by associating voluntarily with the powers of hell, and Mephostophiles declares that he himself would have avoided this path, had he been given the option.

With the second section, the chapbook becomes more diverse. It begins with Faustus asking questions of a more general nature about the sun and the planets, the origins of summer and winter, thunder and lightning. All answers accord with the knowledge or suppositions of the time, giving the book the function of an almanac or science textbook. The devil takes his pupil on a virtual tour of hell and the stars, with the author emphasising that this was made possible through visual deception and sensual disorientation. A rapid tour of the world follows, with Faustus visiting Paris, the Rhineland, Rome, Constantinople, Britain, Crete, the Caucasus Mountains and many other places in rapid succession, before ending up back at home in the vicinity of Erfurt. There then follows another lesson in astronomy, with questions raised and answered about the nature of comets, shooting stars and the like.

The third and final section of the chapbook is the most problematic. Faustus now appears at the Imperial court of Charles V (suggesting a date between 1530 and 1556), where he carries out a number of feats both admirable and pathetic. He is able to conjure up the shades of dead heroes such as Alexander the Great, but he also fools around with the assembled knights, making one of them grow antlers on his head, and plays practical jokes on horse-dealers, inn-keepers and money-lenders, figures who counted among the pet hates of sixteenth-century society. Intertwined with such seemingly carefree exploits are reflections on the perpetrator's impending damnation, nowhere more obviously so than when an old religious man comes forward and attempts to persuade him to abandon heresy and return to the Church. Faustus seems torn, half-inclined to obey, but is reminded, rightly or wrongly, that God will show no mercy towards one so deeply immersed in sin as himself. Helen of Troy is displayed to a group of inquisitive students, a little 'gem set in lead' in the eyes of anyone expecting the icon of female beauty to be treated with more ceremony than she receives at this narrator's hands. The doctor's end is in sight, he knows his time is nearly up and assembles his friends around him to hear his final oration. Curiously for one so steeped in wickedness, he pleads with them not to follow his example and urges them to avoid all association with demons and evil spirits. His death is gruesome and a warning to all. After his death he is spotted lurking in his house, staring from the window, a sure sign of an unquiet spirit that cannot find rest even in the afterlife.

The debate as to the artistic merits of the slender volume has been confused by our knowledge of the myriad continuations and re-workings of the original. It is hard to condemn as inadequate a work that proved so fruitful to later writers. Nonetheless, there are many who admit that it comes across as 'a cheap production' (Hatfield, 464), 'a crude piece of compilation of no literary value' (Palmer/More, 129), 'a miserable construct', and the work of 'a bungler who lacks just about every quality that one might demand of the most modestly talented narrator' (Petsch, Scherer; both cited by Allen, 584). Others have praised it in the highest terms, as 'one of the greatest inspirational books' of the post-classical period (Butler, 338).

Whatever its defects, the volume was soon reprinted, extended, imitated and translated. Four or more editions appeared during 1587 (Jones, 9). Many people will have read it as 'fact', and a hunger developed for further information. New authors set themselves up to write sequels. Additional material was added by upgrading the figure of Christopher Wagner, Faustus' *famulus* ('assistant', 'house-boy') who was generally assumed to have been privy to some of his master's secrets. The first Wagner Book appeared in 1593, and, in response to the latest discoveries, incorporated an account of a voyage to the New World. Later on, Wagner himself was credited with an assistant, Johann de Luna, whose further escapades spawned material for yet more stories. These cannot all be considered here; suffice it to say that what began as the product of a locally based cottage industry rapidly became a global brand-name.

The History of Doctor John Faustus

Two years after the Faust Book had appeared, its hero had attained sufficient notoriety in England for a ballad about 'the life and deathe of Doctor FFAUSTUS the great Cunngerer' to be registered in February 1589. The ballad, now lost, may have itself been derived from a lost source (Greg, 6f.). The English translation of the chapbook by 'P.F. Gent[leman]' cannot be dated. One copy from 1592 survives, but it does not appear to be a first edition. The phrase 'newly imprinted' in the title indicates the existence a previous edition, perhaps from as early as 1588, that has perished. It is generally held to be an improvement on the Spiess text. Jones speaks of 'the work of an obscure but brilliant translator' (Butler, 32-41; Noll-Weimann, 105-111; Jones, 1, 11-34). As a translation of the German, it is more reliable in some respects than in others. In the following extracts, it will be used to convey a flavour of the original German, as it is similarly archaic and therefore

THE

HISTORIE

ofthe damnable

life, and deſerued death of

Doctor Iohn Fauſtus,

Newly imprinted, and in conueni-

ent places imperfect matter amended:

according to the true Copie printed

at Franckfort, *and tranſlated into*

Engliſh by P.F.Gent.

Seene and allowed.

Imprinted at London by Thomas Orwin, and are to be

ſolde by Edward White, dwelling at the little North

doore of Paules, at the ſigne of the Gun. 1592.

12. *Title page of the earliest surviving copy of the English translation (amended in 1592).*

reproduces the 'woodcut' effect that subsequent generations of readers found attractive. The full title reads: *The Historie of the damnable life, and the deserved death of Doctor John Faustus, Newly imprinted, and in conuenient places imperfect matter amended: according to the true Copie printed at Franckfort, and translated into English by P. F. Gent. Seene and allowed. Imprinted at London by Thomas Orwin, and are to be solde by Edward White, dwelling at the little North doore of Paules, at the signe of the Gun. 1592.*

An entry in the Court Book of the Stationers' Company for December 1592 shows that two publishers, Orwin and Jeffes, both claimed the text as theirs (Jump, xxii). There are major deviations from the German original which are important for two reasons: they show how the material was developing from a fairly crude tract into a more subtle investigation of psychological drama, and they also give us an indication of the translator's identity. It is obvious that the travelogue section (Chapter 22 in P.F., chapter 26 in Spiess) omits places that are mentioned by the German author, while adding others that are not. But it is also surprisingly accurate in many respects, despite a tendency to look down upon the 'rude German author' (Chapter 21; Rose, 119).

The German text lists the following countries as having been visited by Faustus within the space of twenty-five days:

> *Pannoniam, Osterreich, Germaniam, Behem, Schlesien, Sachssen, Meissen, Düringen, Franckenlandt, Schwabenlandt, Beyerlandt, Littauw, Liefflandt, Preussen, Moscowiterlandt, Frießlandt, Hollandt, Westphalen, Seelandt, Brabandt, Flandern, Franckreich, Hispaniam, Portugall, Welschland, Polen, Ungern, vnnd dann wieder Düringen* (Chapter 26; Henning, 64: 'Pannonia, Austria, Germany, Bohemia, Silesia, Saxony, Meissen, Thuringia, Franconia, Swabia, Bavaria, Latvia, Lithuania, Prussia, Muscovy, Frisia, Holland, Westphalia, Zealand, Brabantia, Flanders, France, Spain, Portugal, Italy, Poland, Hungary, and back again to Thuringia')

In the English version, Faustus has the same short time-span of twenty-five days at his disposal for his tour, and despite misunderstanding many of the place-names, the translator manages to fit in countries in which the German author showed no interest and of whose existence he may not have known.

> Pannonia, Austria, Germania, Slesia, Saxony, Missene, During, Francklandt, Shawblandt, Beyerlandt, Stiria, Carinthia, Poland, Litaw, Liefland, Prussia, Denmarke, Muscovia, Tartaria, Turkie, Persia, Cathai, Alexandria, Barbaria, Ginnie, Peru, the straits of Magelanes, India, all about the frozen Zone, and Terra Incognita, Nova Hispaniola, the Isles of Terzera, Mederi, S. Michael's, the Canaries, and the Tenorrifocie, into Spaine, the Mayne Land, Portugall, Italie, Campania, the Kingdome of Naples, the Isles of Sicilia, Malta, Majoria, Minoria, to the Knights of the Rhodes, Candie or Crete, Ciprus, Corinth, Switzerland, France, Freesland, Westphalia, Zeeland, Holland, Brabant, and all the seventeen provinces in Netherland, England, Scotland, Ireland, all America, and Island, the out isles of Scotland, the Orchades, Norway, the Bishopric of Breame, and so home again; all these Kingdoms, Provinces and Countries he passed in twenty-five days, in which time he saw very little that delighted his mind (Chapter 22; Rose 122f.).

While the German author sends his character off towards central and eastern Europe, covering many of the places that are described in Hartmann Schedel's *Weltchronik* ('Chronicle of the World', 1493), the British translator directs him to other continents. Evidently misunderstanding place-names such as Swabia ('Shawblandt') and Thuringia ('During'), he has Faustus journey out to the west and across the ocean, as far as Guinea and Peru. For obvious reasons, Madeira, the Azores and Canaries were closer to the sea-faring Elizabethans' hearts than the provinces of central and eastern Europe. In the process, the 'English' Faustus becomes something of an adventurer in the mould of Drake and Raleigh. Marlowe was to build on this element by presenting him as longing not just for wisdom and beauty, but also for an Empire-building role.

When the translator names places that are not among the stations on the German Faustus' itinerary, we may have an indication of his identity. For while the German *Historia* has Faustus travel from Nuremberg to Munich, Vienna, Prague, and eventually Cracow, the English text gives a more detailed description of the latter, suggesting that the English translator was more familiar with Prague and Cracow than the author of the first chapbook had been (Rohde, 5f).

As to his identity, this may be guessed at on the basis of the geographical descriptions; it seems likely that only someone who had personally visited Cracow and Prague would extend the topographical data on these places. John Dee, a multi-talented advisor to Queen Elizabeth I, is a not improbable candidate. He was in Poland in 1584 and thereafter in Prague. He spent several years in Germany (Kassel, Erfurt, Leipzig), before returning to England in 1589, and was thus in German-speaking Europe when the chapbook was published. Dee was himself accused of conjuring and of many other forbidden practices; he and his associate Edward Kelley were viewed with a mixture of admiration and suspicion and interrogated by the papal nuncio in Prague. It is highly probable that Dee will have read the chapbook and been well qualified to translate the topical publication into English, but as a controversial favourite of the reigning monarch he needed to conceal his identity. It is equally possible that Dee commissioned the translation, as Henry Jones suggests, which does not rule out the possibility that he had a hand in it (Rohde, 14f; French, 120–3; Empson, 201).

The English version is frequently more forgiving of Faustus than the German author had been. The latter continually stresses his arrogance, while the emphasis on religious duty is considerably lessened in translation. Here Faustus is much less inclined to blame himself for turning his back on God. In chapter 14, P.F. makes him regret 'had not I desired to know so much, I had not been in this case [...] now therefore must I be rewarded accordingly'. Spiess's chapter 15 paints a far more explicit image of sin: *hette ich Gottselige Gedancken gehabt, vnd mich mit dem Gebett zu Gott gehalten, auch den Teuffel nicht so sehr bei mir einwurtzeln lassen, so were mir solchs Vbel an Leib vnnd Seel nicht begegnet* ('If only I had had thoughts that were pleasing to God and had held on to Him in my prayers and not allowed the Devil to take root in me, the evil I am experiencing in body and soul would not have happened', Henning, 36; Rose, 92). The chapters in which Mephostophiles mocks Faust for his ungodliness are toned down, and in one case, chapter 65, omitted altogether.

There are other ways in which the English Faustus comes off better than his original model. While the German Faustus gets *täglich gekochter Speiss* and *guten Wein* ('cooked food every day', 'good wine'), the translator grants him 'such meat as Faustus wished for' alongside 'the best wine' (Henning, 27; Rose, 80). His gluttony is played down. The peasantry are also treated differently. In German, *Bawern* ('farmers') are regularly used as victims; they become 'clowns', 'clumsy fellows without sophistication', in translation. Finally, Helen of Troy is far more alluring, as the following comparison will show:

Als er wider hinein gehet, folgete jm die Königin Helena auff dem Fuss nach, so wunder schön, dass die Studenten nit wusten, ob sie bey jhnen selbsten weren oder nit, so verwirrt vnnd innbrünstig waren sie. [...] sie sahe sich allenthalben in der Stuben vmb, mit gar frechem vnd bübischem Gesicht [...]

Literal translation: 'When he returned, Queen Helen was following behind him, so wonderfully beautiful that the students did not know whether they were beside themselves or not, such was their confusion and lust. [...] she looked all round the room with a quite cheeky and knavish expression [...]'

PFG's translation: 'Returning presently again, after whom immediately followed the fair and beautiful Helena, whose beauty was such that the students were all amazed to see her, esteeming her rather to be a heavenly than an earthly creature. [...] she looked round about her with a rolling Hawk's eye, a smiling and wanton countenance [...]' (Spiess, chapter 49, Henning, 106; P.F., chapter 45, Rose 178f.)

In the original, there is no mention of Helena's 'heavenly' qualities; such an analogy would have been considered blasphemous. The terms 'cheeky' and 'knavish' are expanded into 'smiling' and 'wanton', which helps to tone down the mischief and focus on her sexual allure. Jones has analysed P.F.'s style and concluded that, in contrast to his German source, he had 'a flair for pungent expression, a vivid visual imagination and a taste for ironic humour' which results in 'vigorous descriptive prose, informed by mental precision, startlingly fresh, and inevitably quickening the characters of Faustus and Mephostophiles by improving their rhetoric.' (Jones, 12) The following extracts, beginning with the pact, are taken from P.F. Gent's version and give an impression of the main elements in the narrative:

I, Johannes Faustus, Doctor, do openly acknowledge with mine own hand, to the greater force and strengthening of this Letter, that since I began to study and speculate the course and order of the Elements, I have not found through the gift that is given me from above, any such learning and wisdom, that can bring me to my desires: and for that I find, that men are unable to instruct me any farther in the matter, now have I Doctor John Faustus, unto the hellish prince of Orient and his messenger Mephostophiles, given both body & soul, upon such condition, that they shall learn me, and fulfil my desire in all things, as they have promised and vowed unto me, with due obedience unto me, according unto the Articles mentioned between us.

Further, I covenant and grant with them by these presents, that at the end of twenty-four years next ensuing the date of this present Letter, they being expired, and I in the mean time, during the said years be served of them at my will, they accomplishing my desires to the full in all points as we are agreed, that then I give them full power to do with me at their pleasure, to rule, to send, fetch, or carry me or mine, be it either body, soul, flesh, blood, or goods, into their habitation, be it wheresoever: and hereupon, I defy God and his Christ, all the host of heaven, and all living creatures that bear the shape of God, yea all that lives; and again I say it, and it shall be so. And to the more strengthening of this writing, I have written it with mine own hand and blood, being in perfect memory, and hereupon I subscribe to it with my name and title, calling all the infernal, middle, and supreme powers to witness of this my Letter and subscription (Chapter 6; Rose, 76f.).

The reasons for the prominence of the pact were suggested above (24). Literary devils in mediaeval morality plays had been growing restless with their victim's attempts to release themselves from bondage to Satan after their wishes had been fulfilled. The story of Giles of Portugal, for example, depicts a man eager to give over his soul to Satan in exchange for knowledge, yet the devils had to release him when he called upon Mary for assistance (Meek, 123f.). The written pact was a device that turned the tables on the victim and ensured the triumph of evil over good, something the mediaeval authors were extremely reluctant to envisage. The pact effectively disables divine grace and destroys Faustus. It is the product of a post-mediaeval world now unable to accept the simple formula of transgression-repentance-forgiveness that was central to earlier morality plays and saints' legends. Strong arguments have recently been advanced to suggest that the written contract with Hell was given added relevance by the proliferation of early modern credit transfer documents, such as the 'Fugger bills', paper 'bonds' which circulated as currency in the sixteenth century (Wilson, 167–73).

There are many reasons why Faustus should sign a pledge rich in legalistic formulations. The concept of secret pacts with the devil was a sixteenth-century commonplace and is often seen in satirical woodcuts. The paper record resembles

13. *The Pact as the devil's final resort. Woodcut by Günther Zainer, c. 1471. The repentant sinner cannot be saved if the devil produces written evidence supporting his claim.*

baptismal, marriage and land ownership documents, and therefore gives the relationship between man and devil an apparent legitimacy and finality that replicates established forms of ownership and commitment, such as the feudal oath of allegiance. As a man of considerable learning, Faustus must be familiar with the legalistic procedures and terminology, here used to confirm his own perpetual enslavement to evil. There is thus a sense in which he is hoist by his own petard, in that the experienced doctor, a proven master of the written word, is now trapped by a scroll that has the power to seal his fate forever. It is the doctor's own world of logic, legal procedures and the entire classical heritage on which university education was based that is now turned against him in the provisions of a single document.

14. Luther concludes a pact with a fool and a devil. Satirical illustration from Thomas Murner, Von dem Grossen Lutherischen Narren, *1522.*

When the pact is concluded, Faustus begins to ask Mephostophiles to fulfil his part of the deal. He attempts to extract knowledge of the real and the spiritual world by asking about astronomical and meteorological phenomena, and receives answers which accord with the conventional wisdom of the time. In the eighth year he is deluded by trickery into assuming that the devil can take him into hell itself; the text makes it clear that all Faustus is experiencing is a kind of virtual reality trip ('Mark how the Devil blinded him'; Rose, 111). Elsewhere, Faustus often fails to get what he requests. There are certain wishes that Mephostophiles cannot grant. One of these is the task of providing his recruit with a wife.

Doctor Faustus continued thus in his Epicurish life day & night, and believed not that there was a God, hell, or Devil: he thought that body and soul died together, and had quite forgotten Divinity or the immortality of his soul, but stood in his damnable heresy day and night. And bethinking himself of a wife, called *Mephostophiles* to counsel; which would in no wise agree: demanding of him if he would break the covenant made with him, or if he had forgot it. Hast not thou (quoth *Mephostophiles*) sworn thyself an enemy to God and all creatures? To this I answer thee, thou canst not marry; thou canst not serve two masters, God, and my Prince: for wedlock is a chief institution ordained of God, and that hast thou promised to defy, as we do all, and that hast thou also done: and moreover thou hast confirmed it with thy blood: persuade thyself, that what thou dost in contempt of wedlock, it is all to thine own delight. Therefore *Faustus*, look well about thee, and bethink thyself better, and I wish thee to change thy mind: for if thou keep not what thou hast promised in thy writing, we will tear thee in pieces like the dust under thy feet. Therefore sweet *Faustus*, think with what unquiet life, anger, strife, & debate thou shalt live in when thou takest a wife: therefore change thy mind.

Doctor *Faustus* was with these speeches in despair and, as all that have forsaken the Lord, can build upon no good foundation: so this wretched *Faustus* having forsook the rock, fell in despair with himself, fearing if he should mention Matrimony any more, that the Devil would tear him in pieces. For this time (quoth he to *Mephostophiles*) I am not minded to marry. Then you do well, answered his spirit. But shortly & that within two hours after, *Faustus* called his spirit, which came in his old manner like a Friar. Then *Faustus* said unto him, I am not able to resist nor bridle my fantasy, I must and will have a wife, and I pray thee give thy consent to it. Suddenly upon these words came such a whirlwind about the place, that *Faustus* thought the whole house would come down, all the doors in the house flew off the hooks: after all this, his house was full of smoke, and the floor covered over with ashes: which when Doctor *Faustus* perceived, he would have gone up the stairs: and flying up, he was taken and thrown into the hall, that he was not able to stir hand nor foot: then round about him ran a monstrous circle of fire, never standing still, that *Faustus* fried as he lay, and thought there to have been burned. Then cried he out to his Spirit *Mephostophiles* for help, promising him he would live in all things as he had vowed in his handwriting. Hereupon appeared unto him an ugly Devil, so fearful and monstrous to behold, that *Faustus* durst not look on him. The Devil said, what wouldst thou have *Faustus*: how likest thou thy wedding? what mind art thou in now? *Faustus* answered, he had forgot his promise, desiring him of pardon, and he would talk no more of such things. The Devil answered, thou were best so to do, and so vanished.

After appeared unto him his Friar *Mephostophiles* with a bell in his hand, and spake to *Faustus*: It is no jesting with us, hold thou that which thou hast vowed, and we will perform as we have promised: and more than that, thou shalt have thy heart's desire of what women soever thou wilt, be she alive or dead, and so long as thou wilt, thou shalt keep her by thee.

These words pleased *Faustus* wonderful well, and repented himself that he was so foolish to wish himself married, that might have any woman in the whole City brought to him at his command; the which he practised and persevered in a long time (P.F., chapter 9, Rose 81–4).

Faustus' abortive attempt to persuade the spirit to provide a wife for him is interesting for a variety of reasons. It shows Faustus asking for something specific and yet failing to receive it – an indication of the limitations of the devil's powers and a sign that Faustus will be short-changed all along the line. However, its position so early in the narrative has the effect of highlighting this request, and the reader is obliged to consider why marriage should be so offensive to Faustus' new master. The answer to this goes some way beyond the initial explanation that Faust, as a sworn 'enemy to God and all creatures', cannot commit himself to loving one such creature in the form of a wife. The biblical argument that a man 'cannot serve two masters' (Matthew 6:24; Luke 16:13) takes us closer to the heart of the problem. This formulation was regularly cited in conjunction with the rule of celibacy for priests and monks of the old faith. When Faustus summons Mephostophiles to re-state his desire, it is thus entirely consistent that the latter should appear before him attired 'like a Friar', dressed like a monk who was pledged to remain single. Lutheran theology had moved on; the influential pamphlet by Johann Eberlin, *Wie gar gfarlich sey, So ain Priester kain Eeweyb hat, Wye Unchristlich, Vnd schedlich aim gmainen Nutz Die menschen seynd, Welche hindern die Pfaffen Am Eelichen Stand* ('How very dangerous it is, if a Priest has no Spouse. How Unchristian and Harmful to the general well-being those People are, who prevent Priests from attaining the State of Matrimony') appeared in 1522 and put forward many arguments supporting the marriage of priests. The provocative title page shows such marriages being conducted by a reformed clergy. Mephostophiles is clearly unreconstructed and therefore a 'dangerous' opponent to marriage, which is why we find him filling the house with wind and ashes, and encircling his victim with a ring of fire. Faustus is soon intimidated. Shortly thereafter he is offered a substitute: the possession, for as long as he wishes, of any woman, alive or dead. The devil may have little say in marriage, but he is the master of the sinful alternative. From this point on, up to the most recent movies, sexual frustration will play a major part in persuading men to bind themselves to the diabolical powers. Yet the constant love of a virtuous woman offers the most effective promise of escape from the pact, as later versions will also demonstrate.

After Doctor *Faustus* had a while pondered and sorrowed with himself of his wretched estate, he called again *Mephostophiles* unto him, commanding him to tell him the judgement, rule, power, attempts, tyranny and temptation of the Devil, & why he was moved to such kind of living: whereupon the spirit answered, this question that thou demandest of me, will turn thee to no small discontentment: therefore thou shouldst not have desired me of such matters, for it toucheth the secrets of our kingdom, although I cannot deny to resolve thy request. Therefore know thou *Faustus*, that so soon as my Lord *Lucifer* fell from heaven, he became a mortal enemy both to God and man, and hath used (as now he doth) all manner of tyranny to the destruction of man, as is manifest by divers examples, one falling suddenly dead, another hangs himself, another drowns himself, others stab themselves, others unfaithfully despair, and so come to utter confusion: the first man *Adam* that was made perfect to the similitude of God, was by my Lord his policy, the whole decay of man: yea, *Faustus*, in him was the beginning and first tyranny of my Lord *Lucifer* used to man: the like did he with *Cain*, the same with the children of *Israel*, when they worshipped strange Gods, and fell to whoredom with strange women: the like with *Saul*: so did he by the seven husbands of her that after was the wife of *Tobias*: likewise *Dagon* our fellow brought to destruction 30,000 men, whereupon the Ark of God was stolen: and *Belial* made *David* to number his men, whereupon were slain 60,000; also he deceived King *Solomon* that worshipped the Gods of the heathen: and there are such Spirits innumerable that can come by men and tempt them, drive them to sin, weaken their belief: for we rule the hearts of Kings and Princes, stirring them up to war and bloodshed; and to this intent do we spread ourselves throughout all the world, as the utter enemies of God and his Son Christ, yea & all those that worship them and that thou knowest by thyself *Faustus*, how we have dealt with thee. To this answered Faustus, why then thou didst also beguile me. Yea (quoth *Mephostophiles*) why should not we help thee forwards: for so soon as we saw thy heart, how thou didst despise thy degree taken in Divinity and didst study to search and know the secrets of our kingdom; even then did we enter into thee, giving thee divers foul and filthy cogitations, pricking thee forward in thine intent and persuading thee that thou couldst never attain to thy desire, until thou hast the help of some Devil: and when thou wast delighted with this, then took we root in thee & so firmly, that thou gavest thyself unto us, both body and soul the which thou (*Faustus*) canst not deny. Hereat answered *Faustus*, Thou sayest true *Mephostophiles*, I cannot deny it: Ah, woe is me miserable *Faustus* how have I been deceived? had not I desired to know so much, I had not been in this case: for having studied the lives of the holy Saints and Prophets, & thereby thought myself to understand sufficient in heavenly matters, I thought myself not worthy to be called doctor *Faustus*, if I should not also know the secrets of hell, & be associated with the furious Fiend thereof; now therefore must I be rewarded accordingly. Which speeches being uttered, *Faustus* went very sorrowfully away from *Mephostophiles* (Chapter 14; Rose, 90–2).

It is curious that, as well as deluding and cheating Faustus, the devil presents many matters from an orthodox point of view and goes further than one might expect in reminding his charge how grave his situation has become. Thus Faustus' life is by no means one of untrammelled pleasure; he is depicted as anxious, sorrowful, and plunged into despair. Well before his twenty-four years are up, he must suffer the knowledge of his wrong-doing, and in this respect the devil is not so much his partner in crime as a malicious tormentor motivated by a fair dose of *Schadenfreude*. Mephostophiles wastes few opportunities to acquaint Faustus with the magnitude and consequences of his transgression, and he does this from a respectable mainstream theological perspective: Faustus has voluntarily damned himself through his own arrogance and folly, and his punishments will be those that await the other great sinners. This devil is a double-sided creature, paradoxically given to encouraging and deprecating vice in one breath, nowhere more obviously so than when he has recourse to quoting mediaeval theologians on the subject of the duration of hell's torments. After asking about his chances of redemption, Faustus receives the following reply, which could have proceeded from the lips of any fire-and-brimstone preacher of the day.

Therefore know *Faustus*, that the damned have neither end nor time appointed in the which they may hope to bee released, for if there were any such hope, that they but by throwing one drop of water out of the Sea in a day, until it were all dry: or if there were an heap of sand as high as from the earth to the heavens, that a bird carrying away but one come in a day, at the end of this so long labour; that yet they might hope at the last, God would have mercy on them, they would be comforted: but now there is no hope that God once thinks upon them, or that their howlings shall never be heard; yea, so impossible, as it is for thee to hide thy self from God, or impossible for thee to remove the mountains, or to empty the sea, or to tell the number of the drops of rain that have fallen from Heaven until this day, or to tell what there is most of in the world, yea and for a Camel to go thorough the eye of a needle: even so impossible it is for thee *Faustus*, and the rest of the damned, to come again into the favour of God. And thus *Faustus* hast thou heard my last sentence, & I pray thee how doest thou like it? But know this, that I counsel thee to let me be unmolested hereafter with such disputations, or else I will vex thee every limb, to thy small contentment. Doctor *Faustus* departed from his Spirit very pensive and sorrowful, laid him on his bed, altogether doubtful of the grace and favour of God, wherefore he fell into fantastical cogitations: fain he would have had his soul at liberty again, but the Devil had so blinded him, & taken such deep root in his heart, that he could never think to crave God's mercy, or if by chance he had any good motion, straightways the Devil would thrust him a fair Lady into his chamber, which fell to kissing and dalliance with him, through which means, he threw his godly motions in the wind, going forward still in his wicked practices, to the utter ruin both of his body and soul. (Chapter 15; Rose 97f.)

The terrors of hell everlasting are an enduring instrument of indoctrination. James Joyce (132) recalls the effect of a similar homily in *A Portrait of the Artist as a Young Man*. The much-cited analogy of the little bird that picks up a single grain of sand and yet cannot shift the smallest part of a mountain representing eternity derives from the mystic illuminations of Henry Suso (circa 1296–1366). It soon became a mediaeval commonplace and appears to have spread to the inmates of hell itself. No less strange is the devil's use of parables taken from the Bible in furthering his argument. The question here raised is whether, ultimately, there can be some kind of co-operation between the forces of good and evil. This co-operation has a negative effect in the chapbook where Faustus is surrounded by enemies on all sides and neither the Bible nor his nefarious companion can assist him; small wonder that he seeks solace in the arms of fair ladies. In later versions of the Faust material, the possibilities of a more beneficial interaction between God and devil are raised.

On other occasions, Faustus surveys the sights like a tourist:

From thence he went to *Norenberg*, whither as he went by the way, his Spirit informed him that the Town was named of *Claudius Tiberius* the Son of *Nero* the Tyrant. In the Town are two famous Cathedral Churches, the one called Saint *Sabolt*, the other Saint *Laurence*; in which Church hangeth all the reliques of *Carolus Magnus*, that is his cloak, his hose and doublet, his sword and Crown, his Sceptre, and his Apple. It hath a very gorgeous gilden Conduit in the market of Saint *Laurence*, in which Conduit, is the spear that thrust our Saviour into the side, and a piece of the holy Crosse; the wall is called the fair wall of *Norenberg*, and hath five hundred and twenty-eight streets, one hundred and sixty wells, four great, and two small clocks, six great gates, and two small doors, eleven stone bridges, twelve small hills, ten appointed market places, thirteen common hothouses [public baths], ten Churches, within the

Town are thirty wheels of water-mills; it hath one hundred and thirty-two tall ships [*Hauptmannschafft*, meaning unclear, but not 'ships'], two mighty Town walls of hewn stone and earth, with very deep trenches. The walls have one hundred and eighty Towers about them, and four fair platforms, ten Apothecaries, ten Doctors of the common law, fourteen Doctors of Physic. (Chapter 21; Rose 134f.)

This example represents the extensive 'gazetteer' section of the chapbook. Faustus is not just a wizard and sinner but also a great traveller, and in this portion of the book he provides the author with an opportunity to reel off factual material of general interest. It is characteristic of the literature of the time that books should have more than one focus. That the chapbook should aim to be instructive as well as entertaining and morally edifying is not exceptional. Yet there is something odd about these descriptions of localities. A surprising amount of space is devoted to ancient shrines and relics – precisely those items that one might expect the Protestant author to ignore or even denounce as abominations. Surely, in a Lutheran tract there would be no references to Longinus' spear and pieces of the Holy Cross, the focus of types of veneration Martin Luther sought to suppress? The answer to this apparent contradiction is that the author had copied sections from earlier travelogues, such as Hartmann Schedel's *Weltchronik* of 1493, still a standard work on the on the geography of the world when the Faust Book was committed to paper (Milchsack, xviii–lxxiv). The German text contains evidence of the Protestant author's scepticism; here we read of 'a very gorgeous golden fountain in the marketplace, therein is or is said to be the spear that Longinus thrust into our Saviour's side, and a piece of the Holy Cross'. This, and much else, is lost in the garbled translation. The phrase *darinnen ist oder sol seyn der Sper, so Longinus Christo in die Seyten gestochen* ('therein is or is said to be the spear that Longinus thrust into Christ's side', Henning, 71) is an intriguing instance of the author's belated attempt to question what he is reporting while ultimately leaving the matter open to the reader's personal judgement; the spear 'is or is said to be' genuine!

A different side to the doctor is revealed in the anecdotal sections, where Fausus acts like a clown among clowns:

Doctor Faustus being in a Town of *Germanie* called *Zwickau*, where he was accompanied with many Doctors and Masters, and going forth to walk after supper, they met with a Clown that drove a load of Hay. Good even good fellow said *Faustus* to the Clown, what shall I give thee to let me eat my belly full of Hay? The Clown thought with himself, what a mad man is this to eat Hay, thought he with himself, thou wilt not eat much, they agreed for three farthings he should eat as much as he could: wherefore Doctor *Faustus* began to eat, and that so ravenously, that all the rest of his company fell a-laughing, blinding so the poor Clown, that he was sorry at his heart, for he seemed to have eaten more than the half of his Hay, wherefore the clown began to speak him fair, for fear he should have eaten the other half also. *Faustus* made as though he had had pity on the Clown, and went his way. When the Clown came in place where he would be, he had his Hay again as he had before, a full load. (Chapter 35; Rose, 164)

Faustus' prank in eating a load of hay belonging to a 'clown' (the German is *Bawer*, a farmer, a term generally regarded as synonymous with folly) must mark the lowest ebb of his career. Yet he performs this inane prank in the company of 'many Doctors and Masters'. Previously, he had associated with Emperor Charles, and yet shortly thereafter he carries out cheap conjuring tricks for no other purpose than to raise a laugh at some poor fool's expense. The author has taken it upon himself to entertain, and in this respect the chapbook has overt affinities with many other popular publications that turn out to be compilations of anecdotes surrounding a named figure, such as Till Eulenspiegel ('Owlglass'), or Fortunatus.

> When Doctor *Faustus* called to mind, that his time from day to day drew nigh, he began to live a swinish and Epicurish life, wherefore he commanded his Spirit *Mephostophiles*, to bring him seven of the fairest women that he had seen in all the time of his travel: which being brought, first one, and then another, he lay with them all, insomuch that he liked them so well, that he continued with them in all manner of love, and made them to travel with him in all his journeys. These women were two *Netherlanders*, one *Hungarian*, one *English*, two *Wallons*, one *Francklander*: and with these sweet personages he continued long, yea even to his last end. (Chapter 53; Rose, 192)

Thoughts of his impending doom may have had an influence in turning Faustus towards pleasures of the flesh, persuading him to end his days leading a 'swinish and Epicurish life'. The two terms are close synonyms in the author's parlance, and yet they bridge the divide, so important for this text, between the vulgar idiom, in which Faustus is no better than the beasts, and the academic tone of a treatise in which the sinner is a follower of the philosopher Epicurus, famous for his doctrine, not, as implied here, of excess, but of freedom from turmoil. Faustus himself is poised halfway between ribald anecdotes and informed reflection. He mingles with peasants and with dons. English readers may be pleased to note that one of the seven beauties selected for the 'swinish' man's delectation is from England, although the two 'Wallo[o]ns' are two ladies from Swabia in the German original, making Germany the outright winner in the beauty stakes. These carnal delectations turn out to be short-lived.

> My trusty and well-beloved friends, the cause why I have invited you into this place is this: Forasmuch as you have known me this many years, in what manner of life I have lived, practising all manner of conjurations and wicked exercises, the which I have obtained through the help of the Devil, into whose Devilish fellowship they have brought me, the which use the like art and practice, urged by the detestable provocation of my flesh, my stiff-necked and rebellious will, with my filthy infernal thoughts, the which were ever before me, pricking me forward so earnestly, that I must perforce have the consent of the Devil to aid me in my devices. And to the end I might the better bring my purpose to pass, to have the Devil's aid and furtherance, which I never have wanted in mine actions, I have promised unto him at the end and accomplishing of twenty-four years, both body and soul, to do therewith at his pleasure: and this day, this dismal day those twenty-four years are fully expired, for night beginning my hour-glass is at an end, the direful finishing whereof I carefully expect: for out of all doubt this night he will fetch me, to whom I have given myself in recompense of his service, both body and soul, and twice confirmed writings with my proper blood. Now have I called you my well-beloved Lords, friends, brethren,

and fellows, before that fatal hour to take my friendly farewell, to the end that my departing may not hereafter be hidden from you, beseeching you herewith courteous, and loving Lords and brethren, not to take in evil part any thing done by me, but with friendly commendations to salute all my friends and companions wheresoever: desiring both you and them, if ever I have trespassed against your minds in any thing, that you would all heartily forgive me: and as for those lewd practices the which this full twenty-four years I have followed, you shall hereafter find them in writing: and I beseech you let this my lamentable end to the residue of your lives be a sufficient warning, that you have God always before your eyes, praying unto him that he would ever defend you from the temptation of the Devil, and all his false deceits, not falling altogether from God, as I wretched and ungodly damned creature have done, having denied and defied Baptism, the Sacraments of Christ's body, God himself, all heavenly powers, and earthly men, yea, I have denied such a God, that desireth not to have one lost. Neither let the evil fellowship of wicked companions mislead you as it hath done me: visit earnestly and oft the Church, war and strive continually against the Devil with a good and steadfast belief on God, and Jesus Christ, and use your vocation in holiness. Lastly, to knit up my troubled Oration, this is my friendly request, that you would to rest, & let nothing trouble you: also if you chance to hear any noise, or rumbling about the house, be not therewith afraid, for there shall no evil happen unto you: also I pray you arise not out of your beds. But above all things I entreat you, if you hereafter find my dead carcass, convey it unto the earth, for I die both a good and bad Christian; a good Christian, for that I am heartily sorry, and in my heart always pray for mercy, that my soul may be delivered: a bad Christian, for that I know the Devil will have my body, and that would I willingly give him so that he would leave my soul in quiet: wherefore I pray you that you would depart to bed, and so I wish you a quiet night, which unto me notwithstanding will be horrible and fearful. (Chapter 63; Rose 202–4)

Faustus' departure from this world is preceded by a studied oration to his students which serves several purposes. Firstly, it helps to authenticate the narrative by placing it in a context. These students are witnesses, as is the doctor's named assistant, who is given the task of compiling his master's biography. The students afford the repentant sinner an opportunity to express his contrition and to go over the main points of his career, drawing a sober conclusion about the depravity into which he had sunk. They are his target audience, the congregation to whom this sermon is addressed. They are the flower of youth and the ones most immediately at peril, since they too have chosen to study and will be exposed to similar temptations. They need to search their consciences as to whether to read the classics or the Bible, whether to follow the gospels or Aristotle, and whether to tempt fate by seeking to invoke the devil. But in another sense the students form part of a body of disciples, they are the followers, the ones who have learnt and whose mission it is to spread the word. This is made clear by the setting, which is that of a Last Supper or Eucharist, in which a goblet of wine is circulated, and the one shortly to meet his death shows his love for them by warning them of what is to come.

The Students lay near unto that hall wherein Doctor *Faustus* lay, and they heard a mighty noise and hissing, as if the hall had been full of Snakes and Adders: with that the hall door flew open wherein Doctor *Faustus* was, then he began to cry for help, saying: murther, murther, but it came forth with half a voice hollowly: shortly after they heard him no more. But when it was day, the Students that had taken no rest that night, arose and went into the hall in the which they left Doctor *Faustus*, where notwithstanding they found no *Faustus*, but all the hall lay besprinkled with blood, his brains cleaving to the wall: for the Devil had beaten him from one wall against another, in one corner lay his eyes, in another his teeth, a pitiful and fearful sight to behold. Then began the Students to bewail and weep for him, and sought for his body in many places: lastly they came into the yard where they found his body lying on the horse dung, most monstrously torn, and fearful to behold, for his head and all his joints were dashed in pieces. (Chapter 63; Rose, 206f.)

The scene could be from a Hollywood 'splatter' movie. The gory death suffered by the sinner confirms that the devil has claimed his prize. Mutilation of the body is a sure sign that the infernal powers have been allowed to have their way with him, for the moment at least. From a strictly Christian point of view, the final verdict would not be pronounced until the Day of Judgement, which is presumably why Faustus is not seen on his way to hell, but lurking at the window of his former abode: 'The same night Doctor *Faustus* appeared unto his servant lively, and shewed unto him many secret things the which he had done and hidden in his life time. Likewise there were certain which saw Doctor *Faustus* look out of the window by night as they passed by the house' (Rose, 207). He has become an 'undead' shade awaiting his final condemnation, something the narrator could not presume to anticipate.

The story concludes with an assurance that Faustus' disciple would write down everything that had happened, thus conveying greater authenticity to the proceedings. Given the work's success, it is hardly surprising that 1594 saw the publication of a Wagner Book, supposedly written by the same assistant and adding more titillating detail to the plot. It is attributed to a certain Fridericus Scotus Tolet [Frederick Schott from Toledo?], who took it upon himself to add new features which he considered would satisfy a popular interest. The book consists of a 19-page preface, followed by 297 unnumbered pages. Scotus claims to have translated it from the Spanish, having received it from a Brother of the Benedictine Order, presumably in Toledo. Although this makes little sense, what is interesting is that Scotus adopts a more conciliatory attitude to the Catholic Church and claims his work was motivated by a desire to acquaint all people with the ways of the devil (Richards, 5).

The Wagner Books demonstrate the vitality of the new myth. A mere six months and six days after publication of the German Wagner Book, a translation appeared in London; in fact, two separate Wagner Books were issued in London during that year, which differ both from one another and, substantially, from the German. From the earliest days, there were times when the English obsession with Faustus exceeded that of his German compatriots. This is what, in an English sequel, becomes of the students who would not listen:

But the most lamentable sight of the seven Scholars utterly torn in pieces, their blood having changed the colour of the ground into a dark Crimson, all their bodies as black as any coal as if they had been scorched with a material fire, their flesh violently rent from the bones, and hanging down in morsels like the skirts of a side coat, their bones all broken, their veins cut in sunder, and their bowels broad shed upon the earth, their brains poured out and covering the red grass all over, their noses stumped, their eyes thrust out, their mouths widened and slit up to the ears, their teeth dashed out, and their tongues staring out betwixt their gums, their hair clean singed off, in brief imagine with your selves in your minds, and propound a picture in your thought, the most deformed, torn and ill favoured that you can think on, yet shall it not compare to the most lachrimable sight and show of them, surpassing as much all credit as my skill duly to describe them, whom when they had buried without tarriance, razed the house to the ground, and filled up the moats with earth, heaping upon the place of this murder the stones of the house defaced, then they returned home discoursing with lamentable judgement upon the high and severe revenge of God's indignation upon them which durst presume to tempt his glorious Majesty. (*English Wagner Book*, 38f; Richards, 84f.)

Much of the rest of the Wagner Books is taken up with Wagner's journeys in the company of Faustus' unquiet shade, Mephistopheles and the spirit Auerhahn (Akercock in the English version), the latter a kind of monkey bequeathed to Wagner by the doctor (Fritz, 9). In the German versions, Wagner behaves very much as Faustus had done. He visits Prague, where he sells a Hebrew-speaking parrot to a Jew at an enormous profit. From there he continues to Italy, Lapland, and the Canary Islands, before meeting a death no less gruesome than that of his erstwhile master. The device of having him die in Spain was a convenient way of explaining why his story had not been disseminated in Germany. A bogus claim to authenticity is made when Scotus states that Wagner's account had been published seventy years earlier in Spanish.

The areas receiving most emphasis in the English Wagner Books are new. Here the ex-disciple joins the Imperial troops that are locked in battle with the Turks at the gates of Vienna. Faustus returns in spirit form and enables Wagner to play numerous tricks on the enemy. The Turkish Sultan is fooled by Faustus' ghostly appearance into believing that he is Muhammad (Richards, 92), and battles between the Christian cavalry and Turkish elephants give the text a topical interest. Wagner is treated surprisingly positively; Faustus, Akercock, Mephostophiles and Wagner being described at one point as 'four honest fellows' (Richards, 112). There is a happy ending to the narrative when the Turks are defeated through Faustus' intervention:

So the Duke of Austria rid of his enemies, gave him self to his forepassed life, and the other princes with great joy caused general feasts and triumphs to be performed in all their kingdoms, provinces, and territories whatsoever. (Richards, 118)

There are substantial variations between the surviving Wagner Books, which were published in Germany in 1593 and 1594, in England in 1594 (two separate editions) and in Dutch in 1597 (Fritz, Introduction, xx). Later German authors, including Widmann and Pfitzer, drew heavily on these sources which continued to be published until the late eighteenth century. An anonymous example dating from 1799, *Leben, Thaten und Höllenfarth Wagners* ('Wagner's Life, Death, and

Descent into Hell'), is prefixed (iii) by an assurance that it was written for pure entertainment only. Translations into Dutch, French and Czech are also extant. But the crucial development was to be provided not by the many continuations in prose but by the transition to a different medium, when the material was taken up by an English dramatist.

The Villain as Hero

Christopher Marlowe's adaptation confirms the story's status as one of the foremost international best-sellers of its day. Despite heavy reliance on one or several sources, his version is no mere clone of the German Faust Book, but an independent *tour de force* that provides evidence of its contemporary relevance and inspirational power. Structurally, it is somewhere half-way between the mediaeval morality play and the Elizabethan dramatisations of remarkable but torn and destructive characters. In Shakespeare, the outwardly wicked Macbeth and Richard III occasionally strike a note of sympathy, while the more benign Lear and Hamlet show a violent and destructive streak. Marlowe's *Doctor Faustus* is a 'bridge-piece' between theatrical images of mediaeval and modern man (Cole, 121), in which the author exploits the dramatic potential of the despairing scholar's descent into vice and presents the outcome, against the grain of the original, as something conducive to empathy as well as revulsion. His Faustus is tragic, and tragedy requires a heroic streak. Audience reaction is hard to gauge. In some quarters, Faustus may have been felt to deserve contempt rather than pity. This is the response one might legitimately expect from the church-going audiences of the time, and is actively encouraged by the poet's many critical references to necromancy and other heinous malpractices. Yet in a wider sense, the play invites reflection on many other matters that were being debated at the time of its composition.

> With occasions for idolatry appearing wherever they looked and in whatever they read or thought, and disputants occupying every conceivable point in a spectrum that stretched from 'idolatrous' to 'iconoclastic', Englishmen of the Renaissance lived amid a chaos of contention. The struggle was pervasive enough to touch the lives of all and bitter enough to end careers, close theatres, demolish works of art, sunder families, and lead, on occasion, to bloodshed. [... T]here is a strong reason to suggest that the issues that vexed society at large would have been of concern [to Elizabethan audiences]. (Siemon, 44)

It is only when Faustus is set, incongruously perhaps, against the ancient heroes that his plight becomes truly tragic. He faces a greater ordeal than the ancients, who with very few exceptions – Tantalus and Sisyphus come to mind – were sent to a place only slightly worse than earth in their afterlife. The theme of hell and its torments is double edged: non-tragic for those who bow to the supreme wisdom of God – for how could He be wrong in condemning the wilful sinner? – but utterly catastrophic for those able to see both sides and to question the compatibility of eternal damnation with divine love and mercy. To be certain that the sinner will indeed go to hell, s/he must be evil through and through – otherwise there is always the potential of forgiveness and redemption, even in the most narrowly dogmatic view. Seen from this angle, the life of Doctor Faustus, part hellish genius, part superman, provides an case-study of a titanic loner whose life appears to demonstrate all those qualities that deserve to forfeit divine pardon, yet whose psychology is sufficiently well drawn as to hint at a better man behind the contorted façade.

Several reasons may have combined to interest Christopher Marlowe in the figure of a man beyond the pale. Marlowe himself entered the University of Cambridge in 1580 to study divinity and obtained a BA in 1584 and an MA in 1587. Although he spent a total of six years as a student and was a member of a group of writers known as 'University Wits', it was noted that he was often absent on government service. Since details are lacking, there is a strong suspicion that he led a double life and was possibly involved in some form of espionage. There is evidence of his having spent time abroad, in Reims and in the Netherlands. Given the turbulence of the age, it is not surprising that he should have died early in a tavern brawl, though the circumstances remain opaque and some argue that he must have been killed for political reasons, as his murderer was granted a free pardon almost immediately.

It is not known exactly when Marlowe composed *Doctor Faustus*. It is assumed that he knew the Faust Book and may have had had access to a manuscript version, and possibly to 'better and richer Faust sources for his drama than the German book or its English translation could offer him.' (Jantz, 152) Marlowe's text was not published until after his death. The delay may have been due to concern that the play would be less attractive to paying audiences once it was available in print and therefore also to the 'pirates' in the publishing trade. It could have been written at any time between 1587 and 1593, though the later date seems more probable. The oldest copy of the printed text dates from 1604, and a longer and rather different text dates from 1616. These two unstable versions are known as A (1517 lines) and B (2121 lines). Editors have tended to favour one over the other. W. W. Greg argues for the superiority of 'B', Roma Gill for 'A', which in Greg's view is a 'bad' or corrupt quarto, 'prepared for the less critical and exigent audiences of provincial towns [...] by memorial reconstruction from the London performance' (Greg, 29; 60). Until recently, the 'B Text' was seen as superior, because it appears more polished and provides more useful material for performances, but 'A' is closer in time to Marlowe, and 'B' was evidently revised in order to satisfy the Act of Abuses of 1606, which forbade the profane or jesting use of religious names and epithets. The 'A Text' refers to 'God' and to 'Christ's blood', while 'B' omits what had become proscribed blasphemous phrases. With less incidental material, the 'A Text' has the advantage of concentrating more directly on the central Faustian predicament; 'most of the additions of the B text are trivial' (Gill, xxii; see below,

195). We shall refer to the 'A Text' which has thirteen as opposed to nineteen scenes. 'A' favours the spelling Mephastophilis while 'B' uses Mephostophilis.

The chapbook describes Faustus' upbringing as a peasant's son, brought up in a town by a wealthy uncle or cousin; Marlowe's chorus merely hints at his background (I, 12-14), and the play goes rapidly into the opening monologue, which shows Faustus as a successful scholar who is well versed in the classics. But his 'university education' is not enough; he bids farewell to the Bible and turns to 'lines, circles, schemes, letters and characters' (I, 51). Encouraged by the episodic figures Valdes and Cornelius, Faustus determines to invoke the devil that very evening. Arrogance may be the driving force, but as such it is closer to theatrical *hubris* than to mere folly. There is a serious undercurrent to this speech, which marks him as a man of sensitivity.

> How am I glutted with conceit of this?
> Shall I make spirits fetch me what I please,
> Resolve me of all ambiguities,
> Perform what desperate enterprise I will?
> I'll have them fly to India for gold,
> Ransack the Ocean for orient pearl,
> And search all corners of the new found world
> For pleasant fruits and princely delicates;
> I'll have them read me strange philosophy,
> And tell the secrets of all foreign kings;
> I'll have them wall all Germany with brass,
> And make swift Rhine circle fair Wittenberg;
> I'll have them fill the public schools with silk,
> Wherewith the students shall be bravely clad;
> I'll levy soldiers with the coin they bring,
> And chase the Prince of Parma from our land,
> And reign sole king of all our provinces;
> Yea, stranger engines for the brunt of war,
> Than was the fiery keel at Antwerp's bridge,
> I'll make my servile spirits to invent. (I, 78-97)

Faustus has developed, in the few short years since the publication of the chapbook, into a more modern character who with clarity of purpose shows signs of knowing where he is headed. He is well on the way to becoming what he was to the eighteenth century, an example of an admirable hunger for knowledge, as a 'striver' who aspires to stand on his own two feet and work out his own salvation. The above extract reveals ambitions remarkably similar to those of the colonial power into which the author was born. Marlowe knows of his country's desire to ransack India, to plunder gold and seek out pearls, not to mention the tropical fruits that would be handsomely rewarded if placed as a delicacy on some princely table. There is something of the rude soldier of fortune in him: he longs to reap the earth's riches 'As Indian Moors obey their Spanish lords' (thus Valdes, scene 1, line 121). This seemingly casual phrase draws a specific analogy between the hero's quest for wisdom and the military campaigns of the colonial powers who conducted their brutal conquests claiming to ensure the spread of Christianity. And the line 'I'll levy soldiers with the coin they bring' shows knowledge of how to raise an army. An awareness of what was happening overseas appears to have increased Faustus' sense of adventure; Marlowe has him reach out beyond the ambitions of a mere scholar.

Faustus' concerns are not merely those of a conquistador; he is well aware of the Spanish encroachment on the Low Countries. The Prince of Parma is mentioned as a threat (scene 1, 93); he had been imposed by Spain as Governor of the Netherlands, as Marlowe will have known when he was arrested in Vlissingen in 1592. Numerous later plays and films have Faustus engage with the Duke or Prince of Parma, and he often seduces the Duchess. The tragedy of his situation is that he cannot properly employ the political power he seeks, even after he has obtained unlimited licence from the devil. As Jane K. Brown puts it, 'One of Faustus' prime motivations for his turn to magic is a desire for power; yet it is never clear in the play what Faustus intends to do with his power. He appears, appropriately, at the courts of the Pope, the emperor, and the Duke of Anhalt, but his desire for power remains an empty dream.' (Brown (1987), 61) But this Faustus is far from indifferent to the moral and theological implications of the career on which he is about to embark. He proves to be full of questions which he does not hesitate to put to his interlocutor. Yet his response to this 'intelligence' is very different from that of his model in the Frankfurt chapbook.

FAUSTUS:	Was not that Lucifer an Angel once?
MEPHASTOPHILIS:	Yes, Faustus, and most dearly lov'd of God.
FAUSTUS:	How comes it then that he is Prince of devils?
MEPHASTOPHILIS:	O, by aspiring pride and insolence,
	For which God threw him from the face of heaven.
FAUSTUS:	And what are you that live with Lucifer?
MEPHASTOPHILIS:	Unhappy spirits that fell with Lucifer,
	Conspired against our God with Lucifer,
	And are for ever damned with Lucifer.
FAUSTUS:	Where are you damned?
MEPHASTOPHILIS:	In hell.
FAUSTUS:	How comes it then that thou art out of hell?
MEPHASTOPHILIS:	Why this is hell, nor am I out of it.
	Think'st thou that I who saw the face of God,
	And tasted the eternal joys of heaven,
	Am not tormented with ten thousand hells,
	In being deprived of everlasting bliss?
	O Faustus, leave these frivolous demands,
	Which strike a terror to my fainting soul.
FAUSTUS:	What, is great Mephastophilis so passionate,
	For being deprived of the joys of heaven?
	Learn thou of Faustus manly fortitude,
	And scorn those joys thou never shall possess.
	Go bear those tidings to great Lucifer:
	Seeing Faustus hath incurred eternal death,
	By desperate thoughts against Jove's deity,

> Say, he surrenders up to him his soul,
> So he will spare him four and twenty years,
> Letting him live in all voluptuousness,
> Having thee ever to attend on me,
> To give me whatsoever I shall ask,
> To tell me whatsoever I demand,
> To slay mine enemies, and aide my friends,
> And always be obedient to my will.
> Go and return to mighty Lucifer,
> And meet me in my study at midnight,
> And then resolve me of thy master's mind. (III, 64–100)

These lines were written no more than five years after the Faust Book, yet the change of perspective and purpose is startling. Marlowe's Mephastophilis is painfully conscious of his own damnation, and aware, too, that hell is not some remote underground location but a state of mind that torments the living. He is more sympathetic but also more tragic than his antecedent in the Faust Book. There is also a marked difference in the doctor's response to this challenge. Renaissance man that he is, the English Faustus not only stands his ground but mocks the devil for his impassioned self-pity ('is great Mephastophilis so passionate [...]?'). The curious confession ('Thinkst thou that I who saw the face of God [...] am not tormented with ten thousand hells') cuts no ice with him; instead of lapsing straightway into despair, as his predecessor had done, Marlowe's Faustus sends his visitor back to where he came from with a message for Lucifer himself stating that he, Faustus, will lay down the terms and fix the hour of their next assignation. Marlowe designed him as an assertive entrepreneur and conscious risk-taker. And yet here, too, there is scope for frivolity and slap-stick.

[*Enter* MEPHASTOPHILIS *with devils, giving crowns and rich apparel to* FAUSTUS, *and dance, and then depart.*]

FAUSTUS: Speak, Mephastophilis, what means this show?
MEPHASTOPHILIS: Nothing, Faustus, but to delight thy mind withal,
And to show thee what magic can perform.
FAUSTUS: But may I raise up spirits when I please?
MEPHASTOPHILIS: Ay, Faustus, and do greater things then these.
FAUSTUS: Then there's enough for a thousand souls.
Here, Mephastophilis, receive this scroll,
A deed of gift of body and of soul;
But yet conditionally, that thou perform
All articles prescribed between us both.
MEPHASTOPHILIS: Faustus, I swear by hell and Lucifer
To effect all promises between us made.
FAUSTUS: Then hear me read them: On these conditions following.
'First, that Faustus may be a spirit in form and substance.
Secondly, that Mephastophilis shall be his servant, and at his command.
Thirdly, that Mephastophilis shall do for him, and bring him whatsoever.
Fourthly, that he shall be in his chamber or house invisible.
Lastly, that he shall appear to the said John Faustus at all times, in what form or shape soever he please.

John Faustus of Wittenberg, Doctor, by these presents, do give both body and soul to Lucifer prince of the East, and his minister Mephastophilis, and furthermore grant unto them that 24 years being expired, the articles above written inviolate, full power to fetch or carry the said John Faustus body and soul, flesh, blood, or goods, into their habitation wheresoever.
By me John Faustus.'

MEPHASTOPHILIS: Speak, Faustus, do you deliver this as your deed?

FAUSTUS: Ay, take it, and the devil give thee good on't.

MEPHASTOPHILIS: Now, Faustus, ask what thou wilt.

FAUSTUS: First will I question with thee about hell;
Tell me, where is the place that men call hell?

MEPHASTOPHILIS: Under the heavens.

FAUSTUS:. Ay, but whereabout?

MEPHASTOPHILIS: Within the bowels of these elements,
Where we are tortured and remain forever,
Hell hath no limits, nor is circumscribed
In one self place; for where we are is hell,
And where hell is, there must we ever be:
And to conclude, when all the world dissolves,
And every creature shall be purified,
All places shall be hell that is not heaven.

FAUSTUS: Come, I think hell's a fable.

MEPHASTOPHILIS: Ay, think so still, 'til experience change thy mind.

FAUSTUS: Why? Think'st thou then that Faustus shall be damned?

MEPHASTOPHILIS: Ay, of necessity, for here's the scroll,
Wherein thou hast given thy soul to Lucifer.

FAUSTUS: Ay, and body too, but what of that?
Think'st thou that Faustus is so fond,
To imagine, that after this life there is any pain?
Tush; these are trifles and mere old wives' tales.

MEPHASTOPHILIS: But, Faustus, I am an instance to prove the contrary
For I am damned, and am now in hell.

FAUSTUS: How! Now in hell? Nay and this be hell, I'll willingly be damned here; what? walking, disputing, &c.? But leaving off this, let me have a wife, the fairest maid in Germany, for I am wanton and lascivious, and cannot live without a wife.

MEPHASTOPHILIS: How, a wife? I prithee, Faustus, talk not of a wife.

FAUSTUS: Nay, sweet Mephastophilis, fetch me one, for I will have one.

MEPHASTOPHILIS: Well, thou wilt have one. Sit there 'til I come; I'll fetch thee a wife in the devil's name.

[Enter MEPHASTOPHILIS *with a devil dressed like a woman, with fire works*]

MEPHASTOPHILIS: Tell, Faustus, how dost thou like thy wife?

FAUSTUS: A plague on her for a hot whore!

MEPHASTOPHILIS: Tut, Faustus, marriage is but a ceremonial toy;
If thou lovest me, think no more of it.
I'll cull thee out the fairest courtesans,
And bring them every morning to thy bed.
She whom thine eye shall like, thy heart shall have;
Be she as chaste as was Penelope,
As wise as Saba, or as beautiful
As was bright Lucifer before his fall. (V, 83–161)

The resemblances with the German prose account of the pact are superficial. Faustus is a more active agent and is ready to challenge some of the threats with which Mephastophilis confronts him. To speak out robustly 'Come, I think hell's a fable' is a sign of something more than arrogance; it shows that the author was willing to allow a 'hero' to serve as a mouthpiece for views so heretical that they run counter to the very essence of the widely practised Christian faith. Faustus has ceased to be an example of an aberration and has taken the first brave steps towards becoming a spokesman for free thought, though the devil still insists that it is the signed pact rather than Faustus' general predisposition to sin that has damned him:

FAUSTUS: Why? Think'st thou then that Faustus shall be damned?
MEPHASTOPHILIS: Ay, of necessity, for here's the scroll,
                 Wherein thou hast given thy soul to Lucifer. (V, 129–31)

The subsequent call for a wife is also handled very differently. Mephastophilis does not refer to the rule of celibacy or quote the biblical passage about serving two masters; he dismisses marriage outright as a mere 'toy', and promises courtesans whose qualities rival those of the ancient paradigms of chastity and wisdom.

There are various ways in which Marlowe exploited the underlying drama of the situation. Faustus is often accompanied by two angels, one good and one evil, who whisper admonishments and advice into his ears at every opportunity. This is psychologically effective in revealing the 'spilt' in Faustus' personality, and is also more theatrical than monologues and less repetitive than successive discussions with Mephastophilis would be. The 'wife' is not merely talked about but seen. Accompanied by fireworks and with a diabolical leer she would have been frighteningly off-putting as a 'hot whore'. She has become a representation of the dangerously seductive rather than of the wholesome and godly side of marriage; here, too, is a glimpse of the future development of the legend, where lascivious temptresses vie with pure maidens for the doctor's affection.

Another important feature of Marlowe's text is the more effective integration of comedy. Many critics have disputed that the texts that have come down to us are an exact record of what Marlowe wrote, and modern audiences are often disappointed by this aspect. A recent reviewer of the 2002 production at the Young Vic in London wrote:

> The biggest problem for a contemporary staging of Marlowe's 16th Century play is how little Faustus exploits his new power.
>
> The entire middle section is a succession of juvenile hi-jinks, with [Faustus] playing pranks on a horse dealer, performing magic tricks or splatting the Pope with a custard pie.
>
> Director David Lan wisely races through these unrewarding scenes, spanning 24 years in an hour so he can concentrate on the hero's climactic anguish.
>
> And he achieves a moment of lasting power by having Helen of Troy appear to Faustus in a looking glass, further highlighting the character's obsessive narcissism (Neil Smith, 'Natural Law for Doctor Faustus', *Friday*, 22 March 2002).

Several critics have spoken of the work as 'a cathedral hit by a bomb'; but they tend to cherry-pick the surviving text, arguing that Marlowe should be credited with the 'covenant' or 'pact' scenes, and with the 'punishment' scene at the end, but that large portions in between, particularly the humorous adventures of Faustus, were written by others (McAlindon, 129; Covella, 201). Empson implies that the good parts of *Doctor Faustus* are very good and that the bad parts remain a mystery. It is known that two men, William Byrde and Samuel Rowle, were paid £4 in 1602 for supplying 'adicyones' to the text of 'docter fostes'. It is usually assumed that these will have consisted of the more light-hearted parts. Particularly the anti-Papal sections involving the Pope (in both texts) and the papal pretender Bruno (in the 'B' Text) are felt to detract from the earnest purpose of the plot, in which Doctor Faustus' immortal soul is at stake. Empson and others claim that such lightweight scenes have 'practically nothing to do with Faust'. There is a sense of outrage that after sensitively written, profound verses, 'one is dropped abruptly into bilge, as through a trap door'. Empson claims that Marlowe's greatest fault – if Marlowe's it is – is that he shows indifference to the feelings of the audience: 'all through the middle of the play Faust is assumed to be a popular character, a great source of fun, and yet his enormous punishment at the end is accepted as a matter of routine.' (Empson, 40) This is a thoroughly modern comment, and one that ignores the possibility that Marlowe's audiences might have looked for comic ingredients with greater enthusiasm than for moral edification. Elizabethan audiences were famous for receiving great tragedies with a liberal dash of humour and even, on occasions, slapstick. The combination appears to have been attractive to them. Empson is patently wrong when he argues that such episodes have 'practically nothing to do with Faust'; the chapbook in its original form was a compendium of material from many sources: the Bible, travelogues, elementary science manuals and, not least, joke books, and the following the scene with the Pope is of central importance rather than an add-on provided by an incompetent collaborator.

[*Sound a sonnet. Enter the* POPE *and the* CARDINAL OF LORRAINE *to the banquet, with* FRIARS *attending*]

POPE:	My Lord of Lorraine, wilt please you draw near.
FAUSTUS:	Fall to, and the devil choke you and you spare.
POPE:	How now! Who's that which spoke? Friars, look about.
FRIAR:	Here's nobody, if it like your Holiness.
POPE:	My Lord, here is a dainty dish was sent me from the Bishop of Milan.
FAUSTUS:	I thank you sir. [*snatches it*]
POPE:	How now! Who's that which snatched the meat from me? Will no man look? My Lord, this dish was sent me from the Cardinal of Florence.
FAUSTUS:	You say true; I'll ha't. [*snatches it*]
POPE:	What again? My Lord, I'll drink to your grace.
FAUSTUS:	I'll pledge your grace. [*snatches the cup*]
LORRAINE:	My Lord, it may be some ghost newly crept out of purgatory, come to beg a pardon of your Holiness.
POPE:	It may be so. Friars, prepare a dirge to lay the fury of this ghost. Once again, my lord, fall to.

[*The* POPE *crosses himself*]

FAUSTUS: What, are you crossing of your self?
                     Well, use that trick no more, I would advise you.

[*The* POPE *crosses himself again*]

FAUSTUS: Well, there's the second time, aware the third,
                     I give you fair warning.

[*The* POPE *crosses himself again, and* FAUSTUS *hits him a box of the ear; and they all run away*]

FAUSTUS: Come on, Mephastophilis, what shall we do?

MEPHASTOPHILIS: Nay, I know not. We shall be cursed with bell, book, and candle.

FAUSTUS: How? Bell, book, and candle, candle, book, and bell,
                     Forward and backward, to curse Faustus to hell.
                     Anon you shall hear a hog grunt, a calf bleat, and an ass bray,
                     Because it is Saint Peter's holy day (VII, 57–85).

These jibes will have gone down well in many circles during the reign of Queen Elizabeth, when the anti-papal parties were gaining influence in England. The humour, as in the scenes with Rafe and Robin, with horse-coursers and ostlers, is crass. Nonetheless it would be unwise to read the play or its source entirely along Lutheran lines. G.M. Pinciss has shown that Cambridge was one of the battle-grounds between continental Protestantism along Calvinist lines and the English variant, which derived from Cranmer's 42 (later reduced to 39) articles. William Perkins was a lecturer and university fellow who propounded a rigorous form of Calvinism; contemporaries say 'he was able to make his hearers [sic] hearts fall down and hairs stand upright'. Perkins describes the sin of witchcraft as peculiar to those 'not satisfied with [...] knowledge, wit, understanding, memory' (Pinciss, 254). It is easy to see Marlowe as engaging directly with these controversies. The influence of an academic environment on *Doctor Faustus* is far greater than it was on the Faust Book of 1587, where the university is largely ignored. But Marlowe's Faustus is demonstrably the product of an ancient seat of learning, he is a scholar, he knows Latin and Greek, he has studied not only law, medicine, theology, but – unlike his German model – logic, too, and it is this knowledge that is now seen to have made him vulnerable. An excessive interest in the classics, in that very world that gave us tragedy, produces a tragedy of a more modern kind – the damnation of an individual as a result of what has been termed 'academic alienation' (Watt, 44).

Yet in this respect, too, Marlowe has given the story a new twist. The university is satirised, not because it is a hotbed of heresy, but for other reasons. The Cambridge graduate poet paints a satirical picture of an overblown don who quotes semi-intelligible chunks of Latin (scene 3, lines 16–22, etc.), whose fawning assistant mimics him without being able to understand what he is saying, and who 'disputes' with the diabolical emissary as though he were in a private tutorial. Uncouth hangers-on like Rafe and Robin imitate him, but like the sorcerer's apprentice in the folk-tale, the magic runs away with them.

What began as a battle between good and evil, divine certainty and human arrogance, as nurtured by the hothouse of academic learning, rapidly became a satire of university life for its own sake. The lure of classical antiquity which Faustus tries to bring to life as one of his star turns is an important part of the theme. Marlowe recognises more clearly than the chapbook's author had done that Faustus is the product of an age that was deeply torn between whether to follow the Greeks and Romans or to abandon them and follow only the Bible. The Humanists urged the former, the radical iconoclasts wished to destroy the legacy of the past and to base their lives on the scriptures alone. Many great thinkers were caught in the crossfire. Erasmus tried to use reason while not dismissing the revealed scriptures out of hand. The outcome of such an endeavour cannot be other than tragic. The central question posed in *The Tragical History of Doctor Faustus* is: must Faustus be damned because he goes against God, or because he fails as a scholar to understand what he is meant to be teaching? Is his greatest flaw that he parades the spirits of Alexander and Helen around as though they were trophies, instead of learning something from them about the value of harmony and humanity? Is his love for Helen a sign of sensitivity and emotion ('make me immortal with a kiss', scene 12, line 83), or an aberration, in which he falls for the superficial, sensually exciting charms of classical beauty, but fails to appreciate its deeper qualities? And it is all too easily forgotten that Helen herself, far from being an unsurpassed paragon of womanly excellence, was seen as a highly ambivalent figure from classical times onwards (Gill, xxxi).

Faustus' death is a double punishment. In religious terms, it is a fitting indictment of a man who has sinned against God. On a moral plane, it brands him as a man who has failed to absorb what he professed to teach and was therefore fundamentally untrue to himself, putting personal pleasure before scholarship when exercising the powers he acquired through his magic.

FAUSTUS:	God forbade it indeed, but Faustus hath done it. For vain pleasure of four and twenty years, hath Faustus lost eternal joy and felicity. I writ them a bill with mine one blood; the date is expired, the time will come, and he will fetch Mephastophilis.
1. SCHOLAR:	Why did not Faustus tell us of this before, that divines might have prayed for thee?
FAUSTUS:	Oft have I thought to have done so, but the devil threatened to tear me in pieces, if I named God, to fetch both body and soul, if I once gave ear to divinity. And now 'tis too late. Gentlemen, away, lest you perish with me.
2. SCHOLAR:	O, what shall we do to save Faustus?
3. SCHOLAR:	God will strengthen me; I will stay with Faustus.
1. SCHOLAR:	Tempt not God, sweet friend, but let us into the next room, and there pray for him.
FAUSTUS:	Ay, pray for me, pray for me, and what noise soever ye hear, come not unto me, for nothing can rescue me.
2. SCHOLAR:	Pray thou, and we will pray that God may have mercy upon thee.
FAUSTUS:	Gentlemen, farewell. If I live 'til morning, I'll visit you, if not, Faustus is gone to hell.
ALL:	Faustus, farewell. [*Exeunt* SCHOLARS. *The clock strikes eleven*]
FAUSTUS:	Ah Faustus,
	Now hast thou but one bare hour to live,
	And then thou must be damned perpetually.

Stand still you ever moving spheres of heaven,
That time may cease, and midnight never come.
Fair Nature's eye, rise, rise again, and make
Perpetual day, or let this hour be but a year,
A month, a week, a natural day,
That Faustus may repent, and save his soul.
O lente, lente, currite noctis equi!
The stars move still, time runs, the clock will strike.
The devil will come, and Faustus must be damned.
O, I'll leap up to my God! Who pulls me down?
See, see where Christ's blood streams in the firmament;
One drop would save my soul, half a drop, ah, my Christ –
Ah, rend not my heart for naming of my Christ,
Yet will I call on him – Oh spare me, Lucifer!
Where is it now? 'Tis gone,
And see where God stretcheth out his arm,
And bends his ireful brows!
Mountains and hills, come, come, and fall on me,
And hide me from the heavy wrath of God.
No no, then will I headlong run into the earth;
Earth gape! O no, it will not harbour me.
You stars that reigned at my nativity,
Whose influence hath allotted death and hell,
Now draw up Faustus like a foggy mist,
Into the entrails of yon labouring cloud,
That when you vomit forth into the air,
My limbs may issue from your smoky mouths,
So that my soul may but ascend to heaven. [*The watch strikes*]
Ah, half the hour is past: 'twill all be past anon.
O God, if thou wilt not have mercy on my soul,
Yet for Christ's sake, whose blood hath ransomed me,
Impose some end to my incessant pain;
Let Faustus live in hell a thousand years,
A hundred thousand, and at last be saved.
O, no end is limited to damned souls.
Why wert thou not a creature wanting soul?
Or, why is this immortal that thou hast?
Ah, Pythagoras' *metempsychosis*, were that true,
This soul should fly from me, and I be changed
Unto some brutish beast.
All beasts are happy, for when they die,
Their souls are soon dissolved in elements,
But mine must live still to be plagued in hell.
Curst be the parents that engendered me.
No, Faustus, curse thyself, curse Lucifer,
That hath deprived thee of the joys of heaven!
[*The clock striketh twelve.*]
O it strikes, it strikes! Now, body, turn to air,
Or Lucifer will bear thee quick to hell.
[*Thunder and lightning*]
O soul, be changed into little water drops,
And fall into the ocean, ne'er be found.
My God, my God, look not so fierce on me!

83

[*Enter* DEVILS]

> Adders, and serpents, let me breathe a while!
> Ugly hell gape not! Come not Lucifer!
> I'll burn my books! Ah, Mephastophilis.

[*Exeunt* DEVILS *with* FAUSTUS] (XIII, 39–117)

This is the most powerful Faustian monologue ever written (Schirmer-Imhoff, 156). Tragedy is dependent on scenes of misery, crescendos of despair, be they Lear weeping over Cordelia or Othello over Desdemona. Yet the situation of Faustus at the end of his life cannot be matched; it is the final outcry of a man knowing that he will suffer in hell for all of eternity, not just for the space of one thousand nor just for one hundred thousand years. The rhetorical force is great, as is the range of knowledge seen in these lines; from the classical (*lente, lente, currite noctis equi* refers to Ovid's *Amores*, in which the lover begs the 'horses of the night to run more slowly' so that he may taste the delights of amorous dalliance for longer) to the biblical 'Let the rocks and mountains fall on us and hills cover us' (Luke 23:30). Faustus displays the full gamut of his erudition, from the Pythagorean spheres of heaven and the transmigrating of souls (*metempsychosis*) to the conceit of the sun as 'Nature's eye', and the 'gaping' mouth of hell as depicted in mediaeval morality plays. Beneath this now redundant learning is the apparently sincere plea for mercy that goes unheard by a God whom some would see as supremely just, others as wantonly cruel. Faustus admits that he craved to utter God's name and call on him for mercy, but was prevented by the antagonist to whom he had pledged himself; is this not sufficient proof of a fundamentally moral orientation? Yet the Saviour to whom he appeals did not hear him then and will not hear him now. The devils are seen on stage, visually embodying clearer proof of his ruination than even the chapbook's author had been willing to offer.

The pathos, though heart-rending, leads to a strangely muted promise: 'I'll burn my books!' Not, perhaps, the most convincing of turning points, but one which pinpoints the source of evil decisively. Faustus has not been corrupted by the devil directly, nor by the example of others. Nor is the root of evil submerged deep down in his own heart, as a kind of 'original' sin. No; it was the fault of the books. Whether this is a pathetic excuse for a misconstructed life or a final point of recognition, is in the end perhaps less important than that it is there, in the text, as a marker; as evidence that books, academic books, learning, scholarship, a classical education, are identified as the bed from which this tragic plot arose. Without the university and its temptations, there would be no Faustus, without the sixteenth-century dilemma of whether to follow Aristotle or Evangelist, there would be no tragedy of the desperate, disoriented doctor who placed his faith not in the fountains of all knowledge and the wisdom of his own conscience, but in a mere medium: the unreliable leaves of a book. His belated promise to burn them is thus both a final acknowledgement of error and a pathetically inadequate redress, for who could, even then, imagine that evil could be banished by destroying the medium rather than the source of misfortune?

The subsequent development of the Faustian material during the years between these early publications and its rediscovery by Lessing and Goethe in the late eighteenth century was not linear. The reception of the chapbook and of Marlowe's play appears to have been positive, if only to judge by the number of reprints both works were to give rise to in Germany and England. Versions of Marlowe's *Doctor Faustus* were seen in Graz in 1608, in Dresden in 1626, and in Prague in 1661. The extent to which the text was diluted on these occasions is not known. From the early seventeenth century onwards, the fortunes of Faustus are frustrating to trace and frequently obscure. Literature is adversely affected by the Reformation in both countries. In London, theatres were closed in 1642, which effectively put an end to revivals of Elizabethan drama; and when they re-opened under Charles II, it was under very strict control. In German-speaking Europe, the Thirty Years' War (1618–1648) had a devastating impact on cultural life, with the destruction of public buildings, and the impoverishment of the burgher class. Yet Faustus does not entirely disappear from sight. The main landmarks are the puppet plays based loosely on the chapbook and on Marlowe. These were accompanied by sporadic attempts by German authors of the Baroque period to gloss and extend the narrative, emphasise its moral import, and add detail in places where such was felt to be lacking. Finally, a much-reduced storybook version was produced in 1725 by a man styling himself *Der christlich Meynende* ('The Christian Thinker') in which the over-long Baroque versions are trimmed back and the plot is restored to its essentials. Each of these will be considered briefly, as they all contain some pointers forward to Goethe, who drew on several traditions when he made his own contribution.

It is odd to think of the lofty tale of Faustus' pact with the devil being re-enacted by mechanical puppets on strings in temporary booths at fairgrounds, but such displays were common at a time when fixed-base installations were thin on the ground and reserved for members of the nobility. The lively tradition of Elizabethan drama was not entirely suppressed by the Puritans or muzzled by the Restoration; puppeteers were widely welcomed at a time when books, too, were often sold by itinerant salesmen. We know that following the devastation of wide swathes of Germany in the Thirty Years' War, so-called 'English Comedians' made their way across the Channel and performed to German audiences, often in rural settings, at fairs and on other occasions. It was also easier for puppet plays to evade censorship and to be given impromptu performances without the knowledge of the authorities, which meant that controversial themes could be discussed with greater impunity in this format than if presented by live actors.

A version of *Faustus* with Punch-and-Judy-like additions was one of their favourites. These playlets have not survived, as they were not published but kept as manuscripts and updated according to location and topical events. Some details can be deduced from the programmes and notices, as well as from a few diary entries. There was often a council of devils which determined to target Faustus, an opening monologue, the pact and court scenes, magic tricks, failed repentance and the devils dragging their victim off to hell. Farcical elements were not uncommon, particularly as Faustus tended to be accompanied by a servant

(Hanswurst, Kasperl, Pickelhäring) whose job it was to mimic the great man as Rafe and Robin do in Marlowe, and to let off fireworks and get up to all sorts of mischief. These will be examined in more detail in the chapter on 'Faust on Stage', below (197–200; 208–11).

Faust in Prose

Three prose versions will be mentioned, in which the material is first expanded to around 600 pages in conformity with the Baroque love of detail, then considerably reduced in size by the 'Christian Thinker', whom we may presume to have been influenced by a more sober brand of Christian Pietism.

After several authorised and unauthorised reprints of the chapbook, a new, identifiable author produced a second, greatly augmented and diluted prose account of Faustus' life. In 1599, Georg Rudolf Widmann's three-volume compendium appeared entitled *Der Warhafftigen Historien von den grewlichen vnd abschewlichen Sünden vnd Lastern/ auch von vielen wunderbarlichen vnd seltzamen ebentheuren: So D. Iohannes Faustus Ein weitberuffener Schwartzkünstler vnd Ertzzäuberer / durch seine Schwartzkunst / biss an seinen erschrecklichen end hat getrieben. Mit nothwendigen Erinnerungen vnd schönen exempeln / menniglichem zur Lehr vnd Warnung aussgestrichen vnd erklehret* ('True Histories of the gruesome and repellent sins and vices and of many wondrous and strange adventures as experienced through black magic by Dr Johannes Faustus, a well-known sorcerer and wizard, up until his terrifying death. With necessary reminders and splendid examples selected and explained for the benefit of many readers, both to instruct and as a warning'). This was published in Hamburg by Hermann Moller after the author's death, and had quite probably been begun before the 'original' Faust Book came out twelve years earlier. The three volumes add up to a grand total of 671 pages.

Various suggestions have been put forward as to why the Swabian Widmann should have seen fit to expand the original material with so many explanations, warnings and digressions. These include the existence of sources now no longer available to us, the demands of the market-place for ever more 'Faustian' adventures, the need to appeal to an erudite audience, and a supposition that the chapbook was not sufficiently orthodox in its approach to a tricky theological subject: the finality of the sinner's damnation in spite of his private feelings of guilt and repentance. Widmann was known for his fanaticism (Jones, 7). He tries not only to explain and extend, but also to bring the text into an even closer relationship with Luther's Bible, from which he quotes extensively, both in the text itself and in the margins, which are exploited to provide parallels and annotations. The equation of Catholicism with magic is made even more explicit by an allegation that the ritual of Holy Mass is itself a form of magic. Many Popes and other Catholic dignitaries are described as having been in league with Satan. Other polemical digressions of questionable value describe supposed malpractices among Jews.

> Fifty years ago, a baptised Jew came to Breslau, to feed upon the alms of the Christian folk. He was very knowledgeable about Hebrew and supplied the Christians with much information relating to Jewish malpractices, and among other matters he explained why the Jews were so eager to get hold of Christian blood. He always maintained that was a great secret, and only the foremost Rabbis knew the answer [which was that] when a Jew was close to death, they would smear the Christian's blood on him, reciting these or similar words: 'When he who is promised in the Law and by the Prophets cometh, should he turn out to be Jesus, then let this blood of an innocent man who died a believer, help you to attain life everlasting.' (Widmann, 71)

The copy in the British Library contains an interesting handwritten entry at this point, saying 'But you'll be found out straightaway, you can't jump into heaven like that.' This is just one of many instances of gratuitous, prejudicial comment on the part of the author, often with no very obvious connection with Faustus. The victims are Catholics and Jews, as well as professions such as money-lenders, horse-dealers, innkeepers, and peasants. The context shows why it was included; chapter 10 deals with the signing of the pact, and Widmann's extensive commentary (61–77) cites every parallel that comes to mind. Yet the original story is all but lost in the detail, and Widmann could be seen as turning the clock back by treating Faustus as just another faceless victim of devil-worship, rather like the fools in Brant's ship or the nondescript figures in earlier sixteenth-century devil books. Yet it marks a growing thirst for ever more supplementary information about the mysteries of the original. Even the devil's name requires an extensive, if somewhat tortured gloss:

> Thirdly, the above-cited account reveals that the devil calls himself Mephostophiles, which is assumed to be of Persian origin. It is right that spirits should have their proper names. The innocent, holy spirits have names, cf. the angel who called himself Gabriel in the presence of the virgin Mary, and an angel Michael who fought against the devil in Persia, and similarly the angel in Tobias called himself Raphael, so why should the evil spirits not have names of their own? In the Book of Job the Lord God names the devil when He says, 'Satan, from where comest thou?' and in Luke 11 the Jews ask Jesus to drive out Beelzebub etc. (Widmann, 85)

Yet Mephostophiles is very different in Widmann, where Faust makes his pact with the devil in person, and Mephostophiles just happens to be the reluctant go-between chosen to enforce it. Jones (7) characterises him as 'an essentially friendly spirit whose great mischance it is to be subject to Lucifer.' The 'friendly spirit' is not entirely lost in later re-workings of the legend to the point that many subsequent Mephistos appear as friend and foe rolled into one, and some will become interestingly problematic, and not infrequently tragic, in their own right.

Seventy-five years later one Johann Nikolaus Pfitzer, a medical doctor, produced what is best described as an edition of Widmann rather than as an independent re-working of the theme. It runs to 635 pages, an index, and a 96-page sermon by Conrad Wolff. Pfitzer's omissions and additions are substantial. Now, in Nuremberg in 1674, the anti-Catholic propaganda is toned down somewhat, presumably since sales in Catholic Bavaria were envisaged. But the anti-Semitic material in chapter 10 and elsewhere is retained. Those episodes from the chapbook that Widmann had discarded were restored, and, crucially for Goethe, the plot is enriched with the story of Faustus' love for a simple maid from the lower orders. One can only presume that this hint at a misalliance was introduced as a sign of Faustus' dysfunctionality as a man and a lover, but it was later to become an indication of his egalitarian disregard of convention and status.

Seven editions appeared between 1674 and 1726; Goethe read it in 1801. 1725 saw the publication of the third major prose version, attributed to an anonymous 'Christian Thinker' (sometimes assumed to be Conrad Monath, a bookseller and publisher from Nuremberg) entitled *Des durch die gantze Welt beruffenen Ertz-Schwartz-Künstlers und Zauberers Dr Johann Fausts, mit dem Teufel auffgerichtetes Bündnüss, abentheuerlicher Lebens-Wandel und mit Schrecken genommenes Ende, auffs neue übersehen, in eine beliebte Kürze zusammen gezogen, und allen vorsetzlichen Sündern zu einer herzlichen Vermahnung und Warnung zum Druck befördert von einem Christlich-Meynenden* ('The Pact, adventurous life and terrifying end of the world-renowned arch-black magician and sorcerer Dr Johann Faust, revised and reduced to a pleasing length, put into print as a heartfelt caution and warning to all deliberate sinners with the support of a Christian Thinker'). Despite its turgid Baroque title, this is a refreshingly short text by comparison with Widmann and Pfitzer, which may account for its even greater popularity: it ran through no fewer than 33 editions between 1725 and 1820. Surprisingly, too, this 'Christian Thinker' does not set out to preach virtue, but sketches out the bare bones of the plot over a mere 46 pages. There is evidence of a modern mind at work behind the fable, and neither is Faust condemned nor are the events presented with anything more than the detached curiosity of a modern observer. The phrasing of the title (*befördert von ...*) suggests that the 'Christian Thinker' may have been the project's sponsor or financial backer rather than the author. Whether 'deliberate sinners' will have taken much heed of it is a different matter.

> The present pages serve two purposes: either to prove, on the basis of incontrovertible evidence, the truth about the world-famous black magician Doctor Faustus, or, should this not be possible, to demonstrate to the fashionable world of today the falseness thereof, which had originally been my intention. But because there are now innumerable documents both for and against the subject, which are either dedicated to this intricate material or deal with it incidentally, and not unsurprisingly many of the most educated of our contemporaries have been shipwrecked upon it, I have set such matters aside to await a more considered meditation, and am here merely collating the narrated stories of the man, in order to satisfy the desires of those people who wanted a life-story on no more than a few sheets of paper. (Mahal, 3)

It is immediately obvious that this 'Christian Thinker' is writing from an 'enlightened' perspective and for a different audience than Pfitzer and Widmann were. He begins by addressing what by his time had become a dilemma: whether to take the ancient tradition seriously or to retell it in such a way as to cast doubt on the events to which it refers. Since, as he admits, his work is aimed at 'the fashionable world' (*die galante Welt*), it is unsurprising that his attitude is marked by the scepticism of a Rationalist, which is why, when the narrative begins, doubt is introduced from the opening sentence:

> And thus this Johann Faust is said to have been born in the market-town of Sondwedel in Anhalt [Saxony] to pious but impoverished country-folk, though he is said to have had a wealthy kinsman in Wittenberg who was his father's brother, who being childless brought him up as his own on account of his intelligence, and sent him to school so regularly that he was able to attend the academy at Ingolstadt and attain after a few years the title of 'Master' along with eleven other candidates, and this not without a considerable reputation for good conduct. (Mahal, 4)

Here, once again, we have a mistrustful voice, expressing doubt ('is said to have been born'), which is further heightened by many other ambivalent remarks. Thus Faustus' qualifications as a doctor are portrayed in a strangely dubious light. Yes, the University of Ingolstadt has records to prove he graduated there, but even those readers sufficiently credulous to believe the rest of the story 'are in many cases inclined to doubt this particular detail' (Mahal, 5).

After quoting the pact and its conditions in detail, and describing Faustus' opulent dwelling, full of tapestries and paintings, there are the familiar comic episodes: Faustus pawns his leg to a Jew, then demands it back, but the matter ends amicably, as both parties decide not to press their claims. In addition to Jews, peasants and horse-dealers, Faustus also plays tricks on Polish aristocrats (Mahal, 18–21), a group that was now providing stock figures for comedy in the eighteenth century. Another telling comment occurs when the 'Christian Thinker' describes the apparition of Alexander and various other tricks presented to the Emperor (Maximilian I): 'One must be surprised that this otherwise so admirable Emperor did not react to this with revulsion.' (Mahal, 30)

Towards the end of his life, Faust reads the Bible assiduously, but it only serves to remind him of his godless life and to convince him of his impending damnation. Twice he attempts suicide, but without success. There is a brief oration to his students, who are aghast at the news of his apostasy; Faust dies alone. The devil consoles him with the thought that his fate will be no worse that that of the 'heathens, Turks and other godless people' who will join him in large numbers (Mahal, 43). A corrupt priest is persuaded to bury Faust after receiving a handsome tip. There is, as yet, nothing to suggest that this rugged plot will, within a few years, provide a beacon of inspiration for the cultural elite of the nation.

Cited Works and Further Reading

Maria Enrica d'Agostini and Giovanni Silvani (eds), *Faustbuch: analisi comparata delle fonti inglesi e tedesche del Faust dal Volksbuch a Marlow*. Naples: Tullio Pironti, 1978.

Marguerite de Huszar Allen, 'The Reception of the *Historia von D. Johann Fausten*', *German Quarterly* 59 (1986), 582–94.

[Anon.], *Leben, Thaten und Höllenfarth Wagners*. Vienna, 1799.

Peter Boerner and Sidney Johnson (eds), *Faust through Four Centuries. Retrospect and Analysis*.

Vierhundert Jahre Faust. Rückblick und Analyse. Tübingen: Niemeyer, 1989.

Neil Brough, 'Doctor Faustus and "P.F.".', *Notes and Queries* 32 (1985), 15f.

Jane K. Brown, 'The Prosperous Wonder Worker: Faust in the Renaissance', in Boerner/ Johnson, 53–64.

E.M. Butler, *The Myth of the Magus.* Cambridge: University Press, 1948.

—, *The Fortunes of Faust.* Cambridge: University Press, 1952.

Douglas Cole, *Christopher Marlowe and the Renaissance of Tragedy.* Westport: Praeger, 1995.

Francis Dolores Covella, 'The Choral Nexus in *Doctor Faustus*', *Studies in English Literature 1500–1900* 26 (1986), 201–15.

William Empson, *Faustus and the Censor. The English Faust-book and Marlowe's* Doctor Faustus. Recovered and edited, with an Introduction and Postscript, by John Henry Jones. Oxford: Basil Blackwell, 1987.

Peter J. French, *John Dee. The World of an Elizabethan Magus.* London: Routledge and Kegan Paul, 1972.

Josef Fritz (ed.), *Ander Theil D. Johann Fausti Historien von seinem Famulo Christoff Wagner 1593.* Halle: Buchhandlung des Waisenhauses, 1910.

Roma Gill (ed.), *The Complete Works of Christopher Marlowe.* 5 volumes. Oxford: Clarendon, 1987–94. Volume II: *Doctor Faustus.*

W.W. Greg (ed.), *Doctor Faustus 1604–1616. Parallel Texts.* Oxford: Clarendon, 1950.

Otto Heller, *Faust and Faustus. A Study of Goethe's Relation to Marlowe's.* 1931. Rptd New York: Cooper Square, 1972.

Hans Henning (ed.), *Historia von D. Johann Fausten.* Halle/Saale: Verlag Sprache und Literatur, 1963.

Harold Jantz, 'An Elizabethan Statement on the Origin of the German Faust Book. With a Note on Marlowe's Sources', *Journal of English and Germanic Philology* 51 (1952), 137–53.

John Henry Jones (ed.), *The English Faust Book. A critical edition based on the text of 1592.* Cambridge: University Press, 1994.

James Joyce, *A Portrait of the Artist as a Young Man.* 1916. Rptd Harmondsworth: Penguin, 1960.

J.D. Jump (ed.), *Christopher Marlowe: Doctor Faustus.* London: Methuen, 1962.

Paul H. Kocher, 'The English Faust Book and the Date of Marlowe's *Faustus*', *Modern Language Notes* 55 (1940), 95–101.

T. McAlindon, 'The Ironic Vision: Diction and Theme in Marlowe's *Doctor Faustus*', *Review of English Studies*, 32 (1981), 129–41.

Günther Mahal (ed.), *Das Faustbuch des Christlich Meynenden von 1725.* Knittlingen: Faust-Archiv, 1983. (Facsimile of the 1725 edition).

Hans Mayer, *Doktor Faustus und Don Juan.* Frankfurt/M: Suhrkamp, 1979.

Gustav Milchsack (ed.) *Historia D. Johannis Fausti des Zauberers: nach der Wolfenbütteler Handschrift nebst dem Nachweis eines Teils ihrer Quellen.* Wolfenbüttel: Zwissler, 1892–1897. Rptd Berlin: Erich Schmidt, 1963, ed. H. G. Haile.

Catherine Minshull, 'The Dissident Subtext of Marlowe's *Doctor Faustus*', *English*, 39 (1990), 193–207.

Renate Noll-Wiemann (ed.), *The History of the Damnable Life and the Deserved Death of Doctor John Faustus.* Hildesheim: Olms, 1985.

G.M. Pinciss: 'Marlowe's Cambridge Years and the Writing of *Doctor Faustus*', *Studies in English Literature 1500–1900* 33 (1993), 249–64.

J.A. Prietopablos, '"What art thou Faustus?" Self-Reference and Strategies of Identification in Christopher Marlowe's *Doctor Faustus.*' *English Studies* 74 (1993), 66–83.

Eric Rasmussen, *A Textual Companion to 'Doctor Faustus'.* Manchester: University Press, 1993.

Alfred E. Richards (ed.), *The English Wagner Book of 1594.* Edited with Introduction and Notes. Berlin: Felber, 1907.

Richard Rohde, *Das englische Faustbuch und Marlowes Tragödie*. Halle: Niemeyer, 1910. Rptd Tübingen: Dr Martin Sändig, 1973.

Hartmann Schedel, *Chronicle of the World*. Nuremberg. Latin July 1493, German December 1493. Rptd as *Chronicle of the World. The complete and annotated Nuremberg Chronicle of 1493*. Introduction and Appendix by Stephan Füssel. Cologne: Taschen, 2001.

Ruth Schirmer-Imhoff, 'Faust in England', *Anglia* 70 (1951), 150-185.

James R. Siemon, *Shakespearean Iconoclasm*. Berkeley: University of California Press, 1985.

Gerald Strauss, 'The Faust Book of 1587', in Boerner/Johnson, 27-39.

Ian Watt, 'Faust as a Myth of Modern Individualism', in Boerner/Johnson, 41-52.

Georg Rudolf Widmann, *Der Warhafftigen Historien von den grewlichen vnd abschewlichen Sünden vnd Lastern / auch von vielen wunderbarlichen vnd seltzamen ebentheuren: So D. Iohannes Faustus Ein weitberuffener Schwartzkünstler vnd Ertzzäuberer / durch seine Schwartzkunst / biss an seinen erschrecklichen end hat getrieben. Mit nothwendigen Erinnerungen vnd schönen exempeln / menniglichem zur Lehr vnd Warnung außgestrichen vnd erklehret*. Hamburg: Hermann Moller, 1599.

Richard Wilson, '"Why this is hell": Marlowe and the devil's pact', in François Laroque and Franck Lessay (eds), *Enfers et délices à la Renaissance*, Paris: Presses de la Sorbonne Nouvelle, 2003, 159-73.

Chapter Three

An Icon is Born

Faust is a type of whom we are all more or less well-made copies. Faust, that is to say, man in his spiritual and natural essence, can assume all forms that are known to humankind and can display any conceivable character. He can engage in this series of adventures or that, despise his fellow men like Diogenes or curse them like Timon, be as solitary as Byron's Manfred or enjoy a joke with equals in the manner of Alcibiades. He can philosophise like Socrates, Plato and Aristotle, like a mediaeval schoolman or Spinoza or Leibniz; or live for pleasure like one of today's fashionable snobs. He can, if you wish, play the fool like a jester or enthuse like a Theosophist, he can be a Pietist or a pious bigot or a Quaker, a Jesuit or a Franciscan, a Don Juan or a Casanova. He can be a warrior, a poet, a dreamer, a libertine or a freedom fighter; in short, he can be anything that man is capable of being, but he cannot be God Himself. —Johann Leutbecher

Doctor Faustus Recycled

IN THE original reading, Faustus is punished for trying to gain supernatural powers and forbidden knowledge from a pact with the devil, but two centuries later, as the influence of Rationalism spread, the source material acquired a completely new orientation. The man who played a pivotal role in this change of direction was Gotthold Ephraim Lessing, 'the father of modern German drama' and Germany's most innovative dramatist prior to Goethe. His approach to the theatre, for which he produced a small number of idiosyncratic plays, was rigorously performance-oriented. He encouraged high-quality productions and strove to reduce the influence of French culture in his own country. From the point of view of someone steeped in the ideology of French neo-Classicism, Faustus was a barbaric aberration. Yet for Lessing, the barbaric was still preferable to an over-regulated classicism. It is in this context that his *Briefe, die neueste Literatur betreffend* ('Letters concerning recent literature') should be read. For Lessing, there are two ways forward. One is for Germany to turn to English models in general and to Shakespeare in particular, the other is look to the older local traditions for plots and characters that were appropriate for a revived national drama. For him to suggest using Shakespeare and Faustus as icons of progress was not paradoxical but inevitable. Firstly, they were products of the same turbulently creative period, the late sixteenth century, and secondly, the temperament of restless inquiry that Faustus demonstrates was much more relevant to the Germany of Lessing's time than the moral dilemmas of Corneille and Racine would ever be. Faustus was eminently promotable; he could advance to becoming a hero in the Shakespearean mould: torn, tormented, longing for a lofty destiny that was within his grasp but that was denied to him. Thus Lessing formulated his famous seventeenth letter concerning recent literature.

> Even by comparison with the Ancients, Shakespeare is a far greater tragic poet than Corneille, though the latter knew the Classics well, the former hardly at all. Corneille may come closer to them in matters of technical detail, but Shakespeare matches them in the essentials. The English dramatist nearly always implements the purpose of tragedy, no matter how strange and individual his chosen method; the French dramatist hardly ever does so, even though he treads the self-same path that the Ancients had prepared. After Sophocles' *Oedipus* there is no play on earth that is able to captivate our passions more than *Othello*, *Hamlet*, and *King Lear*, etc. Did Corneille write a play that was only half as moving as *Zaïre* by Voltaire? And how far removed is this *Zaïre* from the *Moor of Venice*, whose pale copy it is and from which the character Orosman was borrowed?
>
> It would be easy to demonstrate in great detail that our older plays contain very much that is essentially English. To take just the best-known example: *Doctor Faustus* has a number of scenes that only a genius of Shakespearean dimensions would have been able to create. Remember how enamoured Germany was, and to some extent still is, of its very own *Doctor Faustus*! One of my friends is in possession of an ancient draft of this tragedy, and he sent me a scene from it which undoubtedly contains much that is great. If you would like to read it – here it is. [*Faustus questions seven spirits with a view to finding which of them is the fastest*] What do you think of this scene? You would like to see a German play composed of scenes like this? So would I! (Lessing, V, 72f.)

Many writers and philosophers of the period shared the opinion that English drama was superior to French and that German drama must follow Anglo-Saxon models if it wanted to be true to the Germanic spirit. One of these was Johann Gottfried Herder, who became Goethe's mentor during his Strasbourg period in the early 1770s. Goethe's desire to create a national drama was even stronger than Lessing's, and the idea that Faustus was all but made to measure for this purpose had established itself in his mind from an early age onwards. 'Faustus' became plain 'Faust' (the German means 'Fist'): a symbol of ambition and defiant strength rather than one of vacillation and failed repentance. Whether Lessing, as he claimed, ever wrote more than a few scenes of a Faust drama is uncertain, but there is no doubt that the projected play was to exonerate his hero completely. Despite his mistakes, his treachery towards God, his obdurate sinfulness in the traditional sense, he would be forgiven, since he had worked to employ his rational powers and to achieve ambitions that were ultimately legitimate. He was worthy to be saved, because of his now admirable striving after knowledge. This alone was positive in an Enlightenment context. Little indeed has survived of Lessing's Faust drama, but his publicity campaign on its behalf was soon to have astounding repercussions (Palmer/More, 273–86; Henning (1987), 80f.).

It may seem odd that in a century that saw itself as 'enlightened', the figure of the master-alchemist and soothsayer was still considered relevant as a vehicle for a new awakening in drama. Yet the age of superstition was slow to die. Itinerant confidence tricksters not so very different from Faustus enjoyed a privileged status in the very society that deemed itself to have put naïve faith and superstition behind it. The late eighteenth century was a period in which many latter-day wizards made their appearance in royal households and episcopal palaces. Religious orders still held sway in many parts of Europe, mesmerists, Rosicrucians and other faith-healers plied their dubious trades, and individuals such as the exorcist Father Johann Joseph Gassner, the spiritualist Johann Georg Schrepfer and the womanising swindler Giacomo Casanova met with phenomenal success as astrologers, necromancers and cabbalists. Swedenborg communicated with angels, and as late as 1785, the self-styled 'Count' Cagliostro was making prophesies, including, apparently, one concerning a revolution in France, and intriguing the nobility with talk of 'heaven, the stars, the great Arcanum, of Memphis, of hierophancy, transcendental chemistry' and other such wonders. He had been a novice monk in his youth. He travelled from one European court to another, much as the miracle-working doctor had done two centuries earlier, claiming to be 300 years old, an Egyptian Freemason, a medium, and a magician. His appearances were accompanied by outbreaks of 'Cagliostromania'. He treated the poor for free, but had no compunction about robbing the rich. He died in squalor in 1795, his entire career a challenge to the assumption that the eighteenth century had earned the right to be known as the Age of Reason (McCalman, 128 and *passim*).

Faustus becomes Faust

The transition from Lessing's outline and fragments to the completion of Goethe's life's work was a long and arduous process. As so often with Goethe, each pause in the much-postponed work brought with it an obligation to rethink, recast, and often rewrite passages or even whole scenes. There are no fewer than four versions of his play, beside many fragments and so-called *paralipomena* ('discarded passages'). These are the *Urfaust* (the original draft written down around 1775 and subsequently lost; rediscovered and published 1887), *Faust, a Fragment* of 1790 (a version put together at his publisher's insistence), *Faust, Part I* (published in 1808), and *Faust, Part II* (published posthumously in 1832). While the *Fragment* is rarely performed, *Urfaust* enjoys something of a cult status as an unfinished masterpiece and has often been revived, for example by Bertolt Brecht in Potsdam and Berlin in 1952/3 (see below, 183; 228f.). The existence of these well-documented and much-analysed versions show that Goethe worked tirelessly to re-think, improve, and re-cast the material. Prose passages were transposed into verse, scenes were added, cut and moved around. The long gestation brought with it many contradictions and changes of mood and emphasis. The central character is distinguished by his inconsistency; he moves from heady optimism to bitter pessimism and back, from lovelorn romantic to defiant blasphemer in a matter of lines, and when he meets his sweetheart, Gretchen, we can never be quite sure whether to see him as a cold-blooded seducer or as a passionate worshiper of her unsullied purity (Mason, 218). Goethe saw life as a conflation of opposing forces, of diastolic expansion and systolic contraction, interdependent and synchronous in their effect on the human soul: 'The interplay of diastole and systole determine the action of *Faust I*; it is here that we may claim to have found the organising force that underlies the entire work.' (Requadt, 60)

There has been much debate on the subject of Goethe's putative sources. He may not have encountered Marlowe's work until relatively late in his life, although there may be 'inner evidence' of familiarity (Heller, 94). An intertextual relationship via puppet plays and the extensive oral tradition that derived from Marlowe and the chapbook can be assumed. But the differences are substantial, nowhere more so than in the treatment of evil. Because good and evil forces are both at work in the human heart, they do not contradict each other, as do the unilaterally 'Good' and 'Evil' Angels in Marlowe's *Faustus*; instead, from the very outset, the 'Lord' and Mephistopheles are there, together, in a stage implementation of heaven, jointly plotting out Faust's evolution and betting on his career. The heaven we see here is no more than a dramatist's sketch, carefully made to recall the contraptions that featured in mediaeval morality plays, with elements of a hothouse experiment. Mephistopheles gently chides the Lord for having given man those rational powers that scholars such as Faust can all too easily abuse.

Prologue in Heaven

[*Three* ARCHANGELS *step forward*]

RAPHAEL: The sun, forever undefeated,
             Resounds within its crystal sphere,
             And when its journey is completed
             The heavens thunder far and near.
             The angels gaze in rapt elation,
             And draw their strength from what they see:
             The mighty works of all Creation,
             Unfathomed they must always be.

GABRIEL: And fast and ever faster spinning
             The earth revolves in awesome flight;
             Like paradise the day's beginning,
             While gruesome shadows rule the night.
             Upon the coast the waves are hurling
             Their watery might without surcease,
             And cliffs and crags continue whirling,
             Controlled by laws none can release.

MICHAEL: The hurricane pursues the storm
             From land to sea, from sea to land;
             An endless chain of tasks they form
             That none shall ever understand.
             The lightning's flashes burn and sear

	The earth before the thunder's roar;
	Yet we, your messengers, revere
	The gentle day that dawns once more.
All Three:	We angels gaze in rapt elation
	And draw our strength from what we see:
	The mighty works of Thy Creation,
	Unfathomed they must always be.
Mephistopheles:	As you, o Lord, are once again approaching,
	And now do deign to speak to of all of us,
	And since you never minded me encroaching
	Upon your valued time, you see me thus.
	My formulations won't sound erudite,
	And everyone must think that I'm insane,
	You'd have to laugh at anything so trite,
	Had you not chosen ne'er to laugh again.
	The sun and planets mostly I ignore;
	But human life is an unending chore.
	The little god that rules this world's so mean,
	Unfathomable he has always been.
	He'd have a few more leisure hours
	If you would strip him of his rational powers.
	That thing he calls his 'common sense' he uses
	To outdo every beast with clever ruses.
	And if Your Grace permits, his nature's best revealed
	By them there grasshoppers you see in every field –
	The sort that jumps and tries to fly and hops
	Until, worn out, it simply drops
	Into the grass, to muse and doze
	And then find somewhere else to poke its nose.
The Lord:	Do you have nothing more to say?
	Must you complain the livelong day?
	Does nothing in the world seem right to you?
Mephistopheles:	No, Lord, things are quite bad there, in my view.
	The people down on earth are sorely pained,
	If I torment them now, what's to be gained?
The Lord:	Do you know Faust?
Mephistopheles:	The doctor?
The Lord:	He that serves me true.
Mephistopheles:	Indeed! And in a manner most bizarre.
	The man's a fool; he roams both near and far
	Seeking not earthly drink nor food
	And up to now has but half understood
	His folly in reaching to the heavens above
	And chasing every treasure he can find,
	Be it the gift of everlasting love
	It would not calm his deeply troubled mind.
The Lord:	Although right now he serves me in confusion
	Ere long he'll see things with a clearer head:
	The gardener knows that leaves in great profusion
	Signal a bounteous crop in years ahead.
Mephistopheles:	Are you quite sure? You'll lose him yet,
	If in my company you'll let him thrive
	I'll show him my way; would you care to bet?

THE LORD:	While he's on earth you may contrive
	Whatever you will; I shan't forbid it.
	Man makes mistakes as long as he's alive.
MEPHISTOPHELES:	Then thanks a lot. Dead bodies never did it
	For me, I really do prefer a rosy cheek and smile
	To someone who's been dead for quite a while.
	Show me a corpse and I will grab my hat,
	The mouse that's snuffed it will not please the cat.
THE LORD:	Well then, do what you think is right.
	Divert him from his origins,
	And if you can but clasp him tight
	Lead him astray. Teach him your sins.
	But you'll be put to shame and will confess
	That every good man in his darkest hour
	Knows where to find the path of righteousness.
MEPHISTOPHELES:	You're on! I tremble not, nor shall I cower,
	I'll win the bet and thus enhance my power
	And, when the moment comes, make him devour
	The dust, while I shall reap the glory
	Of a triumph none can match; the fabled story
	About the serpent avenged in one short hour!
THE LORD:	You're free to come and go, for I
	Can feel no enmity for such as you.
	Of all the spirits that deny
	The rascal is the one I'd least eschew.
	For human beings readily lose heart,
	They love to down their tools and take a break.
	I've placed the devil at their side to make
	For stimulation, give them a fresh start.
	But you, true sons of the divinity,
	Bask in the riches of infinity!
	The force that works unto the end of days
	Shall bind you with the power of love's ability.
	Now grasp the thought that fades as in a haze
	And strike it into permanent stability.
	[*Heaven closes, the* ARCHANGELS *disperse*]
MEPHISTOPHELES:	Each time I see the Old One, I'm not bored;
	I never anger him, but wish him well.
	It is so kind of such a wise old 'Lord'
	To chat humanely with the Fiend from Hell. (F 243–353)

The scene opens with a chorus of Angels, intermediary entities whose traditional role is to pass messages between heaven and earth. Here they proclaim a simple truth. It could be summed up as the formula for life itself: interdependence of seemingly opposing forces. Day and night, sea and land, fire and water interact in a terrifying but necessary collusion: 'Like paradise the day's beginning,/ While gruesome shadows rule the night'. Into this fragile but essentially stable setting steps Mephistopheles, a spirit given to contradiction and provocation. 'I am the Spirit that denies!' he will shortly proclaim (F 1338). Here he challenges the viability of the Lord's creation, picking on man's rational faculties as the decisive flaw in his constitution, and suggesting that far from having a beneficial effect (as the utilitarian thinkers of the enlightened eighteenth century maintained), it was Reason that fuelled man's brutality: 'He'd have a few more leisure hours/ If you had stripped him of his rational powers./ That thing he calls his 'common sense' he uses/ To outdo every beast with clever ruses.' To this the Lord retorts, not without a touch of self-satisfied complacency, that all is well on earth, and promptly cites Faust as an example of a true 'servant'. There ensues a bet as to whether Mephistopheles has the ability to lure Faust away from the true path; the phrase 'Divert him from his origins' is no less ambiguous in the original than it is in translation, but it is loosely conceived and so vaguely formulated as to constitute little more than a curiosity. How could an evil spirit hope to win a wager against the Lord of creation – always assuming that this is the 'Almighty' speaking?

What is more important here is that forces which we associate with the extremes of good and evil appear not only to engage in dialogue but to cooperate with one another across a vast moral divide. But while the Lord may give an impression of hostility towards his traditional foe, he quietly reflects on the positive side of having a 'devil' at his side, to act as a stimulus upon man, who all too easily slides into lethargy.

Are they enemies or co-workers in the celestial scheme of things? This question is left open. The heavens close, as they did in many a mediaeval miracle play, more in the manner of pantomime than high tragedy. True to the comic tradition, Mephistopheles steps forward as the curtain falls to muse on how 'humanely' the Lord has spoken. God, man and devil come together in this parting jibe that stresses the close proximity of divine wisdom, human error, and diabolical deceit.

Given the radical innovation of the Prologue and the earlier 'Prelude on the Stage', it is surprising that Goethe provides a first glimpse of Faust precisely where we would expect to find him, in his study, reciting a tirade of discontent which previous dramatisations from Marlowe onwards had used to good effect. This is Faust as the public wanted him to be: arrogant, restless, titanic, yet also anguished in a modern, self-tormenting manner: one of us and yet quite ready to do business with the devil himself.

Night

[*Night. A narrow Gothic chamber with high vaulted ceiling.* FAUST, *restless in his chair by his desk*]

FAUST: Poor me, I've studied Philosophy,
Medicine and Law have been my chores,
And even, worse luck, Theology,
These subjects are such crushing bores.
And here I stand, poor fool, bereft
Of all my wisdom, naught is left.
I may be a graduate, a doctor and master;
My professional career has been a disaster.
These last ten years an endless trance,
When I led my tutees a song and a dance,

To see there's nothing we can know,
Just breaks my heart, but it is so.
Admittedly wiser than all other doctors,
Tutors and scribes, clerics and proctors,
I have cast away doubts, I have no aversion,
I fear neither hell nor the devil in person.–
Yet all of my joys have just withered away,
There's nothing to know and nought to say;
What can I teach, what can I invent
To shape people's minds and make them repent?
I have no property, no gains,
The world ignores me for my pains.
No dog would live a life so tragic,
And so I've turned my hand to magic.
I'm eager to know if spirits there be
To assist in resolving the mystery
Of what this world is all about,
No more to stand there in cold sweat
Explaining things that I don't get.
I need to feel that mighty force
Controlling life's essential course;
To visualise the properties of germination
And end this fruitless speculation.

Ah, that the moon would cast its eye
For one last time on my misery.
So many midnight hours I've spent
Over my books all hunched and bent:
Ah, sorrowful friend, and how remote
Above my lonesome desk you'd float!
If I could but stroll on a mountain path
In your cherished light as in a bath,
I'd weave my way through caverns and shades
Enraptured, entranced by fields and glades.

I'm buried alive in this tomb underground
An accursed hole, decay all around,
Where heaven's wholesome light must pass
Through many a layer of tinted glass.
Here I'm hemmed in by my ancient books,
A collection of tomes for the bookworm to gnaw,
They reach to the ceiling wherever one looks:
Parchment and vellum turned yellow as straw.
With bottles and boxes the shelves must groan,
Instruments, gadgets, scrolls to unfold,
Grandfather's collections and chattels of old:
That is the world you must call your own! (F 354–409)

The opening lines of this scene show Faust swaying between the frustrations of a thwarted demigod and the mawkishness of a modern victim of the midlife crisis. He soon exchanges his devil-may-care attitude for the softer tones of sentimentality when he addresses the moon as the 'sorrowful friend' that floats above his desk.

Here stands a modern, inwardly torn individual, a fitting icon for the new age of sensitivity that was in due course to transform itself into Romanticism. His monologue refers back to his many earlier cousins, who may include Descartes as well as the magician of Wittenberg (Shattuck, 86f.). Faust pities his own alienation from nature, cursing the musty cell to which he is confined, longing instead to walk on mountain paths and bathe in the clear light of the moon. Twice he seems to be on the brink of a great emotional breakthrough. His first experience of elation occurs when he contemplates the Sign of the Macrocosm. This symbol of an all-embracing totality may explain the mysteries of the universe, but it does so in a cold, rational manner that cannot satisfy Faust's thirst for action and personal involvement. His next attempt proves more rewarding; a second sign, that of the Earth Spirit, holds out a promise of interaction, and now Faust succeeds in summoning a terrifying spirit into his study. Yet here, too, disappointment follows on the heels of apparent success; the spirit's mysterious identity is something Faust, as a declared sceptic, cannot hope to comprehend, and as it turns away to reject him, his despair is heightened by the appearance of his mawkishly cerebral assistant Wagner, clad in a dressing-gown and bearing a lamp as if symbolising the dry-as-dust spirit of modern 'Enlightenment'.

There are contradictory indications as to where we are in time. The Age of Luther seems a reasonable point of reference, and when Faust tries, briefly, to translate the Bible, he is actually vying with the Reformer. Yet it is never clear whether we are in the Middle Ages, the Reformation, or the eighteenth century (Braun, 24–30).

Goethe's play is not a tale of defeat, but of man's gradual awakening from the futile pursuit of learning to a richer, more active life far removed from the narrow world of his study. The very fact that the knowledge he so far sought was in books, pored over in solitary labour, was enough to ensure failure. Things begin to improve as he leaves his restricted world behind him on Easter Sunday. With Wagner at his side, he contemplates the refreshing sight of the 'reborn' people out enjoying the warmth of spring (F 921f.). It is here that he is followed by a large black dog of the poodle variety that accompanies him home and takes up residence behind the stove. Its company proves something of a challenge, even to one versed in the ways of spirits, but eventually the learned doctor manages to exorcise the spirit, revealing, it would seem, nothing more exciting than a travelling student.

Faust's Study (1)

[MEPHISTOPHELES, *clad as a travelling student, steps out from behind the stove*]

MEPHISTOPHELES: What's all the fuss? How may I serve your honour?
FAUST: A scholar in a poodle's garb! What next?
This really is a case that makes me chuckle.
MEPHISTOPHELES: I greet you, learned master, with respect.
What you just did was quite close to the knuckle.
FAUST: What is your name?
MEPHISTOPHELES: A question trivial

	For one who shuns the madding herds,
	And, far from thoughts convivial,
	Seeks inner truths, despising words.
FAUST:	With creatures such as you, a name
	Reveals the nature of your game
	And tells us much of your profession dire.
	Are you the Lord of Flies, the Spoiler or the Liar?
	State who you are!
MEPHISTOPHELES:	A humble part of them that would
	Do evil evermore, yet evermore do good.
FAUST:	Pray tell me what this riddle signifies?
MEPHISTOPHELES:	I am the Spirit that denies.
	My role is fully justified, for all
	That rises up in life must also fall.
	'Twould be a better place if nought had been created.
	In short, this planet that with wickedness is sated,
	With evil ways and every type of sin,
	Is the environment I'm best at working in.
FAUST:	You call yourself a part and yet you seem complete?
MEPHISTOPHELES:	Your patience modestly I must entreat.
	If man assumes his knowledge of reality
	Is something that approximates to a totality –
	I know my place, am but a wheel within a wheel,
	Part of the primal darkness that did steal
	The light that shines and shining must contend
	With Mother Night until the universe's end.
	And yet, it cannot win this race
	As long as it collides with bodies out in space
	That may reflect and thus be glamorised by light.
	Every body that it beautifies
	Obstructs it in its journey through the skies;
	Soon, therefore, all will have to end in night.
FAUST:	So you have set yourself a task right royal!
	The wide world is too vast for you to spoil,
	Therefore you've turned to little things.
MEPHISTOPHELES:	Such are, indeed, my humble beginnings.
	This clumsy world offers resistance,
	I've challenged it with some insistence,
	I have employed just about every tool
	And dealt out blows that were extremely cruel:
	Tidal waves and storms and fires,
	Have failed to implement my great desires.
	And when it comes to beasts and humankind
	No matter what campaigns I mount –
	I've buried more than I can count –,
	They go on giving birth and multiply, I find.
	And on and on it goes. It drives me to distraction
	When earth and water limber into action,
	Producing seeds in every bog and mire,
	In every corner, warm or cold, frozen or fried,
	You'll find a living, growing thing, and I'd
	Have nought to call my own except, that is, for fire.
FAUST:	So you intend to deal a blow

	Using your cold and devilish fist
	Against the power that makes things grow,
	And yet the vital forces will resist!
	Can't you find somewhere else to play
	Your games, chaotic son of strife and feud?
MEPHISTOPHELES:	I'll trouble you no more today,
	We'll talk again next time we meet. Now I'll be rude
	And ask permission to depart.
FAUST:	Feel free to do as you require.
	Now I'm acquainted with your art
	You may return when you desire.
	Here is a window, here a door,
	A chimney-stack up which to clamber.
MEPHISTOPHELES:	I must confess that I require more
	Assistance if I am to leave your chamber.
	Yonder symbolic charm you've drawn ...
FAUST:	Is it my pentagram that pains you?
	So tell me then, son of the hellish spawn:
	How did you enter, if that sign restrains you?
	Can spirits be deceived by such as me?
MEPHISTOPHELES:	I'll answer that one readily:
	One corner, pointing to the exit, there,
	The lines do not join up: you left a little gap.
FAUST:	And so I've caught you in a trap?
	And you're a prisoner in my care?
	And all that happened by pure chance?
MEPHISTOPHELES:	The poodle did not deign to glance
	At it when he leapt in. That was his doom.
	So now the devil may not leave this room. (F 1332–1408)

The major problem Goethe faced when, around 1800, he returned to the manuscripts he had been working on some twenty-five years earlier was the requirement that a pact be drawn up between the doctor and the devil. This was not merely a prerequisite, but the actual king-pin of the drama. Faust had to interact with his adversary in a manner that reflected the terms of their written agreement, so vital to all earlier versions. For a man who had long ceased to regard evil as an independent 'absolute' and had hinted as much in the Prologue, this was no easy matter.

In the end, Goethe opted for an unusual but thoroughly characteristic solution. There were to be two scenes, both set in Faust's study, and the roles of protagonist and antagonist were to be reversed in the latter. The first of the pair, reproduced in part above, allows Mephistopheles to adopt his traditionally negative role: 'I am the Spirit that denies./ My role is fully justified, for all/ That rises up in life must also fall./ 'Twould be a better place if nought had been created.' (F 1338–41) Even here, Mephistopheles slips in a curiously ambiguous phrase that caused the critics some headaches: 'A humble part of them that would/ Do evil evermore, yet evermore do good.' This would seem to undermine his boastful assertions; and moreover, if something good is eventually to result from his diabolical machinations, then one might ask oneself about the value of the ensuing 'dramatic' wager, if its outcome is already spelt out at this early stage in the proceedings. A reconciliation may be attempted by assuming that when the devil speaks of 'good' he really means 'evil', as the latter is 'good' in his book; but such controversies merely underline the fundamental ambiguity that forms the basis of the relationship (Seidlin, 170–75; Brandes, 134–42).

Their roles are quickly reversed, for while Faust managed to maintain the upper hand in his debates with Mephistopheles in the first of the two study scenes, so much so that the devil has to escape from him by means of a trick, the situation is reversed in the second scene in the group. Here Faust is in the depths of despair, cursing his life, his erstwhile optimism, and all the virtues that provide hope for humankind. Only now can Mephistopheles step in and offer him a pact.

The wording of this document is, unsurprisingly, withheld from view. Faust is obliged to sign it in his own blood, but what he signs remains a mystery. At first glance, it looks like the traditional formula:

> While over *here* I'll take the utmost care
> To carry out the orders you decree.
> But come the day we meet up over *there*,
> Then you shall do the very same for me. (F 1656-9)

But this agreement is quickly superseded by a supplementary clause that Faust adds, verbally, and in virtual contradiction to the traditional formulation. If ever he is satisfied, lulled into contentment, to such an extent that he asks for time to stand still, then the devil may claim his prize without further ado:

> If to the fleeting moment I should say
> 'Stand still, thou art so blithe and fair',
> Then shackle me and have your way,
> I'll gladly meet my doom right there. (F 1699-1702)

These lines may mark the termination of the 'pact' and the beginning of a private 'wager' between the two, but in a way that precludes a clear unscrambling of the one from the other. Is the pact invalidated by the wager, or do pact and wager co-exist, or does the wager, since it seems not to have been included in the signed document, ultimately carry less or no weight? It would be convenient if we could answer this with reference to the later action, but we cannot, as the signals continue to be in conflict. Faust dies when he envisages a moment of contentment in the future (F 11585f.), but having already expressed satisfaction at several earlier junctures. This detail alone does not prove the point beyond doubt.

Faust's Study (2)

FAUST:	A knock? Come in! Who's here to cause me pain?
MEPHISTOPHELES:	'Tis I.
FAUST:	Come in.
MEPHISTOPHELES:	Say it just once again.

FAUST:	So enter, then.
MEPHISTOPHELES:	Well done. You've made a start.
	I've come to you, dressed as a noble lord,
	And aim to cast your worries overboard,
	We fit together like a horse and cart.
	Turned out in clothes with golden stitches,
	Did ever man espy such wondrous riches?
	A silken waistcoat and, in this my headgear,
	A cockerel's feather, not to mention
	This long and pointed handsome rapier.
	I would suggest you copy my invention,
	And with no further care or strife
	You're set to taste a grander life.
FAUST:	In each and every garment I could hire
	I'll feel the pain of this my life on earth.
	I am too old to chase about in mirth,
	Too young, alas, to cast off all desire.
	How could the world enchant me so
	When everybody says: 'Forgo, forgo'?
	That never-ending, cruellest of commands
	Rings out in every human ear,
	And counters each of my demands
	And fills my throbbing heart with fear.
	I wake in terror in the morn
	My face in tears of longing drenched;
	I plod through life alone, forlorn,
	No lust of mine is ever quenched.
	And every pleasure that I've ever fancied
	Once in my mind, it very soon disperses;
	And thoughts turn all my yearnings rancid,
	Marred by a thousand inner curses.
	And when dark night enwraps the human nation
	And I recline in slumber on my bed
	Nay, even then I find no rest or relaxation,
	As nightmares charge and chunter through my head.
	The God who yet inspires my emotion
	Can stir tumultuous thoughts within my breast,
	The power that directs my every motion
	Has left me paralysed, unable to contest.
	My life is now a burden I won't bear,
	I long to exit from this cruel snare.
MEPHISTOPHELES:	But Death is not the kind of guest you'd welcome here.
FAUST:	I envy any hero whom, victorious,
	Grim Death with laurel leaves can bind and charm;
	And would it not be something rather glorious
	To expire, still wildly dancing, in a fair maid's arm?
	If only I, before that lofty apparition,
	Had quit my life in rapturous delight!
MEPHISTOPHELES:	And yet someone in that self-same condition
	Was loath to drain his phial that very night ...
FAUST:	You have the manners of a master spy.
MEPHISTOPHELES:	Though not omniscient, things rarely pass me by.
FAUST:	While in the hour of my confusion

A wondrous tune did charm my ear,
And memories in great profusion
Seduced me with their tempting leer:
I place a curse upon the charming,
Seductive forces that ensnare
The soul with lullabies disarming,
And trap it in its sombre lair.
I curse above all else inflated
Opinions people hold of values spiritual,
I curse the senses too, for they are fated
To be deceived by images unreal.
A curse upon the flattering attraction
Of power and enduring fame,
A curse upon domestic satisfaction
With wife and child and family name.
A curse on Mammon and its treasures
That stimulate us to be brave,
A curse on all the idle pleasures
That it provides in order to deprave.
A curse on wine that brings relief,
A curse on love that does enthral!
A curse on hope and on belief,
A curse on patience most of all!

A CHORUS OF SPIRITS: Alas and alack!
You have caused it to crack,
This world fairer than all,
Under your fist
It must crumble and fall.
A demigod has destroyed it.
Yet bit by bit,
We shall carry the pieces into the void,
Be they forfeit,
We'll save what we can.
Mightiest one
From the Land of Man,
Magnificent son,
Put together again
In your heart what we found!
That's how you can start
To turn the clock back,
No songs shall you lack;
Make your music again
Peal out all around.

MEPHISTOPHELES: Wasn't that pretty –
My private committee?
There's hardly a matter
On which they won't chatter,
Their advice is meant to
Coax you and tempt you
Towards carefree actions,
Not morbid refractions.
You must not revel in your sorrow
Which hacks at you like some great bird of prey,

Quite ordinary people you could meet tomorrow,
To help rebuild your self-esteem each day.
Yet it is hardly my intention
To drag you screaming into mediocrity,
I am no member of the infernal aristocracy
And yet I have a plan I'd like to mention:
If you would care to join up forces
Our lives could take the self-same courses
We could travel together
With me as your fellow
A companion most brave,
Your servant and slave!

FAUST: What recompense must I fulfil?

MEPHISTOPHELES: That time is still a long way off.

FAUST: No, not at all. The selfish devil loves to scoff,
He'd render no favours from sheer good will,
Or simply to make other men better off.
So spell it out clearly: what must I perform?
A servant like you might cause me great harm.

MEPHISTOPHELES: While over *here* I'll take the utmost care
To carry out the orders you decree.
But come the day we meet up over *there*,
Then you shall do the very same for me.

FAUST: Such speculation's hardly to my taste,
Should you succeed in laying all to waste
Whatever follows on, we'll wait and see.
The present world is my delight,
The present sun shines on my plight,
And when I quit this life outright,
I shall accept what comes to me.
I simply do not wish to hear
If in the next place it is love
Or hate that dominates that sphere,
Be it below, be it above.

MEPHISTOPHELES: That's the spirit; take a risk,
Come join with me and I can whisk
You to a place to overcome your spleen;
I'll give you things no man has ever seen.

FAUST: What could you offer me, poor devil!
Was ever a noble attitude, sublime travail
Grasped by the likes of you? Can you supply
A tasty meal for me, unable to satisfy
My hunger, gold that vanishes when in
My hand, a game I cannot win,
A maiden fair, who when within my arms
On other men has trained her eyes?
Honour and such most worthy charms,
That fade away like empty lies?
Show me a fruit that, not yet picked, will rot,
And trees that grow green leaves each day anew!

MEPHISTOPHELES: Such a commission scares me not.
I can provide such treasures, too,
Yet there must come a time to seek, good friend,

106

	Enjoyment at a pace more leisured.
FAUST:	When I lie down content and fully pleasured,
	That's when I want my life to end.
	If you can flatter and deceive me
	So that I'm happy, feeling grand,
	Lulled by distractions that relieve me,
	That day shall be my last, you understand.
	That's what I bet you.
MEPHISTOPHELES:	Done!
FAUST:	Give me your hand!
	If to the fleeting moment I should say
	'Stand still, thou art so blithe and fair',
	Then shackle me and have your way,
	I'll gladly meet my doom right there.
	Then may the bell toll out for me
	And you may quit your duties all,
	The ticking stops, the glass runs empty,
	The hands upon the clock shall fall.
MEPHISTOPHELES:	Ponder it well, we shan't forget.
FAUST:	That is your right and duty, too.
	I have done nothing I regret,
	And when I stop, I'll follow you
	Or someone else I know not yet.
MEPHISTOPHELES:	I shall indeed this very night
	Wait on you by the College's High Table.
	Just one more thing, as soon as you are able:
	A couple of words I'd have you write.
FAUST:	You need a written scroll, confounded bureaucrat?
	Can't you accept my word and leave it all at that?
	Is it not quite enough for you
	That I have offered up my life;
	So won't my spoken pledges do?
	You know I risk great woe and strife.
	We only know what our ancestors knew,
	Cannot divest ourselves of ancient lore;
	Happy the man whose heart is true –
	He's ready for commitment evermore.
	But parchment stamped in black or blue
	Is like a ghost whom men abhor.
	The very word dies on the quill,
	Leather and wax have power still.
	What would you make me write out, then,
	With stylus, chisel, awl or pen?
	On copperplate, parchment or paper?
	The choice is yours, I do declare!
MEPHISTOPHELES:	How eloquent! But is it fair
	To let off so much steamy vapour?
	Some tiny chit should serve us well,
	A droplet of your blood will make the contract gel.
FAUST:	If that is all you need in hell,
	What a harmless little caper!
MEPHISTOPHELES:	Blood is a juice that has its use.
FAUST:	Fear not that I'll forget my undertaking,

I'll do my best and give you all your dues,
A solemn promise I am making.
My overweening pride has burned me,
I'm only fit for creatures low,
The Spirit I invoked – it spurned me,
And Nature thwarts me wherever I go.
The thread of thought snapped long ago,
I am revolted by all that I know.
Let us plumb the depths of sensual lust,
Let us slake our passions so hot that they boil,
We'll hide within an invisible foil
Where magical pranks are an absolute must!
Let us blow off this all-enveloping dust
And shape the future, gain everyone's trust.
Pleasure and pain,
Misery and gain,
Will alternate as best they can,
Restless action makes the man.

MEPHISTOPHELES: No goal I shall prescribe, nor moderation,
Wherever you choose to bite or to nibble
Or grab your prey, I shall not quibble;
You're free to pursue your fascination.
Just help yourself freely and don't be coy!

FAUST: Have you been listening? I don't ask for joy.
I give myself to passion, painful love, and hate
Combined with joy, despair that shall invigorate.
Once my heart is purged of the desire for knowledge,
I'll bear whatever pain yet comes my way,
Forever ready to acknowledge
The fate of all mankind, be what it may,
I'll access highs and lows in all my dreams
And live my life between such great extremes
That while I thrive on such a grand instruction,
The consequence will be my very own destruction.

MEPHISTOPHELES: Believe me, I have chewed this crust
These many thousand years gone by
And no one from their birth to when they're dust
Can say it has the power to satisfy.
And all the many wonders you can see
Were made for no one else but Him up there.
Darkness is the abode to which He exiled me.
He lives in everlasting light without a care
And you get night and day in equal share.

FAUST: And yet I will!

MEPHISTOPHELES: That's what we like to hear.
And yet there's something I would say is wrong:
The time is short, the art is long,
You need instruction, so I fear.
Seek a poet's company
Let him ramble on full tilt;
Every noble quality
Will cover you like fertile silt.
A lion's courage does you proud,

>   Like a stag you'll scurry forth,
>   With fiery Latin blood endowed,
>   And steadfastness from way up north.
>   Let someone work to find a trick
>   To make opposing motives tick,
>   Let someone find a way to ration
>   A love affair that's full of passion.
>   I'd like to clasp him to my bosom
>   And call him 'Mister Microcosm'.
> FAUST: What am I, if there is a force that does debar
>   Me from attaining what I wish, the crown
>   Of all humanity to which I'm drawn?
> MEPHISTOPHELES: You are precisely – what you are.
>   Cover you head with a wig or a million quilts,
>   Set your feet on a pair of extended stilts,
>   You'll always be just what you are. (F 1530–1809)

The scene is punctuated by mood-swings that signal Faust's familiar instability, so much so that at one point ('The fate of all mankind, be what it may,/ I'll access highs and lows in all my dreams,' F 1770f.) a total reversal of roles takes place. From being frustrated and refusing to believe that Mephistopheles can deliver anything worthwhile, Faust changes tack and speaks of increasing his knowledge and pleasure. His antagonist, by contrast, changes his role too, from one who urges Faust on to one who derides his aspirations. It has never been clear whether Goethe wished him to undergo a change of heart at this point or whether the switch was due to the poet inserting material he had written much earlier.

The most radical innovation of all is yet to come: Faust's infatuation with a young girl from a humble background. Here he reveals his credentials as a product of eighteenth-century ways of thinking. The misalliance that was a social stigma in previous epochs, so much so that is was referred to as a symptom of Faust's debauchery by Pfitzer, has suddenly become a mark of distinction. Oblivious to class barriers and social niceties, Faust offers his arm to a young girl he meets by chance in the street, addressing her as though she were a highborn lady. Opinions vary as to whether this fateful encounter has taken place with or without some backstage work by Mephistopheles.

A Street

> FAUST: My pretty lady, if I may,
>   I'll walk you home – please step this way.
> MARGARET: I'm not a lady and I'm not pretty,
>   Can find my own way round the city. [extricates herself and exits]
> FAUST: Heavens, what a beauty, that's for sure.
>   She seems so modest and so demure,
>   Yet not without a seductive streak,
>   I looked at her and I went quite weak.
>   Her lips so red, her cheeks so fair,
>   All I can do is stand and stare.
>   It plucked at my heart-strings just to see

Her avert her glance in front of me.
And how she flared up and spoke out loud,
That girl stands out in any crowd.

[MEPHISTOPHELES *appears*]

FAUST: Listen, I want you to get me that girl.
MEPHISTOPHELES: Which one, then?
FAUST: That little mistress.
MEPHISTOPHELES: That one's set your heart in a whirl?
She's just returned from seeing a priest,
From every sin she's been released.
I stood beside the box and listened in:
The girl's too pure to commit a sin.
With the likes of her, what can I do?
FAUST: She's fourteen years, plus a month or two ...
MEPHISTOPHELES: Good grief, it's a raunchy so-and-so
That won't permit sweet flowers to grow
But will insist on his right to pick them
Even if it means he's got to trick them.
Terribly sorry, but no can do.
FAUST: Listen here, your Honour, you
Would do me a favour if you say no more
About underage sex. So just shut up
And listen to me: if that sweet pup
Is not in my arms by the time we sup,
Then come midnight I shall show you the door.
MEPHISTOPHELES: Consider it well. It may amaze
You to hear that I'll need some fourteen days
To spend on preliminaries alone.
FAUST: If I had but seven hours to play with
It would give me pleasure to do away with
The devil and seduce the wench all on my own.
MEPHISTOPHELES: I like your French; but have you debated
How much fun you can have if you hang about
Instead of just rushing in and out?
Your pleasure would be much inflated
If up and down the garden path
You soften her up as in a bath
And lead her a bit of a song and dance
As they do in tales from Spain and France.
FAUST: I don't need those; I'm raring to go.
MEPHISTOPHELES: I'll tell you straight. You have to know
This pretty lass is not the sort
That in a whirlwind you may court.
You will get nowhere, I esteem,
Unless we come up with a crafty scheme.
FAUST: Then find some trinket to whet my delight,
Show me the place where she rests at night,
A scarf from the angel's bosom pure;
My raging passion needs a cure.
MEPHISTOPHELES: To demonstrate my good intent,
My helpful nature and friendly bent,
I'll take you straight to her private room,
That should help you to shake off your gloom.

110

FAUST:	I'll see her and have her straight away?
MEPHISTOPHELES:	No. There will be a short delay.
	She'll be next door on a visit to a neighbour,
	And thus you will simply have to labour
	In reverent awe and anticipation,
	If you wish to relieve your pent-up frustration.
FAUST:	Let's go, then!
MEPHISTOPHELES:	It's too early now.
FAUST:	Then find a gift for her somehow. [*exit*]
MEPHISTOPHELES:	He's talking presents on the very first day?
	Then he's bound to score. I know some spots
	Where treasure lies buried in vacant plots,
	I'll do my homework straight away! [*exit*] (F 2605–77)

The character introduced as Margaret in these early scenes, and later referred to by the informal diminutive Gretchen ('Little Madge'), partakes of a Faustian ambiguity. She is not his soul mate or in any way his equal; if a woman is to fulfil that function, it must be Helen of Troy, as she appears in the third act of *Faust II*, though she, too, is remote and culturally alien. Margaret is initially evasive and brusquely rejects Faust's offer to accompany her, but she is soon captivated by the handsome, dashing stranger whom she recognises to be her social superior (F 2680–83). Who might he be? she asks herself once she returns to her room. From that point on, her fate is sealed.

The question as to whether or not Mephistopheles foresaw, intended or engineered this encounter with Gretchen has been raised many times, and was frequently answered in the negative by critics of the old school, some of whom saw her as the 'dearest creature in the world' if not as a saintly figure (Mason, 216; Williams, 100). How could the disciple of evil have wished to provide such a pious, innocent companion for Faust, who would be likely to be won over and redeemed by her pure and godly ways? Yet the text makes it clear that Margaret is very young. How young? All we are told is that she is over fourteen, though apparently not by much (F 2627). Later, she will protest that she is too young to be married or have a boyfriend (F 2945, 2949). Here, there is evidence that Faust knows he is on the wrong side of the law and I have tried to bring this out in my translation: 'say no more/ About underage sex'. The German *Lass er mich mit dem Gesetz in Frieden* ('Say no more to me about the law'; F 2634) is euphemistic; the context indicates that the 'law' in question concerns relationships between adults and minors. What is astonishing here is the extent of critical self-deception about the unappetising subtext to the scene. This is another instance of the icon's ability to separate itself from the published text.

As things work out, Mephistopheles remains in control of the situation, stubbornly refusing to supply the girl immediately, whetting Faust's appetite and suggesting that the affair will be even more delicious if it is spun out at length. If Margaret is to be used to provide pleasure, the ground must first be prepared: 'Your pleasure would be much inflated/ If up and down the garden path/ You soften her up as in a bath/ And lead her a bit of a song and dance/ As they do in

111

tales from Spain and France.' (F 2648–52) Only then will the experience be fit for the true connoisseur. So off they go to find presents and then shower stolen goods on the girl until her head is completely turned by these unexpected attentions. By the time we see her at her spinning wheel, she has 'lost her peace' and has been completely swept off her feet by uncontrollable emotions.

Gretchen's Room

GRETCHEN [at her spinning-wheel, alone]:
> My heart is heavy,
> My peace destroyed;
> I can find no rest
> In this awful void.
>
> When he is gone
> I'm so alone,
> There's just no place
> That I can face.
>
> My poor head feels
> It's going mad,
> My poor heart reels,
> I'm just so sad.
>
> My heart is heavy,
> My peace destroyed;
> I can find no rest
> In this awful void.
>
> It's only to greet him
> That I stare through the pane;
> It's only to meet him
> That I go out again.
>
> The way he strides
> And holds himself high,
> The way he smiles
> And flashes his eye,
>
> The sound of his voice
> Is magical bliss,
> The touch of his hand
> And ah, his kiss ...
>
> My heart is heavy,
> My peace destroyed;
> I can find no rest
> In this awful void.
>
> My body yearns
> To clasp him tight;

If I could but grasp him
With all my might

And hold him and kiss him
As I long to so much,
I would surely expire
When our lips touch!
(F 3374–3403)

Rarely has a literary female revealed the depth of her innermost feelings with such intensity. Hers is a blinding passion. Gretchen is feminine sensuality incarnate, and even more so in the *Urfaust* version of this scene, where she speaks of her *Schoss* ('lap', 'womb') being drawn towards her lover. The somewhat monotonous rhythm echoes both the spinning-wheel and the beating heart, which speeds up in time with her accelerating excitement. Yet such is her contradictory nature that surprisingly soon after she has revealed the depths of her infatuation in these suggestive lines, half love song, half masturbation fantasy, we find her, as Margaret, berating Faust for his ungodly behaviour, and blaming him for associating with a companion who strikes terror into her very soul. 'I've seen him by you as your mate,/ He is the one I'll always hate.' (F 3471f.) She proceeds to interrogate Faust about his beliefs, only to be dazzled by an impressive display of verbal fireworks. Her confusion is nicely illustrated by the heavily ironic phrase, 'And our priest I have heard / Talk just like you, in a slightly different way' (F 3460f.) It is so easy to pull the wool over her eyes. Faust's mind is on other things: he is already clutching the sleeping potion that is designed to keep their secret tryst from her mother.

When she hears of his intentions, Margaret shows little surprise and puts up no resistance. The girl who had moments previously argued that sacraments and church law must be honoured, now proves ready to dishonour them herself with no further objection than that her mother might be disturbed and catch them in the act. 'I'd gladly leave the door unlocked at night' (F 3506) is enough to show that what follows is neither rape nor seduction, since both parties are set on a single purpose. Their dialogue must stand as one of the most remarkable in literature for the manner in which it rolls together the religious fervour and the amorous excitement that are raging within the girl. Though much is packed into it, the opening lines show the scene to be a fragment, and we are left in complete ignorance of how this uncomfortable conversation began.

Martha's Garden

MARGARET: Promise, Heinrich!
FAUST: Whatever I can.
MARGARET: What's your religion, do tell me?
              You are good, kind-hearted man
              But I would say it's not your cup of tea.
FAUST: Say no more, child. You know that I mean well –
              For those I love I'd go through fire and hell
              And I don't belittle any creed or church.

113

MARGARET:	But as regards belief you're somewhat in the lurch.
FAUST:	Am I?
MARGARET:	Yes, you are. If only you would listen.
	You do not honour the sacraments like any Christian.
FAUST:	I honour them.
MARGARET:	But where's the passion?
	How long since you last went to church or to confession?
	Do you believe in God?
FAUST:	My sweetheart, who dare say
	They really do?
	Ask anyone you may
	Priest or sage, and all will laugh at you
	For asking.
MARGARET:	So you don't believe then, right?
FAUST:	Listen well, you charming mite:
	Who am I to name him
	Or to claim him
	For myself?
	Who is so bold
	Whose heart so cold
	To say 'I have no faith' outright?
	He holds us all
	Keeps us in thrall
	Holding and keeping
	You, me, and himself.
	Isn't heaven's vault above us,
	And the earth spread out below?
	Don't the stars appear to love us
	As their eternal splendours show?
	And when I look into your eye,
	Doesn't everything around us start
	To sway your head and move your heart
	In eternal secret motion
	Ever invisible beside you?
	Fill your heart now to the point of bursting
	When you're satisfied, no longer thirsting
	For the truth, give it whatever name
	You choose: joy or heart, love or God!
	I can find none; emotion is what counts
	For me, the name's an empty word
	That blinds us to heaven's bliss.
MARGARET:	That's not something I would miss.
	And our priest I have heard
	Talk just like you, in a slightly different way.
FAUST:	It's what everyone says every single day
	In places far apart and many tongues,
	They fill their hearts and fill their lungs
	Why should I not do the same?
MARGARET:	When I hear you speak, I cannot claim
	To disagree; and yet it's empty vanity,
	For you have no Christianity.
FAUST:	Sweet child!
MARGARET:	For some time it has been a pain

114

	To see you with that man again.
FAUST:	How come?
MARGARET:	I've seen him by you as your mate,
	He is the one I'll always hate.
	There's no one else that I discern
	Can give me such a heartfelt turn
	As when I see the face he's got.
FAUST:	Little puppet, fear him not.
MARGARET:	His very presence chills my soul.
	To love all people is my goal,
	But much as I admire your features
	That one's the scariest of creatures,
	I thought him a rascal all along.
	May God forgive me if I am wrong.
FAUST:	Such oddball types have a right to life.
MARGARET:	I'd never ever be his wife!
	And when he enters through the door
	He seems to mock me, and what's more
	He's rather grim.
	You can see there ain't no love in him.
	It's written on his forehead clear
	There's not a soul that he holds dear.
	I feel so safe when it's you and me,
	So warm and sheltered and so free,
	But when he's there I clam up straight away.
FAUST:	An angel's prophesy, I'd say.
MARGARET:	It's such an all-consuming fear
	That when he joins us any day,
	I feel that I can't love you, dear.
	And suddenly I cannot pray.
	And that gnaws away at me,
	It must be the same for you, Henry.
FAUST:	You just don't like him.
MARGARET:	I must go now.
FAUST:	But can't we somehow
	Spend an hour together in deep embrace,
	Join hearts and souls in a quiet place?
MARGARET:	I'd gladly leave the door unlocked tonight
	If I had my own room in which to hide you.
	Yet mother often wakes, and what a fright
	She'd get if ever she found me beside you;
	I'm sure the shock would cause me to drop dead!
FAUST:	There is no reason for your dread.
	Here is a bottle, three drops stirred
	Into her drink, and she will soon
	Sink into pleasant dreams; we won't be heard.
MARGARET:	Is there a thing I would not do for you?
	But is it harmful I would like to know?
FAUST:	If there were any risk, dear, I'd say no.
MARGARET:	When I look upon you, my good man,
	I don't know what draws me to you,
	I've given you so much, done all I can,
	There's almost nothing left for me do.

[*Exit.* Mephistopheles *appears.*]

Mephistopheles:	The little monkey! Has she gone?
Faust:	You've spied again!
Mephistopheles:	I heard it all. From what I understood,
	The learned sage was put right through the mill!
	I am convinced it did a world of good,
	The girls are keen to find out if you still
	Believe and follow all the old commands;
	For if you do, you'll honour *their* demands.
Faust:	A monster if you fail to see
	That this good soul, so blithe and fair,
	Pure as the lamb,
	Can through her faith but think of me
	In her despair
	As someone whom that very faith must damn.
Mephistopheles:	Are you her lover or her priest?
	A little girl has got you hooked.
Faust:	You flaming cur, you filthy beast!
Mephistopheles:	Did you not see the way she looked
	At me and read my personality?
	My cover blown, she thought that she could see
	Signs of a brilliant rationality:
	Indeed, the Devil incarnate – could be me?
	And so, tonight?
Faust:	What's it to you?
Mephistopheles:	I'll get my kicks from what you'll do! (F 3414–3543)

Many unresolved questions emerge from a close reading of this scene. Why does Margaret refer to Faust as 'Henry' ('Heinrich'), when George and, more commonly, John, were the names by which he was known both to his contemporaries and in all subsequent literary derivatives? Does the doctor travel under an alias, or did Goethe merely wish to move away from the hackneyed 'Johann', a name then common among domestic servants? Is Faust truthfully propounding a sincerely held belief in 'joy or heart, love or God' or is he deliberately hoodwinking the untutored girl with learned-sounding but ultimately vacuous terminology? Is Margaret a narrow-minded church-going hypocrite who turns her back on religion when the occasion demands, or is she genuinely concerned about Faust's spiritual well-being, and led by her accommodating nature to go against the commandments she defended so vigorously in the opening lines of this scene?

Whatever the answers, the reappearance of Mephistopheles hints very strongly at his approval if not at direct complicity in the rapidly evolving relationship. Faust's occasional outbursts of sentimentality sit uncomfortably with his earlier desire to possess the maiden come what may. Critics may argue that Faust is on a learning curve, now much more appreciative of her as a person than he had previously been, but future developments will speak louder than words. He will impregnate and abandon her, not before killing her brother Valentine, an act for which he is forgiven by those readers who point out that the deed is actually done by Mephistopheles. Her mother, into whose nightcap Gretchen is instructed to stir three drops from a mysterious bottle, is also to die. Did Faust, a medical man, know this would happen? Was the bottle provided by Mephisto? Did Margaret exceed the stated dose? We do not find out. She is the principal victim, and 'Cathedral', the final scene of *Faust, A Fragment* of 1790, reveals her unenviable plight (F 3776–3834). Religion is scant consolation at this point; instead of offering hope and solace, the choir recalls her guilt, oppressing her further with terrifying visions of hell. The very same punishments that awaited earlier Fausts are now threatened for his victim. An evil spirit whispers malicious taunts into her ear, much as Mephostophiles had done when tormenting the original Faustus with painful reminders that he had forfeited his chance of salvation.

It is a long time before Faust returns to his erstwhile beloved. After dancing among witches on Mount Brocken in the operatic Walpurgis Night scene, he is suddenly reminded of her in a vision. She has been imprisoned and is awaiting execution for infanticide. How and why she came to face this charge is not revealed. Explanations range from a premature delivery to the stresses of their unequal relationship or even a selfless desire to protect her outlawed lover from further shame. The text provides hints, but no direct answers.

At the eleventh hour, Faust reappears and confronts the girl, who here reverts to the name Margaret, at least in the stage directions. He shows a determination to rescue her and has the power to do so. She seems to have lost her mind, but quickly responds to his voice. Although he offers her the opportunity to escape, she delays the process when she implores him to kiss her. Eventually, Mephisto-pheles appears and orders the lovers to hasten. Margaret refuses to obey him, and is abandoned to her fate. A 'Voice from Above' announces that she has been saved.

A Prison Cell

FAUST [*holding a bunch of keys and a lamp, by an iron gate*]:
        A long-forgotten shudder numbed me
        As I beheld her prison's humid cell;
        Mankind's pain and suffering have stunned me,
        I know that in her crime she still meant well.
        And yet, I am afraid to visit,
        I fear the sight of her. What is it?
        A delay could spell lingering death for the girl.
[*He takes hold of the lock. Singing is heard from within*]
        My mother the whore
        Has killed me stone dead,
        My father the rascal
        On my flesh he has fed.
        My sister, so small,
        Found my bones, one and all,
        And hid them away
        And I was a wonderful bird that day,
        Fly away, fly away from them all.
FAUST [*unlocks the gate*]: She does not realise that her love is near.
        The clanking chain, the rustling straw I hear. [*enters*]

117

MARGARET [*hiding on her bunk*]: Alas, alas, they've come to do the deed.
FAUST [*softly*]:   Hush, hush, I'm here to get you out.
MARGARET [*crawling towards him*]: Have mercy, man, in this my hour of need.
FAUST: You'll wake the sleeping warders if you shout.
   [*seizes the chains and tries to unlock them*]
MARGARET [*on her knees*]: Who gave the hangman this great power
                 Over me, how come?
                 It's not long past the midnight hour!
                 Have mercy. I'm still so young.
                 Tomorrow will be soon enough. [*stands up*]
                 I am so young, I do not bluff,
                 Too young by far to die!
                 I was a beauty too, that's why
                 It happened. My friend was near, he's gone away
                 The garland's torn, the flowers in disarray.
                 Don't use such brutal force on me.
                 What have I done to anger thee?
                 Do not let me plead in vain,
                 I have not seen you or caused you pain.
FAUST: Such misery drives me insane.
MARGARET: I'm in your power, there's no doubt,
                 But let me feed my child once more.
                 I cuddled it last night. They took it out
                 Of my embrace just to offend me, that's for sure.
                 They say I've killed it, but without
                 My child I'll never see a happy day.
                 They're singing ditties, mocking me. It is no good.
                 An old fairy tale ends that way.
                 What have they understood?
FAUST [*throws himself down*]: Your lover's at your feet, you see?
                 To free you from this misery.
MARGARET: O let us pray to all the saints.
                 The Lord of hell taints
                 These flagstones
                 And groans
                 Underground,
                 And all around
                 He moans.
FAUST [*raising his voice*]: Gretchen! Gretchen!
MARGARET [*listens attentively*]: That was my friend's sound.
   [*She leaps up. Her chains fall away*]
                 Where can he be? I hear him call.
                 I'm free and no one can forestall
                 My flight. I'll clasp him tight,
                 All will come right
                 When I am in his arms. He called for me
                 From the doorway. In all the raging of hellish hordes
                 I could hear his sweet and adoring words.
FAUST: It is I.
MARGARET: It is you. Speak to me, lover. [*embraces him*]
                 It is he, it is he. My torments are over.
                 I have no fear of prison and chain
                 You have come to put a stop to my pain.

	At last I am free! –
	The street is back in my mind's eye
	Where that first time you passed me by
	And the charming little garden, too,
	Where Martha and I would wait for you.

FAUST [*imploring her to leave*]: Come away, come away.

MARGARET: Stay awhile, stay.

I long to linger when I'm with my love. [*She caresses him*]

FAUST: Let us hurry away.

If you don't make a move
A chance will be missed.

MARGARET: What? You don't want to be kissed?

My friend, who recently did go away,
Forgets to kiss his love today?
And in your arms, what is this anguish?
Remember when you spoke or gazed at me
Heaven itself would seem to vanquish
Me and your fiery kisses would all but smother me.
Please kiss me, now,
Or I'll show you how! [*She holds him tight*]
Woe upon me. Your lips are like ice,
They do not move.
How in a trice
Could you lose all your love? [*She turns away*]

FAUST: Be brave, my dear, and come away.

I cherish you more than I can say;
Just come away; that's all you have to do.

MARGARET [*turning to face him*]: And can I be sure that it's really you?

FAUST: It is. Come quick.

MARGARET: You have undone this very chain,

You hold me in a close embrace again.
And yet you fear me not – so it would seem –,
You do not know, friend, whom you would redeem.

FAUST: Come, come, the night is on the wane.

MARGARET: 'Tis my own mother I have slain.

And it is true that I was driven
To drown the child that you and I were given.
'Twas yours as well. And here you stand.
No empty dream. Give me your hand
So dear to me. It's moist, not dry.
Wipe it clean. I can't deny
There's blood on it too,
My God, what did you do?
And be so good, please, as to cast
That sword of yours away.

FAUST: What is past is past.

You'll be the death of me this day.

MARGARET: No, you are the one who must live.

A description I shall give
You of every tomb,
Please tend them soon.
The best place for my mother
And beside her, lay my brother,

Myself you must hide
Nearby, not too far aside.
The little babe at my breast
Where none else shall rest.
To cuddle and hold you was bliss
But it seems you want to reject me
In a way that must cruelly affect me,
There is something about you I miss.
And yet it's you, and your kind trusting eyes.

FAUST: If you feel it is I, then you must arise!

MARGARET: Leave my cell?

FAUST: And be free!

MARGARET: The grave is well
And truly there, it's where death hides.
Come; to where we may rest in peace
And not one step beyond, understood –
You wish to depart? Heinrich, if only I could!

FAUST: Just try. The door is open; we must elope.

MARGARET: I may not leave, I cannot hope.
And if I escape they'll be lying in wait.
It's a miserable fate to beg for one's bread
With guilty thoughts going round in one's head,
It's a miserable fate to keep moving around,
And in the end I just know I'll be found.

FAUST: I'll stay by your side.

MARGARET: Run, run wild,
To save your child.
Follow the track
Along the stream
Don't look back,
Go into the wood,
Find the landing stage
Where the lake is dank
Grab hold of the plank,
It's beginning to move,
It's wriggling, I swear,
Save the poor thing!

FAUST: Have a care!
Just one tiny step and you're free!

MARGARET: Come round the mountainside with me.
There's my mother sat on a stone,
I feel a nameless dread!
There's my mother sat on a stone,
And up and down she wiggles her head.
She makes no sign; her head's a weight.
She sleeps forever, she slept so late.
For our enjoyment she did sleep,
Fond memories for us to keep.

FAUST: There's nothing left to do or say,
I'll have to carry you away.

MARGARET: Let go of me! I'll not be abused.
Don't grab at me in a murderous style,
I've loved and cherished you all the while.

FAUST:	The day is dawning. My darling, my dear!
MARGARET:	Yes, the dawn breaks, night fades away,
	This was to be my wedding day.
	Don't tell them you've been with your Gretchen.
	My wreath, it did fall,
	It just happened that way.
	We shall meet some day
	But not at the ball.
	Silently the mass of people rolls
	Down the streets towards the square,
	Till there's no space even there.
	The signal sounds, the great bell tolls,
	Now someone grabs and binds me.
	Now my head is on the block
	And the very blade, when it finds me,
	Must seem to stun them and shock
	Them all. The world shall be my graveyard.
FAUST:	If only I had never been born.
MEPHISTOPHELES [appears from outside]: Make haste, or the plan is torn.
	Why waste your time in chatting and prating?
	My shuddering stallions grow tired of waiting.
	The morning star has risen.
MARGARET:	How did this man get into the prison?
	Not him, not him! He's a disgrace
	In this holy place.
	It's me he's after.
FAUST:	You shall live, my love.
MARGARET:	I commend myself to God's judgement above.
MEPHISTOPHELES [to FAUST]: Come with me or else you'll be lost.
MARGARET:	Yours I am, Father, whatever the cost.
	Save me, angels, gather around,
	Take me to where salvation is found.
	Heinrich, you fill me with abject fear.
MEPHISTOPHELES:	She has been judged.
VOICE [from above]: Has been saved.
MEPHISTOPHELES:	Follow me. [leaves with FAUST]
VOICE [from within, fading]: Heinrich, Heinrich! (F 4405-4612)

The complex closing scene is here reproduced in its entirety. It was begun in prose, but repeatedly reworked and transformed into verse for publication. Some would argue that Goethe would have done better to leave it in the rough-hewn form it was given in *Urfaust*, traces of which remain in uneven rhythms and colloquial touches. It is richly symbolic and yet also gruesomely realistic in its treatment of the jilted teenage mother, whose songs and chanting reveal a tormented psyche but also fill in some of the gaps in her story. It creates an unattractive image of a Faust who allows his sense of urgency to get the better of him and in the process rides roughshod over his traumatised victim's emotions. He appears desensitised after the revelry on the Brocken. There Faust enjoyed some temporary respite, but Goethe chose to abandon his plans to let him meet Satan face to face, as he had originally intended. Instead, a satirical intermezzo was added, the so-called

'Walpurgis Night's Dream'. After this, we return to Margaret in a scene that is both harrowingly tragic and conciliatory; tragic in that her reward for loving Faust is humiliation and death; tragic also in that Faust fails to free himself from Mephistopheles, although this will eventually enable him to move into the wider world of politics in a much later continuation of the drama.

Yet Goethe was always reluctant to conclude his works on a bleak or despairing note. Faust is, in some ways, intent on doing his best. Outbursts in previous scenes had shown that Gretchen was far from forgotten. Finally realising what has become of her, he returns to do what he can. Shying away from her tormentor, Gretchen is redeemed, and a celestial voice appears to confirm that she has been judged and approved worthy of salvation. No better fate could await her; this is the very opposite of tragedy.

Faust's role is therefore both one of saviour and, since the girl has to reject him in order to achieve salvation, her tempter. His action, or inaction, in this scene is puzzling. No longer the passionate lover of previous scenes, he cannot even bring himself to kiss the girl he is trying to save. She, by contrast, notices immediately how much his responses have cooled: 'Woe upon me. Your lips are like ice,/ They do not move./ How in a trice/ Could you lose all your love?' (F 4493–97) Here she has completely overcome her temporary insanity, if such it was, only to discover that the man who came to save her is no longer the one she believed she knew. Faust's love was cursed from the outset and could not be sustained, perhaps because all Fausts are denied the ability to love. His verbal cruelty towards Gretchen, especially 'What is past is past./ You'll be the death of me' (F 4518f.), is remarkable for its lack of feeling, and as though this were not enough, he seems ready to manhandle her ('Let go of me! I'll not be abused./ Don't hold me in such a murderous style,/ I've loved and cherished you all the while.' F 4576–78). The reference to his 'murderous style' shows that she has not forgotten his part in the death of her mother and brother.

The text ends as it had begun, with a mixture of psychological verisimilitude (Faust's love has worn off and he makes unsuccessful attempts to conceal the fact) and symbolism (the shadow of Mephistopheles hangs heavily over the scene, as it does over the ill-fated relationship and everything else Faust does). It is tempting to debate whether it is admissible to blame Faust for anything in all of this, since he is manifestly in the thrall of a destructive power. Yet man must turn to evil if he is to achieve good, a point made with some insistence in the Prologue. The second part of Faust (see below, 141–53) will show a gradual process of recovery in which the principles of classical harmony will assert themselves as guiding forces in parallel to Mephisto's influence. It will first be convenient to examine some of the 'Romantic' Fausts that were being written by other authors of the period.

Cited Works and Further Reading

The text of Goethe's *Faust* is cited, here and elsewhere in this volume, as 'F' plus line number(s) based on the following edition: Albrecht Schöne (ed.), *Johann Wolfgang von Goethe: Faust. Texte*. 2 volumes. Frankfurt/M: Deutscher Klassiker Verlag, 1994. English translation by Osman Durrani.

Other English translations include

Dan Farrelly, *Urfaust by Johann Wolfgang von Goethe in Brechtian mode. A new version*. Dublin: Carysfort Press, 1998.
Barker Fairley, *Goethe's Faust*. Toronto: University Press, 1970.
Cyrus Hamlin (ed.), Johann Wolfgang Goethe: *Faust. A Tragedy. Translated by Walter Arndt. With Interpretive Notes, Contexts, Modern Criticism*. New York: W.W. Norton, 1976. 2nd edn, 2001.
David Luke, *Johann Wolfgang von Goethe. Faust Part I*. Oxford: University Press, 1987.
—, *Johann Wolfgang von Goethe. Faust Part II*. Oxford: University Press, 1994.

Secondary literature

Stuart Atkins, *Goethe's Faust. A Literary Analysis*. Cambridge/Mass: Harvard University Press, 1958.
Benjamin Bennett, *Goethe's Theory of Poetry. Faust and the Regeneration of Language*. Ithaca: Cornell University Press, 1986.
Paul Bishop (ed.), *A Companion to Goethe's Faust: Parts I and II*. Rochester/NY: Camden House, 2001.
Peter Boerner and Sidney Johnson (eds), *Faust through Four Centuries. Retrospect and Analysis. Vierhundert Jahre Faust. Rückblick und Analyse*. Tübingen: Niemeyer, 1989.
Peter Brandes, *Goethes Faust. Poetik der Gabe und Selbstreflexion der Dichtung*. Munich: Fink, 2003.
Hanns Braun, *Hier irrt Goethe – unter anderen*. Munich: dtv, 1966.
Jane K. Brown, *Goethe's Faust. The German Tragedy*. Ithaca: Cornell University Press, 1986.
—, Meredith Lee, Thomas P. Saine (eds), *Interpreting Goethe's* Faust *Today*. Rochester/NY: Camden House, 1994.
Charles Dédéyan, *Le Mythe de Faust dans la littérature européenne*. 4 volumes. Paris: Lettres Modernes, 1954-61.
Osman Durrani, *Faust and the Bible. A Study of Goethe's use of Scriptural Allusions and Christian Religious Motifs in* Faust I *and* II. Berne: Herbert Lang, 1976.
—, 'The Character and Qualities of Mephistopheles', in Bishop, 76-94.
Lilian R. Furst, 'The Problem of Gretchen', in Douglas J. McMillan (ed.), *Approaches to Teaching Goethe's Faust*. New York: Modern Language Association, 1987, 48-54.
Ulrich Gaier (ed.), *Johann Wolfgang Goethe: Faust Dichtungen*. 3 volumes. Stuttgart: Reclam, 1999.
Barker Fairley, *Goethe's Faust. Six Essays*. Oxford: Clarendon Press, 1953.
Otto Heller, *Faust and Faustus. A Study of Goethe's Relation to Marlowe's*. 1931. Rptd New York: Cooper Square, 1972.
Hans Henning, 'Lessings Faust-Pläne und -Fragmente', in Boerner/Johnson, 79-90.
Gotthold Ephraim Lessing, *Werke*. 8 volumes. Munich: Hanser, 1970-79.
Werner Keller, 'Faust. Eine Tragödie', in Walter Hinderer (ed.), *Goethes Dramen*. Stuttgart: Reclam, 1992, 258-329.

Johann Leutbecher, *Über den Faust von Göthe. Eine Schrift zum Verständniss dieser Dichtung nach ihren beiden Theilen für alle Freunde und Verehrer des grossen Dichters.* Nuremberg: Renner, 1838.

Iain McCalman, *The Seven Ordeals of Count Cagliostro. Count Cagliostro, Master of Magic in the Age of Reason.* London: Century, 2003.

Eudo C. Mason, *Goethe's Faust: Its Genesis and Purport.* Berkeley: California University Press, 1967.

Peter Matussek, 'Faust I', in Theo Buck (ed.), *Goethe-Handbuch. Band 2: Dramen.* Stuttgart: Metzler, 1997, 352–90.

Eike Middell and Hans Henning (eds), *Faust. Eine Anthologie.* 2 volumes. Leipzig: Reclam, 1967.

Paul Requadt, *Goethe's "Faust I". Leitmotivik und Architektur,* Munich: Wilhelm Fink, 1972.

Friederike Schmidt-Möbus and Frank Möbus, *Who is Who in Goethe's Faust? Kleines Lexikon der Personen und mythologischen Gestalten in Johann Wolfgang von Goethes Faust I und II.* Leipzig: Edition Leipzig, 1999.

Rüdiger Scholz, *Goethes "Faust" in der wissenschaftlichen Interpretation von Schelling und Hegel bis heute: ein einführender Forschungsbericht.* Rheinfelden: Schäuble, 1983.

Albrecht Schöne, *Götterzeichen, Liebeszauber, Satanskult. Neue Einblicke in alte Goethetexte.* Munich: Beck, 1982.

Oskar Seidlin, 'Das Etwas und das Nichts. Versuch zur Neu-Interpretation einer Faust-Stelle', *Germanic Review,* 19 (1944), 170–75.

Roger Shattuck, *Forbidden Knowledge: From Prometheus to Pornography.* New York: St. Martin's Press, 1996.

Fritz Strich, *Goethe and World Literature.* London: Routledge and Kegan Paul, 1949.

Ann White, *Names and Nomenclature in Goethe's 'Faust'.* London: IGS, 1980.

John R. Williams, *Goethe's Faust.* London: Allen & Unwin, 1987.

Chapter Four

Romantics to Realists

I am not put off by the fact that Goethe wrote a Faust. Faust is the common property of all mankind, not a monopoly held by Goethe. If that were the case, you would not be able to write an ode to the moon, because such and such an Old Master had already done so. And besides, the subject can be treated in so many different ways that there will never be a conflict.—Nikolaus Lenau

Restless Titans

The figure of the damnable doctor received a remarkable and enduring facelift when it became known that Goethe, by then a celebrated author of fiction (his sensational novel *The Sufferings of Young Werther* appeared in 1774), was working on the same topic that Lessing had recently recommended. No longer would Faustus be seen as a benighted alchemist with leanings toward black magic and a penchant for mildly entertaining clownish tricks. The gross mockery of secular scholarship that had been a characteristic of the chapbook, parts of Marlowe, and most of the puppet plays was incompatible with an age which thirsted after fresh insights into man's spiritual roots. The intellectual tone of the time was set by a new generation of holistic thinkers, among them Johann Gottfried Herder and Jean-Jacques Rousseau, who argued that a more sympathetic understanding of man's predicament would return people to a more naïve and therefore more natural way of life.

Faust needed to outgrow his role as a warning to Christians if he was to become something more than a historical oddity of severely restricted appeal. Once this had been achieved, his name became associated with progress, with striving, with the rightful quest for ever more knowledge, qualities which had been glimpsed periodically in Marlowe's dramatisation, but had been eroded and travestied in countless puppet plays and harlequin shows. From the 1770s onwards, Faust will appear in a new guise: as a radical, an innovator, a man who occupies a position on the fringes of society and whose powerful inner dynamism ensures that his intentions are at least partly altruistic. Progress rather than pleasure has become his lodestar. Scholarship for its own sake continues to be suspect, not because it is antagonistic to scripture, but because from now on all theory is perceived as hostile to life itself.

Even before Goethe's *Faust. A Fragment* appeared in print in 1790, fellow members of the Enlightenment and *Sturm und Drang* ('Storm and Stress') schools had taken up the theme. Paul Weidmann (1748–1801) has the distinction of completing the first modern play on the Faust theme. *Johann Faust. Ein Allegorisches Drama* ('John Faust. An Allegorical Drama') was shown, according to its title page, at the Royal Theatre in Prague, and published 'with the permission of the Royal and Imperial Censor' in 1775, albeit anonymously. This was the first time since Marlowe that a serious play about Faust was performed with human actors rather than puppets or harlequins in a regular theatre. It transferred to Munich in 1776, and was later seen in Nuremberg, Cologne and Vienna (Černý, 397f.). Weidmann's introduction asserts that he had not chosen this topic to please the masses or to vie with 'Chakespear' [sic] or Voltaire, but because the subject itself was so bleak and disturbing as to present a challenge to any dramatist (Weidmann, iv).

In deference to the 'three unities', Weidmann's play begins at six in the morning and ends at midnight. Faust is introduced as a listless dreamer, surrounded by examples of mediocrity, failed poets, jealous officers and vain courtesans. His role is essentially to see through all these false friends whom he had encouraged and supported with the assistance of Mephistopheles. The parallels with Marlowe include a good spirit (Ithuriel) beside the evil Mephistopheles. Ithuriel attempts to save Faust, but Helena, Faust's paramour, intervenes. She does not know of his secret liaison with Mephistopheles. There are allegorical figures like 'Raufgern' whose names and demeanour anticipate the three strong men of Goethe's *Faust II*.

Faust's inability to find happiness (Weidmann, II, 8; 34), and his confrontations with *Sorge* ('Care') are further parallels with *Faust II*. The ethos is a thoroughly bourgeois one, with Faust's mother and father appearing as hand-wringing bystanders, and Faust rejecting all the pretty maidens whom Mephistopheles has tirelessly been providing, except for his true love, Helena, and her son, Eduard. He accepts the good advice of his mother in his heart, but when faced with a choice between Helena and his son, or his well-intentioned parents and Ithuriel, he rejects the latter (*Op. cit.*, III.6; 48–50). The mood becomes increasingly lachrymose. After a ballet in Act IV, the parents are back yet again, but Mephistopheles has evolved a gruesome plan; Helena must murder Theodor, Faust's father. When Helena hesitates to commit murder, Mephistopheles argues in Goethean fashion that his role is to stir things up, albeit with more serious consequences:

> Humans can harm themselves only too well, and we can only cause them to fall through their own actions. We allow you to carry out our counsels. We arm you against each other. If we decide to spark off a war, then we instil conflicting opinions into your leaders and inspire the conquering soldiers with ambitions that make them throttle millions for the sake of one acre of barren soil. But if we desire to exterminate entire nations, then we inspire religious fervour, and brother takes up arms against brother. The father impales his son, the mother tears her daughter to pieces: such are our victories. (*Op. cit.*, IV, 5; 61)

Act V appears to end as befits a tragedy, when Faust poisons himself and Helena stabs first Theodor and then herself after realising that she has made the situation worse. But Theodor forgives them and they die reconciled. Ithuriel has the final word: although they were found wanting, an infinitely merciful power has forgiven them, and Mephistopheles is rightly defeated (*Op. cit.*, V, 7; 79f.). Weidmann made many characteristic changes to the traditional material in order to conform to the bourgeois drama of the period. The action is now rooted in a single day. Faust is not an isolated loner, but he has parents, a wife and even a son. This circumstance alone contravenes one of the important terms of the original pact: that domestic pleasures, and specifically marriage, are not for him. He is not shown as an old man at the end of his days, nor as a frustrated scholar, but as a successful public figure who has been involved in many a shady deal. What is remarkable is that Weidmann has seen through the paradox that had frustrated all previous attempts by earlier Fausts to escape from their snare: that man is free to repent, and that if Faustus does so in his dying hour, mercy and forgiveness must needs come his way. Weidmann's Catholic faith and the eighteenth-century climate of rationality combine here to suggest a conciliatory conclusion resembling that of a pre-Reformation morality play.

In 1776, the painter and dramatist Friedrich Müller, also known as 'Maler Müller' ('Müller the Painter'), published a short fragment, *Situation aus Fausts Leben* ('A Situation taken from Faust's Life'), and this was followed by *Fausts Leben dramatisirt* ('Faust's Life Dramatised'), in 1778. Another contemporary of Goethe's, Friedrich Maximilian Klinger, published a prose account of *Fausts Leben, Taten und Höllenfahrt* ('Faust's Life, Deeds and Journey to Hell') in 1791. These texts, too, are close to the new, positive spirit. Even so, until well into the nineteenth century it was widely assumed that Goethe's hero would suffer defeat; why else would the first part have been designated a 'tragedy'?

Maler Müller's *Situation aus Fausts Leben* is dedicated to 'Shakespeare's Spirit'. It begins with an assembly of devils, Satan, Moloch and others lamenting the lack of a 'great individual' on earth. Twelve years have passed since the pact was signed, and the 'situation' or episode herein described is a point of recognition for Faust. Just as he is all set to snatch the Queen of Aragon from the arms of the King of Spain, Mephistopheles descends on him to remind him that he is entering the second phase of the contract, and the day of his damnation is now drawing ever closer. Faust may believe that he can find a loophole ('Yet do I belong to myself – I can renounce you – I shall renounce you', Müller (1776), 33), but his antagonist is determined not to forfeit his prize:

> If it were a question of your soul! A breath! I would grab hold of you while you were breathing your last, were it halfway to heaven – but our hell is not so empty as to need you. Go, crawl away, you deserve to be a slave, you braggart, we despise the likes of you. [*He draws out the contract*] Faust, I am talking to you unseen by all the rest – very well, then, take this drivel [*holds out the sheet of paper*, FAUST *attempts to seize it*] You see that I'm laughing, for the very moment you touch it with the tip of one finger, you will revert to what you were: the hunched-up, miserable, famished beggar

in a frayed cloak that I picked up on the steps of a monastery twelve years ago. And then, to pay you back in jest for twelve years' service, I'll humiliate you to such an extent that the servants in this palace will force you out with their hobnailed boots like a mangy dog and the proud queen whom you adore shall avert her gaze when she tosses a coin in the direction of this pathetic mound of rags. – Go on, take it! (*Op. cit.*, 33f. See Act VI, 7, Leuschner, I, 448)

It was typical that this one fragmentary episode should see the light of print in a single, 36-page volume that was published ahead of the competition. Müller was well aware that Lessing and Goethe were working on the same topic (Müller (1778), 9) and clearly wished to stake his own claim before the others published anything of substance on it. He had been attracted to Faust since his earliest childhood, and what he appears to have admired most was the *grosser Kerl* ('a man of great power') in him. It is this notion that commended the figure of Faust to a whole generation of playwrights. Müller attempts a definition of his 'superhero':

A man who can feel his range of powers, aware of the bridle that fate has placed upon him by way of restraint, though he would fain break it, and is struggling to find the means to do so, a man with the courage to beat back all obstacles, a man with sufficient warmth in his soul to ally himself lovingly with a devil who approaches him openly and with affection. (*Loc. cit.*)

1778 then saw the completion of Müller's first two acts in prose. Faust loses the money he has deposited with a dubious goldsmith as a result of financial trickery. Wagner brings the disturbing news to him while he is in a trance. Lengthy legal debates reveal the extent of corruption and the effects of what appears to be a general prejudice against the doctor. The 1778 text remained a fragment, but later in his life, possibly as a result of the publication of Goethe's *Faust I* in 1808, Müller decided to turn these scenes in to a verse drama known as the 'Metric Faust'.

As befits its Faustian subject, the final reworking of Müller's play is wide-ranging, amorphous, and unstageable. Based on a manuscript of 2,155 pages, it comprises eight acts and two epilogues. It is rich in thoughts on matters that concerned most German writers at the time: *Fürstenerziehung* ('the education of princes'), the role of the army, and the purpose of art (Leuschner, II, 10; 52). Faust loses what little money is left when he agrees to gamble with some no-good types. A number of Jews are implicated in his downfall. At the eleventh hour, just before his arrest, a stranger offers him a book that will help him to escape, which he promptly accepts. (II, 4) The conjuration follows in Act II, 9, about 140 pages into the text (out of 726).

The first acts take place in Ingolstadt, Bavaria, but eventually Faust leaves Germany and crosses Europe to Gascony, the Pyrenees, and North Africa. In the final scene (VIII, 13), Lucifer comes close to regretting the time wasted by himself and his minions in pursuing someone as trivial as Faust. The devil's grandmother (*die Höllengrossmutter*) has the final say. She and Satan embrace him and pull him down with them. To the bitter end, Faust bravely stands his ground, forever the epitome of the titanic individual:

Why do you yet pursue
Your playful mocking game; I know full well
What now awaits me, am prepared, and if
My soul as you declare is mortal still,
Then brief will be your triumph, brief no less
My agony! Yet nay, my inner voice
Tells me it cannot be. I shall survive.
I do not fear your wildest greed, you cannot
But obey the Power on high! I shall
Survive. Just hear me out and stand ashamed,
The spark that He implanted in me cannot
Expire, not ever. It is you that cleanse
The sinner of his remaining sins, and brighter
Then he soars, light as the air, and journeys
Back towards his origins. (Leuschner, I, 704)

And yet this eight-act marathon ends in an epilogue in which Faust reawakens, having been asleep for just twenty-four hours. He thinks that he is in hell, but his friends are able to convince him that he is still very much alive, and the subject of his extended nightmare might well be fashioned into a half-serious, half-comic drama.

Despite its author's tireless attempts, the completed work remained unpublished when Müller died in 1825. The long and complex plot is summarised by the author himself in a letter to Count von Seinsheim. Müller claims that he was not concerned with the generation of theatrical effects, but 'to investigate the motives of our actions in the inner recesses of the human spirit and to pursue these to the point of their visible emanation'. (Leuschner, II, 247–55)

A few words need to be said about the inclusion of at least four caricatures of Jewish moneylenders in this play. The first Faust Book had contained an episode in which Faust deposits his leg as collateral with a Jewish pawnbroker who disposes of it, only to have Faust return with the money and demand his leg back. The Jew is mightily amazed and has to forego repayment of his loan. In Müller, this motif is taken much further. The Jews have unpleasant-sounding names (Izick, Schummel, Mauschel), their language is caricatured and they are presented as instrumental in driving Faust into the devil's arms. Müller himself provided a title-piece depicting the ragged-looking threesome. The effect of these crude devices is moderated – slightly – by the fact that other social groups (police, doctors, professors) are made fun of in no less unsympathetic terms (Och, 213).

Friedrich Maximilian Klinger's early drama touched a nerve: *Storm and Stress*, published in 1776, may be forgotten today; not so the movement whose name it provided. *Faust's Life, Deeds and Journey to Hell* of 1791, a 'diverse and tumultuous work' (Dédéyan, II, 76), is typical of the bombastic approach no less than of the multifarious political, social and psychological concerns of its youthful members. But as the first modern novel about Faust, it has a special position in the history of the material. A pointer as to the author's intentions is offered by the English-language dedication:

All this with indignation have I hurl'd
At the pretending Part of the proud World,
Who, swollen with selfish vanity, devise
False Freedoms, holy Cheats, and formal Lies
Over their Fellow-Slaves to tyrannize.
(John Wilmot, Earl of Rochester, 1647–1680, 'A Satyr Against Mankind')

Klinger (3) also claims, somewhat perversely, that he neither made use of nor wanted to make use of anything that had previously been published on the theme. Written partly in narrative prose and partly in short dramatic scenes, possibly because it was begun as a tragedy, it is a work of epic dimensions and great imaginative power. There are picaresque elements that invite comparison with Swift, Lesage, and Voltaire (Dédéyan, II, 41). It echoes and anticipates aspects of Goethe's work. There is a scene in hell, in which the devils serenade Germany as one of the last remaining feudal states in the world. The printer Faust, here identified with Gutenberg's financial backer and later rival Johann Fust (1400–1466), has through his invention spread more misery across the world than it had ever seen before. When, from the second book onwards, Faust and the devil Leviathan undertake their journey across the country in order that Faust may see man 'naked, as he really is' and be freed of the prejudices of his youth and his reading (III, 7; Klinger, 114), they encounter corruption and deceit at every turn. Whenever Faust believes he has found an example of human goodness, the devil is able to prove that seemingly good men will readily yield to any temptation that comes their way.

After many voluptuous kisses and much passionate sighing, she [the temptress, disguised as a pilgrim] whispered even more quietly into his [the hermit's] ear, pressing her hot bosom against his beating heart, 'Their swords are on the table, you kill one of them, I'll take the other, put on his clothes, take their money, we'll set fire to the hermitage and escape to France.'

The terrifying thought of committing murder filled the hermit with horror, but lust tore through his heart, he stumbled, trembled, gazed at the charms of the sorceress, and, imagining that he could possess her, as well as the treasure, without risk to himself, all his previous reservations dispersed and he forgot heaven and his vocation. The pilgrim girl pushed the delirious man into the cell, he picked up one sword, she the other, and as he was about to strike out at Faust, the devil began his hellish laugh, and Faust observed the hermit kneeling at his side with the drawn sword in his hand.

Faust: You damnable man, who would slay your guests while wearing the mask of piety.

The hermit sank quivering onto the ground. The pilgrim girl, a construct of hell, revealed her terrifying form to him and vanished.

Faust ordered the devil to set light to the hut and to burn it down along with its deceitful occupant. The devil was happy to obey him and the hermit's abode went up in flames. The next morning, the local peasants lamented the passing of a just man. They collected the hermit's bones and venerated them as objects of devotion. (II, 5; Klinger, 72f.)

Faust's quest continues in this vein. Instead of inspiring him and broadening his mind, the journey brings Faust face to face with the most outrageous instances of corruption among judges, bishops and other supposedly upright citizens. People from all walks of life allow themselves to be seduced, even when the devil brings no magical powers to bear on them. Klinger's depiction of society is an unrelieved panorama of cruelty and exploitation. Faust is so often moved to tears – as in Book III, chapter 1, by the peasant woman whose abused husband was forced to kill himself – that the devil spends more time righting the world's wrongs at his master's request than perpetrating crimes. Yet these apparent acts of mercy turn out to be the catalysts for yet greater disasters. Court intrigues within the German states are the subject of several episodes, with Faust growing increasingly horrified by the malpractices that go on behind the closed doors of Germany's princely palaces. Faust is finally obliged to ask the devil for an explanation.

> FAUST: If man is obliged to act in a certain way from necessity, then all his actions must be ascribed to the Superior Being and therefore cease to be punishable. Can anything other than goodness and perfection flow from a perfect being? In that case, our actions have the same quality, however revolting they may seem, and we are all victims, without being able to understand why. If our actions should indeed be punishable and as revolting as they appear to be, then the Being is unjust, for it punishes us for those very misdeeds of which it is the cause. So, devil, resolve this conundrum for me, as I would fain know why the just must suffer while the wicked receive rewards?
> DEVIL: Faust, you have named two examples, but what if there were a third? That you have been cast out like dust, like worms, carelessly and indiscriminately. You yourselves are caught up in a dark entanglement, something like an insoluble knot which you are obliged to unravel, and yet just imagine that a strict lord or judge were to indict you for not managing this impossible achievement? Just imagine for a moment that, rather like some despot, he had impressed such ambiguous laws and conflicting yearnings upon you, only to withhold an explanation of their deeper significance, and to punish and reward you at random? (III, 7; Klinger, 112f.)

After many a dubious adventure, Klinger's Faust becomes increasingly morose. The good he does is made worthless by the complexities of the ensuing intrigues: many innocents perish as he takes revenge on the wicked. Virtue turns out to be short-lived, and episodes such as that of the miserly father who sells has 16-year-old daughter to Faust, only to asphyxiate after accidentally locking himself into his secret treasure-chamber, could serve as the basis for a horror film (IV, 3; Klinger, 147–52). The world tour becomes a virtual history lesson, as Faust visits some of Europe's most cruel monarchs and despots (Louis XIV of France, Richard III of England). The Pope in Rome sells him forgiveness before attempting to seduce him (IV, 15–18; Klinger, 180–94). Having seen all the evil the world has to offer, Faust returns to visit his hometown, where his son has been sent to the gallows and his starving daughters have become prostitutes. The devil claims his prize, and Faust is dragged off to hell, where he receives a special curse from Satan.

> Go and float around alone and lost, cut off by burnt-out cliffs in a land where there is no hope, no consolation and no sleep. You shall live only in the past, remembering your madness and your transgression. The future, which you men are inclined by

virtue of your pride and vanity to depict in rosy hues, will be nothing but the terrifying thought that your misery shall never cease but be an unchanging and painful self-knowledge. Your only pleasure will be to exchange this unending torment for yet another torment. Those self-same doubts that tormented you during your life shall gnaw away at you forever, and you shall never solve any of the mysteries whose resolution shall be your role in this place. That surely must be the most painful punishment for a philosopher of your bent, and I have specially reserved it for my disciples. Hell is full of such as you, and your seed will help to populate my empire. Drag him hence and torture him. As for this Pope, find a different corner for him. There are none like these anywhere else in hell. (V, 8; Klinger, 226f.)

The question with which the author began his narrative is therefore not answered, except with reference to predestined evil: 'He gnawed away at the question: what was the reason why the competent brain and the noble man were constantly suppressed and neglected, left to languish in misery, while the rascal and the idiot became wealthy, happy and respected.' (I, 1; Klinger, 9f.) The book was successful and went through many editions, though it has been noted that, despite having conceived it as an attack on oppressive authority, Klinger increasingly toned down or removed offensive passages (Gilman, xvi).

Impassioned Romantics

By the early years of the nineteenth century, Faust had not only been 'romanticised' but had come to stand out as a distinctive emblem of Romanticism. The erstwhile catalogue of wicked deeds that had been compiled as a deterrent now commended itself to a new generation of authors for a new set of reasons. Faust was eager to extend the frontiers of knowledge; he was brave, single-minded, and passionately committed to going his own way, even if that way appeared irrational, immoral, and fraught with unforeseen dangers. Goethe had hinted at a tormented individual who desired to enrich his life to the fullest extent, through a blend of inner passion and increasing experience. All his endeavours were directed towards maximising his potential at whatever cost. Even those who end up damned, as Klinger's does, had shown superhuman courage in trying to right the wrongs of the world and uncover the causes of human misery. This aspect of Faustian endeavour appealed to a generation of poets who shared a belief in tearing down barriers and replacing social norms with their own subjective aspirations.

Yet Faust's development is fraught with frustrations, and none of the Romantic constructs achieves satisfaction. Only Goethe, at the end of his second part of the drama, published posthumously in 1832, allowed his hero a satisfying glimpse of success, albeit in an indistinct vision. The Romantic writers movingly convey their hero's longing and despair, but then home in on the process of self-destruction.

Louis Charles Adélaïde de Chamisso de Boncourt (1781–1838), the son of a French count exiled to Germany during the French Revolution, was not the most obvious author to turn his hand to the Faust material, but it was a subject that fascinated him and that found its way into several of his later works. Chamisso

had left his native France at the age of ten, and while he took a strong interest in
Germany and its culture, he never lost his French accent and remained a marginal
figure, viewed as a Protestant by Catholics, as a Catholic by Protestants, as a
German in France but as a Frenchman in Germany, as a democrat by the
aristocracy and as a nobleman by the people. His Faust reflects his own rootlessness,
and in his first monologue, a resignation is to be felt that is clearly at odds with
the self-reliance of the 'Storm and Stress' authors of the previous generation. In
fact, most Romantic Fausts will replace the Goethean desire for action with a fair
share of morose sentimentality:

> What art thou, human, hungry, all-consuming,
> Reckless suitor to the universe itself,
> Yet blind, benighted, trapped within a twofold
> Everlasting darkness, thou seest nought
> And must remain a mystery to thyself.
> And thou who hast created thy entire
> World, art not thyself created by that world,
> So wherein lies thy power, trifling worm?
> A god in shackles, or a grain of dust?
> Hast thou command of time and space, the all-
> Embracing ones, and of their products too?
> What lies beyond, outside, infinity?
> And what is god, the first, uncomprehended
> Link within a chain which he himself sustains?
> 'Tis but an empty image of the mind. (Chamisso, 304)

These lines strike a new and sombre tone that looks forward to disillusioned
Romantics such as Byron and Lenau. There is nothing to be gained from a pact,
and so the essential constituent of the Faust theme is undermined from the outset.
Man's thought-processes are the 'vipers that you create and that devour you' (*Op.
cit.*, 305); reality is, as Kant and the empiricists had argued, our own personal
construct and conceit. And since a pact is of no value to Faust, there is no
development in Chamisso's version, only a rising tide of despair. The voice of the
tempter becomes the voice of scorn as soon as Faust has signalled, by breaking the
rod of justice that magically appeared in his hand, that he accepts the evil spirit's
terms. All that Faust can hope to learn through the pact is that man is a ship
without sails or anchor, let loose on an infinite sea of doubt:

> Doubt is the limit set upon your knowledge
> Which only blindly trusting faith may cross.
> I banish you to err upon the hostile ocean
> Without the benefit of sail or anchor
> And where no land or shore will ever comfort
> The man condemned to strive, devoid of hope [...] (*Op. cit.*, 313)

The circularity of human thought is emphasised here; the search for truth leads to
those answers that fit the questions we have chosen to pose, as happened when
the first Faustus interrogated the devil about hell. Locke and Kant argued, similarly,

that we construct a reality for ourselves out of the building blocks with which are provided by experience. Faced with this insight into the ultimate futility of man's quest for transcendental knowledge, Chamisso's Faust does not even bother to live out the terms of the pact, but chooses suicide as the only way of escaping the human dilemma. The work remains a fragment and has not been performed.

The poet was to return to the Faust theme in 1814, when he wrote what was to be his most celebrated novella, the story of Peter Schlemihl (*Peter Schlemihl's Remarkable Story*) who sells not his soul, but his shadow, to a mysterious stranger, thereby becoming an outcast. But in this intriguing variant of the pact theme, Schlemihl manages to benefit from the transaction, gaining wisdom, self-reliance and fortitude while becoming less dependent on a society whose failings are traced to increasing commercialisation. The Faustian motifs are replaced by a highly realistic portrait of contemporary society. Schlemihl is not located in a distant fairy-tale past but in Chamisso's own time. Another aspect of *Peter Schlemihl's Remarkable Story* is the ease with which the protagonist can be viewed as a cipher for the artist. This is the way Thomas Mann read the story; and it is no coincidence that an increasing number of Romantics identified their Fausts less with profligacy and sinfulness than with artistic aspiration.

August Klingemann's *Faust* dates from 1815 and was written with the aim of satisfying the public's demand for staged versions of the play. So far, despite the great interest commanded by the theme and fuelled by the publication of Goethe's as yet unfinished work, the actual stagings had been few. Weidmann was out of tune with the times, Klinger and Chamisso had not written for the stage; the absence of a performable text was only too obvious. So Klingemann produced his in 1815, falling back on a variety of older traditions and constructing a spooky tale in the Romantic manner. Faust's blind father Diether is seen staggering round Faust's cellar (in the company of Faust's wife, the innocuous Käthe) amongst all the skulls and skeletons. Faust has many arguments with his god-fearing father, Käthe defends him, but both are terrified by his wild demeanour and bizarre experiments. Faust's left hand shows a worrying tendency to shed blood. His encounter with Helen of Troy is melodramatic in the extreme, as Faust must choose between her and his bourgeois wife. Helen, aware of the conflict, departs, whereupon Faust's mental state rapidly deteriorates. He poisons Käthe, who then announces that she is carrying his child. In the fifth act, Käthe is dead and Faust is cursed by his father, whom he shoots. He has a final meeting with Helen, who turns out to be a skeleton in disguise, a motif that goes back as far as Calderón. Despite these melodramatic setbacks, Faust remains defiant till the end, when he disappears from view in the company of a mysterious stranger. Joseph Carl Bernard's *Faust* dates from the same period; it was first performed in Prague, 1816, and formed the basis of Louis Spohr's very successful opera, which was of some significance in the development of musical implementations of the theme.

In the year in which Goethe's *Faust I* was finally given its first public performance, the dramatist Christian Dietrich Grabbe attempted to combine two of literature's most distinctive figures in a single four-act drama, *Don Juan und Faust*.

There is an obvious thematic attraction in attempting to fuse the tragedy of intense spirituality with that of excessive sensuality (Smeed (1976), 161–96; *Ibid.*, (1990), 75–90; see also Meyer and Csobádi). Grabbe combines their destinies by making Don Juan and Faust love the same woman, Donna Anna. Both are accompanied, and frequently hampered, by trouble-making assistants, Don Juan by Leporello, Faust by a Mephistophelean 'Knight in Black'. The work was first performed in Detmold with a musical accompaniment by Albert Lortzing in 1829.

Byron, Pushkin, Lenau, and many other Romantic authors were intrigued and preoccupied by both figures. The idea of combining Don Juan with Faust into a 'new myth' of the type demanded by Friedrich Schlegel in his 'Discourse on Mythology' of 1800 was therefore typical of the exploratory strategies of the generations that followed Goethe and, while admiring his genius, were positively obsessed with finding ways of outdoing him. Grabbe's strategy of linking the operatic brilliance of Mozart's *Don Giovanni* with the stagecraft of Goethe was intended to bring the extremes of humanity face to face. In terms of their exemplary status, one was obviously over-sensual while the other was over-intellectual, but another polarity is no less significant: that of the coldly rational, 'Nordic' Faust and the hot-blooded 'Mediterranean' Juan. While Goethe's Faust becomes a Don Juan after his rejuvenation, the legendary Juan himself has been described as the 'Faust of Music' by David Friedrich Strauss (cited Smeed (1990), 76).

The basics of the plot are as in Goethe: Faust is both a sage and a lover. The Knight in Black is unable to corrupt Faust by showing him the grandeur of the world; but after tempting him with an image of Donna Anna he secures Faust's interest in a desperate adventure. Faust intervenes somewhat comically in the plot of Mozart's opera, killing Anna's father himself rather than letting Don Juan do the deed, and subsequently whisking his beloved off to his palace on Mont Blanc, a point equidistant from northern and southern Europe. Here, Faust faces defeat at the hands of the fabled smooth-talking womaniser. He has to realise that Anna does not love him, but only Don Juan, who has scaled the mountain in pursuit of her. Juan and Leporello are banished to Rome, but since Anna cannot love Faust, reckless as ever, he murders her. Their reactions are significant: Faust is tormented by anguish, but Juan remains cheerful in the knowledge that other beauties are there for the grasping. The devil finally claims both men as his victims. The tragedy deteriorates into intentional farce at several points. Faust and Don Juan may argue about the point of knowledge if it cannot win you the heart of a woman you love, while Leporello is preoccupied about losing his cap in the wind:

FAUST: Flee, I say, in the face
                      Of my consuming power.
DON JUAN: Of your power?
                      Of something that cannot even manage to
                      Provide a bit of satisfaction for a weakling
                      So feeble that he longed for the flames of hell
                      While he was surrounded by the pleasantly burbling
                      Waters of life?

FAUST:	The slave may well take pleasure in his chains
	As long as he remains ignorant of *freedom*!
DON JUAN:	Which of us is in chains?
	Who has been trying by superhuman means
	To win Anna's heart, and still can't conquer
	That tiny spot? – Why the superhuman effort
	If you are human like the rest?
FAUST:	Why remain human,
	If you won't pursue superhuman goals?
DON JUAN:	A superman, devil or angel, is a complete
	Stranger to woman's love, just like any other
	Subhuman thing, a baboon, maybe,
	A frog, or ape. – Yes, my friend, 'tis *I* that
	Have taken possession of Anna's heart!
LEPORELLO:	We are lost, my lord, you have gone too far –,
	Let me grab your coat tails, there's a thunderstorm
	And a tempest coming out of his eyes!
FAUST:	Ha, if what I have long suspected is true
	Then I must tear Anna's heart with all it roots
	From my imagination. But you I cast
	Upon the tomb of the dead Governor,
	The only remaining spot on earth, where
	You must shudder to face the spirit world.
DON JUAN:	You are mistaken. I shudder not
	Before you, nor before the spirits!
FAUST:	Spirits, cast
	Him down!
LEPORELLO:	Take me with you, my lord – look, clouds and winds,
	And I'm about to lose my pretty cap
	As well!
	[DON JUAN *and* LEPORELLO *are removed at* FAUST'S *bidding*]
	(III, 3; Grabbe, 481f.)

Grabbe moves the story forward not least by giving it a series of comic twists. The association with the notorious womaniser does not enhance Faust's dramatic stature but rather brings him down to a mundane level. He is involved in petty-sounding bickering with an unreflective rival. All earlier Fausts had found it easy to ensnare a maiden, be she Helen of Troy or Little Madge. But now, even the hero's powers of seduction are curbed. Mephistopheles, too, has been diminished. He is a pale shadow of the urbane dandy of earlier versions: a reluctant Leporello to Faust, a servant of limited ability who must carry out his protégé's wishes, secure in the knowledge that he will in the end outwit him. His role remains theatrical rather than dramatic (Nicholls, 138f.). It was presumably not lost on Grabbe that Mozart's Leporello had begun his operatic career with the aria *Non voglio più servir* ('I wish to serve no more'), an echo of Satan's declaration of rebellion against God.

Another point worth considering is that Grabbe's hero makes a conscious attempt to underline his Germanness. The association of Faust with Germany will gain in importance over the century. Grabbe's equation of Don Juan with

Mediterranean, non-German qualities brought him dubious success one hundred years after these lines were written:

FAUST: What could be dearer than my *Fatherland?*
    Only my home can be my inspiration,
    And treachery it is to choose a foreign land.
    I would not be *Faust*, were I not *German!*
    O Germany, my fatherland! A tear forms
    On my eyelash, every time I think of you!
    No land on earth is more magnificent, no people
    Have greater fortitude and virtue than yours. Proud
    And strong, surrounded on all sides by vines,
    The mighty Rhine begins his undeserved decline
    Towards the sands of Holland, yet with a shout of joy
    The Danube cuts a path through towering mountains –
    Innumerable arteries provide channels for our blood
    That flows as straight and proud as our great rivers! Lo,
    High above the icy indentations of Tyrol's Alps
    That's where the eagle rises up to greet the sun
    As if it were his lofty nest, the mountains shrink
    Beneath his gaze, as though they were no more
    Than specks of dust, – yet down below him, in the Tyrol's
    Narrow vales, that's where hearts beat
    Higher and more loftily for yonder Emperor
    Than any eagle dares to rise – (I, 2; Grabbe, 424)

The line in which Faust states 'I would not be Faust, were I not a German!' is an early indication of how the material was providing a platform from which to investigate the German mind and temperament. It gives Grabbe an opportunity to pen a speech in praise of the free German spirit, given to soaring with eagles (the national symbol), and bursting the prison house of Rome, as Luther did from distant Wittenberg. His Faust is clearly a Protestant and in this respect, too, the mirror image of Don Juan.

Despite enjoying some popularity at various stages in recent history, if for narrowly patriotic reasons, Grabbe failed in his ambition of superseding what Goethe had written. He created a play that is rich in action but lacking in cohesion. Faust and Don Juan may have been kindred spirits, but on stage they rarely exchange meaningful dialogues. In fact, they only meet four times. What unites them are their eventual damnation and their desire to continue their rivalry in hell itself. Opportunities are missed that might have led to high drama, yet precisely for this reason, Grabbe might be seen as ahead of rather than behind his times. Don Juan and Faust, the polar opposites of lust and learning, are wrapped in their own personal microcosms to such an extent that they cannot communicate effectively on stage. They talk at cross purposes and it is inevitable that they should ignore rather than understand, let alone challenge, each other's mind-sets and values. The influence of Byron is evident, and the play has points of contact with *Manfred* and *Cain* in its treatment of the solitary exile and outcast. Grabbe's Faust sees the world as empty, but when he turns to lust in imitation of the iconic seducer, he gains even less contentment than Goethe's. The monologue is his favoured mode of expression.

Born Nikolaus Franz Niembsch, later ennobled as Edler von Strehlenau, Nikolaus Lenau was another tormented, rootless Romantic mind drawn irresistibly towards the emblem of lonely desperation that Faust had become. He had ancestral links with Hungary, and spent much of his life travelling. He worked on *Faust. A Poem*, effectively a fragmentary mélange of verse drama and narration, during 1833–1835, and the text was published in book form in 1836, although no attempt was made to stage the incongruous work until 1954. Like several others before him, Lenau resented what he saw as Goethe's 'monopolising' of the Faust theme and intended his work as a challenge, declaring 'Faust is the common property of all mankind'. The view that every poet should shape his own personal version was the moving force behind this and other dramas of the period.

Lenau shows the doctor dissecting corpses in the vain hope that he will learn the secrets of nature and the universe through anatomical enquiry. Mephistopheles presents himself, as he had done in Goethe, in the guise of a travelling scholar, ready to mock the ineffective professor and willing to promise untold delights that will result from embracing the extremes of pleasure and pain. These take their toll on him in due course, and he soon becomes embroiled in jealousy and murder. The culmination of Faust's restless travels is an ocean crossing – Lenau himself had travelled to America and back in 1832 – which ends in a shipwreck from which Faust can only be saved through the agency of his partner. Once on dry land he is confronted by an emblem of self-sufficiency in the form of the sailor Görg, whose shallow contentment makes him all the more aware of his own restless pursuit of an elusive truth. A clear grasp of man's utter insignificance runs through Lenau's work. It reveals a Romantic agony in which all Faustian achievements, be they unique insights or vile misdeeds, are no more than confused dreams in the mind of a sleeping God.

> Yet is not all of this a pale reflection
> Which leaves me quite alone and bans affection?
> So be't: forever bound to that one Entity
> The God of whom a part inseparable
> I am eternally and ever stable.
> Faust therefore cannot be my true identity.
> The Faust who laboured all alone
> And gave his soul unto the Evil One;
> But he and all of humankind
> Be they virtuous or full of strife,
> The devil too, to whom Faust sold his life,
> Are but disturbances within God's mind.
> A dream sent to confuse the Maker in his sleep,
> Like froth thrown up from distant oceans deep.
> Yet if, as Faust has done, a child is made
> And born into the world, new dreams invade
> The land, and when the sky glows red,
> They stimulate the Maker's mind in great profusion

And every time Faust strikes his brother dead
That dream is stirred into confusion.
And should the earthling take delight
To plumb the secrets of the universe
And study hard by day no less than night
Plagued by doubts and by his Maker's curse
Then maybe God knows that his dream shan't last
But must dissolve before another day
As morning is approaching fast
And slumbers all must fade away.
Come now, Fiend, with whom the pact I made,
I mock you and your paper document,
Concluded by a shadow and a shade.
To break that pact is now my firm intent!
I'm too far gone for you to terrify,
So, like a dream, out of your trap I fly.
I am a dream, racked by guilt and lust's enduring dart
I dream a knife, and thrust it through my heart!
[FAUST stabs himself] (Lenau, lines 3380–3415)

Lenau's *Faust: A Poem* is marked by irreconcilable contrasts. The outward form is unstable, vacillating as it does between lyrical descriptions of great power and caustic dialogue between the scholar and his companion-tormentor. The ethos is one of unrequited longing; Faust is both a god-seeker and a god-hater; the misery of the world makes no sense to him, yet he never quite abandons his search for meaning. This Faust, perhaps more than all others, embodies the disillusionment of the later Romantics, who lacked the rational optimism of the enlightened eighteenth century but who recognised that the established faith that sustained earlier Romantics was utterly insufficient to provide satisfying answers to the questions by which they were tormented. Grim (I, 1–15) argues, somewhat paradoxically, that Lenau's *Faust* was both more modern and closer to the chapbook than Goethe's. What Chamisso had hinted at in his unfinished sketch is here worked out and brought to its logical conclusion.

Heinrich Heine (1797–1856) was without doubt the most creative and original of all late Romantics, a man so far ahead of his time that many of his works, while seeming to encapsulate the spirit of Romanticism in its purest form, are shot through with the irony and scepticism of a modern intellect. He, too, produced the synopsis of a play on the Faust theme. It had been commissioned as a ballet, and the plan was for Benjamin Lumley to show it at Her Majesty's Theatre in London and Heinrich Laube to arrange a staging in Vienna. Both schemes came to nought, but the book version of *Der Doctor Faust. Ein Tanzpoem, nebst kuriosen Berichten über Teufel, Hexen und Dichtkunst* ('Doctor Faust. A Ballet, together with Curious Reports about Devils, Witches and the Art of Poetry', 1851) attracted attention for its radical departure from tradition (Heine, 88–97).

Heine breaks new ground in many different ways. Part libretto, part prose narrative, part commentary, the text he produced is not easy to classify. Mephistopheles is replaced by an alluring female spirit, Mephistophela. This is a

139

15. Title page of Heine's Der Doktor Faust, 1851.
Designed by Richard Georg Spiller von Hauenschild.

striking departure that has been much emulated. And Heine exploits the resources of the stage through the use of ballet. Not content with the ballet routines that had been seen in the early eighteenth century, he privileges dance as the central theme; one of Mephistophela's first tasks is to teach her victim to express himself more effectively through this medium.

Faust's adventures with Mephistophela take in visits to several of the traditional stages of his world tour: the corrupt aristocracy (Act II), the orgiastic Witches' Sabbath (Act III) and the realms of classical antiquity (Act IV). But despite superficial resemblances with the trajectory of Goethe's work, Heine handles these episodes in an unconventional manner. The ducal court is itself a den of blasphemy and witchcraft, where Faust, rather than conjuring up the Greek heroes, is obliged to make King David dance before the Ark of the Covenant, a symbol of Jewish subservience to Christian masters desirous of mocking the Old Testament.

Eventually, Faust tires of the witches' antics and flees to a remote, idyllic island with Helen of Troy. Here he experiences a moment of fulfilment, before the satanic Duchess of Act II reappears to cast a spell on Helen, turning her into a skeletal old hag. In Act V, Faust reverts to the role of itinerant huckster, travelling up and down the country peddling miraculous potions. He arrives in the Netherlands, where he is struck by the beauty of a wealthy patrician's daughter. All seems to be going his way, he persuades her to marry him, and, ludicrous though the idea of a settled bourgeois existence may seem, is on his way to church for this purpose. At this point, Mephistophela appears to claim her prize. She turns herself into a serpent and devours Faust on the steps of the cathedral.

A resident of Paris from the early 1830s onwards, Heine places less emphasis on the speculative than on the sensual side of Faust, whose preoccupations revolve around the pursuit of beauty rather than the quest for knowledge. This implementation consciously rejects the ponderous, Nordic-Germanic elements of the story in favour of a lighter, less deadly-serious approach. His devil appears not as a monk but in female attire, in order to emphasise the centrality of eros; and Faust's career is destroyed not by self-torment and doubt but by the jealousy of others. In his annotations, Heine rebukes Goethe for having imposed a conciliatory outcome, complete with pseudo-Catholic amoretti, on what had once been a powerful expression of human fears of punishment in a world dominated by ascetic ideals. These notes are, like so much else in Heine's work, at best semi-serious. It is typical that while he finds fault with Goethe for turning Faust into a ballet, his own Faust is presented as precisely that: a ballet intended for public performance that subverts both Goethe and the popular musical. There have been some highly successful productions, for example in Australia in 1941, and even a circus version in Hamburg. Werner Egk's ballet *Abraxas* of 1947 also shows Heine's influence (Niehaus, 56f; Clasen, 370; Borchmeyer 171–7).

Goethe's *Faust* Revisited

The completion of *Faust* took up much of the latter years of Goethe's life. The text was begun as a single entity, albeit in two parts, and the first half, culminating in Gretchen's death, was offered to the public in 1808 as the 'First Part of the Tragedy of Faust' (*Der Tragödie erster Teil*), a label that implies an eventual catastrophe. It is understandable that many of those who read it assumed that a continuation would follow in which the hero was to receive the traditional punishment for his misdeeds. The devil might even be allowed to triumph, as Germaine de Staël speculated in her enthusiastic and generally perceptive comments on the work (*De l'Allemagne*, 1810–13). But the public had to wait for precisely twenty-four years for the second part to appear in print, and when it did, following its author's death in 1832, it was greeted with incomprehension and derision. Not only was Faust unrecognisable in the sequel, but the problems with which the play had begun were brushed aside and what came in their place was something so utterly different

141

from what was expected, both in form and in content, that the public felt tricked and let down.

The first thing to note is that the old Faust of Part I emerges refreshed after the troubles of his adventure with Gretchen. There is no hint of rebuke or penance; rather, it is as though the sins of the past are washed away, with conciliation replacing judgement. Far from seeking further adventures, Faust now seems inclined to turn his back on the turbulent experiences of his earlier days, and expresses his resolution in measured *terze rime* that recall Dante:

> Long may the sun remain behind my back.
> It gives me ever greater joy to see
> The thundering waterfall create a track
> Through every rocky obstacle there be
> And separate into a thousand courses
> That hurtle downwards, down into the valley,
> Each prancing up and up again like horses.
> Behold, an arc of colour is created
> From this tumultuous exchange of forces.
> Sometimes you see it clear, sometimes it's fated
> To slip away, dissolved by cooling air.
> Its meaning ponder, and your mind be sated:
> In such reflecting hues all life is there. (F 4715–27)

With the sun behind him, the rainbow, a mere reflection of the ultimate source of illumination, is what this new Faust aspires to contemplate, accepting that life in all its richness is an unstable mirror of things we cannot and should not investigate. Moments of clarity are rare; the images are as deceptive and insubstantial as what we see in the cascading droplets of a waterfall. We are, as in Plato's cave, denied access to the sources, we can only perceive the shadowy reflections of a higher world. The rainbow may be more beautiful than Plato's shadows, but it is less stable and more fleeting. All these are indications of the predominantly symbolic representations that will follow: a few fragmentary glimpses of Faust's experiences in a world far wider than that of his early adventures. There is no linear plot to Part II, nor does it link up well with the preceding drama. Liberated from the desire to pursue the knowledge he sought so passionately in Part I, the revived Faust embarks on the second stage of his journey, which takes him not back into the mediaeval world of provincial Nordic Christendom from which he has escaped, but to three different time zones in which he will seek and find activity: the Baroque Emperor's Court, home to an unremitting festival culture, the realms of classical mythology, and a war-torn present/future, in which Faust will strive, but ultimately fail, to establish a productive province on a reclaimed sea-shore. At each of these three stages, Faust attempts to share his knowledge with representatives of humanity, but each time he experiences frustrations, not least because his forward-looking knowledge ultimately derives from Mephistopheles. In Act I, the cash-starved Emperor is offered the 'gift' of paper currency.

A Pleasure Garden

CHANCELLOR:	To whom it may concern on any grounds:
	This piece of paper's worth a thousand pounds.
	And surety thereof, should you require,
	Rests underground. The Emperor, your sire,
	Owns treasures yet unclaimed beneath the earth:
	Just dig, and they'll ensure this money's worth.
EMPEROR:	This must be fraudulent, a huge deceit,
	My signature was copied by a cheat.
	Is there no way to punish such a villain?
TREASURER:	No, sire. 'Twas you yourself, dressed up as Pan,
	Who signed what you were given yesterday.
	All that the Chancellor had to do was say:
	'Permit yourself a favour, take this pen,
	You will restore the people's wealth again.'
	And so you did, and by the midnight oil
	Your clever copyists began their toil.
	Magicians can do things that no one queries,
	And at our bidding they ran off the series.
	When Tens and Thirties, Fifties, Hundreds had
	Been printed out, the populace went mad!
	The city had been mouldering half-dead,
	It's come alive; now pleasure rules instead.
	Although your name was well received before,
	From this day forth they worship you much more.
	The alphabet has been extended now:
	This is the sign to which all people bow.
EMPEROR:	And everybody treats it just like gold?
	The soldier and the courtier, young and old?
	If this be true, I surely can't complain.
STEWARD:	They ran away so fast, no one could rein
	Them in; quick as a flash they crossed the land,
	And then, at every moneylender's stand
	The banknotes were converted by and large
	To gold and silver for a modest charge.
	Thence to the butcher, baker, pub they raced
	As people sought out dainty things to taste.
	Desire for fancy garments likewise grows:
	The merchant cuts the cloth, the tailor sews.
	In every cellar people drink your health,
	They cook and roast and wash away their wealth.
MEPHISTOPHELES:	Sauntering along the terrace you will see
	A beauty all decked out in finery.
	She'll coyly hide behind a peacock feather,
	While smilingly she'll try to discern whether
	You have a currency that's to her taste.
	On her your flattering words would go to waste.
	Don't take your wallet when you chase the skirt,
	Just tuck a piece of paper in your shirt.
	It fits into a *billet doux*, just look!
	The priest can hide one in his prayer-book,
	The soldier making his escape in haste

	Prefers a lighter belt around his waist.
	Your Majesty, don't think that I deride
	It by alluding to its trivial side.
FAUST:	Superabundant treasures you will find
	Deep underground, just waiting to be mined,
	All still untapped. Dare to pursue this notion
	And open up your heart to the emotion
	Of owning such vast wealth. Your mind, unshackled,
	Must train itself to do what none has tackled.
	To face the deepest challenges you must
	Confront infinity with endless trust.
MEPHISTOPHELES:	This paper outperforms your pearls and gold:
	It's handy, you can tell how much you hold.
	You do not need to barter or to trade,
	Your night of love, your cask of wine are paid.
	If yellow metal sets your heart on fire,
	Your paper money ought to find a buyer;
	If not, just dig, and auction off a chalice
	And that will show the doubters in their malice
	That paper is so easy to redeem.
	They'll want no more; it's fast become the dream
	Ticket. The Emperor's lands are in good health,
	And rich in trinkets, gold and paper wealth.
EMPEROR:	The Empire owes this new resource to you
	And an appropriate reward is due.
	The treasures that reside within the soil
	They shall be yours to exploit and despoil.
	You know where they are hid; 'tis my command
	The digging may begin when you demand.
	Collaborate as masters of our treasure
	And execute this noble task with pleasure,
	In which the upper and the lower realm
	Shall be united, as you take the helm.
TREASURER:	There shall be neither quarrel nor debate,
	While yonder sweet magician is my mate.

[*Exit with* FAUST] (F 6057–6142)

This scene reveals a Faust deeply embroiled in the affairs of the state. He has arrived at the court of an Emperor who may, in a bizarre conflation of Maximilian, Charles V and Napoleon, be taken as a parody of a grandiose yet ineffective despot, keen to please his courtiers by staging elaborate carnival processions, but permanently beset by financial worries. Only Mephistopheles knows the answer, and it is one of great historical importance: to shift the currency away from inert metals like gold and silver to the humbler but more versatile medium of paper. The Emperor cannot believe his luck ('And everybody treats it just like gold?', F 6083) The fiscal problems of the state appear to have been resolved at a stroke. Yet it is equally clear that a demonic force is at work here and in much of what follows. Faust, acting as ever in close partnership with his companion, devises schemes to titillate a corrupt court. It is a sad comment on a world dominated by an idle aristocracy that employs the best brains for self-gratifying purposes. Thus

Faust is prevailed upon to summon up Helen and Paris, and although he appears to succeed, the spirits are mere shades that explode on contact: proof, if such were needed, that the pursuit of ideal beauty is incompatible with the shallow mass entertainment shown in Act I. The masquerade eventually culminates in what would nowadays be called a 'virtual reality' spectacle, which comes to an abrupt end in a power overload and something very similar to a short circuit.

Help of a kind is at hand in the form of another dubious creation: the *homunculus* ('artificial man') produced in Wagner's alchemist's laboratory. Yet this creature turns out to be wiser than his maker and takes it upon himself to help Faust return to the fountainhead of beauty by accompanying him back in time to the world of Greek mythology. Whether this is an unqualified success is also open to debate. The scene has been read as a failed attempt to manufacture a new understanding of antiquity by desperate means (Schlaffer, 109).

A Laboratory

HOMUNCULUS: What's to be done?
MEPHISTOPHELES [*pointing to a side door*]: There's work for you right there!
WAGNER [*still looking at the test tube*]: You are a handsome lad, I do declare!
    [*The side door opens and* FAUST *is seen stretched out on a couch*]
HOMUNCULUS [*appears surprised*]: This could be important!
    [*The test-tube slips out of* WAGNER'S *hands, hovers above* FAUST *and illumines him*]
                A pretty spot,
                Ladies disrobing by a crystal stream,
                A copse surrounds them, things are getting hot!
                Yet one of them stands out who, it would seem,
                Descent from heroes or from gods may claim.
                Her foot she places in the watery swirl:
                Around her perfect body's living flame,
                Cooling, caressing waves begin to curl. –
                Yet suddenly a pair of wings come crashing
                And churning up the waters with their splashing,
                The terrified handmaidens run for cover,
                And only one, the Queen, watches it hover
                Nearby; and with a woman's pride she sees
                The prince of swans now nestling by her knees.
                Brazen yet docile by the Queen he lies,
                Until the moment when a pale
                But closely woven swirling veil
                Shields this entrancing scene from prying eyes.
MEPHISTOPHELES: Strange tales you tell. And though you are so small
                In fantasies you outdo one and all.
                I can see nothing of the sort.
HOMUNCULUS: That's true:
                Your northern mind is blinkered, too,
                By fogs and knights and priestly ways;
                You could not ever free your gaze!
                Yours is a world of gloom and doom. [*looks around*]
                These walls are grimy, musty, crude,
                Low vaults and tracery in Gothic mood!

145

16. Wagner creates a Homunculus. By Franz Xaver Simm, c. 1880.

And if perchance this sleeping man should wake
He'll drop dead straight away, make no mistake!
Forests, swans and undraped flesh:
Such was his prophetic vision,
This world of yours cannot refresh,
I loathe it too, despite my cosy prison.
Take him away!

MEPHISTOPHELES: An exit may delight.
HOMUNCULUS: Command the soldiers into battle,
Let the girls dance through the night,
Then all is well; you'll show your mettle.
And yet today, if I remember right,
It's Classical Walpurgis Night:
A splendid sight, a wondrous chance
That will release him from his trance.
MEPHISTOPHELES: I've never heard of this event.
HOMUNCULUS: How could you when you are forever bent
On seeing ghosts in a romantic fantasy;
A genuine ghost must have a classic pedigree.
MEPHISTOPHELES: So we must travel further by some leagues?
I must confess I loathe antique colleagues.
HOMUNCULUS: You, Satan, can but thrive in north and west,
We shall sail south and east, where things are best. (F 6901–6951)

Faust plays no direct part in the genesis of the artificial man. For large sections of Acts II and III, he remains relatively passive, which has led some readers to assume that he is asleep and merely 'dreams' his adventures, thus acquiring a 'sympathetic understanding of the universal harmony of Nature' (Atkins, 183). But this passivity began in Act I. Faust was a bystander when Mephistopheles introduced the Emperor to paper currency, and to obtain the shades of Helen and Paris for the Emperor's delectation, he needed to descend to the mysterious realm of the 'Mothers' on instructions from Mephistopheles (F 6173–6306). The birth of the new man occurs while he is unconscious following the explosion that he caused by attempting to make physical contact with Helen's shadow. It was his assistant, Wagner, who generated the creature with evident help from Mephistopheles. Yet the product is not, as one might expect, a mindless robot or monster, but a sensitive creature capable of reading Faust's spiritual needs. He is able to interpret the dream of Queen Leda's impregnation by Zeus in the form of a swan, the mythological account of the immaculate conception of Helen of Troy, as a sign of Faust's inner longing to break away from the Nordic world of Gothic art and Christian bigotry, and suggests a journey through time and space to Ancient Greece. Mephistopheles is reluctant to follow, but eventually does so in the guise of Phorcyas, an embodiment of ugliness. But the *homunculus* proves unstable and unwilling to live in the 'real' world. His destiny becomes the focus of the final scene of Act II, in which he sacrifices himself to the beautiful goddess Galatea.

Rocky Inlets in the Aegean

[GALATEA *approaches on a scallop-shell chariot*]
NEREUS: Welcome, my daughter!
GALATEA: My father is here!
Linger, ye dolphins, the sight is so dear.
NEREUS: They're passing on in circles wide,
Passing me by without a care.
What does it matter that I'm in despair?
Could I but ride to the other side!
The memory of a glance so dear
Will have to suffice throughout the year.
THALES: Greetings, greetings to you all,
How your presence does enthral;
Truth and beauty are our guiding forces,
Life itself derives from watery sources!
Water is that which sustains the living,
May Ocean persist in his gift-giving,
You give us clouds to make the rain
That irrigates the thirsting plain,
Adding to the rivers' gain,
Guiding them towards the main.
Without you there'd be no hill and no dale;
It's through your kind gift that life can prevail.
ECHO [*A chorus from all sides*]: It's through your kind gift that fresh life shall prevail.
NEREUS: They twist and turn, now far, now near,

	And yet our eyes won't meet, I fear.
	Festive is the path they take,
	Releasing spray into their wake,
	Everyone in motion.
	But Galatea's chariot-scallop
	In and out of view does gallop.
	It shines like a star
	Among the crowd
	My loved one afar
	I can make out
	She shines bright and clear
	And remains true and near.
HOMUNCULUS:	Whatever I illuminate
	In this delightful watery state
	Is marvellous to see.
PROTEUS:	The lamp with which you illuminate
	This life-enhancing, watery state
	Resounds most splendidly.
NEREUS:	What is this newest and latest surprise
	That yields itself up to enquiring eyes?
	Something's on fire near the Goddess's feet,
	Around her scallop, so lovely, so sweet
	As if animated by pulses of love.
THALES:	Proteus caused the New Man to dissolve.
	These are the symptoms of majestic yearning,
	Loud is his anguish, his passionate burning
	As he cracks his glass on the shining throne;
	It's flaming and sparkling; the deed is now done.
SIRENS:	The wonder of fire transfigures the waves
	Now flashing together, the ocean raves,
	Now gleaming and hovering, they've made a new light
	Like miniature bodies traversing the night.
	And all around us a new fire is rife;
	Let Eros command us, creator of life!
	Praise the sea, the wave that churns,
	Encircled by a force that burns.
	Praise the fire and water too,
	Give praise for this adventure new!
ALL TOGETHER:	*Praise the gently sighing air!*
	Praise the ever-secret lair!
	Celebrate them evermore:
	The vital elements all four!

The final scene of Act II reaches a climax of orgasmic proportions. The Greek gods are minor deities often depicted in the Renaissance and Baroque in richly ornamental settings; Raphael's *Triumph of Galatea*, which Goethe admired in the Villa Farnesina in Rome and of which he owned a copy, is generally held to have inspired the spatial arrangement of this scene, which has the God Nereus take leave of his daughter Galatea amid a general celebration of the watery element, recognised by the philosopher Thales and most of the participants as the source of all life. A scientific thesis is put forward by the poet and given greater rather than

148

17. Raphael's Triumph of Galatea *is commonly regarded as having inspired the scene in the Aegean.*

less validity for being phrased in poetry within a dramatic context, much as he did in his 'Metamorphosis' poems. But the scene is neither pure drama nor scientific tract in disguise, but a fusion of many styles, including those of opera and ballet. This accounts for the chorus and for the references to circular motion reminiscent of dance. It marks a climactic point in *Faust II*, in part on account of the veiled parallels with the Eucharist that become obvious as the *homunculus* sacrifices himself in an act of love, in part for its visual qualities, including a waning moon that shines on a 'Twilight of the Gods', and not least for the linguistic versatility and elegance of this symphony for ethereal voices (Canisius, 92f.).

The play then turns to Faust's union with Helen of Troy, which is finally achieved in Act III, although their consummation proves to be of limited duration. In a remarkable scene Faust manages to teach Helen to speak in verse, something she had previously been unable to do, given that the rhyme is a post-classical innovation.

Inner Courtyard

HELEN:	Many miracles I hear and see,
	In my amazement much I long to know.
	I would desire to learn why this man's speech
	Sounds unfamiliar to me and yet kind.
	Each sound unto the next adjusts itself,
	And when the ear has taken in a word
	A partner clasps it in a firm embrace.
FAUST:	If you admire the speech of our nations
	You're sure to love their singing even more.
	It satisfies the ear and soul in equal
	Measure, and we'd do well to practise now.
	A dialogue will coax and call it forth.
HELEN:	So tell me, then, how this fair speech should start.
FAUST:	It is so easy, just involve your heart.
	And when it overflows in loving fashion
	You look around and ask –
HELEN:	Who shares your passion?
FAUST:	The spirit knows no future, can't profess
	To know the past; what's here –
HELEN:	Is happiness.
FAUST:	This treasure is a pledge, a gift and sign.
	Confirmed by whom?
HELEN:	But by this hand of mine. (F 9365-9384)

The idyll does not last. Wars need to be fought, and as the drama moves forward from the sacking of Troy to the present, both the Crusades and the War of Liberation against Turkish domination are hinted at. Faust's son, born of Helen, is named Euphorion, and enjoys a secret affinity with the *homunculus* of Act II; he also comes to resemble Lord Byron, author of the Faustian poem *Manfred* and champion of Greek independence, with whom he shares a self-destructive tendency. Eventually Helen dissolves with the words 'Joy and beauty cannot be permanently allied.' (F 9940) Act IV details the wars fought by Faust to gain land for the Emperor and for his own projects, which focus on reclaiming land from the sea, Faust's main preoccupation at the time of his death in Act V. This may sound like a noble venture, but philanthropy is clearly subordinated to the pursuit of 'lordship' and 'property' (F 10187). To the last, Mephistopheles is heavily implicated as Faust's advisor. He even brands Faust's work as madness, claiming that poets will be found to use Faust's folly to inspire others to further acts of folly (F 10189-91). Mephistopheles has a hand in destroying the idyllic existence of an old couple, Philemon and Baucis, and since Faust deludes himself about the outcome of the land reclamation project, it bears a diabolical stamp and strongly suggests that even in his dying days, Faust's labours will be futile. Mephistopheles believes he can claim Faust's soul when he hears the fateful words that suggest Faust has finally found contentment, albeit in a conditional formulation.

Large Outer Courtyard of Faust's Palace

FAUST:

A swamp that skirts the mountainside
Besmirches all that I have gained;
I'll look upon my task with pride,
When this foul bog is cleared and drained.
Millions could live in lands I have created.
Dangers there'd be, but they'd be liberated
And active in green pastures free from strife
The men and beasts would share a pleasant life.
We'll settle them beside a mighty hill
Constructed by the powerful people's will;
Here, where I stand, we'll make a paradise,
Though at the fringes, waters will still rise,
And should they ever threaten my defences,
Good people will rush forth to mend the fences.
This is my final statement, come what may,
It is the truth that has eluded me:
He that must fight for freedom every day,
Has earned the right to live unharmed and free.
Thus in a place where dangers lurk so near
Children and men will labour year by year.
A swarming multitude I long to see,
All liberated in a land that's free.
Then to the fleeting moment I might say:
'Stand still, thou art so blithe and fair.'
Thereafter untold generations may
Recall what I accomplished here.
Anticipating such exceeding pleasure,
This is the moment I supremely treasure. (F 11559–86)

At this point, Mephistopheles would seem to have won his wager. Things do not look much better for this Faust than they did for the majority of his antecedents. He has accomplished little, despite great effort on his part and great cost to others. His dealings with the Emperor had been dubious from the outset. The pageants, culminating in the public display of Helen and Paris, were ephemeral distractions. Paper money led to gross self-indulgence and over-consumption. The *homunculus* chose self-sacrifice in place of integration. The three-thousand-year journey into a Hellenic/mediaeval/recent past provided a tantalising glimpse of Helen and Faust in harmony, but this came to an end following Euphorion's death in circumstances reminiscent of the siege of Missolonghi. Thereafter, Faust is active in northern Europe as a military general, supporting an Emperor who is at war against a rival; Faust is also hard pressed for tithes and taxes by a ravenously greedy Archbishop. The lands he attempts to colonise may stand, allegorically, for territorial expansion in the nineteenth century. Here Goethe seems to want to emphasise the negative side of colonialism. It must not be forgotten that he deprecated mass culture and remained an elitist who would have muzzled if not banned the press (Schlaffer, 143–157; Rothe, 134–59). Faust dies in delusion as to the merits of his final venture. His failure is emphasised by many attendant circumstances: the lands he plans to colonise do not exist; if his plans should be fulfilled, they would still be continuously threatened by tides and destructive natural forces; the workmen whom he believes he has engaged to drain the swamp are skeletal lemurs, Mephisto's sepulchral minions, digging Faust's grave; and, finally, Faust's speech is in the conditional mood: 'Then to the fleeting moment *I might say*' (F 11581; my italics).

For these and other reasons, it was something of a shock for the early readers of *Faust II* to discover that Mephistopheles was to be cheated of a prize he had worked so hard to win, while Faust was welcomed into an area of 'mountainous ravines' peopled by ecstatic, saintly, and even angelic figures. The jovial Lord of the Prologue does not reappear, but instead there are seraphic beings, angels, blessed boys, and female figures from the scriptures: a great sinner (Luke's Gospel), the Samaritan Woman (John's Gospel), and Mary of Egypt (Acts of the Apostles). A 'Mater Gloriosa' enjoins Faust to follow a transfigured Gretchen to 'higher spheres'. The endless debates concerning the validity and significance of these iconic figures cannot be rehearsed here. Two points are of key importance. The conclusion is presented in powerfully visual, operatic, and even, as some have argued, in filmic terms: 'The images have taken control and determine the action through combination, collage and superimposition [...] The effect of this technique of combination and dissolving can only be shown in a film [...].' (Gaier, 134-6) This is in keeping with Goethe's privileging of visual effects and does not represent a radical departure. Secondly, the scene in the 'mountainous ravines' (*Berg-schluchten*) is located in this world and shot through with ironic devices. The female figures are part of a wider celebration of life in its entirety, and the play itself ends with an acknowledgement that the 'eternally feminine' (*das Ewig-Weibliche*, F 12110) is the driving force behind all human endeavour. This can be read in moral, biological and artistic terms, and Goethe would not have wished his readers to separate out one of the strands at the expense of the others. Like so much else in *Faust*, the final scene aims to replicate the strategies of painting, opera, ballet, choral music, church ritual, while suggesting, on a more rational, scientific plane, that human life is not destroyed and not wasted at the point of death. Continued activity, be it through a return to fast-moving metamorphic elements, is not the least likely of our future trajectories. The 'eternally feminine' principle promises rebirth, and while there are no certainties, the potential is infinite.

ANGELS [*hovering in the higher reaches of the atmosphere, bearing* FAUST's *immortal part*]
        The spirit world's distinguished son
        Henceforth no more depraved.
        'He who relentlessly strives on
        May finally be saved.' (F 11934-11937)

These lines, so often quoted, so rarely understood, are anything but a libertine's charter. The angels may be supernatural beings, but they are within the earth's atmosphere and thus terrestrial mediators. They extend an indirect promise of salvation without explicitly offering it; the phrase 'may finally be saved' is conjectural and does not guarantee anything other than that a range of unknowable potentialities await man, be he good or wicked, after his departure from life. Goethe would go no further than to offer this tentative outlook on the future. Many would-be exegetes overlooked the speculative tone and assumed that Faust was in the process of being taken straight to heaven. Their readings involve wishful thinking and a considerable extrapolation from the text. Before we consider the ultimate consequences of these adulatory reinterpretations, a humorous response to *Faust II* will be examined.

A Literary Parody

Goethe was well aware of the scorn that his *Faust II* would engender; he delayed publication until after his death and predicted, in the last letter he ever wrote, that it would lie buried like a wreck in the sand for some considerable period of time (Letter to Wilhelm von Humboldt, 12 March 1832). This proved accurate. Public incomprehension combined with frustration at being deprived of a recognisable narrative link-up with Part I. The supposed sequel was widely ignored or treated with scorn. The first attempts to continue and parody the text of Part I had appeared years earlier, during Goethe's lifetime. One of these was Carl Christoph Ludwig Schöne's *Faust Part II* of 1823 which appears to have met with the poet's approval and was proudly offered to the public with Goethe's endorsement ('Your applause, Master, was granted to me'; Schöne, ix). This turgid work, spanning 379 pages, attempts to complete the drama in Goethe's spirit. Faust feels that he is about to be saved, Mephistopheles attempts to drag him down to hell, whereupon we are transported to an 'Epilogue in Heaven', where, amongst the familiar archangels, the Lord reappears to proclaim his salvation in trite rhyming couplets:

> I know that Faust has sinned for many a day
> And from the path of virtue far did stray.
> Yet ever faithful to his origin,
> The reckless man was ne'er enslaved to sin.
> A spirit large and free was granted him,
> Who always sought the source where life doth start,
> And strove to find it with a passionate heart! (Schöne, 375f.)

This was a sincere if extremely wooden attempt to imitate Goethe's style and to second-guess the eventual ethos of the work. A 'Winter Night's Dream', a journey to Italy, a scene in St Peter's are all part of a huge pageant intended to show Faust's insatiable nature and to justify him as he appears in the play. A parody of a more ambitious kind was devised by Friedrich Theodor Vischer, who had previously written critical essays on *Hamlet* and even on *Faust* itself. What he objected to was that Faust, instead of supporting the cause of democracy, was content to pursue self-aggrandisement and personal wealth. He opted for a creative approach in his hugely successful *Faust. Der Tragödie dritter Theil. Treu im Geiste des zweiten Theils des Goethe'schen Faust* gedichtet von Deutobold Symbolizetti Allegoriowitsch

Mystifizinsky ('Faust. The Third Part of the Tragedy, faithfully rendered in the Spirit of the Second Part of Goethe's Faust by Elucidor Symbolizetti Allegoryevich Mystificinsky') of 1861.

A major objection to Goethe's sequel had been the charge that the ending employed Roman Catholic ideas about purgation and redemption that were wholly at variance with the source material. The myth had been deliberately stood on its head. It made use of those very concepts that the original author had tried to attack: last-minute conversion, forgiveness of sins after a life of debauchery, rewards for iniquity. Vischer therefore takes this further by locating his sequel in Purgatory, where Faust meets up, not with Gretchen but with another dubious character, the spiteful Lieschen ('Little Lizzie') who had gossiped at the well in Part I (F 3544–86). Together they must do penance until pardoned by divine grace. Not only is Faust denied the hearty meals he so much desires, but his punishments include a trial version of community service: he is given the task of initiating a class of extremely unruly schoolboys into the mysteries of Goethe's play! They are allowed to play pranks on him with impunity, and he must not beat them – the humanitarian regime of the nineteenth century is slowly taking effect.

FAUST: Homunculus is our topic for today,
                     It's quite obscure, so don't let your attention stray!
[reads from a manuscript]
                     'Homunculus, a diminutive artificial human produced by my erstwhile assistant and subsequent Professor, Wagner, by chemical means, is at once both a representative of unthinking scholarship, concerned only to garner the treasures of knowledge without the least ability to convert them into productive mental properties, while also representing the quest for beauty in a clear-thinking, targeted and self-reliant manner; thus he is to be seen both as an emblem of that kind of scholarship that reaches out beyond itself towards the love of a beauty that is the guiding light to mankind in its quest to find the land of beauty; yet also, since he collides with Galatea's scallop-shell chariot and disintegrates into liquid fire – '
                     No, let's stop there, a break is due
                     So that I may examine you
                     And praise your work. Now, Charlie, tell us how ...
[tries to stand up, but sticks to his seat; then tears himself free]
                     What's happened now? –
                     I'm thunderstruck –
                     What's all this muck,
                     This sticky stuff?
                     I've had enough!
                     It's tar and thick!
                     Who played this trick?
[gets down from his desk and walks around the classroom. It is obvious that his trousers have sustained some damage in the process]
                     Who did this? I shall make you cry!
SCHOOLBOYS: Not I, not I, not I!
FAUST: Don't you go make fun of me,
                     You cruel, diabolical, yet in some

Way blessed and heavenly
Troop of scholarly scum,
At last you are going to feel the weight
Of my rod, I shan't delay, it's not too late
For me to do that deed for which I long!
First one and then the next I'll apprehend
Until I've dealt with all that can offend,
Unless perchance someone denounces me and I am done!

[goes resolutely to his desk to fetch a cane, but then stands still and reflects]
Could it but be done, what need be done, 'twere
Well done, and pat; yet would a beating
Attract, as in a net, the consummation of a thousand
Chances, all a-mocking my success,
And with a single stroke I'd have to pay
Perchance for all my sins right here, just here
Upon this desk, among the schoolboys all
My future hopes I'll risk, defiantly.

[The door opens quietly and LIESCHEN is seen]
LIESCHEN [whispering]: Henceforth, dear man, forgo such wild
Pursuits, but try to educate each child.
If untamed bears were to cavort with men,
Just think how sensitive folk would suffer then.
Remember your humanitarian preaching:
Abandon the rod and return to your teaching.
In total contrast to Lady Macbeth
I'm here to ensure that you overcome death.

[closes the door and exits] (Act I, scene 7; Vischer (2000), 26-8)

Successive printings of Vischer's *Faust III* reveal just how successful this pastiche was with the public. The author continued to refine his material, and numerous revisions appeared between 1862 and his death in 1887. The many mysteries to which Faust was exposed in Goethe are travestied in the following scenes, which include a visit to the 'Mothers' in the company of Gretchen's brother, Valentin. Ironically, Vischer probably had a clearer understanding of the aesthetic principles around which *Faust II* was constructed than most of his contemporaries, and his parodies are less the result of ignorance than of a kind of grudging admiration for the sheer complexity of a heavily symbol-laden artefact. The attempted definition of the *homunculus* in the passage cited above is evidence of a good grasp of Goethe's aesthetic strategy, yet rather than explain the text, Vischer remained content to play to the gallery for the reward of a few laughs. Readers will have noticed the parody of Hamlet (III, 3) in Faust's dithering over whether to use his cane (Borchmeyer, 177-80).

The Social Novel

Although Goethe's play ends with high praise for the 'Eternal Feminine' (F 12110), there have been few female Fausts. Precisely ten years before Heine's Mephistophela proved that the devil could equally well present as a woman, Germany's most popular female author of the day, Countess Ida von Hahn-Hahn, published her social novel *Gräfin Faustine* ('Countess Faustine') in which the protagonist emerges as an aristocratic lady torn between her own conflicting desires. This was the first attempt to apply the Faustian model to the biography of a woman in pursuit of emancipation, and the result was both a parallel to and a questioning of the assumptions on which the myth is based. True to the Biedermeier ethos of the work, there are no midnight encounters with satanic emissaries and no pact, and it is the gradual unfolding of personalities within a realistic setting that constitutes the central interest. Yet it remains an intriguing attempt by a middle-brow writer to convert some of Faust's ambitions and dilemmas into conflicts that would strike a chord with a largely female readership. These are, inevitably, the choice of a suitable partner and the conflicting attractions of career, social life and family.

From such meagre Faustian rudiments and against the background of a weak story-line, Hahn-Hahn managed to construct a delicately balanced picture of her heroine, the ambitious and sensitive Countess Faustine Obernau, a lady whose career resembled her author's at least in so far as she was a talented artist able to enjoy free love with relative impunity. She knows of her affiliation with Faust and is proud to bear his name, aware that her fate lies in a continuous, restless striving, motivated by a constant yearning for satisfaction. Her second husband sums up this vital aspect of her character:

> At times she was relaxed, like a pleasure-seeking odalisque, and would spend many hours reclining on her divan with her eyes half-shut, dreaming, thinking, composing verses, without getting bored – and then she would complain of soul-destroying boredom, when I least expected it, and turn to learning or creating things through cogitation or enthusiasm as a means of escape. Once she had demonstrated her genius in some great work that found general recognition, she would turn to minor, practical matters in order to test her ability in these areas, but she only continued to amuse herself with these until she had mastered them, and then turned to something different. Everything that she had completed became a matter of indifference to her – she was not one to keep, to possess, to enjoy things. Her sole delight was to strive, and the moment in which she touched the object of her desire was utter bliss. If she was to hold on to anything, her hand would soon tire and release its grip (Hahn-Hahn (1986), 222).

Her insatiable restlessness provides the Faustian credentials and renders her vulnerable. After a failed first marriage she teams up with the understanding and devoted Baron Anastasius Andlau in whom, it would seem, she finds the perfect companion. Her unmarried status, something of an anomaly at the time, attracts unwanted attentions. Separated for a time by family obligations, she is pursued by two suitors, the suicidal Clemens von Walldorf and the passionate Count Mario Mengen. She succumbs to the latter and spends several outwardly carefree years in Italy before tiring of her own happiness and mindful of the harm she has inflicted on others. She is finally persuaded, reluctantly, by her own personal 'demon' to withdraw from the world and enter a convent, having lived out all of the identities available to a woman at the time and found satisfaction in none (Kaiser, 78; Doering, 170–99).

This was not the last attempt to invest a woman with Faustian qualities. More than a dozen are discussed in a recent study by Sabine Doering, who traces the female Faust figure back to Pope Joan and Mary of Nijmegen (see above, 24f.). Wilhelm Schäfer's six-act play *Faustine* of 1898 is a much less sympathetic portrayal of a woman as Faustus. The structure recalls Goethe. It begins with a Dedication, a 'Prelude on Stage', and a 'Prologue in Hell'. The devils decide to seduce Faustine, a female student who is outwardly committed to studying but secretly longs to fulfil her natural biological role. The spirits *Lebenstrieb* and *Unabänderlichkeit* ('Life-force', 'Immutability') appear to her, then comes Professor Schabholz, a pedant in the manner of Wagner. She willingly follows Praktinski, her tempter, around the familiar locations, until she meets the man of her dreams, the erudite Musarion. He, torn between the simple but alluring Innocentia and Faustine, the erudite, commanding blue-stocking, makes the obvious choice yet Innocentia feels threatened by her rival and seeks the advice of her neighbour, Hertha. The devil Praktinski falls in love with the student, murders Musarion, and whisks Faustine off to a laboratory, in order to generate a new kind of light with her assistance. Together they produce the child Elektra, but when they try to embrace her, they are destroyed by an explosion. Schäfer uses the female figure mainly to deliver a scathing comment on the education of women from a chauvinist viewpoint, and while the play amounts to an interesting counterpoint to its male-oriented models, it does little more than demonstrate that the Faust-figure was amenable to being updated as an icon of questionable erudition. Like the many *Faustas* and *Faustines* discussed by Doering, it is no more than a curiosity. Carl Winderlich's *Faust und Faustina*, an ambitious historical drama dating from 1921, features a 'Faustina' who is groomed to seduce Luther. It was dedicated to 'the first theatre director to stage it in whole or in large part', an aspiration that has remained unfulfilled to this day (Doering, 225).

The eighteenth century may have favoured drama over prose, but the nineteenth century saw fiction assert itself as the dominant literary genre. In this convenient medium, countless authors created convoluted plots in which social issues were discussed against a background that was recognisably realistic. Germany's contribution to this genre is less well known internationally than that of France and Britain, but it was rich and varied nonetheless: Freytag and Raabe, Keller and Stifter are still read with interest today, and Theodor Fontane has maintained an international reputation with gently critical works in the mould of his most famous study of the causes and effects of adultery, *Effi Briest*. Friedrich Spielhagen (1829–1911) was, in his day, one of Germany's most popular authors, and his novel *Faustulus* of 1898 confirms the shift from drama to prose for our theme that began with Klinger and Hahn-Hahn.

Spielhagen's novel is set in an unnamed coastal town peopled by dull, small-minded provincials. Only the local doctor, Arno, shows any sign of genius, but he, too, is all but paralysed in this mediocre environment, caught up in a sordid affair with the chemist's wife, Lora, while working himself into the ground dealing with the epidemics and accidents that strike the small community at regular intervals.

His towering intellect, his wide-ranging aspirations make him a Faustian figure, as does his dissatisfaction with his professional life. This modern genius is also engaged in writing a play about Faust in whom he recognises an alter ego. In a series of letters to a friend, Arno explains what Faust means to him and how he himself intends to advance the theme.

> But for heaven's sake do not think of him as an uncouth libertine in the mould of Caligula, Heliogabalus *e tutti quanti!* He is, like the Prince of Denmark, a philosopher, a thinker and scholar, who with hot-blooded assiduousness has studied in Rome and Athens, sat at the feet of the priests in Memphis, admires the faith of the Christians he tortures to death and speculates earnestly about the invisible god whom they worship. Yet all the while – and herein lies my problem, for I must prove this to be the case – this man of violence is not just capable of tender emotions and generous actions – no, he really does feel them himself and acts accordingly. And what I hope to be able to achieve is that every reader, every member of the audience is compelled to admit that this is no mere product of a poet's imagination but actual, truthful reality. This man might have lived. Indeed he does, albeit as a dark reflection, in us all. (Spielhagen, 86f.)

The man who sees the paradox so clearly is, in the unhealthy atmosphere of small-town Germany, unable to combine his own overarching ambition with the tender feelings he nurtures for a sailor's daughter, and plunges himself into misery, loving and abandoning the innocent creature much as Goethe's hero did. The wisdom he gains from this experience leads to the completion of his play, which receives its première while its author, 'a mere travesty of my hero' (Spielhagen, 286) is punitively murdered by a jealous rival.

By the time this cautionary novel was published, the positive readings of Goethe's play were increasing. The ignominious defeat of France in the Franco-Prussian War of 1870/1 and the subsequent proclamation of a 'German Empire' in 1871 led to the call for a 'national poet', someone who would serve as a cultural beacon for the enlarged nation. Goethe was the obvious choice and *Faust* the obvious work to be serenaded as his greatest achievement. Not only was it the one that had occupied him most, from his youth until the year of his death, but it was undeniably also his most 'German' work, born of the great Age of Martin Luther and the Reformation, and nurtured by a multitude of poets, major and minor, over the centuries. Some of its lines had a prophetic ring to them; 'He who relentlessly strives on/ May finally be saved.' (F 11936f.) seemed to indicate that Germany's increasingly vociferous demands for what Emperor Wilhelm II described as 'a place in the sun' would eventually be met. National unity was the first step in this direction. Faustian endeavour, involving an element of bravado and recklessness, was a motivating factor, and positive references to the drama now became frequent in cultural and political discourse. By 1880, Paul Haffner could remark, 'no one would deny that Faust is the high point of modern German literature.' (Haffner, 1) While it was undoubtedly right that Goethe's treatment of the Faust legend should eventually find favour with the public and become a repertory favourite, not least on account of its poetic and dramatic innovations, the public's tendency to overlook the hero's faults was a more worrying development. It was not until the following century that the nation's revisioning of this myth was to have consequences which none of its earlier supporters or detractors could have remotely foreseen.

Cited Works and Further Reading

Kurt Adel, *Die Faustdichtung in Österreich*. Vienna: Bergland Verlag, 1971.

Peter Boerner and Sidney Johnson (eds), *Faust through Four Centuries. Retrospect and Analysis. Vierhundert Jahre Faust. Rückblick und Analyse*. Tübingen: Niemeyer, 1989.

Dieter Borchmeyer, 'Fausts Wege im 19. Jahrhundert', in Boerner/Johnson, 169–83.

Claus Canisius, *Goethe und die Musik*. Munich: Piper, 1998.

František Černý, 'Die erste deutsche Bearbeitung des Faust-Stoffes in der Form des "regelmässigen" Schauspiels (Paul Weidmann, Kotzen-Theater, Prag 1775)', in Csobádi, 397–404.

Adelbert von Chamisso, *Faust. Ein Versuch*, in Karl Georg Wendriner (ed.), *Die Faustdichtung, vor, neben und nach Goethe*. 4 volumes. Berlin: Morawe & Scheffelt, 1913. Rptd Darmstadt: Wissenschaftliche Buchgesellschaft, 1969, III, 310–18.

Herbert Clasen, *Heinrich Heines Romantikkritik. Tradition, Produktion, Rezeption*. Hamburg: Hoffmann & Campe, 1979.

Peter Csobádi *et al.* (eds), *Europäische Mythen der Neuzeit: Faust und Don Juan*. 2 volumes. Anif/Salzburg: Müller-Speisel, 1993.

Roy C. Cowen, *Christian Dietrich Grabbe*. New York: Twayne, 1972.

Charles Dédéyan, *Le Mythe de Faust dans la littérature européenne*. 4 volumes. Paris: Lettres Modernes: 1954-61.

Sabine Doering, *Die Schwestern des Doktor Faust. Eine Geschichte der weiblichen Faustgestalten*. Göttingen: Wallstein, 2001.

Osman Durrani, 'Lyrisches Drama, dramatisches Gedicht. Erwägungen zur Form von Lenaus Faust', in Alexander Stillmark and Fred Wagner (eds), *Lenau zwischen Ost und West*. Stuttgart: Heinz Akademischer Verlag, 1992, 69–82.

Ulrich Gaier, *Fausts Modernität*. Stuttgart: Reclam, 2000.

Sander L. Gilman, see under Klinger.

Christian Dietrich Grabbe, *Don Juan und Faust*, in *Ibid.*, *Werke*. Ed. Roy C. Cowen. 3 volumes. Munich: Hanser, 1975, I, 407–512.

Ida Gräfin von Hahn-Hahn, *Gräfin Faustine*. Berlin: Duncker, 1841. Rptd Bonn: Bouvier, 1986.

—, *The Countess Faustina*. Translated from the German by H. N. S. London: H.G. Clarke and Co., 1844.

Reinhold Grimm and Jost Hermand (eds), *Our Faust? Roots and Ramifications of a Modern German Myth*. Madison: University of Wisconsin Press, 1987.

Paul Haffner, 'Goethes Faust als Wahrzeichen moderner Cultur', *Frankfurter zeitgemässe Broschüren* 1 (1880), 1–40.

Heinrich Heine, *Der Doctor Faust. Ein Tanzpoem, nebst kuriosen Berichten über Teufel, Hexen und Dichtkunst*. Ed. Joseph A. Kruse, Stuttgart: Reclam, 1991.

Arthur Henkel, 'The "Salvation" of Faust – by Goethe', in Boerner/Johnson, 91–98.

David Hill, *Klinger's novels: the structure of the cycle*. Stuttgart: Heinz Akademischer Verlag, 1982.

Henrice van Ierland-Teodoruk, *Die Rolle des Teufels in den Faustbüchern von Lessing, Klinger und Goethe*, PhD Dissertation, Ann Arbor, 1982.

Michael Jaeger, *Fausts Kolonie: Goethes kritische Phänomenologie der Moderne*. Würzburg:

Königshausen & Neumann, 2004.

Nancy A. Kaiser, 'Faust/Faustine in the nineteenth century: Man's Myth, Women's Places', in Grimm/Hermand, 65–81.

Friedrich Maximilian Klinger, *Faust's Leben, Thaten und Höllenfahrt*. 1791. (anon.) Cited as *Ibid.*, Ed. Sander L. Gilman. Tübingen: Max Niemeyer, 1978.Volume IX of *Werke. Historisch-kritische Gesamtausgabe*.

August Klingemann, *Faust. Ein Trauerspiel in fünf Acten*. Leipzig: Brockhaus, 1815.

Detlev Kopp (ed.), *Christian Dietrich Grabbe – ein Dramatiker der Moderne*. Bielefeld: Aisthesis, 1996.

Nikolaus Lenau, *Faust. Ein Gedicht. Mit Dokumenten zur Entstehung und Wirkung*. Ed. Hartmut Steinecke. Stuttgart: Reclam 1971.

Ulrike Leuschner (ed.), Friedrich Müller genannt Maler Müller, *Der dramatisirte Faust. Text, Entstehung, Bedeutung. Aus dem Nachlass herausgegeben*. 2 volumes. Heidelberg: Carl Winter, 1996.

Ladislaus Löb, *Christian Dietrich Grabbe*. Stuttgart: Metzler, 1996.

— (ed.), *Grabbe über seine Werke*. Frankfurt: Peter Lang, 1991.

Willy Mathern, *Maler Müller 1749–1825. Leben und Werk des Malerdichters Friedrich Müller*. Bad Kreuznach: Raab, 1974.

Renate Möhrmann, *Die andere Frau: Emanzipationsansätze deutscher Schriftstellerinnen im Vorfeld der Achtundvierziger Revolution*. Stuttgart: Metzler, 1977.

[Friedrich] Ma[h]ler Müller, *Situation aus Fausts Leben*. Mannheim: Schwan, 1776.

—, *Fausts Leben dramatisirt. Erster Theil*. Mannheim: Schwan, 1778.

—, (1996), see under Leuschner, above.

Roger A. Nicholls, *The Dramas of Christian Dietrich Grabbe*. The Hague: Mouton, 1969.

Max Niehaus, *Himmel, Hölle und Trikot. Heinrich Heine und das Ballett*. Munich: Nymphenburger Verlagshandlung, 1959.

Gunnar Och, *Imago Judaica. Juden und Judentum im Spiegel der deutschen Literatur 1750–1812*. Würzburg: Königshausen & Neumann, 1996.

Wolfgang Rothe, *Der politische Goethe. Dichter und Staatsdiener im deutschen Spätabsolutismus*. Göttingen: Vandenhoeck & Ruprecht, 1998.

Wilhelm Schäfer, *Faustine, der weibliche Faust. Tragödie in sechs Aufzügen nebst Vorspiel und Prolog*. Zurich: Cotti's Wittwe, 1898.

Carl Christoph Ludwig Schöne, *Fortsetzung des Faust von Göthe. Der Tragödie zweiter Theil*. Berlin: Mauersche Buchhandlung, 1823.

J[ohn] W. Smeed, *Don Juan. Variations on a Theme*. London: Routledge, 1990.

—, *Faust in Literature*. London: Oxford University Press, 1975.

Friedrich Spielhagen, *Faustulus. Roman*. Leipzig: Staackmann, 1898.

Robert E. Stiefel, 'Heine's Ballet Scenarios. An Interpretation', *Germanic Review* 44 (1969), 186–98.

Friedrich Theodor Vischer, 'Zum zweiten Theile von Göthe's Faust', in: *Kritische Gänge*. NF, 3 (Stuttgart 1861), 135–178.

—, *Faust. Der Tragödie dritter Theil. Treu im Geiste des zweiten Theils des Goethe'schen Faust* gedichtet v. Deutobold Symbolizetti Allegoriowitsch Mystifizinsky, Tübingen: H. Laupp, 1862, 2nd edn 1886 (Rptd Hildesheim: Olms, 1963; Fritz Martini (ed.), Stuttgart: Reclam, 2000), 3rd edn 1889.

Oskar Walzel, *Heines Tanzpoem Der Doktor Faust*. Weimar: Gesellschaft der Bibliophilen, 1917. Rptd Hildesheim: Olms, 1962, 1978.

[Anon.] Paul Weidmann, *Johann Faust. Ein Allegorisches Drama von fünf Aufzügen*. Prague: Diesbach, 1775.

Gerhard Weiss, 'Die Entstehung von Heines "Doktor Faust". Ein Beispiel deutsch-englisch-französischer Freundschaft', *Heine-Jahrbuch* 5 (1966), 41–57.

Georg Zilk, *Faust und Antifaust. Eine Studie zum Denken und Dichten Friedrich Maximilian Klingers*. PhD Dissertation, Munich, 1965.

Chapter Five

Humanists versus Brown Shirts: Fausts for the Twentieth Century

But success shall crown my endeavours. Wherefore not? Thus far I have gone, tracking a secure way over the pathless seas: the very stars themselves being witnesses and testimonies of my triumph. Why not still proceed over the untamed yet obedient element? What can stop the determined heart and resolved will of man?—Mary Shelley, *Frankenstein, or the Modern Prometheus.*

The Collective Ideal

THE NINETEENTH century may have ended with faint, bittersweet echoes of the Faustian pact in works as diverse as Friedrich Spielhagen's *Faustulus* and Oscar Wilde's *The Picture of Dorian Gray*, but far from petering out in fin-de-siècle decadence, the image of the magus was about to experience its most radical transformation since the time of Goethe. For the generation that had been sucked into the Great War and lived through its devastating consequences, there could be no return to the serenely aesthetic preoccupations of the past. Nor could the powerfully suggestive figure of Faust be extricated from the political context that was rapidly becoming a touchstone against which cultural achievements were measured.

The most immediate result was a shift from the private preoccupations of individuals like Spielhagen's doctor or Hahn-Hahn's countess towards the wider public arena. The Fausts of the early twentieth century differ from their predecessors in that they seek not only wisdom and enlightenment, but social involvement and political influence. One of the earliest twentieth-century examples was *Faust der Politiker* ('Faust the Politician'), written by Johann von Leyden in 1907. It features a hero determined to wrest power from a corrupt town council, and is thus symptomatic of those modern Fausts no longer content with temporary triumphs over the ageing process or the easy seduction of provincial maidens. Instead, he strives to influence the revolutionary processes that could be observed in a world that was rapidly reshaping itself. After the revolution of 1917 in Russia, it was only too obvious that a modern Faust would have to consider aligning himself with advances in social organisation, if only because these were being vociferously demonised in many quarters. The way had been prepared by earlier attempts to achieve political influence. Goethe made Faust play a political role when he introduced paper currency and supervised land reclamation. Klinger put forward a Faust maniacally anxious to right social ills, though his plans invariably failed as the devil contrived to twist potentially good works into malpractice and chaos. But in all these accounts, Faust had been hampered by one factor: he was obliged to work on his own, with the devil as his only, exceedingly unreliable accomplice. This was to change in the twentieth century, where, with the spread of the collective ideal, Faust tends to seek accomplices among other radically minded groupings. Yet it is symptomatic of the moral confusions of the time that Faust was used as a rallying point at both ends of the political spectrum. Heinrich Mann could speak of him as a 'militant humanist' at the same time as Kurt Engelbrecht was serenading 'Faust in the brown shirt', suggesting that his modern-day equivalent would readily don the paramilitary uniform favoured by the fascists (Jasper, 163, 216).

Between 1910 and 1921, Ferdinand Avenarius, a nephew of Richard Wagner, wrote a trilogy of dramas entitled *Der Wachsende Gott* ('The God of Growth'), which focuses on Faust, Baal, and Jesus. The first of the series, *Faust. Ein Spiel*, was published in 1910 with a dedication to *Den Werdenden* ('Those coming into Being'). It takes up Goethe's *Faust I*, beginning a mere two weeks after Margaret's execution. Helen of Troy is summoned by Mephistopheles and presented to the Pope. This clever idea of confronting the emblems of beauty and religion taps yet another undeveloped potential and produces an amusingly anachronistic clash of values. Faust, meanwhile, uses his trip to Rome to converse with Michelangelo. Back in Germany, he is caught up in the political events of the day: the Peasants' War of 1525, notorious not only for the violence with which the peasants were put down but also for Luther's controversial endorsement of the Princes' right to crush them. Avenarius makes Faust align himself with the revolutionary peasants and students, pleading for tolerance and for civil rights. Later authors such as Hanns Eisler will show him siding with Luther in this matter at least. But Avenarius makes him speak for many Germans disillusioned with the Hohenzollern Empire and Prussian domination when he implores the Emperor to end the rioting and confusion and become a *Volkskaiser*, a true 'Emperor of the People':

FAUST [*pleading intensely, forcing himself to his knees*]:
>Lord, see me kneel before you
>Not me alone; as with a thousand brothers
>And more, you see your subjects all in me.
>You are so young, and yet your subjects all
>Implore you as their father, so help your child!
>You are so young, and like a brother we all beseech you
>Whose heart is beating with the blood of youth
>As in the springtime of your days, and love itself
>Must sing with every voice for freedom and for light.
>Once you yourself declared you'd be the People's Emperor:
>Fulfil your pledge and lo, the hopes in all our hearts
>Will be contained in you as in a stream of joy,

> Do it, and all the world will flower as in springtime ...
> FOOL: [*laughs*] (IV, 1; Avenarius, 104f.)

In this respect, too, Faust is ahead of his time, but circumstances conspire to frustrate his progressive aspirations. Not only does the Fool ridicule his programme, but the establishment intervenes before Faust can persuade the Emperor to share power with the people. It is left to the Chancellor to voice the often-recited arguments against collectivisation and communism. Like so many would-be revolutionaries of the time, Faust is imprisoned on orders from above, although by the fifth act he has freed himself and becomes privy to a vision of a better future. The phantom that appears to him bears none other than Goethe's features:

> APPARITION [*has changed into an exceedingly noble countenance, which appears to resemble that of*
> *Goethe in the period of his maturity*]:
> Each separate thought
> An ancestor of old
> Struggles and strives
> To break the mad mould –
> As darkness falls
> In the creative womb
> As light shines out
> The truth shall loom
> I am the *Godhead* that is *born of mankind*
> . [*The* APPARITION *slowly retreats into the darkness, and in its place the stars begin to emerge*]
> (V, 1; Avenarius, 132; see also Butler, 282f.)

These and other grandiose effects reveal a contemporary relevance, not only of subject, but also of style. There is an affinity with the fervent Expressionism of film-makers like Friedrich Wilhelm Murnau, Fritz Lang, Sergei Eisenstein, and the impassioned social dramas of their contemporaries Bertolt Brecht and Ernst Toller. Lunacharsky's *Faust and the City* will be discussed in the context of Faust's significance for revolutionary Russia (see below, 368f.). Faust now emerges as a reformed rake converted into an emblem of workers' and peasants' rights and student revolt, a supporter of democracy, but in Avenarius, the time is not ripe for his vision. Mephistopheles does not actively harm his endeavours but is powerless to assist him in his struggle against reactionary secular forces. Many subsequent authors will place Faust within the context of the Peasants' War but will tend to see him as indifferent if not hostile to the oppressed masses. Avenarius' Faust is a good man struggling to influence a corrupt world. Just how closely Faust came to be allied to its perversions was to become evident as the twentieth century came under the growing influence of totalitarian dictatorship. The change that was occurring can be gauged from several writers whose influence on the mind of twentieth-century Germany was considerable, particularly Oswald Spengler, who in the years following World War I attained fame and notoriety with a sweeping history of culture undertaken from a new perspective, and Alfred Rosenberg, sometime Head of Nazi Germany's Foreign Ministry and self-appointed prophet of her cultural identity.

163

18. Oswald Spengler, inventor of 'Faustian Man', 1910.

The Invention of 'Faustian Man'

Oswald Spengler's two-volume survey of past cultures, *Der Untergang des Abendlandes* ('The Decline of the West', 1918–22), is Faustian in its scope. The original sorcerer had, after all, begun his career as a discontented scholar, determined to fathom the deeper secrets of life and the universe. In the first chapbook Faustus asks one question after another and is eager to learn more. Goethe had depicted him as a man of considerable learning who needed to go further still. Spengler aims to present a definitive history of human culture, taking in Egypt, China, Greece and modern history, not in the form of dates and facts, but organised into a 'morphology of culture' with the emphasis on a common development. Every culture has a central preoccupation arising out of a set of distinctive aspirations; and for Western culture this is what Spengler identifies as the 'Faustian soul'. Its main feature is an unquenchable longing for the unattainable which causes it to reach upward and beyond itself:

> The Magian and the Faustian souls built high. Their dream-images were set as vaultings above significant inner-spaces, structural anticipations respectively of algebra and analysis. In the style that radiated out from Burgundy and Flanders rib vaulting with its lunettes and flying buttresses emancipated the contained space from the sense-appreciable surface bounding it. In the Magian interior 'the window is merely a negative component, a utility-form in no wise yet developed into an art-form – to put it crudely, nothing but a hole in the wall.'[1] When windows were in practice indispensable, they were for the sake of artistic impression concealed by galleries as in the Eastern basilica. The *window as architecture*, on the other hand, is peculiar to the Faustian soul and the most significant symbol of its experience of depth. In it you can feel the will to emerge from the interior into the boundless. The same will that underlies contrapuntal music is inherent in these vaultings. The incorporeal world of this music remained that of the first Gothic period, and even when, much later, polyphonic music rose to great heights in the *St Matthew Passion*, the *Eroica*, and in *Tristan* and *Parsifal*, it became of necessity *cathedral-like* and returned to its home, the stone language of the Age of Crusades. To strip out every trace of Classical corporeality required the full force of a deeply significant Ornamentation, which defies the delimiting power of stone with its weirdly impressive transformations of vegetal, animal and human bodies (St. Pierre in Moissac), which dissolves all its lines into melodies and variations on a theme, all its façades into many-voiced fugues, and all the physicality of its statuary into a music of folded drapery. It is this spirituality that gave their deep meaning to the gigantic glass-expanses of our cathedral windows with their polychrome, *translucent and therefore wholly bodiless*, painting – an art that has never and nowhere repeated itself and forms the completest contrast that can be imagined to the Classical fresco. It is perhaps in the Sainte-Chapelle at Paris that this emancipation from the purely physical is at its most evident. Here the stone practically vanishes in the gleam of the glass. (Spengler, I, 199)

This is a new and very different use of the Faustian motif. It marks an ingenious attempt to distil the essence from the icon, and the result is remarkable in its broad sweep, encompassing all branches of knowledge: art, architecture, music and science. Faust's universalism is exemplified by Gothic architecture and can be experienced in its purest form in the vast cathedrals of this type, in their vertical lines and lofty structures that reach up into empty space, no less than in the magnificent windows, now empowered to function as gateways to the infinite. 'Faustian Man' is an aspirant, but also, in order to achieve what he seeks, he must become a commander. This in turn explains why Christianity developed from its origins as a religion of meekness and submission into a militant, crusading faith that usurped power, spread out across the globe and sought to rule the world. Here, too, Spengler sees the Faustian spirit at work:

> In the world as seen through Faustian eyes, everything is motion with an aim. He himself lives only under that condition, for to him life means struggling, overcoming, winning through. The struggle for existence as the ideal form of existence is implicit

even in the Gothic age (of whose architecture it is the foundation) and the 19th Century did not invent it but merely put it into a mechanical, utilitarian form. [...] It is quite wrong to bind up Christianity with the moral imperative. It was not Christianity that transformed Faustian man, but Faustian man who transformed Christianity – and he not only made it a new religion but also gave it a new moral direction. The 'it' became 'I', the passion-charged centre of the world, the foundation of the great sacrament of *personal* contrition. (Spengler, I, 344f.)

Spengler tends to consider any post-classical and dynamic artefact as 'Faustian'. The Gothic columns of the High Middle Ages are early indications of a restlessness that was to be the hallmark of modernity. A passion for the unattainable and indefinable is an essential constituent of the 'Faustian' spirit, which embraces the cult of the Virgin and the *Art of the Fugue*, *King Lear* and Nietzsche as somewhat disparate partners who share the questing principle. In literature, this 'Faustian soul' is discernible in the Arthurian knights Percival and Tristan, in Hamlet, Don Quixote, Don Juan, Faust and Werther, and beyond these figures, in the heroes of 'the modern urban romance' (Spengler, I, 13, note 1). In contrast to his more narrowly Eurocentric imitators, Spengler recognises Faustian traits in Islam and the 'Magian' culture of the East, which share a hunger for expansion and totality.

What distinguishes Spengler from later imitators is that his was not a celebration of the Faustian spirit. Rather, he sees culture as doomed. It arises, it flourishes, it declines in accordance with the same ultimately tragic blueprint that determines the rise and fall of all empires of the spirit. 'Faustian Man' recognises this and is characterised by a sense of isolation that had not been known to previous or parallel nations; he is constantly and painfully reminded of his solitude (Dabezies, 124–56).

Spengler might have chosen to opt for Dante or Columbus. But Faust's name helped to spread the doctrine, and a number of lesser authors soon followed suit, ascribing to Faust all the major achievements of German culture, from her great cathedrals to the sermons of the mediaeval mystic preacher Meister Eckhart. Suddenly, Faust was everywhere. From the early days of World War I, it had been noted that an inordinate number of German soldiers were carrying copies of *Faust* in their rucksacks (Dabezies, 89–105). Following the crushing demands of the Treaty of Versailles, Germany sank to a level of demoralisation not experienced since the Napoleonic Wars – which is precisely when Goethe's *Faust I* saw publication. Now again, that figure was available to be exploited as a rallying post for nationalists eager to redefine their country's grandeur. It is hardly surprising that 1919 saw a flood of anonymous volumes with titles like *Faust as Führer. A Book for Thoughtful People.*

Ernst Kratzmann's novel *Faust. Ein Buch von deutschem Geist* ('Faust. A Book of the German Spirit') was typical of its time. Coming from the pen of an Austrian schoolmaster with strong leanings towards National Socialism, this action-packed adventure novel reflects a period in which Faust was hailed as the epitome of all things positive and Germanic. The few dates that are given suggest that we could be anywhere between the early fourteenth century and the Thirty Years' War in the seventeenth. The villains speak French; the good are German peasants, whom Faust assists in their struggle for self-determination. Historical sources are used *en passant*: these include Eckhart's and Suso's sermons, Dante's appeal to Emperor Henry VII, references to the flagellants and the Inquisition. Faust is an itinerant doctor who helps the poor and inspires the mystics. He challenges the high and mighty to act in the service of the people and preaches socialism of a nationalist variety. Like Avenarius' hero, he pleads with the monarch of the day to recognise that he has a duty towards his people, a duty to serve and protect them:

> 'You fail to see the signs of the time, your Majesty. The German Reich, as things now stand, does not rely on the swords of its counts and dukes ...' - he steps up close to the king and looks him in the eyes - 'it relies on labour, your Majesty! On the labour of peasants, the townspeople, and the fighting power of men. But no longer, as in ancient times, does the peasant and citizen have to provide financial support for wars, but the fighting force is there to protect the peasants and citizens.'
> He fell silent. The king walked away from him and leaned against the window ledge. He was very pale, and everything grew blurred around him as in a swirling mist. He felt his anger throb in his temples, but he had lost his voice. (Kratzmann, (1938), 57).

The sense of work to be done to unite the Reich, the need for a strong army and the portrayal of French, Habsburg, and papal elements as inimical to the well-being of the state are the telling hallmarks of this novel. Faust's magic is the result not so much of scholarly learning as of folk wisdom. He travels from town to town, helping artists to draw the human body accurately by showing them how to dissect corpses, and teaching the German mystics how to experience the divine through the medium of passion and thus more immediately than by wearisome study or protracted prayer (*Op. cit.*, 144–152). A black mass is performed (*Op. cit.*, 170–73), and there are powerful diatribes against the church and the papacy. Faust is tried by the Inquisition, a corrupt and hypocritical force that eventually succumbs to his influence (*Op. cit.*, 205–10). Religious bigots murder his free-thinking mistress as a witch. Faust renounces the devil early on this work, which recognises a 'God' but rejects all churches and intermediaries:

> Faust stood facing the peasants. 'Men, kneel down and ask God to forgive his servants. And ask for the strength to believe in him in solitude - for whenever men construct a faith that is meant for the many, it turns into a church. Men, know that many churches will come, just as there have been many in the past ... and every church will become an Inquisition ... You homeless ones, pray for a solitary faith, in order that you may become truly human!' (*Op. cit.*, 212)

Faust rejects the church and all foreign influences, persuading an architect, Meister Johannes, to abandon his plans for a Gothic cathedral as being non-German:

> 'You propose to build something in this city in the French style of the *opus francigenum* ... Have you never felt that the meadows and flowers of Germany are different from those of other lands, as are the sounds of the forests, the song of the birds, the way the mountains rise into the sky? So how is it with your *opus francigenum* that is alien to our land, not born of you, or of our soil?'

Johannes broke down at Faust's feet, clasping his knees. 'I was blind, I was a fool. You have made me see ... How can I build the cathedral now? I have no wish to do so. I'll tear up the plan and leave the city – I cannot build it! ... You – you are the one to build it!'

Faust looked down at him with a distant smile. 'You will not build it and nor shall I. Time itself builds the great cathedrals, not one man, not even the greatest master-builder!' (*Op. cit.*, 233)

This author is interesting as an example of Germany's increasing rejection of its 'Gothic' past under National Socialism. Gothic architecture was beginning to be recognised as having been influenced by French models to a greater extent than was comfortable for the nationalists, and was thus incompatible with the spirit of an age that sought to define itself along strictly partisan lines. The novel culminates in a chapter entitled *Der deutsche Gott* ('The German God', *Op. cit.*, 247–328), in which the German mystic Eckhart preaches a new kind of religion intended to empower the individual at the expense of organised faith. What matters from now on is private experience, an inner vision. The implication is that the true German knows what is right and wrong in his heart and does not need any intermediary to tell him what to do. Faust's whole life is an embittered battle against the Church and its influence in Germany: 'I have up to now seen the church as the very essence of evil on earth and have fought against it for this reason and shall continue to fight against it for as long as I live, as it is fundamentally alien and hostile to the German nature' (*Op. cit.*, 338). This Faust does not die an ignominious death, but his soul dissolves in joy. In an epilogue, Kratzmann explains that his novel was completed in 1927 and published in 1932. In 1936 it was banned in Austria, where it was reissued in 1938 following the *Anschluss*.

Alfred Rosenberg, sometime editor of the Nazi organ *Völkischer Beobachter* and right-wing ideologue, likewise saw in Faust a blueprint for the German soul, claiming that his great monologues were emblems of German culture on a par with Nordic sagas, Prussian marches, Bach's compositions and Eckhart's sermons, all of which he sees as different forms of expression of a single identity.

> The German soul had to take a different pathway from that prescribed by the Church. It chose art. When Eckhart fell silent, German painting developed, the soul of J.S, Bach rang out, followed by Goethe's *Faust*, Beethoven's 'Ninth', Kant's philosophy [...]
>
> In a succession of new forms, Goethe excels himself in tirelessly drawing attention to vitalising activity, be this in the shape of the most modest handicraft. The greatest hymn to human activity is *Faust*. After he has transformed and penetrated all known sciences, all love and hate, Faust is liberated through action. The spirit that continued to strive for the infinite found its crowning achievement in a limiting activity, in the construction of dykes to protect people against floods. This was the last step on the road into the unknown. The nobility of action culminates in the work of art. 'The teachings of the true artist open up meaning, for where words fail, the deed will speak.'[2] [...]
>
> No race on earth has sent more explorers across the globe than northern Europe has. They were not merely discoverers, but uncoverers in the fullest sense of the term, that is to say, men capable of transforming what they had found into a new image of

the world. The darkest continents, the coldest polar regions, tropical jungles and empty steppes, the remotest oceans and the most secret rivers and lakes have been found and the highest mountains have been conquered. The age-old longing of all people to be able to fly through space became a driving force for the people of Europe and not before, and this yearning gave them the strength that led to new inventions. No one can understand an important aspect of the Germanic-European soul unless he is aware, in a car or an express train, of the effect of Lucifer, driving us on to overcome time and space by force, or unless he has experienced the very pulses of an empirical transformation of the world while standing amongst the machines of a steel-works, surrounded by a thousand interlocking cog-wheels. Those who have not experienced this will never comprehend the other - mystic - side. One need only think of Faust's sudden exclamation, at the age of one hundred:

> Those few trees that are not mine
> Ruin the Empire I call my own.[3]

This is not the voice of greed, eager to extend possession for the sake of greater comfort; this is the master who experiences bliss in giving orders. (Rosenberg, 257–63)

This shows the obvious influence of *The Decline of the West*, while denying the broad sweep of Spengler's comparative morphology and restricting the Faustian to 'Nordic' Europe alone. Rosenberg specifically refutes Spengler's thesis that Faustian elements could be found in Arabian culture: 'Our so-called philosophers should cease trying to uncover an "Magian soul" in the Arabesque or to detect in it something resembling a Faustian soul striving for infinity.' Rosenberg contends that Faustian culture is strictly limited to Germanic Europe, and all instances of Arab or Indian parallels are systematically refuted, often by the counter-claim that they arose by contact with Germanic peoples (*Op. cit.*, 368, 403 f.).

Faustian Man does not merely strive for the limitless and most profound things in life, but is also truly isolated. – That is only sustainable because he alone can experience inwardly an immortality that is specific to himself, as he is not only able to distinguish himself from his surroundings as a person, but because he is a personality, by virtue of his immortal, unique soul and his strength that is forever active, dominant, seeking, independent of time and space, and no longer tied to the earth. – Herein lies the secret of the Germanic-Nordic soul, the primal phenomenon, as Goethe would call it, which we cannot and should not explore, analyse or explain, but which we should simply venerate in order to allow it to take possession of us. (*Op. cit.*, 389)

This quotation from Rosenberg's 700-page *tour de force* is symptomatic of the ideology that its author was trying to promote on behalf of the National Socialist movement. Rosenberg was the principal, perhaps the only would-be architect of an 'ideology' that could inspire the masses who had turned to Hitler in their despair over Germany's defeat in World War I. Here, he promises a kind of immortality to the 'Faustian' German, while simultaneously warning that isolation will be his ultimate destiny. He shares a deep antagonism towards the Catholic Church and all derivatives of 'popish' and 'Roman' influence with the author of the first Faust Book. Literary scholarship was becoming extremely defensive about its 'German' Faust. A large number of German literary scholars who extolled the 'Faustian spirit' were subsequently found to have been members of the Nazi Party and even officers of the SS. The most notorious of these was Hans-Ernst Schneider, who had been a high-ranking SS officer before he reinvented himself after the war. Writing as Hans Schwerte, he published an admittedly perceptive history of Faust-adulation and Faust-criticism, *Faust und das Faustische. Ein Kapitel deutscher Ideologie* ('Faust and the Faustian. A Chapter of German Ideology'), and went on to become 'Rektor' of Aachen University before being exposed by a Dutch journalist as recently as 1995 (Mayr, 94–7; Conrady). It is for reasons such as this that Richard Alewyn deprecated those who 'praised Goethe while denying Hitler' and found it paradoxical that Goethe was being celebrated in 1949 'as if nothing had happened or as if what had happened could be undone in this manner.' (Alewyn, 685–7) One need only look at the relatively modest claim made by Robert Petsch, editor of the major collected edition of Goethe's works from the inter-war period, to appreciate the feelings that led to the fashionable view that only German readers were able to fathom out their own national drama:

> Faust was written for the whole of mankind and has long since entered into 'world literature', but only a German will be able to comprehend it in its entirety – the more he repeatedly grapples with it in order to enter into its spirit, the more successful he will be. The aim of this edition is to assist in this process. (Petsch, 52)

However much scholars attempted to present Faust as 'emblematic of the evolution of the German genius' (Gabler, 73), there was yet another surprising side to the Goethe-adulation of the interwar period. In 1931, the right-wing Ludendorff publishing house brought out Else Rost's *Goethes Faust, eine Freimaurertragödie*, ('A Freemason's Tragedy') whose underlying thesis was that *Faust* was nothing other than a veiled celebration of a 'Freemasons' Plot' to place the world in the hands of international Jewry. Mephistopheles thus becomes a Brother of the Lodge who initiates Faust into full membership. One required rite is the seduction of a German girl – who would serve this purpose better than Gretchen? (Belgum *et al.*, 157f.). What underlies these bizarre controversies is the simple fact that Goethe's polyvalent, open-ended work posed a huge problem for the nationalist ideologues of the Third Reich, no less than for most other exegetes. On the one hand, he was the creator of the most poetic, 'iconic' Faust in the German language, on the other, he was far too cosmopolitan in his outlook to be abused for nationalistic purposes. There was thus no consensus; frenzied eulogies of the Faustian temperament co-exist with cautionary observations that Faust fails to accept his limitations (Dabezies, 285–308).

Nor should it be assumed that German historians were alone in attempting to instrumentalise Faust in accordance with their own perceptions of history and their national destiny. The foremost British historian of the age, Arnold Toynbee, was not only indebted, directly and indirectly, to Spengler's morphologies for his own classification of societies, but he also gives pride of place to Goethe's *Faust* when it comes to illustrating his theory of 'challenge and response' as the motor that drives historical progress. Thus *Faust* represents what he calls 'the infinitely multiple ordeal of man' (Toynbee, I, 274). The world that Faust inhabits is perfect in its abundance, until Satan instils distress or discontent or fear or apathy. To make his point, Toynbee finds it convenient to cite Goethe's work at considerable length, before reaching the conclusion that 'Through Faust's dynamic act and Gretchen's act of resignation, the Lord has been enabled to make all things new' (*ibid.*, I, 276–98). Toynbee returns to Faust again and again in the course of his twelve-volume *Study of History*, reminding readers, for example, that the work of the Spirit of the Earth, who weaves and draws his threads through the loom of time, 'is the temporal history of Man as this manifests itself in the geneses and growths and breakdowns and disintegrations of human societies'. (*ibid.*, VI, 324)

Faust and Führer

The theme of Faust's compact with the devil had great appeal to the ideologues of the Third Reich and was to prove more prophetic than even they had imagined. The positive components of Faust's restlessness, his striving disposition, his pursuit of knowledge and success, his questing spirit were easily accommodated within a doctrine of nationalism that involved a desire for domination and actively sought to challenge other cultures. Here, too, the questionable features of his career could be absorbed. Faust had to sin, because it was his destiny to excel, to beat back all opposition, to take risks and to ignore the papery wisdom of a past that had been held back by its self-imposed preoccupation with conventional morality. He could be employed as a ready-made emblem of Germany's expansionist ambitions.

There were many revivals, not just of Goethe's but of many other *Fausts* dating from the 'Storm and Stress' and Romantic periods. Grabbe proved to be one such favourite whom German theatres attempted to rescue from oblivion. In Bochum alone, there were eight separate productions of Grabbe's plays in 1941 (Steffens, 80). The theme of Don Juan and Faust commended itself particularly to the *Zeitgeist* on account of the distinction it drew between the 'Nordic' scholar and the decadent southern libertine. The German scholar seeks knowledge and intellectual fulfilment, the Mediterranean hedonist only personal pleasure: this juxtaposition meshed well with the rampant chauvinism of the day.

Yet dissenting voices were quick to make themselves heard. As early as 1933, a scholar by the name of Wilhelm Böhm had attempted to show that Goethe's Faust was quite different from the by now virtually uncontested image of the relentlessly striving scholar whose inner dynamism excused his vices and whose focus on self-determination was a laudably Germanic trait. Böhm took issue with the fashionable perfectibility theory of the period and attempted to show the other side of the argument, knowing full well that he was taking on an increasingly powerful and inflexible establishment:

> I am not oblivious to the fact that pronouncements about 'Faustian Man' have recently acquired a *cultural mission*, and missions need to avail themselves of *legends!* –

> But it seems to me that scholarship is best able to serve the interests of the people if it does not keep re-orienting itself and sweeping away the old, *however much this may give offence*. (Böhm, 2)

Böhm's Faust was, at the other extreme, a reckless, uncaring criminal, who did not fight shy of sullying his hands with the blood of innocents, as episodes such as the murder of Gretchen's brother and the brutal eviction of Philemon and Baucis showed. Here was a man who waded knee-deep through the blood of his victims and lacked the capacity to learn from his mistakes (*Op. cit.*, 63–6).

By challenging the conventional model, Böhm had shown, once again, that Faust was too complex a construct to be pinned down to specific values, whether praiseworthy or not. The model was therefore liable to be misread. It was not long before satirical texts began to appear in which the vulnerability of the new icon was revealed and turned against its leading proponents. Faust's pact with the devil was tailor-made to be employed in unmasking the hidden agenda behind National Socialism: the unleashing chaotic forces that would prove uncontrollable by rational means.

The most sustained attempt to equate Faustus with the wayward genius of Germany was undertaken by the leading novelist of the period, Thomas Mann, between 1943 and 1947. What is less well known is that Thomas' son Klaus had prepared the ground for this analogy when he worked on the same topic some eleven years prior to the publication of his father's novel. Klaus Mann's *Mephisto. Roman einer Karriere* ('Mephisto. Novel of a Career') was the first émigré novel of any distinction, and the first to go for the jugular in its deconstruction of Nazi pomp and propaganda. Its influence on Thomas Mann's subsequent novel *Doctor Faustus* is beyond dispute (Malcolm, 248–90). Published in Amsterdam in 1936, *Mephisto* commanded attention for two reasons: firstly, because of the extremely sharply drawn portraits of many leading figures from Germany's innermost cultural scene, and secondly, because of its keen focus on the political changes that were occurring in the 1930s. From the point of view of Faust's status as a byword for Germany's destiny, the novel marks a turning point and achieves in narrative mode what Böhm had already suggested in academic terms.

Mephisto concentrates on a talented but vainglorious careerist in the person of actor Hendrik Höfgen, a rising star who is quick to shake off his past contacts with the Communist party in order to curry favour with the fascist regime that has recently established itself in Germany and taken control of cultural life. His past is an embarrassment from which he must cut himself off at all costs. This involves disowning his former friends, avoiding acquaintances of non-Aryan provenance, and imposing self-discipline and censorship on his every word and gesture. Höfgen, a consummate actor, finds compliance easy and quickly ascends to the pinnacle of success through the intervention of a minister's wife. His greatest triumph occurs when he stars as Goethe's Mephistopheles in the presence of the Nazi elite.

> When Hendrik walked into the box of the distinguished spectators, the fat general was sitting in front, stroking the red velvet of the balustrade with his thick fingers.

172

Hendrik stood at the door. How ridiculous that my heart should be beating so hard, he thought; and he remained standing there a few seconds longer. Then Lotte Lindenthal saw him. 'Hubby,' she cried, 'let me introduce my distinguished colleague Hendrik Höfgen.' The giant turned in his direction. Hendrik heard himself addressed in a fairly high, oily but grating voice, 'Aha, our Mephistopheles ...' This was followed by a burst of laughter.

In his entire life Hendrik had never felt so disturbed, and the shame of this agitation only increased his anxiety. To his blurred gaze even his colleague Lotte seemed to have undergone a fantastic change. Was it only the dazzling jewels, which gave her an intimidatingly regal appearance, or was it the fact that she was in such affectionate proximity to her lord and protector? Whatever the cause, she suddenly appeared to Hendrik as a fairy queen – a well-fleshed charming fairy queen, but one that was not without a certain menace. Her smile, which had always struck him as good-natured and somewhat stupid, now seemed obscurely treacherous.

But so great was his anxiety that Hendrik registered almost nothing of the stout giant in his coloured uniform, the demigod. A veil seemed to hang in front of the great man's face – that mystic veil that has always hidden the faces of the prophets and the gods from the frightened gaze of mere mortals. Only one medal blazed through the mist: the frightening contour of a bulging neck was just discernible. And then the sharp and oily parade-ground voice said, 'Come a little closer, Herr Höfgen.'

Members of the audience who had remained chatting in the orchestra became aware of the group in the prime minister's box. They whispered and craned their necks. No movement that the prime minister made escaped the curious congregating between the rows of seats. They saw that the expression of the air force general became ever more benevolent and amused. Now he was laughing. The people below watched with fascination the huge man guffawing. Lotte Lindenthal let her pearly coloratura laugh ring out; and the actor Höfgen – decoratively swathed in his black cape – displayed a smile that on his Mephisto mask had the appearance of a triumphant and painted sneer.

The conversation between the man of power and the entertainer became increasingly animated. The prime minister was having a good time. What wonderful stories Höfgen must be telling for the air force general to appear almost drunk with good humour! Everyone in the orchestra tried to glean the words that Hendrik's blood-red lips were forming. But Mephisto spoke softly; only the potentate caught his delectable jokes.

With an expansive gesture Höfgen threw wide his arms under his cloak, making it seem that he had grown black wings. The man of power slapped him on the back. A respectful murmur went around the orchestra. Then, like the music at a circus before the most dangerous act, it fell silent in deference to the extraordinary happening that followed.

The prime minister had risen. There he stood in all his magnitude, his shining bulk, and stretched out his hand to the actor. Was he congratulating him on his magnificent performance? It looked more like the sealing of a pact between the potentate and the actor.

In the orchestra people strained their eyes and ears. They devoured the scene in the box above as though it was the most exceptional entertainment, an entrancing pantomime entitled 'The Actor Bewitches the Prince.' Never was Hendrik so passionately envied! How happy he must be!

Did anyone watching have an inkling of what was really going on in Hendrik's mind as he bowed deeply over the fleshy, hairy hand of the grandee? Was it happiness and pride alone that made him tremble? Or did he feel something else as well – to his own astonishment? In fact what he felt was something close to nausea.

Now I have contaminated myself, thought Hendrik. Now there is a stain on my hand that I can never wash off... Now I have sold myself - Now I am marked for life. (Klaus Mann, 179f.)

The novel is based on meticulous research. The corpulent, jovial 'Prime Minister' (*Ministerpräsident*) is modelled on Hermann Göring, while Lotte Lindenthal is based on the actress Emmy Sonnemann, who became Göring's wife in 1935. Werner Rieck has investigated these and other parallels (697–709). Höfgen's real-life model, Gustaf Gründgens (1899–1963), enjoyed the patronage of the Nazi leadership and was director of the Berlin State Theatre from 1934 to 1945. Mephistopheles was one of his star roles, both before and after the Second World War. He had been married briefly to Klaus Mann's sister Erika, which gave the satire an extra bite. The book was banned in West Germany between 1966 and 1981 on the grounds of personal defamation.

What makes Höfgen share Faust's tragic qualities is that he knows full well that what he is doing is morally wrong and socially despicable. Chapter 7, entitled 'The Pact with the Devil', makes this clear in its final paragraph, cited above ('Now I have sold myself - Now I am marked for life'). His careerism is so powerful a force as to drive him knowingly into a compact which he perceives as wrong. The next chapter of the novel, headed 'Over the Bodies of Corpses', actually takes its title from Böhm's study. Höfgen now reaps the benefits of his pact, enjoying the high life reserved for members of the Nazi elite and their favourites.

> The actor Höfgen was allowed to take part in the private life of the gods. While sitting with Lotte in her beautiful home in the Tiergarten after the evening performance, playing cards or chess, sometimes the prime minister would burst unannounced into the room making a great din. Did he not then seem the most amiable man in the world? There was no sign either of the hideous transactions he had just concluded or of those he was planning for the following day. He joked with Lotte and drank his glass of red wine; he stretched his enormous legs out in front of him and spoke with Höfgen about serious things. His favourite topic was Mephistopheles.
>
> 'You're the first person to make me understand this character,' said the general. 'He really is splendid! And isn't there a little of him in us all? I mean, hidden in every real German isn't there a bit of Mephistopheles, a bit of the rascal and the ruffian? If we had nothing but the soul of Faust, what would become of us? It would be a pushover for our many enemies! No, no - Mephisto, too, is a German national hero. But it's better not to go around telling people that.' (Klaus Mann, 189)

The obvious symbolism might been seen as a flaw, but the author did no more than convert the sustained panegyrics of Germany's 'Faustian' destiny into their opposite by revealing the Mephistophelean component that has always gone hand in hand with the Faustian. If Germany's character is 'Faustian', then it must also be diabolical, since from the time of the pact onwards, Faust spends his life in the sway of the devil and all his actions become tainted in consequence.

No invention of Klaus Mann represents the lure of Mephistophelean nihilism more accurately than the character Benjamin Pelz, based on Gottfried Benn (1886–1956), a poet and doctor who attracted a following with his powerfully written

Nietzschean contemplations of decadence in modern society. His poems show us a world without values, full of glinting promise and a profound shallowness that masks human suffering and ignorance. As Mann insinuates, Benn briefly aligned himself with National Socialism before joining the ranks of inner émigrés who maintained a position of passivity during the war. Benn/Pelz is one of those who were fascinated by the apocalyptic vision of decay and decadence found in the writings of Spengler and Rosenberg, ready to welcome the triumph of the irrational over political reaction and bourgeois apathy. Mann hints that he may, for a time, have genuinely believed that Hitler's proclaimed synthesis of socialism and nationalism would rescue the country from moral stagnation.

> Pelz cast a fond look at Hendrik, and then continued: 'Life again begins to have a certain rhythm and charm. It awakes from its torpor and soon it will rediscover – as in the times of our buried past – the violent movement of the dance. For people who don't know how to use their eyes and ears, this new rhythm must seem like the well-drilled stamp of marching feet. Fools allow themselves to be deceived by the outward severity of the ancient militant life-style. What a crude mistake! In reality, we are not marching forward, we are reeling, staggering. Our beloved Führer is dragging us toward the shades of darkness and everlasting nothingness. How can we poets, we who have a special affinity for darkness and the lower depths, not admire him? It is absolutely no exaggeration to call our Führer godlike. He is the god of the Underworld, who has always been the most sacred of all for those initiated in black magic. I have a boundless admiration for him, because I have a boundless hatred of the dreary tyranny of reason and the bourgeois fetish of progress. All poets worthy of the name are sworn enemies of progress. Poetry itself is in any case a reversion to the sacred primitive state of humanity, before it became civilised. Poetry and slaughter, blood and song, murder and hymns – they are inseparable. Yes, I love catastrophe.' Pelz pushed forward his melancholy face with its pouchy cheeks and smiled as though his thick lips were tasting sweets or kisses.
> 'I am hungry for doomed adventure, for the depths, for the experience of extreme situations that place a man beyond the pale of civilization, in that region where no insurance company, no police, no comfortable hospital can protect him against the merciless power of the elements or a beast of prey. We are going to experience all this, believe me. We are going to be gorged with horror. And, as far as I am concerned, it can never be too horrifying. We are still too soft. Our great Führer can still not do everything he would like. Where is the *public* torture? Why don't we burn all those humanitarian gabblers and rationalist imbeciles at the stake?' Whereupon Pelz tapped impatiently with his spoon on the side of his coffee cup as though summoning a waiter. (*Op. cit.*, 203)

Although Faust is not mentioned by name, this entire diatribe is a grotesque echo of rabidly nationalistic eulogies of the Faustian spirit, reinterpreted as an invigorating challenge to the drab world of reason and utilitarianism. The new god may well be the god of the Underworld; what matter, as long as a new world order emerges at the end of his struggle? Klaus Mann was later to explain that his book was not aimed at a particular person, but at the careerist, the German intellectual who sold and betrayed the German mind and spirit. Höfgen – both as a type and as a symbol – places his talent at the disposal of a ruthless and blood-bespattered power. His antics as an actor reflect the stage-management of a political regime that was deeply 'untrue and unreal' (Klaus Mann (1958), 357f.). Here, too, there is a Faustian opposition between the striving individual and the intangible might of the state.

Höfgen is not the only culturally active personality to be unmasked and blamed. Pelz speaks for the Faustian apologists when he confesses to 'a boundless hatred of the dreary tyranny of reason and the bourgeois fetish of progress'. This is Faust's opening monologue rephrased and updated to echo a specifically twentieth-century mindset. The poet states his belief in risk-taking while fully acknowledging that the consequences will be disastrous: 'We are going to experience all this, believe me. We are going to be gorged with horror. And, as far as I am concerned, it can never be too horrifying. We are still too soft.' This is the paradox of the clear-sighted individual who, intoxicated by the myth of self-damnation, staggers willingly towards his own doom. By the time the book was published, Benn had seen the error of his ways, and after the war he admitted that Mann had understood the menace to civilisation at a time when he only saw the promise (Spangenberg, 100). It is sometimes hard to believe that Klaus Mann wrote this novel so early in the history of the National Socialist movement and that it remained relatively unknown and unrecognised for so long. After being banned as libellous in West Germany, it was re-discovered by Arianne Mnouchkine in France and performed to great acclaim in Paris. Thereafter, its success was ensured by Isztván Szabó's film starring a very slippery Klaus Maria Brandauer in the title role (see below, 331).

It was more than coincidental that some eleven years later, Klaus Mann's father Thomas supplied what is now seen as the definitive refutation of Rosenberg's model: *Doctor Faustus. The Life of the German Composer Adrian Leverkühn, Narrated by a Friend*. For Thomas Mann the pact was not an allegiance entered into for practical gain or personal glory, as it had been for the actor and social climber whom his son had portrayed so convincingly in *Mephisto*. The pact that Adrian Leverkühn, Thomas Mann's supremely talented creative musical genius, concludes is far more insidious: it is in his blood, and he binds himself to the devil by the device of knowingly engaging in sexual relations with an infected prostitute. His 'pallid Venus' is a less obvious but ultimately lethal companion to the genius by comparison with Juliette, the 'dark Venus' to whom Höfgen had temporarily been subservient.

This act of self-pollution is significant in many different ways. It is an immoral act, a deliberate flouting of bourgeois codes of behaviour, unmasking the 'Faustian' drive as something both deeply sordid and socially isolating. Faust's self-destructive baseness is made explicit, as is the danger to others that he carries within himself. If Faust in the guise of Adrian Leverkühn is to be equated with Germany, then it is as an apolitical figure motivated by an awareness of his cultural mission, which he inwardly knows will result in paralysis and death. There are numerous portents and premonitions that, far from acting as warnings, plunge him into an ever closer relationship with the force of evil.

At university, Adrian Leverkühn attends lectures by two university professors whose teachings are marked by a peculiarly old-fashioned and prejudice-ridden line of argumentation. Ehrenfried Kumpf looks like an incarnation of Luther, a robust 'man of the people' who acts as though his relationship with the devil were a personal one based on feelings of familiarity as well as loathing. Like Luther, he receives a diabolical visitor; like Luther, he strikes back by hurling a missile at his uninvited guest: not an inkpot but a bread-roll, whereupon the apparition vanishes. Leverkühn's second tutor is more sinister still when he proclaims a gospel of misogyny and obscurantism to his assembled students. Here is an extract from one of Eberward Schleppfuss' lectures:

> But from whom came the temptation? Who was to be cursed on its account? It was easy to say that it came from the Devil. He was its source, but the curse had to do with its object. The object, the *instrumentum* of the Tempter, was woman. She was also, and by that token, indeed, the instrument of holiness, since holiness did not exist without raging lust for sin. But the thanks she got had a bitter taste. Rather the remarkable and profoundly significant thing was that though the human being, both male and female, was endowed with sex, and although the localization of the daemonic in the loins fitted the man better than the woman, yet the whole curse of fleshliness, of slavery to sex, was laid upon the woman. There was even a saying: 'A beautiful woman is like a gold ring in the nose of the sow.' How much of that sort of thing, in past ages, has not been said and felt most profoundly about woman! It had to do with the concupiscence of the flesh in general; but was equated with that of the female, so that the fleshliness of the man was put down to her account as well. Hence the words: 'I found the woman bitterer than death, and even a good woman is subject to the covetousness of the flesh.'
>
> One might have asked: and the good man too? And the holy man quite especially so? Yes, but that was the influence of the woman, who represented the collective concupiscence of the world. Sex was her domain, and how should she not, who was called *femina*, which came half from *fides* and half from *minus* – that is, of lesser faith – why should she not be on evil and familiar footing with the obscene spirits who populated this field, and quite particularly suspect of intercourse with them, of witchcraft? There was the instance of that married woman who next to her trusting, slumbering spouse had carried on with an incubus, and that for years on end. Of course there were not only incubi but also succubi, and in fact an abandoned youth of the classical period lived with an idol, whose diabolic jealousy he was in the end to experience. For after some years, and more on practical grounds than out of real inclination, he had married a respectable woman, but had been prevented from consummating his marriage because the idol had always come and lain down between them. Then the wife in justifiable wrath had left him, and for the rest of his life he had seen himself confined to the unaccommodating idol. (Thomas Mann, 103f.)

Schleppfuss ('Dragfoot') is the most sinister of Thomas Mann's many satanic prefigurations. Immersed as he is in long-forgotten tales of witchcraft, he is no political animal, nor even a theologian, since what he preaches is a scarcely veiled anti-Feminism. Even his biblical quotations are travesties of the original texts. The assertion 'A beautiful woman is like a gold ring in the nose of the sow' misrepresents Proverbs 11:22: 'A beautiful *but empty-headed* woman is like a gold ring in the nose of the sow.' [My italics] The choice of this figure as one of several devils in Adrian Leverkühn's life calls for further comment.

Schleppfuss is essentially a creature of the sixteenth century. He is steeped in the world of late mediaeval demonology and utterly oblivious of the preoccupations of the present. For Thomas Mann, this represented a remarkable characteristic of his country. Unlike other nations, Germany had not moved with the times. Adrian Leverkühn's birthplace was near the town of Kaisersaschern ('Emperor's Ashes'), in which despite railway lines and modern industries, something survives of the spirit of schisms and heresies familiar from the Middle Ages. It is this world that Schleppfuss represents, not the visible manifestations of Nazi Germany, but a Germany of the soul, trapped in old-fashioned beliefs and outdated ways of looking at things, arrogant yet clumsy at the same time. This is how Thomas Mann perceives the nation's 'Faustian' legacy. Chasing the impossible, thrilled by a sense of danger, the nation cut itself loose from the world community in the manner in which Faust renounced the Christian community when he sought out the devil. It is a grand and a miserable destiny at the same time. Faust/Leverkühn goes his own way, caring little for how he is viewed by others. He achieves a pleasure that few can hope to experience. Yet the price he pays is as monstrous as the transgression: increasing isolation; inability to love in a way that warms; paralysis; damnation. These are the rewards that Leverkühn reaps in his capacity as a latter-day Faustus. Yet his punishment has a basis in reality; he contracts syphilis through contact with the prostitute Esmeralda. His sexuality was both stimulated and restrained by Schleppfuss' diatribes, and became perverted to the extent that Leverkühn eschews relationships with real women, preferring the company of men and the elusive, diseased Esmeralda.

Exactly half-way through the novel, Leverkühn records a visit from a shape-shifting stranger who claims to inform him of the deal he has already struck with the forces of evil when be became infected with syphilis. This visit confirms the pact years after the event. The devil combines the traits of his antecedents Kumpf and Schleppfuss and expresses himself in a bizarre Lutheran German that recalls the era of witch trials. The meeting is incorporated as a document into Leverkühn's biography.

> HE: 'To make an end and a conclusion will be agreeable to you. I have devoted much time and tarried long to entreat of this matter with you – I hope and trust you realise. But also you are an attractive case, that I freely admit. From early on we had an eye on you, on your quick, arrogant head, your mighty *ingenium* and *memoriam*. They have made you study theology, as your conceit devised it, but you would soon name yourself no longer of theologians, but put the Good Boke under the bench and from then on stuck to the figures, characters, and incantations of music, which pleased us not a little. For your vaine glory aspired to the elemental, and you thought to gain it in the form most mete for you, where algebraic magic is married with corresponding cleverness and calculation and yet at the same time it always boldly warres against reason and sobriety. But did we then not know that you were too clever and cold and chaste for the element; and did we not know that you were sore vexed thereat and piteously bored with your shamefast cleverness? Thus it was our busily prepensed plan that you should run into our arms, that is of my little one, Esmeralda, and that you got it, the illumination, the *aphrodisiacum* of the brain, after which with body and soul and mind you so desperately longed. To be short, between us there needs no crosse way in the Spesser's Wood and no cercles. We are in league and business – with your blood you have affirmed it and promised yourself to us, and are

baptised ours. This my visit concerns only the confirmation thereof. Time you have taken from us, a genius's time, high-flying time, full twenty-four years *ab dato recessi*, which we set to you as the limit. When they are finished and fully expired, which is not to be foreseen, and such a time is also an eternity – then you shall be fetched. Against this meanwhile shall we be in all things subject and obedient, and hell shall profit you, if you renay all living creature, all the Heavenly Host and all men, for that must be.'

I (*in an exceeding cold draught*): 'What? That is new. What signifies the *clausula*?'

HE: 'Renounce, it means. What otherwise? Do you think that jealousy dwells in the height and not also in the depths? To us you are, fine, well-create creature, promised and espoused. Thou maist not love.'

I (*really have to laugh*): 'Not love! Poor divel! Will you substantiate the report of your stupidity and wear a bell even as a cat, that you will base business and promise on so elastic, so ensnaring a concept as love? Will the Devil prohibit lust? If it be not so, then he must endure sympathy, yea, even caritas, else he is betrayed just as it is written in the books. What I have invited, and wherefore you allege that I have promised you – what is then the source of it, prithee, but love, even if that poisoned by you with God's sanction? The bond in which you assert we stand has itself to do with love, you doating fool. You allege that I wanted it and repaired to the wood, the crosse-waye, for the sake of the work. But they say that work itself has to do with love.'

HE (*laughing through his nose*): '*Do, re, mi*! Be assured that thy psychological feints do not trap me, any better than do the theological. Psychology – God warrant us, do you still hold with it? That is bad, bourgeois nineteenth century. The epoch is heartily sick of it, it will soon be a red rag to her, and he will simply get a crack on the pate, who disturbs life by psychology. We are entering into times, my friend, which will not be hood-winked by psychology ... This *en passant*. My condition was clear and direct, determined by the legitimate jealousy of hell. Love is forbidden you, in so far as it warms. Thy life shall be cold, therefore thou shalt love no human being. What are you thinking then? The illumination leaves your mental powers to the last unimpaired, yes, heightens them to an ecstatie of delirium – what shall it then go short of save the dear soul and the priceless life of feeling? A general chilling of your life and your relations to men lies in the nature of things – rather it lies already in your nature; in faith we lay upon you nothing new, the little ones make nothing new and strange out of you, they only ingeniously strengthen and exaggerate all that you already are. The coldness in you is perhaps not prefigured, as well as the paternal head paynes out of which the pangs of the little sea-maid are to come? Cold we want you to be, that the fires of creation shall be hot enough to warm yourself in. Into them you will flee out of the cold of your life....'

I: 'And from the burning back to the ice. It seems to be hell in advance, which is already offered me on earth.'

HE: 'It is that extravagant living, the only one that suffices a proud soul. Your arrogance will probably never want to exchange with a lukewarm one. Do you strike with me? A work-filled eternity of human life shall you enjoy. When the houre-glasse runs out, then I shall have good power to deal and dole with, to move and manage the fine created Creature after my way and my pleasure, be it in life, soul, flesh, blood or goods – to all eternity!' (Thomas Mann, 241f.)

Here Thomas Mann goes back directly to the Faust Book of 1587, ignoring much of what Goethe and others since contributed to the tradition. Adrian is credited with 'a quick, arrogant head, [a] mighty *ingenium* and *memoriam*', just as Doctor Faustus was by the sixteenth-century author whose language Mann takes great pains to emulate. Adrian studied theology, but abandoned it in favour of music, his consuming interest and one which he advances through the invention of new a method of composition. But a terrible price is exacted. No 'crosse way in the Spesser's Wood' and no magic circles are required of him, but he is bound by a pact no less severe than that of the original doctor: he cannot love, he cannot marry, he will be granted a twenty-four-year lifespan, 'a genius's time, high-flying time, full twenty-four years', but thereafter he will suffer the extremes of heat and cold, as in traditional visions of the sinner's torments in hell. Adrian is quick to recognise that the punishments with which he is threatened are merely an extension of his 'extravagant' life on earth: 'And from the burning back to the ice. It seems to be hell in advance, which is already offered me on earth.' The devil concurs: 'It is that extravagant living, the only one that suffices a proud soul. Your arrogance will probably never want to exchange with a lukewarm one.' His only achievement is in the advancement of modern music: atonal compositions in the manner of Arnold Schönberg are described with sentimental, possibly misdirected enthusiasm by the narrator. They are all desperate expressions of his personal torment: an unshakable belief in his own damnation. The crowning achievement of his career is 'The Lamentation of Doctor Faustus', a symphonic cantata during whose introductory performance in front of a group of friends he suffers his final breakdown, as Faustus had done after his cautionary 'oration' to his students.

Thomas Mann's novel is less narrowly political in its approach to the infected genius than Klaus's had been. Adrian Leverkühn is both a representative German, convinced of his vocation, his genius, his superiority over ordinary mortals, but he is also an artist, and as such a distant cousin of the many artist-figures who peopled the Faustian literature of the nineteenth century. So Thomas Mann is ultimately pointing a finger at several groups whom he sees as responsible for the moral as well as the political crisis of the twentieth century. These include passive aesthetes and inner émigrés beside the more vocal apologists for the Reich's cultural triumphalism in the wake of Richard Wagner and Alfred Rosenberg.

Trapped in a Meaningless Universe

Mon Faust is Paul Valéry's only play, begun in 1924 and left unfinished when he died in 1945. It is in two parts, described as sketches (*Ebauches*). The first part, *Luste or the Crystal Girl*, sub-titled a comedy, begins after Faust has read every book and experienced all there is to experience through the devil's services. The play is more of a rough draft than a polished drama and consists of only three characters: Faust's secretary, the image of the eternal feminine, a disciple given to repeating Faust's mistakes, and a helpless, obsolete and infirm Mephistopheles – the pact is somewhere in the distant past. Interaction with him is therefore limited, and Faust can and does deride him for his lack of fervour. The second sketch, *Le solitaire ou Les malédictions d'univers* ('The Solitary One or The Curses of the Universe'), a farce, has Faust abandon Mephistopheles and seek out a Solitary Sage who, poised between pure intellect and utter contempt for humankind, provides him with an answer to the problems that continue to torment him. His nihilistic diatribe gives the seeker scant comfort.

THE SOLITARY ONE: I too believed for a long time that the spirit was something that towered above all else. But then I observed that mine gave me scant service indeed, and was of almost no use in my everyday life. Everything I knew, everything I thought – certainties no less than curiosities – only played a negligible or negative role in the decisions and activities that mattered most to me ... Whatever is truly important affects, reduces or suppresses our thoughts, and that is actually a way of measuring their importance ... Thinking, yes, thinking is what destroys our pleasure and adds to our pain. Seriously, pain sometimes enhances the spirit. How can you deny that the product of suffering is also a product of degradation and chaos? By thinking? ... No, neither love nor sustenance becomes any easier or pleasanter. What is the use of intelligence if it cannot play a part in such important activities? Not only does it not play its part, but thinking actively infects, sullies, corrupts, and speeds up the pleasure of each succulent embrace ... I too was once very intelligent. I was more intelligent than I needed to be to make an idol of the mind. My own mind (which, incidentally, worked well enough) offered me no more than the enervating distillation of its wicked activity. The incessant activity of a force that invents, struggles, keeps trying, pushes itself to the limits in the narrowest confinement of the here and now, has no other effect than to produce incoherent desires, vain hypotheses, absurd problems, pointless regrets and imaginary fears.... (Valéry, 386)

There have been debates as to whether this lonely, contemptuous figure is sane or mad, diabolic or divine; or a caricature of our attempts to explain the universe through the medium of logic alone (Smeed, 77; Weinberg, 46-9; Dabezies, 321-60). His position is perhaps closer to that of an Existentialist in the mould of Camus and Sartre, sharing the former's perception of an absurd universe and the latter's icy disdain for the 'pure' but uncommitted intellect. It comes as no surprise that, having disposed of the spirit, the Solitary One dismisses love, creativity and science as worthless:

Even if words could communicate, they would be of precious little value. Whatever can be put into words is worthless. You know full well what people do with everything that can be put into words. Words generate their own vile currency, an instrument with which to mislead or seduce, dominate and exploit. But nothing that is pure, nothing of real substance or value can be transmitted. Reality cannot be communicated, absolutely not. Reality is what resembles nothing else, and which nothing can represent or explain. Reality signifies nothing, has no duration, no place in this world or in any other order – for duration, place, is what one being gives to another which is alien to it, and the world order demands that whatever is subject to it must result from an agent or force that is indifferent and extraneous to it ... Just look at the disorder of the heavens ... The way those little fires travel conveys a false idea of an ordered system. People just haven't quite worked it out as yet! But the little diagrams they draw are the work of someone who has noted their constituents, extrapolated from them, and constructed a trajectory from average positions that are mutually exclusive. Yet the star cannot be both here and there at the same time, no matter that the diagram shows it in all positions at once. So who has created this order? Human desire. But all it boils down to is a plot between him that sees and wants to see, and the object which he sees. (Valéry, 388f.)

Having escaped from the clutches of Mephistopheles, Faust now finds himself in the company of an utter nihilist. Language fails utterly in its job to communicate. Wittgenstein's *Tractatus logico-philosophicus* attempted to prove as much at roughly the same point in time. Goethe's Mephistopheles had proclaimed this same message to the Student in *Faust I*:

> [...] For at the point where concepts let you down
> A simple word pops up and serves you well.
> The word's a trusty ally in debate;
> The word enables each and all to state
> Their system of belief, their personal creed:
> Each jot and tittle's place is guaranteed. (F 1995–2000)

Neither nature, nor language, nor science serve any purpose in the frozen universe of pure logic. Contemplation may have been superior, in Valéry's eyes, to the vanities of literary production, but the insights produced by contemplation alone are frightening. The seeming order of the universe is quickly reduced to chaos when it is realised that the planetary orbits and astral constellations are the result of diagrams that create imaginary locations rather than marking actual positions. Chaos theory and entropy determine the twentieth-century universe, the classical models of physics have been subverted, and Faust has nothing to learn at the end of his journey. All that remains is for the Solitary One to toss him off the mountain, disdainfully, *comme une ordure* ('like a piece of rubbish', Valéry, 392). The deep pessimism of this work anticipates the spirit of a postwar generation that would orientate itself by Camus and Kafka rather than by the works of a less troubled 'classical' past. This Faust is an extreme example of a modern inquiry into the meaning of life; having exhausted all possibilities, action is replaced by experiments with rhetoric. The final dialogue propels him towards Nihilism and, however much this may run counter to the thrust of Valéry's productive career (Suckling, 193f.), the author can do no more than show his defeat at the hands of an enigmatic mastermind isolated in the barren wastes of a remote glacier.

Faust under Socialism

The end of the war in Europe saw, initially, a great debate as to the value of Goethe's work for German readers and thinkers. Thus the philosopher Karl Jaspers declared, in 1947, 'The cult of Goethe has had its day [...] The pleasure we freely took in admiring his greatness, our submission to the power of his love, our willingness to inhale his air should not stop us from doing what he himself refrained from: to look into the abyss' (reprinted *Welt am Sonntag*, 20 March 1949). Jaspers was attacked in many quarters for daring to criticise the icon. The controversy dragged on for years, with Ernst Robert Curtius citing Goethe as 'a force that will help Germany's youth to recover and grow strong' and Richard Alewyn delivering an inaugural lecture entitled 'Goethe as Alibi' in which he declared 'It is not acceptable to praise Goethe and deny Hitler' (*Die Zeit*, 2 July 1949; Alewyn, 686; Dabezies, 407–34). All this did not stop a renewed flourishing of revivals on stage, which initially culminated in Gustaf Gründgens' Hamburg production of 1957/8, subsequently filmed with Gründgens himself playing Mephistopheles opposite Will Quadflieg as Faust. In common with some postwar film directors, Gründgens alludes to topical fears of a nuclear holocaust in the witches' dance scene on the Brocken (Walpurgis Night).

While West German productions remained faithful to the traditional reading of the hero as a sincere but misguided philanthropist, attitudes to Faust polarised much more sharply in the German Democratic Republic, where, from the earliest days, more radical attempts were made to present Faust in a new light. Bertolt Brecht and Hanns Eisler attempted in different ways to revisit and probe the aura of classical serenity that had long covered Goethe like a suffocating blanket. Brecht attempted a production of *Urfaust* in Potsdam and Berlin in which he dared to sully the image of the doctor – who, one remembers, was in league with the devil – when he stressed that it was 'parasitic love, fixated on pleasure without regard for the consequences' that determined Faust's interaction with Gretchen, claiming that 'The entire first part of the tragedy will never come alive without the presence of a sinister note' (Brecht, XXVII, 332). This was specifically rejected by the press, with the official newspaper rebuking the dramatist for falsifying the classical source by foregrounding Faust's negative qualities (*Neues Deutschland*, 14 May 1953). When Eisler produced a libretto entitled *Johann Faustus* in 1952, portraying the doctor as a renegade who threw in his lot with the princes for the sake of fame and fortune, the reaction was several degrees sharper.

The reasons for the paradoxical traditionalism that prevailed in the socialist 'Workers' and Peasants' State' have been much debated; essentially, they spring from a desire to preserve the heritage of German culture and to interpret what is best within that heritage as pointing forward to a higher humanity – just such a humanity as the emerging state was attempting to implement. Goethe had therefore to be seen as foreshadowing socialism if he was to survive as an icon. And this could not be achieved unless the text itself was treated in upbeat fashion, as optimistically exuding an air of constructive humanitarianism. Even Walter Ulbricht, Party Secretary and effective Head of State, found it convenient to stress the legacy of 'Weimar' (where Goethe wrote his play), and its importance for the country in which the town of Weimar found itself after the division of Germany. He, too, saw Faust as a 'positive hero' and Goethe as anticipating the situation of the GDR at the end of *Faust II*. This marked a curious departure from the pre-war position of many socialists, who had tended to deride Goethe as 'the very essence of German philistinism' (thus the GDR's later Minister for Culture, Johannes R. Becher, back in 1928). The process that led to the eventual acceptance of the German classics of the eighteenth and nineteenth centuries as models for the future of Communism was a complex and laborious one. It was in no small measure due to the writings of veteran ideologue Georg Lukács in the 1930s and 1940s, who had consistently presented Faust as a self-sacrificing ideal hero. Ernst Bloch, likewise, was inclined to view him as a 'Promethean' figure. It is thus obvious that, however much Brecht and others tried to undertake a re-evaluation of the icon, the radical approach was neither favoured nor, in the majority of cases, tolerated, and from the time of Wolfgang Langhoff's production in Weimar in 1949 the image of Faust in the GDR remained coloured by a heavy-handed and over-reductive didacticism (Vietor-Engländer, 8, 17, 66-77, 135-73; Dabezies, 440-4).

The most significant contribution to the Faust legend to be attempted in the GDR, after Hanns Eisler's ill-fated opera (see 257-9, below), came in the form of a play by Volker Braun entitled *Hans Faust*. This was performed in 1968 to commemorate the 20th anniversary of the re-opening of the National Theatre in Weimar. It was surprising that Braun was chosen for this purpose, since he, too, had tampered with the cultural heritage of the nation, and the result was both radical and curiously ambivalent. It was not only a new Faust, but also the first attempt to put a GDR worker on stage with the intention of analysing and even questioning his heroism. Regrettably, the original text appears not to have survived. Despite generally positive reviews, Braun, like Brecht and Eisler before him, was made to feel that he was trespassing on the sacrosanct soil of Germany's cultural treasures. He had produced something more ambitious than a mere reworking: his *Hans Faust* – allegedly inspired by Ulbricht's speech of 1962 – was to provide the legend with a conclusion: a '*Faust, Part III*' in which the two canonical versions by Marlowe and Goethe were superseded by a third that was appropriate to the present. Ulbricht had actually claimed that the GDR would turn out to be the final part of Goethe's work, a *Faust III* ending in a hymn to collectivism. Braun's play was to be neither the tragedy of damnation nor the drama of salvation, but would distance itself in equal measure from the iconic repositories of sixteenth- and eighteenth-century values. The following synopsis has survived:

> This is the story of a marvellous friendship that came about in the darkest hour of the country that had been liberated for the benefit of mankind. That is when a man called Faust – a bricklayer, previously self-reliant – ran way ahead of Kunze, a locksmith who had been in a concentration camp and was now an official of the workers' party. Faust does not want change to come about 'step by step', but 'all at once'. He does not get far on his own. Kunze catches him at a moment of impotent despair. Faust becomes, unconditionally, a partner in a pact that is to last for as long as both are discontented with the new world, for as long as this new world needs their input to reshape it. Thus Kunze takes Faust to places where he must prove his social worth: a mine, a university, a village about to be collectivised. Supported by the power of the working class, Faust finds his strength greatly increased and carries out historic achievements. Kunze recognises his half-fantastic, half-realistic dreams as worthwhile goals, but Faust is still no more than an executor, incapable of independent thought and not yet a conscious member of his class. He fails as foreman of a building site at a chemical works. The relationship with Kunze breaks down. Faust withdraws to pursue scientific inquiries in solitude. These are not put to use. Kunze is thus obliged to doubt his previous methodology and turns instead to administrative work. At the instigation of Schliwa, Kunze recruits Faust to the council for scientific work. Faust now finds a task that maximises his social responsibility. He recognises it as political in all its implications and carries out his duties in conjunction with the full co-operation of his co-workers. Now it dawns on him that he is also

doing Kunze's work and that he and Kunze have become one. At the moment when he gains his most important insights into society and at the beginning of a state of harmony within it, Faust's powers desert the man who had wasted many years in a state of idleness. His tragic death is relativised by the prospect of a succession of 'new Fausts', who grew up side by side with him and will continue to grow. (Synopsis published by Ingrid Seyfarth in *Theater der Zeit*, 23/1968; cited Berghahn, 302)

Braun himself remained sceptical about the qualified optimism of this text, which though performed with some success was quickly subjected to major revisions. This may have been done in response to the public reception of the play, or may reflect personal disillusionment after the tragic events in Czechoslovakia in 1968, which were followed by the re-imposition of a heavy-handed censorship. Over a period of ten years, he re-wrote it several times, changing the title to *Hinze und Kunze* (roughly: *Tom and Dick*). The second version of 1973 is generally regarded as representing his intentions most accurately as well as providing the most convincing variation on the Faust theme (Berghahn, 313). It is the least optimistic, the central question being: is progress really worth all the sacrifices it demands? The Hans Faust of the 1968 text has become Hinze, Mephistopheles is represented by a fervently progressive party activist, Kunze, and Margarete is discernible in the figure of Marlies. Hinze's attempts to educate himself recall Faust, his graduation ceremony is an echo of Auerbach's Cellar. Marlies' abortion obviously recalls Margaret's pregnancy.

The fable becomes, under Braun's hands, an account of the proletarian struggle to create a worker's paradise in postwar East Germany. Hinze, a humble bricklayer, is close to despair at the beginning, delivering a short opening monologue expressing the utter hopelessness of his situation.

HINZE: To see at last
What will become of this ruined barren bloody stretch of land:
Nothing, I
Stand here one year in the mud and hammer
Stones in return for my grub
And for half a bed I beat my two
Arms sore and can do
No more, for here
There's nothing to be done. (Braun, 161)

A democratisation has taken place in so far as Hinze is no scholar, no learned sage, but a simple construction worker concerned more about his daily bread than about philosophic issues. And yet this play, too, will raise far-reaching questions about modern man's role in a changing environment. Braun's Mephisto is a political activist whose role it is to motivate the workers who are disillusioned after repeated wars and deprivations. He is a locksmith, and the hell from which he has recently emerged was a concentration camp. He offers nothing but more hardship, though there is a promise that if Hinze accepts his 'plan' they can work together towards a better tomorrow. Again, his tentative, self-deprecating overtures are modelled on the cryptic words spoken by Goethe's Mephistopheles:

Hinze:	Who are you?
Kunze:	I? What is a man, next to
	Nothing, why speak about me? Locksmith.
	I come from hell: the camp. There are
	Some like me I know, but these ones
	Don't know themselves.
Hinze:	You are a locksmith, I am a bricklayer. – What does this fellow think he
	can achieve? – So they took you? You're not exactly popular in this place,
	you know. Who are your comrades? They locksmiths too? Or joiners?
Kunze:	You are the one I might need.
	If you can do what is in our plan –
Hinze [interested]:	A plan?
Kunze:	I know what you are thinking: Perhaps
	I'm being tricked, sold down the river
	One more time. That's understandable.
	All of this can happen, if you listen to
	Those in high places, Hey, thinks he's Jesus,
	Thinks he knows it all? The devil's out to get me?
	That's what you think. Me, why listen? [Hinze *remains silent*]
	But those in high places have fallen. The plan will only have force if it
	inspires the masses. Grabs them by the neck. Many need to be forced
	into happiness. So you will come with us?
Hinze:	Where to?
Kunze:	You see the point now? Clearing rubble. No more.
Hinze:	Is that your plan? [Kunze *remains silent*]
	You can say it three times, but I
	Disagree. That's not
	What I'll assist you for.
Kunze [shouting]:	No, you just stand and stare, gobbling
	Potato peelings! On the free earth,
	Covered in rubble, a free people
	Mingle in their filth.
	You want to change things? In your dreams. All
	You understand is yourself, but wrongly. Go
	Back to your comfy lounge, throw yourself
	Into your armchair, wait
	For things to get better!
Hinze:	Yes! You dog! [*runs off*] (Braun, 166–168)

The dialogue is full of reminiscences of Goethe. Kunze's reluctance to reveal his identity, his seductive talk of a better future, a way out for man, while presenting himself as either Jesus or the devil, are distant reminders of the first scene in Faust's study. Other parallels include the entreaty to 'say it three times' and especially the reference to 'free people in their filth', a clear perversion of Faust's final vision (F 11579f). Braun's most audacious stroke was to equate Kunze with the devil; yet Goethe's was too often the advocate of social progress for the role to seem inappropriate here. It was he, after all, who ridiculed aristocratic privilege in Auerbach's Cellar. And if Hinze is reluctant to strike a bargain with his future comrade at this point, one is again reminded of the time taken by Faust to accede to his interlocutor in the study scene that cost Goethe so much effort two hundred years earlier. The 'pact' will be concluded shortly, in a scene that identifies the two men's relationship as such in the original terminology: 'Hinze concludes a pact with the power.' (Braun, 169)

The role of Margaret/Marlies is radically altered. Braun begins where Goethe finished. Marlies is, at the start, a weak, pregnant, soon-to-be abandoned ex-girlfriend of the hero, whom Hinze leaves behind, on Kunze's express instructions, when he embraces the socialist work ethic and departs for the mines. Yet Braun's *Faust* is not only a socialist *Faust* but also a feminist one, at least in so far as Marlies refuses to let her life be ruined by a faithless lover. She aborts her child and asserts herself by working her way up in the chemical plant until she is able to perform as well as Hinze.

Like other seriously meant parodies from the GDR (Ulrich Plenzdorf's *Werther*, Peter Hacks' *Tassow*, and, on the Faust theme, Rainer Kirsch's *Schlaghand*), Braun's is an experimental essay with provocative undertones. Written in the year of the Prague Spring, it took liberties not only with Goethe but also with the ideals of socialism. Marlies' abortion is not exactly a humanitarian act, and, more significantly still, the party functionary playing the part ascribed to the devil was not lost on reviewers in West Germany. Faust's quest for knowledge is replaced by a desire for change. The knowledge he gains is that not all tasks in life can be achieved by individuals working on their own; this was inoffensive enough, and to put it across did not require a laboured analogy with Faust. The authorities advised the 29-year-old author to distance himself from Faust, which he did.

Many other versions of Faust produced in the GDR are discussed by Deborah Vietor-Engländer in *Faust in der DDR*. They have one thing in common: they failed to satisfy the authorities, no matter how cleverly inventive or subtly parodistic they were. This applies no less to the operas by Hanns Eisler and Rainer Kunad than to Volker Braun and to Rainer Kirsch's *Heinrich Schlaghands Höllenfahrt* ('Henry Schlaghand's Descent into Hell'), as well as to the directors who staged innovative productions of Goethe. Kirsch's bitterly satirical comedy was published in 1973 but never performed. Walter Ulbricht and his successors did not live to see 'Faust III' enacted on German soil; that the conditions were not right was largely of their own making.

A Postmodern Faust

When Werner Schwab arrived on the German literary scene in 1990, the influential journal *Theater heute* declared him to be the young talent of the year. He changed the face of German drama with one *succès de scandale* after another before his early death in 1994. His 'radical comedies' with their mock-Baroque titles often referred to the classics of the German and Austrian stage. They are much more than mere parodies or updates. Schwab created a new language in which to convey his seemingly absurd plots, a language of which he remarked, 'Language pulls the characters along with it: like a tin can that has been tied to a dog's tail' (Schwab

(1993), 181). He has been commended for his excellent but unintelligible prose, which Julian Preece sees as worthy of an adjective, Schwabian, to go with Brechtian or Kafkaesque. Arguing that 'Language and the comic potential of word play were his overriding concerns', Preece claims that

> Schwab is at his funniest and most satirical [...] when he creates a gap between what is said and what is meant and when the way it is said is farcically inappropriate. In addition to the comic effect, this technique demonstrates once again how speakers are alienated from their speech, and how what they say does not belong to them. (Preece (1996), 269, 271)

Faust :: Mein Brustkorb : Mein Helm ('Faust :: My Thorax : My Helmet') opened in 1994 at the Hans-Otto Theatre in Potsdam, accompanied by music courtesy of punk group 'Einstürzende Neubauten', who used instruments constructed from tables, chairs and books for this purpose. It proved to be a work in which language is always centre stage. The following extract from scene 6 recreates Faust's first meeting with Margaret.

[*A street now runs through* FAUST'S *study. Several shadowy figures walk past in the background. Somewhere there is a telephone booth.* MARGARET *comes along, stops beside the booth and rummages around in her handbag, looking for a phone number. A slip of paper falls out but she doesn't notice it.* FAUST *approaches her tentatively and stares in complete confusion alternately at* MARGARET *and at the slip of paper*]

FAUST: If you would graciously excuse my lukewarm audacity, young lady, but would you grant to myself a retrospective permission that would enable me to raise up the slip of paper recently having emerged from your handbag back to the level of your protective handbagness?

[MARGARET *looks wearily at her bag, foully at the paper and revoltedly at* FAUST]

MARGARET: You are evidently and shamelessly in possession of blotches on the surface of your thought capacity, my fat friend, are you not? Otherwise you would already have picked up the anyway meaningless paper without wasting a word or you would have used your senseless eyes to automatically forget it.

FAUST: Wha-at? Without wings, you are able to overlook me as if I were an overeating person, notwithstanding I may be as delicate as a lung steak, able for the moment to gratuitously body forth a third world?

MARGARET: Tinged with death, without a doubt, Sir.

[MEPHISTO *sneaks up to them, picks up the paper and casually inserts it into* MARGARET'S *handbag.* MEPHISTO *and* MARGARET *contemplate one another at length and with detachment.*]

FAUST [*turning to* MARGARET]: You are certain to live in and experience this location
Which maybe I shall become acquainted with in your presence
I could meet you here and myself too
First it would be no more than auto-mimesis
But I could check myself until
In the end it would be Poetry itself
That would grab us like the devil on high
Umm don't you think that all of this might take on a thrilling façade
that is lucrative in the manner of high economics, were one to write it
off as a principle from the reality of possibilities and translate it into

the reality of realities, which would then, hungry for experiences, collect sediments that would quickly dispense with crutches in the reality of possibilities, such that it may deposit in the future that which the reality of realities might yet again precipitate. But can A SOMETHING precipitously precipitate something?

MARGARET [*turning to* Mephisto]: Does this unbrazenly grotesque person occupy a position of friendship in regard to yourself?

MEPHISTO: He is my flamethrower, the one that throws my flame, equally short-lived and conceited. Or turning to water: he is my as yet unconquered Hydra. People invented me in retrospect as a strong character, but they underestimated my hydrostatics. You may yet have to recognise all this in yourself.

MARGARET: Then strike yourself and allow yourself to be thrown, though it will all probably come to pass in a different way, as ever happens and must happen in boredom. (Schwab (1994), 102f.)

Schwab simultaneously parodies Goethe and extends the theme in the direction of a kind of postmodern absurdity, which involves a critique of our cosy relationship with language. Miesbacher's study of the Schwabian idiom shows how this is achieved through features which include misplaced modal verbs, inappropriate prefixes, excessive use of the passive voice, personification of objects, pleonasms, bureaucratic formulations and many other dislocations which can at best be rendered imperfectly into clumsy-sounding English (Miesbacher, 87–239). Underlying Schwab's re-working of the plot is a kind of love-hate relationship with Goethe that produces intriguing parallels set in the linguistic frame of pure parody; but behind the virtuosity of the elaborate façade, Faust, more phantom than real, is still recognisable as a seeker after new insights. The action is located in what Schwab designates as his 'Study-Room-Brain', and is best read as a sequence of interesting possibilities passing through his mind. After the encounter at the phone box, it is Mephisto and Margaret, his mental creations, who strike up the relationship that Faust desired for himself but which he is denied. Only by acknowledging his iconicity can Faust eventually cease to be Faust; the play suggests that this will ultimately liberate him from his traditional role.

Notes

1. Georg Dehio, *Geschichte der deutschen Kunst*. Berlin: De Gruyter, 1919, I, 16.
2. Goethe, *Wilhelm Meister's Apprenticeship*, VII, 9.
3. F 11241f.

Cited Works and Further Reading

Alexander Abusch, 'Faust - Held oder Renegat in der deutschen Nationalliteratur?' *Sinn und Form* 5 (1953), 179–94.
Richard Alewyn, 'Goethe als Alibi', *Hamburger Akademische Rundschau* 2 (1949), 685–87.
Anon., *Faust als Führer. Ein Buch für nachdenkliche Menschen*. Munich: Faust-Verlag, 1919.

Ferdinand Avenarius, *Faust. Ein Spiel.* Munich: Callwey, 1910.

Kirsten Belgum, Karoline Kirst-Gundersen, and Paul Levesque, '"Faust im Braunhemd": *Germanistik* and Fascism', in Grimm/Hermand, 153-67.

Klaus L. Berghahn, 'Den Faust-Mythos zu Ende bringen: Von Volker Brauns *Hans Faust* zu *Hinze und Kunze*' in Gerd Labroisse and Gerhard P. Knapp (eds), *Literarische Tradition heute: Deutschsprachige Gegenwartsliteratur in ihrem Verhältnis zur Tradition.* Amsterdam: Rodopi, 1988 (*Amsterdamer Beiträge zur neueren Germanistik* 24), 297-315.

Eric A. Blackall, '"What the devil?!" - Twentieth-Century Fausts', in Boerner/Johnson, 197-212.

Peter Boerner and Sidney Johnson (eds), *Faust through Four Centuries. Retrospect and Analysis. Vierhundert Jahre Faust. Rückblick und Analyse.* Tübingen: Niemeyer, 1989.

Wilhelm Böhm, *Faust der Nichtfaustische.* Halle: Niemeyer, 1933.

Volker Braun, *Texte in zeitlicher Folge.* 9 volumes. Halle: Mitteldeutscher Verlag, 1989-92; Volume VII: *Berichte von Hinze und Kunze; Der Eisenwagen; Schriften.*

Bertolt Brecht, *Grosse kommentierte Berliner und Frankfurter Ausgabe.* Ed. Werner Hecht *et al.* 30 volumes. Berlin: Aufbau/ Frankfurt/M: Suhrkamp, 1988-1992.

E.M. Butler, *The Fortunes of Faust.* Cambridge: University Press, 1952.

Karl Otto Conrady, 'In den Fängen der Vergangenheit. Der neue Streit über Germanisten und ihre Mitgliedschaft in der NSDAP', *Die Zeit* 50/2003, 49f.

André Dabezies, *Visages de Faust au XXe siècle. Littérature, idéologie et mythe.* Paris: Presses Universitaires de France, 1967.

Kurt Engelbrecht, *Faust im Braunhemd.* Leipzig: Klein, 1933.

Detlev Felken, *Oswald Spengler. Konservativer Denker zwischen Kaiserreich und Diktatur.* Munich: Beck, 1988.

Karl Gabler, *Faust-Mephisto der deutsche Mensch. Mit erläuternder Darlegung des romantischen und des Realinhalts von Goethes 'Faust'.* Berlin: Theodor Fritsch, 1938.

Claude Gandelman, 'The *Doctor Faustus* of Thomas Mann as a Drama of Iconicity', *Semiotica* 49 (1984), 27-47.

Reinhold Grimm and Jost Hermand (eds), *Our Faust? Roots and Ramifications of a Modern German Myth.* Madison: University of Wisconsin Press, 1987.

Sigfrid Hoefert, 'Die Faust-Problematik in Volker Brauns *Hinze und Kunze*: Zur Erbeaneignung in der DDR', in Gerd Labroisse (ed.), *Zur Literatur und Literatur-wissenschaft der DDR.* Amsterdam: Rodopi, 1973 (*Amsterdamer Beiträge zur neueren Germanistik* 7), 147-63.

Willi Jasper, *Faust und die Deutschen.* Berlin: Rowohlt, 1998.

Hans Keller, 'Figures in the *Rumpelkammer*: Goethe, Faust, Spengler', *Journal of European Studies* 13 (1983), 142-63.

Ernst Kratzmann, *Faust. Ein Buch von deutschem Geist.* Vienna: Artur Wolf, 1932. Rptd Vienna: Luser, 1938.

Johann von Leyden, *Faust der Politiker. Trauerspiel in vier Akten neben einem Nachspiel.* Heidelberg: Carl Winter, 1907.

Lothar Lohs, '"Es ist alles unmöglich, solange man am Leben ist"', *Die Bühne*, December 1991, 94-99.

Klaus Mann, *Mephisto.* Translated by Robin Smith. New York: Random House, 1977. Rptd Harmondsworth: Penguin, 1995.

—, *Der Wendepunkt.* Frankfurt/M: Fischer, 1958.

Thomas Mann, *Doctor Faustus. The Life of the German Composer Adrian Leverkühn as Told by a Friend.* Trans. by Helen Tracy Lowe-Porter. London: Martin Secker & Warburg, 1949. Rptd Harmondsworth: Penguin, 1968.

Walter Mayr, '"Ich bin doch immun." Walter Mayr über das zweite Leben des SS-Mannes Hans Schneider', *Der Spiegel* 49 (1995), 94-97.

Harald Miesbacher, *Die Anatomie des Schwabischen: Werner Schwabs Dramensprache.* Graz: Literaturverlag Droschl, 2003.

Ariane Mnouchkine (ed.), *Mephisto, le roman d'une carrière d'après Klaus Mann*. Paris: Solin, 1979.

—, *Mephisto, geschrieben für des Théâtre du Soleil nach Klaus Mann: 'Mephisto, Roman einer Karriere'*. Munich: Ellermann, 1980.

Robert Petsch (ed.), *Goethes Faust*, Leipzig: Bibliographisches Institut, 1925.

Lucie Pfaff, *The Devil in Thomas Mann's 'Doktor Faustus' and Paul Valéry's 'Mon Faust'*. Berne: Herbert Lang, 1976.

Constanze Pollatschek, 'Ein neuer Faust', *Wochenpost*, 9 August 1968.

Julian Preece, 'Form, Structure, and Poetry in the Varied Plays of Werner Schwab', in Frank Finlay and Ralf Jeutter (eds), *Centre Stage: Contemporary Drama in Austria*. Amsterdam: Rodopi, 1999, 15-30.

—, 'The Use of Language in the Dramas of Werner Schwab: Towards a Definition of "das Schwabische",' in Arthur Williams, Stuart Parkes, and Julian Preece (eds), *Contemporary German Writers, Their Aesthetics and Their Language*. Berne: Lang, 1996, 267-82.

Werner Rieck, 'Hendrik Höfgen: Zur Genesis einer Romanfigur Klaus Manns', *Weimarer Beiträge* 4 (1969), 697-709.

Alfred Rosenberg, *Der Mythus des 20. Jahrhunderts. Eine Wertung der seelisch-geistigen Gestaltenkämpfe unserer Zeit*. 1930. Munich: Hoheneichen Verlag, 1936.

Else Rost, *Goethes 'Faust', eine Freimaurertragödie. Verusch einer Klärung – kein Kommentar*. Munich: Ludendorffs Verlag, 1931.

Peter Schmitt, *Faust und die 'deutsche Misere'. Studien zu Brechts dialektischer Theaterkonzeption*. PhD Dissertation, Erlangen, 1980.

Werner Schwab, *Faust :: Mein Brustkorb : Mein Helm*. In *Ibid., Dramen III*. Graz: Literaturverlag Droschl, 1994, 75-134.

—, *Mein Hundemund*. In *Ibid., Fäkaliendramen*. Graz: Literaturverlag Droschl, 1993, 179-235.

Hans Schwerte, *Faust und das Faustische. Ein Kapitel deutscher Ideologie*. Stuttgart: Klett, 1962.

Eberhard Spangenberg, *Karriere eines Romans: Mephisto, Klaus Mann und Gustaf Gründgens. Ein dokumentarischer Bericht aus Deutschland und dem Exil 1925-1981*. Munich: Ellermann, 1982.

Oswald Spengler, *The Decline of the West*. Authorised Translation with Notes by Charles Francis Atkinson. 2 volumes. London: Allen and Unwin, 1926.

Wilhelm Steffens, *Grabbe*. Velber: Friedrich, 1966.

Fiona Malcolm, *The Literary Relationship between Klaus and Thomas Mann*. PhD Dissertation, University of Kent, Canterbury, 2004.

Norman Suckling, *Paul Valéry and the Civilized Mind*. London: Oxford University Press, 1954.

Arnold J. Toynbee, *A Study of History*. 12 volumes. London: Oxford University Press, 1934-1961.

Hans Rudolf Vaget, 'Amazing Grace: Thomas Mann, Adorno, and the Faust Myth', in Grimm/Hermand, 168-89.

Paul Valéry, *Mon Faust*. In *Ibid., Oeuvres*, ed. J. Hytier. 2 volumes. Volume II, Paris: Gallimard, 1960, 276-403.

Deborah Vietor-Engländer, *Faust in der DDR*. Frankfurt/M: Peter Lang, 1988.

Kurt Weinberg, *The Figure of Faust in Valéry and Goethe*. Princeton: University Press, 1976.

Chapter Six

From Bare Boards to Computer Graphics: *Faust* in Performance

Faust has every element: wit, pathos, wisdom, farce, mystery, melody, reverence, doubt, magic and irony; not a chord of the lyre is unstrung, not a fibre of the heart untouched.—George Henry Lewes

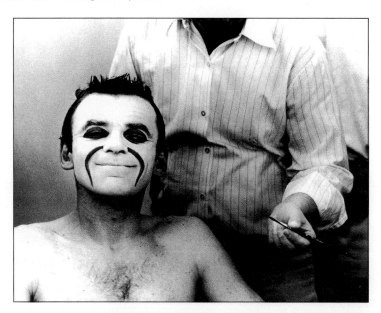

19. *Branko Samarowski is transformed into Mephistopheles, Stuttgart 1977. Photograph by Abisag Tüllmann*

JOHN HOUSEMAN, co-producer of the 1937 adaptation of Marlowe's *Doctor Faustus* in which Orson Welles made his acting début, used his autobiography *Run-Through* of 1972 to comment on a parallel between the actor and the character he played:

Orson was always, at heart, a magician [...] The truth is that the legend of the man who sells his soul to the devil in exchange for knowledge and power and who must finally pay for his brief triumph with the agonies of eternal damnation was uncomfortably close to the shape of Welles' own personal myth. Orson really believed in the devil. This was not a whimsy but a very real obsession. At twenty-one Orson was sure he was doomed. [...] There were moments when Faustus seemed to be expressing some of Welles' personal agony and private terror. (Houseman, 233-35)

Anyone studying Faust's many incarnations on the modern stage will be struck by the number of times critics and casual observers have noted a resemblance between the literary characters and the lives of those who represent them. From Henry Irving to Orson Welles, from Gustaf Gründgens to Richard Burton, the great impersonators of the lead roles have been credited with Faustian or Mephistophelean traits. This is just one of the remarkable facets of the history of Faust on stage, demonstrating as it does the ready adaptability of the 'icon' as a cipher for qualities that are all too familiar in the modern world: thirst for knowledge and power, the lure of the forbidden and the dream of a richer alternative life. How these themes were put across to theatre audiences over the centuries is a key aspect of Faust's continuing resonance.

First on the Stage: Marlowe in London

The first spectators to witness the unfolding of the 'tragical history' of Dr Faustus on stage resided at a considerable remove from the land in which he originated. The religious issues that shaped the Faust Book were of importance to all Christians at the time, yet theological dilemmas are not primarily what brought in the crowds to watch Marlowe's play. Quite the reverse; the Lutherans whose views the chapbook set out to disseminate were, ironically, the first to register their opposition when Faustus made his début on the London trestles. A keen interest in watching plays of all sorts motivated the relatively sophisticated and broad-minded London audiences to flock to this spectacle in the 1590s in defiance of the rising tide of iconoclastic Puritanism. In Germany the situation was quite different. There, very few permanent theatres had evolved in the turbulent post-Reformation phase, and those that had were for the most part either makeshift venues dependent on the itineraries of travelling players, or court institutions given over to such entertainments as appealed to the nobility of the day.

Little is known of how, when, and why Christopher Marlowe came to dramatise a story that had only recently begun to circulate as a moral tract in Germany. There is evidence that *Doctor Faustus* attracted interest in England almost as soon as the Faust Book appeared in Frankfurt. A ballad circulated in broadsheet format just two years later, and by 1592, the translation of the entire chapbook had been printed not once but several times. This may have first appeared at any time between 1587 and 1592. Marlowe's dramatisation is hard to date, as there are no records of a production during his lifetime. The critics disagree; Wraight suggests

1589 as the year of composition, 1592 as the year of revision; Greg claims that Marlowe wrote *Doctor Faustus* 'during the last year of his life'. (Wraight, 158; Greg, 6) Given the uncertain dates of the translation and of Marlowe's *Tragical History*, it cannot be determined whether the latter is based on the English chapbook, the German original, oral tradition such as that of the ballad, or on other sources no longer available to us. All that is certain is that Marlowe's adaptation of comic episodes such as the horse-courser (scene 10 in the 'A' text) reveals familiarity with the prose chapbook or with one of its sources, from which he must at some time have drawn inspiration.

20. First Faustus: Edward ('Ned') Alleyn, inscribed 1626.
By permission of the Trustees of Dulwich Picture Gallery.

Plays by Marlowe were performed at the Rose Theatre by the Admiral's Men in 1593, the year of the poet's death, but there is no proof that *Doctor Faustus* was among them. Greg's views on performance are highly conjectural: 'It was performed, presumably on the London stage, by some unidentified company, no doubt before the plague of 1592–4 reached its height and put a stop to all acting.'

194

He also surmises that a different group, the Earl of Pembroke's Men, performed *Doctor Faustus* in London during January 1593 and in other parts of the country later that year. (Greg, 60f.) 1593 was a bad year for the London theatre on account of the plague in February, which led to the closure of many public venues. It was not until the following year that a recovery set in, due in part to the increasing involvement of William Shakespeare and in part to the tireless efforts of Philip Henslowe, the entrepreneurial London impresario. Readers may recall Geoffrey Rush's flamboyant portrayal of this character in the 1997 film *Shakespeare in Love*. Henslowe was the most successful of Elizabethan theatre managers. His diary records that 'docter ffostose' earned him three pounds and twelve shillings in 1594, more than any other production in that year. (Foakes/Rickert, 25–7)

The earliest indisputable performance was on 30 September 1594. Henslowe's meticulous accounts show that the play continued to attract large audiences for several years, with Henslowe's son-in-law, Edward ('Ned') Alleyn, who along with Richard Burbage was considered the most accomplished actor in Elizabethan England, appearing in the title role. Alleyn was both Faustian in his commitment to education (he founded Dulwich College) and Mephistophelean in his patronage of blood sports and the ownership of brothels in London's Bankside. Twenty-four performances by him are recorded between 1594 and 1597, as are some of the props used: 'I dragon in fostes'; 'faustus ierkin and clok', and perhaps also 'the sittie of Rome' as a backdrop to the 'B' text's third act. (Greg, 11) It has been suggested that Alleyn may have owned the text of *Doctor Faustus*, though it is pure speculation that the declining income from this play in 1597 was due to a farewell 'benefit' performance for him on his retirement. (Wraight, 211) A printed version was promised in 1601 but appears to have been withheld for several further years, if only to ensure that the stage version would continue to draw in the crowds. By 1602, we have evidence that the text was being altered; Henslowe notes that he paid the relatively large sum of four pounds to a William Byrde and a Samuel Rowle for their 'adycions' on 22 November of that year.

These 'additions' have been explained variously as being due to public demand for new material, censorship, Alleyn's retirement from acting, the transfer of the Admiral's Men from the Rose Theatre to the Fortune Theatre, and to changing tastes following the accession of James I to the English throne, factors discussed in detail by Sharpe and Wraight. It is assumed that the 'B' text incorporates the additions, although a rival theory claims that 'B' is the original, and 'A' is a shortened version, either reconstructed from memory or curtailed for the purpose of a less encumbered play. It would be convenient to argue that 'B' is Marlowe's text plus the Byrde/Rowle material, were it not for the fact that their lines had been completed and paid for some two years before 'A' was printed, suggesting that 'A' itself was a dilution of Marlowe's original. The absence in the 'B' text of most references to 'God' and 'Christ' and their replacement by the more neutral term 'heaven' must be attributed to the Act of Abuses of 1606 which prohibited players from using 'the name of God or of Christ Jesus, or of the Holy Ghost or of the Trinity' on stage.

Although specific dates are hard to establish, and the Admiral's Men change their names with confusing frequency, becoming the Earl of Nottingham's Men, Prince Henry's Men, and the Palgrave's Men as they switch patrons, interest in *Doctor Faustus* did not diminish, as can be seen from the nine separate printings of the text between 1604 and 1631. By 1666 the number had increased to thirteen. The available data is sufficient to indicate that what audiences saw of Faustus' career in 1616 was very different from what had been represented by Ned Alleyn just a few years earlier. The anti-papal scenes were extended, the humour became more slapstick. Yet after all the ribald jokes and tomfoolery, there is also greater emphasis on Faustus' punishment and suffering; and the audiences will have left the theatre with a final reminder of how the magus died, having seen the scholars return to the scene of his death and contemplate his dismembered body:

1 SCHOLAR:	Come gentlemen, let us go visit Faustus,
	For such a dreadful night was never seen
	Since first the world's creation did begin;
	Such fearful shrieks and cries were never heard.
	Pray heaven the doctor have escaped the danger.
2 SCHOLAR:	O help us, heaven! See, here are Faustus' limbs,
	All torn asunder by the hand of death.
3 SCHOLAR:	The devils whom Faustus served have torn him thus;
	For 'twixt the hours of twelve and one, me thought
	I heard him shriek and call aloud for help,
	At which self time the house seemed all on fire
	With dreadful horror of these damned fiends.
2 SCHOLAR:	Well, gentlemen, though Faustus' end be such
	As every Christian heart laments to think on,
	Yet, for he was a scholar, once admired
	For wondrous knowledge in our German schools,
	We'll give his mangled limbs due burial;
	And all the students clothed in mourning black,
	Shall wait upon his heavy funeral.

(According to Jump, 103f., this is Scene 20. Gill lists it as 13a)

As Jump has shown, we can gain a few tantalising glimpses of early seventeenth-century productions of *Doctor Faustus* from contemporary commentators. One of these was John Melton, whose *Astrologaster* of 1620 describes a visit to the Fortune Theatre in Golding Lane. 'There indeede a man may behold shagge-hayr'd Deuills runne roaring ouer the Stage with Squibs in their mouthes, while Drummers make Thunder in the Tyring-house, and the twelue-penny Hirelings make artificiall Lightning in their Heauens.' (Melton, 31) But the success of such productions was short-lived. Increasingly, we find Puritan authorities condemning the light-hearted representations of demons on stage. William Prynne, for example, objected to 'the visible apparition of the Devill on Stage' in profane enactments of the life of Doctor Faustus, which to the English Puritan pamphleteer seemed a true story. There is even an account of a production of *Doctor Faustus the Conjurer* at Exeter, when the actors were said to have taken fright in mid-play, believing that 'there was one devell too many amongst them'. They stopped the performance and sent the audience home, and in sharp contrast to their normal custom spent the evening in prayer before hastening out of town. This account exists in several versions and may well be a fabrication. Increasing pressures from Puritan quarters led to the closure of theatres throughout England in 1642. They reopened following the Restoration of the monarchy in 1660, and during the next fifteen years there were several revivals. Samuel Pepys records seeing a 'wretchedly and poorly done' performance of *Doctor Faustus* on 26 May 1662. A new, extended edition appeared in 1663, but this did not help the play to regain its earlier popularity, and after a few years it disappears from the British stage, not to be seen there for a period of just over two hundred years. (Jump, lviii–lxiii)

Return to Continental Europe

Continental revivals of Marlowe's play, in severely truncated adaptations, prevented Faustus from sinking into oblivion and enabled him to re-emerge as Faust when the time was ripe. Germany had been weakening due to internecine strife ever since the late Middle Ages. This process was exacerbated by religious wars. Yet her very lack of cultural cohesion kept the story alive in an unexpected format. A market existed for itinerant entertainers, some of whom used glove or string puppets; many were English actors who specialised in providing a service to the theatre-starved audiences of central Europe. Thus we have a production of *Doctor Faustus* in Graz, Austria, in 1608. This, the earliest performance recorded in continental Europe, is mentioned in a letter by the Duchess Magdalena to her brother Ferdinand in Regensburg. Listing the activities of a group of English Players, she states tersely 'On Sunday they performed Doctor Faustus'. (Mahal *et al.*, 87)

Throughout the next 150 years, this was how the memory of the pact was kept alive in the popular imagination. There are many references to Faustian spectacles in various parts of the continent, but hard and fast details are lacking. Performances were given in Bremen (1688), Hanover, Hamburg, Berlin (1703), Danzig (1668), Dresden (1626), Prague (1651), Basle, Munich and Graz (1608). (Scheidig/Theens, 102) Not a single authentic script has survived from this period, though several reconstructions have been attempted, showing Faustus in dialogue not only with the devil, but also with the figure of Punch – 'Kasperle', 'Pickelhäring', or 'Hans Wurst', as he was know in different parts of the country.

> At the outset, Pluto emerges from hell and calls upon one devil after another: the tobacco devil, the whoring devil, but also, among many others, the cunning devil, and gives them orders to cheat and trick people wherever possible. Thereupon it happens that Doctor Faustus, dissatisfied with conventional science, acquires magical books and summons devils to serve him, which he does by testing their speed and choosing the one that is fastest. It is not enough to be as fast as a deer, a cloud, or the wind, but he wants a spirit that is as fast as the thoughts of men, and as soon as the devil has presented himself to Faustus as such, he desires him as his servant for 24 years and offers to be his on these terms. This the devil does not immediately grant,

but he refers the matter to Pluto, and with the latter's approval he concludes a pact with Faustus, which is signed in his blood. Thereupon a hermit warns Faustus to renounce it, but without success. Faustus manages to conjure up all spirits, he sees Charlemagne and the fair Helen of Troy, with whom he takes his pleasure. Eventually his conscience awakens, and he counts out the hours till twelve o'clock, and talks to his servant and warns him against magic. Then Pluto appears and commands his demons to fetch Doctor Faustus. This happens and they throw him into hell and tear him apart. It is also shown how he is tortured in hell, where he is pulled up and pulled down and the following words are seen writ in fire: *Accusatus est, judicatus est, condemnatus est*. (Report by Georg Schröder, Danzig, 1668; cited by Scheidig/Theens, 87; Palmer/More, 245f.)

This synopsis indicates that not all performances of the time were necessarily dominated by jesters and harlequin figures. The essence of the story is there in outline, with Pluto appearing as a diabolical overlord whose function was to obscure the theological context. Fusions between classical and Christian topics were not uncommon in the Baroque period, with Pluto rather than Lucifer appearing as the tempter-in-chief. As in previous versions, the devil who serves Faust is a servant in two senses; he obeys Faustus, but is also subservient to a higher power. A further characteristic of these later productions is the notion of speed as the distinguishing quality of Mephistopheles. It offers a rational explanation for the apparent miracles. Thus in several eighteenth-century versions, including Lessing's, various devils are mustered and tested by Faust for their agility, and the one that is as quick as the thoughts of man is eventually given the contract. The following poster is the oldest surviving advertisement for a theatre production on the Faust theme, given at Bremen in 1688. It provides an outline of a much-watered-down tragedy, in which the harlequin figure *Pickelhäring* plays a central role.

Today, Friday 18th May, the Saxon High German Comedians will present at their venue the unforgettable and world-renowned play, known as: The Life and Death of the great arch-conjurer Dr Johannes Faustus, excellently performed in full, with entertainment afforded by Pickelhäring. The following scenes are offered for the admiration of the public:

1. Pluto rides in the air on a dragon.
2. Doctor Faustus performs magic and conjures the spirits.
3. Pickelhäring wants to gather money but is tormented by all sorts of magic birds in the air.
4. Doctor Faustus gives a banquet at which the main dishes are transformed into all kinds of wonderful figures.
5. Wonderful to behold how human beings, dogs, cats, and other animals come out of a pastry and fly through the air.
6. A fire-breathing raven comes flying though the air and announces to Faustus his approaching death.
7. Faustus is carried away by the spirits.
8. Finally, hell itself is represented with the aid of beautiful fireworks.

In conclusion, the whole action shall once again be presented in silhouettes in the Italian style, in an unusual manner that is certainly worth twice the admission price. This will include a masquerade of six persons, a Spaniard, two jugglers, a schoolmaster, a farmer and a farmer's wife, all of whom will dance in an uncommonly humorous manner. (Palmer/More, 246 f.)

This bombastic advertisement is as close as we get to a synopsis of the kind of spectacle that built up around the name of Doctor Faustus one hundred years after Marlowe. The spectacular features are typical of the Baroque theatre, in which, originally under Italian influence, glittering detail was viewed as essential. Fire-breathing ravens and dancing peasants may have little to do with the original chapbook, but they point forward to the rich embellishments with which the plot was endowed in the eighteenth and nineteenth centuries. Goethe included a peasants' dance, talking animals and fantastic visual effects in his version. His first contact with the theme was at a spectacle such as that outlined above.

There have been many other types of event involving shadow puppets and even performing dogs. In 1716 the Augsburg brewer Rudolph Lang trained his two black hounds 'Mosche' and 'Hanswurst' to perform tricks. They were first presented in public in 1717. The show included a somewhat truncated version of 'Doctor Faust'. (Lang, 102; Andreas Meier, 62f.) Following a successful appearance in his hometown, Lang travelled through southern Germany and Austria with these performing beasts between 1718 and 1721. Although he was suspected of wizardry, his shows were much praised and evidently lucrative.

21. Performance of Doctor Faustus by Rudolph Lang's dogs, circa 1720.
Source: Lang, illustration nr. 50.

Karl Simrock's attempt to reconstruct the puppet plays dates from 1846. It gives an impression of the versions that were circulating in Germany one century earlier, but cannot be relied on for authenticity. The connection between Faustus and puppets is nonetheless very strong, not only because of its visual effectiveness, but also because Faustus himself acts in a mechanical way and functions as the devil's puppet. So while it may seem slightly grotesque that the titanic struggle between Faustus and hell's minions should be represented by mere puppets, recent attempts to recreate these productions have been well received. There are many. Henning lists 62 puppet plays in German and a further 23 in other languages in his bibliography, to which Theens adds 31 dating from the twentieth century. Most of these appeared in limited editions and are difficult to trace; some were performed to commemorate specific events and were soon forgotten (Henning, I, 342–53; Scheidig/Theens, 94).

From Scene Selection to Total Theatre

Marlowe's *Doctor Faustus* was repeatedly re-written for the stage; Lessing's remained a fragment, but the status of Goethe's *Faust* is far more ambiguous. Its stage history is chronicled in detail by Bernd Mahl, to whom I am indebted for much information on the subject. Although several of Goethe's other works were performed almost as soon as they were written, *Faust* remained a closet drama for many years. The author talked and wrote about his plans, but rarely exposed his drafts to public scrutiny in any detail. When the 'first part' was finally printed in 1808, Goethe was approached with a view to arranging a public performance. A letter to the composer Carl Friedrich Zelter of 1810 is both encouraging and sceptical on the question of staging the work in its published form.

> Finally [I can] report that we are faced with a strange enterprise, namely to perform *Faust* is it stands, insofar as that should prove at least partially achievable. Would that you might provide us with some assistance in composing music, especially for the Easter chorus and the lullaby song [...] (Goethe to Zelter, 10 November 1810)

An attempt was made, with Goethe's approval, to adapt the play to the conventions of the day; this involved dividing it into five acts, as befitted a tragedy. Act I was to have contained no more than the 'Dedication' and the two prologues, which were subsequently destined to be omitted from most nineteenth-century productions. Act II was to comprise eight scenes, from 'Night' to the first 'Study' scene in which Mephistopheles appears, Act III would run from the pact scene to Faust's first visit to Gretchen's bedroom, and Act IV would end with the Evil Spirit taunting Gretchen in the cathedral. Goethe's own illustrations may give an idea of how one might resolve the problem of putting spirits and celestial beings on stage (see 284–6, below). But the plan to stage *Faust* in Weimar did not come to fruition and Goethe made no further attempts to promulgate it as a stage work. Moreover, the volumes of illustrations produced over the years by many artists (Cornelius, Retzsch, Seibertz and others) may also have put a dampener on the would-be producer: they seemed to confirm the view that the play was best approached visually and read in book form, while at the same time providing evidence of the complexity of scenes such as 'Walpurgis Night'. The view gained ground that these could never be adequately represented in a conventional theatre.

Not only artists but musicians, too, were involved in producing accompaniments to the play. The Berlin nobleman Anton Heinrich Radziwill provided music for a melodramatic implementation of the early scenes. He recited his work to Goethe, accompanying himself on the cello. The poet was impressed and the temptation to see how it would work was great. Karl Graf von Brühl has the distinction of attempting the first production before a private audience with minimal publicity, albeit with numerous additions and musical effects. Zelter directed the choir. The première, which followed three years of rehearsals, was on 24 May 1819. Little has been published on this production, since the general public were excluded and there were no press reviews. Some accounts of the rehearsals have survived, as have sketches of the scenery (Mahl, 11–15). The score was recently rediscovered in Minsk, Belarus, and, in combination with other fragments found in Cracow, was staged in the local language by the National Opera of Belarus.[1]

The productions undertaken in many parts of Germany ten years thereafter are often assumed to have been intended to honour the poet's 80th birthday. This was not entirely true, as Mahl and Parenth have shown. The circumstances were fortuitous. Dr August Klingemann, director of the court theatre at Brunswick, had written a *Faust* of his own (see 134, above) and had it performed anonymously in the autumn of 1828. He explained to his patron, Archduke Karl, a regular theatre-goer, that his work was not Goethe's, and the Archduke insisted that Goethe should also be performed at Brunswick. Klingemann, alarmed at the prospect, commented that Goethe's *Faust* had not been intended for the stage. The Archduke demanded to see a copy and returned it to Klingemann with the scribbled instruction 'To be performed' (Mahl, 16).

Klingemann sought Goethe's approval for the première at Brunswick on 14 January 1829, and was told that the poet no longer had any interest in the theatre, but since the published text was now common property, he was free to do as he pleased with it (Parenth, 48). Klingemann took many decisions that were later imitated elsewhere. Despite massive cuts, the spectacle lasted for four and a half hours. The following principles were adopted: to strip out the prologues and short stand-alone scenes (Gretchen at the spinning-wheel, Gretchen at the well with Lieschen), to follow the illustrators (especially Retzsch and Cornelius) meticulously, both in terms of layout and of costume, and to end with Faust being bundled off the stage as if to suggest that Mephistopheles had triumphed. This tied in with the opinion that Faust would be damned and involved no great inconsistency, as the Prologue in Heaven had been omitted. The play was well received in Brunswick and, in sharp contrast to other venues, remained on the programme for many years (Mahl, 16–20).

Klingemann showed that *Faust* could make money at the box-office. Productions followed at Weimar with the reluctant involvement of the author, as well as in his native Frankfurt, in Dresden and in Leipzig. Klingemann rendered his emulators a further service by offering his director's notebook for sale; Ludwig Tieck relied heavily on it at Dresden in a production marred by savage cuts and bowdlerising. Anything to do with the church, religion, or physical intimacy was ruthlessly excised, often with amusing results and always to the detriment of Goethe's verse. Similar things happened in Goethe's hometown, where the poet noted laconically in his diary on his eightieth birthday, 'Evening alone. *Faust* performed at the theatre'; he evidently preferred not to witness the local première of his greatest work. His reaction to the original plan had been far from positive:

> Herr von Müller put the matter to him calmly, but as previously mentioned, he appears to have used the expression 'It has been decided'. Goethe responded as if a hornet had stung him: 'Do people think that if I had been minded to do so I could not have put *Faust* on stage myself? Is it fair to dispose of my works without enquiring into my own intentions? Am I not still alive? *It has been decided*, has it? So people have *decided* without troubling to consult me?' His friends found themselves in a most embarrassing situation. Yet the matter took its course, like so many other things that had originally met with his opposition but were carried out notwithstanding. Goethe became accustomed to the idea and eventually expressed the following opinion to his daughter-in-law Ottilie, who had played a mediating role: 'If they have really decided to do a production of *Faust*, then the least one can hope for is that it will be done as I would wish and not as they fancy!' (Conversation, December 1828; cited Mahl, 27f.)

The Weimar production was, despite Goethe's indirect participation, no less of a reworking of the canonical text than the Brunswick and Dresden versions. Klingemann's manual again served as a basis, and Goethe's friends von Müller, Eckermann, and Riemer recommended numerous economies. The three prologues were passed over, as were Walpurgis Night and Lieschen at the well. Other episodes were conflated in order to avoid shifting scenery. Yet this was not all. In view of the poet's apparently rigorous determination to defend his work against incursions from outside, it is little short of amazing that he himself should have written comic-sounding verse commentaries. For example, just as Faust is about to sign the pact, a chorus is heard singing:

> *Will he sign it?*
> *Yes, he will sign it.*
> *He will not sign it.*
> *No! no! no!*
> *He's signing, he's signing,*
> *And using a liquid most rare.* (Mahl, 28)

Allegorical dances and ballets were inserted and some music was specially composed by Karl Eberwein. It is known that Goethe spent much time with the actor who played the part of Mephistopheles, Karl von La Roche, and went through all his speeches with the utmost diligence. He also instructed August Durand, who took on Faust, to modulate his bass voice into a 'youthful tenor' after contemplating the mirror in the Witch's Kitchen. (Mahl, 30)

The nineteenth century saw a gradual shift from scrupulously edited productions to the modern mystery plays that were handled with extreme veneration at the end of the century. The Weimar production remained on the books until 1873, though it was performed only 37 times in 44 years. Yet it had an important effect; from this date onwards, no self-respecting theatre in the German-speaking world could ignore a piece that was rapidly acquiring the aura of a national treasure. *Faust* was now *the* German drama. Towns vied with one another to offer it to the public, no matter how much truncation this might entail. In 1839, Mozart's chamber music was to be heard between the acts in Vienna, but Faust was not permitted to regret having studied 'theology': the term 'astrology' was coyly substituted in defiance of a three-hundred-and-fifty-year-old tradition. Aged over 30, Julie Rettich must have struggled to embody Gretchen, a young lass of fourteen. It is clear that a tradition was establishing itself that ran counter to the spirit of the play. *Faust* had become a kind of elaborate costume drama in which artists laboured to outdo each other in the production of ornate backdrops depicting baronial castles beside the gabled houses and city walls of a bygone era. All this was happening as the city walls were being dismantled and railroads were being driven through Germany's ancient towns. Faust and Gretchen appeared as unsullied icons of the good old days, dance sequences were added and choreographed with meticulous attention to detail, producing an almost Wagnerian effect. There are indications that the public of the time would have preferred a simpler fare; critics complained not only about the unnecessary opulence but also about the confusing, a-historical mixture of styles: 'There is a lack of mental engagement and concentration; the entire project is lost in the midst of operatic effects', was said of the monumental 1878 production in Dresden. (Mahl, 39)

Things did not change substantially until, thanks to the efforts of logical positivism with its respect for original data, efforts were made to strip off the additions and accretions and return to the text itself. This involved abandoning the five-act structure, re-instating the deleted scenes, bolting on the vital prologues, and cutting the ballets and musical intermezzi. These operations paled into insignificance in the face of the challenge of *Faust, Part II*, which was both notoriously obscure and extremely demanding in terms of technical resources.

Although viewed by many as a whimsical add-on incorporating the philosophy of the aged poet in symbolic form, *Faust II* had its place in the earliest conception of the work, as its author repeatedly affirmed. A first attempt was undertaken at Dresden in 1849, the year of the poet's hundredth anniversary. Karl Gutzkow's *The Rape of Helen* was a condensation of Goethe's Acts I through III. Gutzkow made a crucial alteration to his production, which many would regard as controversial. He treated the entire 'Helen of Troy' episode as a dream experienced by Faust as he lies unconscious in his study after the explosion at the Emperor's Court. This is an interpretation that has its champions, including Stuart Atkins. Gutzkow explained that it would make the play intelligible to lay audiences. There were budgetary considerations that required him to cut the cost of casting nymphs, sphinxes, and dragons in speaking roles. By all accounts, it was an elaborate affair, in which music was again used to impart a mythical flavour. The third performance is said to have ended with Faust becoming trapped in the elaborate machinery that was to hoist him off the stage out of the winged Helen's arms. This was probably a fabrication on Gutzkow's part designed to explain why the costly and unpopular production was abandoned after three nights. (Brandt, 209)

That *Faust II* nevertheless found its way onto the German stage was the result of a laborious process involving many false starts. The difficulty is that while making technical demands that the nineteenth century theatre was unable to fulfil, its content arose from eighteenth-century preoccupations with which modern generations found it hard to empathise. The prime example of this is the marriage of Helen and Faust as a brave but doomed synthesis of Nordic and Mediterranean elements.

Five years after Gutzkow's unsuccessful experiment, Anton Wollheim da Fonseca attempted the first full production of *Faust II* in Hamburg. Wollheim imposed bizarre, seemingly arbitrary interpretations on individual figures and events; thus the *homunculus* was the child that Gretchen had borne Faust, reconstituted by Mephistopheles after it had been drowned by its mother:

> I thus assumed that [Mephistopheles] collected up the life-sustaining elements in which Gretchen's drowned child [...] dissolved and evaporated, and, through the addition of fiery substances, revitalises it by virtue of his own negative spirit. In this manner, Mephistopheles is able to regenerate a creature that is related to Faust's life and spirit in various ways. [...] I inserted all this into the magical pageant for the sake of obtaining yet another point of contact between the first and second parts of *Faust* in a general sense, but also in order to place the hero in a relationship to both Helen and Gretchen, which is ultimately to lead to the triumph of the divine element in human nature. (Wollheim, 10)

Wollheim's alterations serve a similar purpose: to streamline the action and to make it more plausible in terms of character development. The masquerade at Court, the Classical Walpurgis Night and Philemon and Baucis are sacrificed, the latter replaced by a single hermit. Many people may have objected to these truncations, yet as Mahl shows, there was also a general acknowledgement that Wollheim succeeded in demonstrating the stageworthiness of a play hitherto deemed unmanageable. There followed several other attempts to reduce *Faust II* to what different experts considered to be its essentials; these include Johann Peter Eckermann's *Faust at the Emperor's Court* (Weimar, 1856) and Albrecht Marcks' monumental musical (in today's terminology) of 1880. This Dresden spectacular required Faust to be accompanied by 166 knights and camp followers, while Helen, not to be outdone, was attended by a grand total of 215 handmaidens.

These opulent and melodramatic approaches to the text led to demands, both from artists such as Richard Wagner and from directors such as Otto Devrient, that if *Faust* was to be performed in total, this would have to be done within the framework of a commemorative festival. This is essentially what has happened ever since. *Faust I* and *II* enjoyed their first joint production in Weimar in 1875/6 to celebrate Goethe's arrival there 100 years earlier. More than Wollheim's contrived attempts to link the two parts through the imposition of a heavy-handed symbolism, the juxtaposition of the two parts with the same actors was what cemented their continuity in the public eye. An integral musical score played its part in this process. The trend established itself rapidly, the most recent combined productions being staged by Peter Stein at Hanover's World Fair ('Expo 2000'), Barry Yzereef at Calgary's 'Faustival' in 2003, and Wilfried Hammacher (Dornach, 2004).

National Drama of the Reich

Photographic documentation of actors and actresses begins around 1875. Costumes and sets as well as plentiful newspaper reviews, posters, playbills, programmes and directors' notes are now accessible. The Theatre Museum in Cologne mounted an exhibition in 1982, when the organisers estimated that around 900 major productions had taken place since 1819 (Grosse/Vogelsang). It is possible to trace a development from the lavish Faust festivals of the late nineteenth century all the way to the scaled-down Hamburg production of 1957/8, which was also the first stage version to be released on film. A few milestones will have to suffice for a rich and enduring tradition incorporating several hundred pseudo-mediaeval stage sets in the neo-Gothic tradition.

Otto Devrient set new standards in Weimar when he designed a triptych-like stage that helped to turn *Faust* into a timeless mystery play. There were steps to the left and right of a central bridge; beneath this was a pit, which served as the

22. *Otto Devrient's mystery-play, 1876, was staged on three levels.*

entrance to hell, a doorway, a prison; while the bridge above it could be used variously as heaven, a stage, or Helen's throne room. Played over two days, Devrient's *Goethe's Faust als Mysterium in zwei Tagewerken* ('Goethe's Faust as a two-day Mystery Play'), with Devrient himself as Mephistopheles, soon established itself as the centre-piece of a an almost mythical cult of the national poet. The Prelude on the Stage and Prologue in Heaven were given their due, and although music by Eduard Lassen was frequently heard, this was no longer felt to be intrusive. Visual tricks, such as Faust riding on a barrel out of Auerbach's Cellar, were now viewed with awe where previously they had caused amusement and uproar. Devrient's version was an enormous success, and actors, designers, critics and scholars came from all over Germany and many parts of Europe to admire and to learn from it; his designs were copied in Berlin, Leipzig and Cologne.

After the two-day event with substantial cuts, it was almost inevitable that others would try to include most, if not all of the work, a labour that could not be accomplished in less than four very intensive days. Hermann Müller's four-day *Faust* at Hanover, involved, for the first time, minimal cuts, despite chopping the text into four full-length plays of four, five, three and four acts respectively. It fell

23. Adolf Sonnenthal before and after his transformation from hoary sage to dashing cavalier, Vienna, 1883. Costume and scenery are typical of the period.

to Vienna, a city as proud as any of its theatrical traditions, to commission a three-day event, devised by Adolf Wilbrandt with Adolf Sonnenthal in the title role. It required Part I to be split into two halves. Some excellent photos survive of this production from 1883. Here, too, attempts were made to render the plot intelligible, and to whitewash the role of the protagonist. The director left a detailed account of his interventions, which included showing exactly how Mephistopheles turns the sleeping draught that Faust provides for Margaret into a lethal potion. (Wilbrandt, viii, 163)

From now on, productions became ever more lavish. Bernd Mahl illustrates many of these amazingly detailed attempts to create scenery worthy of the national drama. In Munich, where Jocza Savits attempted in 1895 to preserve Goethe's original as far as was possible, six people were employed at the Königliche Hofbühne as set designers. The surviving shots of Part II show just how much trouble was taken to create pseudo-classical verisimilitude in the manner of great art – one is reminded of Thomas Cole's series of grandiose paintings, *The Course of Empire*. Yet behind the façades created for the final act's 'Palace and Canal' scene, there is evidence of German industrialisation in the tall, smoking chimney that is set among a collage of Gothic-looking arches and gables.

History was made, again, in 1909, when *Faust* became the first play to be transferred by Max Reinhardt to the recently introduced 'revolving stage', which enabled a large number of very different settings to be seen in rapid succession, a technique from which *Faust* benefited on account of its many short episodic scenes.

24. *Paul Wegener, star of many early horror films in the Expressionist style, appearing as Mephistopheles in Max Reinhardt's 1909 production in Berlin.*

One of the longest periods of theatrical gestation in history was that of Marie and Rudolf Steiner's complete version of *Faust I* and *II*, the first completely uncut production of both parts. Rehearsals began in 1913. Individual scenes were shown in 1919. After Rudolf Steiner's death in 1925, his wife Marie continued working on her husband's vision of a 'eurhythmic' production, in which the actors' words and movements would be in complete harmony with nature. Steiner traced many of his ideas back to Goethe's thoughts on the 'primal plant', which he saw as one of the fundamental notions around which the career of Faust was arranged. Here, too, a kind of mystery play was being envisaged. Until Peter Stein's production in 2000, the Goetheanum in Dornach was the only theatre ever to have attempted an uncut version. Singing, dance, rhythmic motion, but also colours and tableaux-like use of space were distinctive features. The actors and actresses were obliged to cultivate an array of artistic and physical skills, including elaborate speech training, poetry, painting, and Greek-style gymnastics, which included running, jumping, wrestling, discus- and javelin-throwing. They appeared at the World Exhibition in Paris in 1937 to great acclaim as the official Swiss entry, and finally staged their first production in the Swiss village of Dornach in 1938. Since then it has been modified only slightly and is still revived from time to time. The production was last seen, by around 6,000 spectators, in 1999 and again in April 2004. Rehearsals involve around sixty players and take approximately eighteen months. (Mahl, 114–18; Dabezies, 109–123; see also *Faust am Goetheanum*)

From Farce to Spectacle and back: English-language Productions

The last recorded production of Marlowe's *Doctor Faustus* in 1675 had been followed by watered-down versions involving harlequin figures, much as had been the case in the German-speaking world. A farce by William Mountford was produced in Dorset Gardens, London, between 1684 and 1688, and this was followed by John Thurmond's *Harlequin Doctor Faustus* and John Rich's *The Necromancer, or Harlequin Doctor Faustus*, both of 1723, and many others, up to a *Harlequin and Faustus* of 1793. The harlequin had been imported to Britain and Germany from Italy via France, and soon became an indispensable concomitant of popular comedy. The title of the following pamphlet speaks for itself:

THE / LIFE and DEATH / OF / Doctor Faustus, / Made into a / FARCE. // By Mr MOVNTFORD // WITH THE / Humours of *Harlequin* and *Scaramouche*, / As they were several times Acted / BY Mr *LEE* and Mr *JEVON*, / At the Queens Theatre in *Dorset* Garden. // Newly revived, / At the Theatre in *Lincolns Inn Fields*, / With *Songs* and *Dances* between the ACTS. // LONDON, / *Printed and sold by E. Whitlock near Stationers Hall*, 1697./ *Price 6d.*

William Mountford [or Mountfort], born 1660, used Marlowe's text as his point of departure, introducing Faustus seated in his chair and reading in his study, but before we are more than one page into the text, Scaramouche, a chimney sweep and thus acquainted with the 'black art' already, has appeared and been taken on as the doctor's apprentice, in order to dilute Marlowe's plot with scatological material and cheap laughs. Despite a superficial resemblance to Rafe and Robin in Marlowe, Scaramouche and Harlequin extend the vulgar potential of these scenes in new directions. Some of this will strike viewers of today's Whitehall farces as familiar.

SCARAMOUCHE: Now have a care of another Proverb: We go without our Supper.

HARLEQUIN: Nay, now I know the Devil's humour; I'll hit him to a Hair: pray, Mr Doctor, cut up that Pasty.

SCARAMOUCHE: I can't get my Knife into it, 'tis over-baked.

HARLEQUIN: Ay, 'tis often so; God sends Meat and the Devil sends Cooks. [*Table flies down*]

SCARAMOUCHE: Thou Varlet, doest thou see, what thy Proverb has done?

HARLEQUIN: Now could I curse my Grand-mother, for she taught 'em me: Well, if sweet *Mephostopholis* will be so kind as but to let us and the Table come together again, I'll promise never to say Grace, or speak Proverb more, as long as I live. [*They are let down to the Table*]

SCARAMOUCHE: Your Prayers are heard, now be careful; for if I lose my Supper by thy Negligence I'll cut thy Throat.

HARLEQUIN: Do, and eat me when you have done; I am damnably hungry; I'll cut open this Pasty, while you open this Pot of wild Fowl. [HARLEQUIN *takes of the Lid of the Pasty, and a Stag's Head pops out, and out of the Pot of Fowl flies birds.* HARLEQUIN *and* SCARAMOUCHE *start back, fall over their Chairs, and get up.*]

HARLEQUIN: Here's the Nest, but the Birds are flown; Here's Wine though, and now I'll conjure for a Supper. I have a Sallad within of my own Gathering in the Fields to Day.

SCARAMOUCHE: Fetch it in; Bread, Wine and a Sallad may serve for a Collation.

[*Enter* HARLEQUIN *with a Tray of Sallad*]

HARLEQUIN: Come, no Ceremony among Friends. Bon, fro.

SCARAMOUCHE: *Sallad mal adjuste*; here's neither Fat nor Lean.

HARLEQUIN: O Mr Doctor, neither Fat nor Lean in a Sallad.

SCARAMOUCHE: Neither Oyl, nor Vinegar.

HARLEQUIN: Oh! I'll fetch you that presently. [HARLEQUIN *fetches a Chamber-pot of Piss, and a Lamp of Oyl; and pours on the Sallad.*]

SCARAMOUCHE: O thy Sallad is nothing but Thistles and Netles; and thy Oyl stinks worse than *Arsefetito*.

HARLEQUIN: Bread and Wine be our Fare. Ha! the Bread's alive.

SCARAMOUCHE: Or the Devil's in't. Hey! again. [*Bread sinks*]

HARLEQUIN: My Belly's as empty as a Beggar's Purse.

SCARAMOUCHE: And mine as full of Wind as a Trumpeter's Cheeks.

[*Table sinks, and flash of Lightning.*]

But since we can't eat, let's Drink: Come, here's Doctor *Faustus's* Health.

HARLEQUIN: Ay come; God bless Dr *Faustus*. [*Bottles fly up, and the Table sinks.*]

SCARAMOUCHE: What all gone; Here's a Banquet stole away like a City Feast. [*Musick.*]

HARLEQUIN: Ha, here's Musick to delight us.

[*Two Chairs rise.* HARLEQUIN *and* SCARAMOUCHE *sit down and are caught fast.*]

SCARAMOUCHE: Ha! the Devil, we are lock'd in.

HARLEQUIN: As fast as a Counter Rat.

[*Enter several Devils, who black* HARLEQUIN *and* SCARAMOUCHE's *faces, and then squirt Milk upon them. After the Dance they both sink.*]

SCARAMOUCHE AND HARLEQUIN. O', o', o' –

[*The End of the Second Act.*] (Mountford, 15f.)

Crude terms like 'belly' and 'arse' are used, and salads are dressed in unconventional fashion, with 'A chamber-pot of Piss, and a Lamp of Oyl'. Conjuring tricks were much appreciated, pies opened to reveal the head of a stag, and live birds emerged from pots, much as happened in some of the early Faust-films by Georges Méliès (see below, 314f.). Not everyone was enthralled by the favour such works found; as Nicholas Rowe put it:

> Must Shakespeare, Fletcher, and laborious Ben,
> Be left for Scaramouch, and Harlequin? (Francke, xxxvii)

Thurmond's implementation of 1723 was one of several: he also produced a Wagner pantomime a few years later. Faust captures two farmer's wives, takes them off to his castle, where they are terrified by Mephistopheles, who appears in the form of a dragon. The farmers sprout horns, a motif familiar from Marlowe, and are prevented by these horns from climbing in through the window to rescue their wives. Scaramouch, Punch and Pierrot feature as drunken students, and are entertained by a dancing Helen of Troy. Faust tricks a brothel-keeper by paying him money that later turns into thin air. After various other tricks and transformations, Faust is consigned to the fires of hell, and a final chorus of antique gods and goddesses express their joy at the demise of the arrogant magus.

> The Music changes, and the Scene draws, and discovers a Poetical Heaven with the Gods and Goddesses rang'd in order on both sides of the Stage, who express their joy for the Enchanter's Death, (who was suppos'd to have power over the Sun, the Moon, and the Seasons of the Year). (Thurmond, 13)

Thurmond himself, an accomplished dancer, played the part of Mars on the London stage. Sophisticated machines were used to create pantomimic entertainment, though several fatalities occurred when one of these malfunctioned during a performance of *Doctor Faustus* at Lincoln's Inn Fields in 1724 (Stumme, 12–17; Butler, 61). John Rich's pantomime of the same year is quite different. The text is closer to Marlowe, with Faust appearing more often in his capacity as teacher and necromancer than as a womaniser or cheap conjurer. And many further implementations were to follow. Thomas Merrivale published *The Necromancer; Or Harlequin Doctor Faustus. A Poem Founded on Gentile Theology* in 1724, in which he expresses his admiration for Rich's production and apologises for adding yet another pantomime on the same theme. Merrivale, a student of Trinity College, Oxford, shows greater erudition in his work, including scenes from Ovid and references to contemporary events such as the Jacobite Rebellion. Despite the farcical elements, it contains much that foreshadows Goethe: an opening scene in heaven, with the gods in disarray before Jupiter commissions Harlequin, here a kind of messenger figure, to seek out Faust. The doctor produces wine which turns into fire when drunk carelessly. He is in awe of Helen of Troy, yet also pursues a simple woman, a miller's bride. Merrivale's play is mentioned by Pope and Hogarth; it entertained packed houses over a period of forty days. Throughout the eighteenth century, English representations of Faustus in such dance-dramas or pantomimes enjoyed no less popularity then the puppet-plays of the previous century (Jump, lxi). These comedies quickly became fashionable on the continent. A programme dating from around 1730 shows that Faust was performed in Vienna in a combination of styles:

> Today, Saturday the 9th June, to be performed for the first time at the Theatre at the Kärtner-Tor, which enjoys the patronage of His Royal and Imperial Catholic Majesty: Dr Faust, arranged in the style of German Comedy, English Pantomime and Italian Music. Note that the action will take place in a form never previously witnessed, and will be unique on account of its many machines and incomparable décor. (Stumme, 29f.)

The author of this hyperbolic advertisement was intent on maximising the play's attraction with reference to German, English and Italian traditions, all of which had their adherents in Vienna. These productions were still in vogue in nineteenth-century London, as the following report from a Dresden evening newspaper in 1824 shows:

> Doctor Faust and the black demon, or Harlequin and the Seven Fairies. Chinese slaves, conjurers, fairies and magicians, a princess with diamond eyes, a prince with ruby lips cause each other joy and delight, grief and misery; the characters are, according to ancient tradition, transformed into Harlequin, Pantalon and Columbine etc. There is no lack of transformations, machinations, scene-changes and humorous effects; in short, everything you might expect is delivered. Mrs Searle was the cutest and most witty Columbine who had ever teased Pantalon and Harlequin and all other men on the London stage. – The most impressive machine was an umbrella that was pumped by means of a bellows until it became a balloon which lifted the villain into the air. One of the most attractive decorations was a panorama of the siege of Algiers. (Stumme, 29)

The task of producing Goethe's *Faust* in Britain was initially far from uncontroversial. Although Percy Bysshe Shelley had translated extracts of Part I, including the supposedly offensive 'Prologue in Heaven', many critics opined that the work was ill-attuned to notions of propriety as entertained in that country, and went so far as to argue that Goethe's text should not be imported into Britain. (Hauhart, 26) In defence of such seemingly narrow-minded outbursts, it must be added that Goethe's native land launched its fair share of diatribes against his work and that many German theatres placed their own embargos on controversial scenes.

English productions based more or less loosely on Goethe begin with George Soane's *Faustus. A Romantic Drama in three Acts*, shown in Drury Lane in April 1825, with music by Bishop, Horn and Cooke. *The Devil and Doctor Faustus*, adapted by Leman Rede, dates from the same year and was a more lavish affair, incorporating music by Carl Maria von Weber. Both preceded the German première of Goethe by some four years, as did the three-act adaptations by Marie-Emmanuel-Guillaume Théaulon de Lambert (first performed at the Théâtre des Nouveautés, 27 October 1827) and by Antony Béraud (first performed at the

FAUST;
OR, THE DEMON OF THE DRACHENFELS.
A ROMANTIC DRAMA, IN TWO ACTS. BY H P. GRATTAN.
First Produced at Sadler's Wells, Sept. 5th, 1842.

25. Grattan's Faust, or the Demon of the Drachenfels *was performed at Saddler's Wells in 1842.*

Théâtre de la Porte St.-Martin, 29 September 1828) in Paris. Henry Willoughby Grattan Plunkett, writing as 'H.P. Grattan', produced a *Faust, or the Demon of the Drachenfels* for the Saddler's Wells Company in 1842, in which Faust inadvertently poisons Marguerite and stabs his own father, Ernest, before being handed over to the Inquisition by Mephistopheles. On 27 June 1852, Charles Fechter performed Goethe's *Faust* in the presence of the Royal Family, apparently at the request of the Prince Consort. (Heinemann, 318) William Robertson's *Faust and Marguerite* of 1854 was an adaptation of Michel Carré's French revision, which became more widely known when it was subsequently adopted as Gounod's libretto. In 1854, Dion Boucicault's *Faust and Margaret* was shown at London's Princess Theatre in a production by Charles Kean. W.S. Gilbert also wrote a four-act play, *Gretchen*, which ran for a fortnight at the Olympic Theatre in 1879. Here, Faust is a young monk, but there are Goethean features, for example in the comic dialogue between Mephistopheles and Martha (see below, 348–50).

The most spectacular *Faust* ever seen on English soil was the lavish undertaking by Henry Irving at the London Lyceum Theatre. Irving, in partnership with Ellen Terry, was the most vibrant force in the British theatre of the late Victorian period, the first actor ever to be knighted, and, one may safely presume, the only Briton to receive from the Duke of Sachsen-Meiningen the Order of the Komthus Cross of the Ducal Saxon Ernestine House, if only its 'Second Class' variant. *Faust* was the pinnacle of the couple's 'intensity school' of acting. Terry, as Margaret, was 37 years of age on the opening night, but 'brought tears into the eyes of the most hardened in the audience' in a deep, pleading voice half-choked with sobs

(Clement Scott, *The Daily Telegraph*, 21 December 1885). This melodramatic adaptation in blank verse by William Gorman Wills, first shown in December 1885 after months if not years of preparation, required 350 stage hands, an orchestra of 36 musicians and a chorus of 43 singers (see Booth, 97–126, for a very full account of the event). Irving made a special journey to Nuremberg and Rothenburg, both for inspiration and in order to purchase large quantities of Germanic-looking bric-à-brac, while the artist Hawes Craven was summoned to paint the scenery *in situ*. The result was performed 577 times in London, 128 times in the provinces and 87 times in America, with takings in excess of £250,000.

Wills reduced the play to a lengthy prologue which squeezed, into seventeen pages of text, Faust's opening monologue, the pact, a scene in the tavern with students, and the initial encounter with Margaret, here effected in Nuremberg's Lorenz-Platz. Only then does the five-act tragedy begin, though Irving re-arranged the scenes after comments about the cluttered prologue. As so often, attention was divided between Margaret and Mephistopheles, with Faust receiving little interest. Tall, lean and unapproachable, Irving was well qualified to incorporate the diabolic as his public wished to see it. The sets were breathtaking, and the special effects were state-of-the-art. The duel between Faust and Valentine involved flashes of electricity, conducted from iron plates on the stage floor into their swords, which sparked whenever they crossed, at no inconsiderable risk to the actors. The Prince and Princess of Wales were at the première, although the future Queen of England, eighteen-year-old Princess May, was forbidden to attend for fear that that the story might adversely affect her morals. The play was widely discussed in Germany (Heinemann, 318–22) and was seen by Germany's Crown Prince Frederick, as well as by the leading politicians of the day, such as William Gladstone and Joseph Chamberlain. German content was stressed. Music by Beethoven, Berlioz, Lassen, Meredith Ball and Hamilton Clarke played continuously, and scenes were modelled on Old Masters such as Rembrandt and Dürer. As in German productions of the period, very precisely drawn scenery was used, with Faust and Mephistopheles 'not only as the chief characters in the tragedy, but as the principal figures in a picture rich in color, vigorous in composition. Their every pose is a subject for a painter.' (Pennell, 309) Irving himself took the decision to reject Leipzig in favour of Nuremberg as the visual source. Beecham the Chemist produced a copy of the text, price one penny, containing adverts for its medicines on each page. More than 100,000 copies were shifted during the first season alone, and a fashion was started for 'Margaret shoes' and 'Mephistopheles hats'. The Boston production took $4,582 in a single night, the highest sum ever attained for a single event in the USA at that time. Bram Stoker notes that the play fared much better in God-fearing areas like the Quaker stronghold of Philadelphia than in liberal areas like Chicago (Booth 124; Brereton, II, 85–96; Stoker, I, 175–84; Stumme, 130–33; Irving). The following reviews will exemplify the range of opinions no less than the heated emotions this production was able to inspire.

Pictorial successes of Mr Irving's "Faust"

Of the many pictures of Faust and Margaret that have been painted, not one has equalled this of the Lyceum, when, in the tender light, Margaret, the daisies in her hand, tells Faust the simple story of her life. In her garden the scene is fairer, as indeed it should be, as here love grows sweeter and passion more intense. In broad daylight one wonders would Margaret's heart be so heavy without her lover? O heart of lead! And her little Nuremberg world still so fair about her! The red fades, and the luminous green, that never comes but in the evening, covers the sky beyond the spires, and Faust returns. Students pass in a neighbouring street singing, and three girls come running in the gate, to stand still and watch, and then shut it softly, only to open it a second time and watch again. Someone within the little house lights the evening lamp. It is as real and beautiful as life itself. In just such a garden many a trusting maiden has been wooed and won in Nuremberg.

On the Brocken Mr Irving could not be realistic [...] When the curtain first rises it is dark along the labyrinth of vales and rocky ramparts. Great crags are to the right; to the left is an abyss overshadowed by rude fir-trees. As Faust and Mephistopheles appear to climb toilsomely upward from the cavern to the crag, the moon with its belated glow breaks through the clouds. Weird, uncanny figures fly through the air. The tempest raves, the forest grinds and cracks, but above the whistling and surging of the storm voices ring high, singing now near, now far, until along the mountainside the infuriatedly clamouring song sweeps as the witches, young and old, horrible and beautiful, in strange unearthly draperies, come slowly winding up from the depths below. They groan and push and roar and clatter. Faust and Mephistopheles stand apart on the high cliff, and away above all loom up their shadows on the sky beyond, great spectres of the Brocken. One dance ends only that another may begin, but at last Mephistopheles leaves the apes he has been caressing and bids the revellers begone. There is nothing more powerful than this single scene, – one minute a wild shrieking singing crowd of misty shapes, moving hither and thither, clambering over the rocks and trees, dancing and turning; the next, after one last shriek, wilder, shriller than the rest, a silent, storm-beaten mountain-top deserted but for one flaming form. Then, summoning them once more, he himself plunges into the midst of the revelling. Now the dreary light, that has been strangely glimmering, here glows through film and haze, there sweeps in rolling vapor; now creeps like a thread, now leaps and plays, lighting up the great mountain and all the rugged slopes, and finally gushes forth, a shower of fiery rain, over the wild and howling crowd of witches, while the rocky ramparts on all their heights are set ablaze. Thus is the ideal Brocken of the poem realized on the stage, and, hardened play-goer that you are, you cannot but shudder as the curtain falls. (Pennell, 310f.)

The acting in Mr Irving's "Faust"

We may as well express frankly that we attach the most limited importance to the little mechanical artifices with which Mr Irving has sought to enliven "Faust". We care nothing for the spurting flames which play so large a part, nor for the importunate lime-light which is perpetually projected on somebody or something. It is not for these things that we go to see the great Goethe, or even (for we must, after all, allow for inevitable dilutions) the less celebrated Mr Wills. We even protest against the abuse of the said lime-light effect: it is always descending upon someone or other, apropos of everything or of nothing; it is disturbing and vulgarising and has nothing to do with the author's meaning. That blue vapours should attend on the steps of

Mephistopheles is a very poor substitute for his giving us a moral shudder. That deep note is entirely absent from Mr Irving's rendering of him, though the actor, of course, at moments presents to the eye a remarkably sinister figure. He strikes us, however, as superficial – a terrible fault for an archfiend – and his grotesqueness strikes us as cheap. We attach also but the slenderest importance to the scene of the Witches' Sabbath, which has been reduced to a mere bald hubbub of capering, screeching and banging, irradiated by the irrepressible blue fire, and without the smallest articulation of Goethe's text. The scenic effect is the ugliest we have ever contemplated, and its ugliness is not paid for by its having a meaning for our ears. It is horror cheaply conceived, and executed with more zeal than discretion.

It seems almost ungracious to say of an actress usually so pleasing as Miss Terry that she falls below her creation, but it is impossible for us to consider her Margaret as a finished creation. Besides having a strange amateurishness of form (for the work of an actress who has had Miss Terry's years of practice), it is, to our sense, wanting in fineness of conception, wanting in sweetness and quietness, wanting in taste. It is much too rough-and-ready. We prefer Miss Terry's pathos, however, to her comedy, and cannot but feel that the whole scene with the jewels in her room is a mistake. It is obstreperous, and not in the least in the poetic tone. If the passages in the garden fail in their effect, the responsibility for this is not, however, more than very partially with Margaret. It is explained in the first place by the fact that the actor who represents Faust is, as we have explained, not "in it" at all, and for the second by the fact that the conversation between Mephistopheles and Margaret is terribly overaccented – pushed quite out of the frame. (James, 313)

Irving was a close friend of Bram Stoker, and a picture of Irving as Mephistopheles in *Faust* graces the cover of the Norton Critical Edition of *Dracula* as well as that of the Penguin edition, demonstrating the ease with which Mephistopheles can be

26. 'In Martha's Garden' by W. H. Margetson *was clearly inspired by the Lyceum production of 1885.*

recycled as a replacement for any of his infernal cousins. Irving's fame lives on, not only in Royal Doulton china figurines, but on stage. Robert Poulter recently produced a puppet play, *Faust Fantasy*, for his own toy theatre, which focuses on Irving acting the part of Mephistopheles (Webb).

The success of Gounod's opera had fuelled a demand for other, more authentic, versions of *Faust*. There was even a cynical attempt to fuse the works of Goethe and Gounod into a single entity, entitled *Mephisto on the Horns of a Dilemma between Herr von Goethe's Faust and Monsieur Gounod's Marguerite. A potted version of the two masterpieces rolled into one unhappy concoction.* This features two Mephistos, and was seen at the German Officers' Club in London in 1912. (Dabezies, 49) Spectacular *Fausts* continued in London right up to the eve of World War II. The Fairbairn Pageant Choir, for example, produced what was billed as a 'spectacular pageant ballet version' at the Royal Albert Hall from 14 to 26 February 1938.

Marlowe was ultimately, if indirectly, responsible for Goethe's interest in the Faust material, and Goethe was responsible for the revival of Marlowe's *Faustus* on the British stage. The phenomenal success of the Wills/Irving adaptation led to a demand for the English 'source' of that imported work to be enacted on home territory. William Poel's Elizabethan Stage Society was the first group to revive *The Tragical History of the Life and Death of Doctor Faustus* in St George's Hall in July 1896, using for this purpose a stage that had been modelled on that of London's seventeenth-century Fortune Playhouse (Stumme, 22–27; Speaight, 113–119). According to Jump (lxii), the first German production occurred at Heidelberg in 1903, and the earliest American one on record was at Princeton University in 1907. The Marlowe Memorial in Canterbury was part-funded by subsequent productions in London. British interest increases during the interwar years and beyond, with *Doctor Faustus* appearing at the Old Vic (1944) and at Stratford-upon-Avon (1946, 1947).

The most successful production of Marlowe's *Doctor Faustus* was directed by Orson Welles and produced by John Houseman at New York's Maxine Elliott's Theatre on West 39th Street. This opened on 8 January 1937, with Welles, just twenty-one years of age at the time, playing Faustus as his first major role. Lighting director Abe Feder made a major contribution by utilising Expressionistic effects created by black-outs, innovatory ellipsoidal bulbs and multiple 1,000-watt downward-pointing spotlight cones that defined both space and characters. The stage was not cluttered as in the familiar opera, but completely bare, surrounded by black drapes and divided into distinct pools of light. The costumes, too, were minimalist: black robes with a sixteenth-century look to them, purple robes for the clergy. A play without props or scenery was an innovation that was welcomed by audiences and critics; it ran for six months and was a landmark event not only for *Doctor Faustus* but also for American theatre: 'A brilliantly original production. Goes a long way towards revolutionizing the staging of Elizabethan plays. A Dr Faustus that is physically and imaginatively alive, nimble, active – heady theatre stuff,' thus Brooks Atkinson in the *New York Times*. The production notebook and much supplementary information has been deposited in the New York Library of

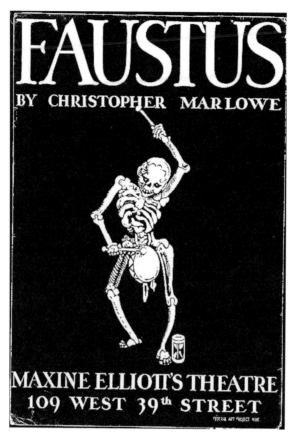

27. Eye-catching 'skeleton poster' for the Federal Theatre Project presentation of Orson Welles' 1937 production of Doctor Faustus. The Federal Theatre Project was one of the first U.S. Government programmes to support the arts.

Congress and affords a useful insight into all aspects of the lighting, stage design, costumes and musical score, while Tim Robbins's 1999 movie *Cradle will Rock* examines the turbulent conditions in which Welles enjoyed his early successes.

This production was so successful that many other cities quickly followed suit; for example, New Orleans, June 1937, directed by William Armitage; Boston, November 1937, directed by Eliot Duvey, music arranged by Charles Frank; Detroit People's Theatre, July 1937, directed by Verner Haldene; Detroit, January 1938, directed by Verner Haldene; Atlanta Theatre, July 1937, directed by William Armitage. What is less well known is that Welles re-wrote the Faustus plot in a script of his own devising, *Time Runs*. This was produced in Hamburg in 1950, in English, and has John Faust, inventor of the atomic bomb, destroy the world, whereupon a few survivors, now reduced to living in caves, recollect the story of the sometime 'Superman' (Dabezies, 479f.). There was another, less immediate follow-up to Welles' enactment of Faustus. In 2002, the Genesis Representative Company revived Christopher Marlowe's *Doctor Faustus* at the Raw Space Theatre on 42nd Street with a production (directed by Mary Elizabeth Micari and Michael Fortunato, 10 July – 5 August 2002) that was clearly intended to investigate the chain of events behind the production of 1937. The programme stated Time: 1937–1962, Place: New York, California, Hell. What New York audiences saw in 2002 was a curious fusion of Elizabethan drama and American stage history, in which Faustus surfaces as a power-hungry New York director (portrayed by Jay Michaels, a virtual dead-ringer for Orson himself) who bargains his soul to the demons of Hollywood in return for fame and power. The text by Jay Michaels, an adaptation of several previous adaptations of Marlowe, transforms the legendary doctor into a monomaniac actor who pursues the glittery attractions of Hollywood; where Welles used cones of light-beams, Micari and Fortunato employ the flickering white light of a movie projector to obtain a similarly ghostly effect while reminding viewers of the cinematic medium that will eventually imprison the actor just as effectively as the spirits imprisoned Faustus (Shandell, 5).

The most recent production of Marlowe to be considered here was done at the Young Vic in London, 2002, produced by David Lan, with Jude Law as Faustus and Richard McCabe as Mephistopheles. Lan's production, writes one reviewer, is 'never less than good, sometimes very good, and, on more than one occasion, diabolically good' (Paul Taylor, *The Independent*, 19 March 2002). The following review, by Michael Billington in *The Guardian*, is worth quoting in full.

Audiences, it seems, can resist everything except temptation – which is one reason that Christopher Marlowe's *Doctor Faustus* is being revived at London's Young Vic, starring Jude Law. But behind this lies a difficult question. Why is it that modern, secularised audiences should relish an apparently broken-backed play that depends upon a medieval belief in heaven and hell? Are we not supposed to be beyond that kind of thing?

One has to accept that the Faust legend of a man who sells his soul to the devil exerts a mythic appeal. It starts with stories of a real-life practising magician, who became the hero of the German *Faustbuch*, published in 1587, and then of Marlowe's play. This led to pantomime and puppet-play versions seen in Frankfurt by the young Goethe, who between 1770 and 1832 produced his own monumental two-part Faust, recently staged in its exhausting, exhilarating entirety by Peter Stein.

But what is striking about the Faust industry is that each artist mines the myth for his own purposes. Gounod turns it into 19th-century romantic opera, while in the 1920s *Doktor Faust*, Busoni discovers a metaphor for artistic creativity. Thomas Mann's novel *Doctor Faustus* deals with the artist's relation to Nazism, while Vaclav Havel's play *Temptation* is clearly about life under communism. And even the American musical has got in on the act. Adler's and Ross's *Damn Yankees* (1955) revolves around a baseball nut who sells his soul for the chance to play ball with the Washington Senators. This being America, however, the hero is eventually returned to his long-suffering wife.

Power and temptation are themes that clearly fascinate us all. But this still leaves the question of why we so frequently revive Marlowe's imperfect play. It contains some sublime poetry, but the long central section – in which Faustus plays practical jokes on the pope, a sceptical knight and a horse dealer – suggests that the hero did

218

not get much for his devilish bargain. And do we still believe that eternal damnation awaits those who, in the play's final words, 'practise more than heavenly power permits'?

Popular as the play has been over the past century, it has not lacked detractors. Shaw, reviewing William Poel's mock-Elizabethan revival in 1896, describes Marlowe as 'childish in thought, vulgar and wooden in humour and stupid in his attempts at invention'. Having said that, Shaw, in one of his great, swashbuckling reviews, broadens his attack to include the full panoply of Elizabethan dramatists – 'the whole obscene crew of these blank-verse rhetoricians' – not excluding Shakespeare himself, with 'his bombast and drivel'. But even allowing for Shaw's excesses, other critics have also wondered what Marlowe's play says to us now. 'Leave the Ghost out of Hamlet,' wrote James Agate in 1925, 'and you impair the play very little, whereas the whole of Faustus is bound up with the belief in the actual existence of hideous things with tails.'

But is it? I would argue that modern directors have grasped the point that Marlowe's play is much more than a Hieronymus Bosch floor show book-ended by great poetic passages of desire and damnation. For me the turning point was a brilliant John Barton production for the Royal Shakespeare Company in 1974, starring Ian McKellen. Barton beefed up the text with 550 lines from Marlowe's source. But his main innovation was to set the entire action inside Faustus's study and, by implication, his mind. All the play's illusions, from the Seven Deadly Sins to Helen of Troy, were embodied by life-sized puppets. The result was that the real drama – the contest between power and penitence – seemed to be taking place within Faustus himself, an idea dazzlingly executed by McKellen, whose arching, cat-like body seemed full of unrealised desires.

Barton threw much of the onus on to his star. And one reason for the play's popularity is precisely the opportunity it affords to actors, at least in the two main roles. In recent times it has attracted heroic performers who seem to find in it a self-fulfilling prophecy of destruction. The supreme example is Orson Welles, who in 1937 staged and starred in his own Broadway version for the Federal Theatre Project (he did a later version in Paris with music by Duke Ellington, and with Eartha Kitt as Helen). Simon Callow in his classic biography points out the chilling resonance of the Prologue's opening lines for Welles's whole career. Comparing Faust to Icarus, Marlowe writes: 'Till swoll'n with cunning, of a self-conceit,/ His waxen wings did mount above his reach/ And melting, heavens conspired his overthrow!'

When Richard Burton played Faustus at the Oxford Playhouse in 1966, with Elizabeth Taylor as Helen and an undergraduate supporting cast, people were not slow to point out the disquieting parallels between the performer and the role. Burton could command any part in the classical theatre, but had chosen riches, fame and, ultimately, the path of self-destruction. I never saw his stage performance, but in the filmed version he reveals a melancholia that seems to stem from self-awareness. Law seems a much more level-headed fellow, but even he must be aware that the play contains its own inbuilt metaphor for the modern actor. When Mephistopheles cries: 'Why this is hell, nor am I out of it', he might well be referring to a long-term Hollywood contract.

But the ultimate fascination of Marlowe's Faustus is that the play acquires a different meaning for each age and each new generation. When it was revived at Stratford's Swan Theatre in 1989, Simon Trussler wrote an excellent critical commentary in the comprehensive programme book. One of his key points was that Faustus was modern man, the ultimate consumer believing that he could work miracles, but who was in fact switched on to a satanic TV set 'tuned into Channel Seven for the Deadly Sins or to the Helen of Troy Show'.

It was a perfect metaphor for the Thatcherite era, one in which we sold our souls for the sake of conspicuous consumption, and in which there was supposedly no desire that we could not, given sufficient wealth, realise. This, I suspect, is the final appeal of Marlowe's play. It is a volatile scenario in which we find our own personal meaning. It may use the devices of the medieval morality play, with its good and bad angels and prospect of damnation. But it is set in an eternal present in which material wealth, scientific knowledge and sexual fantasy become the objects for which we trade our own integrity. I know about my temptations. What are yours? (Michael Billington, 'Carry on Doctor', *The Guardian*, 13 March 2002)

Marlowe's play will continue to fascinate audiences through the astonishingly modern, torn and unreconstructed figure of Faustus. Less polished but more radical than Shakespeare, this author gave his hero all those qualities that we associate with modernity: speed, volatility, blind superficiality, lust and greed. Faith in his subjective right to ignore established rules of conduct combines with faith in his books, which he belatedly promises to burn, as though the feeble gesture of the cornered tyrant in his desperation could ever bring release from the prison-house he has constructed for himself. It is perhaps for this reason that the most recent German translation of Marlowe's *Doctor Faustus*, by Wolfgang Schlüter, has him start his monologue with the words, 'Switch off thy laptop, Faustus, and begin/ To sound the depth of that thou wilt profess.' (Schlüter, 338)

While there has been an explosion of Faust-derivatives in the English-speaking world, full-length productions of Goethe are rare and combinations of the two-part drama rarer still. In 1984, the East German Berliner Ensemble brought a four-hour uncut *Urfaust* to the Edinburgh Festival, and a year later, the Citizens' Theatre in Glasgow staged the first-ever implementation of both parts on the British stage. A radio version had been attempted by Louis MacNiece in 1949. The Glasgow *Faust* was a crisp new version translated somewhat idiosyncratically (*Das Ewig-Weibliche* comes out as 'The woman in all of us') and directed by Robert David MacDonald. With severe cuts and textual liberties including passages written by the director and frequent use of the expletive 'Oh, Goethe!', it ran for just three hours in total, 90 minutes for each of the two parts.

The stage was bare as in Welles' New York *Faustus*, but painted a contrasting white. Anglepoise lamps, bentwood chairs and a draped statue were in evidence. The heavenly spheres were represented by waiters bearing tin trays, the Emperor emerged as a spoilt brat in shorts who made a grandiose entrance but was denied access to the stage and spent much of his time confined to a kind of playpen. Helen of Troy was accompanied by a muzzled dog. When it came to finding suitable garb for Mephistopheles to wear, the director opted for rapid changes: an aviator modelled on Biggles, a cricketer in white flannels, salesman, clown, and drag queen in a silk body-stocking. Gretchen first appeared as a waitress in Auerbach's Cellar. Despite the evident gimmicks, reviews were overwhelmingly positive; MacDonald had proved that 'Goethe can be staged as well as studied', in the words of Michael Billington (*The Guardian* 11 November 1985). The following assessment appeared in the magazine *Theater heute* in January 1986.

Goethe a Go-Go. *Faust I* and *II* done in English for the First Time

After Proust's *Remembrance of Things Past* and Kraus' *Last Days of Mankind* – is there no end to the megalomania of the Citizens' Theatre and its director Robert David MacDonald? It was another hair-raising venture. British audiences have less stamina than their German counterparts, and one cannot expect any degree of familiarity with the key works of German classicism in this country. *Faust II* has never been performed on a British stage, and MacDonald had only sixteen actors and three extras at his disposal, all more at ease in fast-moving comedies than in weighty verse dramas.

And yet MacDonald was able to make a virtue of necessity. His own translation condenses Goethe's 12,000 lines into a neat, breezy entity of just three and a quarter hours' duration. Although disjointed and fragmentary in the manner of an episodic Expressionist drama, this epic journey to the mythically elevated realms of mankind's potential is held together by a single strand of action. Instead of confusing his non-specialist public with a multiplicity of parts in a fruitless quest for fidelity, MacDonald has preserved only a few of the minor roles and used them to give the work coherence. These are, in particular, a group of individuals who appear in Auerbach's Cellar as a bunch of idiotic boozing, belching and flatulating aristocrats, a prince in lederhosen and loden hat, accompanied by a cleric in red silk and three ministers in evening dress. The prince becomes the Emperor of *Faust II*, where he gets to amuse himself with tin solders in a playpen, clad in Bermuda shorts and purple velvet.

The scenes all take place on a uniform, open-plan, sepulchrally white stage designed by Kenny Miller. There are steps, a draped statue, lecterns, and some bookshelves and skulls for Faust's study. This enables one scene to lead into the next without interruption, in what is an action-packed, party-size implementation of Goethe's play. The stage is periodically subdivided by a shoulder-high white curtain that serves, for example, as a screen onto which the encounter between Helen and Paris is projected as a shadow play. The scenes involving Helen are, however, the least convincing, with the plot becoming blurred at this point and Helen's mythical aura not exactly enhanced by a conventional-looking outfit from C&A.

As ever, MacDonald has managed to be both entertaining and disrespectful in his eclectic approach to the text. He quotes not only Shakespeare but also Gilbert and Sullivan. All this in the interests of putting across the contradictory spirit of the original to the British public of today without indulging in trendy anachronisms. He has retained the unpolished verse form and used it to illustrate the tension between lofty pathos in some parts and vulgar comedy in others. The tragic images thus become even more poignant, such as when a white-as-chalk Gretchen, in her madness, drags her foetus across the stage by its umbilical cord.

Mark Lewis was a convincing Faust, alternately tormented by his restless intelligence, desire, despair, world-weariness, passion, and a hunger for action and power. In his dream about land reclamation, with its faint echoes of the Nazi *Lebensraum* ideology, he starts playing around with that alchemist's tool of the present, a word processor. Mephisto, played by Andrew Wilde, remains the highlight, as in many other productions. Certainly not a hellish bogeyman, but rather – such is his diabolical nature – a kind of Figaro, a jack-of-all-trades and facilitator who is constantly undermining the pathos of the other characters. This leads to the only major flaw in the production, as it prevents Faust's predicament from being viewed in serious terms.

The first walkout occurred when the Witch, attired as a Nazi girl, began to stroke Mephisto's gigantic phallus with a dreamily affectionate look in her eye, although what she did was in strict compliance with the 'obscene gesture' that Goethe's text demands. When the Lamiae, played by men made up to look like grotesque tarts with huge blonde wigs and corsets, waddled onto the stage, there was another exodus. Yet here, too, I thought that MacDonald's reading was close to the original with its obvious mockery of unthinking sensuality. 'An entertaining evening – but was it Goethe?' asked a local theatre critic. It was an unfair accusation. By reading Goethe thoroughly and taking him on his own terms, MacDonald was able to persuade his team at the Citizens' to convert a play that many see as heavily Teutonic and indigestible into something quite different: entertaining and moving theatre, in which all the disparate amusing, melancholic, crude, sublime, earthy, metaphysical, absurd, erotic, cynical and romantic elements of both parts of *Faust* were made to coalesce. (McGowan, 61. Translation by Osman Durrani)

28. *Prison scene from the 2003 production of Faust I and II at Calgary.*
Guillermo Urra as a deliberately non-professorial Faust,
Jamie Konchak as Mephistopheles and Nicole Dunbar as Gretchen.

The most recent attempt to put Goethe's play before an Anglophone audience in something resembling its entirety was in 2003, when Barry Yzereef directed both parts in versions that lasted for three and a half hours each at the Reeve Theatre in Calgary. These were staged on separate evenings during a two-week period, except on the closing night, when they were shown in succession in what was to be a seven-hour marathon. The translation was by Howard Brenton. It was hailed as the first-ever production of *Faust II* in Canada, where even *Faust I* had not been seen since the 1960s. Twenty-one actors and actresses from the local drama department shared a total of 219 roles in this ambitious amateur production whose budget was a mere 7,000 dollars. Mephistopheles was played, as often happens these days, by an extremely energetic actress, Jamie Konchak, who found it easy to slide in and out of male, female, hetero- and homosexual attitudes. She was complemented by an altogether unacademic-looking Faust. But then, as Yzereef observed, 'In Alberta, people don't find it easy to sympathise with professors' (Conversation with Osman Durrani). Much use was made of masks, the correct application of which had been very carefully rehearsed over seven months by the company's mask coach, Brian Smith. Audience response indicated that Yzereef and his team had succeeded in their aim of 'reaching the summit of the Mount Everest of German literature', and they did this by converting the two parts into two distinct story-lines: the love theme in Part I and the quest for a perfect world in Part II.

New German Minimalism

Gustaf Gründgens' *Faust* at the Deutsches Schauspielhaus, Hamburg, in 1957 was a major breakthrough in several respects. As it was later filmed by Peter Gorski, some of the technical aspects will be discussed in the chapter on screen implementations (see 326f., below). Some reviewers went so far as to claim that this was the first truly appropriate staging of Goethe's masterpiece (Melchinger, 214). In fact, as Mahl has shown, it was less of a breakthrough than the result of a careful, gradual stripping away of the cluttering accoutrements of earlier productions; Gründgens had, after all, been playing the part of Mephistopheles ever since 1919. Teo Otto, who was responsible for the décor, went against the conventional thirst for ever more opulent artefacts; his stage was empty, his approach minimalist. Will Quadflieg was a clean-shaven and comparatively youthful Faust. The sparse props indicated a modern rather than a mediaeval world. Faust's study was not bursting at the seams with dusty parchments and stuffed animals; instead, a labyrinthine construction of tubes and globes reminded the viewer of the 'Atomium', a modernist sculpture that was being assembled in Brussels for the World Exhibition of 1958, with its sinister implications.

Gründgens based his version on the often neglected 'Prelude on the Stage'. Seen from its perspective, the rest of the drama is nothing other than an attempt, by a small troupe of players, to create the illusion of great drama with minimal resources. This has profound implications both for the reading of the text and for its implementation. The anti-illusionist stance that Gründgens adopted derived its impetus from this prefatory look behind the scenes at a poet conversing with an actor and a manager about how best to create a box-office success. The rest of the play then becomes a practical essay in the art of the possible. Gründgens explained his approach as follows:

29. Will Quadflieg in Gustaf Gründgens' 1958 Hamburg production breaking with tradition by appearing from the outset as a clean-shaven Faust, surrounded by a structure reminiscent of the Brussels Atomium. Photograph by Rosemarie Clausen.

Nothing was more repugnant to me than the idea of repeating a production that had already been shown. I inspected photographs of earlier productions that had, without exception, been hailed as successful, and was horrified at the excessive use of cardboard, plywood, platforms and scenery. Then, while reading the Prelude on the Stage (which I had always omitted), I hit on the idea of using that as my point of departure.

I sat down with Teo Otto, and by dint of taking the poet quite literally, just like schoolboys, line by line, we arrived at a solution that strikes me as so natural that I would regard any attempt to perform *Faust* without the Prelude as fraudulent. For it is here, precisely, that Goethe releases us from the need to view his heaven as heaven, his imperial court as an imperial court, his Greece as the real Greece. No, the entire world, heaven, hell, the wide world and the small world, all these derive from the world of the theatre.

From that point on, there was no need to take up the poet's express instruction to make use of technical devices. It really was possible to encompass the whole of creation on the narrow planks of the stage and to focus on the opportunities that these very planks offered to us. It was most interesting to observe that, having been, as we thought, amazingly Spartan in our approach, we were able to reduce the intended décor by a further half after the initial rehearsals, and when, a few months later, Caspar Neher saw the production, yet more items were dropped. The idea of making Faust's study and Wagner's laboratory approximate to contemporary notions of a scientist's workshop was so obvious as to need no further explanation.

After locating all scenes involving Faust and Mephistopheles in abstract space, as I did in Berlin, because I saw no reason why people who were capable of flying through space on a magic cloak had to meet at an elaborately Gothic street corner, I went even further in Hamburg, and was encouraged to do so by the raised platform on the stage. (Cited Mahl, 141f.)

From this day on, German productions lost their overloaded, 'Gothic' appearance. They could ill afford to drop the 'Prelude on the Stage', nor could they overlook the affinities between Faust and the nuclear scientist, which had been explored in René Clair's film some ten years previously (see 323–5, below). The theme of the 'mad scientist' as a literary commonplace has itself been traced back to Faustus and the alchemist tradition. It had been growing in importance for the German (and international) stage since Brecht's *Life of Galilei* had raised questions about scientific self-interest; like Faustus, Galilei is both a seeker of truth and a seeker of pleasure. The years following the trial of master spy Klaus Fuchs in 1950 saw the production of a spate of dramas and films that portrayed the modern scientist caught up in a Faustian pact with his political minders (Haynes, 9–19, 300–12). In 1962, Friedrich Dürrenmatt went one step further in *The Physicists*; here the scientist, if not truly mad, must feign madness if the world is to be protected from the consequences of his discoveries. Faust continues to be presented as a power-crazy virtuoso in recent fiction, for example, in Michael Swanwick's novel, *Jack Faust* (see 354–7, below).

30. Gretchen (Therese Affolter) goes the Full Monty, in accordance with Goethe's stage directions (Stuttgart, 1977, directed by Claus Peymann). Photograph by Abisag Tüllmann. The minimalist décor recalls life in a 1970s student commune. A few years later Affolter was seen as Ulrike Meinhof in Reinhard Hauff's film Stammheim *(1985).*

Gründgens' influence is to be felt in much subsequent work that was done for the German stage, where new milestones were set by a series of outstanding directors, among whom were Claus Peymann (Stuttgart, 1977), Dieter Dorn (Munich, 1987), and Peter Stein (Hanover, 2000). Although Peymann cut 50 per cent of the text of Part I and 70 per cent of the text of Part II, his two-night version kept audiences in their seats for a total of eleven hours and was generally well received. It was colourful and light-hearted. The Student was a radical, the Lord a humorous old man with a very overdone flowing beard. Faust ended up as a shipping magnate with a private swimming pool. Reviewers commented that Peymann had tried, among other things, to provide a history of the theatre in this production, which moved on from mediaeval box-like effects in Part I via Baroque and Romantic traditions to conclude with a modern scenario reminiscent of Eugene O'Neill. Young people flocked to see this event which was sold out for years and would have run for much longer, had not unforeseen circumstances arisen. Two years after the première, Peymann was hounded out of conservative Stuttgart for having attempted to collect money for terrorist Gudrun Enslin's dental treatment. His production thus came to an abrupt and unexpected end, despite the advance bookings. It had been an important one for a number of reasons. Peymann had succeeded in creating a unique scenography involving huge puppets and other visually powerful devices; unlike Gründgens, he also retained the irreverent perspective adopted by Brecht in East Berlin. The result was animated, fast-moving, and full of appeal, especially for younger audiences for whom this approach to the classics was something of an eye-opener. (Rühle, 18–25; Mahl, 159–66; Beil *et al.*)

Peymann stimulated subsequent directors whose work continues to stress neglected aspects: Faust's solitude and isolation (Klaus Michael Grüber in Berlin, 1982), and the age-gap between the senile scholar and his teenage partner (Michael Degens, Munich, 1977). In 1987, Dieter Dorn surprised Munich audiences with strangely sinister six-hour version, using stark lighting to create bright yellow, red, blue or green backdrops to a box-like stage, the restricted format of which has the effect of making audiences feel they are watching a kind of human puppet show in a severely confined environment. Only the spirits are able to break through the flimsy walls of this enclosed theatrical space. Humans enter and exit via a series of rickety ladders, or are completely hemmed in, as in Auerbach's Cellar, where blood flows freely as the boozers hack off each other's noses in conformity with Mephisto's 'Note the way the devil jests.' (F 2320) Among the special effects was a reclining Goethe, modelled on Johann Heinrich Wilhelm Tischbein's 1787 painting of the artist in the Roman Campagna, for the Lord in the Prologue. A huge Madonna figure dominates Gretchen's bedroom, signalling her subservience to the mediaeval world-view. The production was not universally welcomed. The lighting effects and scenery (or lack of it) were praised, Romuald Pekny was viewed as a melancholic dandy proudly showing off a whole gamut of pyrotechnic tricks, Helmut Griem as Faust fluctuated, in his reviewers' eyes, between a retired general, a village schoolmaster, and Dr Caligari. Sunnyi Melles as Gretchen was little more than a precocious tomboy who would have leapt into bed with anyone, had Faust not done the honours at the opportune moment. (Mahl, 187–90; Kaiser, 16)

31. *Faust (Bruno Ganz) and Mephistopheles (Adam Oest) arguing about the pact in Faust's study. Each character was played by two actors in Peter Stein's production, Hanover 2000. Photograph by Ruth Walz*

The most recent major production, by Peter Stein, Director of the Salzburg Festival from 1991 to 1997, was heralded as the 'première' of Goethe's life's work, the first attempt to produce the 12,110-line play without any cuts. Later it emerged that this feat had been accomplished in Dornach 62 years earlier. Stein insisted on a full year of rehearsals. The unlikely venue for this historic event was the huge Trade Fair Hall Nr 23 in Hanover, a building that closely resembled a run-down airport terminal and was so large that actors had to use roller-skates and bicycles during rehearsals. It was performed there for two months in July to September 2000 during EXPO-2000, then for nine months in Berlin, followed by three months in Vienna. It was offered in two variants, the 'marathon' over two nights, and the 'sushi' squashed into six hours. All aspects of this production have been meticulously documented in a volume by Roswitha Schieb, who attended the rehearsals and recorded her observations on each of the play's scenes, concentrating on the problems they threw up for the actors and ancillary staff. The film, almost 21 hours in length, was initially made available for viewing on the Internet, in 300 separate segments shown in such a way that the texts scrolled down in a separate window of a split screen.[2] A scaled-down 13-hour version was broadcast on television during February 2001. A series of excellent colour photographs were taken by Ruth Walz, and these may be examined and indeed ordered for personal use from the project website.

A team of around 80 people collaborated, including 35 major performers, though only a few of these were well-known acting professionals, 15 assistants and a technical staff of around 30. It also involved many different types of stage. The team had access to huge arenas beside puppet theatres, tents and Baroque palaces, with the audience walking from one to the next during the intervals. The technical effects were breathtaking, sometimes quite literally. Euphorion's death was taken by some to have been produced by a backstage accident, a not unreasonable assumption, as both Stein and Ganz were in fact seriously injured during rehearsals. (Schieb, Krippendorff, Kümmel)

The Socialist Stage

The 199th anniversary of Goethe's birth in 1948 was chosen for the première of Hans Robert Bortfeld's *Faust I* and *II*; this was the first staging of both parts in postwar Germany. The venue was the German National Theatre in Weimar. The aim was to 'transform classical into socialist humanism', in the words of the theatre's director, Wolfgang Langhoff. This involved stressing the cohesion of the work, retaining Goethe's original text (with the consequence that *Faust I* lasted for almost six hours), and yet making it relevant to the present while hinting at a better, more humane future. Unsurprisingly, a number of problems arose, nowhere more so than in regard to the figure of Mephistopheles, played by Lothar Müthel, who followed Gründgens and others in assuming that he, not Faust, was the star of the show. Gretchen was no longer the heroic blonde beauty queen, but a demure representative of bourgeois qualities, and Marthe Schwerdtlein revealed her proletarian credentials as a washerwoman. Prudishness led to some toning down of the sensual aspects. (Vietor-Engländer, 136–8)

Brecht's production of *Urfaust* was mentioned above (183). It premièred in Potsdam in 1952 and later transferred to Berlin, where it was shown three times to matinee audiences and three times in closed sessions to invited guests only, before being taken off the programme. The ban occurred for a variety of reasons. Faust revealed his limitations as an enlightened scientist who was also a criminal. Mephistopheles was small and fat, a coarse and robust servant equipped with tiny golden horns. Instead of impersonating the professor in the scene with the freshman student, he draped his cloak over a skeleton and let the skeleton conduct the interview, a detail that was viewed as critical of the Republic's educational policies. Gretchen was anything but an icon of romantic sensitivity. She had a vulgar streak and presented herself as both stupid and vindictive, naïve but not inexperienced. Some scenes were recorded and were incorporated into Hans-Jürgen Syberberg's film *Nach meinem letzten Umzug*. (Vietor-Engländer, 144–49; Syberberg/Mayer)

Brecht was understandably unhappy about the official response to his production, which was characterised by a lightness of touch and much satirical humour, such as is often lacking in German stagings of indigenous classics. In

1954, he penned an essay entitled *Einschüchterung durch die Klassizität* ('Intimidation by Classicism') in which he highlights the absurdity of demanding 'heroic' behaviour from a man who has recently concluded a pact with the devil.

> A false kind of greatness was generated which was simply boring. The marvellous quality of Goethe's humour in *Urfaust* did not fit in with the measured, dignified pace that one associates with the classics, as though humour were incompatible with genuine dignity! The wonderful details of the plot were exploited merely in order to give rise to powerful declamations, that is to say, they were completely neglected. The bowdlerising and falsification were taken to such extremes that – in the case of *Urfaust* again – the pact which the great Humanist concludes with the devil was rapidly passed over in a dismissive manner [*einfach 'weggespielt'*], regardless of its importance for the Gretchen tragedy, which would not have happened without it or would have happened in a completely different way. This was done because they obviously took the view that a hero can only do heroic things in a classical work. (Brecht, XXIII, 318)

This passage should be read in the light of the no less serious debate about Hanns Eisler's opera *Johann Faustus* in which Brecht also had a hand and which will be considered below (see 257-9). Subsequent productions in the GDR proved less controversial. Fritz Bennewitz's use of the National Theatre in Weimar (1965-7) was predictably conventional. Faust was to exemplify man's ability to re-shape his environment and function as an omni-directional problem-solver. He was a second Christopher Columbus, ready for action, not the world-weary representative of a decadent mindset. This was Faust as the GDR wished to have him: a practical worker who succeeded in harnessing his creativity for the good of mankind, a synthesis of the principles of scholarship and comradely devotion. Gretchen, if one is to believe the critics, combined the qualities of Shakespeare's Juliet with those of Joan of Arc, and was labelled a 'revolutionary in love', while Mephisto's role was reduced to that of Faust's obliging assistant. (Vietor-Engländer, 155-7)

A more dynamic approach was taken by Wolfgang Heinz and Adolf Dresen in Berlin's Deutsches Theater in 1968. On the morning after the première, on 30th September, six weeks after the Soviet invasion of Czechoslovakia, the Minister for Culture intervened and ordered cuts to be made. Five performances later, the play was withdrawn for 'corrections', but a third version remained on the programme for approximately eighteen months, playing to full houses but with tickets hard to obtain. Here Faust is a neurotic, frustrated, doubt-ridden intellectual, weighed down by inhibitions that disqualify him from attaining 'Faustian greatness' in any form whatsoever. The theatre director of the prelude wore a dressing gown, and Mephisto stepped out of a huge inflatable poodle. Gretchen was an average teenager with the moral values of a small-town secretary. The censor may have robbed this production of its satirical edge, but it succeeded in blowing off the dust that was accumulating on the Republic's attempts to revive the classics. Press comment was largely negative; few reviewers dared to remind their readers of the close parallels with what Brecht had done fifteen years earlier. The importance given to official and unofficial interpretations of *Faust* in the playhouses of the GDR is shown by the fact that the Republic's Council of State debated this production at length. (Vietor-Engländer, 157–64)

When, after many agonising debates, the winds of change began to blow across Eastern Europe, the cultural icons were quick to feel the effect. The final implementation to be mentioned here is Horst Sagert's *Urfaust* in East Berlin 1984. The taboos that had frustrated his predecessors were not enforced. Faust appeared on stage carrying a chamber pot, while Wagner dissected the corpse of a small child. The Earth Spirit was a robot; Faust was given an enema. It was as though the team wished to compensate for years of frustration by inserting every childish prank they could imagine into this enterprise. In four hours, the public received a series of lessons in what had now become possible to achieve with impunity. In its dying days, the state had more important matters to debate than what was being done to the classics on the nation's stages. (Reviewed in *Neues Deutschland*, 4 April 1984; *Frankfurter Rundschau*, 9 April 1984)

Puppet Shows, Experimental Theatre, *Commedia dell'arte*, Laser Spectacular

The puppet controlled by strings or other methods has proved an endurable medium for the presentation of Faust's career. There are many reasons for this, not least the fact that this medium comes closest to what many Germans still regard as the essence of Faust: the *Volksdrama* ('drama of the people') which the glitzy productions in downtown playhouses regularly fail to capture. A recent critic speaks of the 'people's Faust' as a fabled Loch Ness Monster that everyone talks about but no one has actually seen. (Kreutzer, 29) The extraordinary effectiveness of Jan Švankmajer's film *Faust* may be due to its adoption of human actors and wooden, clay or *papier mâché* figures that recall and privilege this tradition (see below, 338–345). Yet the use of puppets does not signal radical experimentation. Some of the oldest puppet-plays are still being shown in this format, for example by the 'Fundus' Theatre in Dresden under the directorship of Dr Olaf Bernstengel.

Bernstengel's outfit describes itself as a 'Museum on Wheels'. It was founded in 1982 with the aim of employing the recources of the Dresden Theatre Museum to revive and preserve the travelling theatres of nineteenth-century Saxony and Bohemia. He was well qualified to undertake this task, having gained a doctorate for research into the use of marionettes in travelling theatres in Saxony. In his productions, Bernstengel uses a variety of texts from German and Czech sources. These are taken to festivals, schools, cultural centres and other venues at home and abroad. The play *Johannes Doctor Faust* received the Mayor's Prize at Ostrava in 2001.

Many companies have adopted an approach that involves combining humans, masked actors and puppets. Ophaboom, founded in 1991 by Howard Gayton and Geoff Beale, is a leading UK-based developer of experimental theatre along *commedia dell'arte* lines, to which they add a contemporary flavour by improvising wordplay and encouraging audience backchat. Here, too, there is an attempt to keep past traditions alive: in this case the travelling mountebanks and street

32. Dr Olaf Bernstengel at work: Faust in his study. Photograph by Osman Durrani

peddlers as well as carnival masques and borrowings from Greek and Roman drama. Ophaboom's version of *Faustus* received much acclaim following its première in Kingston-on-Thames in 2000. During 2003/4 it toured Europe. Four performers play seven characters, wearing striking masks designed by Ninian Kinnear-Wilson. This is a spectacle which combines physical theatre with Punch and Judy, elements of slapstick, audience involvement, and contemporary references. A modern, part-comical, part-serious update, it successfully maintains the combination of tragedy and hilarity that that provided the winning formula for the original.

> Doctor Faustus is a provincial psychiatrist who lives with his wife Gretchen and their servant Wagner. Constantly being berated by his wife for his lack of status and career, he is turned down for the post of Psychiatrist to the Royal Court. It is at this point that the flamboyant Mr Mephistopheles has one of his minions deliver an incantation to Dr Faustus promising him wealth and fame if he were to call on the name of Mephistopheles. When he does and Mr Mephistopheles appears, Dr Faustus demands

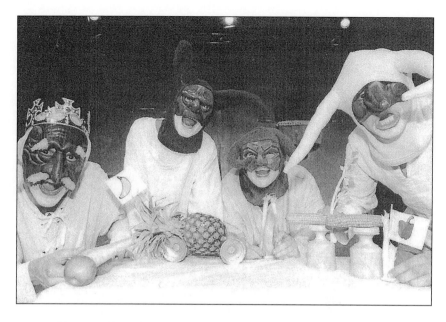

33. *The Vegetable battle scene from Ophaboom's* Faustus *(2000): Howard Gayton
(Faustus), Geoff Beale (devil), Sarah Ratheram (devil) and David Bere (devil).
Photograph supplied by Howard Gayton.*

proof of the supposed abilities of the mysterious man, so Mephistopheles tempts
Gretchen with an apple, uncovering her passionate desires. On seeing this Faustus is
about to sign, but at the last minute he notices the small print – the price is his soul.
He chases Mephistopheles away. Not one to give up, Mephistopheles bewitches
Wagner and turns Gretchen into Helen of Troy, whereupon Faustus is made to watch
the scene of Wagner wooing Gretchen as a piece of theatre. As the two are about to
embrace in a passionate kiss, Faustus is drawn into the devilment, and ends up being
left alone by the two lovers who disappear on a wooden horse. Saddened, Faustus
accepts Mephisto's offer of comfort, and he is soon tricked into signing the pact. The
scene returns to the start, but this time Faustus is not rejected by the Court. He is
made a Prince and informed that the King is to stay at his house that night. Gretchen
encourages Faustus to murder the King in order to seize the throne. No sooner have
they done this than Mephisto's devils take over the court and start to advise Faustus
to wage war on a duke who, they claim, has abducted Queen Gretchen. A vegetable
battle ensues during which Faustus dies and goes at first, and very briefly, to heaven,
but then is dragged off to hell. In trying to repent, he is given a last chance to save his
soul by Mephistopheles by playing the game show 'Win your Soul Back'. In order to
do that he has to name the deadly sins that are being acted out in front of his eyes.
He gets six, but Mephistopheles falters on the last one. Faustus helps him to remember
– it is Pride. It seems that the entire play was an elaborate ruse by Faustus to cure Mr
Mephistopheles of his psychiatric problem of pride, and so we are back in the clinic
with Nurse Gretchen and Wagner. Or are we? As Faustus goes off to celebrate the
fact that he has finally been made Court Psychiatrist, Gretchen and Wagner go off
hand in hand, and there is a devilish laugh resounding out from the dark. (Summary
provided by Howard Gayton)

A different approach was taken by the Basement Theatre's production at the Oxford Playhouse in May 2003. This involved a team of eleven puppeteers operating complex, lifelike puppets requiring three people apiece to control them and therefore capable of producing convincing and life-like movements and subtle gestures. Rebecca Ting describes this much-applauded production as 'a stunning and memorable performance, touching in its sadness, yet supremely witty.' (*The Oxford Stage*, May 2003)

Amy Trompetter's *Faustus: A Puppet Opera*, adapted from Marlowe and performed at New York's Minor Latham Playhouse during April 2002 in collaboration with students from the Barnard/Columbia Theater Department, served as a constant reminder of the evil that the play was meant to represent. Large and small puppets traversed human and demonic spheres within a brightly painted proscenium stage. Contrasts between extremes of human behaviour, between goodness and vice, are more easily represented through wooden dolls than through people of flesh and blood. For example, when Mephastophilis brought a wife for Faustus, at Faustus's request, the female puppet initially looked kind and good. However, the wickedness soon became apparent when the woman proved to be yet another spirit dredged up from hell. Even today, puppets may be the more effective medium for this play in its original form. (*Barnard College Campus News*, New York, April 2002)

Timothy Gosley's *Faust through the Shadows* closely follows Goethe's *Faust 1*, incorporating actors, light puppets, shadow puppets and live video. It was created for the Merlin's Sun Theatre, Quebec, in April 2003, and was shown in venues across Canada during that year and at Bishop's University in Lennoxville, Quebec, in 2004. The objective that Gosley set himself was to combine the media in order to create an environment similar to that of the early German Expressionist film. The result is something of a Witch's Kitchen in which light and dark are balanced and contrasted on a shadow screen, using a technique developed by puppeteer Marcelle Hudon from Montreal. This involves three-dimensional objects held at different distances from the screen, and a light source that can be employed in creating variegated effects. The actors move from one medium to another, and, when not on stage, remain in contact with the audience through the shadow screen and the video. A typical use of the light puppet is in the appearance of the 'Earth Spirit' as a laser light refracted through glass creating a throbbing ghostly energy. By using mobile light sources, the traditional shadow show is greatly expanded in a manner that accords well with the Faustian source material.

The script of *Faust through the Shadows* combines humour and social commentary while reflecting aspects of Goethe's original. It is seen through the minds of two human actors: the Puppet, based on Kaspar as seen in Jan Švankmajer's *Faust* who, in turn, is based on the Kaspar of the Faust puppet tradition, and the Actor, a visual derivative of silent film characters such as Nosferatu. The Puppet is direct, impulsive, earthy and thoughtless. The Actor is convoluted, retentive, cerebral and pretentious. Human actors perform the puppet characters in the play. The Actor (male) is God and Faust along with secondary characters. Ultimately the Actor, God and Faust are different extensions of the same essence. The Puppet (female) plays Mephistopheles, Wagner, and Gretchen along with secondary characters. The Puppet, Mephistopheles and Wagner are inextricably linked. In the end the Puppet and its derivative characters maintain the upper hand over the Actor/Faust/God.

34. Faust confronted by the devil in dog form, from Tim Gosley's Faust through the Shadows (2003), an implementation rich in Expressionistic effects. Photograph by Tim Gosley.

It is difficult to think of Gretchen as a defenceless fourteen-year-old. In Gosley's version she desires Faust's riches and never properly falls in love with him. She has a strong sense of self and does not suffer Faust's doting lightly. Her character arcs back to Goethe's as soon as her mother and brother fall victim to Mephisto's manipulations. Social commentary peppers the script to connect the sins of yesterday to today. Reference is made to current drugs ('You'll come like Niagara with Satan's Viagra.') And there is mention of the Iraq war of 2003 ('I feel the push. In a future life [Faust's] name will be Bush.'). A short extract will help to exemplify the fast-moving timbre of this innovative production.

SCENE 9: STREET SCENE

[MARGARETA *enters singing.* FAUSTUS *arrives and stares at* MARGARETA'S *breasts*]

FAUSTUS:	Those are the most voluptuous … eyes.
MARGARETA:	Oh kind sir, you must be from a different land. 'Eye' is not the word we use for that particular gland. [MARGARETA *exits.* MEPHISTO *enters*]
FAUSTUS:	I must have her.
MEPHISTO:	Who?
FAUSTUS:	Her. The one with the voluptuous … eyes.

234

MEPHISTO: Eyes, thighs, they're all the same. Not her sir. She frequents church and is light on sin. Let's find a dame that sucks back gin.

FAUSTUS: I want her. I am in love. [FAUSTUS exits]

MEPHISTO: Oh suffering Satan, and all for a bet. Now when he dreams the sheets will be wet. [FAUSTUS enters]

FAUSTUS: Deliver her a token of my love. Something special. Tonight. [FAUSTUS exits]

MEPHISTO: Yes sir, I feel the push. In a future life, your name will be Bush. [MEPHISTO exits. MARGARETA enters]

MARGARETA: I don't like gin. I prefer scotch. And both those jerks look light in the crotch. [MARGARETA exits]

SCENE 10: MARGARETA'S BEDROOM
[Music: ZAPPA: Catholic girls]

MARGARETA: There once was a king from Thule with the virility of a mule. [stumbling noises] Someone's coming. [MARGARETA hides. MEPHISTO's clawed hand reaches in, delivering a jewel]

FAUSTUS: Shhhh ...

MEPHISTO: Shhh ... We'll leave this here. [They exit]

MARGARETA: That is so Baroque. But at least the guy's got cash. All I can get around here is a headache and a rash.

SCENE 11: A WALK
[Music: ZAPPA: Catholic girls]

FAUSTUS: Oh, beautiful Margareta, to feel the softness of your bed.

MEPHISTO: Tie not your testes in a knot. Your gift of love was soon forgot. She gave the jewels to the local parson, who doubles as a fence, and she negotiated a very tidy recompense.

FAUSTUS: Beautiful and intelligent! Quick, give her more, even better then before. [FAUSTUS exits]

MEPHISTO: A true cliché 'Love is blind': Love turns a brain to a sow's behind. (Unpublished manuscript)

Faust continues to inspire new generations of actors and directors to explore innovative methods of representation. These cover all aspects of traditional theatre: characterisation, sets and scenography, music, lighting, seating arrangements and many others. It will clearly not be possible to document everything that has been attempted in this respect, particularly as modern theatres tend to be meeting-places of music, film, and various forms of digitised presentation. Key developments are evaluated in Hans-Peter Bayerdörfer's study of 2002. In conclusion, the work of 66b/cell in Japan is worth considering as an extreme example of what is being done with (and to) Faust on the contemporary stage. Founded jointly in 1994 by Tetsutoshi Tavata (Osaka, Japan) and Maria Adriana Verdaasdonk (Melbourne, Australia) as a result of work combining body movement and multimedia, Tokyo-based performance and media network 66b/cell use live acting as well as pre-recorded computer graphics and animation, expanding the performance potential of the human body. Some of this is executed by a real-time graphics engine from

235

genemagic.com in the interests of creating different moods, texturing, lighting and motion. The group present their work in theatres, warehouses, galleries and nightclubs, maintaining an open framework in which the relationship between body, visuals and sound is a unifying principle.

Inspired by Goethe's *Faust II*, 66b/cell's approach has evolved through a series of presentations in Tokyo, New York, Berlin, Vienna, Linz, Melbourne and Sydney since its première at the East Gallery, Tokyo, in 1998. The aim is to access individual characters of the play and make them come to life through adaptation and mutation in a fusion with spirits from Far Eastern tradition.

> *Faust II* developed from an initial staging held at a small studio in 1997 where movement together with extracts of text elucidated several of the scenes, while projected images enabled multi-layered realms of reality and illusion. This was followed in 1998 at a much larger performance venue where the fragmented texts of Heiner Müller were spliced with the 'mind pictures' of Goethe, presenting the opportunity for an experimental juxtaposition of text, movement and visual projections. The audience, seated in a central pit, was surrounded on all sides. Twisting and craning their necks to follow the action, people were made to experience the fragmented nature of the performance through physical exertion.
>
> The approach in 1999 to 2002 involved short remixes and 'hybrid versions' through successive live performances in studios, night clubs and event spaces in Japan and Australia, as well as in New York, Berlin, Linz and Vienna. The text became the departure point for characters derived from *Faust II*: Mephistopheles, Faust, Homunculus and the Mothers, as well as from mythical creatures taken from the play and from other sources.
>
> *Faust II* is seen as a kind of literary cubism or layering, reflecting the changing thoughts and perceptions of the age in which Goethe lived: the concept of an evolving world as distinguished from a pre-ordained one was a distinction that separated eighteenth-century European thought from that of the nineteenth, in the differing perceptions of reality and in the way of representing reality in art. Goethe himself thought that *Faust II* was more suited to a different age. In the last letter he wrote before his death (to Wilhelm von Humboldt, 17 March, 1832), he described the second part of his *Faust* as a text 'shattered like a wreck [...] covered over with the debris of the hour', ill rewarded in his own time, but waiting to be discovered by a future generation.
>
> Among the many often perplexing themes of the text is the parallel of Faust's search for an ideal with the search of Homunculus (a creation of life by scientific means) for a form. The concept of Homunculus is significant in this age not only in regard to bio-engineering but also as a new alchemic creature in terms of information and artistic technologies, ever-expanding synthesised 'life forms'. Mephistopheles is not the devil of old, or even merely the principle of evil, for this is not a realm of absolutes. Rather, s/he is a catalyst prompting action and reaction and in the 66b/cell approach represents not negation, but the urge towards creativity. (Summary supplied by Maria Adriana Verdaasdonk)

Characters include Mephistopheles, a devilish trickster spirit with laser gloves and platform boots; Mother, symbol of the goddess in her various aspects, who wears platform shoes and various headpieces, representing the Mater Gloriosa and a hybrid version of Helena of Troy; the Tulip Women, or Mothers, with lantern-like headpieces, cosmic spirits dwelling in a realm beyond time and space; Homunculi,

35. *Faust's salvation by the Mother/Mater Gloriosa figure. (66b/cell) Tetsuji Yamazaki (Faust), Maria Adriana Verdaasdonk (Mother), 1998. Photograph by Shibasaki.*

friendly alien-like creatures with elongated white heads; finally, Buku Buku, Gorgons or intergalactic gate-keepers with bright orange suits and large spotlight head-beams.

The subject of this volume provides an inexhaustible quarry for dramatists and direc-tors, producers and actors, lighting experts and sound recordists. This is due in large part to the 'open' quality of the material, and notably to its uncertain, waver-ing ethical standpoint that has permitted a multitude of contradictory interpreta-tions to gain favour among its recipients. Even when restricting oneself to the Faust Book, Marlowe and Goethe, one notes that they share a distinct lack of linearity. Chapters and scenes do not proceed logically from one another and are often tenuously linked, if at all. The narrative flows in an unstable rhythm around the central figures, illuminating them from new angles and confusing the audience by presenting not so much a plot as a series of mind pictures that produce ever-shifting images. Faust's exploits demand to be continuously re-evaluated, his predicament cries out to be investigated further, yet his mysterious personality resists close analysis. Theatre, opera and ballet, mystery plays and harlequinades, puppets and shadow images have not resolved matters but merely contributed additional layers to an essentially elusive figure. More will be said about the manner in which other visual media, such as the cinema, have played their part in this process, and the present chapter must necessarily overlap with others. Of all artistic media, music enjoys the most intimate relationship with Faust by virtue of an inherent affinity with the theme. Yet despite the enormous popularity enjoyed by operatic, vocal and instrumental treatments of the subject, the quest for the perfect musical setting has frustrated successive generations of composers, whose work will be examined in the following chapter.

Notes

1. Premièred on 20 July 1999; ARD (German television) 26 July 1999; Anton Heinrich, 'Radziwill der Autor der ersten Musik zu Goethes Faust', DRS2 (Swiss radio) 30 December 2002.
2. See http://www.faust-stein.de/ (information on the project); http://faust.zdf.de/ (playable internet version). Accessed May 2004.

Cited Works and Further Reading

Stuart Atkins, *Faust. A Literary Analysis.* Cambridge/Mass: Harvard University Press, 1957.
Hans-Peter Bayerdörfer (ed.), *Im Auftrieb. Grenzüberschreitungen mit Goethes Faust in Inszenierungen der neunziger Jahre.* Tübingen: Niemeyer, 2002.
Hermann Beil, Achim Freyer, Bernd Mahl, Claus Peymann and Vera Sturm (eds), *Faust. Der Tragödie Erster und Zweiter Teil. Die Aufführung der Württembergischen Staatstheater Stuttgart. Eine Dokumentation.* Stuttgart: Belser Verlag, 1979.
Michael Billington, 'Carry on Doctor', *The Guardian*, 13 March 2002.
—, 'The Salvation of Dr Faust', *The Guardian*, 11 November 1985.
Michael R. Booth, 'Henry Irving's *Faust*, Lyceum Theatre, 1885', in Ibid., *Victorian Spectacular Theatre 1850–1910.* Boston: Routledge & Kegan Paul, 1981, 93–126.
Heinrich Brandt, *Goethes Faust auf der königlich sächsischen Hofbühne zu Dresden. Ein Beitrag zur Theaterwissenschaft.* Berlin: Emil Ebering, 1921.
Bertolt Brecht, *Grosse kommentierte Berliner und Frankfurter Ausgabe.* Ed. Werner Hecht *et al.* 30 volumes. Berlin: Aufbau/ Frankfurt/M: Suhrkamp, 1988–1992.
E.M. Butler, *The Fortunes of Faust.* Cambridge: University Press, 1952.
Austin Brereton, *The Life of Henry Irving.* 2 volumes. London: Longmans, 1908.
Heinz-Rudi Brunner and E. Peter Moosmann (eds), *Johann Wolfgang von Goethe – Faust – Erster und Zweiter Teil. Ausgewählte Inszenierungen auf Bühnen der Bundesrepublik Deutschland.* Exhibition at the Goethe-Institut, Munich. Frankfurt/M: Goethe-Institut, 1982.
Faust am Goetheanum. Stuttgart: Urachhaus, 1982.
R.A. Foakes and R.T. Rickert (eds), *Henslowe's Diary,* Cambridge: University Press, 1961.
Otto Francke (ed.), *The Life and Death of Doctor Faustus, Made into a Farce by Mr Mountford.* Heilbronn: Henninger, 1886.
W.W. Greg, *Marlowe's Doctor Faustus 1604–1616. Parallel Texts.* Oxford: Clarendon Press, 1950.
Dieter Görne (ed.), *Faust in Weimar. Dokumente.* Weimar: Deutsches Nationaltheater, 1975.
—, *Wolfgang Engel inszeniert Goethes Faust am Staatsschauspiel Dresden 1990.* 2 volumes. Berlin: Zentrum für Theaterdokumentation, 1990.
Helmut Grosse and Bernd Vogelsang (eds), *Faust und Mephistopheles. Goethes Dramenfiguren auf dem Theater.* Cologne: Theatermuseum der Universität, 1983.

Joseph Hatton, *The Lyceum 'Faust'. With Illustrations and Drawings*. London: J.S. Virtue, 1885.

William Frederic Hauhart, *The Reception of Goethe's Faust in England in the First Half of the Nineteenth Century*. New York: Columbia University Press, 1909.

Rosalynn D. Haynes, *From Faust to Strangelove. Representations of the Scientist in Western Literature*. Baltimore: Johns Hopkins University Press, 1994.

W. Heinemann, 'Faust auf der englischen Bühne', *Goethe-Jahrbuch* 7 (1886), 318–22.

Hans Henning (ed.), *Faust-Bibliographie*. 3 parts, 5 volumes. Berlin: Aufbau, 1966–76.

John Houseman, *Run-Through. A Memoir*. New York: Simon and Schuster, 1972.

L. Hughes, 'The Date of Mountfort's *Faustus*', *Notes and Queries* 192 (1947), 358f.

Henry Irving, *Faust*. Lyceum Theatre Programmes, 19 December 1885 and 17 May 1886. Templeman Library, University of Kent.

Anon. [Henry James], 'The Acting in Mr Irving's "Faust",' *The Century Magazine* 13 (12/1887), 301–13.

John D. Jump (ed.), *The Tragical History of the Life and Death of Doctor Faustus*. London: Methuen, 1962.

Joachim Kaiser, 'Faust – ein Schreihals ohne Zentrum?', *Süddeutsche Zeitung*, 3 May 1987, 16.

Hans Joachim Kreutzer, *Faust. Mythos und Musik*. Munich: C.H. Beck, 2003.

Ekkehart Krippendorff, 'Die Moderne auf dem Prüfstand', *Freitag*, 3 November 2000.

Peter Kümmel, 'Augenblick, beeil dich', *Die Zeit*, 31/2000.

Rudolph Lang, *Kurz-verfasste Reiss-Beschreibung Oder: Offt-beschuldigte aber niemals erwiesene Zauberkunst, so in zweyen künstlichen Hunden bestunde, welche Rudolph Lang, Bürger und Bier-Brauer, dermassen künstlich abgerichtet, dass auch die grossen Herren nicht begreiffen konnten, wie diese Kunst beschaffen wäre [...]*. Augsburg: Andreas Jacob Maschenbauern, 1739.

George Henry Lewis, *The Life and Works of Goethe: with sketches of his age and contemporaries from published and unpublished sources*. 2 volumes. London, 1855. Rptd London: Dent, 1906, ed. Havelock Ellis.

Moray McGowan, 'Goethe a go-go. Am Glasgower Citizens' Theatre "Faust I & II" erstmals auf Englisch', *Theater heute*, 1/1986, 61.

Günther Mahal, Brigitte Bruns and Ottmar Maier (eds), *Faust Museum Knittlingen. Exponate, Materialien, Kommentare*. Stuttgart: Paul Daxer, 1980.

Bernd Mahl, *Goethes Faust auf der Bühne (1806–1998). Fragment, Ideologiestück, Spieltext*. Stuttgart: Metzler, 1999.

Christopher Marlowe, *Doctor Faustus*. Ed. Roma Gill. London: Black, 1989.

——, Basil Ashmore (ed.), *Christopher Marlowe's The Tragical History of Doctor Faustus, including the 1592 edition of The History of the damnable life and deserved death of Doctor John Faustus*. London: Blandford Press, 1948.

Andreas Meier, *Faustlibretti: Geschichte des Fauststoffs auf der europäischen Musikbühne nebst einer lexikalischen Bibliographie der Faustvertonungen*, Frankfurt/M: Peter Lang, 1990.

Siegfried Melchinger, *Theater der Gegenwart*. Frankfurt/M: Fischer, 1958.

John Melton, *Astrologaster or the figvre-caster*. London: Barnard Alsop, 1620. Reprinted Los Angeles: Clark Memorial Library, 1975, ed. Hugh G. Dick.

Thomas Merrivale, *The Necromancer; or Harlequin Doctor Faustus. A Poem Founded on Gentile Theology*. London: J. Roberts, 1724.

Martin Morrow, 'Giving the devil his proper due', *The Globe and Mail*, 31 March 2003.

John Mountford, *The Life and Death of Doctor Faustus, made into a Farce*. London: E. Whitlock, 1697.

Hermann Müller, *Erklärung der Faust-Vorstellungen am Königlichen Theater zu Hannover*. Hanover: Helwing, 1877.

Carl Niessen (ed.), *Faust auf der Bühne. Faust in der bildenden Kunst. Zur Jahrhundertfeier der Uraufführung des ersten Teiles in Braunschweig*. Berlin: Fritz Klopp, 1929.

Ulrich Parenth, *Wie Goethes 'Faust' auf die Bühne kam. Eine Dokumentation über die Welt-Uraufführung in Braunschweig.* Brunswick: Holtzmeyer, 1986.

Joseph and Elizabeth R. Pennell, 'Pictorial Successes of Mr Irving's "Faust",' *The Century Magazine* 13 (12/1887), 309–11.

Günther Rühle, 'Faust oder der leichte Traum', *Theater heute*, 4/1977, 18–25.

Kurt Scheidig and Karl Theens, *Doktor Fausts Höllenfahrt. Das Puppenspiel vom Doktor Faust.* Stuttgart: Faust-Gesellschaft, 1971.

Roswitha Schieb (ed.) in collaboration with Anna Haas, *Peter Stein inszeniert Faust von Johann Wolfgang Goethe. Das Programmbuch Faust I und II.* Cologne: DuMont, 2000.

Wolfgang Schlüter (trs. and ed.), Christopher Marlowe, *Sämtliche Dramen.* Frankfurt/M: Eichborn 1999.

Jonathan Shandell, 'The devil is in the details. *Faustus* by Christopher Marlowe', *oobr, the off-off-broadway review*, 9 (2002), 5.

Robert B. Sharpe, *Real War of the Theatres: Shakespeare's Fellows in Rivalry with the Admiral's Men.* Boston: Modern Language Association, 1935.

Karl Simrock (ed.), *Doctor Johannes Faust: Puppenspiel in vier Aufzügen.* Frankfurt/M: Brönner, 1846. Rptd Stuttgart: Reclam, 1991, ed. Günther Mahal.

George Soane, *Faustus: a romantic drama in three acts.* London: J. Miller, 1825.

Robert Speaight, *William Poel and the Elizabethan Revival.* London: Heinemann, 1954.

Bram Stoker, *Personal Reminiscences of Henry Irving.* 2 volumes. London: Heinemann, 1906.

Gerhard Stumme, *Faust als Pantomime und Ballett,* Leipzig: Poeschel & Trepte, 1942.

Hans-Jürgen Syberberg and Hans Mayer, '1971 – Nach meinem letzten Umzug.' *Drucksache* 4 (1993), 97–116, 141–51.

Paul Taylor, 'With a little more contrast, Law could be devilishly good', *The Independent,* 19 March 2002.

John Thurmond, *Harlequin Doctor Faustus with the Masque of the Deities, with Additions and Alterations.* London: W. Chetwood, 1724.

Deborah Vietor-Engländer, *Faust in der DDR.* Frankfurt/M: Peter Lang, 1987.

Laurie Webb, 'Report on Preetzer Papiertheatertreffen No. 14', *British Puppet & Model Theatre Guild News Letter* 480, October 2001.

Manfred Wegner (ed.), *Die Spiele der Puppe,* Cologne: Prometh, 1989.

Adolf Wilbrandt, *Faust. Für die Bühne eingerichtet und in drei Abende eingetheilt.* Vienna: Verlag der Literarischen Gesellschaft, 1883.

William Gorman Wills, *Faust in a prologue and five acts. Adapted and arranged for the Lyceum Theatre, from the first part of Goethe's tragedy.* London, 1886.

Anton Eduard Wollheim da Fonseca, *Erläuterungen und Gesänge zum zweiten Theil von Göthe's Faust.* Hamburg: Lehmann und Birkmann, 1854.

Annie Doris Wraight, *Christopher Marlowe and Edward Alleyn.* Chichester: Adam Hart, 1993.

Simon Williams, 'Performing Mephistopheles,' *Goethe Yearbook,* Special Volume 1 (1994): *Interpreting Goethe's Faust Today,* 94–100.

Chapter Seven

Musical Fausts: From Broadsheet to Rock Opera

There can hardly be a single dramatic work in world literature that is filled with so much inaudible music and which, despite innumerable attempts and despite the obviously operatic structures of Part II, is ultimately as hostile to musical composition as *Faust*.——Dieter Borchmeyer

36. *Gounod's opera* Faust *as staged at Covent Garden, 1864, with Jean-Baptiste Faure as Mephistopheles, Giovanni Mario as Faust and Adelina Patti as Marguerite. Even Mephistopheles had become quaintly picturesque rather than menacing.*

The Devil's Tunes

T HE DEVIL, according to the English proverb, has all the best tunes. He uses music to divert and to seduce his victims. No sooner has Faustus begun to invoke him than he is overcome by doubt as to whether he should continue with his conjurations, 'whereupon the devil made him such music of all sorts, as if the Nymphs themselves had been in place: whereat Faustus was revived and stood stoutly in his circle [...]'; the German text speaks of 'many admirable instruments, music and singing' (Henning, 15; Rose, 68f.). Goethe has his Mephistopheles perform music on many occasions, either in person, such as when he entertains the drinkers in Auerbach's Cellar, or indirectly, by summoning subordinate spirits to do his work for him. Dancing and chanting are a feature of the Walpurgis Night revelry, and it is easy to imagine Faust learning some new dance-steps on that occasion, as he does in Heine's ballet. There are so many other points at which music plays a central role that it is possible to see *Faust* as embodying a history of music, beginning with the celestial music of the spheres, and returning to its 'transcendental base' after exploring all points between. Its inherently operatic qualities are often noted. 'Music in *Faust* is as ubiquitous as the sea in novels by Conrad' (Borchmeyer, 334; Green, 47). The Romantics continued to foreground its musical potential. Nikolaus Lenau's Mephisto rebukes the village orchestra for not playing their instruments passionately enough and demands to be given a violin in order to liven things up:

> Dear folk, as the bows of your violins
> Scrape lazily across the strings –
> Your waltzes are best suited to
> The flagging arm, the lame man's shoe,
> But not to youth's impassioned ways.
> Pass me your instrument and stand amazed
> How soon the tavern will resound
> To a merrier note as you leap around! (Lenau, lines 818–25)

There are traditions that represent the devil as a musician, and specifically as a violinist. This may explain why it used to be rumoured that great violinists such as Niccolo Paganini can only have obtained their outstanding gift though some kind of diabolical compact. The theme continues in a number of films – including *Crossroads* and *O Brother, where art thou?* – which suggest that blues musicians regularly acquire skills in this manner (Grim, I, 4; see 313, below). Faust is so closely bound up with music that Thomas Mann claimed, 'If Faust is to be a representative of the German soul, he must be a musician [...]' (Mann, 1131). There are ballads, *Lieder*, arias, and drinking-songs, piano suites and chamber music, cantatas, oratorios, ballets and operas galore, symphonies, popular songs in many styles, musicals, rock albums and rock ballets that have used Faust's career as their point of departure. In addition, there are by-products like music-hall operettas and burlesques in which up-market compositions are travestied. The most productive genres have been, unsurprisingly, those with a strong vocal and dramatic component. There are well over forty operas that can claim to have been inspired by the theme. Those that make use of Goethe's play tend to restrict themselves to selected aspects of Part I. The chapbook and puppet plays contributed to many of the twentieth-century compositions. Several Faust operas reached iconic status and were among the most successful examples of their type and of their age; this is especially true of the nineteenth-century works by Louis Spohr and Charles Gounod. Goethe may have provided the inspiration, but the subject was avoided by German composers, some of whom appear to have been reluctant to vie with the national genius by recasting his greatest work.

Operas have allowed artists to explore the sidelines of the story, sometimes exposing quite minor figures to the limelight and shaping them into distinct personalities – thus Siebel, whom Goethe sketches briefly in the Leipzig tavern scene, becomes a key figure for Gounod. Margaret's brother Valentin looms large as an offended party whose thirst for retribution meshes as well with the stock-in-trade of grand opera as it does with that of 'revenge' tragedy. Large-scale musical settings on the Faust theme continue to be written; Kunad's *Sabellicus* of 1974 opens up new aspects, Schnittke's *Historia* of 1995 follows the chapbook, and Volz's rock opera, Part II of which was completed in 2002, claims to be the first operatic work of any description based directly and entirely on Goethe's *Faust II*. Many twentieth-century composers, including Busoni, Eisler, and Schnittke, have moved away from Goethe and returned to the puppet plays and chapbook. In fact, with the exception of Boito and, latterly, Volz, most operas depart from Goethe and follow other sources, not least because of the unconventional structure of Goethe's drama.

The second area in which Faust has been fertile is that of the *Lied*. It is here, rather than in opera, that native German talent comes into its own. Certain passages from Goethe's work seemed tailor-made for short musical settings of the type known as *Kunstlieder* ('through-composed songs') that were so appealing to nineteenth-century music-lovers. They range from reflective, lyrical romances such as Gretchen's 'King in Thule' to lively satirical ballads like Mephisto's 'Song of the Flea', best known in its setting by Beethoven (Opus 75 nr. 3). Faust has continued to inspire modern song-writers in the popular vein. Chamber music has, by contrast, been thinner on the ground, although a variety of instrumental essays, including symphonies, have been woven around the theme, many of these enriched by a vocal component.

The following survey will not only demonstrate the versatility of the theme but will track its relationship to those art-forms that were most in demand at the time of writing. To follow Faust's fortunes through public performances over the past four hundred years is to trace the history of the supporting media. In music, this extends from broadsheet ballads to harlequin ballets, and thence from the *Singspiel* to grand opera, light opera, the music hall, and on to twelve-tone and chromatic experimentation, and eventually to punk and rock. Beyond the musical medium, there are literary descriptions of compositions that do not exist: in his novel *Doctor*

Faustus, Thomas Mann supplies a moving description of an opus entitled 'Doctor Faustus' Lament' by the fictitious composer Adrian Leverkühn.

Ballads and Ballets

The earliest music associated with Faust was composed almost before the ink had dried on the Faust Book of 1587. Fritz Beer's 'Faustus conjures twelve students' and 'Faustus silences the howling peasants' were set to music in 1588 (Bolte; Mertens). The former tells of students who were brawling in two groups of 7 and 5. Faustus considers the larger group to have an unfair advantage and makes them blind, so that they cannot recognise who is fighting against whom. The noisy peasants are given a similar lesson in civic virtue: they have their jaws fixed wide open as a punishment for their unruly behaviour. The tunes to these two moral ditties were by two prominent Mastersingers, Heinrich Frauenlob and Heinrich Mügling (Aign, 15).

An English ballad was granted permission by Bishop Aymler in the same year. Walter Aign assumes it was identical with 'The Just Judgment of God shew'd upon Dr John Faustus', a ballad printed on a broadsheet around 1670 and believed to be based on a much earlier source. It begins:

> All Christian Men give Ear a while to me,
> How I am plung'd in Pain, but cannot see:
> I liv'd a life, the like did none before,
> Forsaking Christ, and I am damn'd therefore.

This, too, was not an original composition, but sung to the tune of 'Fortune my Foe'. A number of similar items have been preserved from later years. The ballads normally purport to illustrate a single episode from the magician's life; they were sometimes accompanied by a woodcut image and usually sold as broadsheets.

More ambitious musical compositions were supplied in connection with the pantomimes and ballets that were popular in the early eighteenth century. Johann Ernst Galliard is the author of *Dr Faustus or the Necromancer. A Masque of Songs as they were perform'd at the Theatre in Lincolns Inn Fields* (London, 1724; two surviving copies are in the British Library, London and in the Library of the Brussels Conservatory). The eighteenth-century harlequinades that were staged in London by Thurmond, Mountfort, Rich and others also made extensive use of music and dancing.

Goethe's personal musical ability was limited. There is no record of whether he could sing or recall a tune, although his interest in musical theory was considerable (Kreutzer, 49; Canisius). Maybe this explains why he was sceptical as to whether music could be written to *Faust* without giving offence, commenting to Eckermann on 12 February 1829 that 'the repulsive, unpleasant and terrifying qualities that it would in some places require are out of tune with our age.' And yet, somewhat perversely, he remarked in the same conversation that '*Faust* should have been set to music by Mozart.' Despite such reservations, operas and ballets were quick to establish themselves alongside drama. The first production in Paris, at the Théâtre de la Porte St.-Martin, was a three-act adaptation in a setting by Antony Béraud, the high points of which were Lemaître's mocking laughter and fascinating dance steps (Baldick, 66). The *Original romantisk Ballet i tre Akter* by August Bournonville, a central figure in Danish culture, who fought tirelessly to improve the social status and security of dancers, opened on 25 December 1832. The plot follows Goethe closely, though in common with theatre productions of the time, the scenes in Heaven and on the Brocken are omitted, the latter being replaced by a fairground display. There are some amusing touches, such as Martha boxing Mephisto's ears when he is about to embrace her. The ballet ends with Gretchen's salvation; when Faust tries to follow her upwards towards the heavenly light, the angels push him away and he sinks into the abyss with Mephistopheles (Stumme, 95–100).

Adolphe Adam produced a score for a ballet written by Deshayes in 1833, and this was performed in February of that year in the King's Theatre, Haymarket. Later ballets include Antonio Montirini's *Cardenuto*, which Fanny Lewald saw in Milan in 1845 and describes in her *Italienisches Bilderbuch*.

> It was inevitable that the tragedy would have to be changed, and this for two reasons. Firstly, the Italians find it difficult to appreciate that anyone could feel as miserable as Faust does solely because he cannot comprehend the universe in its entirety and cannot solve the riddles of existence. The happily contented people of southern Europe are not riven by such inner torments [...] Secondly, Goethe's play is unable to provide sufficient technical and theatrical splendour for a ballet. Its marvellous effects cannot be displayed in Faust's modest study or in Gretchen's peaceful bedchamber. Thus the following alterations were called for.

37. *In Giulio Perrot's ballet, 1851, Gustave Carey as Mephistopheles tempts Gretchen by giving her a box of presents and showing her Vanity, the third of the seven deadly sins (Stumme, 120).*

The intellectually resolute, manly Faust is changed into the aged, weak sculptor Cardenuto, after whom the ballet is named. His creative powers are in abeyance and he looks in vain for the ideal of beauty. Thereupon the devil, whom he summons, shows him a vision of Helena, the daughter of the princess of Magdeburg, whose mother has promised her to Vormos, a relation of the Duke of Brunswick. (Lewald, I, 43f.)

The reception was ecstatic and Lewald ends her account of it by regretting that such moving, light-hearted ballets, which accord so well with the spirit of Goethe's work, are not likely to be seen in Germany (*Op. cit.*, I, 42–51).

Of those that were, one of the most successful was produced by Giulio Perrot in Vienna, in 1851, with Fanny Elsler in the role of Gretchen and music by Giacomo Panizza. The entire Viennese court attended the première and the reviews were ecstatic. The same ballet was also performed in Milan and possibly also in London (Stumme, 122f.).

Lied and *Singspiel*

Willi Schuh's index of *Lieder* derived from Goethe's works contains a total of 735 entries. Only one hundred of these are from *Faust*, although Aign claims to know of at least 300 others. The commonest of these is Gretchen's song about the 'King in Thule'. Music is indispensable at this point: a stage direction specifies that Gretchen sings it as she takes off her clothes (F 2759). Aign estimates that there are 100 *Lieder*-type settings of this one poem from the play, plus approximately 15 versions from musical dramas and operas. He distinguishes between three types of *Faust-Lied*: strophic compositions, combinations of strophic and through-composed, and entirely through-composed songs, counting around 50 of the first and 20 each of the second and third types for the 'King in Thule'. Carl Friedrich Zelter, a close friend of the poet, actually produced a version for a bass voice. Goethe himself observed the paradox: 'Our friend Zelter has admittedly produced a fine setting for the song, but it would be more appropriate to the powerful bass voice of a suitably endowed Viking than for a sweet child of nature like Gretchen'. But, as Aign rightly points out, Gretchen is to be imagined as remembering a song she heard, not as its author; the bass is thus appropriate. Others went so far as to rework the poem for male choirs, and the song served as the basis for no fewer than three operas in its own right, including Georg Wilhelm Rauchenecker's apocalyptic *Die letzten Tage von Thule* ('The Last Days of Thule') of 1889 (Aign, 43–5). Goethe preferred strophic compositions and would not have approved of Liszt's use of 97 bars where Zelter was able to make do with nine.

The second most popular *Lied* is the heart-wringing 'Spinning-Wheel' song (F 3374–3413). Aign registers 53 compositions of this, of which the undoubted favourite is Schubert's. There has even been debate as to whether the spinning-wheel is to be thought of as revolving, or whether the girl is too deeply immersed in her reveries to continue with this chore; no fewer than 33 of Aign's examples do appear to recreate the sound of the wheel in motion, but the compositions range from sombre and soulful adagios to lively, impassioned *vivace e agitato* settings. Carl Loewe's implementation, *tief bewegt, mit glühender Sehnsucht* ('Deeply moved, with a glowing yearning') comes close to the mood of the original.

The 'Prayer to the Virgin' (F 3586–3619) is the third favourite with 45 compositions (Aign, 48). The most ambitious of these is by Josef Dessauer, whose version extends to 172 bars. They were by no means the exclusive work of German musicians; Verdi, Glinka, Tomaszek among other non-German composers turned their hands to this material. Yet the most prolific was Conradin Kreutzer (22 songs from Faust), and Richard Wagner wrote seven in 1832 when he was nineteen, ostensibly for his sister Rosalie, who was then playing the part of Gretchen in Leipzig. They were not used, and opinions vary as to their merit, something that cannot be said about another young prodigy, Franz Schubert, whose preoccupation with Goethe dates from 1814, when he was seventeen. Schubert set a total of 73 poems by Goethe, and the five that are based on *Faust* appeared in 1821. Schubert's passion for Goethe knew no bounds; he dared not dedicate them to his idol without his permission, and thus he used an intermediary to plead for this privilege. Goethe never responded. Two years after Schubert's premature death, however, he praised a recital of the latter's 'Erlkönig' ('The King of the Elves') when sung for him by Wilhelmine Schröder-Devrient (Aign, 90).

The Oxford Dictionary of Opera lists twenty-one Faust operas based on Goethe and a further fourteen operas deriving from other sources (Warrack and West, 234). There are many obvious omissions in this. Andreas Meier's bibliography of 'Faustlibretti', by contrast, runs to 135 pages, though his list includes much in the way of 'incidental' music. The many harlequinades from the early eighteenth century have hardly begun to be investigated, nor have the pieces that were specially commissioned for theatre productions in more recent times. As in literature and film, the operatic repertoire includes many works with distinctly Faustian traits, from Weber's *Der Freischütz* to Stravinsky's *L'Histoire du soldat*, which cannot be considered here as Faust is neither named nor specifically alluded to.

Following publication of Goethe's *Fragment* in 1790, composers were quick to work on large-scale musical settings. One of the first was Johann Friedrich Reichardt's *Musik zu Göthes Faust* of 1790. A year later, hopeful of an early production, both Anton Radziwill and Karl Eberwein were working on compositions intended for the theatre. It was not long before operas were written: Johann Ignaz Walter composed his *Doctor Faust* in 1797, from which one or two songs are remembered. Ludwig (or Louis) Spohr's *Faust* (libretto by Joseph Karl Bernard) dates from around 1813; this was first performed in Prague in 1816 and was much played during the early nineteenth century. Torn between two women, Röschen and Kunigunde, the hero relies heavily on Mephistopheles for protection against their various understandably jealous suitors. After several amorous adventures, he decides to withdraw from the world and devote himself solely to Röschen, but she drowns herself when she realises how unfaithful he has been. It amounts to little more than a moral tale with romantic elements, but this, com-

38. A production of Spohr's Faust, *Royal Italian Opera, London 1852,*
Illustrated London News.

bined with its tunefulness, ensured its popularity at a time when Spohr was rated
a greater composer than Beethoven. It was performed in London in May 1840 to
celebrate the marriage of Queen Victoria to Prince Albert (Marinelli, 1; Kreutzer,
28-45). The British Library in London holds no fewer than 67 volumes of libretti,
translations, piano arrangements, and 'admired airs' deriving from this work.

Symphonic Fausts

Robert Schumann's *Scenes from Goethe's Faust* were written between 1844 and 1853
and first performed in Cologne in 1861. The composition has remained
underrated, despite being Schumann's most ambitious, featuring eight vocal parts,
three choruses and a full orchestra. Something of a hybrid in its final form, it was
planned as opera but executed in the manner of an oratorio in three sections. The
original title claimed that it was intended for 'voices, choir and orchestra', placing
it on the margins of the recognised genres. There is no doubting Schumann's
sincerity in trying to transpose Goethe's drama directly into the musical medium.
Yet he made changes to the style and ethos that reflected personal religious
perceptions. He began at the end of *Faust II*, with the 'Mystic Chorus', never
previously set to music, and completed what he called 'Faust's Transfiguration' in
1848, a noble choral piece with ecclesiastic leanings. He then worked backwards,
completing three scenes from Faust's affair with Gretchen ('Garden', 'Prayer to
the Virgin', 'Cathedral'), three from Part II, and, finally, the grand overture.
Schumann's achievement was to combine the two parts of play and provide music

248

that not only fitted the action-rich first part, but was also appropriate to the second and addressed the significance of Faust's struggle for self-fulfilment. The pact scenes and the Mephistophelean elements are sidelined. The dreamy nature of Schumann's music, combined with the composer's enduring interest in religious questions, is thus only partially appropriate to the Faustian material, and the work can be criticised for Schumann's unwillingness to exploit the dramatic qualities of the text on which it is based. It shed its theatrical qualities in favour of a new attempt at fusing words, music and ethical content, the latter being transmuted into a personal theory of salvation (Grim II, 161–81; Kreutzer, 85–101).

Curious affinities have sprung up between Faust and certain countries that originally had no direct connection with the story. One of these is Hungary. Lenau's Romantic Faust is one example; and it was from Lenau that Franz Liszt drew inspiration for his 'Mephisto Waltz' and 'Der nächtliche Zug' ('Nocturnal Procession'), which were published together as *Two Episodes from Lenau's 'Faust'* in 1860. Liszt also composed a *Faust Symphony*, in which he attempted musical representations of the three central figures, Faust, Mephistopheles and Gretchen, apparently in preparation for a fully-fledged opera, which may explain why the *Chorus Mysticus* was attached to the symphony. Although untexted, the symphony of themes associated with the play's three main characters provides an accompaniment to a drama which is acted out in their minds. By Liszt's reasoning, what Goethe attempted to do in drama may be impossible in that medium but achievable in music (Grim II, 186f.).

Wagner also worked on a Faust symphony between 1839 and 1855. What remains is an overture, Opus 59, that has some similarities to *The Flying Dutchman* (Hafner, 131). The only other great 'Faust Symphony' was written by Gustav Mahler as his Eighth Symphony, known as the 'Symphony of a Thousand'. Its musical sources include the above-mentioned pieces by Liszt and Schumann, as well as Beethoven's Ninth (Grim II, 194–210). It shares the hybrid qualities of the latter, being a choral work composed around two separate cantatas, one a Catholic prayer ('*Veni creator spiritus*'), the other the finale to *Faust II*. Both evoke the idea of a universal brotherhood and seek to invest it with an ideal of continuity. That a Christian prayer for love, peace and knowledge should be answered by Faust's inner illumination, ironically after being blinded, gives the work a more rounded and more universal quality than it would possess, had Mahler restricted himself to purely literary or ecclesiastical sources.

All stage productions of Goethe's play also required music to be borrowed, invented or specially commissioned. Spoken theatre with no musical effects whatsoever is a relatively new invention, at least in Germany, where few directors would have dared to emulate Barry Yzereef in asking the cast to make up their own tunes for the songs. Hedwig Meier has shown that incidental compositions often had a major role in ensuring the success of a production. Eduard Lassen, for example, provided music for the 1876 production at Weimar with the specific intention of unifying the two disparate parts of the play through a non-verbal medium capable of sustaining variations on a single motif. Lassen's thematic approach was finally replaced by a more operatic composition by Felix von Weingartner in 1908, reflecting a tendency that was establishing itself in other theatres at the time (Hedwig Meier, 129–151, 178–182; Ballstaedt, 364–79).

Grand Opera

Radziwill's efforts to provide a fitting score for Goethe's text extended over many years and led to the composition of around 25 arias. It is seldom performed, and the composer was accused of lifting part of the overture from Mozart (Green, 57). Hector Berlioz was strongly attracted to subjects that exuded what he took to be the spirit of Romanticism. He read *Faust* in 1828, at the age of 24 ('I could not put it down, I read it incessantly, at meals, in the theatre, in the street, everywhere'), and began to compose scenes from it, beginning, as so many had done, with the 'King in Thule'. These were published in 1829 as *Huit scènes de Faust* ('Eight Scenes from *Faust*') and constitute his Opus 1. He sent them to Goethe, who cruelly observed, 'Certain individuals can signal their presence of mind and attention only through loud coughing, snorting, crowing and spitting; Mr Hector Berlioz appears to be one of these. The sulphuric odour of Mephisto attracts him, so he must sneeze and splutter to make all the instruments of the orchestra arise and haunt about – but not a hair of Faust moves.' Berlioz may have agreed, for he soon destroyed as many of the published copies as he could find. After working on *Rob Roy* and *King Lear* as well as on his *Symphonie fantastique*, he returned to the theme in 1845 while on tour in central and eastern Europe, completing *La Damnation de Faust* in the following year, having written much of the libretto himself. This deeply personal and idiosyncratic 'dramatic legend in four acts' was performed at the Paris Opéra-Comique on two occasions during 1846 to a half-empty house. Berlioz was later to write, 'Nothing in my career wounded me more deeply than this unexpected indifference' (*Berlioz and the Romantic Imagination*, 123; Heidelberger, 535–48).

There is no overture and no strictly logical sequence of scenes. Set somewhat incongruously in the plains of Hungary, the first part incorporates an adaptation of the Hungarian national march, the Rákóczy March. After the appearance of Mephistopheles, Faust sets off on his journey which takes him to Auerbach's Cellar and thence, by-passing the Witch's Kitchen, to the banks of the River Elbe, where he experiences a dance of the sylphs and a dream vision of Marguerite. The encounter with the life-enhancing maiden, so important in most other versions, is played down by Berlioz, reduced in effect to the 'King in Thule', a love duet with Faust, and an moving lamentation of her loss after Faust has departed. This is followed by Faust's rapturous soliloquy to nature and, in a final vista of pandemonium, his ride into the abyss with his infernal companion. The salvation of Marguerite is hinted at but does not constitute a major element.

This was not the kind of *Faust* the public was expecting. As its title suggests, it portrays a figure doomed from the start and a Mephistopheles noticeably more malevolent than Goethe's. In sharp contrast to what Gounod was to make of the same material just a few years later, Berlioz excises those elements that take us away from Faust himself: the scenes set in the cathedral and prison, for all their dramatic qualities, depict Margaret rather than Faust and were thus of little interest to him. By ignoring these dramatic moments, he deprived his work of those qualities which were to commend Gounod to a sensation-hungry public. Berlioz had chosen a half-way house between oratorio and opera, an *opéra de concert* without décor or costumes, located not in physical surroundings but in the realms of an imagined reality, resistant to staging without major adaptive effort. Underlying this composition are a passion for Goethe as read and reread in Gérard de Nerval's translation of 1827, Berlioz's experiences on his own travels in Hungary and elsewhere, and his friendship with German exiles in Paris, most notably Heinrich Heine. It suffers from having been written piecemeal, while on tour. Yet all *Fausts* are of necessity fragments of a whole that can at best be dimly glimpsed, and in its rapid transitions from darkness to light, in its changing moods and explorations both of terror and of beauty, it came much closer to the 'Faustian' spirit as conceived by the Romantics than did any other of the period. It incorporates the centrally Faustian experiences of the unfulfilled ideal, his pantheistic worship of nature and a terrible sense of isolation, yet the public must have expected a neater package with fewer disharmonies of the type Berlioz placed even into Marguerite's vocals when he associated her with Mephistopheles via the tritone known not inappropriately as *diabolus in musica* (Cairns, 354-65). This is a profoundly Romantic Faust, a lonelier individual than his counterpart in Goethe, and full of immense longing:

FAUST [*alone in the fields, at sunrise*]:
> Spring makes the world look young again,
> Winter has been cast out to die:
> A shower from heaven's dome on high
> Brings sparkling flames like drops of rain.
> Fresh breezes woo the waking air,
> My burning heart begins to stir.
> The birds' fair chorus echoes all around
> And plants and waters rustle on the ground.
> Ah, it is sweet to wrap oneself in solitude
> Far from all human strife, far from the multitude! (Scene 1)

The specific difficulties of performing this work were acknowledged in characteristically robust terms by George Bernard Shaw, who showed just how easily *The Damnation of Faust* could be subverted into something far more anodyne:

> Berlioz's *Faust* is a particularly stiff subject for Albert Hall treatment. To comb that wild composer's hair, stuff him into a frock-coat and tall hat, stick a hymn-book in his hand and obtain reverent applause for his ribald burlesque of an Amen chorus as if it were a genuine Handelian solemnity, is really a remarkable feat [...] Instead of the brimstonish orgy in Auerbach's cellar we have a soirée of the Young Men's Christian Association; the drunken blackguardism of Brander is replaced by the

decorous conviviality of a respectable young bank clerk obliging with a display of his baritone voice [...], Faust reminds one of the gentleman in Sullivan's *Sweethearts*; the whiskered pandoors and the fierce husars on the banks of the Danube become a Volunteer corps on the banks of the Serpentine; and all Brixton votes Berlioz a great composer, and finds a sulphurous sublimity in the whistles of the piccolo and clashes of the cymbals which bring Mr Henschel, as Mephistopheles, out of his chair. This does not mean that Berlioz has converted Brixton: it means that Brixton has converted Berlioz. (Cited by Bentley, 98)

After Berlioz, the public did not have to wait long before another, less demanding and more pleasing Faust was to appear before them through the obliging agency of Charles Gounod, who combined a skilful staging technique with flowing and sensuous melodies that were easy on the ear. His opera of 1859 was one of the most successful of all time. It astounded the public, initially in 58 performances at the Théâtre Lyrique, later at the Opéra, where it reached 500 performances in 1887 and 1,000 by 1894 (Demuth, 29). It was published and republished, the music being transcribed for every type of instrument. It was the first opera to be performed at the inauguration of the New York Metropolitan Opera in 1883. Years later, a rumour surfaced that Gounod had stolen the score from a young genius who had died in a lunatic asylum. So strong were nationalist sensibilities at the time that a German reviewer argued that the music was so quintessentially Teutonic that the composer could not have been a true Frenchman, but was probably Flemish by descent. On the question of its morality, Gounod fared substantially better in England than Goethe had done, with churchmen declaring 'The interests of religion and morality are never compromised but are substantially promoted by such a work as Gounod's *Faust*' (Budden, 21; Harding, 113f., 132).

Like Berlioz before him, Gounod had been inspired by Nerval's translation. But his libretto was the work of Jules Barbier and Michel Carré, who based their plot rather loosely on Goethe, concentrating again on the romantic theme. There is, indeed, a shift of emphasis, both in Faust (who merely seeks youth and pleasure) and away from Faust, towards concentration on Marguerite, which has led many in Germany to refer to the work not as *Faust* but as *Margarete*. In fact, it has been performed as *Faust*, as *Margarete*, and as *Faust et Marguerite*. It has also been subject to major changes and revisions, so that no two productions are alike – the 'Flea Song', a 'scarab' in Gounod's original, was considered particularly offensive and was quickly replaced by a 'Song of the Golden Calf'. The opera is in five acts, beginning with the bargain, which Faust concludes when he is shown an image of the fair Marguerite. The second act concentrates on Valentine, who entrusts his sister to his young friend Siebel as he goes off to war. Siebel is the name given to one of the inebriated hooligans in Goethe's Auerbach's Cellar, so things do not bode well for the girl, least of all after Mephistopheles has prophesied that all flowers touched by him will wither. This comes true in a literal and in a metaphorical sense, as the remaining scenes show, with Faust murdering Valentine, cavorting on Mount Brocken, and returning too late and unable to save the imprisoned Marguerite. Satan claims his soul, but she is transfigured and saved.

Gounod's *Faust* was not only the crowning achievement of its composer's career, but the most successful opera on the international stage for nearly three quarters of a century. From 1863, when it was first performed in England, to 1911 it was played annually to enthusiastic audiences and affectionately referred to by the nickname of 'Daisy Faust'. Marinelli (43–6) lists twenty separate gramophone recordings. Its success lies in the application of a light, Gallic touch to the more ponderous Germanic substratum. What this means in practice is that the spirits are largely removed or turned into ballet routines, then *de rigueur* at the Paris Opéra; Mephistopheles is a witty, non-threatening cavalier; Siebel is propelled from the murky shadows of Auerbach's wine-cellar to the open air, where he figures as the bashful lover equally deserving of praise and pity; and Marguerite becomes a more rounded character in her own right, genuinely overwhelmed by her conflicting responsibilities towards her brother Valentine, her rustic boyfriend, and the mysterious stranger who accosts her. Thus in her long soliloquy preceding the 'Jewel Song', Goethe's 'King of Thule' is not rendered straight but cleverly punctuated by little asides expressive of her deepest fears and longings.

Faust has here, more consistently than elsewhere, been accommodated to the traditional mould of the operatic genre, and soon people were saying, 'it is a sorrowful triumph for music over drama that when Faust is mentioned now, among ordinary English folk, the title is taken as referring to the opera' (Cole, 186). Contemporary lithographs show that the décor was regularly based on the models supplied by visual artists like Cornelius and Delacroix. Gounod's success led to numerous burlesques and parodies, such as Hector Crémieux's and Adam Jaime's *Le petit Faust* with music by Florimond Ronger, alias Hervé. This was performed on 23 April 1869 in the Théâtre des Folles Dramatiques. It was full of humorous travesties of Gounod and Goethe, which led German critics to speak of sacrilege. Stumme mentions with evident distaste the transformation of the King of Thule's goblet into a pair of exploding braces containing state secrets, yet it survived to be recorded on vinyl twice during the 1960s and was revived in Metz as recently as 1990 (Stumme, 127; Marinelli, 65–7). Other parodies include *Faust du Faust, pas trop n'en Faust* and *Saf'aust et Marguerite* (Harding, 154). London even saw the production of a piece entitled *Faust on Toast*, music by Willie Redstone and Melville Gideon, text by F. Firth Shephard and Adrian Ross, which gives us a useful hint as to how the name of the magus was pronounced in England. Stumme recounts the experience of a comic opera in Geneva in 1905, in which, with the exception of Valentin, all roles were played by women. Here Valentin entrusts his 16-year-old sister to the 65-year-old professor Faust, who agrees to look after her while the former goes off to the wars. Mephistopheles promises Faust eternal youth and possession of Margeret if Faust will sign a pact. He agrees, and Valentin is slain. Margaret's love saves Faust and the two ascend to heaven. Henry Irving's Lyceum *Faust* produced many musical parodies, such as F. C. Burnand's *Faust and Loose*, and G. L. Gordon's *Faust & Co*, both performed in 1886. In 1888, London witnessed a two-act opera, *Faust up to Date*, by George R. Sims and Henry Pettitt, with music by Meyer Lutz. This was performed at the Gaiety Theatre, with Faust, a lovelorn dandy, Gretchen, a merry damsel, brought together by Mephistopheles, an Irish newspaper vendor (Stumme, 127–32). *Faust on Toast* of 1921 was one of the last such productions; the type went out of favour with the decline in Gounod's popularity.

As Peter Conrad put it, 'Gounod makes the philosophical questor languishing and love-sick and turns Mephistopheles into a moustache-twirling dandy with a plume in his cap.' And William Grim rightly observes, 'Even the greatest music cannot compensate for a shoddy text' (Conrad, 71; Grim, I, 26). For such a 'shoddy text', it has had a remarkable after-life in literature, serving as the cause for Emil's and Marie's murder in Willa Cather's novel *O Pioneers!* and as the basis for Estanislao del Campo's humorous poem *Fausto. Impresiones del gaucho Anastasio el Pollo en la representación de esta ópera* of 1866, in which a gaucho named 'Anastasio the Chicken' struggles to retell the plot to one of his friends. His enjoyment of the spectacle is marred only by the circumstance that a pickpocket, 'probably a gringo', steals the knife that was essential equipment for a visit to the Buenos Aires Teatro Colón, where Gounod's *Faust* was indeed performed in 1866 (Grim II, 11–37; Csobádi, II, 427–36; Dabezies, 46–9).

The last of the grand operatic Fausts of the nineteenth century was the single completed work of Arrigo Boito, an accomplished novelist, poet, journalist, translator and librettist who supplied Verdi with the texts for his *Otello* and *Falstaff*. This, too, was to be much revised. It had three separate premières, in 1868, 1875 and 1876, and was based on a palimpsest of manuscripts on which Boito worked for more than ten years. Its grandiose concept was unrivalled in Italian opera of its time. The 1868 première lasted for five and half hours and led to battles in the streets which were considered so serious that subsequent performances were temporarily banned.

Set in heaven, Frankfurt, and ancient Greece, Boito's *Mefistofele* is an ambitious transposition of Goethe into a musical idiom that amalgamates French grand opera and middle-period Verdi with touches of Beethoven and Wagner (Arnold, I, 238f.). With Boito responsible for the words as well as the music, it conforms to Wagner's theory that true opera must involve the composer as a poet. Berlioz had placed Faust at the heart of his work, Gounod had concentrated on Margaret, thus it was almost inevitable that the next composer to treat the material would place the devil centre-stage. Faust is, from the moment he concludes the pact, a passive figure whom Mephistopheles can manipulate at will, right up to the final moment of recognition. The all-powerful enabler comes into his own as a ferociously active deep-bass role, chanting, howling, laughing, whistling, and yet displaying a *scherzoso* levity that counterbalances his infernal gravity. Witty and urbane in the Goethean mould, yet not lacking mediaeval grotesqueness, he is a delightfully contradictory figure who appears drawn to Faust rather than summoned by him as in all previous versions. Boito took on challenges that his predecessors had avoided: he conceived his opera as a single entity, and in four acts and an epilogue sought to encompass the gist of Goethe's narrative from the heavenly prologue through the tragedy of Margherita and on to the Vale of Tempe, the encounter with Helen of Troy (a soprano part usually taken by whoever played Margherita), and from there back to Faust's study, where by falling on his knees in prayer the doctor finally defeats his antagonist. Only in this way could the dramatic outcome of the pact be appreciated, Boito reasoned. If the action stops with Margherita's death, the fate of Faust remains unresolved. Boito therefore incorporates both the scene in heaven and Faust's union with Helen of Troy. The pact has a more obviously religious focus than in Berlioz or Gounod: Faust risks his soul for a single moment of pure happiness. Old favourites like the 'Song of the Flea' and the 'King in Thule' are avoided; Boito cut out all those scenes that actually require some form of musical setting or accompaniment. His departure from the familiar path was probably what deprived this work of the success it merited. As one influential authority has stated: 'When it strays into Part II of Goethe's drama, the main thread of the action suddenly seems broken rather than restored. That is why one of the most profound works for the lyric stage, one of the most beautiful scores that has come out of Italy, figures comparatively rarely in programmes outside its native country' (Kobbé, 672).

From Chromatic Scales to Rock Musical

The Wagnerian influence led to several more operatic works appearing in the final two decades of the nineteenth century in Germany. Thus Heinrich Zöllner's extensive output includes a four-act *Faust*, seen in Munich in 1887. A better-known and decidedly anti-Wagnerian composer who straddled the German-Italian divide, Ferruccio Busoni, produced in his tightly controlled *Doktor Faust* – composed between 1914 and 1923, left unfinished but premièred posthumously, Dresden 1925 –, a remarkable synthesis of styles, ranging from late mediaeval essays in polyphony that recall the age of Faustus to powerful experiments with chromatic harmonies. *Doktor Faust* is acknowledged as his masterpiece, and as a modern treatment of the theme provides yet another example of a work in which ancient traditions are preserved while new techniques are simultaneously pioneered. Busoni's interests are manifold, not only in combining and contrasting harmonic microworlds, but also in exploring Faust's psychology and the creative mind. It is a sombre work, reflecting its composition during the First World War and Busoni's periods of depression and ill-health. Like other twentieth-century operatic depictions of artists (Pfitzner's *Palestrina* and Britten's *Death in Venice*), an autobiographical subtext may be discerned, most notably in Faust's performance at the court of the Duke of Parma. The storyline is discontinuous, but the three principal figures, Faust, Mephistopheles and the Duchess of Parma, are bound by close, psychologically significant ties. The text of this 'Poem for music' derives from the legend, Marlowe and some puppet material as well as from Lessing's fragment. It begins with a direct address to the audience in which the poet explains why he chose Faust in preference to his plans for Merlin and Don Juan.

255

When as a child I watched a play, entranced,
To see the devil speak and get his due,
That figure that before my eyes had danced –
When fully grown, I knew it to be true.
Yet truth alone gives out, except I chanced
The freshly germinating seed to view
That guides the vision which the child possessed
Until the work of art with life is blessed.
(Busoni, 1)

The parallels with Goethe's 'Dedication' (F 1–64) are obvious; here, too, childhood memories have nurtured a 'freshly germinating seed' to maturity. After two preludes showing how the doctor came to sign a pact with Mephistopheles, Faust elopes with the Duchess of Parma. Back in Wittenberg, he learns of her death while discussing the Reformation with a group of Catholic and Protestant students. Mephistopheles tosses a bundle of straw at Faust – the remains of his child. The bundle ignites; a vision of Helen is glimpsed. Faust cannot grasp her, as 'Mankind is not yet ready for perfection.' The Duchess returns to haunt him in the guise of a beggar woman clasping the corpse of a child. Faust offers his own life if the child can be brought back from the dead. As he expires, the child revives, and a naked youth steps forth into the night, clasping a blossoming branch. Thus Mephisto is transcended by the combined efforts of his two antagonists; Helen, the devil's 'trump card', is ineffective because unattainable (Beaumont, 311–54; Grim, I, 51–71; Fischer, 559–71).

Like Thomas Mann and an increasing number of modern composers, Busoni deliberately eschewed the Goethean plot-line that had been done to death by their nineteenth-century predecessors. He returns to the oldest traditions, uses Wittenberg as the main location and makes reference to the pro- and anti-Lutheran factions who were clashing intellectually and literally at the time. Busoni's students turn from chanting – the Catholics in Latin, the Lutherans in German – to fisticuffs in convincing fashion. The Gretchen episodes that were so important in previous versions are briefly alluded to as a misadventure that happened in the past; Grim (I, 62) relates her insignificance to Nietzsche's objection to her role. Perhaps the most astounding and new feature about this version is the end, in which Faust is neither consigned to the flames of hell nor explicitly pardoned. Rather, good and evil are cancelled out and the opera ends with an unanswerable question from the mouth of a Mephistopheles turned Night Watchman: 'Could this man's death have been an accident?' An unpublished fragment from Faust's final address to heaven and hell spells out the position: 'Upon this highest insight of my wisdom / is your malice now broken to pieces / and in my self-won freedom / expire both God and Devil at once' (Beaumont, 325).

Henri Pousseur's opera Votre Faust ('Your Faust'), written jointly with Michel Butor, was seven years in the making, from 1961 to 1968. It consists of five plots and six epilogues, so that it can be performed in a total of thirty versions. It is rightly subtitled a 'variable play in the manner of an opera.' This makes it difficult to summarise. Henri is a composer who is commissioned to write an opera. He is given as much time and money as he needs by a theatre director, the Mephistophelean Mondor. Henri's affair with the waitress Maggy ends with her arrest and imprisonment. In one version, indicated as the route to salvation, the project is never completed, Henri turns his hand to writing sacred music instead and is eventually dismissed by the director. In another, Henri damns himself by agreeing to write the opera. Similarly, Maggy may survive or die. By holding up red or green batons, the audience can decide on the progress. This opera is, among other things, a parody of those compositions that do not permit of variation. It presents itself as a kind of 'mobile' which can be viewed from any number of angles, rather like Karlheinz Stockhausen's cycle *Aus den sieben Tagen*; chief among the influences are not only Goethe and Marlowe, but also Pirandello and Gertrude Stein. One could say that Pousseur and Butor did no more than exploit the underlying ambiguity of the existing material. A recording, accompanied by copious instructions, was released in 1972 (Marinelli, 114–8).

Luca Lombardi's *Faust. Un Travestimento* ('Faust. A Travesty') was performed in Basle in 1991 and in Weimar two years later. It was awarded the S.I.A.E. Prize by the Italian Authors' and Publishers' Association. Unlike the operas by Giacomo Manzoni (1989) and Konrad Boehmer (1983) who used Thomas Mann's *Doctor Faustus* as their source, Lombardi based his three-act composition on Goethe's *Faust I* in an adaptation by Edoardo Sanguineti. The result of its alienating devices is serious and burlesque at the same time, crude and artistic, trivial and profound. Lombardi describes his music as 'inclusive'. The percussion instruments used in the Witch's Kitchen include copper cauldrons, saucepans, wooden barrels, wine bottles, whetstones, graters, whisks and washboards. The music, which involves two string quartets as well as electronic devices, hovers perpetually between tradition and a-tonality. Mephisto's 'Flea Song' is replaced by the Rolling Stones' 'Sympathy for the Devil'. However, Valentine is given an old-fashioned tuneful air, and Greta's 'King in Thule' is similarly regular, while betraying its artificiality in a self-parodying manner. The work ends with Greta shouting *Enrico, mi fai schifo* ('Henry, you make me sick'), and a twelve-tone chord which could equally well signal despair or salvation (Wiesmann, 576–81). A plurality of approaches produces an unstable result; this was evidently Lombardi's intention. It is the musical equivalent to the postmodern revisions such as that by Werner Schwab, whose text was accompanied by a punk group using a similarly unconventional collection of instruments.

Two operas on the theme were written in the GDR: Hanns Eisler's embarrassingly controversial *Johann Faustus* of 1952, and Rainer Kunad's *Sabellicus* which premièred in 1974. Eisler's stalled at the libretto stage; the composer did not write the music after the authorities expressed their displeasure. It created an even greater stir than Brecht's production of *Urfaust* during the same year, and both works can be and have been discussed in parallel, the more so as the two authors were in close contact during the period. It is probable that Brecht had a hand in Eisler's libretto (Vietor-Engländer, 174–201).

Eisler was the GDR's foremost composer and had provided the emerging country with its national anthem. He was drawn to Faust through having seen a puppet version complete with harlequin or *Hanswurst*. His opera was to be a true *Volksstück*, a play that addressed the concerns of ordinary people and aspired to be an emblematic work, perhaps even the GDR's answer to Goethe. It is located at the time of the Peasants' War of 1525 but makes reference to the present, for example when Faustus journeys to the wealthy capitalist state of Atlanta. A direct connection is established between Faustus and the failed peasants' uprising, the first revolution ever attempted on German soil, as Friedrich Engels had shown. Eisler's Faustus embodies the tragedy of the German people, attributable to a combination of arrogance, bad conscience, sloth on the part of the rulers and intellectuals, and also to myopic self-interest across the entire spectrum. Eisler took his cue from Thomas Mann and used Faustus to demonstrate Germany's failings. But he went further in assimilating aspects of Brecht's Galilei, an early example of a scientist with an ill-functioning conscience; Eisler intended to make people reflect on how intellectuals should respond to the problems of the day. Unlike Clair, with whose film (see below, 323–5) there are numerous parallels, Eisler has Faustus fail in his duty to himself and to humanity.

> The son of a peasant, went to school with the priests, and thence to Luther, because Luther exposed the abuses of the church, but when Luther defended the lords against the servants, crossed over to Thomas Müntzer, but when the violence and the looting began, returned to Luther, who now preaches violence against the peasants. Tried medicine, law, theology, then black magic, must now perish miserably, because he lacked the courage to stand up for what he knew to be right. (Vietor-Engländer, 179; Bunge, 83–87)

Thus Faustus' confession, which was much admired by Brecht. This Faustus is a negative icon, a central impersonation of German misery, a humanist who fears the Revolution, a half-hearted traitor to a great cause. His pact with the devil is a result of social irresponsibility. That Goethe's erstwhile 'hero' – if such he ever was – should have degenerated into an embodiment of hypocrisy in what aspired to become the new German national opera was a prospect too awful to contemplate, especially as Luther was to be tarred with the same brush. At one point, the *Hanswurst* figure is seen eating cakes and remarking 'Here I sit, I can do no other' in evident mockery of Luther who used a similar formula before the Imperial Court at Worms. The work was heavily criticised for its revisionism at the time, and neither Brecht nor Arnold Zweig nor Helene Weigel could reverse the ministerial decision to ban the opera, following heated discussions in the Academy of Arts, of which Eisler was a founding member, during May and June 1953. *Petit-bourgeois* ideas about the inherent superiority of the classics and their continuing relevance to the working classes, who, coincidentally, were involved in anti-government demonstrations during June 1953, led to its suppression. Specially commissioned readers' letters appeared in the official organ *Neues Deutschland* on 2 June 1953, objecting to 'such a frivolous mockery of what was perhaps the most inspired masterpiece beloved of all Germans'. Zweig made the not entirely facetious remark that, had the hero been named 'Knaust' or the title been *A False Faust*, there would have been no talk of banning it. The entire debate has been documented in a 385-page volume by Hans Bunge, which illustrates the extent to which Faust was able stir up passions in modern times. Spoken versions were performed in Tübingen in 1974 and West Berlin in 1977. Some music has survived and was added to by the composer's friend and pupil Wolfgang Hohensee (Betz, 217–225; Bunge, 63 and *passim*; Schnell, 119f; Schartner, 158–69). In the GDR, it was finally seen in 1982, twenty years after the author's death. It was the subject of a specially convened conference at Knittlingen (November 2003), and the most recent production was in Kassel in 2004, in a version containing music by Friedrich Schenker.

A second opera that associates the magus with the Peasants' War of 1525 had its première in the GDR in 1974: Rainer Kunad's *Sabellicus*, whose title derives from one of the names Faustus is alleged to have bestowed on himself according to Tritheim's letter of 1506. This, too, is a pessimistic reading of Faust's life that accords ill with the official ideology of the state and was clearly inspired at least in part by Eisler, whom Kunad was careful not to mention in the accompanying programme booklet (Vietor-Engländer, 211–15; Andreas Meier, 570–80). His Sabellicus is a scientist who finds employment at court, hoping to work towards the achievement of a paradise on earth. He creates a system of wheels that is intended to make life easier for the country's hard-pressed labourers. These are wrecked by marauding peasants. Sabellicus becomes a kind of jester, 'with an almost mad look and frightening aspect'. After pleading with the Duke to lighten the peasants' burden during a drought, Sabellicus is thrown into jail and eventually executed, while the Mephistophelean Chancellor puts about the myth that he was in the devil's thrall:

> It is hereby publicly made known to all,
> That George Sabellicus was, in recompense for his dastardly deeds,
> Sinful life and abominable heresy, taken by the devil
> At midnight, whereupon he met his gruesome end. (Cited by Vietor-Engländer, 213)

Like others who turned to the material in the forty years of the GDR's existence, Kunad failed to satisfy the authorities, who were determined to gauge all cultural artefacts by their level of compliance with the official ideology. Admittedly, *Sabellicus*, also known as *Die Versuchung des Sabellicus* ('The Temptation of Sabellicus') was staged at the Berlin State Opera under the direction of Harry Kupfer during 1974 and was commended for portraying the aristocracy as the socialist regime wished to see it: corrupt, deceitful, misanthropic. Kunad's Sabellicus is more of a role model than Eisler's Johann Faustus, at least in so far as he supports the underdogs and works for an improvement in their lives. But Kunad was rebuked for treating the peasantry with contempt. To make the 'progressive forces within society' into wreckers and Luddites was unpardonable, in the words of *Neues Deutschland* (27 December 1974). Kunad was a member of the GDR's

Academy of Arts between 1974 and 1985, when he effectively ended his career by applying for leave to emigrate to West Germany. It remains largely unknown in Germany today, Kunad 'having fallen victim to German disintegration in a manner almost unparalleled in art' (Sadie, II, 1058).

Since then, there has been a veritable boom of Faust operas. At least two television operas have been broadcast. Luboš Fišer's *Eternal Faust* will be discussed below (334). Mario Nascimbene's *Faust in Manhattan*, libretto by Luigi Candoni, was composed in 1962-3 and broadcast in 1965. Here it is not Faust who sells his soul to the devil in exchange for youth, but rather Faust (as 'Johnny Faust Lerriman') who sells his youth to 'Mefis' in order to find his true soul (Marinelli, 112f.). Alfred Garriyevich Schnittke's [also Shnitke; 1934-1998] controversial, wildly eclectic *Historia von D. Johann Fausten* (1994), an unfinished opera in three acts, was first performed in Hamburg in 1995; it was preceded by a *Faust Cantata* for soloists, mixed chorus and orchestra (1983), based on chapters 67 and 68 of the chapbook. The composer faced difficulties similar to those encountered by Eisler and Kunad when it came to having the work performed in the Soviet Union. The authorities disliked the printed programme, which they considered pro-religious. But the work was a success in Russia, almost too much so. The pop-star Alla Pugacheva was to take the role of Mephisto in Moscow, but became over-enthusiastic. She improvised the five-minute tango for just over half an hour and had to be replaced by someone more appreciative of the underlying ethos of the work. Schnittke stresses the view that Faustus is a heinous sinner, yet he is not punished unconditionally at the end. Ivashkin (174) relates it to the 'Passions' composed by Bach and Schütz, describing it as a 'negative Passion'. The opera ranges in style from atonality in Act I to *bel canto* and rock. Faustus' death is accompanied by Mephistopheles walking though the auditorium to the strains of a tango, singing mocking couplets into the microphone. Alex Ross, in the *New York Times*, says 'His accomplishment in *Faust* is singular; no composer before him has come so close to the story's primal terror', while Andrew Clark of the *Financial Times* wrote, 'Schnittke's third opera is his best [...] his version of *Faust* is a major contribution to twentieth-century music theatre, and deserves the widest possible hearing. It is approachable but highly original, thought-provoking as well as entertaining, spiritual and worldly in the same breath' (Ivashkin, 173-80; Vietor-Engländer, 207-14; Gratzer, 595-620; Kreutzer 155-65).

It is something of a paradox that while Goethe could remark to Eckermann that it was 'quite impossible' that appropriate music would ever be composed for Faust, the most recent bibliography lists upwards of a thousand items in 135 pages of 'Compositions relating to Faust' (Andreas Meier, 685-820). Songs such as 'Sympathy for the Devil' of 1968, written by Keith Richards and Mick Jagger, are not altogether unrelated. Jagger's devil introduces himself as 'a man of wealth and taste,' and insinuates that he is no different from anyone else. But in true Mephistophelean style, the singer shifts from cultured gentleman ('Pleased to meet you') to anarchic scoffer ('I made damn sure that Pilate washed his hands and sealed his fate') and back again, claiming credit for many of history's greatest crimes:

39. *Recording of the Hamburg production of Schnittke's* Historia.
Poster designed by Heinz Baltes.

'I rode a tank, held a general's rank, when the blitzkrieg raged and the bodies stank'. The emphasis on outward respectability, the repeated taunt 'Can you guess my name?' seem to demand a response, an admission of complicity with the diabolical force behind this song. The Faustian pact and the sum of its consequences are laid before us in a three-minute track.

Songwriter Randy Newman produced a musical based on Goethe's *Faust* as his tenth album in 1995. A kind of shotgun wedding between Lloyd Webber and rock spectacular, for which Newman also wrote the lyrics (with David Mamet), this was given a full production at La Jolla Playhouse in San Diego and at the Goodman Theater in Chicago. In the Warner Music recording, which differs in some respects from the above-mentioned productions,[1] James Taylor plays God, who in his opening number 'Glory Train' claims that all is well in the world 'like a Bing Crosby or Arnold Palmer kind of golf-playing white guy, a little bit full of himself' (Notes accompanying the Warner Music CD, 5). One of his numbers is called, tellingly, 'Relax. Enjoy Yourself.' Randy Newman, as the Devil, butts in: 'In all my life I don't believe I've ever heard such bullshit. Even from you, a master of bullshit. You know it's a lie, it'll always be a lie. The invention of an animal that knows he's going to die.' When the action shifts to earth, there is a cameo appearance by Elton John as an embittered Archangel who for no obvious reason laments the passing of Britain's greatness. There are the predictable jokes played to the gallery: Lucifer meets with the Lord on the heavenly golf course, where God drives a white golf cart and carries golden clubs. God lights his pipe, asking, 'Do you mind if I

261

smoke?' to which Lucifer replies, 'Go ahead – I'm used to it.' Don Henley plays Faust not as a scholar but as a profoundly dislikeable, insensitive and self-absorbed freshman at Notre Dame College, Linda Ronstadt plays the virginal Margaret, Faust's girlfriend, and Bonnie Raitt plays Martha, the girl from the other side of the tracks who runs with the Devil and ends up not in hell but in Costa Rica. Despite the humorous additions, Newman follows Goethe, for whom he shows evident admiration, in many details, including the eventual infanticide. Margaret is convicted of murder and sentenced to die in Indiana State Prison in Michigan City. Here she sings the lullaby 'Sandman's Coming' to the empty blanket in which she wrapped her baby. The final scene has her borne off by angels. Henry is mortified. He drinks the rest of the poison that he gave to Margaret's mother, but tries to vomit as it begins to take effect. Then the Lord decrees that he is saved. The devil has again been cheated of his prize, but soon begins to think of new torments he can unleash on his victims; as the curtain comes down, he is heard intoning 'I've got Las Vegas on my mind.' The show was not particularly well received, and Newman went on to write the soundtrack to *Toy Story* which earned him the acclaim that eluded the more ambitious *Faust*.

This is by no means the only attempt to convey the theme of Faust to a contemporary mass audience using the musical idiom most favoured by the young. The popular groups that use the name of Faust on their labels are too numerous to mention. They come from various backgrounds, including one from Russia, and frequently present themselves as embracing a 'Gothic' element. Among the more interesting attempts to set texts from *Faust* to modern music are Bernd Kauffmann's 2-CD compilation *Rosebud. Songs of Goethe and Nietzsche* (Mastermind Publications, 1999), and punk group 'Einstürzende Neubauten' ('Collapsing Tower Blocks') who provided a musical accompaniment to Werner Schwab's play *Faust :: My Thorax : My Helmet* (Our Choice, 1996). Composer and violinist Leroy Jenkins wrote a jazz-rap-opera, *Fresh Faust*, commissioned by the late Gillian Levine, which was performed in workshops in Boston at the Institute of Contemporary Arts. Jürgen Rosenthal, sometime percussionist with the 1970s rock groups Scorpions and Eloy, devised a 'rock ballet' whose music is credited to 'Shade'; it was choreographed by Ewa Wycichowska and performed by the Ballet of the Grand Theatre of Lodz, Poland. Here, Faust is torn between Mephistophela, who offers him 'sex, drugs and rock'n'roll', and his true love, Helena. Though he chooses to destroy himself, salvation eventually comes his way. One of the most ambitious projects of recent years has been Rudolf Volz's two-part rock opera, which closely follows Goethe and was premièred in 1997 (Part I) and 2002 (Part II). This demonstrates clearly that Faust is still perceived as a musical icon of central importance. We therefore conclude this survey of musical Fausts with a detailed case study of this work.

'You'll always be the one you are.' Faust as Rock Opera by Paul M. Malone

From Concept Album to Rock Opera

Rudolf Volz holds a doctorate in mathematics from California's Claremont Graduate University. In 1994, he set himself the task of 'packing old, traditional intellectual property in new and modern forms, in order to revive it for the present and future.'[2] After three years' work, the result was to set Part I of Goethe's drama, using the original text, into the idiom of popular music, as *Faust: Die Rockoper* ('Faust: The Rock Opera').

The rock opera form has little connection with classical opera other than the name. It arose at the end of the 1960s, in a convergence of rock and theatre: in 1967, the so-called 'concept album' began to displace the collection of singles after the Beatles released *Sgt. Pepper's Lonely Hearts Club Band* and the Rolling Stones quickly replied with the darker *Their Satanic Majesties Request*. Meanwhile, other rock bands were creating ever more theatrical forms for their concerts, be it the Grand Guignol-inspired antics of American Alice Cooper—which led to KISS and eventually to Twisted Sister—or in England, the art school-influenced dramatics of Genesis and flashy but classically-grounded musicianship of the Nice and Yes. At the same time, the legitimate theatre was being invaded by musicals devoted to a rock aesthetic rather than the old-fashioned sounds of Tin Pan Alley: in 1967, *Hair* premiered off-Broadway, as did *Your Own Thing*, a rock musical based on Shakespeare's *Twelfth Night*. These stage shows, aided by dialogue, had a surer sense of plot than the still disjointed concept albums, but their songs were written by outsiders to rock culture and earned little respect from the rock critics, one of whom labelled *Hair*'s creators 'the Francis the Talking Mule of rock'n'roll' (Anon., 52).

1968 saw efforts to construct concept albums around actual plots, with the Kinks' nostalgic *Village Green Preservation Society* (which by 1974 had spawned a triple-album sequel, *Preservation Acts I and II*) and the Pretty Things' seminal *S.F. Sorrow*, a dystopian fantasy now acknowledged as the first true rock opera. Inspired equally by the latter album and by eastern mysticism, The Who's Pete Townshend created the classic *Tommy* in 1969. Like *S.F. Sorrow*, *Tommy* is really an oratorio or cantata rather than opera, and though its music is brilliant compared to its precursor, its plot is little clearer. The story, on the other hand, was the strong point of Tim Rice's and Andrew Lloyd Webber's hit album *Jesus Christ Superstar*, also released in 1969 as a 'rock opera'. More truly operatic in form, and with the advantage of a well-structured and well-known plot, *Superstar* became a stage success in 1971. *Tommy* was briefly staged as an all-star musical the following year, but remained incoherent despite Townshend's attempt to act as narrator.

The success of *Superstar* as an album had forced rock critics to acknowledge, if not to accept, the existence of the rock musical. Jonathan Cort, describing the classically-trained Webber's efforts in the popular idiom, wrote in *Rolling Stone*: 'Italian nightclub imitation rock music adjoining strings and horns create a melodious but embarrassing scene.' Webber himself professed little love for the form, informing Cort: 'Melody in rock is unoriginal for the most part. Intervallically it's not very interesting' (Cort, 10). By the time *Rolling Stone* investigated Broadway's interest in rock in 1971, both rock musical and rock opera seemed to have had their day after a brief commercial success. Stephen Sondheim opined: 'Rock is much too monotonous for a musical [...] You can't have twelve, or twenty, songs like that' (Topor, 3). One can only wonder what constituted a rock album, or a rock concert, in Sondheim's view.

Nonetheless, both the 'rock musical' and the 'rock opera' refused to fade away. While Webber soon progressed to writing music in a more conventional idiom, other composers and musicians continued to expand the stylistic palette of rock music, to integrate rock features into classically-inspired works and to explore rock in the context of theatrical performance. The successful re-emergence of The Who's *Tommy* (now officially renamed *The Who's Tommy*) as a fully-fledged Broadway musical in 1992 with a reworked and more comprehensible book may have seemed an emasculation of the original to rock purists, but it demonstrates the hardiness of the form and was only one sign of a resurgence. Only a year before Volz began his labours, Boston Rock Opera had been formed in Massachusetts to maintain the tradition, reviving *Jesus Christ Superstar* (2000) and *The Rocky Horror Show* (1997), and even attempting to stage *Sgt. Pepper's Lonely Hearts Club Band* in 1995.

Volz's choice of this medium for the popularisation of Goethe's *Faust* is thus quite fitting; though it seems curious that he claims, 'There are indeed several classical operas on this theme, but absolutely no popular materials in music and film.' Leaving aside the question of film, which will be the subject of a subsequent chapter, there are many rock songs about the devil, though relatively few of them could be labelled 'Faustian', and Volz is clearly speaking narrowly of interpretations of Goethe. Besides 'Sympathy for the Devil,' one might also name Black Sabbath's 'N.I.B. (Basically),' in which Ozzy Osbourne pines for love: 'my name is Lucifer, please take my hand.' More often than not, however, in rock the devil appears as a cardboard villain at best – as in Alice Cooper's 1976 concept album *Alice Cooper Goes to Hell* – when not reduced to a metaphor for dissipated living or hard-hearted women. The occult trappings of so-called 'black metal,' 'death metal,' or 'doom metal,' on the other hand, are usually couched in such nihilistic terms as to minimise the Faustian element of temptation.

The major exceptions to these generalisations have in fact been produced by figures peripheral to the rock scene: most notable of these is Randy Newman's

Faust, described above. Like most of Newman's output, his *Faust* has been praised but was not commercially successful, and perhaps because of this and its relatively late appearance in 1995 Volz overlooks it. Equally marginal, and arguably more deservedly so, is Paul Williams's music for Brian De Palma's 1974 horror-comedy film *Phantom of the Paradise*. Williams himself appears in the film as the evil record producer Swan, who steals the 'pop cantata' Faust from its composer, Winslow Leach, in order to plagiarise it for music to open his new concert venue, the 'Paradise'. Leach, framed for theft, escapes from prison to revenge himself, falls into a record-press and is horribly scarred, becoming the eponymous phantom; Swan turns out to be invulnerable, however, having sold his soul years ago for eternal youth and fame. The film attempts to satirise both rock opera and theatrical rock, but its confused mélange of elements from *Faust*, Gaston Leroux's *The Phantom of the Opera* and Oscar Wilde's *The Picture of Dorian Gray* descends into a final chaotic bloodbath. The signature rock ballad 'Faust' appears twice on the soundtrack, sung once as a piano-only 'demo' by William Finlay as Leach and again with full band backing by Williams. Most of the songs, however, are parodies of 1970s rock styles that fall far short of their targets. As a model for rock versions of *Faust* it sets an ominous precedent, but its association of the theme with both hard rock and theatrical rock does anticipate Volz's endeavours.

The Faust Rock Opera

On the website devoted to his adaptation of *Faust*, Volz first offers a conventional interpretation of the story, claiming that the theme is 'independent of historical period, since it deals with crossing the border between ignorance and knowledge, and the automatically associated question of good vs. evil.' Goethe's version marks the transition from the old Faust legend of a quest for earthly wealth to 'the drive for knowledge and wisdom in order to achieve [...] a religious path to God via knowledge of the world and the cosmos.'

Having invoked Goethe's authority, Volz makes a claim that 'The rock opera is true to Goethe's texts'—although he quickly qualifies this statement: 'However, it is confined to Part I, and many cuts have been made. The remaining texts have been reduced to songs by repeating some passages as a refrain.' The cuts are indeed substantial: gone are the so-called 'Easter Walk,' Goethe's famulus Wagner, Mephisto's twitting of the visiting student, the scene in Auerbach's Cellar, and Gretchen's brother Valentin; so that, even more than in Gounod's opera, the plot rushes toward the tragic love story. Moreover, to compensate for the cutting, visual aids are employed:

> Between the songs there are spoken passages to make the plot clear. Sections that are difficult to understand from the text, such as the poisoning of Gretchen's mother, are clarified by mimed scenes and lively video inserts. (www.Faust.cc website)

Additional changes include the modernisation, often to humorous effect, of the play's milieu: Faust calls up the Earth Spirit on his computer; Mephisto gives Faust a lift on a bicycle and later in a miniature space shuttle made of CDs; the two plotters stay in contact by cellular phone; and the Walpurgis Night festivities include a robot and machine-gun wielding criminals.

Having claimed his participation in 'high culture,' Volz now also attempts to establish the 'street credibility' of his opera in terms of rock culture, clarifying his choice of musical genre as follows:

> The production takes the form of a contemporary rock concert. This is stylistically appropriate, because in recent years such diabolical variants as black metal and death metal have become popular. Mephisto is also a 'devilish fiddler,' who indeed sounds more like Jimi Hendrix than Pagganini [sic]. Even Faust sometimes plays electric guitar and enters into a duet with Mephisto [...] Not only the music, but also the lighting, videos and costumes correspond to those of a contemporary rock concert. (Loc. cit.)

40. Mephisto (Falko Illing) as 'devilish fiddler', accompanied by attractive she-devils, 1997. Note heavy metal's influence on makeup and T-shirt. The women's costumes are demure by current rock standards.

As Volz points out, the black and white makeup worn by Mephisto (a role already associated with whiteface in the German theatrical tradition) is 'similar to the painted faces of the rock band KISS'—and in its design even more similar to those of such Scandinavian death metal rockers as King Diamond, former lead singer of Mercyful Fate, and the groups Emperor and Immortal. The similarity, however, is deceptive.

Volz describes the music for his *Faust* as heavily indebted to the British band Deep Purple and Germany's Scorpions, whose involvement in Jürgen Rosenthal's rock ballet was noted above (262). It is therefore mainly in the category of 1970s-style hard rock or heavy metal. In general, both of these musical genres—the latter is sometimes considered a subcategory of the former—are characterised by extreme volume, produced by screaming vocals, distorted electric guitar and heavy bass; an adherence to the basic musical form of the blues, including the pentatonic blues scale; and themes of youthful rebellion, generational conflict, and sexuality. Hard rock usually expresses these themes in a quotidian, naturalistic context, and in a major key; whereas heavy metal is more frequently played in a minor key and set against a backdrop of fantasy, science fiction, or Gothic horror, and thus more suitable for *Faust*. Heavy metal is also more likely than hard rock to be influenced by classical music. Some bands produce music in both styles, or are categorised differently in different sources. Deep Purple, for example, are not usually considered a heavy metal band, despite their sheer volume and clear classical influences (keyboard player Jon Lord's music often quotes Bach, Holst or Elgar, while guitarist Ritchie Blackmore is a devotee of Renaissance music). Nor is KISS generally accepted as heavy metal rather than hard rock. Scorpions, on the other hand, are often classified as heavy metal thanks to their reliance on two guitarists and lack of keyboards. All of these groups peaked artistically and commercially in the late 1970s or early 1980s, and thus there is an element of nostalgia in using them as reference points.

This sense of nostalgia is also conveyed in the music itself: the use of keyboards, and particularly the sound of the Hammond organ, in the score of *Faust* recalls Deep Purple, while the electric guitars make use of such well-tried effects as distortion, compression, phasing/flanging, the vibrato unit (also known as the 'tremolo arm' or 'whammy bar'), and the 'wah-wah' pedal (a foot-controlled band pass filter) with its Jimi Hendrix associations, in a manner common to both Deep Purple and Scorpions, as well as to many other bands of the period. In fact, Volz's statements to the contrary notwithstanding, the more contemporary sound of death metal, with its typical barrage of industrial-noise guitar chords, throat-wrenching guttural vocals and determinedly repulsive themes, as evidenced in songs like Deicide's 'Satan Spawn, Caco-Daemon' or Cannibal Corpse's 'Necro-pedophile,' is almost nowhere evident in this rock opera.

The relatively safe ground of old-fashioned rock facilitates Volz's essentially domesticating strategy of marrying popular music with high culture:

> The synthesis of classical theatre and rock music creates a new art form. In music such forms have already existed, e.g. in the [1970s German] rock group Novalis.
> Similar to the Hegelian principle of creating a synthesis from thesis and antithesis, an old classic theatre piece and a musical form are combined to produce a new product from these hitherto independent and contiguously situated elements.
> This synthesis reaches its climax in the song 'Du bleibst doch immer' ['You'll always be the one you are', F 1806ff.], which uses the same music as 'Born to be Wild.' At first glance it seems impossible that a classic text by Goethe could be reconciled with a classic motorcycle song. (*Loc. cit.*)

Perhaps not coincidentally, 'Born to be Wild,' the 1968 Steppenwolf hit penned by Mars Bonfire (né Dennis McCrohan), contains the phrase 'heavy metal thunder,' allegedly the first occurrence, and therefore often suggested as the origin, of the term in rock music (for varying degrees of credulity on this latter point see Christe, 10; Weinstein, 18–20; Stuessy (1994), 321). The seminal importance of 'Born to be Wild' within rock is indicated by the fact that the song, which quickly became a biker anthem, remains instantly recognisable over thirty years after its release, and has been covered, particularly in concert, by artists as diverse as American heavy metal bands the Blue Öyster Cult and Slayer, instrumental surf rock band The Ventures, southern rocker Duane Allman, British glam-rock band Slade, the Muppets' Miss Piggy (in duet with Ozzy Osbourne), the West German art-rock group Grobschnitt, and veteran East German rockers, Puhdys. The last two, incidentally, were among the most popular live acts in their respective sections of the divided Germany. This song's inclusion in the score of *Faust*—with appropriate authorisation from the composer and publisher—is therefore clearly a programmatic choice.

The line numbers accompanying the following excerpt from *Faust: Die Rockoper* reveal the manipulation of Goethe's verses necessary to adapt the text to the form of the popular song, including abridging lines or repeating sections of lines (both indicated here by an asterisk), and transposing or interpolating lines or whole passages. In this case, the fact that the text has to be adapted to a pre-existing piece of music adds to the difficulty of the task. Perhaps as a result, in this example there is no consistent rhyme scheme in the verses and no attempt at rhyme at all in the third verse (in 'Born to be Wild,' every second line in the verses rhymes in an AABB scheme; the chorus preserves the original rhyme scheme).

Here the phrase *Du bleibst doch immer, was du bist* is sung wherever the phrase 'Born to be wild' occurs in the original; this is possible thanks to the melisma of 'wild,' which stretches over four notes, so that *immer, was du bist* can be sung in almost the same space (in fact, the 'bist' takes up one additional beat, overlapping the instrumental repetition of the vocal phrase).

MEPHISTOPHELES:

Du bist am Ende, am Ende was du bist	1806*
Doch willst du mit mir	1642*
Deine Schritte durchs Leben nehmen	1643
So will ich mich bequemen,	1644*
Dein zu sein, auf der Stelle,	1645
Und mach' ich dir's recht,	1647
Bin ich dein Diener, dein Knecht!	1648*

CHORUS (SUNG BY BOTH):

Setz dir Perücken auf von Millionen, Millionen Locken.	1807*
Setz deinen Fuß auf ellenhohe Socken,	1808
Du bleibst doch immer, was du bist.	1809
Du bleibst doch immer, was du bist.	1809

FAUST:

Der Teufel ist ein Egoist	1651*
Und tut nicht leicht,	1652*
Was einem andern nützlich ist.	1653

Was willst du armer Teufel geben?	1675
Sprich die Bedingung deutlich aus;	1654
Was willst du böser Geist von mir?	1730
Erz, Marmor, Pergament, Papier?	1731
Ich gebe jede Wahl dir frei.	1733
CHORUS:	
Setz dir Perücken auf ...	
MEPHISTOPHELES:	
Du unterzeichnest dich mit einem Tröpfchen Blut.	1737
Ich will mich hier zu deinem Dienst verbinden.	1656
Blut ist ein ganz besondrer Saft.	1740
Wir gehen eben fort.	1835*
Ich gratuliere dir zum neuen Lebenslauf.	2072
CHORUS:	
Setz dir Perücken auf ...	

Volz's adaptation achieves a degree of intertextuality: at the same time as Mephisto assures Faust that he will stay as he is, the well-known music supplies the subtext of temptation, promising the aged scholar that he is, after all, destined to live life to the fullest! The original text is just as confusing at this point, as was noted above (109).

41. The attempt to corrupt Gretchen with jewels having failed,
Mephisto (Falko Illing) plans a new strategy – involving a cell phone, 1997.

Many of the other songs in the adaptation fall into the same hard rock vein, so that the music for *Du bleibst doch immer* is not conspicuously different. Mephisto's *Tierischer als jedes Tier* ('Beastlier than any beast,' sung to the Lord in the prologue), *Das Böse* ('Evil,' in which Mephisto introduces himself to Faust), and *Kein Teufel wär* ('Were I not a devil,' expressing his frustration that Gretchen has given his first gift of jewels to the priest) are skilfully executed hard rock songs based on

269

solid riffs—brief ostinatos originating in the blues, usually chord-based, that underpin most successful rock songs—as are Faust's opening monologue *Der Magie ergeben* ('Turned to magic') and his *Das Leben mir verhasst* ('Life hateful to me,' Faust's contemplation of suicide, conflating scenes before and after Mephisto's appearance).

Faust's *Mondenschein* ('Moonlight,' a continuation of his opening monologue) takes the slower form of the so-called 'heavy ballad,' building from a simple acoustic guitar intro to the verse, in which Faust's lines alternate with an echoing electric guitar solo in classic call-and-response fashion (another legacy of the blues and ultimately of African music forms) before the chorus brings in the bass guitar and drums to propel the song forward dynamically. Culminating in an orgasmic guitar solo with strong Ritchie Blackmore overtones, *Mondenschein* is a classic example of the hard rock combination of sonic bombast and unabashed emotionality.

Volz also uses generic differences within contemporary music to aid both plot and characterisation: 'While Faust's and Mephisto's songs vary from heavy metal to death metal [sic], Gretchen's songs are ordinary pop songs' [in the English translation on Volz's website, 'ordinary pop songs which you can hear on the radio at any time']. A key contrast is thus set up between the two main male characters—in fact, they are the only remaining male characters in this heavily reduced version of Goethe—and Gretchen, who is offhandedly relegated to the lesser sphere of 'pop,' recalling Robert Pattison's definition:

> Pop is the most contemptuous term among the rock cognoscenti. Pop is what the mass public buys. Pop is pap. [...] The adjectives used in rock criticism to define pop are *tired, formulaic, unoriginal, boring.* The Sex Pistols, Iggy Pop, the Fall—the groups and performers who have been scorned by the mass market—are the heroes of rock precisely because their work is the opposite of pop. For these heroes, pop is the dreary foil to their misunderstood genius, which straight culture mistakes for confusion or depravity. (Pattison, 190)

And in fact, although Gretchen's 'King in Thule' cannily combines folk-rock stylings with the dynamics of the heavy ballad, and her complaint about Mephisto's influence on Faust, *Heimlich Grauen* ('Nameless Terror'), is equally clever in delaying the entrance of the electric guitars until the final section to signal the Evil One's presence, she otherwise does not fare particularly well musically in comparison to the dynamic, if equally derivative, nature of the numbers given to Faust and Mephisto. When, for example, she finds the jewels in her closet to *Am Golde hängt doch alles* ('Everything depends on gold'), the combination of synthesised marimba and strings with syncopated pop-funk rhythm guitar straight out of a Falco disco tune creates an almost unbearably saccharine effect; while her duet with Faust, *Er liebt mich* ('He loves me'), perfectly reproduces that 'melodious but embarrassing scene' of which *Rolling Stone* had complained in *Jesus Christ Superstar* three decades before (though here, at least, one could argue that the mawkishness is dramaturgically justified). *Meine Ruh ist hin* ('My Peace is Gone'; see 112f., above), meanwhile, which inspired *Lieder* by Schumann and Spohr, is turned into a rather dreary slow rock waltz with a slight country-pop flavour—somewhat reminiscent of early 1970s-era Olivia Newton-John—which a brief but blistering guitar solo in the last section fails to enliven. A similarly slow power ballad treatment of the opera's last real song, *Meine Mutter hab' ich umgebracht* ('I killed my mother'), is arguably the score's nadir, with heavy guitar chords bathetically underpinning the title phrase in the chorus, as if Gretchen's confession of murder is to be accompanied by the audience waving their cigarette lighters in the air.

Among the other rock styles in evidence in *Faust*, particularly noteworthy are the songs *Erdgeist* and *Walpurgis Nacht*. The former is sung by the Earth Spirit as an appropriately earthy rock boogie with requisite piano solo. This lively number combines elements of the Acid Queen's song from *Tommy* with an arrangement that would not be out of place in the *Rocky Horror Show* (to which Volz refers on his English website, but not in the German, where he merely claims that *Faust* has already become a 'cult musical'). The song performed by the Walpurgis Night revellers, on the other hand, aspires to *Rocky Horror*-style novelty but misses the mark, and oddly suppresses the slightly obscene references in the song about the apple tree, apparently because Goethe himself struck them out of his manuscript. Given the alleged intent to 'mirror old literary goods in the garment of modern rock and pop music' and the tameness of these references for a contemporary audience, leaving gaps in the lyrics of this song seems contradictory, and is apparently motivated by a combination of reverence for the original text—a reverence that nonetheless proves extremely flexible elsewhere in the adaptation—and perhaps a desire to keep the adaptation suitable for school groups (interestingly, the English-language version of the song, available for download on the website, is abysmally translated but fills in the gaps in the text; presumably English-speaking audiences can take this sort of thing without flinching).

The derivative quality of much of the music in *Faust: Die Rockoper* should not be considered a serious flaw (even though one of the press reviews posted on the website contains what I presume is a typo: *Rock-Opfer*—'victim of rock'); much of the music produced by rock writers and performers from the 1950s to the present exists in an ongoing intertextual dialogue that swings between homage and plagiarism. The digital sampling typical of rap and hip-hop is only the latest, automated manifestation of this dialogue. In fact, much of the opera's hard rock music is competent in its idiom, largely thanks to very skilful arrangements. It remains questionable, however, whether Volz's work lives up to its explicit claim to be faithful to Goethe's text—as opposed to the plot, at least in its barest outline—given the amount of cutting and transposition undertaken.

Volz's project has an additional dimension, moreover, through which he intends to trump all previous operatic and musical interpretations: not content with confining his work to the first part of Goethe's tragedy, Volz has gone on to adapt the second part of *Faust* (which Volz rather bizarrely describes as 'hardly known') into rock musical form as well. In addition to his original claim of fidelity, Volz now adds the further claim of historically unique completeness: 'This is the first adaptation of this theme into operatic form.'

This claim too is not entirely true: as we have seen, Boito's *Mefistofele* works sections of Part II into the plot, as do several other works; and Alfred Brüggeman in fact composed a trilogy of operas covering both parts of the tragedy in the early 1900s, although the third opera, *Faust and Helena, Faust's Redemption*, was never performed (Kelly, 104–6). Thus Volz's claim is also not utterly false either. In any case, *Faust II: Die Rockoper* premièred in October 2002; like its precursor, it has been greatly abbreviated, but in contrast to Part I, the second part contains at least fragments of all the major scenes, and hence runs much longer than Part I. Moreover, although the influence of hard rock is still present, as in the Emperor's song *Gegenkaiser* ('Anti-Emperor,' very much in the Deep Purple mould), it is now counterbalanced by explorations of the classical elements of Goethe's text through the medium of another musical form that rose to prominence in the early 1970s, so-called 'progressive rock' or 'art rock' in the style of Yes, Procul Harum, Renaissance or the above-named Novalis. Accordingly the sounds of the Hammond organ and the piano prevalent in Part I are now by supplemented by a greater variety of synthesised sounds, including those of the stereotypical 1970s art-rock instrument, the Mellotron. Classical music itself also appears: the 'Promenade' from Mussorgsky's *Pictures at an Exhibition* (shades of Emerson, Lake and Palmer!) appears as a fanfare for the Emperor, and Faust's death is marked by Chopin's 'Funeral March.' The music is more complex, freely mixing styles and giving the expanded cast greater opportunities for harmony, background vocals and choral work—and more interesting parts for women's voices (Helen, Ariel and Homunculus, among the named roles). Indeed, the singers, especially the women, are often hard pressed to rise to the challenge of the higher notes. Of particular interest is the Emperor's and Mephisto's *Es fehlt an Geld* ('Money is lacking'), which segues from Mussorgsky into a number of styles, ranging from 1950s-style syncopation to a driving funk bass rhythm to eerie free-form wash of synthesisers and back again. *Rechnung* ('Reckoning,' about Mephisto's invention of paper money), on the other hand, mimics the style of David Bowie; *Hier knie nieder* ('Here kneel down,' Faust's order to the watchman Lynkeus to submit to Helen's punishment) is based on a twangy Byrds-style arpeggiated guitar riff that somehow evokes Gerry and the Pacemakers' 1964 hit 'Ferry across the Mersey'; and *Grablegung* ('Burial') alternates Mephisto's rage at being cheated of his prey, growling and screaming over irregular Metallica-inspired power chords and thus coming as close as *Faust* ever does to true death metal, with the angelic choir backed by synthesiser—a juxtaposition that, no doubt coincidentally, recalls the contrast between the voices of the virtues and that of the devil in Hildegard of Bingen's mediaeval work *Ordo Virtutum*.

Both a greater degree of confidence and a larger budget are evident in the second part, and the recent appearance of a new song for Part I, *Grau ist alle Theorie* ('Gray is all theory,' from Mephisto's scene masquerading as Faust for the Student), on the *Faust* website, may well indicate that the first part is now being enlarged to take advantage of the increased resources. A Spanish-language touring company has now been formed, and an English-language version is available for download on the website; the existence of these versions, combined with the offer of limited free performance rights for educational institutions in English-speaking countries, indicates the scope of Volz's ambition for his interpretation.

Unfortunately, the English translations are not only incompetent but also suffer from the handicap of not scanning correctly to fit the music—and matters are not helped by the fact that many of the German cast are clearly uncomfortable singing in English. This may prove, however, to be only a minor obstacle in the dissemination of Rudolf Volz's *Faust: Die Rockoper*. As the conclusion of Part II demonstrates: 'Whoever aspires unweariedly/ is not beyond redeeming' (F 11936f.).

Notes

1. I am grateful to Joachim Lucchesi for drawing my attention to some of the differences between the stage version and the recording.
2. This and all subsequent quotations from Volz are taken from his website at www.faust.cc in July 2003. All translations are by the author, ignoring the less complete English versions on the same site.

Cited Literature and Further Reading

Walter Aign, *Faust im Lied*, Stuttgart: K. Theens, 1975.

Anon., Review of the album *DisinHAIRited*, *Rolling Stone*, 21 February 1970, 52.

Dennis Arnold (ed.), *The New Oxford Companion to Music*. 2 volumes, Oxford: University Press, 1983.

Robert Baldick, *La vie de Frédéric Lemaître*, Paris: Denoël, 1961.

Andreas Ballstaedt, Ulrike Kienzle and Adlof Nowak (eds), *Musik in Goethes Werk – Goethes Werk in der Musik*. Schliengen: Edition Argus, 2003.

Jean-Pierre Barricelli, 'Faust and the Music of Evil,' *Journal of European Studies* 13 (1983), 1–26.

Alexander Beaumont, *Busoni the Composer*. London: Faber & Faber, 1985.

Eric Bentley (ed.), *Shaw on Music*. London: Applause, 1996.

Berlioz and the Romantic Imagination. London: The Arts Council, 1969.

Albrecht Betz, *Hanns Eisler. Political Musician*. Cambridge: University Press, 1982.

Peter Boerner and Sidney Johnson (eds), *Faust through Four Centuries. Retrospect and Analysis. Vierhundert Jahre Faust. Rückblick und Analyse*. Tübingen: Niemeyer, 1989.

Johannes Bolte, 'Ein Meisterlied von Doktor Faust,' *Euphorion* 1 (1894), 787f.

Dieter Borchmeyer, '*Faust*. Musikalische Thematik und Dramaturgie', in Ballstaedt, 325–34.

Clive Brown (ed.), *Selected works of Louis Spohr*. 10 volumes. New York: Garland Publishing, 1990. Volume I: *Faust*. Ed. Jonathan Stracey.

Julian Budden, 'Gounod's Faust over the Years', Notes to EMI recording, 1991, 17–25.

Hans Bunge (ed.), *Die Debatte um Hanns Eislers 'Johann Faustus'. Eine Dokumentation*. Berlin: BasisDruck, 1991.

Ferruccio Busoni, 'Doktor Faust. Dichtung für Musik', *Die weissen Blätter* 5 (4/1918), 11–29.

——, *Doktor Faust. Dichtung und Musik*. Leipzig: Breitkopf & Härtel, 1925.

Michel Butor and Henri Pousseur, *Euer Faust. Variables Spiel in Art einer Oper. Vorläufige Fassung*. Munich: Biederstein, 1964.

David Cairns, *Berlioz. Servitude and Greatness 1832–1869*. Harmondsworth: Allan Lane, 1999.

Claus Canisius, *Goethe und die Musik*. Munich: Piper, 1998.

Michel Carré, *Faust et Marguerite, drame fantastique en 3 actes*. Paris: Bibliothèque dramatique, 1849.

Ian Christe, *Sound of the Beast: The Complete Headbanging History of Heavy Metal*. New York: Harper, 2003.

Douglas Cole, 'The Impact of Goethe's *Faust* on Nineteenth- and Twentieth-Century Criticism of Marlowe's *Doctor Faustus*', in Boerner /Johnson, 186–96.

Peter Conrad, *Romantic Opera and Literary Form*. Berkeley: University of California Press, 1977.

Jonathan Cort, 'Jesus Christ Sings an Aria,' *Rolling Stone*, 2 December 1970.

Hector Crémieux and Adam Jaime, *Le Petit Faust. Opera-bouffe en 3 actes, 4 tableaux*. Paris: Au Ménestrel, 1869.

Peter Csobádi, Gernot Gruber, Jürgen Kühnel, Ulrich Müller, Oswald Panagl and Franz Viktor Spechtler (eds), *Europäische Mythen der Neuzeit: Faust und Don Juan. Gesammelte Vorträge des Salzburger Symposions 1992*. 2 volumes. Anif/Salzburg: Ursula Müller-Speiser, 1993.

André Dabezies, *Visages de Faust au XXe siècle. Littérature, idéologie et mythe*. Paris: Presses Universitaires de France, 1967.

Norman Demuth, *Introduction to the Music of Gounod*. London: Dennis Dobson, 1950.

Hanns Eisler, *Johann Faustus. Oper*. Berlin: Aufbau, 1952. Rptd *Johann Faustus. Fassung letzter Hand*, ed. Hans Bunge, Berlin: Henschel, 1983; ed. Jürgen Schebera, Leipzig: Faber & Faber, 1996.

Hermann Fähnrich, *Faust in Kantaten, Oratorien, Symphonischen Dichtungen und Symphonischen Kantaten*. Stuttgart: K. Theens, 1978.

Jens Malte Fischer, '"Ich, Faust, ein ewiger Wille." Ferruccio Busonis Faust-Komposition in seiner unvollendeten Oper', in Csobádi, II, 559–71.

Johann Ernst Galliard, *Dr Faustus or the Necromancer. A Masque of Songs as they were perform'd at the Theatre in Lincolns Inn Fields*. London: I. Walsh and Ino. & Ioseph Hare, 1724.

Wolfgang Gratzer, '"Eine negative Passion". Alfred Schnittkes Faust-Kantate als Paradigma postmoderner Mythenrezeption', in Csobádi, II, 595–620.

Richard D. Green, 'Music in Goethe's Faust: Its First Dramatic Setting', in Grimm/ Hermand, 47–64.

William E. Grim, *The Faust Legend in Music and Literature*. 2 volumes. Lewiston/NY: Edwin Mellen Press, 1987–92 (Studies in the History and Interpretation of Music, 5, 36).

Reinhold Grimm and Jost Hermand, *Our Faust? Roots and ramifications of a modern German myth. 16th Wisconsin Workshop Papers*. Wisconsin: University Press, 1987.

Ottfried Hafner, 'Richard Wagner zwischen Faust und Don Juan', in Csobádi, I, 129–35.

James Harding, *Gounod*. London: Allen and Unwin, 1973.

Petra Hartmann, *Faust und Don Juan. Ein Verschmelzungsprozess, dargestellt anhand der Autoren: Wolfgang Amadeus Mozart, Johann Wolfgang von Goethe, Nikolaus Lenau, Christian Dietrich Grabbe, Gustav Kühne und Theodor Mundt*. Stuttgart: Ibidem-Verlag, 1998.

Hans Henning, *Faust-Bibliographie*. Berlin: Aufbau-Verlag, 1966–1976. Volume III: *Das Faust-Thema neben und nach Goethe*. 1976.

Frank Heidelberger, 'Die Faust-Kompositionen von Hector Berlioz. Untersuchungen zum Verhältnis von literarischer Adaption und musikalischer Deutung', in Csobádi, I, 535–48.

Aleksander Ivashkin, *Alfred Schnittke*. London: Phaidon, 1996.

James William Kelly, *The Faust Legend in Music*, PhD Dissertation, Northwestern University, 1960. Bibliography updated 1974. Detroit: Information Coordinators, 1976.

Kobbé's Complete Opera Book. Ninth edition, London: Putnam, 1976.

Hans Joachim Kreutzer, *Faust. Mythos und Musik*. Munich: C.H. Beck, 2003.

Nikolaus Lenau, *Faust. Ein Gedicht. Mit Dokumenten zur Entstehung und Wirkung*. Ed.

Hartmut Steinecke. Stuttgart: Reclam 1971.

Fanny Lewald, *Italienisches Bilderbuch*. 2 volumes. Berlin: Alexander Duncker, 1847.

Thomas Mann, 'Deutschland und die Deutschen', in *Ibid.*, *Gesammelte Werke*. 13 volumes. Frankfurt/M: Fischer, 1974, XI, 1126-48.

Rainer Kunad, *Sabellicus. Oper in neun Bildern. Libretto vom Komponisten*. Berlin: Henschel, 1974.

Carlo Marinelli, *Faust e Mefistofele nelle opere teatrali e sinfonico-vocali*. Discografia. Treviso: Istituto di Ricerca per il Teatro Musicale, 1986.

Andreas Meier, *Faustlibretti: Geschichte des Fauststoffs auf der europäischen Musikbühne nebst einer lexikalischen Bibliographie der Faustvertonungen*. Frankfurt/M: Peter Lang, 1990.

Hedwig Meier, *Die Schaubühne als musikalische Anstalt. Studien zur Geschichte und Theorie der Schauspielmusik im 18. und 19. Jahrhundert sowie zu ausgewählten "Faust"-Kompositionen*. Bielefeld: Aisthesis, 1999.

——, 'Die erste Gesamtaufführung des *Faust* aus dem Geiste der Musik', in Ballstaedt, 364-79.

Stefan Melle, 'Der Teufel kommt nach Moskau', *Berliner Zeitung*, 11 July 2000.

Volker Mertens, 'Doktor Faust im Meisterlied', in Franz V. Spechtler (ed.), *Lyrik des ausgehenden 14. und 15. Jahrhunderts*. Amsterdam: Rodopi, 1984, 97-114.

Ralph Müller, *Das Opernlibretto im 19. Jahrhundert*. Winterthur: Schellenberg, 1965.

Robert Pattison, *The Triumph of Vulgarity: Rock Music in the Mirror of Romanticism*. New York: Oxford University Press, 1987.

Julius Perrot, *Faust. Grosses phantastisches Ballet in drei Acten*. Vienna: A. Pichler's selige Witwe, 1851. Reviewed in *Bäuerles Wiener Allgemeine Zeitung für Theater, Musik und Kunst*, 27 May 1851.

Jürgen Rosenthal, *Faust. Rockballett*. Hanover: Edition Kröpcke, 1986.

W. Rösler, 'Zur musikalischen Dramaturgie der Oper *Sabellicus* von Rainer Kunad', in Hirst Seeger (ed.), *Jahrbuch-Musikbühne 75: Probleme und Informationen*. Berlin: Henschel, 1975, 67-81.

Stanley Sadie (ed.), *The New Grove Dictionary of Opera*. 4 volumes. London: Macmillan, 1992.

Irmgard Schartner, *Hanns Eisler, Johannes Faustus. Das Werk und seine Wirkungsgeschichte*. Frankfurt/M: Peter Lang, 1998.

Ralf Schnell, *Geschichte der deutschsprachigen Literatur seit 1945*. Stuttgart: Metzler, 1993.

Willi Schuh, *Goethe-Vertonungen. Ein Verzeichnis*. Zurich: Artemis, 1952.

James Simon, *Faust in der Musik*, Berlin: Bard, Marquardt, 1906.

G. R. Sims and H. Pettitt, *Faust up to Date. Burlesque opera, with incidental Songs written & composed by R. Martin, E. Solomon, A. Chapman, S. Smith & F. Bowyer*. London: E. Ascherberg & Co, 1889.

Hans Heinz Stuckenschmidt, 'Es muss ein "Faust" sein', *Frankfurter Allgemeine Zeitung*, 20 January 1969, 20.

Gerhard Stumme, *Faust als Pantomime und Ballett*, Leipzig: Poeschel & Trepte, 1942.

Joe Stuessy, *Rock and Roll: Its History and Stylistic Development*. Englewood Cliffs/NJ: Prentice Hall, 1990. Revised 1994, 2003.

Alexander Tille, *Die deutschen Volkslieder vom Doktor Faust*. Halle/Saale: Max Niemeyer, 1890.

Tom Topor, 'Rock and Roll, Dead, Takes Over Broadway,' *Rolling Stone*, 23 December 1971.

Rainer Wagner, 'Der Teufel tanzt Tango. Alfred Schnittkes "Historia von D. Johann Fausten" in Hamburg uraufgeführt', *Opernwelt* 8/1995, 26f.

John Warrack and Ewan West (eds), *The Oxford Dictionary of Opera*. Oxford: University Press, 1992.

Deena Weinstein, *Heavy Metal: A Cultural Sociology*. New York: Lexington, 1991.

Sigrid Wiesmann, '"Mi fai orrore." Einige Bemerkungen zu Henri Pousseurs *Votre Faust* und Luca Lombardis *Faust. Un Travestimento*', in Csobádi, II, 574-81.

Chapter Eight

From Woodcut to Manga: 100 Images of a Magus

He was born in Deutschland, as you would suspect,
And graduated in magic from Cracow
In Fifteen Five. His portraits show a brow
Heightened by science. The eye is indirect,
As of bent light upon a crooked soul,
And that he bargained with the Prince of Shame
For pleasures intellectually foul
Is known by every court that lists his name.
> Karl Shapiro, 'The Progress of Faust'

Early Illustrators

ONE HUNDRED faces of Faust the magician are shown on a poster designed by E. Peter Moosmann and distributed by the Faust Museum in Knittlingen. The earliest is taken from an ancient woodcut, the most recent from Osamu Tezuka's *manga* comic *Neo-Faust*. A similar number may be admired on the walls of the entrance to the 'Goethe Room' at Auerbach's Cellar in Leipzig, an establishment which claims to own illustrations dating from as early as 1525 showing the doctor carousing with his students. Yet amidst all these ancient and modern counterfeits, there is not one demonstrably authentic record of the doctor's appearance. Instead, we have editions of the play that are lavishly illustrated by one or several artists, from Peter Cornelius and Moritz Retzsch via Eugène Delacroix to Harry Clarke, Ernst Barlach, Max Slevogt, Rockwell Kent, Max Beckmann and other, more recent artists. The first attempt to record the images was undertaken by Glasgow-based Alexander Tille in 1899. His 'catalogue' lists 543 German portraits of Goethe's Faust beside 111 from France and 46 from English sources. Franz Neubert's anthology of 1932 contains 236 pages of illustrations covering all aspects of the myth. Numerous exhibitions on the general topic of 'Faust in the figurative arts' have attempted to bring together the diverse images, leading to voluminous catalogues such as those issued by Carl Niessen in

42. *Detail from* One hundred faces of Faust. *Poster designed by E. Peter Moosmann, 1991.*

1929 and E.P. Moosmann and Carl Paschek in 1991. A further landmark was provided in 1924 by Max von Boehn, whose luxury edition of *Faust* is preceded by a richly illustrated essay on 'Faust in Art'. This later became known as the *Hundertjahrsausgabe* ('Centenary Edition') and is now a sought-after collectors' item. The first doctoral dissertation on Faust illustrators dates from 1930, and the more recent research by Wolfgang Wegner and Sebastian Giesen has gone some way

43. *Andreas Brettschneider, 'Faustus carousing with his friends in a tavern'. Copy of a painting in Auerbach's Cellar, Leipzig. Although dated 1525, it cannot have been painted much before 1620 on the evidence of the clothing worn by the revellers.*

towards illuminating key aspects of this hugely complex subject.

Faust's countenance and physical appearance have intrigued artists from the sixteenth century to the present. Several images have attained iconic status. No medium has remained untouched by their endeavours: Faust has been cast in bronze and moulded in clay, painted on porcelain, canvas and paper, in oils, ink, watercolours, engravings and etchings. This, in itself, is hardly remarkable; the so-called supernatural has had pride of place in the arts from earliest times. There is a clear affinity between Faust's temptation, his miraculous powers, his damnation or redemption, and the biblical and legendary stories treated by artists in sacred contexts and displayed in temples and chapels. The earliest pictures of the doctor served two purposes: to accompany the printed accounts of his life, and to display his alleged adventures in such taverns and other venues that had acquired an association with him. When the legend entered literature, the relationship between text and image grew more intimate. The long delay in having Goethe's work performed led to pressure for visual substitutes. Sketches of what a live production might look like began to appear in tableau form. The public had to wait nearly forty years, from 1790 to 1829, before being able to see actual productions in public theatres, and in the interim, many artists were waiting in the wings all too ready to plug the gap, the more so as Goethe himself had insisted that *Faust I* be published in book form devoid of all illustrations.

> I would think that we should issue *Faust* without any woodcuts or images. It is inordinately difficult to produce something that fits in with the spirit and the mood of a piece of writing. Poetry and copperplate have a tendency to parody one another by turns. I believe the old sorcerer will have to get by without any assistance. (Letter to Cotta, 25 November 1805)

Hence the series of extraordinarily detailed line-drawings intended to make the action burst into life as if in performance. When in due course the play became

278

part of theatre repertoire, these early sketches were not forgotten or superseded. Such was their appeal that they were relied upon as models on which productions had to be based if they were to satisfy audience expectations. This development was not without its negative consequences for subsequent dramatisations. It raised expectations of a certain type of scenery, specific props, clothing and even gestures. The producers' style was effectively cramped by these images, and for one hundred years, productions of *Faust* resembled each other closely in their pseudo-Gothic arcades, flowing robes, and vaulted chambers festooned with almost identical accretions of 'Faustian' paraphernalia. It was not until the 1950s that we see a departure initiated by Gustaf Gründgens, who dared to place a clean-shaven Faust among minimalist props on bare boards. Yet, conversely, the relationship between paintings and enactments of the play was not a one-way process. From the 1820s onwards, artists were guided not only by the written words but also by the playhouses; Delacroix, for example, admits to having been influenced by a version he saw in London, the specific effect of which is visible in his arrangement of 'Faust in his Study'.

M. D. LXXXVIIL

44. The earliest image of Faustus in existence derives from the title page of a chapbook dated 1588 (no publisher shown).

The sixteenth-century chapbooks are sparsely illustrated. They were intended as warnings: the protagonist was not to be emulated, and therefore any pictures showing him on his travels or playing tricks on people would have been counterproductive. The book arose from an iconoclastic tradition that objected to unnecessary imagery and encouraged earnest reflection on the message of the written word. But this did not last. Images help to sell books, and before long, woodcuts of relatively general import began to appear on the title pages, in the Wagner Books, and on broadsheets.

45. Christopher Marlowe: The Tragicall Historie of D. Faustus, *London, 1631, from the title page.*

A more detailed but equally fanciful picture can be seen in a cellar of the Auerbachs Hof tavern in Leipzig, whose university rivalled Wittenberg, where Faustus is alleged to have taught. It seems probable that Leipzig, too, will have cashed in on the story, and some enterprising tavern-owner commissioned a picture illustrating what Faustus got up to there. Although not specifically works of art, the various *Höllenzwänge* ('magic formulae'), some richly illustrated, should also be mentioned here. They purported to contain spells used by Faustus and were the products of a cottage industry that survived until the eighteenth century. The chapbooks indicated that Faustus left books to Wagner that contained detailed spells and *coniurationes*. A professor from the University of Halle, one Johann Ernst Philippi, is said to have produced such documents for cash. As late as the end of the eighteenth century these forgeries changed hands for sums up to 200 talers. Many found their way into monastic libraries (Boehn, 6; Niessen, 30–34).

Christoph van Sichem lived around 1580–1648. In 1608, he published a series of eighteen portraits of famous heretics, false prophets and black magicians; Faust was added to these in the second edition. Sichem's two illustrations represent the earliest attempt by a known artist to provide a detailed portrait of the magician and his personal demon. Faustus is, unsurprisingly, clad in the academic garments of the time and Mephistopheles is depicted as a monk carrying a bell and a distinctive-looking rosary. Faustus had asked him to ring the bell when approaching, so as not to be frightened. Christopher Wagner's picture is also included, probably because of the large number of Wagner Books that were in circulation at the time. He is engaged in a dispute with the simian spirit Auerhahn, his own attendant demon.

46. *Two Illustrations by Christoph van Sichem: Mephistopheles and Faustus; Wagner and Auerhahn. Published in Middelburgh 1677. The engraving was used in reverse by Achim von Arnim in his* Zeitschrift für Einsiedler *('Journal for Hermits') in 1808.*

The earliest image commonly associated specifically with Dr Faustus and bearing a recognisable individuality is by Rembrandt. Of his contemporaries, neither Dürer nor Holbein nor Cranach appears to have shown any interest in the subject. Voices were heard in the eighteenth century to the effect that it was due to Rembrandt rather than Marlowe that Faustus had survived as an entity in the public imagination (Boehn, 11). Yet Rembrandt's image is not a portrait. As Rudolf Payer von Thurn has shown, Rembrandt used the same face in various other contexts, for example, in *Flight into Egypt* where he is the model for St Joseph. It dates from around 1639 and was copied by Jan Joris van Vliet, who worked in Rembrandt's studio in Leyden, and was later recycled by an enterprising Parisian engraver, Jerome David, as a portrait of 'Doctor Faustus'. Many subsequent authors availed themselves of it, down to the so-called 'Christlich Meynender' of 1725.

Payer von Thurn made another interesting comparison, this time with a portrait of one of the great villains from the Scriptures. When he needed a face for Judas, Rembrandt turned again the same physiognomy that provided Faustus and Joseph: that of a care-worn middle-aged man, bowed or bent down to avoid the spectator's gaze. At first sight this affinity seems perplexing. What could the black magician and the betrayer of Jesus have in common with the husband of the Virgin, here portrayed tenderly looking down at the suckling Christ child? If there is a connection, it is that all three are failures who have to content themselves to playing a peripheral role, and not an enviable one, in the divine scheme of things. Joseph is more often pitied than admired; he was married to the holiest woman who ever lived, yet denied carnal knowledge of his own wife. Faustus was frustrated and outwitted by a devil who fobbed him off with false pleasures, and Judas, the most favoured of disciples, ended up having to play the role of traitor, thus ensuring his

281

47. Rembrandt's Faust is a short, hunched-up individual in contemplative mood, 1639.

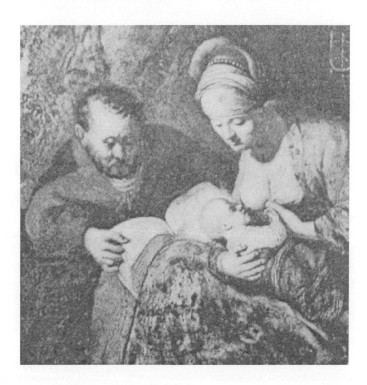

48. Detail of Flight from Egypt *attributed to Rembrandt, c. 1640, shows the Holy Family resting on the journey. Here St Joseph, an unlikely Faust look-alike, is hunched over a book.*

Doct· Faust.
Berühmter Schwartz Künstler

49. *'A stout and coarse libertine, confronting the world with a satiated stare',
the same 'Rembrandt Faust' is recycled in 1725.*

50. Rembrandt, Faust in his Study, 1652. *Goethe used Johann Heinrich Lips' engraving of
this picture (reversed) as the title piece for Volume 7 of his* Collected Works *of 1790.*

own damnation but the redemption of others – a role Faustus, too, must accept with good grace at the end of the chapbook. Another surprise is that the immediate source of the Faustus-Joseph-Judas figure appears to have been Rembrandt's father Harmen Gerritszoon van Rijn. By 1725, the Rembrandt/Vliet/David portrait had come to be viewed as 'a stout and coarse libertine, confronting the world with a satiated stare' (Payer von Thurn, 3–12; Niessen, 15; Boehn 15).

A second portrait of the doctor has been attributed to Rembrandt. Curiously, this considerably more detailed and interesting picture has not been copied as often. It was published by Balthasar Moncornet in Paris some time after 1650. It depicts an alchemist in his study, and a spirit or apparition is discernible, framed by a window. This picture acquired its association with Faustus via a sales gimmick by the French art dealer Edmé Gersaint, who compiled the original *catalogue raisonné* of Rembrandt's etchings in 1751. It was known to Goethe, who used Johann Heinrich Lips' engraving as the title piece and sole illustration for Volume 7 of his *Collected Works* in 1790. It may have provided visual inspiration for his Macrocosm and Earth Spirits.

Substitutes for Drama

From the time of Faust's re-emergence as a literary icon in the late eighteenth century, art and drama became interdependent. Stage productions were few but the effect of illustrations was great. Set-piece scenes like 'Faust in his Study', 'Mephistopheles appears before Faust', 'Faust's Encounter with Gretchen', 'Gretchen at the Spinning Wheel', 'Valentine's Death', and 'Gretchen in Prison' were worked over by countless artists and dilettantes. 'Martha's Garden', with its contrast of the old and shrivelled couple in the background and the young lovers in the foreground was another favourite, not least on account of its redeployment of the Garden of Eden motif. Much later, the political aspects were foregrounded, as Faust came to symbolise the hopes of the recently unified nation (Forster-Hahn, 83).

The importance of the visual image can also be deduced from the many scenes that Goethe based on known drawings or tableaux. These include Raphael's *Triumph of Galatea*, Correggio's *Leda and the Swan* and others so numerous that critics have noted that the play moves from one picture to another almost in the manner of a film: in the last act of Part II, 'the images become the dominant feature and determine the action in their combinations, collages and super-impositions' (Gaier, 134). Goethe himself executed several sketches based on situations from his play. They were found in a folder inscribed 'Theatre drawings' after his death. It is thought that they date from the second decade of the nineteenth century. Maisak argues that they were not intended to depict scenery for a future production, and relates them instead to discussions with the actor Pius Wolff in 1812. The sketches show the Lord in a Zeus-like pose, and the Earth Spirit has a classical grandeur that was obviously intended as a polemical challenge to the moderns. It is conceivable that the 'Heavenly Prologue' scene was based on drawings by Moritz Retzsch, the least Germanic of Goethe's contemporary illustrators; John Flaxman's 'Assembly of the Gods' of 1793 has also been suggested as a possible source (Giesen, 70; Maisak, 249-51).

51. Goethe's sketch of his 'Prologue in Heaven'. Ink on blue paper; undated.

Goethe's sketch of the Earth Spirit is perhaps even more remarkable. Far from being the chaotic alchemist's den that we have come to expect, the setting is comparable to the altar of a Baroque church, with the majestic spirit appearing in a huge alcove. To the left there are objects, books and glass jars, but the lectern beside which the magician stands is an ornate artefact such as one might find in a place of worship. The sketch may be based on a no longer extant sepia drawing by Nauwerck,

52. Goethe's sketch of the Earth Spirit. Pencil on white paper; undated.

285

albeit stripped of the magician's paraphernalia in the foreground (Bergmann, 316).

Early illustrators include Christian Friedrich Osiander and Asmus Jacob Carstens, both of whom produced drawings based on the 'Fragment' of 1790 (Giesen, 15-18). From 1808 onwards, a veritable deluge of pictorial material ensued. Christian Ludwig Stieglitz and Ludwig Gottlieb Carl Nauwerck were among the first; Goethe commented positively on the latter's sepia drawings in *Über Kunst und Altertum*, 1827. Gustav Heinrich Naeke was an early illustrator whose work was well received and set the tone for many who followed. He produced three images for use in *Urania*, an edifying periodical for ladies. These were subsequently engraved by C. A. Schwerdgeburth. Here Gretchen appears very child-like, her maidenly innocence indicated not only in her delicate, hesitant gestures but also by her shining white robe. Faust, by contrast, has pulled up his cloak to reveal his nether regions, a detail, along with his protruding sword, that hints at the theme of innocence traduced. Another remarkable characteristic of the 'garden' scenes is the obvious affinity with the Garden of Eden. Flowers proliferate, the scene is one of temptation, Satan himself hovers in the background, and sometimes the couple are separated by a tree (Giesen, 266-71).

53. Naeke's naïve, childlike Gretchen can be read as a warning against impropriety in a setting that recalls the Garden of Eden, 1812.

The most famous illustrator of *Faust* from this early period is unquestionably Peter Cornelius (1783-1867), who supplied twelve images and a title-piece. They were executed around 1812, engraved by Ferdinand Ruscheweyh, and published as a free-standing series without any accompanying text. Cornelius was a member of the 'Nazarene School' of German painters who congregated in Rome and devoted themselves to the recreation of a neo-mediaeval style in works of religious or Germanic import. Their revivalist aims were pursued by applying the modern techniques of copperplate engraving to historical subjects. The most favoured architectural backdrops, reproduced in great detail, are invariably Gothic, despite having been executed mainly in Italy.

54. Peter Cornelius, First Encounter between Faust and Gretchen, *1816.*

These images are deliberately designed to appear to the viewer like modern Dürers, albeit stripped of the wood-cut effect and focused on a small number of iconic elements. They have a quaint *altdeutsch* ('olde German') quality which at the time conveyed anti-Napoleonic political sentiment; Cornelius actually considered himself to be fighting French influences though the medium of art (Forster-Hahn, 86). Although Goethe disapproved of the *altdeutsch* line of thinking as too narrowly provincial, he was not unimpressed by the outcome. Having been

55. Peter Cornelius, Gretchen in Prison, *1816.*

shown a selection of sketches in 1811, the poet advised Cornelius to study Dürer and classical art, commenting:

> The drawings [...] were a most pleasant reminder of the progress that you, esteemed Herr Cornelius, have made since the last time I had sight of your work. The themes are well chosen and the depictions well thought out, and the inspired treatment both of the topics as a whole and of the details are cause for admiration. As you have transported yourself into a world which you have never seen with your own eyes, but which you know only from images derived from an earlier age, it is truly remarkable that you were able to distinguish yourself not only in respect of costumes and other peripheral matters, but by entering into the very spirit of the work, so that there can be no question but that the longer you proceed in this manner, the more freely you will be able to manoeuvre in this medium. [...] (Letter to Cornelius, 8 May 1811)

More than any other artist, Cornelius had the effect of shaping, and to some extent fossilising, future perceptions of Faust. To him we owe the image of Gretchen as a passive, demure maiden with long flaxen plaits. The significance of his twelve prints was enhanced by a lack of performances. When *Faust* came to be seen on stage from 1829 onwards, theatre directors looked closely at these sketches when planning layouts and scenery and were reluctant to depart from what was already in the public domain (Mahl, 24).

It was not only through his late mediaeval settings and garments that Cornelius' influence on the drama was made manifest. Unlike Dürer, Cornelius and later illustrators prefer the 'landscape' to the 'portrait' format, and many adopt a low, centred perspective similar to that of a viewer sitting in the front stalls of a playhouse. Margaret is depicted as the reactive victim in the six pictures in which she appears. Faust, by contrast, is highly assertive. The 'First Encounter' contains a clear indication of the dynamics of their relationship. True, Faust offers the lady his arm as the text demands, but the gesture is an extravagant, almost threatening one, and her reaction as she walks away is docile, designed to pacify his ardour rather than shun his offer. It is typical that Cornelius should marginalise the devil. Mephistopheles is rarely centre-stage; his position is that of a bystander or voyeur. Faust is bursting with energy, as his bulging thigh and calf muscles indicate. Even on the Brocken, when one might expect Mephistopheles to be in full control of the excursion to the Witches' Sabbath, Faust is the stronger of the two and forges ahead while Mephistopheles clings somewhat precariously to the rocks. In the final scene in the Prison, Faust is resolutely doing his utmost to save the girl, reaching out towards her with his right hand and with his left trying to fend off the devil. She commends herself to an angel, in a manner reminiscent of the penitent Magdalen, a favourite subject of the Nazarene School. One notes the presence of many religious objects strewn on the floor around her: a rosary, a prayer book, and even a skull (Giesen, 40-60).

For many contemporary and subsequent viewers, these twelve drawings represented an unsurpassable level of profundity, comparable to some miracle of Nature. Christian Eckert's monograph of 1906 gives a flavour of the patriotic eulogies that were to be heard at the time:

One must, of course, be able to see these drawings through German eyes if they are to speak to us. Up to this day there has hardly ever been a descendant of the Romans [ein Romane] who was able to appreciate the wholesome magic of the Faust legend or to imagine the secrets that lurk behind the bare facts, those mysterious forces that determine our existence. Peter Cornelius must have been well aware that people of other nationalities would never be able to fathom out his work, which to this day comes closest of all similar attempts to the spirit of the original drama. There are limits to what can be understood and these are determined by racial factors that cannot easily be overcome. The Romance peoples have a keen sense of form, but this lets them down when it comes to understanding the profound psychology of Germanic and Slav poetry and has long caused them to resist the influence of German music. (Eckert, 23)

They were not unique, nor were they universally admired. Mephistopheles, in particular, was seen as weak and effeminate, looking 'more shifty than powerful', in the words of Sebastian Albin, and even 'like a little old woman' (Giesen 55, n. 306). Other artists were waiting to offer their own, strikingly different perspectives on the drama. Moritz Retzsch adopted a diametrically opposite style in his *Umrisse* or 'Outlines to Goethe's Faust'. These were the subject of an early contract with Goethe's publisher, Cotta, dated 10 October 1810, but they did not appear in print until six years later. Like the work of Cornelius, they were submitted to the public in horizontal format, with no text, and from a front-stall perspective. Retzsch used a technique known as styleography to indicate scenes through outlines only. This was a method for which there were classical antecedents, and it therefore gave his drawings an appearance that was in complete contrast to the mediaevalism that distinguished Cornelius and the 'olde German' effects sought by the Nazarenes. Styleographic methods had been used by, among others, John Flaxman, a master of the pure line, whose illustrations of Homer may have had an influence on Retzsch.

While Cornelius had foregrounded Faust, Retzsch gave pride of place to Gretchen, whom he refuses to set in a sombrely Teutonic context. She is given classical features and flowing robes in the antique manner, and a playful smile suggests a level of active participation that other artists of the time hesitated to evoke. Even the background has an Arcadian flavour, and the spirits that sing Faust to sleep as Mephistopheles makes his escape are far removed from the world of Nordic hobgoblins. With wreaths in their hair and seductively waving their arms, they strike poses familiar from Greek mythology. In the Garden and Prison scenes, too, we have few reminders of the German milieu on which other artists of the period concentrated. Gretchen's gestures are very different here; she is not clasping her hands in the manner of a Christian at prayer but opening them wide in an expansive gesture that contrasts strikingly with the pose adopted by Cornelius' figure. Nor is there a rosary, crucifix or prayer-book in evidence. Her cell lacks Gothic encumbrances, but instead contains an urn shaped like an amphora, and is lit by a small oil-lamp in the classical style. She has, throughout the cycle, the appearance of one who has loved, actively, and suffered, rather than been seduced and traduced (Giesen, 63–5).

56. Retzsch's Gretchen in Prison, *1816, dispenses with the Christian pose and accoutrements, substituting classical gestures and details.*

Retzsch's work was criticised for transporting the story away from its mediaeval Germanic roots, but his images sold well and were soon published in France and England, where their reception was more favourable than in their homeland. A further sign of their impact was noted on stage, where a number of leading ladies playing the part of Gretchen chose to model themselves on Retzsch rather than Cornelius (Giesen, 69–74).

Eugène Delacroix produced his series of seventeen lithographs in 1827. They are among the best-known literary illustrations of from any period. The subject is approached in a theatrical manner which brings out the demonic and irrational aspects of the story to a far greater extent than either Cornelius or Retzsch were able to. The suite was first published in 1828 along with a portrait of Goethe in a French adaptation by Albert Stapfer, although the artist had originally intended to place them before the public without any accompanying text (Letter to Philippe Burty, 1 March 1862). His interest in Goethe's play dates from 1824, but it was only after he had seen George Soane's adaptation in the New Theatre Royal, Drury Lane, London in May 1825 that the cycle began to preoccupy him. This adaptation of Goethe was a spectacular event, which the painter describes in the following terms:

> I have seen here a play of *Faust* which is the most diabolical one can imagine. The Mephistopheles is a masterpiece of character and intelligence. It is Goethe's *Faust*, but adapted. The principle has been preserved. They have made it into an opera, mixing together the comic with all the blackness it contains. One sees the scene of the church with the chant of the priest and the organ in the distance. The effect could not be carried further in the theatre. (Letter to Pierret, 18 June 1825, cited by Trapp, 143)

Delacroix may have seen the drawings by Cornelius; it is certain that he was familiar with Retzsch's 'Outlines', which had been lithographed in France. What he may not have known is that the Drury Lane production had utilised Retzsch as inspiration for its stage effects. Even before they were published, Clemens Wenzeslaus Coudray, a German architect, obtained a couple of proofs in Paris and showed them to Goethe, who discussed them in detail with his assistant, Johann Peter Eckermann, and wrote a review based on what he had seen (Conversation with Eckermann, 29 November 1826).

> [Delacroix is] an artist whose major talent is beyond dispute, but his wild ways in putting it to use, the monstrosity of his designs, the profusion of his compositions, the violence of his arrangements, and the crudeness of his coloration cannot meet with approval. Yet it is for precisely this reason that he is the ideal person to enter into the spirit of *Faust* and is likely to produce images that no one else could have imagined. [...] Both pictures are no more than sketches, executed in a somewhat coarse manner, but the conception is spirited and its powerful expression calculated to create a massive effect. The artist will probably succeed in mastering all the other wild, uncanny and strange situations in a similar manner, and if he could somehow muster the ability to submit to the more delicate effects, then we may in the near future expect a wondrous work of art that will enter into the spirit of that paradoxical poetic piece in a harmonious manner. (*Über Kunst und Altertum* 6, 1827)

The pictures have a highly dramatic quality that builds on, yet far exceeds, the quaint, staged impression of Cornelius and Retzsch. True, *Faust in his Study* could be an image of a theatre production, but the restrictive narrowness of the scene looks as though it were set in a broom-cupboard rather than in an alchemist's laboratory. The traditional Faustian paraphernalia, normally seen strewn about his study in vaulted alcoves, are relegated to a single shelf above the actors' heads. There are no large vistas here, as in many of the German sketches. Auerbach's Cellar, too, has this condensed quality, with the revellers placed almost on top of each other as they crowd round the fire that has sprung up out of the spilt wine. This, too, may relate directly to the 'spectacular' London production of 1825. The series is remarkable for its variety; Mephistopheles is at times quietly detached, for example as he watches the incident in the Wine Cellar, while at other times he becomes a violently controlling force, as when he leans over Margaret in church. Delacroix' cathedral is an altogether more threatening environment than Cornelius', in which two babies are glimpsed playing innocently in the foreground. Temptation is more real, as is the ambience created by the French artist by comparison with the sugary pseudo-mediaeval settings favoured by his German contemporaries. The title piece has Mephisto hovering over a grimly outlined city panorama. Faust is a tormented sinner whose lineaments bear a striking resemblance to those of his adversary. The use of the diagonal line helps to underscore the tension and is particularly suited to the 'diabolical', as is the distribution of light and dark areas on the page (Schäfer, 87–91). Generations of art critics have attributed the peculiarities of Delacroix' sketches to the distinctive nature of the French as opposed to the German temperament, not without making themselves guilty of chauvinism in the process; Giesen, by contrast, reads the French artist's work as a considered visual response to Germaine de Staël's three-volume account of Germany, *De l'Allemagne*, published in 1813. Staël was quite clear in her own mind as to where the centre of interest was to be found: 'The devil is the hero of the piece', was a pronouncement with which Delacroix evidently concurred (Giesen, 98).

Nowhere is Mephistopheles more obviously Faust's double than in the encounter with Margaret. Their size, their physiognomy, their expression and even

57. *Faust's study is compact and cluttered in Delacroix, possibly in imitation of the production he saw in Drury Lane, London, in 1825.*

58. *Delacroix's Faust is scarcely less menacing in appearance than his adversary.*

the manner in which their swords stick out in parallel – Faust's partly veiled by his cloak, but no less menacing – are visual echoes; and thus the focus is on Mephistopheles as the sustaining force of the narrative. Instead of reducing it to manageable set-pieces, Delacroix homes in on the tumultuous and startling aspects of the drama. There is, in the three exemplary artists we have considered, a clear preference for one of the three main persons of the drama; for Cornelius it was Faust, the strong, assertive hero; for Retzsch it was Margaret/Gretchen, who lived and died for her love; for Delacroix it was Mephistopheles, as the controlling force over both. He is no longer the 'little old lady' of Cornelius, but has become *le plus diabolique qu'on puisse imaginer* ('the most diabolic that one can imagine'), as the artist had remarked of the actor in London.

From now on, recycling occurs on a large scale. The early line-drawings are engraved, painted, worked in wood and other media in ever-increasing numbers. Paintings of the period include those by Ludwig Schnorr von Carolsfeld and frescoes in the Weimar Palace by Bernhard Neher. The underlying ideas are shared out and expanded; Retzsch's design for 'Prelude on the Stage', for example,

59. August von Kreling's Poet, Manager, Comedian *of 1878.*

included an image of Goethe writing out his text behind the scenes as the curtain was about to go up. This was copied in various increasingly elaborate formats, until August von Kreling perfected the image in 1878. Another interesting detail attributable to Retzsch was Margaret's pose in the 'Spinning Wheel' scene. He has her place two fingers against her forehead, a gesture that was used to signal deep thought and as such is familiar from paintings of the 'philosopher queen' Sophie Charlotte of Prussia.

Here we see the beginnings of experimentation by artists eager to suggest things that were scarcely even implicit in the text. Visual artists enjoyed much more

60. Retzsch's Margareta adopts a pose traditionally associated with philosophers, 1816.

freedom when it came to manipulating the classics than did actors or dramatists. An interesting example is provided by Eduard Grützner's 'Mephisto on and off Stage' (1872), which depicts an actor in Mephistophelean garb chatting in Mephistophelean style to an under-age chorus girl amid the familiar accoutrements of Faust's study.

61. *Eduard Grützner's* Mephisto vor und hinter den Kulissen
('Mephisto on and off Stage'). Pen and ink, 1872.

England, too, had its Faust illustrators, the most important of whom was Theodore von Holst, who arrived as a refugee from Riga and was the most gifted pupil and follower of Henry Fuseli [Johann Heinrich Füssli]. Opium was a major influence on the fantastical dream effect in paintings such as 'Witches' Sabbath' of *c.* 1835. His Fausts do not constitute a complete cycle, but take the form of incidental works, possibly because the British market was already saturated with editions of Retzsch. Between 1828 and 1857, around twenty paintings on the theme were exhibited in London. William Vaughan identifies thirty-five between 1825 and 1860. Most of these have proved untraceable (Giesen, 135; Vaughan, 259–65). A further impetus occurred at the time of the 1885 production of *Faust* at the Lyceum which led to many images, cartoons and other forms of artwork. There are some interesting figurines of Mephistopheles and Margaret that were evidently modelled on Irving and Terry in the Doulton china collection; even the world of fashion experienced a vogue for 'Mephisto hats' and 'Gretchen shoes'.

62. One of Paul Konewka's 'Sihouettes', showing Faust accosting Margaret. From an 1871 American edition.

'De luxe' Editions

By mid-nineteenth century a change had set in. The lavish illustrations continued, but were nearly always issued in combination with the full text, no longer in self-contained collections of sketches with few if any accompanying notes. 'De luxe' editions, *Liebhaberausgaben*, catered for a growing community of bibliophiles. There were also collections dedicated to specific topics, such as Eugen Napoleon Neureuther's *Randzeichnungen zu Goethes Balladen und Romanzen* ('Marginalia to Goethe's Ballads and Romances', 1855), and Wilhelm von Kaulbach's *Goethes Frauengestalten* ('Goethe's Female Figures', 1862). As Faust became the undisputed 'icon' of Germany's spiritual essence, pictures of him grew ever more heroic and began to reflect and inspire other subjects of comparable stature, including Gutenberg, Luther, and even Christ (Giesen, 181–96). The importance of such illustrations can be gauged by the fact that by the 1880s, complaints were being voiced that the public was more familiar with pictures in the luxury editions than with the texts: 'There are certain so-called educated ladies who have never read Goethe's *Faust* or a historical play by Shakespeare but fondly imagine that they know it intimately, as long as it lies, adorned with many colourful pictures, gathering dust upon their coffee-tables' (Mazzoni/Ott, 53).

Such lavish tomes were themselves treated, quite literally, as quasi-religious icons. They were carried through towns on certain holy days, for example, on St John's Day, when Johannes ('John') Gutenberg, inventor of moveable type, was honoured as a hero if not as a saint. They demonstrate the rapid advances being made in printing, such as early experiments in photographic reproduction. One such luxury edition that enjoyed iconic status was produced by Engelbert Seibertz, who was employed for this purpose by Goethe's publisher Cotta when their first choice, Kaulbach, had fallen out with them after submitting some excessively licentious drawings. Kaulbach's attitude to Faust was idiosyncratic; in 1836, his painting 'Mephistopheles appearing from behind the Stove' drew an unmistakeable parallel between the magus and Christ. When his work was belatedly published in 1865 by Bruckmann in Munich, it rapidly became a 'cultural icon of the educated bourgeoisie' (Forster-Hahn, 89).

63. *Wilhem von Kaulbach,*
Mephistopheles appearing from
behind the Stove, *1836,*
attracted comment for its use of
'Semitic' features as well as for its
close resemblance to iconographic
scenes of 'Christ cleansing the
Temple'.

Seibertz attained fame thanks to his elaborate vignettes which accorded well with the taste of the time for overblown, lavishly ornamented line-drawings. They saw the light of print as steel engravings and fine woodcuts. The publisher is known to have intervened to suppress Seibertz's enthusiasm for the nude: 'We are no supporters of prudery, but books are different from paintings; women and even children must be allowed to hold them in their hands, otherwise the commercial success will be severely impaired' (cited by Giesen, 212). Conscious of the strength of the publisher's argument, Seibertz agreed to draw a veil over some of the copulation scenes. The work was prepared with the attention nowadays accorded to the launch of a blockbuster movie. Reviewers were won over and briefed, the volume was well advertised in advance, and political considerations determined the date of publication: scrupulous preparations which ensured that the volume was a commercial success.

As in Cornelius, Faust is at the heart of the illustrations. He develops from scholar to lover, and thereafter by stages to courtier, warrior, father, and local ruler. Seibertz is commonly seen as having transformed Faust into a truly Germanic figure with the attributes of a religious hero. Christian Schulz is another artist who positioned a stately German Faust beside a hunched Semitic-looking Mephistopheles. It was a short step from here to the work of Franz Stassen, a member of the anti-Semitic *Werdandibund*, who completed the transformation of Faust from an obscure late mediaeval quack to a Nordic-Germanic icon purged of all foreign influence (Boehn, 23; Forster-Hahn, 92). Alexander Tille agonised over which is the 'true' Faust in art, the old or the rejuvenated doctor, and derided most attempts prior to Seibertz as failures. Retzsch's Faust comes across as a retired general, Cornelius' as a schoolmaster, and so forth:

> The individual characters of the play have acquired their own particular and peculiar history in the arts. Ludwig [Carl] Nauwerck's old cobbler, Peter von Cornelius' schoolmaster, the retired general depicted by Mortitz Retzsch, Ramberg's terrified misery-man [*der entsetzte Kläglichkeitsbold*], Delacroix' dashing womaniser and Paul Nehrlich's desiccated philistine are all tentative, uncertain essays in transferring Faust to paper. Each of these artists has exaggerated one feature of the hero and used the distortion to represent the essence of the whole man. It was a major step forward when the so-called Berlin Cycle based itself on theatre productions as described by Prince Anton Radziwill and subconsciously returned to Klinger's *Faust*, portraying a male head not unlike Christ's with dark hair and beard. Faust's head is the main achievement, yet it must be given even more prominent national characteristics, and must come to be seen as powerful and restlessly active in accordance with the manner in which this century has progressed from valuing thought to valuing action. [...] Seibertz fashioned him into a powerful man of action, whom we are prepared to see as capable of liberating ideals and as fighting wars and colonising vast tracts of land. (Tille (1899), xxxviii; see also Giesen, 217)

From now on the movement away from the set-piece images – the scholar in his study, Margaret coming out of church – towards the more lurid Witch's Kitchen and Walpurgis Night scenes will gather momentum. While the early artists expended much effort on depicting the miscellaneous utensils that were scattered around the Witch's abode, their successors were more inclined to focus on the vision in the mirror, which now changes from a dimly glimpsed statue to a reclining odalisque in the manner of *salon* painters like Jean-Auguste-Dominique Ingres or Jean-Léon Gérôme. A similar transformation occurred in twentieth-century movies, where Gründgens allows a brief glimpse of a remote, statuesque female, while Dorn's mirror reveals a lusty wench massaging her bosom with evident pleasure. Ever more characters and motifs were thematised, including some who, like the King in Thule and Gretchen's mother's priest, do not appear in the drama other than in indirect references. While Faust and Mephistopheles remained relatively constant iconic presences, with no room for departure from the established prototypes, it was Gretchen who underwent the most profound re-evaluation by artists influenced by movements such as 'Satanic Romanticism'. The image of naïve innocence was gradually replaced by one that indicated a degree of willing

297

64. *Cover illustration of a typical* Prachtausgabe *('de luxe edition'); Stuttgart: Deutsche Verlags-Anstalt, late nineteenth-century.*

complicity and voluptuousness (Giesen, 261–85). Comparing Pecht with Cornelius, one notices a movement away from the Germanic maiden tearfully clutching her prayer-book in front of the Virgin to an elegantly attired courtesan who would not look out of place in a Parisian *salon*.

65. *Gretchen drawn by Friedrich Pecht, steel engraving by A. Schultheiss, 1864.*

Margaret's metamorphosis was both superficial (sensual lips) and essential (greater interest in her mental deterioration and in the tragic plight of the infanticide). There was an increasing interest in dream sequences. By the early twentieth century it was quite common to see the erstwhile innocent depicted as a *femme fatale* if not as a witch. A late nineteenth-century canvas, *Le Rêve de Faust* ('Faust's Dream'), executed by Luis Ricardo Faléro, a Spanish artist who exhibited in Paris and London, is typical of the overblown, fin-de-siècle approach to the theme. Despite a superficial resemblance to a celestial vision, involving flight, clouds, and beautiful bodies, the painting it is shot through with the more disturbing images of the lizard, the black cat, the bat, the broomstick, and at the centre, the goat. Two hideously misshapen human bodies mingle with the otherwise perfect examples of female beauty; Faust himself appears to be borne away in the company of a damsel who in turn is pursued by a succession of increasingly unappealing creatures. The ambiguity of the Faustian experience is well rendered in this combination of bliss and nausea.

66. *Luis Ricardo Faléro,* Le Rêve de Faust, *1878. Exhibited in Paris, 1880.*

The Twentieth Century

Sumptuous bibliophile editions continued to appear, not only in Germany but in Britain (*Faust. From the German by John Anster. Illustrations by Harry Clarke.* London: Harrap, 1925), America (*Faust. A Tragedy. The First Part.* Translation by Alice Raphael. Illustrated by René Clarke. New York: Limited Editions Club, 1932), and France (*Faust*. Ed. Paul Derupt. Illustrated by André Collot. Paris: Jean Delauriere, 1937. 2 volumes), to cite but a few examples. Sculptors had long been attracted to the legendary figures, and Mark Antokolsky's statue of Mephistopheles in the St Petersburg Museum remains one of the finest. The idea of creating the image of Mephistopheles was, paradoxically, the result of the artist's work on a statue of Christ in 1874. A letter sums up his view of the Mephistophelean character:

> He ails and suffers from the idea that he has experienced everything, is falling apart and can no longer live and take pleasure in life like those around him; he is helpless in spirit; he cannot create anything but his hatred is strong, and his self-esteem suffers in recognition of his powerlessness. The warm spring rays of sunlight burn him, irritate and blind his gaze; any joy, laughter or a young kiss only irritates him; he wants everyone around him to be as grim, dead, empty and lifeless as he is; walking in darkness, burrowing in the earth beneath his feet like a mole, destroying and creating luckless beings, seeing blood and tears [...] All this calms and satisfies him, but he still can find no satisfaction because his thirst is insatiable. This is how I see Mephistopheles. We can say that I dreamed up this being, that this is purely my fantasy, or you could ask where I saw such a being? Yes, no one sees him like this, but we sense his breathing, feel his monstrous paw pressing on our chest, sense our inability to cry out, in a word, we see the nightmare. (Letter to E.G. Mamontova, 1883)

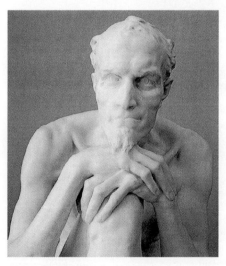

67. Mark Antokolsky's statue of Mephistopheles, 1883. Here the impression is a combination of thoughtfulness and malice.

Faust was now being given the same treatment as poets, generals and politicians. Large-scale monuments sprang up in public places, such as the pair of bronze statues by Mathieu Molitor positioned beside the entrance to the refurbished Auerbach's Cellar in Leipzig. In 1911, Anton Mädler, a wealthy industrialist who made suitcases, purchased the Auerbachs Hof buildings with the intention of demolishing the complex to make way for a new exhibition pavilion. After massive protests, he agreed to preserve the historic wine cellar and embellish it with new paintings and statues. Molitor, who had recently been given the title of Professor

68. *Mephistopheles guiding Faust through a Leipzig shopping arcade. Bronze statue by Mathieu Molitor, 1913. Leipzig, Mädler-Passage. Note the effect of treaing Faust's left foot as a good luck charm. Photograph by Osman Durrani.*

by Grand Duke Wilhelm Ernst of Saxony-Weimar and had produced statues for other locations in Leipzig, accepted the commission and on 24 September 1913 'Faust and Mephistopheles' and 'The Enchanted Students' were unveiled as centre-pieces for an arcade which bore a faint resemblance to the Galleria Vittorio Emanuele in Milan. The doctor is shown in his as yet unrejuvenated state, deep in thought and failing to appreciate the attractions of the gloomy wine cellar. The two statues have become a symbol of Leipzig; touching Faust's left is supposed to bring luck and guarantee a return to the city. Two smaller statues by Bernd Göbel were added in 1999. They depict Faust with a naked Margaret and Mephistopheles with an equally naked Marthe, the two women appearing to resist advances. An imposing statue of Faust adorns the Town Hall in Knittlingen. It was created in 1954 by Hanne Schorp-Pflumm, whose work is well known in southwest Germany (see illustrations nos. 2 and 95).

It was inevitable that leading artists of the Naturalist and Expressionist schools should turn to *Faust* for inspiration, portraying the central figures in ultra-realistic manner, as Käthe Kollwitz did with Gretchen in 1899, showing her in a pose reminiscent of Edvard Munch, hugging her shoulders not merely in grief but shivering from cold. Other pictures show her beside her dead child, in conditions that could have been drawn from life at the turn of the century. *Faust* is one of the very few literary texts which Kollwitz chose to illustrate, concentrating as she did throughout her career on scenes of urban and rural poverty.

The great Expressionists Emil Nolde, Walter Klemm, Ernst Barlach, Lovis Corinth and later Max Beckmann all attempted scenes from *Faust*; these are briefly discussed by Wegner (103–113). Barlach completed several cycles of charcoal drawings

301

69. *Käthe Kollwitz's shivering Gretchen dates from 1899.*

and woodcuts that used Goethe's works as their point of departure. It has been claimed that Goethe is the 'red thread' that runs through the Expressionist's work; as early as 1893, he was spending 'entire evenings meditating on a single line from Faust' (Doppelstein, 10). By 1897, he was drawing scenes from both parts of the play, attempting to approach the work from new angles. Kollwitz was drawn to the economic misery and social marginalisation of Gretchen, while Barlach explored underlying themes such as man's alienation from God and his desperate attempts to beat out a new path to salvation while battling against his own ignorance and impotence. Barlach's cycle, *Walpurgis Night* (1923), represents a return to folk superstitions, and here crude effects seem well able to convey ancient fears and longings. 'In Barlach's woodcut technique with its use of sharp contrasts and in the artist's powerful handling of shapes, the wild activity of the Walpurgis Night comes alive in an uncanny

70. *Ernst Barlach's woodcut 'Walpurgis Night' (1923) is typical of the poster-style favoured by many Expressionists.*

302

manner. Figures and landscape are woven into sinister, nightmarish images, out of which Barlach's dark imagination creates something that goes far beyond the actual textual source' (*Goethe in der Kunst des 20. Jahrhunderts*, 60).

Just as composers were turning to the puppet-play for inspiration, the figurative artists were adapting the seemingly naïve methods of sixteenth-century art to convey

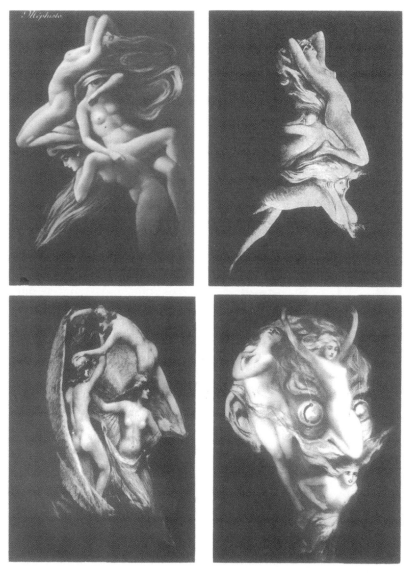

71. *John de Yongh (1856–1917), 'Mephisto'. Published by Edward Gross, New York, c. 1937. The original lithographs date from 1907 and are an optical illusion that can look either like the devil's profile or three naked women.*

303

the primitive aspects of the story. This method proved appropriate to the scenes of barbarism and superstition: Walpurgis Night with its cavorting witches, and the forlorn image of the deserted Margaret in her simple, shroud-like cloak. While in disgrace due to his allegedly 'degenerate' painting, Max Beckmann produced 143 pen-and-ink drawings for *Faust II* which are effective in a child-like manner and incorporate many of the artist's wartime experiences: the horrors of war, the clash of persecutor and persecuted (Perels, 111f.).

The illustrated editions continued to be reprinted, and others were commissioned. The most detailed of these is Max Slevogt's *Faust II*, with a total of 510

72. *Max Slevogt's 'Song of the Flea',*
1908.

lithographs that tend to merge with the written word. Part caricature and part stage designs, they have a relaxed quality that made them well suited to modern mass-consumers' tastes. Slevogt manages to illustrate all aspects of the text in a pleasing, neo-Impressionist style that brings out the fairy-tale elements by using both classical and oriental techniques. What emerges is a wholesome, ultimately optimistic reading of the play in visual terms attuned to Goethe's 'Olympian' serenity and possessed of an operatic quality (Imiela, 238–43).

Harry Clarke was born in Dublin in 1889. He was recognised by contemporaries as both a master of stained glass and as one of Ireland's most outstanding illustrators. His work spans the pre-Raphaelite, art-and-crafts, 1920s 'propaganda art', and Symbolist traditions; his extraordinarily ornate and accomplished *Faust* of 1925 invites comparison with Aubrey Beardsley. The output of his short life was prodigious and ranged from flesh-creeping editions of Poe, Coleridge, Andersen and Swinburne to Shakespeare and Goethe.

Published in 1925 in an edition of 2,000 copies, Clarke's *Faust* was laden with dark and grotesque effects that 'anticipate the psychedelic, drug-induced fantasies of the 1960s' according to his biographer (Bowe, 190). There were twenty-two full-page illustrations (eight in colour), plus 64 vignettes of various sizes in the text, each as idiosyncratic as it is disturbing. The work met with mixed critical success in 1925, but Clarke is said to have considered it his best book. Reviews could be very cruel:

> Delicate ugliness, indeed, is an epithet which seems to sum up Mr Clarke's latest work [...] Here is a very cornucopia of almost bestial creation [...] Every creature depicted is diseased and indescribable abortions people the dim backgrounds of the scenes [...] The clash of pinks and greens in the very colour scheme seems to symbolise the mood of the whole. Every picture shocks, but shocks only as might some horror

of the operating theatre or some untold abnormal thing of a surgeon's museum. [...] We think that no artist of the Beardsley School could hope to capture the rugged, Gothic strength of Goethe's imagery. [...] Goethe's Margaret never resembled the consumptive creature with black-ringed eyes and languid hoopy figure which seems to be the only kind of woman that artists of the Beardsley School can draw (Anon., *Irish Times*, 20 November 1925; cited by Bowe, 274, n. 4).

73. Harry Clarke, Night, 1925. *The aged Faust surrounded by images of youth and decay.*

Other authorities acknowledge that Clarke had used his boundlessly fertile imagination to good effect:

> Take the little drawing which illustrates the heart-rending meditation of Marguerite, who has been listening to the girls' chattering scandal about Hannah [*sic*] and who is all the while conscious of her own secret. Here the distraught soul looks out from a misery from which there is no escape. Long quivering hands with fingers like sharpened fires waver in the air and point to the piteous figure. The hands have eyes in them like vipers that know everything and will forgive nothing. We would like to close the eyes of the soul to shut out that piteous image. How awful, too, is the Despair with head like a bird of prey, which holds the fainting girl in the *Cathedral*, while the choir chants the Dies Irae. It is the soul inside the body rather than the external form which is symbolised in the decoration to the scene in *Auerbach's Cellar*, where one can almost hear grunt or whinny, from creatures already become half animal to the spiritual vision. Clarke is not the artist of men and women, but the seer of forms which their passions and imaginations assume. (AE, in the *Irish Statesman*, 14 November 1925; cited by Bowe, 188f.)

Clarke's *Faust* is heavily influenced by his interest in stained glass. The controlled, sweeping curve of the lines that dominate the work gives it its unique quality. AE (George William Russell) argued that Clarke had finally freed himself from

Beardsley's influence, and that his inspiration had come from a Mid-Earth or Purgatory of the soul where shapes shift in accordance with the beauty or evil of the imagination. Much use is made of hybrid forms – sexually ambiguous figures, witches with skeletal wings that mimic the iconography of heaven, misshapen bodies with tumescent breasts in place of heads. Far from being the work of a beautifying imagination, Clarke's was inspired by victims of malnutrition, disease, inbreeding and neglect, as observed in person on Dublin's streets and in the Tara Street Public Baths (Bowe, 190).

74. Porcelain Mephisto figurines by Karl Tutter, c. 1930.

Faust and Mephistopheles have been favourite subjects in porcelain for many years. From the late nineteenth century onwards, major producers such as Royal Doulton, Dresden, Meissen and others have turned out both humorous caricatures and sombre, at times grotesque or macabre representations of the principal figures from the legend (Eyles/Dennis, 165). Karl Tutter, who worked for the porcelain manufacturer Lorenz Hutschenreuther for many years, created a series of highly expressive Mephisto figurines from 1922 onwards. These contrast with the rather jolly, 'Toby Mug' effects of some, but not all, of the Royal Doulton pieces. Other striking designs have been developed by the Meissen Porcelain Factory. Two slender figures representing the doctor and his adversary designed by Peter Strang, and two solid, block-like ones designed by Jörg Danielczyk, are in their current catalogue.

Relatively few artists have returned to the chapbook for inspiration. An exception is Heinz Zander (born 1939), whose twenty pencil drawings accompany a de luxe GDR edition of the *Historia* dating from 1981. The images are characterised by an overpoweringly detailed, Baroque complexity in which physical and ethereal beings blend effectively with one another. This alone places Zander in the ideal position to illustrate a work written during the period that strongly influenced his style. His Faust is anything other than heroic: he revels in the pleasures that

306

75. Helen of Troy from the chapbook, drawn by Heinz Zander, 1980.

Mephistopheles has put before him and, far from being a tragic figure, is regularly shown enjoying a grossly sybaritic existence.

The well-known Surrealist Salvador Dalí produced a Faust cycle of 21 etchings (Paris: Les Editions Argillet, 1961), at a time when he was busily illustrating many works of world literature, from the Bible and the Divine Comedy to the works of Marquis de Sade and poems by Mao Tse Tung. He based his etchings on the French translation by Gérard de Nerval. The images include some relatively detailed ones (Gretchen, the Witch Baubo astride a pig), and others that are more skeletal sketches and doodles. The Spanish influence is obvious in many details, such as the bull-like appearance of some of the devils.

Paula Rego, born 1935, has been described as a sinister storyteller. She has painted fairy-tales and operas, always attempting to condense complex plots into her paintings, and is acknowledged to be one of the leading figurative artists at work in Britain today. What is remarkable about her painting *Faust* is that she has managed to juxtapose so many elements from the story in a dream-like combination of Surrealism, folklore effects and Disney animation, while preserving a sense of mystery. Her 'Operas' series, which includes *Aida, Rigoletto, La Bohème* and *The Girl from the Golden West* as well as *Faust*, originated as a contribution to an exhibition of English 'Eight for Eighties'. Here she decided to create works based on operas she remembered hearing as a girl from her father. All her paintings tell stories or revamp the ones she heard in childhood; and what they tend to have in common is a girl in conflict with her parents over the man of her choice. Rego has the effect of drawing the onlooker into an uncomfortable world where women's experiences are often of central importance. *Faust* has a personal, instinctive quality, enhanced by the restricted range of colours she uses, beige, brown, umber, black – the same as were used in Ancient Egyptian frescoes and in Attic pottery, but here applied to figures which make leaps in scale from the huge Faust and Mephistopheles at the top, Margaret and her child at the bottom, to the medium-sized Valentine and the black dog, to ever smaller ones representing witches, revellers and animals. The self-importance of the great man is deflated by means of grotesque caricature (McEwan, 121; 53). The symbolic torn flower (bottom right) stands out as a commentary on the lovers' meeting (bottom right) and the wide-eyed mother who holds a limp child that has a tail very similar to Mephisto's. The techniques of children's drawings and Primitive art combine to bring out the essence of the story-line in an unobtrusive but striking manner.

The work of two contemporary painters who have specialised over many years in compiling comprehensive cycles of Faust illustrations will conclude this chapter. Margret Hofheinz-Döring (1910–1994) and Jens Rusch (born 1940) have both had many successful exhibitions and received support from the Goethe-Institut, which promotes German culture across the globe. Hofheinz-Döring's brightly coloured illustrations were exhibited in Weimar (1995) and Knittlingen (1999) and subsequently published in a catalogue introduced by Faust-expert Günther Mahal. Rusch had a major exhibition, 'Auf eigene Faust radiert', at the Düsseldorf Goethe-Museum, in Kiel and in several other venues, including Goethe's house in Weimar. Rusch worked closely with Rosemarie Clausen, who photographed many stage versions of *Faust*, including the Hamburg production by Gustaf Gründgens. This is obvious in many of the exhibited etchings, in which the faces of actors and

76. Jens Rusch: Walpurgis Night. *Pencil drawing on card. 1988.*

77. Margret Hofheinz-Döring, Faust converses with the Earth Spirit. *1969.
Oil. Series F, nr. 15.*

actresses familiar from Gründgens' version are visible amongst symbolic figures and backdrops.

Hofheinz-Döring was a prolific illustrator of *Faust* from 1959 to her death in 1994. Her 'pictorial conversations' with Faust run to some two hundred images, produced over a period of more than thirty years. She is therefore one of a very small group of artists who spent much of her life grappling with ways of transferring her perceptions of the Faustian material onto paper and canvas, using a wide variety of techniques. This fact qualifies her as an appropriate figure with whom to conclude the present chapter. She produced, during a restlessly active career, no fewer than six separate cycles on the theme of Faust, each characterised by a distinctive technique. Her work in oil displays a concentrated use of primary colours. Other media include watercolours, pastels, ink and tempera, as well as mixed media, including textiles. What distinguishes her approach from all others is that there is little or no attempt to retell the story or envisage actors on stage. Rather, a few ideas are selected and presented as abstractions. All her cycles are therefore incomplete fragments, variations rather than narrative entities. For this reason, she speaks of her work as an 'intimate dialogue' with *Faust*. And this, ultimately, would be a fitting description of the work of all artists who have grappled with the theme, whatever the outcome. There will be a return to the artistic depictions of Faust in chapter 11, below, which will refer to an exhibition on the theme during 2003.

Cited Works and Further Reading

Ernst Barlach, *Walpurgisnacht. Mit 20 Holzschnitten.* Berlin: Cassirer, 1923. Rptd Düsseldorf: Droste, 1967.

Max Beckmann, *Goethes Faust II. Teil, Zeichnungen von Max Beckmann.* Prestel. Rptd Frankfurt/M: Büchergilde Gutenberg and Leipzig: Reclam, both 1982.

Alfred Bergmann, 'Goethe und Nauwerck', *Jahrbuch der Sammlung Kippenberg* 6 (1926), 306–17.

Max von Boehn (ed.), *Goethe: Faust. Mit einer Einleitung Faust und die Kunst.* Berlin: Askanischer Verlag, 1924. Rptd 1932, 1938, 1940.

Peter Boerner and Sidney Johnson (eds), *Faust through Four Centuries. Retrospect and Analysis. Vierhundert Jahre Faust. Rückblick und Analyse.* Tübingen: Niemeyer, 1989.

Nicola Gordon Bowe, *The Life and Work of Harry Clarke.* Dublin: Irish Academic Press, 1989.

Harry Clarke (ill.), *Faust by Goethe. From the German by John Anster.* Illustrated by Harry Clarke. London: George G. Harrap, 1925. Rptd London: Harrap, 1985.

Peter Cornelius, *Bilder zu Goethe's Faust von P. Cornelius. Gestochen von F. Ruscheweyh.* Frankfurt/M: Wenner, 1816. Rptd Berlin: Reimer, 1845, 1916.

—, *Zeichnungen zu Goethes Faust.* Frankfurt/M: Städel, 1991.

Salvador Dali, *Literarische Zyklen.* Exhibition Catalogue, Madrid and Schloss Drachenburg, 1982, ed. Hermann Wünsche. Madrid: Subdirección General de Artes Plásticas, 1982.

Jürgen Doppelstein, *Barlach und Goethe.* Leipzig: E.A.Seemann, 1997.

Christian Eckert, *Peter Cornelius.* Bielefeld: Velhagen und Klasing, 1906.

Desmond Eyles and Richard Dennis, *Royal Doulton Figurines.* Stoke/Trent: Royal Doulton Tableware, 1978.

"Faust" in der Malerei. Exhibition catalogue, Weimar: Nationale Forschungs- und Gedenkstätten der klassischen deutschen Literatur, 1969.

Sebastian Giesen, *"Den Faust, dächt' ich, gäben wir ohne Holzschnitte und Bildwerk": Goethes "Faust" in der europäischen Kunst des 19. Jahrhunderts.* PhD Dissertation, Technische Hochschule, Aachen, 1998.

Goethe in der Kunst des 20. Jahrhunderts. Weltliteratur und Bilderwelt. Exhibition catalogue, Frankfurt/M: Freies Deutsches Hochstift, 1982.

Reinhold Grimm and Jost Hermand, *Our Faust? Roots and ramifications of a modern German myth. 16th Wisconsin Workshop Papers.* Wisconsin: University Press, 1987.

Margret Hofheinz-Döring, *Bildgespräche mit Goethes Faust. Werksverzeichnis.* Ed. Günther Mahal. Vaihingen/Enz: IPa-Verlag, 2000.

Françoise Forster-Hahn, 'Romantic tragedy or National Symbol? The Interpretation of Goethe's *Faust* in nineteenth century German Art', in Grimm/Hermand, 82–123.

Hans Henning (ed.), *Goethe, Faust. Der Tragödie Erster Teil. Mit Illustrationen aus drei Jahrhunderten.* Berlin: Rütten und Loening, 1982.

Philip Hofer (ed.), *Some Drawings and Lithographs for Goethe's Faust by Eugène Delacroix.* Cambridge/Mass: Harvard University Press, 1964.

Hans-Jürgen Imiela, *Max Slevogt. Eine Monographie.* Karlsruhe: G. Braun, 1968.

Elmar Jansen, *Ernst Barlach, Käthe Kollwitz. Berührungen, Grenzen, Gegenbilder.* Berlin/GDR: Union Verlag, 1989.

Rockwell Kent (ill.), *Goethe's Faust. A new American translation by Carlyle F. MacIntyre with illustrations by Rockwell Kent together with the German text.* Norfolk/Conn: New Directions, 1941.

August Klipstein, *Käthe Kollwitz. Verzeichnis des graphischen Werkes.* Berne: Klipstein & Co., 1955.

Käthe Kollwitz, *Zeichnungen, Grafik, Plastik. Bestandskatalog des Käthe-Kollwitz-Museums Berlin.* Ed. Martin Fritsch. Leipzig: E.A. Seemann, 1999.

Paul Konewka, *12 Blätter zu Goethes Faust*. Berlin: Amsler & Ruthardt, 1866. Rptd as *ibid.*, *Illustrations to Goethe's Faust*. Boston: Roberts Brothers, 1871.

John McEwan, *Paula Rego*. London: Phaidon, 1992, 2nd edn 1997.

Petra Maisak, *Johann Wolfgang Goethe. Zeichnungen*. Stuttgart: Reclam, 1996.

Gabriel Max, *Faust-Illustrationen*. Berlin: Grot'sche Verlagsbuchhandlung, 1880.

Diana Mazzoni and Ulrich Ott (eds), *Prachtausgaben. Literaturdenkmale in Quart und Folio*. Marbach: Deutsche Schillergesellschaft, 1991.

E. P. Moosmann and Carl Paschek (eds) *Doctor Faustus und Mephistopheles. Bücher, Graphiken und Figuren aus der Sammlung E. P. Moosmann. Katalog zur Ausstellung der Stadt- und Universitätsbibliothek Frankfurt a.M. 16. Mai bis 28. Juni 1991*. Frankfurt/M: Stadt- u. Universitätsbibliothek 1991.

Hans Joachim Neidhardt, 'Gustav Heinrich Naeke: ein Nazarener aus Sachsen', *Zeitschrift des Deutschen Vereins für Kunstwissenschaft*, 47 (1993), 32-48.

Franz Neubert, *Vom Doctor Faustus zu Goethes Faust*. Leipzig: J.J. Weber, 1932.

Carl Niessen, (ed.) *Katalog der Ausstellungen: Faust auf der Bühne. Faust in der bildenden Kunst*. Berlin: Fritz Klopp, 1929.

Rudolf Payer von Thurn, *Der historische Faust im Bilde*. Vienna: Wiener Bibliophilen-Gesellschaft, 1917.

Christoph Perels, 'Max Beckmanns Zeichnungen zu Goethes *Faust – Zweiter Teil*', in Boerner/Johnson, 99-132.

Klaus Popitz, 'Goethes Faust', in *Von Odysseus bis Felix Krull. Gestalten der Weltliteratur in der Buchillustration des 19. und 20. Jahrhunderts*. Berlin: Dietrich Riemer, 1982.

Jens Rusch, *Auf eigene Faust radiert*. Düsseldorf: Goethe-Museum, 1993.

Dorit Schäfer, '"Bilder, an die niemand hatte denken können." Die Faust-Illustrationen von Delacroix', in Klaus Schrenk, Holger Jacob-Friesen, Astrid Reuter and Dorit Schäfer (eds), *Eugène Delacroix. Staatliche Kunsthalle Karlsruhe*. Exhibition Catalogue, Heidelberg: Kehrer, 2003, 86-95; 130-150.

Max Slevogt, *Illustrationen zu Goethe*. Ed. Wilhelm Weber and Norbert Suhr. Mainz: Mittelrheinisches Landesmuseum, 1982.

Willy F. Storck, *Goethes Faust und die bildende Kunst*. Leipzig: Xenien, 1912.

Alexander Tille, 'The Artistic Treatment of the Faust Legend', *Publications of the English Goethe Society* 7 (1893), 151-225.

— (ed.), *Bilderverzeichnis der Bode-Tilleschen Faust-Galerie: Zur Ausstellung im Ausstellungssaale des Archiv- und Bibliotheksgebäudes der Stadt Köln vom 5. bis 30. November 1899*. Cologne: Schmitz, 1899.

Frank Anderson Trapp, *The Attainment of Delacroix*. Baltimore: Johns Hopkins Press, 1971.

William Vaughan, *German Romanticism and English Art*. New Haven: Yale University Press, 1979.

Wolfgang Wegner, *Die Faustdarstellung vom 16. Jahrhundert bis zur Gegenwart. Mit 90 Abbildungen*. Amsterdam: Erasmus, 1962.

Stephan Wünsche, *Margret Hofheinz-Döring. Retrospektive zum 80. Geburtstag*. Eislingen: Verein zur Förderung von Kunst, Kultur und Baudenkmalen, 1989.

Heinz Zander (ill.), *Historia von D. Johann Fausten, dem weitbeschreiten Zauberer und Schwarzkünstler (1587). Mit 20 Bleistiftzeichnungen*. Leipzig: Reclam, 1981.

Chapter Nine
The Moving Image

Film is an heir to fairground attractions and popular crafts. It is sustained by a combination of sentimental and obscene, comic and moral elements, blood-thirst and a spiritual longing for salvation.—Georg Seesslen

78. Mephistopheles (Bret Moe), Faust (Roger Allen Johnson), Witch (Lynette Kraft) in the Witch's Kitchen scene from John Hansen's Faust/The Lost Feminine (2000).

A Challenge for Illusionists

FAUST'S APPEAL to film-makers is unrivalled by any other theme that has evolved in world literature. The plot is inherently unstable (Faust can be young or old, wise or foolish, learned or lascivious) and embraces the vital concomitants of mystery, religion, horror, violence, class conflict, and sex. Goethe himself paved the way for the 'happy end' so beloved of movie-makers by going against the grain of the original and redeeming Faust in spite of his failings. It was also Goethe who provided the hero with that other prerequisite of the box-office success, a tear-jerking romance. Pacts with the devil are now alluded to so frequently on screen that it is hard to determine where 'Faustian' influences begin and end. The resulting narratives can be classified according to the aspirations of the contracting party: personal wealth (*The Devil and Daniel Webster*, 1942), the love of a specific woman (*Bedazzled*, 1967 and 2000), professional success, (*Alias Nick Beal*, 1949; *The Devil's Advocate*, 1997), sporting achievement (*Damn Yankees*, 1958), or artistic talent (*Crossroads*, 1984). Other Fausts of the celluloid variety strive for revenge (*Faust. Love of the Damned*, 2001) or are motivated by a socially conditioned desire for integration (*I was a Teenage Faust*, 2001). The genre is so extremely productive that whenever Faust is specifically named, the permutations are unlimited. This echoes the variations found in literary and operatic adaptations with their diverging approaches to questions such as Faust's inherent merits and eventual fate. The main difference in the movies is that more often than not, Faust manages to extricate himself from the pact by defeating the devil in a battle of wits from which he emerges as the superior party. In this respect at least, the twentieth-century cinema has reclaimed the structure and ethos of the pre-Reformation morality play, in which the devil is easily outwitted.

Within three years of 1895, when Auguste and Louis Lumière patented their device for the manufacture and viewing of chronophotographic prints, several pioneers of the new medium on both sides of the Channel had turned their hands to the creations of miniature vignettes on the Faust theme. Audiences wanted to see something more satisfying than approaching locomotives, walls being built and demolished and workers exiting from factories. Very soon after their first experiments, the Lumière brothers began to look to literary texts to extend their repertoire, and it has even been claimed that *Faust* was the very first book to have served as the basis for a short film (Seesslen, 104). Louis Lumière's catalogue of 1897 lists one as having been directed by Georges Hatot, possibly as early as 1896. It lasted for little more than one minute, and contained the story in a nutshell. There were just two scenes, 'Appearance of Mephistopheles' and 'Faust's Transformation and the Appearance of Marguerite', set out in the tradition of the *tableaux vivants* that had been displayed in fairgrounds throughout the nineteenth century (Prodolliet, 11; Hammond, 7f; Dabezies, 50). Yet what followed was more to do with a curious affinity between Faust's story and the new medium than with the development of the cinema out of the stereoscopes and magic lantern shows of earlier years. The proliferation of cinematic derivatives is explicable not only in terms of the representative role he gained though the public's exposure to him in opera and the arts, but also in terms of qualities inherent in the material. Faust accommodates to celluloid in a way in which the great works of Homer and Cervantes do not; hence the far greater quantity of films about him than about Achilles or Don Quixote, for all their importance as cultural landmarks.

Ulrich Gaier has shown that the supernatural premises on which this legend is based are readily evoked in a filmic medium that itself hovers on the margins between reality and fantasy. Experimental lighting, unstable imagery and trick photography, as exploited from the beginning of movie theatre history, seem calculated to breathe new life into the legend. It is almost as though the dramatists could foresee the strategies of the film-makers in their rapid scene-changes and sudden cuts, in pyrotechnics and fantastic projections. Marlowe pushes Elizabethan theatre to its limits; Goethe anticipates an 'epic' approach with his interacting crowds and groupings and the many spirit choruses and magical dances which were impossible challenges to the theatres of his own day. Musical accompaniments were devised long before the invention of synchronised sound tracks. What the stage did for Faust in earlier times was to play on the audience's imagination by the deft application of theatrical resources, many of which were recent innovations at the time of production. Marlowe's combining of high tragedy with low-life comedy and fireworks and Goethe's disorienting scene-changes reflected progress in the stagecraft of the period while anticipating the evolution of future media, right up to the virtual reality devices of a much later era (Gaier, 109f.). A succession of twentieth-century directors were attracted to Faust not least because of the challenge to develop new cinematic strategies. No longer bound by conventional constraints, they dispensed with tangible props and three-dimensional settings, mixing shadows, cartoons, mechanical marionettes and live actors in vibrant productions that bear the hallmarks of many styles, ranging from the woodcut-like effects of Expressionism to digitisation. Orson Welles was one of those who exploited new lighting effects and other devices in his stage production of *Doctor Faustus* in 1937 (see above, 216). The majority of Faust films were pioneering achievements that occupy a special place in cinema history; this chapter will provide a brief review of the highlights.

For many people, Murnau's *Faust* of 1926 marks the arrival of Faust on celluloid, but there were over thirty earlier silent motion pictures on the same theme, many of them no longer extant. Louis Lumière's first attempt at a *Faust*, directed by Georges Hatot, has been mentioned; it was followed in the same year by Georges Méliès's *Faust et Marguerite* (Hammond, 137). These two pioneers of the cinema represented very different approaches to the new medium. While the former concentrated on the realistic reproduction of tableau scenes from real life, Méliès, an autodidact of delirious imaginative powers, was committed to making the cinema a portal into a dream world in which the audience would be exposed to illusions and magic. He was a practising magician as well as an accomplished actor with a penchant for diabolical roles, and was also the first to portray the 'mad scientist' type on screen (Herbert/McKernan, 94f; Hammond, 111f; Robinson, *passim*; Usai, *passim*). His early life had been devoted to the creation of stage illusions. The 500 films he made between 1896 and 1912 included around twenty-five increasingly complex and ambitious versions of the Faust legend, in which he usually appeared as Mephistopheles himself, among them *La Damnation de Faust* (1897) and *Faust aux Enfers* (1903). While his first attempt, *Le Cabinet de*

Méphistophélès, was little more than an excuse for some clever trick photography using contrived tableaux, it was soon followed by *Faust et Marguerite* (1898) with Jeanne d'Alcy - the world's firm film diva - as the leading lady. The 20-metre strip created a stir wherever it was shown, and encouraged Méliès to compile his ambitious *Faust aux Enfers ou la Damnation de Faust*, pleonastically subtitled *Fantaisie fantastique* ('Fantastic Fantasia', 1903). The latter, in sixteen separate scenes, was inspired by Berlioz's opera. Here Méliès again starred in his favourite role - as Mephistopheles who took a woman down into the deep recesses of hell before opening his cloak to reveal a pair of bat's wings. New methods of suggesting movement by scrolling the background were developed expressly for this subject. His interest in opera continued with *La Damnation du Docteur Faust, ou Faust et Marguerite* in the following year. This consisted of twenty scenes and was coupled to a soundtrack based on Gounod that was played alongside the projection. This lavish production ran for approximately fourteen minutes, involved 500 actors and fifty dancers from the Paris Grand Opera. The Walpurgis Night scene alone took eight days to film and cost 3,200 francs. Méliès rarely managed to produce more than two minutes of film in a single working day. He eventually became bankrupt and 400 of his early his films were sold as scrap and made into shoe soles. The cataloguing of Méliès' Faust films is complicated by the fact that many have similar titles which vary in different catalogues (Deslandes/Richard, 465; Prodolliet, 12–20; Hammond, 80f.).

79. *Georges Méliès posing as Mephistopheles in one of his own films, c. 1908. He appeared in this role in more than twenty silent films.*

It was not only France that took up the theme of the pact. Closer to home, *Faust and Mephistopheles* was a 75-foot strip directed in Britain by erstwhile hypnotist George Albert Smith in 1898. Smith had worked as a mesmerist and medium; having witnessed the Lumière Brothers' display in Leicester Square during 1896, he set about creating short magical scenes. Thirteen of these were produced in his Brighton studio during 1897. *Faust and Mephistopheles* featured a scene of Faust being visited in his study. Mephistopheles appears in a cloud of smoke and offers Faust the gift of youth if he would sign a pact. Faust is tempted to agree by being shown a vision of the young Margaret sitting at her spinning wheel. Thereupon Mephistopheles hides Faust in a cloud of smoke, and when he emerges, he has been transformed into a handsome youth (Herbert/McKernan, 135f; Barnouw, 89).

1902 saw the first woman film director

in history, Alice Guy Blaché, originally Léon Gaumont's secretary, make a serious attempt to intertwine Gounod and Goethe in her film *Faust et Méphistophélès*. She had created the first narrative film, *La Fée aux choux* ('The fairy among the cabbages'), in 1896. Thomas A. Edison produced a *Faust and Marguerite* at the Black Maria Studio in West Orange, New Jersey, in 1900, which shows Marguerite seated before a fireplace, Faust standing by her side. Mephistopheles enters and offers his sword to Faust, commanding him to behead Marguerite. Faust refuses, whereupon Mephistopheles executes her. Faust, then a skeleton, is seated in her place. Another Edison production of the same year, *The Artist's Dream*, features Mephistopheles making painted images come alive (Musser, 578–84). There is little genuine acting in these staged studio productions. Edwin Stratton Porter, now regarded as the inventor of narrative cinema for *The Great Train Robbery* (1903), was drawn to the same material and produced *Faust and Marguerite* in 1909, in which William J. Sorelle attained something approaching stardom for his rendering of Mephistopheles. In the same year, we have a *Madame Faust* from France in which a lady concludes a pact in the hope of retaining her youth and looks. Seesslen (110) regards this as the first anachronistic satire of social mores. One year later, the first of many Faust puppets appeared on screen in *Le tout petit Faust*, created by one of the world's earliest animators, Emile Cohl.

By the second decade of the twentieth century, ever more complex movies were being generated on this productive theme. Henri Andréani and David Barnett III worked on the first international co-production in 1910. With Fernanda Negri Pouget and Tom Santschi in the leading roles, their *Faust*, based once again on Gounod, was the result of collaboration between Great Britain, France and Italy. In 1910, the first German film of Gounod's opera was made by Oskar Messter, with Franz Porten playing Faust beside his daughter, Henny Porten, as Margaret.

80. Oskar Messter's Faust *(1910) with Franz Porten as Faust and Henny Porten as Margaret.*

It was not until 1913 that we get the first German attempt to make a film on the theme of the country's national drama; this was *Der Student von Prag*, starring Paul Wegener. The plot is loosely based on Goethe, with Chamisso, E.T.A. Hoffmann, Alfred de Musset and Oscar Wilde contributing elements to the story of a poor student, Balduin, who sells his mirror image to the magician Scapinelli. There are some structural similarities with Faust, and since the pact has a central function its Faustian ancestry is beyond dispute (Prodolliet, 23–26; Grim, II, 221–26; Dabezies, 79–81).

Der Student von Prag was the first German film of international quality; there were two remakes, in 1926 (Henrik Galeen) and 1935 (Artur Robinson). Less well known today is *Rapsodia Satanica*, directed in 1915 by Nino Oxilia and the first polychrome version, at least in so far as the individual prints were in part hand-coloured. This variation on the Faust myth is typical of the pre-Expressionist phase of extravagant aestheticism and was one of the first films to dispense with wide-angle views in favour of focusing on actors and especially actresses through the use of close-ups. It was shown at the Locarno International Film Festival in 1996. Other famous names who produced early silent films were Cecil M. Hepworth (1911), Edward Sloman (1915), Gérard Bourgeois (1922), and Bertram Phillips (1923). Sloman's *Faust* was applauded especially for the transformation scene in which the doctor is rejuvenated, while Bourgeois used a pioneering technique to create three-dimensional effects. At the same time, ever more parodies were surfacing, particularly in Britain and America, where we see the seeds being sown for comic and slapstick versions, such as the two *Bedazzleds* of 1967 and 2000. They include *Bill Bumper's Bargain* of 1911, a parody of Gounod, *The Devil to Pay*, directed in England by Saunders and Bowden in 1912, *Faust and the Lily* (1913), *The Black Crook* (1915), and *Devilish Business* (1916).

The Golden Age

Of these and many other products of the first two decades of the twentieth century we know little more than the titles. The third decade yields longer and more elaborate versions, including attempts to combine Faust with other themes. In 1922 Marcel l'Herbier directed a visually extravagant version of *Don Juan et Faust* which contrasts the northern Faust with the easy-going southerner and is directly based on the play Grabbe had put on the German stage ninety-five years previously. Here, too, it is interesting to note that a French director was prepared to use a German script that had, until then, found little favour in its native land. It was filmed on location in Spain and attracted an enthusiastic response. The pressure on the German film industry to put the national drama onto celluloid was by now overwhelming. But one attempt after another was fated to stall. The Hamburg Johann-Hagenbeck-Filmgesellschaft went so far as to commission a musical score in 1918, and an impatient Richard Oswald threatened to import a Gretchen from America if local talent could not be found (Prodolliet, 29–32).

81. Faust (1926), directed by F.W. Murnau, is an outstanding example of the German UFA
Studio's output of horror classics during the silent era.

America almost won the race outright. In 1923, Ernst Lubitsch planned to
sign the mega-star of her day, Mary Pickford, as Gretchen. Lubitsch lost his chance,
however, when Pickford's mother took offence at a terse synopsis of the story-line
that had been communicated to her by Lubitsch himself: 'She has a bebby and she
is not married, so she stringles the bebby.' (Seesslen, 115f.) Pickford Senior roundly
forbade her daughter to have a part in any such low-life debauchery, thereby
conceding to Lubitsch's rival Friedrich Murnau, remembered for Nosferatu (1922)
and The Last Laugh (1924), one of the crowning achievements of the age of silent
movies. Lubitsch did, however, eventually produce a movie of his own in which
Faustian motifs are gently parodied: Heaven Can Wait (1943).

Although it was made in the UFA Studios in Potsdam, the film that came out
in 1926, promoted contradictorily both as 'Goethe's Faust' and as 'A German
Folk Legend', was not an all-German product. Even the role of Gretchen had been
offered to Lillian Gish, who made excessive demands and was replaced by the
unknown débutante Camilla Horn. Faust was played by the Swede Gösta Ekman,
Frau Schwerdtlein by a French actress, Yvette Guilbert. Murnau and his scriptwriter
Hans Kyser were able to draw on a long tradition of experimentation and on their
experience of making horror movies. The result displayed Murnau's ability in
harnessing the increasingly sophisticated visual resources available to the camera
operators of the day. The textual basis was a pot-pourri of Goethe, Marlowe, and a
less well-known manuscript Das verlorene Paradies ('Paradise Lost') by Ludwig Berger.
Murnau took no responsibility for the captions. These were sub-contracted to the
celebrated playwright Gerhart Hauptmann, at 64 years the doyen of German

poetry, but what he wrote was considered too ponderous, and his 350 verses were eventually replaced by more snappy captions by Hans Kyser (Prodolliet, 45). Murnau's team follow Goethe at several points, especially in the heavenly prologue (spoken by an angel) and the tribulations of Gretchen, but rewrite large parts of the plot. Apocalyptic shadows chase across the earth; an angel demands an end to strife and pestilence, while Mephisto argues that the world is his to do with as he pleases. Faust is glimpsed instructing his students, while Mephisto is promised sovereignty over the earth if he should succeed in corrupting Faust. He spreads pestilence, hinted at by the dark shadows that engulf the houses. In the face of Faust's despair at his failure to cure the plague victims, Mephisto promises success, eternal youth and the love of Gretchen, in exchange for possession of his soul. Faust is allowed to test the pact for a day; this expires as he is about to woo the Duchess of Parma, and Mephisto finds it easy to obtain Faust's consent to the pact with the help of a mixture of sweeteners and deceit. This devil, played by Emil Jannings, is patently out to trick his victim in the most blatant manner, which he does by reversing the hour-glass during the trial period, and, fatally for the lovers, by spreading malicious gossip about Gretchen to her brother and his drinking-companions, leering meaningfully at the camera as he contrives to wreak disaster. Faust flees after killing Valentine in a duel, and Gretchen is seen struggling to care for her child on a winter's night. No help is offered by the uncaring townspeople, and after the child's death she is sentenced to be burned at the stake. Yet when he hears her cries for help, Faust renounces the devil's gifts and returns to rescue his love through a thick cloud of fire and smoke. As he curses his earlier thirst for knowledge and youth, he is transformed once again to the old man he was at the outset. Yet then, confusingly, Faust becomes young once again and the reunited pair expire together at the stake and are then promptly saved, demonstrating the triumph of love over evil.

The concentration on Gretchen was both a strength and a weakness of the film. Kyser recognised that 'a mediaeval spirit that copulates with succubi and incubi' was no subject for the modern cinema, and commented:

> The most difficult task was to present a figure such as Faust to a multinational audience in a silent film in such a way as to be able to appeal to a totally non-literary spectator not merely by making him intelligible, but by provoking a feeling of kinship without saying a single word. The specifically metaphysical problem of the Faust material, and Goethe's characterisation of Faust as someone who was struggling to understand the innermost workings of the universe, was not something that could be put across through silent images alone, and although Faust does appear in the lecture room of a mediaeval university in his capacity as a metaphysician, he had to be introduced as a doctor and scholar in the tradition of the great alchemists. (Cited by Heining, 47)

Faust is seen as a scholar, then as a lover, with the focus shifting from him to Gretchen as the plot unfolds. Yet the storyline and script, as seen in the captions, were hardly the main attraction. Theodore Huff speaks of Murnau's *Faust* as 'one of the most pictorially beautiful films ever made, a supreme example of German studio craftsmanship, at times seeming like a Dürer or Brueghel come to life.' Eric Rohmer concurs that Murnau owes more to painting than to other forms of imagery (Rohmer, 15, 35). On the subject of its significance for Germany, a matter of great interest at the time, Thomas Elsaesser writes:

> Besides the international cast, the other key ingredient of the film was to be its 'Germanness'. This was not necessarily that evoked by Goethe, and more by Gothic: the film attempted to reinvent a typically 'medieval' Germany, or rather, that of the Reformation, of half-timbered houses, steep cobbled streets in crooked townscapes, of mountain ranges and valleys, deep forests and waterfalls. In other words, a tourist Germany, but one sufficiently saturated with art-historical markers to make it possible that the whole Northern renaissance from Albrecht Dürer to Lukas Cranach, from Matthias Grünewald to Albrecht Altdorfer would be called upon to provide the authenticating iconography. (Elsaesser, 242)

Its chiaroscuro mediaeval settings, so familiar from the golden age of German cinema, were given added effect by the employment of techniques such as the intense spotlighting of the duel with Valentine. Low angles and sloping ceilings were used in the Expressionist tradition for the interiors of Gretchen's and Martha's houses, while strange apparitions and dexterous camera tricks added an almost mystical atmosphere. Jannings, master of the roguish leer, disguised his middle-aged spread with the help of a long cloak; the scene in which he and the rejuvenated Faust fly through the air over towns and villages was a pioneering feat that won universal acclaim. It had been filmed in a 35-metre long hangar, and reflects Murnau's experiences as a fighter pilot in World War I (Elsaesser, 245). It is beyond doubt that the director considered the technical aspects of making this film to be more important than the story-line. He even felt he knew how Goethe might have reacted to his film.

> Murnau bent his huge torso down to the tiny, silent scene [the miniature sets] and smiled: 'If Goethe was alive, he would be interested in the movies. More than the writers are today. And he would be especially interested in this film. But everything, manuscript, acting, actors would not engross him half as much as these [special effects], because they are the only thing that would remind him of his own work.' (Robert Herlth, 'Konturen von F.W. Murnau', *Filmtechnik-Filmkunst*, 18 April 1931, cited by Elsaesser, 258)

Goethe might well have been intrigued by the 'special effects', having anticipated many technical developments. Murnau had his own, unconventional ways of engineering them and took great risks, nowhere more so than in the execution of Gretchen/Camilla Horn, who would later recall how she was almost burned alive when Murnau applied a torch to the stake. In the end, it was Jannings's Mephisto who dominated the picture, while reactions to its hero were uniformly negative: he 'faded from memory as quickly as he faded from view' (Prodolliet, 49). There was good reason for this: Murnau had deliberately foregrounded the suffering masses, the townspeople who are attacked by the plague and the girl who is spurned by her neighbours. In this process, Faust was necessarily pushed to the margins.

82. The unknown starlet Camilla Horn as the suffering Gretchen in Murnau's Faust, *1926. Source: UFA publicity poster.*

The shift of emphasis was anathema to those German viewers who had come along in the not unreasonable expectation that he would emerge as a powerful icon. Lotte Eisner captures the atmosphere of the film well in the following extract from her book on Murnau.

Light and movement: all Murnau's experiments and discoveries in [his] two previous films came to full fruition in *Faust*.

The beginning and the end are fugues of light, orchestrated with incomparable mastery. The clash between the explosive brightness of the archangel and the darkness which surrounds the devil in this 'heavenly prologue' is a piercing vision, an apogee of the art of the silent film. The gentle sunlight which seems to colour the sky at the end becomes the counterpoint which brings promise of redemption.

The visual magic marks everything. Smoky atmospheres wrap around the little medieval town like a great devil's cloak, bringing noxious exhalations of plague. Faust rises up on the screen, powerful, looming out of the mists; the light is diffused when his now immense face leans forward in close-up. Or Faust throws his useless books on to the fire which seems to fill the whole room. Suddenly the pages of the book of witchcraft blaze with an infernal flame. Finally, delivered into darkness, Faust tries vainly to break through the wall of light which blazes out of the door of the cathedral which he can no longer enter.

Light and movement: the huddled town itself, with its complex stairs and alleys, provokes movement: men in cloaks carry coffins, the crowd crushes the steps to bring their sick to Faust. Children come to the church like equivocal Botticelli angels, carrying lilies in their innocent hands.

The journey through the skies on the cloak of Mephisto whirls through gliding landscapes, the mists making the models seem entirely authentic. Gretchen's cry of anguish, represented in a series of superimpositions, comes to us across the mountains and valleys, achieving a sort of three-dimensional effect. This plastic quality, this *volume* gives the film its power: the costumes, still more the heads and the bodies of people sometimes acquire this same three-dimensional effect through their modelling.

> In all these Rembrandtesque tonalities there are few Expressionist elements, apart from some expressively steep roofs and gables which the designers Herlth and Röhrig invented. And when Mephisto becomes a devil once again, and cries out for murder, he spreads himself diagonally across the screen like the complete Expressionist actor. (Eisner, 165)

Other authorities, including Siegfried Kracauer, were less than impressed, arguing that much of the content had been sacrificed on the altar of special effects. It had cost two million reichsmarks to produce and earned barely half that sum. It was more popular outside than inside Germany, where it was eventually given an 'Adults Only' certificate by the Prussian Ministry of the Interior. The verdict of 9 December 1929 reads:

> The confusing impression of the concept of youth that is created by the representation of an unrestrained, pleasure-seeking Faust is [highly likely to produce] a negative influence on the moral development of young people. This effect is intensified by the circumstance that the viewer perceives the sole catalyst of Faust's behaviour to reside in his unrestrained sensuality. In view of the above-mentioned seduction scenes, the love-potion scene and the images used in the seventh act to visualise the death of the child and the ensuing punishment, the film as a whole is designed to damage the moral awareness of young people. Regardless of its intrinsic ethical value, the film will from now on not be shown to minors. (Cited by Prodolliet, 51f.)

There is an obvious clash between the recognition of 'intrinsic ethical value' and the desire to stop young minds from following the example of an unrestrained pleasure-seeker. By the time this edict was enforced, the film had reached the end of its run in German cinemas, and a new wind was beginning to blow. 1929 was the year in which talking pictures suddenly replaced the silent films, sometimes half-way through their production, and this can be seen in James Flood's *Faust*, begun as a silent film but with spoken scenes subsequently inserted during production. It tells of a tycoon who allows himself to be rejuvenated in order to obtain the love of a young woman, but the truth catches up with him as he ages rapidly while attending a production of *Faust*.

Stephen Vincent Benét's short story *The Devil and Daniel Webster* appeared in print in 1937 and was filmed in 1941. Here, too, the devil is cheated of his prey, not by personal empowerment through love or self-sacrifice, as in many other instances, but by the mental prowess of a lawyer, the eponymous Daniel Webster, who raises a number of deceased villains to act as jurymen and manages with their assistance to have the pact between Jabez Stone and 'Mr Scratch' annulled. The film, also released as *Here is a Man* and as *All that Money can buy*, is set in the 1840s, like the book, but transforms the causes of Stone's pact from a purely financial crisis to a typical case of failed rural existence that is vaguely reminiscent of the recent Wall Street Crash, Depression and rural drought as experienced in the 1930s. Webster has the makings of a presidential candidate, while Scratch wears outlandish-looking tweeds. Thomas Mann hailed it as 'an Americanised fable, a patriotic fantasy brilliantly performed' (Mann, 202). Wilhelm Dieterle, who played Valentine in Murnau's *Faust*, directed this movie as William Dieterle. He made many changes to the text in the interests of increasing his film's appeal. The unlucky farmer is turned into a young man and consequently needs no rejuvenation. This also permitted the device of introducing Stone's mother, a domineering woman played by Jane Darwell. Her counterpart is the temptress, a servant-girl named Belle, invented for cinematic effect and given a French accent to underline her un-American provenance. Faust's fortunes in the New World are explored greater detail in chapter 10 of this study.

France continued to produce films on the Faust theme, and during the Second World War some of these were inevitably read as cryptic allusions to Vichy France's pact with Germany. Marcel Carné's *Les Visiteurs du soir* of 1942 is one example. Here, at least, one of the two tempters refuses to carry out the devil's work out of love for a mortal woman. In 1943, Jean-Paul Paulin directed *L'Homme qui vendit son âme*. This much-admired film also has a conciliatory ending, as the banker who sold his soul repents under the influence of true love. The most enduring French contribution, René Clair's *La Beauté du diable*, released in the USA as *Beauty and the Devil*, was produced in 1949 and premièred in March 1950. It is based on Marlowe, Goethe and the folk books, and even on Murnau, and yet it takes the legend further in a way few of the earlier films were able to. This is partly because it was so obviously written with an eye to examining the role of the scientist in the age of nuclear fission.

Like a parody of the very first French Faust films, it begins with a burst of smoke; unlike almost all other versions, it has a comic lightness that separates it from the Teutonic gloom that so often surrounds the tale. Thus Méphistophélès is heard muttering *Quel métier!* ('What a job!') under his breath, not unlike some latter-day Parisian taxi-driver. The old Professor Henri Faust is almost grotesquely senile at the start, defeated more by gout and dementia than by the ungratified quest for truth, mocked rather than revered by his students and colleagues. Yet despite the levity, Clair's film raises interesting technical questions that all previous versions had ignored. How does the rejuvenated Faust get used to his new body? (By limping around initially like a man fitted with artificial limbs). How is it that no one ever expresses surprise at the disappearance of the 'old' Faust? Surely the entire academic community of Wittenberg would want to send out search parties for such an eminent 'missing person'? (Here they do, and the young Faust is almost executed on suspicion of robbing and murdering his older self). Why does Faust rarely ask for samples of his future pleasures before signing the pact? (Clair makes Méphistophélès wait and wait until Faust is finally ready to sign).

In tragicomic fashion, a plot unfolds in which the aged doctor Henri Faust is rejuvenated and makes the acquaintance of a remarkably well turned-out gypsy girl, Marguerite. Nicole Besnard, a fiery Carmencita, comes across as the very antithesis of the *echt-deutsch* Gretchen type; she is more of a remote descendant of the gypsy girl Lyduschka who tried to save Balduin in *The Student of Prague*. Faust is admitted to the aristocracy of the day – Berman (147) places the action in the seventeenth century, but it looks more like the late eighteenth or early nineteenth – through the assistance of Méphistophélès, a somewhat bumbling agent of Lucifer who quickly becomes Faust's controlling mentor. When the young Faust is accused of murdering the doctor, Méphistophélès is able to protect him by assuming the latter's shape. He remains in this guise throughout the film and teaches his pupil the art of alchemy, which binds them closer together, although the people become ever more sceptical about their experiments. After the pair have produced gold by the barrowful, courted the princess and played tricks with time, a pact is finally signed between them. Now Faust makes another obvious request neglected by his previous incarnations: he asks to be shown his own future. Méphistophélès reluctantly shows him all in a mirror. He will have numerous affairs, become a tyrant, and lay waste to the earth, enveloping everything in clouds of contaminated smoke. Horrified by his surrender to runaway progress, Faust orders Méphistophélès to destroy all traces of his scientific labour. Finding that their gold has turned into sand, the people demand revenge, initially assuming that Marguerite is the guilty party. But she saves the situation, for when Méphistophélès tries to add her soul to his collection, she throws the pact into the crowd, who now realise that Faust was behind the scam and turn on him, or rather on Méphistophélès, who is still wearing the old professor's disguise. Henri Faust retains his youth and is free to join the circus caravan with Marguerite under a clear, sunny sky (Dale, I, 390–411 and II, 313–45).

Clair re-employs the motif of the provisional pact that enables Faust to sample the devil's wares without committing himself; this replicates the single day offered in Murnau's version, where Mephisto used it to cheat his victim. In Clair's implementation, Lucifer's permission must be sought for what is clearly an exception to the general rule. The impression is gained that this demon has not progressed very far in the art of winning souls. The figure of the 'inept' devil desperate to obtain his quota of souls becomes a significant theme in later cinema versions (*Bedazzled*; *I was a Teenage Faust*), as it creates a second centre of interest around Faust's antagonist. Clair published the following comment:

> But why a new Faust, you ask, and in our own time? The interest that this legend has elicited for four centuries can be explained in simple terms: Faust personifies the desire for knowledge and the desire for power (which everyone carries within himself, and whose manifestations can be observed even in children). To satisfy his desires, Faust sells his soul to the devil. Couldn't we say that if the devil set that price, more than one man would be tempted to do the same, in order to learn what he doesn't know, or to acquire what he doesn't possess?
>
> The character of Faust is illuminated strangely by the light of our own times. The great current of intellectual activity that pushed alchemists towards the search for the philosopher's stone and the secrets of matter has continued on to the age of atomic discoveries. And our contemporaries have the privilege of watching the strange spectacle of a humanity that, having sold its soul to science, is trying to prevent the damnation of a world towards which its own endeavours are dragging it.
>
> Nevertheless, would we not all like to believe that hellish artifices are not foolproof, that the devil isn't as strong as he believes, that his weapons can occasionally turn back on him, and that he can disappear, ridiculous and vanquished, in a great spurt of flames and smoke? (Clair, 1959, 97f; translated by Dale, II, 345)

83. Michel Simon as Méphistophélès in the company of the gypsy Marguerite (Nicole Besnard) and a rejuvenated Henri Faust (Gérard Philipe), 1950.

Clair's may be the best-known postwar Faust film from France, but there were others. They include his sometime assistant Claude Autant-Lara's *Marguerite de la nuit* of 1955. This places Marguerite centre-stage and explores the shady demi-monde of Montmartre in the 1920s. Méphistophélès is a sinister figure from the Parisian underworld: a drug baron by the name of Léon who has a club foot and can prevent fire from burning. Marguerite is allied to a dealer called Angelo. When the rejuvenated Georges Faust woos her, he has no alternative but to kill his rival. Thereafter he tries to annul the pact, and the terrified Marguerite seeks shelter with her brother Valentine, a young priest, before sacrificing herself for Faust. This she does by entering a symbolic railway carriage that resembles a coffin. Léon recognises that he has no power over her and tears up the pact. This results in her death and the survival of her unworthy partner. Here, finally, the Gretchen figure proves not only to be Faust's equal, but his moral superior. Institutionalised science is also the subject of Louis Pauwel's *Président Faust* of 1974 (Berman 149).

Less than a week after the U.S. release of René Clair's *Beauty and the Devil* a rather different dramatisation came into the movie theatres. It had been produced in 1948 in Italy as *La leggenda di Faust* ('The Legend of Faust'). In the U.S. it ran as *Faust and the Devil* and also as *The Strange Life of Doctor Faust*. In France, it was released as *Et Satan conduit le bal* ('And Satan leads the ball'). It was directed by Carmine Gallone, whose career extended back as far as 1914 and who was responsible for screen adaptations of *Madame Butterfly* and *Carmen*. Gallone's version was a musical on the Faust theme, based on a mélange of Goethe, Gounod and Boito. Gino Mattera appeared as Faust, Italo Tajo as Mephistopheles. The two male stars did their own singing, but Nelly Corradi as Marguerite proved unequal to the task and had to accept the voice of Onelia Finechi in the musical sections, which Corradi was obliged to mime. José Luis Saenz de Heredia's *Faustina* was based on the author's opera *Si Fausto fuera Faustina* ('If Faust were Faustina'); it premièred in Madrid in 1954. It focuses on the comic difficulties encountered by a female 'Faustina' determined to become the most beautiful princess in the world (Prodolliet, 61–5).

Postwar Germany has seen many attempts to transfer successful stage productions onto film. For the most part, these have been recordings of elaborate productions such as Dieter Dorn's and Peter Stein's versions, produced for the Kammerspiele Theatre in Munich and the Hanover Exposition in 1987 and 2000 respectively. However, Peter Gorski's film of 1960, although also based on a theatrical representation at the Deutsches Schauspielhaus, Hamburg, by a leading director, is different at least in so far as it attempted to create a conflation of theatrical and cinematic effects, and, more significantly perhaps, in that it was, to the surprise of many, a commercial success among the rapidly dwindling movie audiences of its day, perhaps because it offered the double illusion of witnessing a great drama on stage from the informal and affordable ambience of the modern movie theatre.

Gustaf Gründgens had enjoyed a long and not uncontroversial career as an actor and producer of plays prior to, during, and after the Third Reich. He himself had been the subject of a novel about the careerist actor under National Socialism. In terms of his German reputation, he was seen by many as the greatest Mephisto of all time, and the fact that his morals no less than his politics were ambivalent in the eyes of many merely enhanced his Mephistophelean aura (see above, 174).

Gründgens and Gorski produced a *Faust* which was neither pure film nor pure theatre but a hybrid located at the middle point between the two. The décor is at times minimalist (Prologues, street scenes), at times prolific (the Witch's Kitchen abounds in accoutrements such as party drinks and a gramophone, and Walpurgis Night resembles a vast postwar dance-hall). The technical effects range from the non-existent (Mephistopheles invisible in dog form, spirit choruses that remain unseen) to the unstageably filmic (the Earth Spirit enveloped in flames; the shattered mirror in the Witch's Kitchen; the atomic explosion at the end of Walpurgis Night). Montage and superimposition are used sparingly. Makeup is also applied inconsistently. Faust is not, as in Clair, a tottering imbecile, but a relatively youthful, beardless scholar at the outset who might not look out of place in a modern Senior Common Room, while Mephistopheles has a chalky whiteness reminiscent both of a Pierrot and a fairground skeleton. When rejuvenated, Faust becomes a close-cropped playboy type with luridly painted lips. But alongside these devices, there are constant reminders of the origins of the play in a bygone age: Gretchen is reassuringly old-fashioned, the bare boards can almost be heard creaking, the curtains have to be wound open and shut by the actors. The amateurish, sometimes almost monotonous recitals of some passages is another factor that could be put down to Brechtian alienation. Nowhere is this more obvious than in the transition from the Prelude on the Stage to the Prologue in Heaven. We actually see the Theatre Manager grab the cloak and false beard that

84. *Will Quadflieg as Faust and Gustaf Gründgens as Mephistopheles in Peter Gorski's Faust, 1960. Photograph by Rosemarie Clausen.*

he will wear as 'The Lord' in the following scene, and when the curtain rises on 'Heaven', where one might expect clouds and celestial music, an empty space is revealed in which three almost laughably carnivalesque figures, attired like peacocks rather than angels, recite their 'hymns' as though auditioning for minor parts in an amateur pantomime. The film's success was unexpected; it played to full houses for many years after its release, and the accompanying volume by Rosemarie Clausen is still in demand.

Postwar Glitz

Bedazzled (1967), starring British comedy duo Peter Cook and Dudley Moore, was a relatively low-key, patchy comedy in the popular vein, full of in-jokes, transparent puns, cross-dressing and other stock-in-trade components of Whitehall farce. In Germany it was released as *Mephisto 68*. The shy and gauche burger bar cook Stanley Moon initially demands no more from life than the courage to talk to waitress Margaret Spencer. When his attempts at suicide fail, the devil, alias George Spigott, offers him seven wishes in exchange for his soul. He agrees, and his first wish resembles Faust's at least in so far as he desires to be an intellectual. This impresses Margaret and brings personal satisfaction, but at the crucial moment she rejects his physical advances. Riches, marriage and fame (as a rock star) bring ever scanter rewards, and even the peaceful happy life with Margaret that he desires

327

is flawed, in that it involves transforming himself into a nun. Throughout the film, George complains about the good works of God, yet his own 'devilry' expresses itself in a series of petty pranks: cutting buttons off new shirts, scratching vinyl records, interfering with parking meters, and, in conformity with the tired conventions of Ealing comedy, removing wet paint signs from park benches. Improbably, he has a kind heart, as is evident when he generously releases Stanley at the end in the belief that he has already achieved his target of 100 billion sinners, only to be denied re-entry to heaven on a technicality. It is this focus on the metaphysical framework that places *Bedazzled* in the tradition of Goethe's *Faust*, for here, too, a contest between the divine and the satanic powers is the catalyst, and here as there, specific reference is made to the Book of Job. In a curious but not entirely un-Goethean bargain, God promised salvation to George if he could corrupt a certain number of humans; but his prize is denied to him on the grounds that he saved Stanley in order to make himself feel good. The film ends in cosmic laughter, as the creator delights in having tricked the 'Evil One', and as in an increasing number of Faust films, a modicum of pity is generated for the proactive devil who has tried so hard, effortlessly displaying intellectual superiority over his victims, yet must accept defeat by a moronic if good-natured mortal.

In 2000, *Bedazzled* was updated and transferred to an American setting by Harold Ramis, remembered for the *Ghostbusters* movies. The Faustian parallels are more difficult to discern. Yet the film is a good indicator of the direction in which theatrical presentations of Faust are moving, in that here, as in many modern stage versions, the devil is feminised. The modern love-affair with the motor-car, which in the 1967 version led to some rudimentary tomfoolery with parking meters, is taken a few steps further when the devil tires of fiddling the meters and manipulates traffic lights in order to cause the pile-ups so beloved of Hollywood. The dark forces have their offices in 'Hell, Purgatory and Los Angeles', and current perceptions of evil are reflected in the thesis that watching TV, playing video games, avoiding homework and waking up late are key priorities in the devil's campaign of corruption. Where Peter Cook was suave and gentlemanly as the devil in Stanley Donen's film, Liz Hurley's evil qualities do not extend much further than a self-satisfied grin and a penchant for revealing red and black PVC. Redemption occurs when the once feeble Elliot makes his final wish, which is for his Gretchen, incongruously named Alison Gardner, to be happy. This altruistic gesture demonstrates his essential goodness and renders the devil's machinations ineffective.

The public had to wait until 1967 before they got to see a film version of Christopher Marlowe's source-drama for all subsequent Fausts. This despite the fact that the earliest British Faust film dates from 1897, and that the local 'House of Hammer' had a virtual monopoly on low-budget but often effective horror movies thronged with devils and necromancers. It was not until seven years after the Gorski-Gründgens film that an attempt was made to commit Marlowe's seminal work to celluloid. The circumstances were similar. Again, we have an actor with a commanding presence, Richard Burton, acting in and co-directing a film of a distinguished theatrical production, the Oxford University Dramatical Society's

1966 version at the Oxford Playhouse, directed by Professor Nevill Coghill. The same problems that confronted the Gorski-Gründgens team were faced by the British team, yet they employed traditional filmic methods in dealing with them. The result was commended in some quarters but derided in others.

Coghill's film focuses on the eponymous character, treating him not as a base conjurer or senile academician, but as a Renaissance scholar born before his time. For this reason Robin, Rafe and Dick are omitted. It remains uncertain whether the decision to incorporate Elizabeth Taylor as Helen of Troy and all other female roles was an enhancement or an irritant. Her image was constantly recycled as a projection of sexual temptation. This happens from the moment that Valdes and Cornelius enter with their crystal ball and view the images that appear in it. Helen provides structural breaks in the narrative by presenting herself as almost every spirit or succubus that is conjured up, including that of Alexander's paramour. Taylor slides from one seductive outfit into another, rather like Liz Hurley in the remake of *Bedazzled*. That is probably closer to Marlowe than many critics enjoying the benefit of knowing their Goethe would care to admit. Grim (II, 232) argues that she represents both the positive (ideal) and the negative (real) aspects of womanhood. When Valdes speaks of women and unwedded maids 'shadowing more beauty in their airy brows / Than have the white breasts of the queen of love', Taylor is there

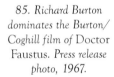

85. Richard Burton dominates the Burton/ Coghill film of Doctor Faustus. *Press release photo, 1967.*

to illustrate what is meant; yet, somewhat disfigured, she is also the woman who, as a 'hot whore', is substituted for the wife Faustus desires. Andreas Teuber as Mephastophilis, after abandoning his hideously misshapen form, becomes a slender and handsome if anaemic young man. Opinions vary as to whether he pales into insignificance beside Burton or steals the show by conveying the agony of hell while rarely moving or speaking above a whisper (Zambrano, I, 190).

There are echoes of Goethe, too, showing how difficult it is to read Marlowe without the benefit of hindsight. One such element is Faustus' rejuvenation, which here takes place as soon as the pact is signed. It is simply implied that this is one of the effects of the compact. The production of the pact out of thin air is also handled in a manner that recalls the German film. The visit to Rome looms large, with mildly entertaining food-snatching, fireworks, and pie-throwing contests unfolding. Faustus is seen to be enjoying these schoolboy pranks; both he and Mephastophilis appear relaxed. And yet the two fail to get a proper purchase on the clerics, as their robes turn out to be empty when Faustus and his companion start to thrash them. Near the end of the movie, Faustus holds up a mirror and cannot see his reflection in it. Eventually, hell opens up in the ground like a fiery trapdoor with hands pulling Faustus down. Thus the story appears to allow of no alternative but damnation – were it not for the promise that Helen/Taylor will escort him through the underworld. Whether this is an echo of Goethe's 'Eternal Feminine' is a matter for speculation.

There is one further parallel between Gründgens and Burton. In both cases, critics were quick to point out the disquieting parallels between the actor and the role he had taken on and played to perfection. Both had played the full gamut of roles in the classical theatre, outshining all other performers of their day. But both, in different ways characteristic of their period, had pushed themselves further, Gründgens by entering into a Mephistophelean alliance with National Socialism, Burton by opting for Hollywood rather than Stratford-upon-Avon, a path that led to riches and beautiful women, but ultimately also to self-destruction. The film of *Doctor Faustus* reveals a melancholia in Burton that can only stem from self-awareness. When Mephistopheles cries: 'Why this is hell, nor am I out of it', he might well be referring to a long-term Hollywood contract (Billington).

Foreign and Arthouse

Ion Popescu-Gopo's rarely seen *Faust in secolul douazeci* ('Faust in the Twentieth Century', 1966), also known as *Faust XX*, shows a scholar dying of an incurable disease. Mephisto conducts a comic transplantation of his soul into a younger body, that of his youthful assistant Wagner, companion to an attractive night-club singer, played by Eva Krzyewska. It is as Wagner that Faust falls in love with Margaret, in whose body Mephistso takes refuge. The film ends with Faust, lodged in Wagner's body, impregnating Mephisto, in Gretchen's body (Prodolliet, 79f.). The body-invasion theme is carried to similar extremes in Paul Wendkos' 1971 film *The Mephisto Waltz*, written by Ben Maddow, in which a dying pianist, stimulated by Liszt's Mephistophelean piano music, lodges himself in the body of a journalist out of an incestuous love for his daughter.

In 1972, Aleksandar Petrović made a film of Bulgakov in a Yugoslav-Italian co-production, *Majstor i Margarita*. Bulgakov uses Margarita to conclude the pact with Voland in order to save the Master. Petrović had read the novel in one sitting and was convinced that he had read a fundamental account of his time. He describes it as 'A book that not only deals with the problems of Russia and the world at large, but also the problems of the milieu in which I live'. The film was a great success in Venice, but caused problems for its director. It was recognised as having some relevance to the situation of Alexander Solzhenitsyn. It can be read on a human or on a political level. The outcast of the sixteenth century had found a worthy parallel in the subversive intellectual of the twentieth.

It would be a serious omission to pass by the one Faust film other than *The Devil and Daniel Webster* ever to have received an Academy Award, István Szabó's *Mephisto* of 1981, the 'Best Foreign Film' of that year. Yet on the whole, it sticks closely to its source, Klaus Mann's novel of 1936, and is more of an adaptation than a filmic creation. The references to homosexuality are excised, the character of Juliette is toned down, and Brandauer is both himself and, when he portrays Mephistopheles, a reminder of the novel's alleged prototype, Gustaf Gründgens. The political edge of this bitterly satirical novel is blunted. Höfgen is not so much the ruthless careerist as the man of the theatre, anxious to modernise and improve the institution whatever the cost in human terms. Thus when he weeps, it is not

86. *Klaus Maria Brandauer as Höfgen in István Szabó's* Mephisto, *1981*

out of self-pity or from unrequited love but in despair at the low quality of the acting. While Klaus Mann attacks National Socialism and its fellow-travellers, Szabó merely deplores the way the State manipulates the arts (Berman 150f.). It is only in the very last scene that Szabó departs productively from his source. Instead of collapsing in his mother's arms as he hears of the death of a former colleague, Höfgen is taken to a stadium, where he is told to perform in the searing glare of searchlights mounted all around its perimeter. Höfgen the actor thus finally becomes, in a single stark image, the celebrated performer whose personality is 'up in the lights' as any actor would wish, and, simultaneously, the hunted animal, caught in the sights of the pursuing huntsmen, trapped within the stadium like the inmate of a concentration camp.

Thomas Mann's *Doctor Faustus* was filmed shortly thereafter, in 1982, by Franz Seitz, although several elements from the novel had previously been incorporated into Luchino Visconti's *Death in Venice* of 1971: the name 'Esmeralda', the brothel experience, and, most strikingly, the transformation of its central character from a burnt-out novelist into a relatively youthful composer of avant-garde music. But unlike *Mephisto* and *Death in Venice*, Seitz's film met with scant success (Kost, 27–46). It was shot in English but never released outside Germany. It follows its source closely, and attempts to make visual reference to the wider issues of the Faust tradition, beginning, for example, with a puppeteer, sixteenth-century images, and newsreel clips from the Second World War. Four hundred years of German history are condensed into a shot of a squadron of Halifax bombers flying over Dürer's *Melancholia*. Esmeralda is given the name 'Lada', and Bratislava is replaced by the more exotic Sarajevo, which allows the director to blend in a shot of a muezzin calling the faithful to prayer, a detail reminiscent of the beginning of the *The Exorcist*. The motif of frost flowers is regularly used. The director borrowed a detail from Mann's earlier novel, *The Magic Mountain*, by having Adrian Leverkühn climb through grandiose snow-fields in bright sunlight for his assignation with the devil, whose diabolic laughter promptly triggers a rather feeble avalanche. Darkly satanic it is not. Seitz struggled to convey a flavour of Adrian's music without either trivialising it as 'film music' or adapting the work of known composers. He opted for a controversial solution: to incorporate excerpts from Benjamin Britten's opera *Death in Venice* as well as a new score by Rolf Wilhelm. The character of 'Lada', here played by a soulful Marie Lebée, is best left invisible, the music unheard. John Fetzer (57, 118–21) emphasises the difficulty of finding expression for a novel already over-rich in visual elements, yet the film fails ultimately because it tries too hard to depict events over which the novelist had cast a veil of mystery and ambivalence.

Written, directed and produced by Andy and Mike Jones of the Newfoundland Independent Filmmakers Co-operative, *The Adventure of Faustus Bidgood* (1986) occupies a distinctive place in the history of Faust films. It was begun in 1977 and took nearly ten years to complete; the budget was a paltry $100,000, and the actors were paid in shares rather than cash. The result was a landmark event in Canadian cinema: 'Possessed of the formal energy of early Godard and the comic daring of Monty Python, *Faustus Bidgood* is an unprecedented event in English Canadian cinema', writes Geoff Pevere on the Cinematheque website. There is much topical relevance in what was the first locally produced full-length narrative film about Newfoundland. The plot is tightly woven and frequently phantasmagorical. It follows a day in the life of the eponymous 'closet human being' Faustus Bidgood (Andy Jones), an outwardly undistinguished and mentally unstable official in the Newfoundland Department of Education who is scorned and ridiculed by his co-workers. Like all Fausts, Bidgood finds his work restrictive and oppressive, yet is prone to moments of vision and genius. In some ways, he resembles the type of the *idiot savant*. His colleagues tease and torment him. A confused dreamer capable of spectacular fantasies, Faustus is mysteriously catapulted into the position of first President of the Republic of Newfoundland, which he believes has been established after a revolution that began as a chance meeting of malcontents in a local bar during which Bidgood is arbitrarily chosen to be the leader. This revolution, shown only in black and white, seems to be a figment of his imagination; but since his colleagues are making grotesque preparations for a benefit night for 'crippled children' [*sic*], his fantasies are only one carnivalesque element among many.

87. Andy Jones as Faustus Bidgood (in shades), in a daze as the people try to prevent him from resigning as President of Newfoundland, 1986. Photograph by Dougal Dunbar.

Vasily Bogdanovich Shagoff plays the part of Wagner in Bidgood's life, attempting to warn him against taking his visions too seriously. In his presidential role, Bidgood faces the dilemma of whether to resign (as he promised when he came to power), or to continue in office (as the people appear to want), or to go back to sleep and finish his dream (as we feel he really wishes). His childhood traumas are explored in depth. But the Mephisto figure, Fred Bonia-Coombs, attempts to use Faustus to blackmail the Minister of Education, Eddy Peddle, into establishing a crackpot policy of 'total education' involving the application of mathematical grids as learning tools. What the blackmailer does not realise is that Peddle has for some time been murdering young girls by feeding them poisoned bubble-gum. It is Bidgood's genius that alerts him to the crime, though he misidentifies the culprit. To complicate matters further, while the Education Department staff are rehearsing their pantomime for the Crippled Children's Benefit Show, the 'real' Premier of the province, the enigmatic poet Jonathan Moon, has gone into hiding, and his whereabouts are the subject of a spoof television quiz entitled 'Find the Poet Premier.'

Bidgood himself takes the Faustian dichotomy to extremes; his 'two souls' are reflected in the two characters he embodies: the Head of an independent People's Republic, and the lowly clerk banished to one of its dysfunctional offices. The film mixes scenes of Bidgood the clerk dreaming of becoming President with scenes of Bidgood the President dreaming that he is still a simple bureaucrat in a provincial office. He unravels Eddy Peddle's secret, but is crushed by the piano in which Premier Moon was hiding. The film is rich in visual puns and clever gags, dispensing pointed comments about Newfoundland's political upheavals while at the same time providing an unsettling depiction of the unravelling of Bidgood's mind. Helen Peters has argued that the root cause of his mental instability lies in church control of schooling in post-confederation Newfoundland. The consequences are graphically illustrated at various points in the film, which exposes a dry-as-dust educational system and creates a positive alternative: a vibrant visual spectacle which both reveals and transcends the restrictive atmosphere of a small-town bureaucracy. In these two respects, *Bidgood* remains true to its Faustian roots.

Directors and composers from Central Europe have continued to be active in producing imaginative material based on the legend, often using indigenous traditions such as puppet plays as their basis. This is true of Jan Švankmajer's *Faust* of 1994, perhaps the most remarkable version, which will be discussed in detail below, and no less true of a little-known television opera, *Věčný Faust* ('Eternal Faust') by the Czech composer Luboš Fišer, libretto by Eva Bezděková and Jaromil Jireš, which was completed in 1985. This short film, broadcast on the 3Sat television channel on 23 December 1990, begins with the Faust (Petr Čepek) and Mephistopheles characters mingling with a rather bored-looking eighteenth-century audience and watching a somewhat overblown performance of *Faust*. The 'spectator' Faust now concludes a wager with the devil, promising that he will never be satisfied with anything that is offered him. He has set his heart on the 'stage' Gretchen, and intervenes in the play. Mephistopheles produces the usual gifts, youth, beauty, political influence, Helen of Troy, paintings that come alive, military power. Whatever Faust sees fails to content him. He therefore succeeds in winning his wager, and the signed document is burnt before his eyes. Faust has won, but he had not foreseen was that he would now be returned to his original form, the wrinkled old scholar he was before his involvement in magic. Gretchen, who was about to embrace him, recoils, not so much in horror as in mirth at the sudden and complete transformation. The visual reference here is to Murnau's ending, where Faust, somewhat incredibly, became old and then young again. With its multiple layers of 'reality' and Faust's failure to distinguish between role-play and real life, *Věčný Faust* also looks forward to Jan Švankmajer's *Faust*, in which Čepek played the last and most complex Faust of his career.

Aspects of the Faust tradition are faintly discernible in the television movie *I was a Teenage Faust*, written and directed by Thom Eberhardt and first shown on premium cable in 2001. This begins with a schoolteacher laboriously introducing her class to Goethe's masterpiece, only to have Brendan Willy inform her that he has first-hand experience of being Faust himself. It transpires that he was tempted by an under-achieving minor demon, 'Mr Five', desperately seeking to increase his quota of damned souls, with the promise of becoming the 'coolest' kid in the extremely uncool environment of Cloverdale, Indiana. The movie gives a mildly entertaining insight into life in small-town Middle America, but the action rapidly branches into several distinct themes. There is Mr Five's dilemma of not finding enough victims to satisfy his vindictive boss, which is reminiscent of George Spiggot's target figures in *Bedazzled*. Essentially a genial buffoon (played by Robert Townsend), Five commands sympathy rather than fear. The second strand involves

88. Poster designed by John Hansen, drawn by Larry Negaard, 2000.

Brendan's struggle to 'deal with the devil' whom he inadvertently summoned and now needs to dispose of. Like Henri in *La Beauté du diable* he plays for time by asking for a temporary contract to test the demonic gifts. Finally, there is the 'teenager learns to accept himself' fable that may owe more to high-school soaps than to *Faust*, as Brendan ends up learning that it's always best to keep things as they are; arguably the central lesson of all Fausts.

Faust/The Lost Feminine (2000), was directed, produced, written, photographed, and edited by John Hansen. It is a short film adaptation concentrating on Faust's painful emotional dilemma, which it places within a contemporary postcolonial context. This art-house movie portrays an overweight Faust as a man successful in thinking and doing, but totally unable to express himself in a relationship. Although only seventeen minutes in length, the source is preserved in a remarkably condensed and effective manner. Faust hesitates to swallow the potion, is twice confronted by his own naked image and its grotesque shadow, leaves his familiar suburban world for an increasingly hostile landscape; gardens give way to a precinct where he is molested by bikers, he then passes an oil depot and ends up falling down a motorway embankment. Mephisto, initially a black poodle, later in various human forms, lures him to the Witch's Kitchen, where he glimpses, in a glass, the defenceless Gretchen briefly rubbing her stomach as if in pain: a nondescript, care-worn twenty-something. Mephisto takes him to her room, where he masturbates over her bed before collapsing in exhaustion. In the final scene, 'The Wounded Feminine', Gretchen returns, undresses, and sees the trinket Faust has left. But her song – and this is perhaps the most sinister detail – is not, as one might expect, 'The King in Thule', but the air from the 'mad' scene in the Prison, 'My mother the whore, who put me to death, my father the rogue who fed on my flesh' (F 4412–20), hinting at her loneliness and eventual ruination by the lover who comes across as morally sordid and utterly self-obsessed. The film premièred in Rotterdam in 2000 and was shown at film festivals in Uruguay, São Paulo, Champaign, Illinois, and at the New Orleans Film Festival 2000. It was also included in the Independent Feature Project's Market 2000 in September of that year. Hansen explains his choice of theme as the following terms:

> Goethe's *Faust* is an image of the western heart and mind. It is a metaphor for life which is successful in thinking and doing, but wanting in feeling and relationship. Dr Faust's error is his attempt to find an external remedy for an emotional challenge which lies solely within him. In the western tradition, conquering indigenous peoples, laying claim to all resource, innovating machines, and producing money are supposed to be, at some time, emotionally fulfilling. For feeling and relationship, they are futile and commonly destructive efforts. (Publicity flyer)

Horror and Pornography

Shape-shifting is the theme of Germany's most recent contribution to the genre, Rainer Matsutani's *666 – Traue keinem, mit dem du schläfst!* ('666 – Don't trust anyone you sleep with'), released in November 2002. Frank Faust is a no-hope taxi-driver who enlists a junior devil's help to get his girlfriend Jennifer back. The film's main selling point is the devil's ability to transform himself into a number of German celebrities, including super-model Claudia Schiffer and tennis ace Boris Becker. The narrative is complicated by a twist in the plot which has Mephisto (Armin Rohde) develop a crush on his victim.

Faust: Love of the Damned (2001) was directed by Brian Yuzna of 'splatter movie' fame. Special effects were entrusted to Screaming Mad George. This low-budget film is based on the Rebel Studios comic books originally written by David Quinn and drawn by Tim Vigil. The storyline runs something like this: John Jaspers is an artist whose muse, an illegal immigrant, is brutally murdered in his presence by a group of gangsters. John is on the point of throwing himself off a bridge when M offers him the power of revenge in return for his soul. John accepts and carries out an act of vengeance, but then tries to renege on the contract. M insists that the commitment is for life; John Jaspers must accept that he is obliged to work for M. After John is buried alive, he re-emerges as 'Faust', equipped with deadly powers and intent on killing everyone who gets in his way. When arrested after killing leading diplomats, he is befriended by Dr Jade de Camp. Jade, who has no womb and has been through her own private trauma when she was raped at the age of eleven, becomes his confidante. The film is a postmodern collage of visual effects lifted from the Alien movies, the Bond movies, Batman comics and *Nightmare on Elm Street*. The Faustian connections are less obvious. The pact grows out of attempted suicide and has consequences from which 'John' Faust cannot extricate himself. He is a Faustian incarnation at least in so far as he cannot be pinned down as wholly good or evil, and this comes out in the visuals, which give him a resemblance to both Superman and Dracula. As in Michael Swanwick's novel *Jack Faust*, with which there are parallels, M is using John's ambition as a means of bringing the world to a rapid end; a briefly glimpsed image of M in the company of Hitler is another reminder of the strong association Faust retains with the political villainy of twentieth-century fascism for writers of the postwar period.

Less well-known in the Anglo-Saxon world is the 'erotic' movie *Faust* (shown in Germany as *Faust im Sog des Seelenfängers*), written by Danielle Morietti and directed by Mario Salieri. The Italian original is described as *Reinterpretazione hard del Faust di Marlowe, il film racconta· il rapporto tra bene e male nelle varie epoche* ('Hardcore reinterpretation of Marlowe's *Faust*, this film describes a contest between good and evil at various points in history'). The German title screen states that the work was inspired by Goethe and Marlowe, but the connections are far from obvious, and the caption on the box actually advises purchasers to 'forget what you learned at school about Goethe's *Faust*.' There is a trimmed-down, mildly pornographic version made for the German cinema, and an uncut version. The narrative begins in the year 1358, when 'Faust Pietro' tires of endless warfare, marries Margareta, and decides to unify Germany. Mephistopheles doesn't like the sound of this and shows Faust what will come of his plans. In this respect, the film is closer to René Clair than to the classics. We now leap forward into 1961, when Germany has won the Second World War and occupied the United States. We see collaborators, such as film producer Richard, whose wife Kathy has her sights on Marilyn, who in turn is having an affair with the leader of the resistance movement. One of the main points is that Mephistopheles used the figure of a double agent called Odette to delay the allied landings and thus ensure a German victory. The plot is wholly unconvincing, and the Faustian elements were manipulated in order to give the confused, sordid and generally inane scenario a veneer of respectability. This, too, is a consequence of Faust's iconicity. As early as 1962, a French film by Georges Franju, *Les Yeux sans visage* ('Eyes without a Face', 1959) was renamed *The Horror Chamber of Dr Faustus* for the North American market for no other purpose than to add an extra frisson of terror. The villain of this piece, Professor Génessier, specialises in removing facial tissue from young women and also carries out experiments on animals. He is thus one of many deranged scientists who have acquired a Faustian label on the strength of a perversion deemed to be diabolical in the popular sense of the word. The marketing potential of the icon has long been exploited in this manner, as will become more evident in an examination of the way in which the name is used and abused in everyday life. This chapter concludes with a detailed analysis of one of the most original films ever made on the theme, Jan Švankmajer's *Faust* of 1994, in which a combination of human actors and puppets is used to emphasise Faust's manipulation by forces he seems unable to resist.

Jan Švankmajer's *Faust*
by Derek Katz

In a profile headed 'Kafka's Heir', Anthony Lane observed that 'the world is divided into two unequal camps: those who have never heard of Jan Švankmajer, and those who happen upon his work and know that they have come face to face with genius.' (Lane, 48) In the intervening decade, the latter group will have increased in size, but the Czech director still remains something of a cult figure. Švankmajer is considered one of the major artistic figures in Central Europe, but the spread of his work has been slowed by a number of factors, most obviously political repression in Eastern Europe, his participation in a specifically Czech surrealist movement, and the fact that he has worked primarily in animated film, a genre with a proud pedigree in the Czech lands, notably in the films of Jiří Trnka and Karel Zeman, but not generally thought of as a vehicle for high art in the West (Holloway, 225–51). Finally, and most importantly for the film in question, his work is closely connected to the traditions of the Czech vernacular puppet theatre, another medium more highly regarded at home than abroad. Švankmajer's *Faust* of 1994 is perhaps the best introduction to his distinctive and highly disturbing world, demonstrating both his virtuoso technique as an animator and his skill at combining different media and types of drama in a single coherent work.

Following some 25 shorts, *Faust* is Švankmajer's second feature-length film, and like most of his films, it combines animation of various sorts with live action featuring both marionettes and human actors. For convenience, I will use the terms 'marionette' and 'puppet' interchangeably, always referring to the jointed wooden figure controlled by strings, not to hand puppets. The film opens with a nameless, trench-coated figure played by Petr Čepek emerging from the Prague subway. Two men on a street corner hand out maps to passers-by. Our protagonist takes a map and eventually follows it to a run-down building, which turns out, improbably, to contain a theatre, an alchemist's laboratory and a puppet stage set, and also to connect to a bar, a busy street and to a variety of outdoor locations. He enters a dressing room, costumes and makes himself up as Faust, opens a beer, and reads a few lines from Goethe to the dressing-room mirror. From this point on, the protagonist plays the role of Faust for the remainder of the film, mostly by participating in staged versions of the story. At times, he plays Faust as a costumed human actor, sometimes on stage, sometimes behind it, at others he is part of a puppet play, eventually becoming literally incorporated into the puppet world and acquiring a puppet body. He is also thrust onto the stage in the leading role of Gounod's *Faust*, lip-synching a scene for a surprisingly untroubled and appreciative audience.

Švankmajer draws on a number of *Faust* settings. Most of the dialogue comes from the Bohemian puppet tradition, but there are also substantial borrowings from Marlowe, a couple of lines from Grabbe's *Don Juan und Faust*, six lines from Faust's first monologue in Goethe, and an excerpt from Gounod's opera. In addition, other elements from the tradition are alluded to in unspoken portions of the film, including a re-enactment of the Auerbach's Cellar scene in a Prague beer garden and an allusion to the episode with the Jew and a severed leg from the chapbook. The different texts are linked to particular modes of representation as well as to particular characters. Unsurprisingly, the marionettes are given material from the puppet play of folk tradition, while the lines from Marlowe, Goethe and Grabbe are spoken by the human protagonist. Mephisto usually appears as a plasticine head, and his dialogues with Faust are taken from Marlowe, while the Harlequin character only appears as a puppet.

Švankmajer's selection of texts aggressively disrupts the familiar canonical hierarchy. The best known of the treatments, Goethe's play, is represented by only a single short excerpt. Even this brief reference is challenged by its presentation. Čepek reads from a partially burnt script, whose physically compromised state suggests the instability of the text he is about to perform. The same charred volume will later prove to contain words by Grabbe and Marlowe. The relatively obscure Grabbe is quoted more often than Goethe, and Gounod's operatic treatment of Goethe, long considered a travesty of the play, is recreated at much greater length than its source. The text which is used most extensively, and which serves as the structural basis for the film, is the Czech puppet play. The relative prominence of Marlowe may be explained by its status as a source for the early indigenous derivatives.

That the Czech puppet play is the most privileged source must be viewed in the light of the prominent role of puppet theatre in the Czech vernacular tradition, and is related to Faust's canonical stature within that tradition as well as to Švankmajer's interest in both puppet theatre and Faust. He studied at the Division of Puppetry of Prague Academy of Performing Arts from 1954 to 1958, where his graduation project, like the Faust film, mixed puppets, actors and actors dressed as puppets. Thereafter he became a director and designer at the State Puppet Theatre in Liberec. His engagement with the Faust puppet play also goes back to his student days. Švankmajer was a puppeteer for Emil Radok's *Johannes Doktor Faust*, which won a prize at the 1959 Venice Film Festival. Three years later, he staged the folk puppet version as masked theatre at Prague's Semafor Theatre, and subsequently prepared a version for the Laterna Magika Theatre in the 1980s which was never performed (Hames (1995), 96–9).

The centrality of the puppet play appears to have caused some problems with the film's reception. Initial reviews often complained about the pacing of the film and its apparent lack of incident. Caryn James wrote in *The New York Times* that 'the result will probably be more intriguing to Švankmajer cultists than to newcomers [...] the idea presents a serious dramatic problem [...] it takes far too long for Faust to make his bargain with Mephistopheles.' Similarly, Philip Strick complained in *Sight and Sound* that 'Švankmajer's contender derives little benefit from his bargain. [...] The promised tour of Heaven and Hell never materialises, there is not so much as a glimpse of the Seven Deadly Sins, and the trip to Portugal signally fails to amuse. It seems odd that Faust's demand to 'live in all voluptuousness' remains unpursued until the cynically explicit coupling with a wooden Helen [...] it is disappointing that Švankmajer finally renders [his] quest so inconsequential, deflecting himself time and again into other rituals and amusements.' (James, 15; Strick, 40f.)

These reactions seem predicated on an assumption that Švankmajer's *Faust*, like Goethe's, Gounod's, or, to a lesser extent, Marlowe's, will follow a dramatic trajectory in which the negotiation with Mephistopheles will be a mere prelude for the real action facilitated by the demonic pact. This is a reasonable expectation, given the many well-known musical and cinematic versions descended directly from the Goethe play. In fact, Švankmajer closely follows the structure of the puppet plays, in which Act I contains the conjuration of spirits and the introduction of a Harlequin figure, the pact with Mephistopheles comes in Act II, the third act is devoted to an adventure with foreign royalty, usually either the Duke of Parma or the King of Portugal, and Faust attempts to repent, and is bribed with Helen of Troy in Act IV. Švankmajer even includes an 'intermission' between Acts II and III, where the curtain drops, the theatre audience applauds, and Faust repairs to his dressing room while members of the audience visit the snack bar.

It is therefore appropriate to view the entire film as a radical staging of the puppet play. This is what provides by far the greatest portion of the script and supplies the structure for its narrative. The strong presence of elements specifically associated with puppet play (and Marlowe) like the Harlequin figure, and the absence of those found in later canonical versions, most notably Goethe's 'Gretchen Tragedy', also emphasise the primacy of the popular derivative. In less obvious ways, even the portions of the film that seem to exist outside of the puppet-theatre world are implicated in a larger statement about the conventions of representation.

Despite the presence of so many different types of theatrical and cinematic technique in *Faust*, Švankmajer obstinately refuses to follow their conventions with any degree of consistency. At the very beginning of the film, before any animation, puppets or theatrical elements have been introduced, the absence of either dialogue or soundtrack music is both striking and disturbing. The first act chorus from Gounod's *Faust* is heard over the opening credits, music that will later prove to have a visible source in the film world. Instead of the expected dialogue, the prosaic noises of everyday life – the scraping of brooms, scuffling of shoes, and crumpling of paper, unnaturally amplified, provide all there is in the way of a soundtrack. Significantly, there are no audible words spoken in the film before Čepek clothes himself as Faust. Speech occurs as part of the various performances of *Faust*, but is absent from the narrative frame. The presence of the spoken word is thus directly linked to Čepek's assumption of the role of Faust. As he sits at a dressing table, partially transformed, his first vocalisation is a mere syllable – 'Eeh!' This vocal, but pre-verbal, utterance marks the beginning of the performed *Fausts*.

340

This moment at the start of the 'dramatic' action of the film, when the unnamed protagonist literally dons the mantle of Faust, is no more theatrical than the introduction was conventionally cinematic. Everything about the beginning of the 'play' is wrong, in some sense. The action begins backstage, in a dressing room, rather than on-stage. We see the process of dressing and making-up in detail, destroying any possible illusion of transformation. Čepek merely throws on a robe over his trenchcoat. The artificiality of the assumption is emphasised at every opportunity, from close-ups of the texture of Čepek's skin as he rubs make-up on it to the laborious application of a false beard and moustache. This also represents a slyly anti-Faustian dynamic – a slow, mechanical transformation into an old man, rather than a sudden, magical transformation of age into youth. Subjective camera work, as when the dressing room is seen from Čepek's point of view, encourages the cinema audience to see the protagonist in a filmic context rather than a theatrical one. Once we are inside Faust's cloak, we are hardly likely to be impressed by his appearance.

The first lines from Goethe are also presented in a resolutely untheatrical manner. Čepek is in costume as Faust, but he reads his lines from a script while sipping a beer, speaking to a mirror rather than projecting them to an audience. His delivery gives no hint that he is expressing his own feelings. He reads as if he has not seen the words before, and pauses in mid-sentence for another swallow of Pilsener, wiping and re-sticking his artificial beard before continuing. While there is no question that Čepek's character is a Faust figure, he can never be identified comfortably with any single instantiation of Faust, be it Goethe's, Marlowe's, Gounod's, Grabbe's or the puppet-theatre's character.

Similar troubling questions of representation persist in the scenes with the puppets. The puppet theatre first appears in an alchemist's laboratory, dropping down in front of a bemused Čepek. While it seems to be a self-sufficient theatrical space, containing some props, backdrops, and puppets, there is no obvious explanation for its sudden materialisation, nor any way to explain where it has come from. And again, there is no audience. Čepek, having removed his Faust costume, at first appears to be a spectator in relation to the puppets, but then violates the boundary between audience and stage by walking onto the puppet stage. The puppets seem to see the human actor as one of them. Puppets playing good and bad angels entreat Faust to follow them. Although both angels address Faust, there is no puppet Faust on stage, leaving Čepek as the only possible target for their speeches. He appears to accept this role and asks the puppets to fetch Cornelius and Valdes.

Despite Čepek's acquiescent entry into the puppet's physical space and dramatic world, the naturalistic potential of the puppets is consistently undermined by Švankmajer's direction, which focuses attention on the mechanical aspects of operating the puppets. We see hands moving the strings that control the puppets, a hand holding the thunder-sheet that announces the evil spirit, and heads being attached to puppet bodies. These are all commonplaces of the puppet theatre, where heads greatly outnumber bodies, but they are also exactly the devices which, in any live production, would be hidden from view in order to protect the illusion that the puppets are animate and individual. At the conclusion of the scene, Čepek, stepping out of character as Faust, kicks a marionette as if to demonstrate that it is an inanimate object.

The existence of a theatrical space in which humans and puppets can interact is disturbing enough, but the fact that there is no consistent physical relationship between the various elements in the scene is even more so. Compared to Čepek, the puppets appear to be enormous, large enough to envelope the human actor; a potential which will be realised later in the film. Compared to the hands that control them, though, the puppets are mere miniatures. The hands never appear in the same shot with Čepek, leaving the physical relationship between the body parts ambiguous. Do the puppets change size from shot to shot, or are they being operated by superhuman limbs? When asked about these enormous puppets, Švankmajer replied:

> The intention was that I wanted to get the marionettes into reality, and therefore I had to increase their size, so that they could function in a correct ration to the actors, to interact with them. The marionettes exist also in small size in a miniature theatre. That way I manage to make the viewer very insecure about the size. One moment you can see them very small, when they are led by a human hand, and in another you see them in life size. So, we are actually approaching a different dimension of reality. (Jackson, 37)

Švankmajer's relentless assault on conventions of representation and on audience expectations continues in the film's one foray into opera. In the middle of the puppet play's second act, after Mephisto has been summoned, but before the contract has been sealed, Čepek finds himself surrounded by stagehands, forcibly costumed as Faust, and pushed onto stage in the midst of a performance of Gounod's *Faust*. The music comes from a reel-to-reel tape player in the wings. We see a finger pushing the play button and setting the tape in motion, and the stage manager uses hand signals to instruct Čepek to lip-synch his part. The scene shifts to a field, where four rake-wielding ballerinas in toe-shoes rake hay amidst obviously two-dimensional stage sets. They break for a meal of soup and fall asleep. A tractor, which has been audible for most of the scene, discharges its driver, who now ogles the sleeping ballerinas.

This bizarre interlude can be read in a number of ways. The incongruous presence of the tractor in the pastoral idyll suggests a parody of Soviet musicals extolling the agricultural proletariat, with the ballerinas as the happy and productive workers.[1] The camera's lingering on individual body parts of the ballerinas (taking the point of view of the dirty old tractor operator as he leers at the sleeping dancers) invites us to see them as an inanimate collection of limbs and joints, and suggests an analogy with puppets. Similarly, Čepek, acting on stage while his voice is provided for him offstage, 'controlled' by the hands of the stage manager, becomes a human puppet of sorts.

Opera's potential for naturalistic illusion is also dealt with ruthlessly. As was the case when Čepek first clad himself as Faust, the action begins backstage, undermining the distinction between the area where theatrical illusion is produced and the wings, where the technical business that makes that illusion possible takes place. The clear separation between the mechanically reproduced voice and its human host makes it difficult to identify Čcpek as Faust, or take the words that he 'sings' as his own. This can also be understood as a comment on the frequent process of filming mimed opera by having actors simulate singing and synchronising their movements to a pre-recorded soundtrack. There was a vogue for this kind of film in Italy in the 1950s, including an *Aïda* with Sophia Loren. Carmine Gallone's *La leggenda di Faust* was mentioned above (see 325f.). More recently, the Czech director Petr Weigl has produced a series of films providing a visual component for noted opera recordings. One is his 1992 film for Mstislav Rostropovich's recording of *Lady Macbeth of Mtsensk* by Dmitri Shostakovich. In Švankmajer's *Faust* the pre-recorded soundtrack is evident, as is its means of projection. Similarly, the movement from stage to field, and the presence of stage sets in that field, conforms to neither of the most common ways of filming opera, producing neither the experience of witnessing a production in an opera house, nor taking advantage of the cinematic medium to open out the opera house and place singers in more naturalistically plausible settings. Examples of the latter type of opera film include Miklós Szinetár's film of Béla Bartók's *Bluebeard's Castle* (Decca, 1992) and Joseph Losey's version of Mozart's *Don Giovanni* (Columbia Tristar, 2002).

The operatic interlude is characteristic of Švankmajer's obsessive repetition of visual and thematic elements. The close-up of a vibrating larynx while Čepek lip-synchs refers back to an analogous emphasis on the clacking jaws of the puppets and forward to similar shots of the ballerina's throats while they eat their midday stew. Meanwhile, the latter shot establishes a link to other representations of eating and drinking in the film, and to the rest of Švankmajer's *oeuvre*, which is well-nigh obsessed with the eating – including an entire short film about eating, *Jidlo* ('Food'), made in 1992.

On a more literal level, Švankmajer stubbornly subverts most of the opera's text and stage directions. The first disturbing element is the presence of the ballerinas. They should, in the context of the opera, be singers, not dancers. Given that they are dancers, clad in stereotypical pink tutus, there is no reason for them to be wielding rakes. A somewhat similar effect was created in Ken Russell's production of Gounod's *Faust* for the Vienna State Opera in 1985, which had a particularly strong ballet component. In the scene in question, a dancer playing a servant girl sweeps out Faust's study while the chorus sings from offstage.[2] As the scene proceeds, this tension between the aesthetic and the utilitarian is reinforced by the sight of the dancers actually raking hay, albeit in stylised synchronisation, and later by the dancers' feet, in toe shoes, squishing through the mud. Instead of the ballerina as weightless, ethereal sylph, familiar from canonical nineteenth-century ballets like Adolphe Adam's *Giselle*, Švankmajer's dancers are not only earthbound, but graphically mired in muck. Even if the dancers were singing, this scene would hardly express the words of the chorus heard during their labours.

Instead of 'day, shining in its golden cloak,' we have a darkening sky, pouring rain and thunder. Instead of the trilling of songbirds, we hear squawks of domestic fowl. The words sung by Gounod's chorus end with an assertion that 'All Nature awakens to love!' The dominant image of Švankmajer's version, conversely, is of the dancers sleeping while the tractor driver lusts after them.

The analogies between human singers and dancers and wooden puppets suggested in the opera scene are just one hint of another structural element in the film. As the film progresses, Čepek becomes more puppet-like and the puppets become more human. Čepek's transformation is accomplished literally. After signing the contract with Mephisto, Čepek emerges from within a wooden case, splitting it open to escape as if from a chrysalis. Even after his emergence, though, he still retains the metal rod, screwed into the top of his head, by which he can be controlled from above. He must unscrew himself from the rod, mercifully with no visible consequences for his skull, before taking part in human activities during the interval, and screw himself back on before the play can continue after the break.

The puppets have some human properties from the beginning. One of the running jokes of the film is that the one backstage lavatory is permanently occupied by a puppet sitting on the toilet and audibly urinating. While easy to pass over as a crude joke, the situation also raises questions about the puppet's autonomy – there are no puppet master's hands in the lavatory –, and the process of excretion implies that the puppet has successfully consumed food and drink. The fact that the puppet is urinating also implies the presence of a sexual organ, an idea that will be taken up later. As the film continues, the puppets become more autonomous, running around without human aid while the tops of the controller rods are visible, and acquiring human legs. They even escape the confines of the puppet theatre, exiting to a Prague street and interacting with human bystanders, the devils rudely jostling past them, while the Harlequin figure earnestly solicits their help.

The most graphic and disturbing consequence of this blurring of the boundaries between human and puppet worlds occurs near the end of the film, when Faust pursues Helen of Troy. We have seen a puppet devil transformed into Helen, complete with a drilled hole for a vagina and a swath of pubic hair (recalling Čepek 's application of Faust's beard at the beginning of the play). When Čepek finally catches Helen, he forces himself upon her, only to discover that she is a devil in disguise, and, in a moment inescapably reminiscent of Neil Jordan's *The Crying Game*, vomits in disgust. While this is a perfectly good realisation of any of the many moments in the tradition where Faust attempts to satisfy his lust with a devil impersonating a human woman, much of the frisson of this particular scene comes from the simultaneous multiple transgressions. Faust/Čepek has had sexual congress with a devil, unknowingly committed a homosexual act, and literally violated the boundary between human and puppet. In the context of the film, this last transgression is the most disturbing.

This blurring of the distinction between human and puppet plays an allegorical role in the film. The original Czech title of Švankmajer's film is *Lekce Faust* ('The Lesson of Faust'). This lesson is, at least at one level, quite clear and is sanctioned by the director. The end of the film circles back to its beginning, suggesting that our Faust is just one of an endless cycle of Fausts, all of whom will have the same experiences, and none of whom will learn from the experiences of his predecessors. Each generation makes its own Faustian bargain. Read as a political allegory, this Faust represents the post-Velvet Revolution Czech Republic, dealing no more successfully with the seduction of free-market capitalism then it had with the oppressions of communism. Faust's transition from human to puppet represents the loss of individual agency inherent in these deals. As Švankmajer put it in an interview:

> There's no great difference between a totalitarian system, which we lived through in the '70s and '80s, and a capitalist society. The manipulations are the same, it's just the methods that differ. So the film is about the degradations of our time, and Faust is manipulated like a puppet. ('A Faust Buck'. Interview with Geoff Andrew, *Time Out*, September 1994. See also Švankmajer, xii)

Beyond this allegorical reading, though, Švankmajer is also clearly just as interested in shaking audience assumptions about cinematic and theatrical conventions as he is in questioning political pieties.

Notes

1. I am grateful to Paul Malone for this observation.
2. My thanks to Jane K. Brown for alerting me to this production.

Cited Works and Further Reading:

Russell A. Berman, 'The Masses and Margarita: Faust at the Movies', in Grimm/Hermand, 139–52.
Erik Barnouw, *The Magician and the Cinema*. New York: Oxford University Press, 1981.
Michael Billington, 'Carry on Doctor', *The Guardian*, 13 March 2002.
René Clair, *Comédies et Commentaires*. Paris: Gallimard, 1959.
—, *Four Screenplays: Le Silence est d'or, La Beauté du Diable, Les Belles-de-Nuit, Les Grandes manoeuvres*. New York: Onion Press, 1972.
Rosemarie Clausen, *Gustaf Gründgens FAUST in Bildern*. Brunswick: Westermann, 1960.
André Dabezies, *Visages de Faust au XXe siècle. Littérature, idéologie et mythe*. Paris: Presses Universitaires de France, 1967.
R.C. Dale, *The Films of René Clair*. 2 volumes. Metuchen/NJ: Scarecrow Press, 1986.
Jacques Deslandes, *Histoire comparée du cinema*. 2 volumes. Tournai: Casterman, 1966–68.
Lotte H. Eisner, *Murnau*. London: Secker and Warburg, 1973.
—, *The Haunted Screen*. London: Thames and Hudson, 1969.
Thomas Elsaesser, *Weimar Cinema and After. Germany's Historical Imaginary*. London: Routledge, 2000.
Elizabeth Ezra, *Georges Méliès. The Birth of the auteur*. Manchester: University Press, 2000.
John E. Fetzer, *Changing perceptions of Thomas Mann's Doctor Faustus: Criticism 1947–1992*. Columbia/SC: Camden House, 1996.
Carl Forch, *Der Kinematograph und das sich bewegende Bild*. Vienna: Hartleben, 1913.
Ulrich Gaier, 'Goethes Traum von einem *Faust*-Film', in *Ibid., Fausts Modernität*. Stuttgart:

Reclam, 2000, 92–136.

Reinhold Grimm and Jost Hermand, *Our Faust? Roots and ramifications of a modern German myth. 16th Wisconsin Workshop Papers.* Wisconsin: University Press, 1987.

Peter Hames, 'Czechoslovakia: 'After the Spring,'' in Daniel J. Goulding (ed.), *Post New Wave Cinema in the Soviet Union and Eastern Europe.* Bloomington: Indiana University Press, 1989, 102–42.

— (ed.), *Dark Alchemy: The Films of Jan Svankmajer.* Trowbridge: Flicks Books, 1995.

Paul Hammond, *Marvellous Méliès.* London: Gordon Fraser, 1974.

Heinrich Heining, *Goethe und der Film. Mit vielen Bildern und Dokumenten.* Baden-Baden: Neue Verlags-Anstalt, 1949.

Stephen Herbert and Luke McKernan (eds), *Who's Who of Victorian Cinema.* London: British Film Institute, 1996.

Ronald Holloway, 'The Short Film in Eastern Europe: Art and Politics of Cartoons and Puppets,' in David W. Paul (ed.), *Politics, Art and Commitment in the Eastern European Cinema.* New York: St. Martin's Press, 1983, 225–51.

Theodore Huff, *An Index to the Films of F. W. Murnau.* London: Sight and Sound, 1948.

Wendy Jackson, 'The Surrealist Conspirator: An Interview with Jan Svankmajer', *Animation World Magazine* 2.3 (June 1997), 34–9.

Caryn James, 'A Passive Faust Goes to the Devil Slowly,' *New York Times*, 26 November 1994, Section C, 15.

Oskar Kalbus, *Vom Werden Deutscher Filmkunst, 1.Teil: Der Stumme Film.* Altona-Bahrenfeld: Cigaretten-Bilderdienst, 1935.

Rudi Kost, 'Dr Fäustchen oder die (De-)Montage der Attraktionen. Gedanken zur *Doktor Faustus*-Verfilmung von Franz Seitz und zu Literaturverfilmungen überhaupt', in Rudolf Wolff (ed.), *Thomas Manns Doktor Faustus und die Wirkung.* Bonn: Bouvier, 1983, 27–46.

Anthony Lane, 'Kafka's Heir', *The New Yorker*, 31 October 1994, 48.

Mira Liehm and Antonin J. Liehm, *The Most Important Art: Eastern European Film after 1945.* Berkeley: University of California Press, 1977.

Martin Loiperdinger (ed.), *Oskar Messter. Filmpionier der Kaiserzeit.* Basel: Stroemfeld, 1994.

Thomas Mann, *Briefe 1937–1947*, ed. Erika Mann, Frankfurt/M: Fischer, 1963.

Charles Musser, *Edison motion pictures, 1890–1900. An annotated filmography.* New York: Smithsonian Institution Press, 1997.

Helen Peters, '*The Adventure of Faustus Bidgood*: Deconstructing Faust', Lecture, Prague, 2003 [unpublished transcript].

Hans Helmut Prinzler (ed.), *Friedrich Wilhelm Murnau – Ein Melancholiker des Films.* Berlin: Bertz-Verlag, 2003.

Ernst Prodolliet, *Faust im Kino. Die Geschichte des Faustfilms von den Anfängen bis in die Gegenwart.* Fribourg/Switzerland: University Press, 1978.

David Robinson, *Georges Méliès: Father of Film Fantasy.* London: BFI/MOMI, 1993.

Eric Rohmer, *L'Organisation de l'espace dans le «Faust» de Murnau.* Paris : Union Général d'Editions, 1977.

Georg Seesslen, *Faust – Materialien zu einem Film von Peter Gorski.* Duisburg: Atlas Film, 1992.

Gabriele Seitz (ed.), *Doktor Faustus. Ein Film von Franz Seitz nach dem Roman von Thomas Mann.* Frankfurt/M: Fischer, 1982.

Philip Strick, 'Faust', *Sight and Sound*, 10/1994, 40f.

Jan Švankmajer, *Švankmajer's Faust: The Script, including a preface by the author and excerpts from his diary during filming.* Translated by Valerie Mason. Trowbridge: Flick Books, 1996.

Paolo Cerchi Usai (ed.), *A trip to the movies: Georges Méliès, Filmmaker and Magician (1861–1938).* Rochester/NY: Eastman House, 1991.

A.L. Zambrano, *Horror in Film and Literature.* 2 volumes. New York: Gordon Press, 1978.

Chapter Ten

Faust Globalised

They also want to mount a production of my *Faust*, to which I respond passively, or rather, in pain. Yet I cannot have any worries about this play, because Duke Bernhard found a copy of it in the possession of a native tribesman in North Carolina.— Goethe, letter to Carl Friedrich Zelter, 28 March 1829.

The Anglo-Saxon World

A SPECIAL RELATIONSHIP between Faust and Britain has existed since earliest times. The original Faust Book was imported and translated within a few years, maybe even within months of its appearance in Frankfurt. As we have seen, its English translator strove to improve on the original, with the result that it quickly became a 'hit' in London, whose sophisticated audiences looked upon Germany as the natural home of weird supernatural and magical occurrences (Herford, 173). It was left to English players to export the new product, as re-fashioned by Christopher Marlowe, back across the sea to its land of origin and there keep it alive in a variety of renderings. England produced its own Wagner Books, which continued the story in a more entertaining and less didactic manner than did the German Wagner Books, and the pantomimes of the early eighteenth century ensured that the doctor's name was remembered in British thespian circles. Both Lessing and Goethe looked to England and emulated the Elizabethan theatre in their efforts to revive drama in their own country. Other figures from English literature, from Robert Greene's Friar Bacon to Lord Byron's Manfred and Cain, owe key features to the tradition. Greene's *Friar Bacon and Friar Bungay* of c. 1590 may actually have been a parody of Marlowe's *Faustus*. Byron was inspired to create his Faustian heroes after Matthew 'Monk' Lewis had visited him in Villa Diodati near Lake Geneva and given an impassioned reading from Goethe's work. The cross-currents are too numerous and too complex to list.

The first public production of *Faust I* was seen in London four years before its German première, and although it must be said that the Drury Lane versions of 1825 were invasive adaptations, so, too, were the later German ones that were mounted, despite initial opposition, from 1829 onwards in Brunswick, Weimar and elsewhere. It was in London that Eugène Delacroix saw *Faust* and was inspired to produce his uniquely effective illustrations. Repeatedly during that century, British theatres and opera houses commissioned new Fausts for their own purposes; Spohr's opera was recast for Covent Garden in 1852, and Gounod's *Faust* was made famous not only in France but also as a result of its success on the English stage.

One of the most elaborate and profitable theatre productions of *Faust* of all time was that devised by Henry Irving for the Lyceum Theatre in 1885, which played to capacity audiences for two years on both sides of the Atlantic. London was also notorious for its gross parodies of the play. These can be traced back to the seventeenth century; and from then to the present there have probably been as many comic re-castings and travesties of Faustus' adventures as there have been serious updates. A large collection of Victorian playbills held by the Templeman Library in Canterbury shows that virtually every theatre in Britain, from those patronised by royalty in the capital to the smallest variety theatre in the provinces, offered an endless string of romps with titles like *Faust and Imogene* (The New Theatre, Greenwich, 1866), *Faust and the Pupils* (Royal Foresters' Music Hall, 1875), and *Faust and Marguerite, or The Devil's Draught* (Royal Olympic Playhouse, London, 1866). The light-hearted tone is evidenced in the way Faust is described in the latter: 'Fond of magical tricks, but left in a fix,/ Why black is not white, and this is not t'other,/ And with all his researches still left in the lurch is,/ About metaphysics and such kind of bother.' The character-list includes not only the familiar Doctor, Marguerite, Martha, Mephistopheles, Brander and the Poodle, but also Brandynose, Froth, and an assortment of young girls calling themselves Miss Prim, Miss Bitemsly, Miss Stuckup and Miss Overnice. One may speculate as to how much or how little these pot-pourris owed to the classics to which they made reference. It is in the nature of the material that parody and adaptation cannot always be distinguished, but complement one another in strange ways. Marlowe, whom we now number among the high-minded adapters, was also the first to travesty the doctor's self-inflicted plight and to furnish bumbling dolts as his would-be disciples. In what follows it will not always be possible to separate satirical from sober re-workings. What remains beyond doubt is that Faust has a global presence and that his endurance as an icon in areas remote from his origins has produced many curious adaptations that cast light on the cultures that adopted the story no less than on the source material itself. The plays by Thurmond and Rich have been mentioned above; they were clearly conceived as light-hearted *divertissements*, but not all English authors used the material for mere entertainment. Soane, Rede, and Plunkett were more serious in their approach to the theme; *Faust, or the Demon of the Drachenfels* by Plunkett ends with multiple murders in the manner of *Hamlet*. Philip James Bailey's *Festus* of 1839 attempted to retell the story in modern, that is to say, Byronic verse, adding a dash of fashionable liberal theology and Victorian social and political aspirations. The final edition of 1889 runs to 39,159 lines, which is more than three times the length of Goethe's two-part drama. *Festus* appeared in 52 editions between 1839 and 1889. A later attempt to fashion a new tragedy out of what Goethe had written was *Gretchen*, a four-act play by William Gilbert, better known today for his collaboration with the composer Arthur Sullivan. It opened to high hopes by the author on 24 March 1879 at London's Olympic Theatre. Despite having recently embarked on his celebrated partnership with Sullivan – *HMS Pinafore* had premièred a year earlier – Gilbert still thought himself to be a serious dramatist in his own right: 'I consider the two best plays I ever wrote were *Broken Hearts* and a version of the Faust legend called *Gretchen*. I took immense pains over my *Gretchen*, but it only ran a fortnight. I wrote it to please myself, and not the public.' (Schirmer-Imhoff, 163–66; How, 339)

In Gilbert, Faustus' dilemma is that he withdrew from the world as a monk when the woman he loved left him for someone richer than himself ('I sickened of the world and woman's love,/ And here sought refuge', Gilbert, II, 157). The monk's cell rather than the scholar's study has become his 'sanctuary', from where he cursed the world and all the women in it. Yet it soon becomes clear that he is no happier in his new vocation:

> No hope! no hope! no hope! For life entombed –
> For life cut off from life – a breathing man,
> Wrapped in a winding-sheet of his own weaving!
> A living heart, inurned and sepulchred! (*Op. cit.*, 156)

He can no longer be happy in either the Church or the secular world since he is out of sympathy with the values of both. His erstwhile friend, Gottfried, draws his attention to a pure young orphan, Gretchen, in the hope that she will help him to transcend his world-weary contempt for life. Mephistopheles, who introduces himself as 'A travelling clock-cobbler, who repairs/ The moral time-piece when it's out of order' (II, 160), confirms what Faustus has heard of Gretchen's purity:

> I know a maid,
> A fair and gentle girl – the pink and bloom
> Of all that's loveliest in maidenhood,
> Whose simple truth and pure and blameless life
> Have done my cause more harm in eighteen years
> Than all the monks in Christendom could mend! (*Op. cit.*, 162f.)

The most obviously Goethean influence in this, other than the girl's name and qualities, is seen in Act II, with its double flirtation scene involving Martha and Mephistopheles in parallel with Faust and Gretchen (II, 174–81). But Gretchen is horrified to learn that Faustus has taken clerical vows and summarily rejects him in favour of Gottfried, who re-appears, determined, like Valentine in Goethe and Gounod, to seek revenge. Faustus is quite willing to let Gottfried kill him for what he has done but the dying Gretchen intervenes to save him from death and to direct his penance:

> Thou shalt atone, for thou hast greatly sinned –
> Thou shalt atone with worthy deeds lifelong;

Thou shalt atone with steadfast, humbled heart,
With faith, and truth, and works of charity.
Atone with life – with brave and blameless life,
And not with coward death. Resign thyself. (*op. cit.*, 200)

The action revolves, in Faustian style, around a dilemma between the spiritual and the secular realms; Faustus is once again the lonely outsider figure who seeks integration into life but cannot achieve it due to powerful inner torments, a cynic who is nonetheless prepared to forsake the world for the life of a hermit, a hermit who retains a sentimental craving for the love of a pure woman.

Dorothy L. Sayers' *The Devil to Pay* of 1939 is a Faust drama that has been likened to Marlowe's and Goethe's work. (Spivack, 946f.) The Angel Azrael intercedes, at the end of Faust's conventionally wicked life, in various unlikely ways, for example by substituting a little black dog for his soul. Eventually, he is handed over to Mephistopheles, but only to do temporary penance in purgatory before his eventual redemption. This is one of a small number of modern plays that attempt to maintain a Christian focus on Faust, albeit from a conciliatory Catholic perspective. Other Catholic writers have found aspects of the theme worthy of attention. Although not strictly on the Faust theme, C. S. Lewis' *The Screwtape Letters* of 1942 makes many references to the tempting of mortals by devils, in this case, a sinisterly benevolent uncle, 'Screwtape', who instructs his young nephew 'Wormwood' in the art of winning souls. A series of letters reveal to the novice where the humans' weakest points may be found and how best to engage with them in the perennial struggle to defeat the 'Enemy' on high. Screwtape's arguments show a not uncommon tendency to associate advances in technology with the diabolical, and pick up the twentieth-century 'Faustian' commonplace that science is ultimately destructive. Speaking of man's commitment to the notion of his own perfectibility, Screwtape observes:

> So inveterate is their appetite for Heaven that our best method, at this stage, of attaching them to earth is to make them believe that earth can be turned into Heaven at some future date by politics or eugenics or 'science' or psychology, or what not. (Lewis, 144)

Ever more vivid examples are provided of the supposed association of sin and science in the 'Fausts' of the postwar period, from René Clair to Michael Swanwick. It is the gentle path that leads downwards to hell, and murder may in the end be no more effective than a game of cards, if cards can do the trick. 'The safest road to Hell is the gradual one – the gentle slope, soft underfoot, without sudden turnings, without milestones, without signposts' (Lewis, 65) – in short, the career of many Fausts whose involvement with Mephistopheles seems so casual as to blind them to the extent of their subservience to him. Yet here, as in an increasing number of modern updates, the tempter fails – in part, because he is a mere apprentice, but in part also because man is stronger than he himself imagines. Goethe's Mephistopheles may have been confident of his own success, but later devils are caught up in bureaucratic processes and will reap revenge from their masters if they fail; here the unfortunate Wormwood must fear not only the 'House of Correction for Incompetent Tempters' (Lewis, 111), but also the sinister designs of his 'affectionate Uncle'.

Some nineteenth-century 'Faustines' were discussed above (155–7), and while these have not exactly flourished during the twentieth century, Irmtraud Morgner in Germany and Emma Tennant in Britain have made efforts to accommodate the genre to the present. Tennant's *Faustine* dates from 1992. Here the narrator's grandmother, a 48-year-old 'sad menopausee' by the name of Muriel Tyman, walks into a television showroom and is offered, casually, a hire purchase contract along with a pact that includes rejuvenation and wish-fulfilment: 'And you can get your youth back. For twenty-four years. Not bad, eh?' This is achieved via the Summerfield beauty farm, the modern equivalent to the Witch's Kitchen. She then becomes the pop idol 'Lisa Crane'. In the dénouement, the devil gets to tell his side of the story and admits that the contract cannot be enforced, as he who was responsible for setting it up must accept that souls such as Muriel's are of negligible value to the infernal powers. It is not possible for a soul to exist within a consumerist universe. (Tennant, 137, 72, 139; Doering, 285–90)

North American Fausts

The Faust legend enjoys a curiously close relationship to North America, and it has recently been claimed that 'nowhere outside Germany has Faust appeared so frequently or in such variegated forms as in the United States' (Grim, II, 141; see also Ziolkowski, 153). It is simultaneously appropriate and inappropriate for an understanding of the American character. The English Faust chapbook was among the most popular books in Puritan areas. Invoices of Boston booksellers show that *The History of the Damnable Life and Deserved Death of Dr. John Faustus* outsold all books other than the Bible, hymnals, and a few school textbooks in seventeenth-century New England (Wright, 121–3). Many still follow Luther in seeing the devil as a real character who is constantly pitted against all that is good, and this belief lives on among several of today's political leaders, as recent talk of an 'Evil Empire' and an 'Axis of Evil' demonstrates. It is in the Puritan heartland of New England that many of America's most 'Faustian' works came into existence. In 1692, Cotton Mather made the following observation:

> The *New-Englanders* are a People of God settled in those, which were once the *Devil's* Territories; and it may easily be supposed that the *Devil* was exceedingly disturbed, when he perceived such a People here accomplishing the Promise of old made unto our Blessed Jesus, *That he should have the Utmost parts of the Earth for His Possession.* [...] We have been advised by some Credible Christians yet alive, that a Malefactor, accused of *Witchcraft* as well as *Murder,* and Executed in this place more than Forty Years ago, did then give Notice of, An Horrible PLOT *against the Country by* WITCHCRAFT, *and a Foundation of* WITCHCRAFT *then laid, which if it were not seasonably discovered would probably Blow up, and pull down all the Churches in the Country.* And we have now

with Horror seen the *Discovery* of such a *Witchcraft!* An Army of *Devils* is horribly broke in upon the place which is the *Center*, and after a sort, the *First-born* of our *English* Settlements; and the Houses of the Good People there are fill'd with the doleful Shrieks of their Children and Servants, Tormented by Invisible Hands, with Tortures altogether preternatural. After the Mischiefs there Endeavoured, and since in part Conquered, the terrible Plague, of *Evil Angels*, hath made its Progress into some other places, where other Persons have been in like manner Diabolically handled. These our poor Afflicted Neighbours, quickly after they become *Infected* and *Infested* with these *Dæmons*, arrive to a Capacity of Discerning those which they conceive the *Shapes* of their Troublers; and notwithstanding the Great and Just Suspicion, that the *Dæmons* might impose the *Shapes* of Innocent Persons in their *Spectral Exhibitions* upon the Sufferers [...] yet many of the Persons thus Represented, being Examined, several of them have been Convicted of a very Damnable *Witchcraft*: yea more than One *Twenty* have *Confessed*, that they have Signed unto a Book, which the Devil show'd them, and Engaged in his Hellish Design of *Bewitching*, and *Ruining* our Land. (Mather, 13-15)

Nathaniel Hawthorne was familiar with such writings, in which there is ample evidence of the morbid fears that assailed the Puritan conscience in much the same way as they pitted themselves against Luther. Over one hundred years later, when Goethe's works became known in North America, they had great influence on the intellectual climate. Longfellow analysed them in depth at Harvard and planned to write a 'New England Faust' in which the old indigenous Puritan tradition would be enriched with Goethean wisdom. The age of witch hunts was over, but in the new conflicts between forces such as Calvinism and Unitarianism, *Faust* seemed to 'shadow forth the soul of the age', as Margaret Fuller put it, and to point a way forward. Hawthorne himself was quick to recognise the dangers of erecting a new temple of faith on the uncertain foundations of a misunderstood idealism imported from Germany. (Fiedler, 125f; Long, 116f; Stein, 23-34)

Although no pacts as such are ever concluded in Hawthorne's stories and novels, they do examine the effect of the Faustian bargain on New England folk, who when tempted to go against God in private bring about their own fall and damnation. Fanshawe is an early example of such an obsession, intoxicated as he is by a dream of all-embracing knowledge and undying fame. In 'Peter Goldthwaithe's Treasure', the figure of 'Old Scratch' is introduced in situations that look back to Irving and forward to Benét; Peter wrecks his uncle's house in search of legendary treasure, only to find it in a form that is of no use. 'Dr. Heidegger's Experiment' ushers the reader into a combination of Faust's study and a witch's kitchen, complete with a magic mirror showing the doctor's deceased patients. A rejuvenation of sorts takes place, but such is the exuberance of the newly restored men that they destroy the very elixir that contained the gift of youth. Even those characters who resist, like Young Goodman Brown, have to learn the bitter truth at the heart of Puritan history: that their fathers and forefathers were in league with evil while posing as upright citizens. Here the devil can claim, 'I have been as well acquainted with your family as with ever a one among the Puritans; and that's no trifle to say. I helped your grandfather, the constable, when he lashed the Quaker woman so smartly through the streets of Salem; and it was I that brought your father a pitch-pine knot, kindled at my own hearth, to set fire to an Indian village, in King Philip's war. They were my good friends, both' (Hawthorne, 136). Brown, too, is ultimately destroyed by his desire for hidden knowledge.

Many other American writers were experimenting with aspects of the Faust theme. Washington Irving's story 'The Devil and Tom Walker' is an example of an attempt to locate the legend in New England, with Walker selling his soul in order to find buried gold (Irving, VII, 393–419). Another New England author, Louisa M. Alcott, wrote a psychological thriller *A Modern Mephistopheles*, which appeared anonymously in 1877. It was clearly influenced by Goethe. Alcott admitted 'It has been simmering since I read *Faust* last year. Enjoyed doing it, being tired of providing moral pap for the young' (Alcott, vi). Felix Canaris, a nineteen-year-old on the brink of starvation, desperate to be a famous poet, comes under the malignant influence of Jasper Helwyze, a mysterious old man who offers him literary success in exchange for total subjugation in a bizarre psychological experiment. Drugs, homosexuality and other practices not normally alluded to by this sentimental children's author feature in what is ultimately an indictment of male domination over women: Canaris' beloved, a radiantly pure girl called Gladys, dies at the end when she recognises the extent to which her friend had been corrupted by Helwyze.

Stephen Vincent Benét's story 'The Devil and Daniel Webster' was first published in the *Saturday Evening Post* in 1936. It is the best-known American re-working of the Faustian tradition; it quickly caught the public imagination and brought its author national recognition. Within five years it had been made into a play, an opera, with music by Douglas Moore, and a film. Here there is little trace of the gloomy, snake-infested swamps of Irving's 'The Devil and Tom Walker'. The attitude exhibited by the local New England folk hero Webster reflects a gung-ho confidence; he easily demonstrates that the devil can be dispatched by receiving a kick in the backside, never to be seen again, at least not in the State of New Hampshire: 'For if two New Hampshiremen aren't a match for the devil, we might as well give the country back to the Indians,' as Webster puts it (Benét, 37). The presiding judge in the trial is called Justice Hathorne, almost certainly a tribute to Nathaniel Hawthorne, one of whose forebears, John Hathorne, had been a witch-hunting judge (Stein, 13). The jury consists of no-gooders with names like 'Teach the Pirate' and 'Murderous Reverend John Smeet'. Patriotic pride in the rightness of the United States' justice system comes out here – such is the power of the legal process that it could even annul a pact with the devil. Yet it also touches on some uncomfortable home truths:

'Well, I never yet heard of the dev – of your claiming American citizenship,' said Dan'l Webster with surprise.

'And who with better right?' said the stranger, with one of his terrible smiles. 'When the first wrong was done to the first Indian, I was there. When the first slaver put out for the Congo, I stood on her deck. Am I not in your books and stories and beliefs, from the first settlements on? Am I not spoken of, still, in every church in

New England? 'Tis true the North claims me for a Southerner, and the South for a Northerner, but I am neither. I am merely an honest American like yourself – and of the best descent – for, to tell the truth, Mr. Webster, though I don't like to boast of it, my name is older in this country than yours.' (Benét, 39)

The story was much expanded in William Dieterle's movie (see 322f., above, and Grim, II, 146–159). The character of Stone comes across as weak by comparison with the magisterial orator in both versions; yet Jabez's – the name is similar to Job's – weakness is also his strength: he sells his soul to the devil not for knowledge, but in order to attain his fair place in the American dream of 'self-made' prosperity. What the story shows is that he cannot achieve this on his own; the strong helping hand of Webster is an essential when it comes to fending off evil. This is brought out even more strongly in the film, where where Stone must choose either to surrender to evil or join a farmer's union or 'Grange'.

The protagonist of Jack Kerouac's semi-autobiographical novel *Doctor Sax: Faust Part Three*, Ti Jean Duluoz, is a quintessential outsider from a French-speaking Canadian background who is searching for an American identity. The quest is not dissimilar to Faust's. Duluoz embodies American culture before the quest begins; as an aficionado of jazz, baseball, and Hollywood movies he would appear to be on track for full integration. But he still feels marginalised. In the company of Dr Sax, a wizard figure modelled in part on Faust and in part on William Burroughs, TJD travels around America in 'road movie' style, moving back into his own childhood and forward towards adulthood and drug-induced visions. Dr Sax is central to the novel, 'a sort of contemporary magus, pitted in cosmological struggle, with the whole conscious universe at stake. To Jack, the Burroughs-Sax figure represented the last incarnation of what Spengler had called 'Faustian man'. TJD and Sax visit a convention of vampires held at Snake Hill Castle in anticipation of the appearance of the Great Snake of the World. At the end, the apocalypse is averted, as the snake is destroyed by a bird in a manner that recalls both Nietzsche and ancient Aztec mythology, whereupon Dr Sax mutters, with characteristic American nonchalance, 'I'll be damned.' (Clark, 110; Grim, II, 39–45; Ziolkowski, 161–4)

Michael Swanwick's *Jack Faust* of 1997 begins in late-mediaeval Wittenberg. Tired of learning and disillusioned by the flaws he has found in Ptolemy, Aristotle and the Bible, 'Jack' Faust does what Marlowe's hero only promised: he sets fire to his accumulated tomes and thereupon commends himself to an invisible spirit who offers him total knowledge. This Mephistopheles presents himself as a devil of a new type: a construct from a parallel universe, commanded by a succession of its inhabitants. This idea derived from science fiction is not at variance with the older traditions. Goethe's and all other demons and spirits come from what can be described as an alternative dimension. They are inherently unstable. They change their shape and their gender. Goethe signals as much in *Faust II*, when Mephistopheles temporarily becomes Phorkyas, and other authors, from Heine onwards, have feminised the devil in whole or in part. Swanwick's Mephistopheles offers a compelling explanation for his rapid shape-shifting. The universe from

354

which s/he derives runs at a faster speed and at a higher ambient temperature than ours, and thus the successive 'devils' are forever burning themselves out and being replaced. The motivation to destroy this world through Faust is provided by the aliens' jealous hatred of our seemingly stable but unknowing contentment. They themselves are so far in advance of Faust's mediaeval learning as to offer him instant knowledge that permits him to transform the world. For the worse, inevitably.

The pact, if such it is, involves a contest between the Mephistophelean aliens who want to see the earth destroyed before they themselves perish and the scholar who hopes that he can use infinite knowledge for betterment of his own species.

> 'If you were dying, Magister Faustus, and a cockroach chanced to scuttle upon the bedside table, an inch from your clenched fist, and you knew it would live to see the dawn denied you – what would you do?'
>
> Faust's eyes felt dry and gritty. It was painful just to keep them open. A ferocious anger rose within his breast at all the human race for having within it the potential to create the grotesquerie before him. Bastards! Weaklings! Were it not for their failings, their undisciplined appetite for cruelty and destruction, he could achieve in an instant such insight and enlightenment as all the philosophers of the ages had sought and been denied. Knowledge without limit was his for a word.
>
> 'Surely,' he cried, 'this is not inevitable. Surely humanity could take the knowledge you offer and use it to ennoble itself. Surely they could apply it wisely and without folly.'
>
> 'They could,' Mephistopheles said dryly. 'But will they?' (Swanwick, 32)

The contest is, as so often in the history of the legend, a grossly unequal one. From the outset Mephistopheles indicates that a transformed world will not be a better one, much as happened in René Clair's film *La Beauté du diable*, but unlike the latter's Henri Faust, Jack perseveres, even when the image of Auschwitz is put before him. As in *Faust II*, a productive industrialised society is his aim; but unlike Goethe, who does not show its implementation, Swanwick makes the mediaeval world change into the modern over a few short years, with horrific consequences. In the end, we have Faust himself transformed into Hitler, in a manner that appears to recycle the Faustian equation with Germany's political destiny as devised by Thomas Mann, except that here it is not his infatuation with art but the pursuit of science, fame and wealth that has motivated him. The novel ends with words similar to those spoken by Mann's narrator '"God help them!" he cried. "God help them all".' (Swanwick, 337)

Swanwick's familiarity with the earlier Faust traditions runs deep, and his is panoramic presentation of a late mediaeval world thrown into chaos by a deluge of new inventions is close to the original theme. (Ziolkowski, 178–81) Plague sweeps across the land, as it did in Murnau's film, and Faust vies with Luther when, in one of the many humorous touches, he brushes aside the theses that are pinned to the door of the Schlosskirche in Wittenberg, replacing them with a labour of his own, his 'Periodic Table of the Elements'. Faust's journey through history has him appear, by turns, as Luther, Leonardo, Darwin, Marconi and

Hitler, while remaining Faust, so much so that Swanwick can offer his own intriguing explanations of earlier 'Faustian' mysteries, such as why the girl he loved should be called 'Margarete' in some scenes and 'Gretchen' in others. Speed is at the heart of this novel, as it was in so many earlier Fausts; indeed, many inventions that were associated with Faust from earliest times (paved roads, printing, fruits out of season, paper money) are attributed to him here, except that Faust's dystopian race through the centuries is incomparably faster and more devastating than ever before.

GEVERS: Your most recent novel, *Jack Faust*, presents an exceedingly grim vision of history and human nature. Are you increasingly a pessimist?

SWANWICK: No, in fact I've grown increasingly optimistic with age. But *Jack Faust* was a grim story, and once the identification has been made of Faust with Hitler, the story's logic flows only in one direction. In some ways this book is my argument with Goethe. On that level, I wanted to accomplish two things: to give Margarete her own voice, and her own tragedy; and to revoke Faust's salvation. Goethe was writing in the Age of Enlightenment, of course, and Faust's divine discontent looks very different to us from the far side of the Holocaust. In Trevor-Roper's *The Last Days of Hitler*, he quoted Hitler as saying, in the bunker, 'Afterwards, one regrets having been so kind.' So he too was unable to find content in the moment. But that fact does nothing to redeem him in my eyes.

GEVERS: It seems to me that in *Jack Faust* you use alternate history much as Bruce Sterling and William Gibson did in *The Difference Engine* (1990), accelerating the rate of technological 'advance' in past centuries as a way of highlighting present and future dangers posed by that tendency.

SWANWICK: Yes, and I have to say that compressing five hundred years of technological history into a single life-span was enormous fun. Doing so makes manifest a lot of trends of the past half-millennium, particularly the fact that a lot of our difficulties with this flood of new technologies arose from the fact that they came up too fast for people to react to them wisely. That's really a lot of what the novel is about – wisdom and its lack.

I'd argue, though, that because it's simply not possible to condense so much industrial development into a single lifetime (and I was deliberately vague about exactly how many years Faust spends in England, for exactly this reason), *Jack Faust* is not really an alternate history, but a fable. I meant it, in part, to be a cautionary tale for scientists. Oppenheimer recorded that when he saw the first atomic blast, at Trinity, he thought about the line from the *Bhagavad-Gita*, 'I am become death, destroyer of worlds.' I found that quite moving, that this physicist would have such a broad educational background, and that it would be of use in putting his experience into perspective. I wanted to write about intellectual arrogance and the wilful blindness to consequences in such a way as to be useful to those who might find themselves in analogous situations.

GEVERS: In adapting the Faust legend for an SF novel, how did you alter it?

SWANWICK: I'm not sure it *is* an SF novel, though I'm as satisfied with that label as any. I wrote it not knowing whether it was SF or Fantasy, and when it came out, its American publisher packaged it as Mainstream, and its British publisher as Horror. What I did was to move the legend into a materialistic universe. Mephistopheles is of course an artificial construct, a fictive device of an alien race living in a radically different universe from ours. That was done first of all to remove God from the equation – and you'll note that once Faust is converted to atheism, the word 'God' disappears entirely from the book, to reappear only on the final page – because in a

Christian universe there can be, properly speaking, no tragedies. Secondly, I wanted to write the story that Christopher Marlowe began but didn't follow through on. I wanted a story about a man who sells his soul for knowledge, and then is by that knowledge damned. So I made the alien race intangible on our plane, able to influence events only through the medium of information. And of course, I played out the story on the stage of the cumulative history between Faust's time and our own.

On a literal level, I took enormous freedoms. I wanted the novel to open in Wittenberg, so Faust could nail the Periodic Table of the Elements to the cathedral door, but the very first thing I discovered in my researches was that Wittenberg was far too small for my purposes. So I multiplied its population by four. You can't do that in non-fabulist fiction. In that genre, however, nothing is forbidden.

The alterations were simple. The adherences, however, were complex. There is an enormous amount of Faust-legendry, and I mined it freely for my own purposes. The quite grotesque scene near the end, where Faust torments a young Jewish couple, is only different from similar scenes in early collections of Faust tales in that it's not meant to be funny. The rhyme scheme in Goethe's Faust was borrowed from Hans Sachs, the author of 'The Wittenberg Nightingale,' propagandiser for Martin Luther, and the man who ended a rhymed history of Nuremberg with the couplet, 'A pleasant thought to end this ditty/There's not a Jew left in the city.' So I took Sachs' 'limping meter' and used it to write the booklet Margarete is given, describing a prostaglandin abortion. Which rhyme is signed 'A.S.' because in the nineteenth century the poet Anna Swanwick translated Goethe into English. All of which is pointless fun, perhaps, but fun nonetheless. ('The Literary Alchemist. An Interview with Michael Swanwick' by Nick Gevers, *Infinity Plus* website)

This novel, beside many other fictional biographies of Faust, not only updates the narrative but also attempts to give explanations for some of the unsolved mysteries in the sources. Several authors have provided their own explanations for some of the curious details of the plot. Goethe's use of two names for Gretchen/Margarete is accounted for by the English novelist Robert Nye by making them twins, although in Nye's well-researched picaresque novel the pair spend more time serving Wagner's sexual needs than they do with Faust. Swanwick, by contrast, makes Gretchen switch between the two names according to her changing moods. Nye relates the story of Faust's death from Christopher ('Kit') Wagner's perspective, turning it into an action-filled travelogue in which a foul-smelling, drunken Faust embarks on a nightmarish pilgrimage to Rome in the company of a sanctimoniously pious Helen, a stray dog called Satan, a clairvoyant monkey, Akercocke, the narrator/diarist Wagner, and seven more or less nymphomaniac ex-virgins, all derived with impeccable authenticity from the chapbook tradition. The object of this journey is one of many mysteries surrounding Nye's Faust, who differs from most of his predecessors in that he is not content to remain in his study and wait for the devil to claim his soul. We are kept guessing as to his strategy. Is the purpose of this journey to try to seek the Pope's blessing and forgiveness, or does Faust intend to murder him in return for an extension to the pact, which is due to run out in a matter of days? In the course of this journey, many traditional events are presented in a new light, including several meta-textual matters such as Tritheim's letter, not to mention the familiar anecdotes about Faust cheating innkeepers and money-lenders. Nye's *Faust* is thus a fast-moving pseudo-historical tale of suspense constructed in irreverent fashion from a close reading of many sources, taking in not only the chapbook, but the life of Luther, Calvin, and several Popes.

Three Irish Fausts

In 1892, William Butler Yeats published a partly symbolic, partly social drama, *The Countess Cathleen*, which gave the Faustian pact a new dimension that related it to the troubled history of Ireland. Starving peasants are tempted to sell their souls to two demons in exchange not for knowledge but for the barest necessities of life. The aristocratic Countess Cathleen comes to hear of what is about to happen and offers up her own soul to the devils not on her behalf but in order to benefit the entire population. Upon her death, with the populace now saved from starvation, she does not forfeit her soul since it was so obviously dedicated to a noble purpose. As in so many modern Fausts, motivation is the key to the outcome, and a pact concluded with the devil for altruistic purposes meets not with a string of catastrophes, as it did in Klinger's version of 1790, but with annulment and a just reward. This moving verse drama is both a tribute to Maud Gonne and a stirring document of Irish nationalism; yet ironically, it was not accepted by the predominantly Catholic audiences until, years later, Yeats was persuaded to remove some of the pagan Celtic elements.

An *Irish Faustus. A Morality in Nine Scenes* was the third play by the highly acclaimed novelist, poet and translator Lawrence Durrell, written at the behest of a German theatre company headed by Luigi Malipiero, an Italian entrepreneur who settled in the small town of Sommerhausen on the River Main, where he ran Germany's smallest theatre, the so-called 'Torturmtheater'. Here, in front of an audience of just fifty people, Malipiero presented a mixture of old and new plays, in which he acted and for which he designed sets and painted scenery. Malipiero had a special interest in *Faust* and produced a further seven versions, from Marlowe to Valéry, in addition to Durrell's. *An Irish Faustus* was given over one hundred performances in a translation by Ursula Schuh during 1966, and was also shown to invited audiences in Heilbronn, receiving praise and criticism at both venues. (Fraser, 109)

Like *The Countess Cathleen*, Durrell's play is set in a mythical semi-Christian, semi-pagan Ireland. Faustus is seen instructing Princess Margaret of Galway in the art of gaining self-knowledge through mystical visions. He seems torn between black and white magic, opting eventually for the latter in contrast to his mentor Trimethius, who had chosen the black arts and been burned at the stake. Trimethius, whose name recalls Faustus' contemporary rival Trithemius, had a magical ring, now in Faustus' possession, and it is this ring that provokes much of the action, ultimately driving the wicked Queen Katherine into madness. Mephisto encourages Faustus to avail himself of the ring's powers, but Faustus destroys it by reciting the 'great formula', terrifying even the devil in the process. He journeys down into 'furnaces such as no alchemist has seen or dreamed of [where] all matter is undifferentiated, burns itself away in an ecstasy of disappointment' (Durrell, 69). In a kind of primal vision of a terrible yet vitally necessary dark centre of the universe, the ring is destroyed and Faustus can return, purified, to a simple life with other recluses, Martin the Pardoner, a harmless local rogue, and Matthew the Hermit, his new mentor. Even Mephisto is allowed to join them, he, too, having become pacified: 'A murderer or felon of sorts. But you couldn't have better company.' (Durrell, 89) This incongruous foursome, the rogue, the scholar, the hermit and the devil, end up plying cards, 'the old game of Fortune', in apparent tranquillity.

Fraser (114) argues strongly that this play is 'a small masterpiece' that represents its author's central beliefs. Unlike Goethe's restlessly active hero, Durrell's does not even try to use evil. He recognises the ring as dangerous, since it has the power to reawaken Eric the Red and drive Katherine to distraction. Many Faustian problems are solved in unexpected ways; this Faustus does not burn his books or abandon them, but passes them on to Margaret when he no longer needs them. In his quiet submission to the cosmic order of things, he is closer to Goethe the man than to Goethe's character, Faust. Some of these themes are continued in Durrell's *Avignon Quintet*, especially in the first volume, *Monsieur, or the Prince of Darkness* (1974).

This play was moderately successful outside Germany. It was translated into French in 1974, where there have been several performances, for example, at the Théâtre de Vanves, as *Un Faust Irlandais* de Laurent [sic] Durrell (programme leaflet). German audiences were often disappointed by the depiction of a small-minded, rational Faust who turns his back on sorcery and ends up contentedly playing cards with his adversary. The Hamburg production, directed by Oscar Fritz Schuh and starring veteran Faust-actor Will Quadflieg, transformed 'Doctor Faustus' into 'Doctor Morienus' and 'Mephisto' into 'Asmodi', and the play was widely interpreted as a commentary on the responsibilities of present-day nuclear scientists. (Althoff)

John Banville is known for his imaginative fiction, which includes the novels *Doctor Copernicus* and *Kepler*. His *Mefisto* focuses on Gabriel Swan, a mathematical genius born into the poverty and misery of small-town Ireland, who is relentlessly mocked as an outsider until he comes under the influence of the sardonic fixer Felix, the doomed businessman Mr Kasperl, and a mysterious deaf-mute girl, Sophie, who is obsessed with marionettes. An underground explosion destroys the latter two, and Gabriel, hideously scarred, enters a post-adolescent, urban world peopled by devious researchers and emaciated drug addicts. In this surreal environment, Gabriel matures to the point of recognising the signs of a system behind the chaos of his experience.

> My head swam. Something surged within me, yearning outwards into the darkness. And all at once I saw again the secret I had lost sight of for so long, that chaos is nothing but an infinite number of ordered things. Wind, those stars, that water falling on stones, all the shifting ramshackle world could be solved. I stumbled forward in

the dark, my arms extended in a blind embrace. On the gravel by the petrol pump a woman squatted, pissing. The fight was still going on somewhere, I could hear cries and groans. Felix rose up in front of me with a dark laugh. (Banville, 183)

The Faustian elements are limited to the tutelary role of Felix, Mr Kasperl as the Punch or Harlequin figure, and details that include Swan's episodic visits to an 'Auerbach's Celler' and a hugely bloated 'Mother' figure. The final pun is just one of many intertextual signals with which the novel is punctuated:

> – Can't tempt you, eh? he said. Well, there'll be another time.
> I gazed away up the road. He touched my arm lightly.
> – Oh yes, he said, there's always another time. (Banville, 230)

Faust in Verse

D. J. Enright, who died in 2002, was a poet, critic and lecturer whose interests straddled European and oriental cultures. Although he taught English literature in various parts of the world, he retained a particular interest in German authors and a commentary on Goethe's *Faust* was one of his earliest publications. His collections of poetry include several cycles, including one based on Milton. *A Faust Book* uses the figure both to illuminate the paradoxes of the story and to comment on educational issues in postwar Britain. Enright places Faust in the context of 'Senior Common Room' culture, featuring a Mephistopheles who dines on High Table and swigs port while predicting the disintegration of the values of Middle England and those of its 'Oxbridge'-style academic culture. Intertextual relationships are manifold; Enright's knowledge of Goethe is intimate; the chapbook, Marlowe, Thomas Mann and other, more obscure sources are frequently discernible, and he recalls even the late eighteenth-century Fausts with upstanding if careworn aged parents in tow. The chapbook/Goethean story-line is preserved in broad outline and embroidered by association with the present, producing what reads like an extended verbal joust between Faust and Mephistopheles, each of whom displays a very English liking for puns, understatement, and subtle *double-entendres*. Faust's treatment of Gretchen skirts the conventions of a crude sitcom, with the absent-minded professor holding a lecture on the meaning of meaning in the presence of a girl fresh from scrubbing away at her mother's laundry.

> Faust and Gretchen walk in the garden
>
> *'No, I don't see much of the priest –*
> *Actually, I'm a Doctor of Divinity myself ...'*
>
> *If Divinity was sick*
> *He was the man to cure it.*
> *'Do I believe in God, you ask.*
> *You're a natural philosopher!*

Can anyone say he believes in God?
What is meant by God?
What is meant by believe?
What is meant by I?
Can we employ these words any more?'

Gretchen felt that she could,
Although in fact she rarely did.

'But when I speak of hand
I know what I mean, I can touch it ...
Ah, let me kiss it!
What do you mean, I don't know
Where it's been?'

It had been in soap and water.
Her mother took in washing.

'You're not very fond of my skinny friend?
I wouldn't want you to be!'

Gretchen shuddered. Her hand moved
To the crucifix round her neck.
'So you are wearing a cross,
You little darling!
I gave it to you?
Yes of course I did.'

He remembered Mephisto grinning
As he handed it over.
'When in Rome ...' the fellow had said.

'It's too good for you?
Nonsense, my sweet – nothing's too good ...
Oh dear, the chain's broken–
Where can the cross have got to?
It can't have gone too far ...'

It went too far. (Enright (1979), 22)

There is nothing here that is not hinted at in Goethe – the dialogue between an erudite scholar intent on seduction and the blushingly self-conscious maiden who says very little and whose relationship is, we feel, already doomed from the moment she attempts to interrogate him about his faith: 'Gretchen is essentially a secondary figure and it is unfortunate for the play as a whole that she should have come to symbolise all ill-done-by innocents.' (Enright (1949), 76) In the next poem we return to the chapbook ('Faust is forbidden to marry'), and then the affair is over ('Faust is soon bored'). The poet fast-forwards to the German question on more than one occasion, with Mephisto asking if Faust has the makings of an internal émigré while himself adopting the language of a Gestapo official: 'Do you hope to emigrate internally?'/ Asked Mephistopheles coldly./ 'We have ways of tearing you to pieces' ('Faust betrays signs of forwardsliding', Enright (1979), 33). There is also more than one cruel aside on the state of contemporary academia, such as when the modern Faust, in emulation of his sixteenth-century predecessor, offers to reproduce the missing comedies of Terence, but the University Senate is too busy with 'minutes, motions and amendments' to take up his proposal ('Faust appears before the Senate', Enright (1979), 56). The cycle of 73 poems represents a sustained interrogation of the legend in not one, but many of its permutations. This transposition into the poetic medium displays a combination of uneasy respect and sly subversion that, like so many contemporary re-workings, is evidence that the modern age, for all its love of irony, is still able and willing to grapple with the legend's underlying premises.

Faust has inspired more poetry than could easily be surveyed here. To select just one further example, Karl Shapiro's 'The Progress of Faust', first published in the collection *Trial of a Poet* of 1947, is an outstandingly melodic attempt to sum up the magician's life in seven stanzas:

> *His frequent disappearances are put down*
> *To visits in the regions of the damned*
> *And to the periodic deaths he shammed,*
> *But, unregenerate and in Doctor's gown,*
> *He would turn up to lecture at the fair*
> *And do a minor miracle for a fee.* (Shapiro, 97)

Shapiro does not leave it at that, but traces the malevolent scientist's progress into the modern world, where he is held responsible for the culture that produced the atomic bomb (see below, 377–9).

Across the Continents

There have, inevitably, been similar updatings in other literatures. Of the hundreds that could be mentioned, the briefest of references to examples from French, Portuguese, Spanish and Arabic will have to suffice before we turn in more detail to a consideration of the special significance that Faust attained in modern Russia. Moving further afield, the specific difficulties Faust encountered in Japan must remain largely unexplored, although they have been discussed in a recent paper by Naoji Kimura (143–55). In the present volume, however, the Japanese treatment of the legend will be limited to an examination of the role played by Faust in the *manga* cartoon (409–16, below).

The French novelist and dramatist Philippe Raulet published *Jean Faust. Histoire d'un pacte* ('John Faust. History of a Pact') in 1987. Purporting to derive from a 'low German text from the late fifteenth century' (cover), this takes the form of a narrative interspersed with dramatic dialogues and diary entries attributed to Faust and Wagner and letters passed between many of their contemporaries. Faust is shown the wonders of the universe, but tires quickly of all the names of the planets and star-systems. His erotic adventures bring him little pleasure, and in the end Mephistopheles appears to regret having agreed to a twenty-four-year pact, as it gave his victim too much time to speculate on his fate (Raulet, 132, 245). The novel ends with Faust's death in the traditional manner, after his friends have quizzed him as to why he could not free himself from the pact. Fernando Pessoa's *Fausto. Tragédia Subjectiva* ('Faust. A Subjective Tragedy'), is an inordinately ambitious, unfinished torso, begun in 1908 when the author was twenty, and worked on from then until his death. Thousands of verses produced a posthumous package of 227 fragments, adding up to an enormous soliloquy that has been described as the tragedy of being oneself. Pessoa was, like Valéry, interested in Faust's intellectual frigidity, and his Faust is another solitary modern incapable of genuine emotion. In conversation with the great minds of the past, Christ, Buddha, Shakespeare and Goethe, he cannot devote himself to the present. His long, reflective monologues are placed beside short, emotionally vibrant exclamations by Maria, whom he claims to love, but in such a cerebral manner that he can only talk about rather than act out his love. He dies, as he has lived, in isolation. The author sums it up: 'The drama in its entirety represents the battle between the intellect and life, in which the intellect is always defeated' (Pessoa, 7). In 2000, the Swiss composer Xavier Dayer achieved a major award for his ballet project entitled *Sept Fragments de Faust* which was inspired by Pessoa's work.

A Faust novel by the Venezuelan author Francisco Herrera Luque, *La luna de Fausto* ('Faust's Moon'), first appeared in 1983. It takes as its point of departure a prophesy allegedly made by Faustus to Philip von Hutten, the adventurous brother of the Reformer Ulrich von Hutten. According to Faustus, the former's expedition to South America, intended to locate the legendary El Dorado, would go disastrously wrong, as indeed it did (see above, 32f.). This becomes the subject of a gripping novel in which German superstitions mingle with the cruelty of the conquistadors and the myth of Eldorado. The moving forces behind this fated expedition, of whose laborious progress Herrera Luque spares the reader few gory details, are the big businessmen of the day, notably the Welser banking concern and Emperor Charles V.

Fausts have been written in many parts of the world; the results cannot be discussed or even surveyed here. André Dabezies lists and comments on several dozen little-known French, English and German novels, films, radio-plays and other spectacles dating from the 1950s. The Brazilian response is discussed by Rosenthal (Dabezies, 467–504; Rosenthal, 157–68). Non-European Fausts in Egypt were recently reviewed in a paper by Moustafa Maher. This reveals a perhaps surprising affinity between the German and European traditions and those circulating in the Arab world. When Goethe's play was translated into Arabic (Part I appeared in Egypt in 1929, accompanied by an introduction by Taha Hussein) it struck a chord and led to several subsequent adaptations. These include Taufiq al Hakim's '*Ahd esh Shaitan* ('Pact with Satan', 1938), influenced both by Gounod and Goethe, whom the author had read in French translation. Muhammad Farid

Abu Hadid wrote a play called '*Abd esh Shaitan* ('Satan's Slave') in 1929 based on Goethe, whom he had read in English translation. Here Mephistopheles (Ahriman) has no difficult in seducing Faust (Toboz), if only because humans now enslave themselves to evil much more readily than they did in Goethe's time. As Satan's instrument, Toboz wreaks destruction in society, commerce, and politics. Toboz does eventually repent, but his conversion comes too late. More recent versions include Yussuf Wahbi's *Ash Shaitan* ('The Devil'), filmed as *Safir Gahannam* ('Journey to Hell'), and *Faust al gadid* ('The New Faust'), a radio play by Ahmad Bakathir, broadcast in 1987. Here, too, we find the familiar variety of approaches; Wahbi's Faust succumbs to Mephisto's promises and gains nothing, while Bakathir's, torn between the attractions of good and evil, recognises that he must work to save mankind and is able to break the pact and strive towards peace and love. Mephisto is powerless and Faust actually thanks him, in his dying moments, for showing him clearly what distinguishes good from evil. (Maher, 437–50)

Faust and the Russian Revolutionary Hero
by Rolf Hellebust

Responding to reviews by Thomas Carlyle, Jean Jacques Ampère, and Stepan Shevyrev of his 1827 publication of the Helena 'Phantasmagoria' from Part II of *Faust*, Goethe wrote, 'The Scot attempts to penetrate the work, the Frenchman to understand it, the Russian to make it his own [*sich es zuzueignen*]' (Letter to Zelter, 28 May 1828). This characterisation of the Moscow critic's approach can be extended to much of the Russian reception of Goethe as a whole – and certainly to that of his most celebrated protagonist. As they tended to do with other literary archetypes such as Hamlet and Don Quixote, Russian artists and thinkers recreated a native version of Faust to reflect their own cultural concerns. Traditionally, the chief exponents of these concerns have been the famous poets and novelists – from Pushkin to Turgenev and Dostoevsky – who imported not only Goethe's masterpiece, but much of the complex of German literary and philosophical ideas that figured in its original composition. The possibility of influence in the opposite direction has been raised by the Russian scholar Mikhail Epstein, who suggests that Goethe's decision to make Faust a city-builder and drainer of swamps was influenced by the historical precedent of Peter the Great, whose utopian vision gave the Russians a new capital city – a northern Venice on the marshes of the Gulf of Finland, the building of which demanded the sacrifice of thousands upon thousands of Baucis and Philemons. Epstein's evidence comes from Goethe's observations on Peter and his daemonic construction project, as recorded in the *Conversations with Eckermann*.[1] For Pushkin, Turgenev and Dostoevsky, Faust remained an ambivalent figure, especially in his relation to that of the Russian *intelligent* ('member of the cultural and progressive political elite') as it evolved over the course of the nineteenth century, from the Hamlet-like *lishnii chelovek* ('superfluous man') to the quixotic political radical. In the figure of the legendary German scholar, Russians recognised both their fondest utopian ambitions and those flaws that, in their opinion, most hampered their realisation.

For Russia the nineteenth century opened with the defeat of Napoleon, of whom Pushkin writes 'To the Russian people/ He showed a lofty destiny' (Pushkin, I, 194). It was the lack of political avenues of expression for this newly-awakened national consciousness that prompted the nascent intelligentsia to work out Russia's destiny indirectly, through literature and literary criticism. Palpable in this development is the role of German thinkers, especially Herder, the Schlegel Brothers, Hegel, Schelling, and Fichte. The most widely cited name is that of Hegel, whose idealism spurred the eminent critic Belinsky to seek the national essence in the field of culture. Yet in the larger perspective, a more important figure is that of Herder, with his focus on the creation of a culturally-centred national identity. In contrast, Hegel's *Endzweck* ('ultimate goal') is in politics, not art. Likewise, he diminishes the role of the individual in history, against Herder's emphasis – especially in his interpretation by the Romantics, on the individuality of both human beings and cultures. From this emphasis there arises the Romantic conception of history as a sum of Carlylian biographies. Finally, Herder's philosophy posits an essential, Faustian duality in the human condition, between the world with its mundane impediments and the infinite realm of our aspirations.

In other words, the Russian intelligentsia believed in their potential as creative *individuals* to influence the nation's fate, in the pursuit of such influence primarily through literary and other cultural means, and in a dualistic reality, in which the darker and mustier one's study, the more glorious the literary alchemy that would inevitably be wrought therein. Thus there was ample motivation for progressive thinkers to see themselves mirrored in Goethe's hero, especially as he emerged in the ostensibly philanthropic builder of utopia in Part II, Act V of the completed work. At the same time, they could not escape the fact that the mustiness, darkness and isolation of their positions with regard to the realm of political action was not so much self-imposed as predetermined by the Tsarist autocracy. So Faust in Russia took on traits of the 'superfluous man', beset with doubts as to the possibility and wisdom of ever taking action.

In 1826 Pushkin published his 'Scene from Faust' (Pushkin, I, 383–86). This brief dialogue begins with the scholar's pronouncement 'I am bored, Devil' and ends with the command that Mephistopheles sink a ship which the world-weary Faust has espied on the horizon. In Pushkin's version, the idealistic energy of Goethe's hero has been overwhelmed by Byronic spleen. His ennui, with its capacity for expression in the form of destructive nihilism, anticipates the mood of generations of Russian literary heroes, beginning with Pushkin's own *Eugene Onegin* (Gronicka, I, 69–71). Faust is all-powerful, the superfluous man relatively powerless. What they do have in common, as will be made explicit by the Russian writers and critics who followed Pushkin, is the tragic flaw of their isolation from the common folk, whether individually, as with Baucis and Philemon, or collectively, as with the passengers of the doomed ship. It is this isolation that subverts their great potential for revolutionary action on behalf of these same people.

It has already been mentioned that the Russian intelligentsia sought support from German philosophy for their belief, conditioned by political reality, in the power of individuals to effect radical social change. The great test of this belief was in the Decembrist revolt of 1825. Part of the reason for the failure of this first abortive Russian revolution was the tendency of its aristocratic participants to see themselves as individuals acting out the parts of popular heroes from history and literature, rather than as members of a conspiratorial organisation (Lotman, 123f.). The validity of the Romantic model of the great history-making individual was an issue that would dominate Russian nineteenth-century political thought, right down to the split between the Bolsheviks, believers in a mass movement directed by a select group of revolutionary talents, and the Mensheviks, believers that the laws of history, not individuals, were what mattered. In literature, various iconic figures were called upon to embody the different sides in this debate. A prominent example is Napoleon, whom the hero of Pushkin's *Queen of Spades* is thought to resemble, whom Dostoevsky's Raskolnikov wants to resemble, and who, in Tolstoy's *War and Peace*, bears no resemblance whatsoever to the quintessential revolutionary individual that history has made him out to be.

Another key figure in this debate was that of Faust, echoes of whose story can be found throughout the Russian classics – though Pushkin's 'Scene from Faust' remains a rare example of direct engagement with Goethe's drama. Of course, there is much in Goethe's protagonist – not to mention the Faust of earlier popular tradition – to make Russian literary and political thinkers hesitate in seeing him as any kind of a model for revolutionary action. On the positive side, we have the endless striving, the utopian engineering, the stance of a non-believer who has risen above religious superstition, and finally the implicit support, crucial in the Russian context, for the possibility of moving from highly abstract theory to revolutionary practice, symbolised by Faust's reinterpretation of the biblical *logos* from Word to Deed (F 1237). On the other side of the balance, we have the problem of Faust's comfortable position within the social hierarchy (one which greatly bothered Russians with regard to the figure of Goethe himself), and his almost complete isolation from the masses. No more complete than the isolation of Russian intellectuals from the peasant majority, but at least the *intelligenty* were constantly bemoaning this fact, whereas the aim of Faust's supposed philanthropy in Goethe's Part II is not to unite with the people, but, as he unequivocally puts it, to gain 'lordship' and 'property' (F 10187). As Turgenev complains: 'For Faust, society and humankind do not exist; he is completely absorbed in himself, and only from himself he awaits salvation' (Zimmermann, 38). It is worth noting that if writers such as Turgenev were reluctant to assign a positive social role to Faust, they tended to show fewer scruples with regard to his alter-ego Mephistopheles – whose radical spirit of 'absolute negation' was viewed by the author of *Fathers and Sons* as a 'positive and a creative impulse ushering in a new epoch' (Gronicka, II, 16).

There are a number of other problems that relate to the sheer complexity and ambiguity of Goethe's version. The Gretchen story was of limited use to Russian revolutionaries, though it did attract attention as a representation of a social problem of contemporary interest (Zimmermann, 40). And while these materialistic idealists were torn by the irresolvable problem of Faust's two souls (F 1112), they did not necessarily want to be reminded of the source. Finally and most importantly, they did not want to deal with the thought that their progressive aspirations might be fuelled by demonic temptation. Despite their atheism, the Russian radicals – like their Bolshevik descendants – tended to be highly moralistic. *What is to be Done?* was the most influential nineteenth-century novel about the revolutionary movement, but was written by the son of a provincial priest, Nikolai

Chernyshevsky. This was a typical pedigree for a radical writer of the time and shows in the depictions of what its author calls Russia's 'new people', whose asceticism and longing for martyrdom recall the saints of Orthodox hagiography rather than Goethe's free-thinking polymath.

On the other hand, the most famous book *outside* of Russia about the nineteenth-century Russian revolutionaries has no qualms about bringing in Faust precisely because its stance is negative. This is Dostoevsky's novel *The Devils* of 1872. In his youth, Dostoevsky was himself a Faustian radical; yet by the time he came to write *The Devils* he had evolved into a radical conservative. The Goethean parallels in this work have been explored by other scholars, and are too numerous to catalogue here. Suffice it to say that Dostoevsky's would-be revolutionaries are parodies of Goethe's hero: in particular, the chief devil, Stavrogin, whom the poet Viacheslav Ivanov referred to as a 'negative Faust,' since, as a typical Russian 'superfluous man', he is incapable of translating his extraordinary potential into any sort of meaningful action (Mann, 240).

Nevertheless, it is also possible to identify positive examples of Faust as a revolutionary role model in Russian literature. Anatoly Lunacharsky is best known for his role as Lenin's Commissar for Culture. Yet well before the 1917 Revolution, he had acquired a reputation as a literary critic and playwright, among other things, for the drama *Faust and the City* (1908–1916), a precursor of Soviet-style 'Socialist Realism'. Towards the end of the nineteenth century, Russian interest in Faust had been revitalised by his identification with the Nietzschean *Übermensch* ('Super-Man'), who was superior to the masses and not bound by ordinary laws. Encouraged by Mephistopheles, Lunacharsky's Faust starts out this way, but eventually joins with the people, those 'great-grandchildren of slaves,' as the demon contemptuously calls them (Lunacharsky, 76). Mephistopheles raises an army of corpses to support the old order, but is defeated. At the end of Lunacharsky's drama, as in Goethe's, Faust dies – and uses his last breath to profess his newfound democratic faith:

> You have taught me to value the genius of the people. For a long time now I have been watching from the height of my tower, and my heart has gone from doubt and confusion to trembling love. Children, brothers! Receive me . . . I am you, completely! . . . I am everybody else . . . I am the many, I am the multitude . . . Let us go, let us go! There is no death. There is life, such a colossal life of which I had never suspected . . .

'Faust is dead,' says the attending doctor. But he is countered by a representative of the masses, who exclaims, in the play's final lines, 'Faust is alive in everyone! Alive with us! Alive forever!' (Lunacharsky, 99f.)

Lunacharsky was to be castigated by subsequent generations of Soviet critics for his attempts to reconcile Marxism-Leninism with fundamentally antithetical philosophical positions – in particular, that of Nietzsche (Tait, 190). In fact, we find a strong Nietzschean undercurrent throughout Russian revolutionary thought of the early twentieth century. At least Lunacharsky is bold enough to confront the contradiction between collectivism and the *Übermensch*, even if we remain unconvinced by his claim that if Nietzsche 'could have overcome his prejudices [...] he would inevitably have come to socialism,' or his optimism that great individuals such as Faust are inevitably drawn to 'build the edifice of culture' rather than merely to pursue their own interests – not out of any sense of altruism, but from the sheer joy of creative activity. It is this same contradiction that Lunacharsky is seeking to confront in his play, when he has his spokesman proclaim: 'There is only one way out – to come to terms with Faust.' (Tait, 198f; Zimmermann, 50–2; Lunacharsky, 42)

89. *Sergei Chekhonin*, Building the Utopian City, *in Anatoly Vasilevich Lunacharsky,* Faust and the City, *1918.*

Faust and the City is probably no immortal classic; but it was influential enough in its time to become an object of parody for a far greater writer than Lunacharsky, whose links with Faust – Gounod's rather than Goethe's –, have been extensively explored. This is Mikhail Bulgakov, author of the tragicomic novel *The Master and Margarita* (1940). Bulgakov's writer-hero is in many ways a positive Faustian figure. From the age of Romanticism onwards, as has been shown in earlier chapters of this book, Faust as scholar is increasingly replaced by Faust as artist; as Boris Pasternak puts it, the latter represents the 'last surviving individualist in a mass-era' (Kopelew, 84). Still, following the nineteenth-century tradition, he is a passive hero in whose salvation Gretchen plays a much more active role than she does in Goethe. The nameless Master is by no means a revolutionary. At the conclusion of the multi-volume study of Goethe in Russian literature of 1937, Viktor Zhirmunsky (1937, III, 630) calls for the 'creation of a Russian *Faust*' by Soviet literature as a task of the utmost importance. One wonders whether he would have considered that he had found an answer to his appeal in the romantic misfit taking shape at that very moment under Bulgakov's pen.

By the time of *Master and Margarita* the positive image of Faust as a builder of utopia and a political radical had been largely subsumed by that of his mythic forebear – Prometheus. Besides the fact that Marx himself declared this Titan the 'most eminent saint and martyr' in the philosophical calendar, and the fact that his story centres on those favourite revolutionary symbols of fire and chains, Prometheus enjoys numerous advantages over Faust as a revolutionary role model. There is no question of isolation from the masses: the philanthropy of Prometheus is beyond dispute. His steadfast endurance of the Gods' punishment is also a crucial model of behaviour for those many revolutionaries who languished in Tsarist prisons. And most importantly, there is no pact with the devil, only a rebellion against gods whose authority for modern Russians, if not for the Greeks of Aeschylus' time, was most certainly in doubt.

Prometheus appears most prominently as a revolutionary icon during the first years of unfettered Utopianism immediately after 1917. For example, there are the mythopœic factory poems of proletarian poets such as Aleksei Gastev, whose work was described by a contemporary as 'a fragment of the worker's fire, taken in its pure essence' and 'a factory whistle, extending its arm from the flames to take the wreath from the head of tired Pushkin – cast-iron leaves, melted in a fiery hand' (Khlebnikov, V, 223).[2] Like Faust, Prometheus was also appropriated by anti-Soviet writers, such as Evgeny Zamyatin, whose dystopian novel *We* of 1920 directly influenced George Orwell's *Nineteen Eighty-Four*. Among other things, Zamyatin's book is a venomous satire on proletarians such as Gastev. Thus its hero, the engineer D-503, cites a piece of verse propaganda in which Prometheus harnesses 'fire in the machine and steel.' He paraphrases it as follows: 'And everything is new and made of steel: steel sun, steel trees, steel people' (Zamyatin, 338). This theme of a metalworking Prometheus has resurfaced more recently in the work of Vasily Aksenov, for example in his novel *Our Golden Piece of Iron* of 1980, or in his story 'The Rendezvous,' which also features a steel-clad version of Mephistopheles playing the part of a fatal muse to a would-be Faust of post-Stalinist Russia.

In the end, although it was Prometheus who won out in Russian political iconography, a Faustian model of revolutionary behaviour remained crucial, especially in the years immediately after 1917, even if the significance of this model was to a great extent unacknowledged. Here we must consider one more individualist hero of the modern age: the engineer. D-503 in Zamyatin's *We* is a prominent literary example of a member of this profession who uses collectivist rhetoric to conceal his elite status and deep-rooted Faustian individuality, even from himself. He is chief designer of the symbolically named *Integral*, a spaceship intended to realise the proletarian poets' dream of exporting revolution throughout the solar system. Supervising the assembly of the rocket, D-503 gazes down at the workers performing the construction. Like the mass-man of a Gastev poem, they move 'smoothly and quickly, in rhythm, like the levers of a single huge machine.' D-503 rushes to join the workers, hoping to be 'welded with them, caught up in the steel rhythm.' But he soon realises he has no place in this dance: his irrepressibly individualistic thoughts have forever sundered him from the collective (Zamyatin, 361f.). Contrast this thwarted desire for union with the smug elitism of the one poet whose industrial fantasies are a match for Gastev: Giacomo Marinetti. In Italian Futurism, the gap between technological aristocrat and suffering masses is clearly demarcated (White, 352). The Russian futurists held a very different view of the collective; yet they too were eager to claim for themselves the role of socialist 'psycho-engineers.' Similarly, a contemporary critic suspected that 'lurking behind Gastev's description of proletarian culture was an elite of engineers, standing above the proletariat and controlling it completely.' Here we recall the defiant declaration made by the blinded Faust: 'To complete the greatest task / One mind is sufficient for a thousand hands' (F 11509f.).

Of course Prometheus is also an engineer. Not only does he bring fire, but he teaches human beings how to use it. And in some versions of the myth he appears as the engineer of the species itself. The crucial difference is that he shares his smith's and potter's expertise with the masses and then lets them get on with the job, whereas Faust is content to remain the one mind directing a thousand hands.

Marxism itself is fascinated by the conflict of bourgeois engineer-hero and proletarian. One could even argue that the former is the real champion of Marx's version of contemporary history. Certainly, it is the bourgeoisie that takes the lead in technological modernisation, a drama narrated by Marx in rapturous, Faustian tones:

> The bourgeoisie, during its rule of scarely one hundred years, has created more massive and more colossal productive forces than have all preceding generations together. Subjection of Nature's forces to man, machinery, application of chemistry to industry and agriculture, steam-navigation, railways, electric telegraphs, clearing of whole continents for cultivation, canalisation of rivers, whole populations conjured out of the ground – what earlier century had even a presentiment that such productive forces slumbered in the lap of social labour? (Marx, 225)

Readers from a backward Russia would be especially eager to master the revolutionary potential of bourgeois technology. They would be further encouraged to focus on the technological side of Marx's revolutionary narrative by a native tradition, harking back to Peter the Great, of viewing technology as a panacea. Finally, let us recall that in less developed countries such as Russia where Communists actually gained power, their revolution did in fact become a revolution of modernisation – a struggle to accomplish the task of the engineer-hero, rather than the indefinable proletarian work of building Communism. Correspondingly, despite the extreme efforts that were made in the Soviet Union to promote a collectivist mentality, it was inevitable that the type of the great, history-making individual would remain no less prominent, as evidenced by the cult of Stalin, and of all the Lysenkos, Michurins and the lesser luminaries of industry and culture who exercised their Faustian powers under his reign.

Notes

1. See www.data.minsk.by/pedal/rus_las_vegas.htm (accessed June 2004).
2. For more on Gastev and the symbols of Russian revolutionary utopianism, see my *Flesh to Metal: Soviet Literature and the Alchemy of Revolution*, Cornell University Press, 2003.

Cited Works and Further Reading

Louisa May Alcott, *A Modern Mephistopheles*. Anon., 1877. Rptd New York: Bantam, 1995. Introduction by Octavia Davis.

Jürgen Althoff, 'Schauspieler retten den "Irischen Faust",' *Abendpost*, 21 December 1963.

Philip James Bailey, *Festus. A Poem*. London: William Pickering, 1839.

John Banville, *Mefisto. A Novel*. London: Secker and Warburg, 1986.

Stephen Vincent Benét, 'The Devil and Daniel Webster', in *Ibid., Selected Works*. 2 volumes. New York: Holt, Rinehart and Winston. Volume II: *Prose*, 32–46.

Peter Boerner and Sidney Johnson (eds), *Faust through Four Centuries. Retrospect and Analysis. Vierhundert Jahre Faust. Rückblick und Analyse*. Tübingen: Niemeyer, 1989.

Tom Clark, *Jack Kerouac. A Biography*. London: Plexus, 1984.

Andrew Crowther, *Contradiction Contradicted: The Plays of W.S. Gilbert*. Cranbury/NJ: Associated University Presses, 2000.

Peter Csobádi, Gernot Gruber, Jürgen Kühnel, Ulrich Müller, Oswald Panagl and Franz Viktor Spechtler (eds), *Europäische Mythen der Neuzeit: Faust und Don Juan. Gesammelte Vorträge des Salzburger Symposions 1992*. 2 volumes. Anif/Salzburg: Ursula Müller-Speiser, 1993.

Sabine Doering, *Die Schwestern des Doktor Faust. Eine Geschichte der weiblichen Faustgestalten*. Göttingen: Wallstein, 2001.

J. Douglas Clayton, 'Pushkin, Faust and the Demons', *Germano-Slavica* 3 (3/1980), 165–87.

Lawrence Durrell, *An Irish Faustus. A Morality in Nine Scenes*. London: Faber and Faber, 1963.

—, *Drei dramatische Dichtungen: Sappho; Actis; Ein irischer Faust*. Introduction by Oscar Fritz Schuh. Reinbek: Rowohlt, 1964.

—, *Un Faust irlandais*. Translated by F.J. Temple. Paris: Gallimard, 1974.

—, *An Irish Faustus*. Adapted by Penelope Durrell Hope. Birmingham: Delos, 1987.

D.J. Enright, *Commentary on Goethe's Faust*. New York: New Directions, 1949. First published in the magazine *Scrutiny*.

—, *A Faust Book*. Oxford: University Press, 1979. Rptd in *ibid. Telling Tales: 'Paradise Illustrated' and 'A Faust Book'*. Oxford: University Press, 1997.

Leslie A. Fiedler, *Love and Death in the American Novel*. London: Jonathan Cape, 1967.

G. S. Fraser, *Lawrence Durrell. A Study*. London: Faber and Faber, 1968.

W.S. Gilbert, *Original Plays*. 3 volumes. London: Chatto & Windus, 1886–1895.

William E. Grim, *The Faust Legend in Music and Literature*. 2 volumes. Lewiston/NY: Edwin Mellen Press, 1987–92 (Studies in the History and Interpretation of Music, 5, 36).

André von Gronicka, *The Russian Image of Goethe*. 2 volumes. Philadelphia: University of Pennsylvania, 1968, 1985.

Nathaniel Hawthorne, *Selected Tales and Sketches*, ed. Michael J. Colacurcio. New York: Penguin, 1987.

Charles H. Herford, *Studies in the literary relations of England and Germany in the sixteenth century*. Cambridge: University Press, 1886. Reprinted London: Cass, 1966.

Francisco Herrera Luque, *La luna de Fausto*. Santiago/Chile: Editorial Pomaire, 1983. Cited as *Ibid.*, *Faustmond. La luna de Fausto*. Trans. by Claudia Sierich, Percha: R.S. Schulz, 1986.

Harry How, 'Illustrated interview with Mr. W.S. Gilbert', *Strand Magazine* 2, October 1891, 339.

Richard Ilgner, 'Goethe's "Geist, der stets verneint," and its Emergence in the Faust Works of Odoevsky, Lunacharsky, and Bulgakov', *Germano-Slavica* 2 (3/1977), 169–80.

Washington Irving, *The Complete Works*. 10 volumes. New York: Putnam, 1854–56.

Viktor Vladimirovich Khlebnikov, *Sobranie proizvedenii*. Leningrad: Izdalelstvo Pisatyelei, 1933.

Naoji Kimura, 'Probleme der *Faust*-Rezeption in Japan', in Boerner/Johnson, 143–55.

Lev Kopelew, *Zwei Epochen deutsch-russischer Literaturbeziehungen*. Translated by Heddy Pross-Weerth. Frankfurt/M: Fischer, 1973.

C.S. Lewis, *The Screwtape Letters*. London: Geoffrey Bles, 1942.

Iurii M. Lotman *et al.*, *The Semiotics of Russian Cultural History*. Ed. Alexander D. Nakhimovsky and Alice Stone Nakhimovsky. Ithaca/NY: Cornell University Press, 1985.

O.W. Long, 'Goethe and Longfellow', *Germanic Review* 7 (1932), 166f.

Anatoly Vasilevich Lunacharsky, *Faust i gorod*. Petrograd: Narodnyi komissariat po prosveshchenyu, 1918.

Moustafa Maher, 'Die Rezeption des Faust-Stoffes in Ägypten und die vermittelnde Rolle des Theaters', in Csobádi, II, 437–50.

Robert Mann, 'The Faustian Pattern in *The Devils*'. *Canadian Slavonic Papers* 24 (3/1982), 239–44.

Karl Marx, *Selected Writings*. Ed. David McLellan, Oxford: Oxford University Press, 1977.

Cotton Mather, *The Wonders of the Invisible World. Being an Account of the Tryals of several Witches lately executed in New-England*. (1692). Rptd London: John Russell Smith, 1862.

Robert Nye, *Faust: Being the Historia von D. Johann Fausten dem weit beschreyten Zauberer und Schwartzkünstler; or, History of Dr. John Faust the Notorious Magician and Necromancer, as Written by His Familiar Servant and Disciple Christopher Wagner, Now for the First Time Englished from the Low German*. London: Hamish Hamilton, 1980.

Hesketh Pearson, *Gilbert: his life and strife*. London: Methuen, 1957.

Fernando Pessoa, *Faust. Eine subjektive Tragödie. Fragmente und Entwürfe*. Translated and edited by Georg Rudolf Lind. Zurich: Ammann, 1990.

Alexander S. Pushkin, *Polnoe sobranie sochinenii*. 10 volumes. Moscow: Akademia Nauk SSR, 1949.

——, 'Stsena iz Fausta,' in *Ibid.*, I, 383–86.

Philippe Raulet, *Jean Faust. Histoire d'un pacte*. Paris: Albin Michel, 1987.

Erwin Theodor Rosenthal, 'Gretchen ganz spesenfrei. Brasilianische Faustvisionen', in Boerner/Johnson, 157–68.

Ruth Schirmer-Imhoff, 'Faust in England', *Anglia* 70 (1951), 150–85.

Karl Shapiro, *New and selected poems, 1940–1986*. Chicago: University Press, 1987.

William Bysshe Stein, *Hawthorne's Faust: A Study of the Devil Archetype*. Gainesville, 1953. Rptd Hamden/CT: Archon Books, 1968.

Michael Swanwick, *Jack Faust*. New York: Avon, 1997.

A.L. Tait, 'Lunacharskii's Russian *Faust*,' *Germano-Slavica* 3 (3/1980), 189–203.

Emma Tennant, *Faustine*. London: Faber and Faber, 1992.

John J. White, *Literary Futurism: Aspects of the First Avant Garde*. Oxford: Clarendon Press, 1990.

Thomas G. Wright, *Literary Culture in New England*. New Haven: Yale University Press, 1920.

Yevgeni I. Zamyatin, *Izbrannoe*. Moscow: Sovremennik, 1989.

Viktor M. Zhirmunsky, *Gete v russkoi literature*. 3 volumes. Leningrad, 1937, rptd Leningrad: Nauka, 1981.

Gisela Zimmerman, *The Revolutionary and the Superfluous Man: Soviet Russian Images of Faust*. PhD Dissertation, University of Kansas, 1992.

Theodore Ziolkowski, *The Sin of Knowledge. Ancient Themes and Modern Variations*. Princeton: University Press, 2000.

Chapter Eleven

The Popular Imagination

Advanced science is indistinguishable from magic.—Arthur C. Clarke

Science and Politics

THE CAREER of Faust is as relevant to the contemporary world as it ever was. Our inquiry into the exploitation of the myth by the movie industry suggested that more films were made on this theme during the last ten years than at any point since the First World War. They had a variety of subtexts: political, social, humorous and psychological, and were the products of profoundly moral as well as of gratuitously titillating agendas. Faust is one of many German figures that have had a major impact on the arts, enriching the imagination of all who have come into contact with his story in one of its many recorded forms. Even those who have no direct knowledge of the sources may still speak of a 'Faustian pact' or a 'Mephistophelean ploy', just as they do of a 'Kafkaesque paradox', a 'Freudian slip' or 'Brechtian alienation effects'. Yet there are sinister undertones to the analogy that are absent from other casual attributions. To speak of Berlin as 'Faust's metropolis', as Alexandra Ritchie does in the title of her historical survey of the city, may impart a pithy edge to her investigations, but it does so by evoking a city in league with the devil, giving Berlin a diabolical association of a type to which residents of Copenhagen or Antwerp would, understandably, object. From here it is a short step to the accusation, recently voiced by Jonathan Petropoulos, that artists such as Emil Nolde, Erich Heckel, and Ernst Barlach who agreed to exhibit work during the Third Reich were involved in a 'Faustian bargain'. The root cause is that, on the evidence of history and in the popular imagination, the world war which devastated nations in the mid-twentieth century was a result of an accumulation of evil so monstrous as to invite and even demand comparison with a Satanic agency. The course on which Germany embarked, at the behest of its leadership and with the apparent compliance of a large part of its populace, was marked by a 'Faustian' disregard for morality such as has rarely been seen in earlier epochs and remains unparalleled in modern history. Here, finally, was the proof that Faust's combination of rationality, ambition, and trail-blazing temerity was an entirely destructive formula. The greater the knowledge he attained, the more devastating the consequences.

And yet, the Faustian association did not come about by chance but grew out of a chosen political and cultural agenda. As shown in chapter 5, there were many who prided themselves on their Faustian destiny, many who believed that the greatest risks would bring the greatest rewards, many who saw Faust's striving as a legitimate response to the humiliation sustained in earlier military campaigns that had ended in defeat. Yet the cautionary voices were not silent, and as early as 1936, Klaus Mann observed the self-destructive side of the pact in his novel *Mephisto*, centred on an actor so determined to play the part of Mephistopheles on stage that he fails to realise that he is playing the very same role in real life. Thomas Mann took his son's idea one stage further, by writing a fictional biography of a different Doctor Faustus whose career tallied chronologically with Germany's pact with evil and also with the life of her greatest modern thinker, Friedrich Nietzsche (Durrani, 111–13). There was thus a consensus between supporters and opponents of Germany's quest for aggrandisement: both parties proclaimed that the process was Faustian, though what the one side saw as heroic the other denounced as a tragic aberration. The status of Faust as a national icon for Germany, already firmly established as such in the nineteenth century, was strengthened in the twentieth by authorities representing the two ends of the political spectrum.

It was, paradoxically perhaps, only in the German Democratic Republic that Faust was still being used by the political and cultural apparatus as a forerunner of its own ideals, demonstrating optimism arising out of bourgeois humanism and proclaiming egalitarianism in a subtly encrypted form. As Alexander Abusch put it in numerous polemical papers, Faust's words at the end of Part II were 'a high point of dialectic thought in classical German literature before Marx' and Engels' dialectic materialism. [...] The humane and humanist elements in Goethe's work were the highest and most complete expression of the ideals of the progressive bourgeoisie of the period' (Abusch, 57; see also Scholz, 104f.). Little attempt was made to analyse Goethe's deep-seated antagonism to what we now understand by democracy (Rothe, 158f.).

New uses were discovered for the Faustian analogy in the postwar period. After the proud identification with Faust and the cautionary warnings not to emulate him, the pact with the devil could be cited both to explain and to excuse the evil that had emanated from within the country. If Hitler was indeed a reincarnation of Satan, how could ordinary individuals hope to resist his snares? The idea of the pact simultaneously illustrated and obscured the true nature of what had happened. Thus Hitler's architect, Albert Speer, comments in his memoirs: 'For the commission to do a great building, I would have sold my soul like Faust. Now I had found my Mephistopheles. He seemed no less engaging than Goethe's' (cited by Petropoulos, 5). Carl Zuckmayer had used the analogy in his controversial drama *Des Teufels General* ('The Devil's General') of 1946, written, like Mann's *Doctor Faustus*, while in exile in America. It was to be the most successful German drama of the 1940s, with over 3,000 performances in the first four years. Zuckmayer's General Harras is trapped by a pact into which he entered for reasons that include a passion for flying and a lack of moral scruples. Yet he has a conscience, helps a Jewish doctor to escape, and recognises his own impending damnation: 'I believe the judgement was written in blood [...] He who became the devil's general on earth and bombed a path for him must prepare a residence for him in hell' (Zuckmayer (1960), 617). With these words, Harras sets off on a final mission which he knows to be suicidal. The play was criticised for its moral ambiguity, but it is in precisely this ambivalence that the Faustian parallel is most obvious. Admirable and despicable at the same time, Harras serves the devil for reasons which he himself knows to be superficial and venal, and yet manages to deliver a warning to his fellow officers and admirers when he puts an end to his life in an act of deliberate sabotage. Like the first Faustus, he dies 'a wicked and a good man'; this may not satisfy the historian or the psychologist, but it demonstrates the continuing applicability of the traditional model in which extremes of morality and immorality co-exist within one man.

From the time of René Clair's film, identifications of Faust with the natural scientist – especially the biologist, nuclear physicist and chemist – have taken hold of the popular imagination. Fictional scientists with Faustian propensities had clearly featured in late Victorian dystopian fantasies such as R.L. Stevenson's *The Strange Case of Doctor Jekyll and Mister Hyde* (1887) and H.G. Wells' *The Island of Doctor Moreau* (1896). These and many other authors ask the same question, a quintessentially 'Faustian' one: are there areas of science that the inquisitive mind should not explore? Mary Shelley had done this in 1818; it is hard not to read her *Frankenstein* novel as a retort to *Faust* (Shattuck, 77–107, esp. 98f.).

Scientists have themselves applied the name for various purposes. One of the most amusing instances to have been recorded was the *Blegdamsvej* spectacle, when the Niels Bohr Institute in Copenhagen witnessed a bizarre showing of *Faust* by the leading astrophysicists of the day. Named after the address of Bohr's institute in Blegdamsvej, this tells the story of Wolfgang Pauli (Mephistopheles) trying to sell to the unbelieving Paul Ehrenfest (Faust) the idea of the neutrino (Gretchen), the particle with no mass and charge. It was written and performed by several associates of Niels Bohr at the Copenhagen Spring Conference in 1932, with Bohr himself playing the part of the Lord, James Chadwick as Wagner, and Paul Ehrenfest as Faust. Bohr was the leading authority of his day on nuclear physics, and Pauli, based in Zurich, one of his fiercest critics. Einstein's repeated revisions of his field theory were the subject of much merriment in Auerbach's Cellar, here renamed Mrs Ann Arbor's Speakeasy, and the Walpurgis Night scene was turned into a series of disputes about quantum physics, in which Dirac, Slater and other theorists were parodied (Göres, 87; Gamow, 190–4).

GRETCHEN [*comes in and sings to* FAUST. *Melody:* "*Gretchen at the Spinning Wheel*" *by Schubert*]:

> *My Mass is zero,*
> *My Charge is the same.*
> *You are my hero,*
> *Neutrino's my name.*

I am your fate,
And I'm your key.
Closed is the gate
For lack of me.

Beta-rays throng
With me to pair.
The N-Spin's wrong
If I'm not there.

My Mass is zero,
My Charge is the same.
You are my hero,
Neutrino's my name.

My psyche turns
To you, my own.
My poor heart yearns
For you alone.

My lovesick soul
Is yours to win.
I can't control
My trembling spin.

My Mass is zero,
My Charge is the same.
You are my hero,
Neutrino's my name. (Gamow, 188f; translation by Barbara Gamow)

Increasingly, the protagonists summon evil spirits out of themselves and not from some other plane of existence. In recent times, several types of scientist, including those who clone life-forms and those who unleash radioactive chain-reactions, have made themselves vulnerable to the accusation of attempting to play God. Few scientists have done more to underline the Faustian responsibilities and Mephistophelean threats to scientific research than Freeman Dyson, sometime Professor of Physics at the Institute for Advanced Study in Princeton, who pays tribute to the influence of Goethe's drama on his thinking in 'The Redemption of Faust', a chapter of his autobiography *Disturbing the Universe* (Dyson (1979), 11–18). He was to acknowledge that he and others like John Robert Oppenheimer, under whom he studied, were guilty of service to a modern devil: 'The Faustian bargain is when you sell your soul to the devil in exchange for knowledge and power. That, of course, in a way, is what Oppenheimer did' (Dyson (1981), 14). The devil may offer the ability to lift a thousand tons of rock into the sky, or, as in I. A. Richards' play *Tomorrow Morning, Faustus*, the instrument of seduction may be nothing more than a tempting research grant argued over in the Board Room of the 'Futurity Foundation'. The connection between the German intellectuals who were expelled in 1939 and those who perfected the engines of destruction is cogently made in Karl Shapiro's poem 'The Progress of Faust', where it is precisely the expulsion of a 'backwardly tolerant' Faustus that leads to Germany's defeat ('the breaching of the Rhine').

> Backwardly tolerant, Faustus was expelled
> From the Third Reich in Nineteen Thirty-nine.
> His exit caused the breaching of the Rhine,
> Except for which the frontier might have held.
> Five years unknown to enemy and friend
> He hid, appearing in the sixth to pose
> In an American desert at war's end
> Where, at his back, a dome of atoms rose. (Shapiro, 98)

Shapiro breaks new ground in depicting Faustus as a victim, not as a symbol or originator of Fascism, but his legacy to the world is far from beneficial; he is now implicated in the American weapons programme, which was based, as many have acknowledged, on Nazi Germany's rocket-building technology. The Faust that tried to be as God, the Faust that strove for mastery of the elements whatever the cost to his moral well-being, is still with us. Yet the case, once made, is apt to be overstated. Not every searching scientist is a clone of the magus. Rolf Hochhuth's recent play about Hermann Oberth describes the physicist as 'Hitler's Doctor Faustus' on the basis of the his research into propulsion systems. John Cornwell's study *Hitler's Scientists. Science, War and the Devil's Pact* of 2003 draws the same parallel. The thousands of doctors, engineers, physicists – in short, any trained professional who aided and abetted the Führer's plans to subjugate Europe – was by definition involved in a Faustian pact with the Nazis, and all scientists who ignored the evil consequences of their discoveries deluded themselves if they pleaded that science could remain morally neutral. The threat has not gone away: 'The Faustian bargains lurk within routine grant applications, the pressure to publish for the sake of tenure and the department's budget, the treatment of knowledge as a commodity that can be owned, bought and sold' (Cornwell, 462). In *Newsweek*, Michael Hirsh arraigns Swiss bankers who made profits out of the war for concluding a 'Faustian bargain' ('Secret bankers for the Nazis', 24 June 1996, 50f.). The list is endless and understandable in the circumstances.

The analogy is not limited to Germany or to science. As recently as September 2003, journalists were putting the question: 'Tony Blair: Dr Faust – Or Mephistopheles?'

> In many ways, Mr Blair looks like a modern-day update on Dr Faust. Just like the 16th century protagonist of that famous tragedy, Mr Blair initially sought to make his mark on domestic policy – including a rebranding of Great Britain as "Cool Britannia." This was much like the knowledge of alchemy that Faust strived for – the way of turning base metal into gold.
> [...] Rather, he is increasingly viewed by the British public as a Mephistopheles who actually convinced his nation to plunge itself into a military campaign – for dubious reasons and with an uncertain exit strategy.
> As a matter of fact, it fits to a T. In Goethe's version, Mephistopheles initially follows Dr Faust home disguised as a poodle.

This is eerily appropriate. Remember how in the run-up to the Iraq war – and continuing today – the British media were fond of portraying Mr Blair as a "poodle" for his willingness to do the bidding of President Bush?

Either way, what matters here is that things didn't quite work out as planned for either of Goethe's characters. Although Dr Faust was transformed into a vigorous young man, his love affair with a maiden, Gretchen, caused nothing but suffering all around. His military prowess turned out badly as well, as he ended up killing the brother of his beloved.

After a number of convoluted misadventures, Faust sought to redeem himself by setting out to improve the lot of mankind. But that too came to nothing. In any case, in the end the hero gained neither knowledge nor happiness, failing to be satisfied even with a fleeting moment. (Richter)

A few days later, the British parliamentarian Menzies Campbell complained that Tony Blair has struck a 'Faustian bargain' with George W. Bush when agreeing to attack Iraq (*The Guardian*, 25 September 2003, 14). Yet we need to remind ourselves that the original doctor sought personal pleasure rather than the conquest of peoples and showed very little interest in exploiting technology for the sake of either progress or destruction.

Another approach has been to see Germany's destiny as 'Mephistophelean' rather than as 'Faustian', as Daniel Goldhagen does when he speaks of Germans emitting 'Mephistophelean laughter' during executions of their victims. He is undoubtedly right that much of the ideology that led to the war and the exterminations was fuelled by a 'prevailing Manichaean idiom', but a radical distinction between good and evil could equally be described as 'biblical' (Goldhagen, 398, 84). The original Mephistopheles was full of regret for the damage he had done to his soul, as was the tempter in Marlowe's play. This is often forgotten. The terms are too complex to serve as blueprints for an ideology or a political programme, and a century of history cannot be shoe-horned into a model based on an inherently unstable, much-revised myth. A national opus does not a national character make, and Germany today is no more 'Faustian' than Spain is 'Quixotic' or Britain a nation of indecisive Hamlets. As the following examples will show, a lingering pride in the heritage serves both to preserve a past legacy and to promote regional tourism, and it is to this altogether more harmless form of provincial self-indulgence that we now turn. The world of commerce is likewise of relevance here and has adopted its own, frequently light-hearted, tongue-in-cheek approach to the 'Faust' brand, which includes a full gamut of gastronomic products, alcoholic beverages, and consumer goods as diverse as medical ointments and computer programs. The 'Faust' logo is even used by seismologists, who have set up an organisation under this acronym, which resolves into 'FAUlts as a Seismologist's Tool'. The aim of this environmental project of the European Union (ENV4-CT97-0528) is to create a database of seismogenic sources and to test the impact of different source models on estimates of seismic hazards.

Faust for Tourists: Museums, Memorials, Festivals

90. Faust's alleged birthplace in the small town of Knittlingen near Stuttgart.
Photograph by Osman Durrani.

Several German towns claim an association with Faust. They can be divided, along regional lines, into two distinct groups: Knittlingen ('Kundling' in various early references), Simmern, Heidelberg, and Staufen are in the South-Western provinces (Baden-Württemberg, Rhineland) while Wittenberg, Leipzig, Stadtroda and Erfurt are in Central Eastern Germany (Thuringia, Saxony). This reflects the contradiction between literary and popular sources. As discussed above (25–7), scholarship tends to favour a South German birthplace, although there is disagreement as to precisely where this might have been. There are oral traditions linking Faust with locations not mentioned in any written sources: these include the monastery of Maulbronn and the area around Batenburg in the Netherlands. The contradictory evidence is examined by Günther Mahal (1997, 13–30), whose evaluations, while compelling, betray the influence of his personal patronage of the Knittlingen Museum. Frank Baron is no less determined to defend his finding of a 'Georg Helmstetter' whom he identifies with Faust. The positive side to these apparent contradictions is that mementos are preserved in different ways in many parts of the country. Tourist attractions in places as far apart as Leipzig in Saxony and Staufen in the Black Forest help to cast light on aspects of a life that is as intriguing as it is elusive. It was easier for Faust to become a national icon than for those many other figures who were based in a single locality.

381

*91. Hotel Zum Löwen, Staufen, one of several locations where Faust is alleged to have died.
Photograph by Osman Durrani.*

Knittlingen and Staufen, both in Baden-Württemberg, have proudly christened themselves *Fauststadt* ('Faust Town'), on not uncontroversial documentary evidence that the legendary figure was born in the former and died in the latter. Room Nr. 5 of Staufen's *Hotel Zum Löwen* ('Lion Hotel') is locally regarded as the scene of the doctor's demise, and is still booked by guests hoping for an extra-sensory experience, although the current management emphatically does not welcome those visitors who wish merely to view or to photograph the location. The local tourist office will point such people in the direction of Mephisto's footprint on the third floor of the Town Hall instead. According to other traditions, Faust died in Rimlich near Wittenberg, in Cologne, in Waerdenberg (where an indelible bloodstain was used to corroborate his demise), and in Pratau on the River Elbe (Niessen, 18f.).

92. Knittlingen Town Logo.

The town most closely related to the doctor's professional life is Wittenberg in the present-day province of Sachsen-Anhalt. Here was the university in which he was said to have lectured and where the devil is supposed to have tempted him to abandon his studies of the traditional subjects in favour of magic. There are no eye-catching relics here and

93. Alleged imprint of Mephisto's huge right foot plus hoof on the third-floor landing of Staufen Town Hall. Photograph by Osman Durrani.

little attempt has been made to attract tourists to the town by offering tours, souvenirs or drama festivals centring on the Faustian experience. This despite the presence of a 'Hamlet House' in the main street, purporting to have been the site of the Danish prince's accommodation when a student at Wittenberg – a chronological impossibility, if only because the university was founded centuries after Hamlet's death. Unlike Knittlingen and nearby Leipzig, Wittenberg does not take pride in its Faustian heritage, if only because it has no need to reinvent itself. It possesses an abundance of other historical relics of great significance. Since 1938, it has been known officially as 'Lutherstadt Wittenberg', and with Martin Luther's monastery, Philip Melanchthon's house and Lucas Cranach's studio still relatively well preserved, not to mention the Schloss and Schlosskirche where Luther's revolutionary theses were posted, it enjoys an abundance of historical sites. Such pageants as are performed there inevitably revolve around the Reformation (a musical rendition of 'Luther's Marriage' was on the programme for 2003), and Faust would be out of place. Yet here, too, there are traditions about the magus, who is said to have resided from 1525 to 1532 in a house at Collegienstrasse 31 and to have taught at the now-defunct Leucorea University during that period. The site where the pact was concluded has been identified as the so-called 'Specke', a grazing area near the town that was much frequented by students. Wittenberg traditions maintain that the magician's death occurred in a tavern called 'Freischütz' in a village by the name of Pratau, some three kilometres from the town. Other local legends speak of a final wager between Faust and Mephistopheles which required the latter to construct a road from there to a town called Kemberg, which the devil did, thus assuring himself of Faust's soul. The road to Kemberg has curious zig-zags in consequence.[1]

The nearby city of Leipzig offers tourists 'Faustian' gastronomic and other experiences at its most famous wine cellar, *Auerbachs Keller* ('Auerbach's Cellar/

*94. Faust-Museum, Knittlingen, established by Günther Mahal in 1980.
Photograph by Osman Durrani*

Tavern') in the Mädler-Passage, said to have been visited by the doctor and to be the site of one of his most famous stunts. A lively trade in souvenirs is done not only in this establishment's gift shop but also in up-market porcelain outlets in the Old Town Hall and elsewhere. The wine cellar, which formed the basement of the Auerbachs Hof complex in the city centre from the sixteenth century onwards, has a long and colourful history. It was built by a professor of Mathematics, Heinrich Stromer von Auerbach, as an investment in the years between 1525 and 1538, which makes it just about conceivable that a person whose dates coincided with those of the legend could have visited it a few years before his death (Benndorf; Anon., *Wirtschaftsjournal*).

The cellar is truly of enormous proportions. Contemporary sources describe it as having 100 vaults, containing shops, picture galleries, accommodation and stabling. It was, from the earliest days, a favourite haunt with Leipzig's students; rumours suggested that Stromer had thoughtfully built a secret passage connecting the nearby university to this popular venue. This, like so much else, is fanciful speculation; so, too, was the attempt by the author of a broadsheet to relate a sensational event to this location. An ancient Leipzig chronicle states that by virtue of his art the well-known Dr Johann Faust rode out of Auerbach's Cellar onto the street on a barrel full of wine that the apprentices were meant to haul up, an event now depicted on the restaurant's table-napkins (Anon., *Wirtschaftsjournal*, 8).

95. A statue by Hanne Schorp-Pflumm dating from 1954 commemorates the legendary doctor outside the Knittlingen Town Hall. Photograph by Osman Durrani

The monastery at Maulbronn, a World Heritage Site, comprises a *Faust-Turm* ('Faust Tower'). Faust is said to have conducted his essays in alchemy here – although the tower was constructed in 1604, long after his death and a full seventeen years after the chapbook was printed. Yet Maulbronn not only has its Faust Tower, first referred to as such in 1840, but also a kitchen and a recess named after him, as well as two bloodstains purporting to be his own (Mahal, 10). There was a Faust House in Roda near Altenburg, also in Bad Kreuznach, where Tritheim has Faust appear in 1507, likewise in Erfurt, which also boasts a *Faust-Gässchen* ('Faust Alleyway'). Altogether, there are well over a dozen buildings in Germany that claim to have been lived in or visited by the doctor in the course of his travels.

Faust would not be a cultural icon in the fullest sense of the term if he did not

96. German postage stamp, issued 14.11.1979

continue to be commemorated across the globe in all the familiar formats, not only in artefacts but in brand names, advertising, postage stamps and drama festivals and other, more ephemeral walks of life. To begin with small-scale mementos, from the early twentieth century onwards, sets of cigarette cards and postage stamps have been depicting famous productions. John Player's tobacco card series, 'Old Stage Actors and Actresses', issued in 1916, shows both Henry Irving as Faust and Ellen Terry as Margaret, splendidly attired for the Lyceum production of 1885.

97. Eight stamps from a set of ten designed by Albert Decaris, each one a masterpiece in miniature, 1969.

Postage stamps have been issued in the most unlikely places. A German example came out in November 1979. The design consists of a red devil holding up a mirror to a traditionally attired Faust with a glass container in his hand. Some elaborate designs were produced by the master engraver Albert Decaris (1901–1988) for the Principality of Monaco in 1969. Decaris has more than six hundred designs to his credit, and helped to shape the distinctive image of the delicately coloured and ornate French postage stamp of his time. The ten images he created for the Faust series were based on Berlioz's opera and are among his finest; each one is a masterpiece in miniature. In 1999, a series of three stamps marking the 250th anniversary of the birth of Goethe appeared in the Caribbean states of Antigua and Barbuda. One of these, a fine design with a face value of $1.75, depicts Faust being borne aloft by angels. In March 2004, the German Post Office issued a 1€ stamp commemorating the 150th anniversary of the first production of both parts of *Faust*.

It can be roughly estimated that on every night of the year some three hundred productions of *Faust* – in one form or another – are staged across the world. There have been drama festivals and Faustian spectacles, sometimes promoted as 'Faustivals', in many towns. The 'Goetheanum' in Dornach, Switzerland, has been staging spectacular productions at regular intervals for the past sixty-five years. Kronach in northern Bavaria is another location that has been hosting outdoor productions during the summer months, using as a backdrop the castle of Rosenberg, one of the largest in Europe. An open-air production takes place here during July and August, with the intention of preserving local colour and historical costume, while making the play appear fast-moving in a filmic manner. It was here that Rudolf Volz's rock opera versions were performed during 2003. A further institution worth mentioning is the time-honoured tradition of vernacular theatre.

98. Faust and Mephistopheles (played by Ulrike Mahr) in Kronach. Ulrike Mahr has been playing the devil here since 1995. Photograph supplied by Ulrike Mahr.

Attempts to transpose Faust into regional dialects, including Hessian, Frisian, and Saarländisch, will be examined below (407); there are many provincial theatre groups that perform *Faust* in the local patois. One such team that has been staging a *Faust* in Bavarian for many years is that headed by Johannes Reitmeier und Thomas Stammberger. Their adaptation *Der Faust* was televised in 1992; it was recently revived as *Der Bayerische Faust* ('The Bavarian Faust') and was performed in Starnberg near Munich during October and November 2003. Despite ingenious renderings of the original into the guttural patois of the area, the 'Lord' speaks his lines in High German, no doubt as a concession to local sensibilities.

Merchandising

Faust has been used for an array of incongruous purposes, perhaps none more so than the election campaigns in the 1930s, for which useful sound-bites, especially the lines in which he speaks of a longing to see 'a swarming multitude [...] on a land that is free' (F 11580) were used to win votes. These verses, stripped of their ironic context, had been employed by early socialists in the 1890s and were recycled many times over by politicians and orators. The first recorded use was by Franz Mehring, on 1 May 1894; and they were quoted again by Walter Ulbricht in his speech 'To all citizens of the German Democratic Republic. To the entire German nation' (*Neues Deutschland*, 28 March 1962, 5).

On a more mundane level, the name, and often the image, too, have appeared on a wide variety of products, ranging somewhat unselectively from instant coffee and salmon to medicinal and alcoholic beverages. The name of Mephisto is associated both with a chess computer and a well-known brand of footwear. Quotable quotes from the play have long been used to sing the praises of meat extracts, champagne, liqueur, margarine, corn removers, typewriters, shoes and even toilet paper (Jasper).

A 'Faust Apothecary' sells medicines in Knittlingen, and several local companies used to produce their own wares under the 'Faust' label: potions, lotions, and even meat products. Beer is another favourite. The 1929 Faust exhibition in Brunswick, a vast affair set up to commemorate the 100th anniversary of the first theatre production of Goethe's work there, had a special room devoted to what was called 'Faust-Kitsch'. It contained many household consumer goods. Carl Niessen, who was responsible for compiling the catalogue, confesses with evident regret that the more lurid exhibits were withheld from the general public. None-theless, pocket handkerchiefs, skeins of wool, and bottles of liqueur were included, all bearing a Gretchen label or image, and nail-polish, cigars, and boxes of chocolate were marketed with the help of Faust's name or profile (Niessen, 197f.).

99. Chemist's shop in Knittlingen. Photograph by Osman Durrani.

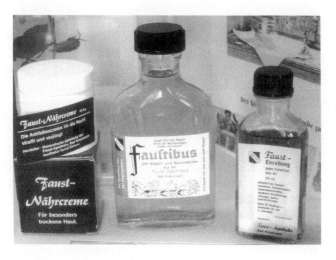

100. A selection of beauty products and embrocations bearing Faust's name (Faust Museum, Knittlingen). Photograph by Osman Durrani.

388

Several breweries have named products after Faust. Since no copyright is infringed, there seems to be no limit to this activity. Faust beer was first brewed in the New World in 1885 by the Anheuser Busch Company, best known for their 'Budweiser' brew. While the beer was named after Tony Faust, a restaurant owner and friend of the brewer Adolphus Busch, it took its marketing strategy from Gounod's opera, then at the height of its popularity; this includes a scary figure clad in red on the label and a very flaxen-haired Gretchen figure beside a barrel. Limited editions of accompanying beer steins were produced, alongside a whole range of accessories, including key rings and tankards; 5,000 of these were issued in 1997. Several European breweries have from time to time also used the name of Faust to promote their product in publicity campaigns, including the Belgian brewing giant Stella Artois. Germany's 'Faust Brewery' is based in Miltenberg on the River Main, near Frankfurt. The name derives from Johann Adalbert Faust, who bought out the local 'White Lion' Brewery in 1895. For some time, the British independent brewer Eldridge Pope of Dorchester produced 'Faust Pils' under licence from the Miltenberg company.

101. *Historic 'Gretchen' advert for Faust Beer as produced by Anheuser Busch. Note the diminutive American Eagle under the barrel.*

102. *Faust brand diet lager, photographed and consumed by Osman Durrani. Brewed under licence by Eldridge Pope, Dorchester, UK.*

103. *Faust Brand Red Salmon*

Other products bearing Faust's name in the old world include tinned meat from a factory that once operated in the vicinity of Knittlingen, and household and gardening equipment. American consumers came to associate the name with a rather different range of products. One of these was salmon. 'Faust' brand choice red salmon from Washington State has been marketed with the aid of a Mephistopheles figure, clad appropriately enough in eye-catching red. Here the connection is easy to spot. In the case of 'Faust Instant Coffee' the relevance may be more difficult to appreciate, until you look at the advertising slogans that were

104. *Napkin from Auerbach's Cellar,*
Leipzig, celebrating the doctor's ride on
the barrel

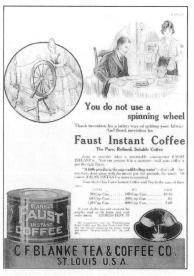

105. *Faust Instant Coffee advert from*
Vogue, 1923

390

used to promote C.F. Blanke's brew from St. Louis. In the 1920s, at a time when most people still ground their coffee beans by hand, Blanke proudly informed its consumers: 'You do not use a spinning wheel', and placed a Gretchen look-alike in the corner of the advert. The pun was immediately grasped by anyone familiar with the relevant scene from the play or opera.

The name of Mephisto(pheles), by contrast, signifies anything that is 'diabolically good'. The fine walking shoes produced in France are one example, and here the name may be suggestive of footwear in which you can quietly sneak up on someone without being heard. The chess computers also require little explanation. Their computational ability has proved itself in many a contest between man and machine.

106. While Faust's name is used to market food, drink and flowers, Mephisto sells shoes and chess programs. Hegener's and Glaser's Mephisto, released in 1981, was one of the earliest chess computers.

The Leisure Industry

Doctor Faust is a relatively abstract strategy game invented by the prolific Göttingen-based games author Reinhold Wittig and marketed by Blatz Games of Berlin from 1994 onwards. It won an award as the 'Most Beautiful Game of the Year'. It is suitable for two players who take the part of a red and a blue devil; their role is to chase the Doctor's 'soul', represented by a crystal pyramid, across a board whose squares are inscribed with quotations from Goethe. In doing so, they can develop strategies by judiciously employing so-called 'soul cards' and 'devil cards' to outmanoeuvre their opponents. Each game lasts for approximately thirty minutes. A full description of the rules will be found on the www.gamecabinet website. The box bears a warning to the effect that it is 'not suitable for children aged below three'.

107. Doctor Faust: the Board Game. The caption reads
'Only those who think like the devil will win.'

Many other producers have used the name more or less loosely for a 'diabolically difficult' adventure or strategy game. The part of Faust is offered to someone who faces great risks. Thus in the PC-based *Jazz and Faust*, developed in Russia by Saturn Plus and currently marketed by 1C Company, an adventure scenario is offered to players who must assume the role of either sea captain Faust or smuggler Jazz and embark on a quest for lost treasure and riches in an ancient Oriental environment. Players must communicate by pointing and clicking on the various inhabitants of the three distinct worlds. Opinions vary as to whether the many marvellously rendered scenes give the feeling of playing inside a living painting, creating a rich and impressive world for players to enjoy, or whether 'ugly, boring, terribly written, and acted out even worse, *Jazz and Faust* is a box with plastic that should be avoided at all costs' (Review by Ivan Sulic, pc.ign.com website).

Better known is *Faust. The Seven Games of the Soul*, marketed by Cryo Interactive and developed by Arxel Tribe, in which the curiously named 'Marcellus Faust' figures as the hero of the game. He is an elderly black man whose function is to guard the entrance to an unused theme park on the border between heaven and hell. At midnight, the 'aristocratic demon' Mephisto appears, and a duel ensues in which the stakes are salvation or damnation. As 'master of illusions', Mephisto sets numerous traps before Faust can enter the park and investigate its secrets. The player's task is to search for clues and reveal the whole history of each of its seven inmates, every one guilty of one of the seven deadly sins, and, as Marcellus Faust, to 'play God' and decide whether they should be sent to Heaven or Hell.

Only when the player, through Faust, has identified which sin the person committed and the motives for his or her actions, and Faust has pronounced his verdict on them, will the mystery unravel. The game is enormously complex. It should be obvious from this that although Faustian figures like 'Homunculus' appear in it, the latter as effeminate genie and side-kick to the hero, *Faust. The Seven Games of the Soul* strays as far away from the original tale as you can get while still retaining the main characters' names (review by Scott Humphries, pc.ign.com website).

108. *Granville Taylor appeared as 'Faust' for many years*

Exhibitions and 'Fringe' Theatre

Faust's name has been used in recent times by conjurors and illusionists. The name was bought by Granville Taylor as a personal trade mark in 1950 for £100; he chose it because he had been a great admirer of the illusionist 'Dante' and was looking for something similarly short and memorable (Letter to Osman Durrani, 24 September 2003). It served him well; over forty years he built up a reputation for spectacular illusion shows, some of which involved up to twenty-four dancers and stage assistants. He appeared in Japan during the 1970s and 1980s, was seen at the Ice Drome, Blackpool, during the summer of 1980 and at the Theatre Royal, Brighton, in 1985–6. Several websites currently document his appearances (www.faust-the-magician.co.uk/; also www.faust.i8.com/).

The contemporary theatre continues to benefit from the influence of the Faust theme, as the Edinburgh Festival, 2003, demonstrates. Here there were no fewer than four plays that claimed to adapt the Faust theme, including *Faust*, by the 'Theatre of Eternal Values', which set out to shed new light on Goethe's play. The intended result was a vibrant, living theatre based on a hope that the essence of Goethe's philosophy could be transmitted through the hearts and minds of the actors and musicians.

> The story of the scholar Faust, a master of philosophy, law, medicine and theology, has fascinated mankind across the ages. The more Faust knows, the less satisfied he feels. As his discontent grows, he begins looking for answers outside the boundaries of conventional wisdom. He calls on the spirit world and Mephistopheles, the Devil, appears. He offers Faust great rewards if he signs a contract with blood. Faust agrees to the bargain and the journey of temptation is born.
>
> Faust is a seeker of truth. He is aware of the uselessness of his own intellectual knowledge and yet he is blinded by the ego he has acquired through his studies. The Devil, who plays with the ego of man, easily finds a doorway into his soul. He creeps in slowly, formulating a complex web of intrigue and temptation until Faust becomes lost. But the Devil meets an unexpected obstacle in the innocent peasant girl Gretchen.
>
> This allegorical poetic drama, set in 18th Century Germany, is the ideal context in which to explore the dangerous path of an awakening consciousness, the exalted ambitions that can lead to self destruction, and the profound impact of innocence and simplicity in the struggle against our darker selves. This performance merges comedic elements with the Faust story giving balance to this powerful drama. (Theatre of Eternal Values, Publicity Prospectus)

Feasting on Faust, by MATE Drama Workshop, was another offering at Edinburgh during the 2003 season. This was a gluttonous fusion of physical theatre, grotesque puppetry and gritty jazz-cabaret, with a full musical score and eight original songs. It was a lively production; as the advert put it, 'You'd have to be dead to miss it!' A third show was *Faust (US)* by HWS Rembiko Project, in which megalomania and sexual depravity beckon in a kind of collage taken from Marlowe's *Doctor Faustus* and Goethe's *Faust*. Finally, *Meat* by Sarah Colvin, set during the Falklands conflict of 1982, turned out to be the tale of a twisted Faustian pact between the unlikeliest of collaborators. The presence of four re-workings of *Faust* at a single festival open to all arts and all themes confirms the material's enduring ability to inspire the most varied groups of performing artists.

Visually, too, the theme is in the limelight. It recently inspired nineteen contemporary artists to exhibit their works in pottery, glass, textiles, oils, watercolours and anamorphic kinetic constructions at The Gallery in the Friars, Canterbury, during October 2003. It was difficult to select a few examples from this array of minor masterpieces with which to conclude this chapter, as each seemed worthy of detailed comment. The following observations are based on interviews with the artists conducted between 5 and 12 October 2003.

The range of exhibits at this, the most recent public display of art produced through the influence of the Faust myth, included a large multi-coloured bowl by Roger Cockram of Chittlehampton Pottery with a starkly contrasting interior and exterior. Cockram considers the form of the bowl to be the most appropriate

109. Artist Roger Cockram holding a ceramic bowl illustrating 'Faust's choice'.
Photograph by Osman Durrani

vehicle to illustrate the opposing forces that vie for Faust's soul. Thus the outside surface represents paradise and the promise of salvation, while the inside shows hell and its destructive fires. A set of ceramic pieces designed by Avis Murray, who works freelance for Dartington Pottery, were, in the words of the artist, 'a personal and creative catharsis'. She now regards the triptych of 'Belcher', 'The Two Angels' and 'My Mephistopheles' as representing a new stage in her work. Clive Soord, known as the 'Master of the Dragons' for his many intricate fantasy sculptures, based his contributions on Victorian grotesques such as those of the Martin Brothers. The theme of Doctor Faustus is well suited to Soord's creative imagination, and the vessels he exhibited comprise a microcosm of demonology.

The illustration in ink and gum Arabic by Felix Zakar that appears on the cover of this volume depicts Doctor Faustus in the guise of Dr Simon Forman ('Devil Forman'), alchemist and astrologer at the time of Queen Elizabeth I. Forman was an occultist, a quack physician and surgeon, who was persecuted for prescribing dangerous potions, yet admired for treating himself during a plague epidemic and surviving. Like John Dee and Christopher Marlowe, he was a shadowy figure who was implicated in murder and served time in prison for occult practices. Zakar cites several reasons why Marlowe may have used Forman as the basis for the character of Doctor Faustus. Apart from his exploits as an alchemist – he is said to have summoned the spirit of a black dog and spent years trying to produce a Philosophers' Stone –, he was devoted to Marlowe's rival, Shakespeare, and was hostile to the more scholarly Dee, whose involvement in the translation of the Faust Book was noted above (60). The painting also shows a little-known Canterbury landmark, the 'Alchemist's Chimney', built in 1804 by the Reverend Thomas Mitchell as an oratory and laboratory. Mitchell was a latter-day alchemist who is said to have treated patients with a set of specially-tuned hand-bells. In using this image on the cover, I aspired to link the old with the new, the light with the dark, the humorous with the tragic aspects of the legend.

110. A selection of Clive Soords' Devil Jugs and grotesque sculptures.
Photograph by Osman Durrani.

Note

1. The information about Wittenberg was kindly provided by Eva Leithoff of the Wittenberg Tourist Information Office.

Cited Works and Further Reading

Alexander Abusch, 'Goethes Humanismus und die Arbeiterklasse' (1949), in *Ibid.*, *Humanismus und Idealismus in der Literatur. Aufsätze.* Leipzig: Philipp Reclam jun., 1973, 38–58.

Anon., '475 Jahre Weinausschank in Auerbachs Keller zu Leipzig', *Wirtschaftsjournal*, Special Supplement, Chemniz: Wirtschaftsjournal Sachsen, May 2000.

Paul Benndorf, *Auerbachs Hof*, in Georg Merseburger (ed.), *Leipziger Kalender – Illustriertes Jahrbuch und Chronik.* Nr 11, Leipzig 1914. Rptd Leipzig: Sachsenbuch Gesellschaft, 1992.

Gunilla Bergsten, *Thomas Manns Doktor Faustus. Untersuchungen zu den Quellen und zur Struktur des Romans.* Tübingen: Niemeyer, 1974.

John Cornwell, *Hitler's Scientists. Science, War and the Devil's Pact.* London: Viking, 2003.

Osman Durrani, *Fictions of Germany. Images of the Nation in the Modern Novel.* Edinburgh: University Press, 1994.

Faust in Kommerz und Kitsch. Exhibition Catalogue. Knittlingen: Faust Archiv, 1999.

Freeman Dyson, *Disturbing the Universe.* New York: Harper and Row, 1979.

——, *The Day after Trinity: J. Robert Oppenheimer and the Atomic Bomb.* Kent/Ohio: Transcript Library, 1981.

George Gamow, *Thirty Years That Shook Physics. The Story of Quantum Theory.* London: Heinemann, 1972.

Daniel Jonah Goldhagen, *Hitler's Willing Executioners. Ordinary Germans and the Holocaust.* London: Little, Brown and Company, 1996.

Jörn Göres (ed.), *Meinungen zu Faust. Handschriften und Porträts aus der Sammlung Theens.* Düsseldorf: Goethe-Museum, 1979.

Roslynn D. Haynes, *From Faust to Strangelove. Representations of the Scientist in Western Literature.* Baltimore: Johns Hopkins University Press, 1994.

Rolf Hochhuth, *Hitlers Dr Faust. Tragödie.* Reinbek: Rowohlt, 2000.

Willi Jasper, 'Der dämonische Held. Der "Faust" und die Deutschen – eine verhängnisvolle Affäre', *Deutsches Allgemeines Sonntagsblatt*, 5 February 1999.

Günther Mahal, *Faust. Und Faust. Der Teufelsbündler in Knittlingen und Maulbronn.* Tübingen: Attempto, 1997.

Carl Niessen (ed.), *Katalog der Ausstellungen: Faust auf der Bühne. Faust in der bildenden Kunst.* Berlin: Fritz Klopp, 1929.

Jonathan Petropoulos, *The Faustian Bargain. The Art World in Nazi Germany.* London: Penguin, 2001.

I.A. Richards, *Tomorrow Morning, Faustus! An Infernal Comedy.* London: Routledge and Kegan Paul, 1962.

Stephan Richter, 'Tony Blair: Dr. Faust – Or Mephistopheles?', *The Globalist*, 19 September 2003.

Alexandra Ritchie, *Faust's Metropolis. A History of Berlin.* London: HarperCollins, 1998.

Wolfgang Rothe, *Der politische Goethe. Dichter und Staatsdiener im deutschen Spätabsolutismus.* Göttingen: Vandenhoeck & Ruprecht, 1998.

Ralf Schnell, *Geschichte der deutschsprachigen Literatur seit 1945.* Stuttgart: Metzler, 1993.

Rüdiger Scholz, *Goethes "Faust" in der wissenschaftlichen Interpretation von Schelling und Hegel bis heute: Ein einführender Forschungsbericht.* Rheinfelden: Schäuble, 1983.

Karl Shapiro, *Collected Poems, 1940–1978.* New York: Random House, 1978.

Roger Shattuck, *Forbidden Knowledge: From Prometheus to Pornography.* New York: St. Martin's Press. 1996.

Carl Zuckmayer, *Gesammelte Werke.* 4 volumes. Frankfurt/M: Fischer, 1960. Volume III: *Dramen.*

——, *Des Teufels General.* Edited with an introduction, notes and a select vocabulary by Charles B. Johnson. London: Harrap, 1962.

Chapter Twelve

Cartoons and Comics

SPIDERMAN: My deadliest enemies – coming thru the very walls at me! Am I going mad?
DOCTOR FAUSTUS: Indeed you are, my boy – and only Doctor Faustus can save you!!
(*The Amazing Spider-Man*, Issue 170, 1977)

Retold in Pictures

THE STORY of Faust's pact with the devil and his life of debauchery was written as a deadly earnest warning to adults and is not the most obvious subject for children's literature, and even less so for illustrated comics. Horror movies have been based on it, and despite some films designed for easy viewing, such as *Bedazzled* and *I was a Teenage Faust*, the industry has frequently endeavoured to exploit the gruesome aspects of the story. Illustrated comic literature in cartoon form has taken a different approach, often bringing lighter aspects to the fore. This approach is not new, as the 'pantomime' Fausts and puppet plays of earlier years have shown. The twentieth century experienced the exponential growth of lavishly illustrated picture books on the theme, some of which were aimed at young readers while others targeted an adult market.

The earliest simplified drawings were the volumes of *Umrisse* ('outline sketches') that retold the story in images alone and were executed by artists such as Moritz Retzsch and Johann Nisle in the first half of the nineteenth century. The comic as such, with its concentration on rapid action and its consignment of the spoken word or expletive to miniature balloons within simplified graphics is a twentieth-century phenomenon. There have been many series of 'Marvel' comics in the United States, in which a 'Mephistopheles' figure wreaks havoc on the world or one of the 'Super Heroes' battles with him or with Doctor Faustus, who in the 'Marvel Comics' context is either naturally evil or perverted by some previous misadventure. 'The Amazing Spider-Man versus Dr. Faustus' or 'Mephisto versus the Fantastic Four' are typical of this type of product. More recently, specialist illustrators have replaced the studio artwork of the 1970s and 1980s. Text-writer David Quinn and illustrator Tim Vigil formed a productive partnership to create a series of twelve extremely gory 'adult' narratives originally published by their

Rebel Studios, and concurrently picked up by Northstar Productions, featuring a
'Faust – Love of the Damned' character with huge extendable metal claws and an
apparently unquenchable blood-thirst. These comics have a following in the USA
on account of their gritty combination of violent crime, sex and the occult. They
appear not to have been imported into Britain or Canada through the regular
channels. Eventually, a semi-coherent narrative was condensed out of the series
and pressed into service as the basis of the film *Faust. Love of the Damned*, which
was directed by Brian Yuzna and scripted in part by David Quinn (see 336f., above).

For Marvel Comics, 'Doctor Faustus' is a crazy German scientist who plots to
destroy the planet. In a sinisterly prophetic episode dating from 1975, 'Captain
America' catches him trying to crash a load of lethal weapons into Manhattan
aboard a jumbo jet operating as 'Flight Nine Eleven'. The only female Super Hero,
'Wonder Woman', easily outshone her German antagonist in 'Fausta, the Nazi
Wonder Woman'. Other authors have stuck closely to the sources when illustrating
the story for their young readers. This in itself is no easy undertaking, given that

111. Stan Lee, Captain America and the Falcon. *Marvel Comics, December 1975, 7.*

even adult readers may disagree about the nature of the pact, the status of Faust's mystical experiences, the rights and wrongs of his interaction with Gretchen; given also that far-reaching questions as to whether or not he merits eternal damnation are incapable of easy resolution.

Attempts to retell Faust's story through simplified pictures fall into three main groups. There are picture-books intended for children; these tend to reduce the story to selected aspects by cutting out a proportion of the action. The majority pursue educational objectives. Comic-type books are aimed at various age-groups which retain more of the original text, and indeed in some cases reproduce it in full. Thirdly, there are the loosely 'Faustian' stories which refer to the original through parody or in some other manner. A brief review of examples will follow.

Kids' Stuff: Educational Comics

112. *Mephistopheles mirrored on the covers of the American and German editions of* Classics Illustrated.

From the 1940s onwards, the 'Classics Illustrated' (sold as 'Classic Comics' prior to March, 1947) series, the brainchild of Albert E. Kanter, a self-educated immigrant from Russia, put a selection of the world's greatest books before young readers in sequences of vivid cartoon drawings. These booklets with their bright yellow rectangles in the top left-hand corner rapidly became household favourites across the world – they were published in distinct editions in no fewer than 36 countries –, introducing children to works of literature through colourful pictorial narratives. The series began with *The Three Musketeers* in 1941, and soon sales figures of around half a million copies per volume were achieved, even at a time when there was a vocal anti-comic lobby led by Frederic Wertham in the USA. Goethe's *Faust* was, as things turned out, the very last literary title to be published by Kanter, in August 1962, bearing the serial number 167. The German series runs to 206 titles, with Faust appearing somewhat earlier, as item number 129.

> In sixteenth-century Germany, there lived a learned man highly respected by the people in all the hills and valleys around for the help he had given them in the time of the plague. His name was Doctor Faust. The famous man often sat in his study after hours, away from the lecture platform where he taught younger scholars. About him were many books and chemical mixtures. But for all his knowledge, he despaired that he had accomplished little. He longed for a different kind of life, richer and more meaningful than the one he had known. (*Faust*, Classics Illustrated, 1)

Alfred Sundel, who adapted *Faust* for the Classics Illustrated comic over 'a weekend and in a few evenings' (Jones, 115), is necessarily highly selective in condensing the 12,000-line drama into just forty-seven pages of images that have very little room for text. It is remarkable that Part II is summarised in addition to Part I, albeit in a total of just ten pages. Many episodes are abridged or omitted. Faust's opening monologue is disposed of in just five images, with no sign of Wagner or the Earth Spirit, despite the obvious potential for dramatic sketching. The next scene, 'Outside the City Gate', gets a generous nineteen images and even shows Faust treating patients with his father, a relatively minor flashback within the play as a whole. The events in Auerbach's Cellar are also dealt with in great detail, requiring a further nineteen images. From then on, the pace speeds up. Key favourites with the nineteenth-century illustrators, like Gretchen at her spinning wheel, are omitted altogether, and others reduced to a single image. 'Martha's Garden', for example, consists of just one very dark picture showing Faust giving instructions to the girl on how to administer the sleeping-potion to her mother.

The pictures have a Disney-like quality. The artist, Norman Nodel, was evidently influenced by Gustaf Gründgens' production, which the publisher had obliged him to attend when it came to New York: the portrayal of Marthe Schwerdtlein clearly recalls Elisabeth Flickenschildt (Jones, 115; Classics Illustrated, 29), and Mephisto's cloak is cut very much like the one worn by Gründgens. The woman in the Witch's mirror could be a Hollywood starlet. She has little in common with Gretchen, who is more modestly attired and distinguished by long, reddish-auburn plaits. The *homunculus*, whose story is left unfinished, is an embryonic Quasimodo. Faust, on the other hand, is modelled on the bearded Junker familiar from countless German steel engravings rather than on Quadflieg. The English-language text breaks down at some points, as was not uncommon in Kanter's comics; William B. Jones' study shows that many of them garbled or misrepresented the stories on which they claimed to be based. Here, the final chorus of angels is paraphrased simply as 'Bear the sleeper to Paradise.' And the little volume ends, as ever, with a well-meant encouragement to children: 'Don't miss the added enjoyment of reading the original, obtainable at your school or public library,' (Classics Illustrated, 47) regardless of whatever difficulty young readers may have experienced in finding it there.

George Haimsohn's *Bedside Faust* dates from 1952. It consists of some 200 crude line-drawings depicting Faust's career in minimalist outline and couched in the slang of the day (Mephistopheles: 'Let's blow this dump and have some real fun!'). The plot adheres more closely to Gounod than any other version and, given its sarcastic perspective, it is hard to say whether the target audience is teen or adult. One of the undisputed children's favourites from this period is 'Tintin', the hero of a string of comics by Hergé. Gounod's *Faust* makes regular appearances here, too, and is the only opera ever to be mentioned by name in the series. The overweight singer Bianca Castafiore specialises in somewhat grotesque renderings of the 'Jewel Song', and opera and reality intertwine in the volume *Les Bijoux de la Castafiore* ('The Castafiore Emerald') of 1963.

Many German writers and artists have attempted to retell the plot for children. Early examples of such books include Else Franke's *Die Geschichte des Dr. Faust* of 1925, which provides a synthesis of various traditions for young readers. More recently, Dr Barbara Kindermann, whose PhD thesis examined the Grimm Brothers' fairy tales, produced two separate editions of *Faust* aimed at children aged seven and above. Her *Weltliteratur für Kinder* ('World Literature for Children') series even includes a *Romeo and Juliet* aimed at precocious seven-year-olds. The first of Kindermann's two *Fausts* appeared in 1995 with illustrations by Christiane Mitzkus. The plot is retold in around 3,000 words. Mitzkus uses dark colours: black, grey and blue seem to dominate this volume. Mephisto is clad in a tight-fitting black cloak, which together with his chalk-white face makes him look like a youthful, athletic and only slightly sinister circus clown. The text describes him as a 'low-ranking devil'. This was soon replaced. Kindermann's second attempt to retell the story was published in 2002 and takes a different approach. In this more gaudy, colourful book, Mephisto is upgraded to 'the devil' in the text, and his appearance is no longer that of a clown. He has graduated to a seedy-looking long-nosed tramp in a tattered overcoat and purple skull-cap. Klaus Ensikat's elaborate drawings betray a fondness for clever little anachronisms: The Lord wears a vulgar-looking Panama hat and the students in Auerbach's Cellar drink their beer, somewhat incongruously, from aluminium cans. They include a typical 'punk' with a Mohican hairdo, an image that clashes somewhat with the focus on 'olde German' architecture and fairy-tale effects. Both of Kindermann's versions go rather coy on the subject of why Gretchen ended up in prison: 'She had expected Faust's child and in her despair had not permitted it to live'. The last page informs the young readers: 'Thanks to his love of Gretchen, Faust finally manages to tear himself away from Mephisto. And Gretchen had been praying so fervently that Faust should be saved from the devil that he was eventually allowed to enter heaven, where she awaited him with joy. Thus the two of them were finally united forever.

But Mephisto was left alone and had lost his wager' (Kindermann (2002), 34). Despite relatively few direct quotes and a tendency to reinterpret or even distort Goethe's work, it was nonetheless commended in many circles and even won an award from *Stiftung Buchkunst* (Thiele).

This book is one among many that set out to illustrate the text in such a way as to introduce children of different ages to the plot while appealing to adult readers as well and offering some new insights into a story with which they might already be familiar. In 1991, the architect and sculptor Christian Schieckel produced a complete version of Part I. It is richly illustrated with one hundred pages of line-drawings that at various points combine the simple interiors of Moritz Retzsch, the landscapes of Caspar David Friedrich and the labyrinthine work of Maurice Escher. The overall effect is powerful and frequently surreal. Martha's Garden, for example, features a maze, and while Gretchen's room is Spartan of appearance, Martha's is opulently furnished with Biedermeier antiques, potted cacti and even a goldfish bowl. This book deserves to be more widely known. Schieckel reproduces the entire text in neat sans serif type. In his treatment of Faust and other characters, there is much variety. Close-ups and head-and-shoulders portraits dominate, but there are also landscapes and wide-angled vistas. The author's stated aim is to achieve on the page what cannot be implemented on stage; witches fly effortlessly through the air, and the frequent metamorphoses such as that of dog to hippopotamus to elephant to Mephistopheles-as-travelling-scholar are deftly visualised, with the transformation of the carousing drinkers into vines presenting no problems, as Schieckel proclaims on the dust-cover. Yet it is precisely here that the artist is apt to exceed his brief as illustrator: there is much in the text that is merely imagined, one such matter being the vineyard episode. At other points Schieckel had to interpret rather than illustrate; thus the figure in the witch's mirror could be Helen, or Gretchen, or some nameless icon of feminine beauty. The image he chose is that of a fully-clad, modest and sexless woman; it fails completely to explain Faust's rapture when gazing into the mirror.

That Schieckel's images are effective is in part due to the black-and-white, lino-cut approach to the graphics. Friedemann Bedürftig's two 56-page volumes *Goethe: Zum Sehen geboren / Zum Schauen bestellt* (1999) take a different approach. This venture, supported by the Goethe-Institut and a website all of its own, currently at www.goethe-comic.de, sets out to narrate the poet's life in pictures, including a number of short extracts from *Faust*. Selectivity was essential, and the team restricted itself to the prologues, the Earth Spirit, Walpurgis Night, Helen of Troy, and Faust's death and salvation.

Comics for Grown-ups

Leaving aside the violent scenarios drawn by Tim Vigil for an exclusively adult readership of nineties 'graphic novels' aficionados, there have been several attempts to picture the story of Faust/Faustus from an unconventional angle. The effects are frequently surreal. Here, too, the 'mad scientist' is rarely far from the surface. A cartoon version of Marlowe's *Doctor Faustus* appeared in 1986, illustrated by Oscar Zarate, an artist from Argentina based in London, also responsible for *Lenin for Beginners* and *Freud for Beginners*. Here, the doctor has been transported into the twentieth century, with the pact still running for twenty-four years, beginning in 1961 and ending in 1985. He appears, in Richard Appignanesi's words, as 'a modern child of the Bomb Culture, a Peter Pan of fantastic pop-scene ambition. Mephistopheles is not a cliché stage devil, but a Ziggy Stardust extra-planetary visitor to earth' (Zarate, 3). Faustus courts the company of John F. Kennedy and General de Gaulle, the Beatles, Andy Warhol, the Pope of the day (Paul VI) and Richard Nixon. He bears a passing resemblance to pop icon David Bowie. Marlowe's text is reproduced exactly, though Faustus' journey takes him through a London populated by glitterati, drug addicts and down-and-outs. The horse-courser is drawn in the likeness of sometime US President 'tricky' Richard Nixon, while the 'Good Angel' is a relatively feeble-looking Salvation Army matron. Background tableaux familiar from newsreel footage (Vietnam, civil unrest in the Paris of 1968, Nelson Mandela) are regularly pasted in. This colourful and brilliantly entertaining comic ends with Faustus – and with him our entire world – on the point of self-destruction, as he is shot into space amidst nuclear weapons, with his finger on the trigger of a lethal missile launcher.

113. Faust among the pop icons of the Sixties. Zarate's adaptation of Marlowe (1986), 41.

Falk Nordmann's edition of Goethe's *Faust* dates from 1996, and despite a superficial similarity to the work of Christian Schieckel, presents a meaner version of the story to an adult audience. There are no pleasing landscapes or beautiful people in this black and white picture book, which gives a very personal, idiosyncratic interpretation of the first half of Part I, but breaks off after 159 pages at the end of the 'Witch's Kitchen' scene. It is unlikely to be continued.

114. Falk Nordmann's doctor confronted by a faceless superhero, 1996.

What is remarkable about Nordmann's *Faust* is that unlike the output of almost all other illustrators, his is not yet another attempt to visualise the play in dramatic terms. His spontaneous drawings range from the simplest lines to elaborate, page-filling pictures that are vibrant with kinetic energy. They do not constitute a set of illustrations in the conventional sense of the term, but a series of accompaniments through which Nordmann interrogates the text from many angles, ignoring the long iconographic history of individual scenes. Thus his work is at the opposite extreme to Schieckel's, with its conscious referencing of previous artists' work. In artistic terms, Schieckel is a modern Cornelius or Retzsch, while Nordmann's approach is akin to that of Paula Rego or Hofheinz-Döring. Nor does he adopt a consistent style, but shifts from the position of a diarist to that of a cartoonist. In the text boxes, Nordmann uses different calligraphic styles to present the speech of the individual figures: these include a childishly cursive hand for the senile Wagner, and a chaotic jumble of upper and lower case letters for the facelessly 'alien' Mephistopheles. But when it comes to the *dramatis personae*, Nordmann's imagination takes him into exciting new areas. The three rival authorities in Goethe's 'Prologue on Stage' are the Director, the Poet, and the Comedian; Nordmann draws them as a baby in nappies, a woman with a black eye, and a nude figure in a carnival mask. The Student mutates into a teddy-bear with a funnel of the type used to fill bottles in place of a head. The backgrounds are no less imaginative: a destroyed, post-nuclear world awaits the ramblers 'Outside the

City Gate'; the 'Witch's Kitchen' is crammed with monitors, and it remains uncertain whether Faust's study is a torture chamber, vivisectionist's laboratory, taxidermist's workshop, library, or boiler room. This Faust effectively challenges our preconceptions by juxtaposing the familiar story with a multitude of disorienting contexts and unstable, mutually contradictory scenarios.

Rewritten for Laughs

115. Bulbous noses and raunchy humour a-plenty in Flix's updated Faust.
© Flix/Ctm-Com GmbH, 2003.

While Zarate, Nordmann and Schieckel adhered rigidly to the written sources, the comic *Who the Fuck is Faust?* by an author writing under the pseudonym of 'Flix' updates not only the graphics but also the plot. The cover text speaks of Faust, Mephisto and Gretchen being 'ready for the new millennium', even promising to turn the Walpurgis Night into 'a drug-induced trip'. Yet the content is firmly if sarcastically rooted in everyday life in the Federal Republic. True, it begins with a contest between a God figure, busily creating new worlds on his computer, and a would-be 'hacker' of a devil intent on engineering a total system shutdown, but when the celestial wager – for a case of beer – is concluded, Heinrich J. Faust turns out to be no more than a moderately accident-prone theology student whose main aim in life is to form a relationship with an apparently equally uninspired salesgirl, Maggy, whom he meets at the local delicatessen. In the German cartoon tradition established by Loriot, they all have bulbous noses. Bawdy humour gets a frequent look-in. Mephisto has all manner of difficulties in arranging a rendezvous between Faust and his chosen woman, but after overcoming skinheads, a mother-in-law from hell and other stereotypical hazards, he seems on the point of winning his wager. If, in the end, he is deprived of his right to triumph, it is because both he and the Lord have cheated on the sly. Compromise is the only solution: 'You get the soul, and I get the beer' is the agreed formula that allows the devil to preserve a modicum of self-respect. 'Flix' is the pseudonym of Felix Görmann, a student who produced this comic at the age of 20. It is used in German schools as a warming-up exercise prior to the classroom study of Goethe. But the story does not end there. Rob Houwer Film & Television in co-operation with the Dutch Cineventura Animation Company have acquired the rights and begun production of a cartoon film, provisionally entitled *Who the* **** *is Faust?* which is expected to run for 72 minutes when completed in 2006 (Interview on www.comicgate.de/flix.htm, accessed June, 2004).

Although not a comic, Michael Swanwick's *Cigar-box Faust* is worth mentioning in the context of humorous adaptations in miniature format. The title piece of this 100-page paperback, first published in 2003, attempts to condense the story into a five-minute tour-de-force, which Swanwick, author of the novel *Jack Faust*, has popularised in live performances. Here Faust appears in the unlikely guise of a cigar, Mephistopheles as a cigar-cutter. The other main player is a box of matches, from which several familiar participants emerge: Helen of Troy, an Angel of the Lord, and the 'Light of Ontology' as the Lord's representative.

There is, in Germany, a market for humorous transpositions of the classics into regional dialects. A Low German rendition was released in 1974 by Friedrich Hans Schäfer. This inspired others to try their hand at similar transpositions. Gerhard Bungert was responsible for a version of *Urfaust* in the dialect of the Saarland which was originally broadcast on local radio in 1980. The text appeared later that year as *Fauschd*, illustrated by Heinz Diesel. This proved so successful – a second printing occurred in 1981 – that others followed. A version in the Hessian idiom with identical illustrations was produced by Harald Schäfer in 1989. These mildly entertaining books present Faust as a disillusioned schoolteacher fed up with his low social status and poor working conditions. The love story is reduced to a string of banalities, delivered in the unpolished vernacular of the relevant provinces.

A different type of picture-book for adults was produced in 1995 by the eminent couturier and photographer Karl Lagerfeld. His *Faust* is a hybrid between a fashion magazine and a film. Composed of some ninety carefully staged portraits of elegantly draped models, and interspersed with captions reminiscent of silent movies, it resembles the storyboard of a film that was never made. Much of its appeal resides in the use of well-known celebrities such as illusionist David Copperfield (as Mephisto) and catwalk queen Claudia Schiffer (as Gretchen). The storyline is only loosely related to tradition. An elderly scholar is offered the gift of eternal youth, a promise overheard by Miss Lucy Fer, proprietress of the 'Martha's Garden' nightclub. Here Faust fails to find the pure girl he desires, so Mephisto introduces him to Gretchen. The two spend the night together, and are then photographed in various prime sites in Monaco. Faust is satisfied by his experience, but Gretchen desires more: she has set her sights on wealth and expensive jewellery. Miss Lucy Fer can provide these, at a price. Gretchen has to work for a living in 'Martha's Garden', and if Faust wishes to see her, he must pay for her services. Like so much of Lagerfeld's work, the combined effect of costumes, hairstyles, lighting and props exudes intellectual sexiness. In his preface, the author claims that 'Money has now taken the place of what used to be called sin – that is why this story differs from the ancient legend and from Goethe's famous tragedy' (no page numbers); were it not for the gruesome horror and fantasy comics, and the violent pornography reviewed above, it would be hard to disagree with the description of Lagerfeld's work as the 'ultimate trivialization' of the legend (Ziolkowski, 5). Yet it is these many re-workings of the basic plot, of which only a small sample has here been presented, that demonstrate its key strengths and point to its importance for the present and, we may safely assume, for the future. Taken together, the cartoons and the adverts, the 'Faust brand' products and the art-house movies, the 'fringe theatre' productions and the locally marketed souvenirs provide a complement to the 'high' art that manifested itself in painting, opera and literature. They prove that Faust is the common property of all, a figure who remains no less accessible to today's youth culture than he was to yesterday's intellectual elite.

Faust through the Eyes of a
Japanese Cartoonist
by Yoko Riley

The objectives of this paper are to introduce three *Faust*-based cartoon stories published by Osamu Tezuka to non-Japanese readers and to show how these cartoons evolved in accordance with the artist's experience and career, reflecting the Japanese cultural and traditional background, the societal changes which Japan was undergoing at the time of their composition, and technological and scientific developments in the rest of the world.

Osamu Tezuka was a giant among Japanese story cartoonists. Hayao Miyazaki, better known to Western audiences as the creator of animations such as *Princess Mononoke* and *Spirited Away*, held him in the highest regard, and commented that 'the death of Osamu Tezuka better represents the end of the Showa era than the death of the Showa Emperor himself' (Miyazaki). To appreciate his importance in modern Japanese society, it is necessary to understand the Japanese phenomenon of *manga*. This term refers to full-length narratives of an almost cinematic type and covering a broad range of topics from children's stories to those for adult readers, from action to the classics and from pure entertainment to an educational medium. They cannot easily be compared to Western comics.

The origins of *manga* are often attributed to the *Chojugiga*, or animal scrolls of the Buddhist Bishop Toba Sojo from the twelfth century (Schodt (1983), 28f.). Toba drew humorous stories of animals acting as humans in order to expose the corrupt Buddhist establishment. Since then they paralleled the development and the course of other art forms and evolved from drawings on temple walls, scrolls, block prints, and eventually to the modern printed page. In the 1950s, I recall that there were over twenty monthly *manga* magazines just for elementary school children. This industry has continued to flourish. In 1995, there were 265 cartoon magazines published, totalling 1.6 billion individual copies (Schodt (1996), 82). Not all *manga* are for entertainment. Often, educational topics such as economics, science, history and the teaching of foreign languages are presented in them, and the topic of this paper is an example of the more serious literary and cultural themes often found in *manga*. Tezuka's early stories were adaptations of world literature or social comments on universal problems. Over his career, he produced *manga* transformations of such classics as *Crime and Punishment*, *The Merchant of Venice*, and *Treasure Island* in addition to the three versions of *Faust* which form the subject of this paper. The Japanese are known to be the most literate society in the modern world, yet *manga* comprise approximately forty per cent of the nation's published media (Schodt (1996), 20). The look and feel of modern *manga* is primarily the offspring of Tezuka's marriage of Western and Japanese styles. Reprints of his works are still popular today. Their effect is based on naïve simplicity, character motivation and themes clearly displayed in black and white terms. He pioneered long narratives of hundreds, even thousands, of pages, bringing a cinematic style and novel-length plots to the medium.

Tezuka's transformation from a PhD-holding medical doctor to a cartoonist started the exploration of a new range of possibilities in the world of Japanese cartoons. His most famous animation is *Astro Boy* and it has recently been argued that Disney's *Lion King* was based upon his cartoon *King of the Jungle* (*Jangaru Taitei*) which was originally published in 1950 as a magazine series. Machiko Satonaka went so far as to publish an open letter requesting that Disney provide 'a few lines paying respect to the origin of the story' (www.eccosys.com/SMN/opinions/ sletter.html; subsequently reprinted on the www.cs.indiana.edu website).

Amongst more than 500 cartoon books are a series of cartoons based on Goethe's *Faust* which are little known in the West. Yet it is a fact that from his twenties till the end of his life, Tezuka was, like Goethe, involved with the idea of *Faust*. His concept of *Faust* grew and transformed over time, and it remained an unfulfilled hope to develop his *Faust* series into animation. Tezuka's interest in *Faust* began at an early age: 'Due to the my exposure to the collection of world-famous stories in my home, I was captured by Goethe's *Faust* when I was a junior high school student and read it over ten times' (cited by Ikeda, 21). This sustained interest is what enabled him to use a different approach every time he attempted to re-structure the cartoon. He was clearly inspired by Goethe's view of metamorphosis and incorporated this theme into many of his *manga*.

Tezuka refers to *Faust* in many of his cartoons as well as actually writing three stories which make use of the plot in some detail. These are *Faust* (1950), which is a relatively closely translated cartoon of the original *Faust*, although intended for young children; *Hyaku Monogatari* ('Story of One Hundred', 1971; sometimes mis-translated as 'One Hundred Stories') is a version of the story of *Faust* set in the mediaeval period of Japan, the era of the *Samurai*; and *Neo Faust* (1988–1989), in which Tezuka locates the Faustian theme in modern Japan of 1970 to 1980, the time of lengthy campus disputes. This remained un-finished.

Tezuka's first attempt to make a cartoon of *Faust* was in 1950 while he was still a medical student and Japan was under American occupa-tion. It involves the Princess Margaret who is told at birth by a heavenly spirit that it would be her destiny to meet a man named Faust and it would be her duty to lead this man into heaven.

Tezuka developed his story within the context of the real world and a spiritual world (spirits, angels, devils, etc) in parallel and ingeniously

116. *Princess Margaret learns of her mission.* Faust, *Tokyo: Fuji Shobo, 1950, 12.*

integrated *Faust I* and *Faust II* together in this children's cartoon. And yet he achieved his intention to stay as true as possible to Goethe's *Faust*, making Faust's agony, his crime and his salvation appeal to the young children who will read his comic. This version of *Faust* ends with a direct reference to Goethe: 'If a man makes continuous efforts, he can be saved' (F 11936f). This was Tezuka's didactic message to Japanese children after the defeat of World War II. The subtext implied that although Japan started the Pacific War at great cost to human life in all the nations involved and gained absolutely nothing, we can be saved as long as we make continuous efforts. It is questionable whether children reading the comic understood the political implications of this message. What is beyond doubt is that after the defeat and with Japan under occupation, Tezuka demonstrated, in his first attempt at *Faust*, a very clear desire to introduce more global stories to Japanese children who had been prevented, by wartime edict, from reading non-Japanese stories.

Twenty-two years later, in 1971, Tezuka published another *Faust*-based story, which could be called Tezuka's *Mon Faust* (Tezuka (2001), 341). He located this cartoon in the lawless period of mediaeval Japan. Between the fifteenth and sixteenth centuries, without any central control, Japan was divided into more than one hundred fiefdoms and local warlords fought each other over the expansion of their territories. This 'Warring Era' lasted for over one hundred years until, in 1600, three consecutive warlords unified Japan. *Hyaku Monogatari* is developed in the context of the Feudal Lord, the *samurai*, *bushido*, *seppuku* and courtly love. If the first book can be called the simplest and the last book the most complex in terms of their ideas, then the second book is clearly the most elaborate in terms of plot and context. It is rarely, if ever, discussed in English. Tezuka divided this story into four chapters. The first chapter is called *A Wanderer*.

An inexperienced man who had not yet accomplished the way of the *samurai*, known as the unwritten code of *bushido*, was charged with being involved in a clan dispute and ordered to commit *seppuku*, a privileged form of death by suicide, allowed only to *samurai*. The devil in female form, Sudama, transforms herself from a white dog into a beautiful female. Sudama promises to buy his soul and, in return, she will grant him three wishes. He signs a contract, in blood, promising that he will end his life when his wishes are fulfilled. They are to experience a new life with full satisfaction, to fall in love and marry the most beautiful woman in the world, and to become the Lord of a territory. The warrior is taken to a cave in the forest by Sudama and given a magic medicine, which makes him young and handsome. He is also given a new name, Fuwa Usuto, which approximates phonetically to 'Faust' and signifies strength. Thus the man who held death in horror, and was willing to sell his soul in exchange for life, is saved from death by Sudama. On a scroll, Fuwa Usuto sees a picture of a more beautiful woman than Sudama and forces Sudama to take him to her and allow him to marry her.

Sudama now explains that this beautiful woman is a witch who is an apparition of a fox. The fox is known to be a mediator between divinity and humans in the *Shinto* religion. Fuwa Usuto has fallen blindly in love with the picture and ignores

Sudama's advice. A young innocent girl, Masago, also falls in love with Fuwa Usuto. A *samurai* who was also in love with her challenges him and Fuwa Usuto kills him. As a result he leaves the girl and heads for the 'Fearful Mountain' to find the most beautiful woman. He encounters a mountain full of evil creatures, and in the end finds the beautiful girl whom he saw in the picture scroll at the Shinto Shrine. With the assistance of Sudama he narrowly escapes the death that was planned by this beautiful incarnation of the fox.

117. *Sudama and Fuwa Usuto fall in love (read from right to left), 1971.*

Eventually, Sudama and Fuwa Usuto fall in love with each other. Meanwhile, Fuwa Usuto saves the young kidnapped daughter of a well-known family and he agrees to work for the Lord of the small fiefdom. With the assistance of Sudama, against all odds and all that the mountain devils can mount against him, he finds a gold mine and brings wealth to the fiefdom. The love relationship between Fuwa Usuto and the devil Sudama is an addition to the legend.

The jealous *samurai* in the fiefdom trick Fuwa Usuto to fall in love with one of the Lord's most beautiful concubines, but he realises that this woman is an

412

incarnation of the fox and kills her. However, the enraged Lord, upon hearing of the death of his favoured concubine at the hands of Fuwa Usuto, tries to punish him with one hundred beatings. Sudama helps him avoid his punishment by creating a substitute.

The fourth chapter, Gekokujo ('The lower defeats the upper'), introduces a concept that was new to Japan at that time. Up until the Warring Era, every position in the traditional, bureaucratic society was hereditary. However, during the Warring Era, this tradition was ignored and gekokujo was introduced on the basis of ability and achievement. Fuwa Usuto, upset due to the Lord's treatment, was determined to fight against the Lord. With the help of Sudama yet again, he wins and becomes the new Lord of the fiefdom.

So far, in the cartoon, he has achieved two of his original conditions, to experience a new life, and to be the Lord of the fiefdom. In Sudama's words, 'I cannot take your life yet, since you failed to find the most beautiful woman.' Fuwa Usuto answers, 'You are wrong, I found you to be the most beautiful woman in the world.'

At the scene of Fuwa Usuto's seppuku, he hears Sudama's voice, 'Say out loud that you do not love me and you will be saved from death'. Fuwa Usuto slits his abdomen with his sword uttering 'Sudama, you are the most beautiful woman in the world.' Sudama, who loves him deeply, breaks the rule as Satan, and sets his soul free saying, 'Go to heaven or wherever you want' (Tezuka (1994), 329).

A female devil accompanying Faust is not new. However, the love between Faust and the female devil, and the fact that that love saves him from falling into hell, is Tezuka's invention. It is a natural phenomenon that when a human being dies, he or she wishes to die in the arms of a loved one. This understanding and sensitivity at the time of death could be offered by Japanese women. Love between the devil and Faust, and salvation by the devil, however, could happen only in Japanese theology (Hasegawa, 256). Sudama's love for Fuwa Usuto is one of extreme, active involvement, while most women appearing in Western Fausts are rather passive. And this is surprising, since, in general, Western women are regarded as more active participants in relationships and society. Tezuka's understanding of Japanese women is clearly shown in his Story of One Hundred.

Hyaku Monogatari was also published for young people around the age of Junior High School students. Tezuka's maturity, as well as the increasing maturity of his readership, cannot be denied twenty-two years after World War II. This shows itself not least in the increasingly open acceptance of erotic art, especially by comparison with the first of Tezuka's Fausts.

Neo Faust was first published in 1988. It appeared in Asahi Journal, a weekly magazine for the intellectual salaryman. This complex work could be described as the crystallisation of knowledge in the fields of medicine, science, the humanities, religion, political science and art that Tezuka had acquired throughout his life. He sets this story in the more immediate present and focuses on the campus disputes, which involved the major universities in Japan from the 1970s onwards. The unrest was caused by students asking for more control of university policy and over the

118. Neo Faust, cover, *Tokyo, 1992*

allocation of resources after a high-level scandal about misappropriated funds.

An old professor, Dr. Ichinoseki (here again, there is a pun on *ichi*/first/Faust), ready to commit suicide due to his realisation that he could not find the fundamental formula for the universe, was tempted by a beautiful she-devil, Mephistopheles. She listens to the professor's wishes and then makes a contract that when the doctor will be satisfied with everything and when he says 'If ever I should tell the moment: Oh, stay! You are so beautiful!' (F 1699f.) the magic will disappear and his life will end.

As a result of an unexplained incident, Ichinoseki comes into possession of an enormous amount of money, and with wealth and an abundance of knowledge in the field of science, he now desires to create a new form of human like life, thus emulating Almighty God.

The idea of cloning appears here and repeatedly throughout the story. After Dr. Ichinoseki becomes an accomplished, successful and powerful businessman, he spends time in the United States to expand his business before eventually returning to his homeland. However, what awaits him at the airport in Japan is the news that his lover Mariko Takada has killed the illegitimate child born to them and is confined to a mental asylum. He rushes to the hospital and attempts

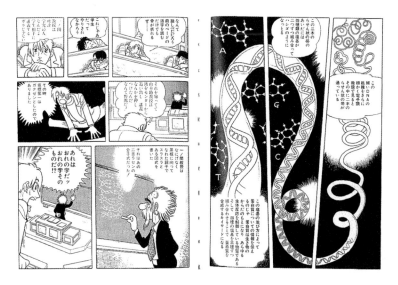

119. Professor Ichinoseki unravels the genetic code, Neo Faust, *234f.*

to save her from the asylum, but she refuses his attempts, sensing the presence of Satan in him. Here again the situation is very close to that at the end of Goethe's *Faust I*.

This is a concise description of *Neo Faust I*. Tragically, a few months after *Neo Faust II* began to appear in weekly instalments from 1989 onwards, Tezuka developed cancer and died at the age of 60. According to his close friend Professor Tsutomu Hasegawa, Tezuka's intention for *Neo Faust II* was to bring the story to the point that Dr Ichinoseki's life-form clone, like the *homunculus*, survives and destroys the world. In other words, the author's fears about excessive biotechnology were the main theme (Tezuka (1992), cover note). But the question of whether he would have eventually introduced the principle of salvation cannot be resolved. The detailed explanation of the cloning, and the possibility of creating a humanoid creature, is central to *Neo Faust*. Tezuka's aspiration to write a cartoon that was ahead of the times is evident from this unfinished story.

Osamu Tezuka's three Faust stories are created not in the European tradition, but as a reflection of Japanese culture. Tezuka, in common with most artists, had a strong individuality and ignored the idea of conformity that was still very strong during the postwar period in which he was active as a cartoonist. He had no hesitation to refer to, and question, the notion of Japanese conformity, traditional ways of thinking, customs and even Japanese humour. He remained an individualist and had no fear of going against established conventions in his cartoons. He also had no hesitation in bringing female nudity into children's cartoons as long as it was aesthetically pleasing.

Because of his independent outlook and personality, Tezuka's treatment of the Faust theme does not result in conformity to local cultural stereotypes. Since the readers are mainly children (with the exception of his last work), Tezuka might have felt that children could be more open to accept nonconformist ideas. He might have hoped that Japanese children could be encouraged to break out of their traditional conformity.

Tezuka's Faust evolved as he grew older. His fundamental idea of a cartoon shifted from the child to the adult reader, and especially to those readers who were brought up with his cartoons in their childhood and youth. He is known to have written a total of over 150,000 pages of cartoons (Ikeda, cover). Children who read his first *Faust* will therefore have been more willing to respond to the complex story of *Neo Faust*.

Within the context of this book, is Faust an icon of modern culture? Peter Salm, in the introduction to his translation of *Faust*, Part I, said of the original chapbook:

> It was a plot made to order to be a warning not to do as Faust did – not to reach for powers that lay beyond one, not to 'speculate the elements' – but to rest content with the approved answers that were provided by the Scriptures and by the inspired and approved ancient philosophers. (Salm, ix)

Tezuka took the concept of *Faust* and rendered it relevant to its original, both in a feudal and in a modern context. Many would argue that Faust might be a more relevant icon amongst the temptations of late twentieth- and early twenty-first century society. In Tezuka's representations, Faust is a cultural manifestation of many generations and centuries and appears in a society and culture fundamentally different from the context of the original. His adaptation of the Japanese background made it more interesting to his readership. However, above all, the Faust-based cartoons by Tezuka are more meaningful due to the author's Faust-like interest in every field of learning. Tezuka remained true to himself and refused to allow himself to be washed out by the Japanese tradition of conformity. It has been claimed that 'Goethe's wide-ranging mind could never be confined to one form or one philosophy. When asked for the theme of his masterwork, *Faust*, he could only say, "from heaven through all the world to hell"; his subject was nothing smaller' (Salm, *loc. cit.*). Tezuka responded to the challenge of this great epic story and transformed it into several new sets of images that were of relevance to his Japanese contemporaries: the fairy tale of redemption and salvation set in the spirit world; the historical image of the steadfast and loyal *samurai* who would never renounce his love in return for life, set in the Warring Period; and finally, the modern, sombre image of Dr. Ichinoseki, in *Neo Faust*, leaves us wanting to know whether salvation, or despair, prevails. In contrast to the *manga* Fausts by Quinn and Vigil, Tezuka's work is much more diverse, subtle, less bloodthirsty, and raises questions that encourage readers to think constructively about their own position in society. The only regret is that these transformations remain unknown in the Western world, where Goethe is so well known.

416

Cited Works and Further Reading

Friedemann Bedürftig, Christoph Kirsch and Thomas von Kummant (eds), *Goethe: Die Comic-Biographie*. 2 volumes. I: *Zum Sehen geboren*. II: *Zum Schauen bestellt*. Stuttgart: Egmont Ehapa Verlag, 1999.

Thomas Bleicher: 'Die gezeichnete Auflösung einer Ikone. Der Hagener Künstler Falk Nordmann verwandelt Goethes >Faust< in einen Comic,' in *Das Hagener Jahrbuch*, 2 (1997).

Peter Boerner and Sidney Johnson (eds), *Faust through Four Centuries. Retrospect and Analysis. Vierhundert Jahre Faust. Rückblick und Analyse*. Tübingen: Niemeyer, 1989.

Gerhard Bungert, *Fauschd. Goethes Urfaust auf Saarländisch. Mit Illustrationen von Heinz Diesel, einem Vorwort von Friedrich Hatzenbühler und einem Essay von Ludwig Harig*. Lebach: Queisser Verlag, 1980.

'Classics Illustrated' *Faust* by Goethe. Volume 167. Illustrated by Norman Nodel. New York: Gilberton Company, 1962.

Uta Claus and Rolf Kutschera, *Bockstarke Klassiker*. Frankfurt/M: Eichborn, 1985.

'Flix' [pseudonym], *Who the Fuck is Faust? Eine Comictragödie in sieben Tagen frei nach Goethe*. Frankfurt/M: Eichborn, 1998.

Else Franke, *Die Geschichte des Dr. Faust*. Oldenburg: Stalling, 1925.

George Haimsohn, *The Bedside Faust*. New York: Coward-McCann, 1952.

Tsutomu Hasegawa, *Majutsushi Faust no Tensei* ('Transformation of Faust as a Magician'). Tokyo: Shoseki Co., 1983.

'Hergé' [pseudonym], *Les Bijoux de la Castafiore*. Tournai: Casterman, 1963.

—, *The Castafiore Emerald*. London: Methuen, 1963.

Hiroaki Ikeda (ed.), *Tezuka Osamu Character Zukan* ('Illustrated Book of Tezuka Osamu's Characters'). Tokyo: Asahi Shinbun-sha, 1998.

William B. Jones, *Classics Illustrated: A Cultural History, with Illustrations*. Jefferson/NC: McFarland & Company, 2002.

Naoji Kimura, 'Probleme der *Faust*-Rezeption in Japan,' in Boerner/Johnson, 143–55.

Barbara Kindermann, *Faust. Nach der Tragödie von Johann Wolfgang von Goethe, mit Bildern von Christiane Mitzkus, nacherzählt von Barbara Kindermann*. Berlin: Kindermann, 1995.

—, *Faust nach Johann Wolfgang von Goethe. Neu erzählt von Barbara Kindermann. Mit Bildern von Klaus Ensikat*. Berlin: Kindermann, 2002.

'Marvel Comics' *Captain America and the Falcon*. Issue 192. New York: Marvel Comics Group, December 1975.

—, *The Amazing Spider-Man*. Issue 170. New York: Marvel Comics Group, July 1977.

Hayao Miyazaki, 'A Eulogy for Tezuka', *Shuppatuten* (Japanese language Internet site).

Falk Nordmann, *Johann Wolfgang von Goethe: Faust. Der Tragödie erster Teil*. Hamburg: Edition B&K, 1996.

Peter Salm (ed.), *Johann Wolfgang von Goethe, Faust, Part I*. Revised Edition, Translated with an Introduction and Notes. Toronto: Bantam Books, 1962.

Friedrich Hans Schäfer, *De holsteensche Faust: eine niederdeutsche Nachgestaltung von Goethes Urfaust mit Ergänzungen aus der Tragödie erstem Teil*. Leer: Schuster, 1974. Revised 1983.

Harald Schäfer, *Urfaust hessisch, frei nach Johann Wolfgang von Goethe und Gerhard Bungert*. Darmstadt: Eduard Roether Verlag, 1989.

Christian Schieckel, *Johann Wolfgang von Goethe: Faust. Der Tragödie erster Teil, gezeichnet von Christian Schieckel*. Cologne: Prometh, 1991.

Fred Schodt, *Dreamland Japan*. Berkeley/CA: Stone Bridge Press, 1996.

—, *Manga, Manga!* Tokyo: Kodansha International, 1983.

Michael Swanwick, *Cigar-box Faust and Other Miniatures*. San Francisco: Tachyon Publications, 2003.

Osamu Tezuka, *Faust*, Tokyo: Fuji Shobo, 1950. Rptd Tokyo: Asahi Shinbun-sha, 1994.

—, *Hyaku Monogatari*, included in *Faust*, Tokyo: Asahi Shinbun-sha, 1994.

—, *Neo Faust*, Tokyo: Asahi Shinbun-sha, 1992.

—, *Faust.* Commentary by Tsutomi Hasegawa, Tokyo: Ashai Shinbun-sha, Tokyo, 2001.

Jens Thiele, 'Die Jury von ZEIT und Radio Bremen stellt vor: J. W. Goethe/Klaus Ensikat "Faust"', *DIE ZEIT*, 46/2002.

Frederic Wertham, *Seduction of the Innocent.* Museum Press: London, 1955.

Oscar Zarate, *Christopher Marlowe: Dr Faustus. Illustrated by Oscar Zarate.* Introduction by Richard Appignanesi. World Theatre Classics Series. London: Abacus, 1986.

Theodore Ziolkowski, *The Sin of Knowledge. Ancient Themes and Modern Variations.* Princeton: University Press, 2000.

120. Faust *and* William Tell *featured on German postage stamps issued on 11 March 2004*

Conclusion

'Faustus and the Potters': A Short Story by Derek Sellen

Potters, glass-blowers, ceramicists.

I have come here tonight to ask you a favour.

Yes, I am John Faustus.

The famous, the celebrated, the notorious Doctor John Faustus.

Wanted for embezzlement, fraud, deception with intent to gain monies, bigamy, assault, trespass, felony, living off immoral earnings, association with organised crime, indecent behaviour in a public place, possession of class A, B, C and D substances etcetera, etcetera, as far as murder.

And that's just in the secular courts. There are several ecclesiastical misdemeanours, little matters of blasphemy, heresy, desecration and profanation – not bad for someone who started out as a cherub-faced chorister in the cathedral choir.

I blame it all on Mephistopheles.

We called him Phiz. He really did fizz along in life. There were all sorts of rumours about him, even as a school-kid. That the money that paid his fees came from the Greek Mafia, that the carefully disposed fringe of his hair covered some disfigurement on the brow, even that the reason he never showered after sports with the rest of us, supposedly on medical grounds, was that he possessed a curled vestigial tail at the base of the spine.

I never had much to do with him in the King's School days or when we met again at university. He was in marketing, selling new courses to overseas students, educational pimping as we called it, I was in theology. He was a sharp dresser and a sharp talker, I was a shy stammerer in charity shop clothes. He was on podiums and in fancy restaurants, I was in library carrels and at cut-price cafes.

I had my problems as a young man. I didn't find it easy to get girls. An intimate knowledge of the schisms among rival episcopal candidates in early medieval Heidelberg is not generally held to be particularly sexy. I lusted at a distance, went on doomed dates in a state of suppressed anxiety and ended up alone at home. I travelled to towns where no-one knew me to buy top-shelf magazines in newsagents and enrolled for assertiveness-building courses by post.

As for my scholastic career, it had brought me examination passes in obscure subjects with unprecedented high grades. I was rewarded by a series of minimal grants which enabled me to peruse disintegrating documents in badly lit and chilly monastic archives before I went home to a supper of tepid beans. I wrote some distinguished papers on twelfth-century heretics – research which was stolen by my professors and published under their names.

Is it surprising that I ended up teetering on the parapet of Bell Harry, looking down on the city of my schooldays and of my abortive academic career? I cursed God in ripe medieval terms I had learnt from the manuscripts, God who had given me intelligence but no wit to gain any earthly pleasures from those brains.

Then I leapt.

Some people say it was freak gusts of wind that saved me. Others that this was a divine miracle. A few that it was the result of demonic arts. All I know is that I floated rather than fell, spiralling down the side of the cathedral like the seed from a tree. Strangest thing of all, as I looked up in wonderment, relaxing in this blissful suspension, this gentlest ease of descent, I saw, even though the tower roof had been empty a few seconds before when I had launched myself, that a sharp-eyed face was watching me from above, chin resting on the flaking stone.

It was Mephistopheles.

After that, I had the devil's luck.

I won the lottery.

Ten times.

I was seen at world premières with divas and actresses and Page 3 girls on my arm.

I answered the million-pound question on television quiz shows, as confident in naming the latest soap opera character or pop-chart celebrity as in dating the dynasties of the ancient Assyrians.

I gave papers at international conferences to standing ovations as I turned the accepted tenets of medieval theology on their heads.

Everyone wanted to know me. The Pope made the mistake of inviting me to the Vatican. I bet all my winnings from lotteries and quiz shows and casinos against the Sistine Chapel ceiling that I could defeat him and his cardinals in metaphysical debate on the existence of the soul.

Who won?

Well, my team are busy at this moment tenderly removing the layers of the fresco, ready to transfer it to the atrium of my Kuala Lumpur offices.

And all the time, Mephistopheles has been beside me.

He was in the studio audience of TV quizzes, supplying far more subtle and undetectable hints than a cough or a sneezing fit.

He was the one who decided the choice of gift, Parisian lingerie or Amsterdam jewels or Istanbul confectionery, that would seal my seductions.

It was his voice that assisted me, whispering his prompts in my concealed ear-piece, as I fenced with the cardinals.

Yes, it has been Mephistopheles, flatterer, go-between, spin doctor, agent, fixer, who guided everything.

In return, he asked for nothing.

Until ...

Until, yesterday, he asked for my soul.

My soul?

But didn't I prove in fourteen days of debate with the Catholic hierarchy that no such thing existed?

'If your soul is non-existent,' says smooth Mephistopheles, 'then it is a nothing to ask you for. Come, roll up your sleeve, cut your arm until the blood spurts and sign this scroll.'

As he speaks, I can almost swear that I see beneath the straight-cut fringe he still wears, as he did when he was a schoolboy, two tiny bud-like horns.

'I'll share my fortune with you,' I say. 'I'll give you all of it, Phiz. I'll sign over my chateaux, my art collections, my library of erotica ...'

'Here is the knife. Here is the pen. Here is the scroll,' he says relentlessly.

I refuse to sign. You can call it superstition if you like, an anachronistic reluctance to give away something that our century no longer believes in, but I shied away from it. The nib will not move.

'My master Lucifer,' says Mephistopheles, 'will possess you one way or another, Doctor John Faustus. Be warned.'

And he disappears in a puff of sulphurous smoke.

I have a little time now before the police arrive. You see, Mephistopheles has kept all the evidence, and has fabricated it where none existed. The plagiarised doctoral theses, the monastic documents we faked together, the marriage certificates that clearly prove bigamy, the DNA samples that link me to the murders of various vice chancellors, archbishops and husbands who inconveniently stood in my way, the forged land deeds that gave me possession of mansions and oilfields and whole countries. He has surrendered them all, anonymously, to the authorities. The warrants are being signed now.

And when I am in the cell, who is it who will appoint himself my solicitor and visit me daily and persuade me to do his bidding?

My soul is in danger.

Potters, glass-blowers, ceramicists.

I come here to you in the last hour of my freedom.

I ask you, with all your skills, to fashion some little well-made flask.

Place my image on its outer surface.

Make a well-fitting stopper for it, with no gap or crack where an essence might escape.

After you have captured in it what I shall give you, seal it with wax and water from a holy spring.

And write in the finest script around the tiny neck:

This bottle contains the soul of John Faustus, for safe keeping.

Hurry.

Do it now.

Thank you.

Postscript: 'Some little well-made Flask'

The story reproduced above is a fitting substitute for a conclusion to a volume as diverse as this, since it illustrates, in a few words and through the use of appropriate images, what the preceding elaborations have attempted to prove over many pages: that Faustus is a living icon capable of evolution and adaptation to new situations. The past twenty years supply ample proof that Faustus' career continues to inspire artists from many countries and cultures, working in media as diverse as opera and oil, potter's clay and printed page. This continuity gives the icon its unique ability to speak to us in the present while beckoning us to investigate and rethink its past. What astounds about this versatility is the fact that the original material, born out of a specific and narrow sixteenth-century dogmatic conflict, has proved so flexible as to be updated and accommodated to cultures across the world, whether for the Elizabethan and later for the European stage, in the Gothic novels of nineteenth-century New England or in the *manga* comics of present-day Japan. Derek Sellen's story was chosen not merely on account of the fortuitous circumstance that, of all the examples I have collected and reviewed, it was the most recent to appear in print, but also because of the way in which its author approaches the theme. Faustus' soul has indeed been preserved over the centuries in a variety of splendid receptacles which, like the potters' art, have survived, timeless and intriguing, to outshine and outlast the deterioration of their original content. Whoever he may have been, whenever and wherever he may have lived, whether or not he practised whatever art or craft: these are topics on which debate will inevitably run on. What counts for later generations are the resulting artefacts. Faustus' soul has been rescued from the flux of time and struck into stability by the creative labour of those who sought to constrain it within what Sellen calls 'some little well-made flask'. This volume is offered as a memorial to their collective endeavour.

Index

Figures in **bold** type refer to pages containing illustrations